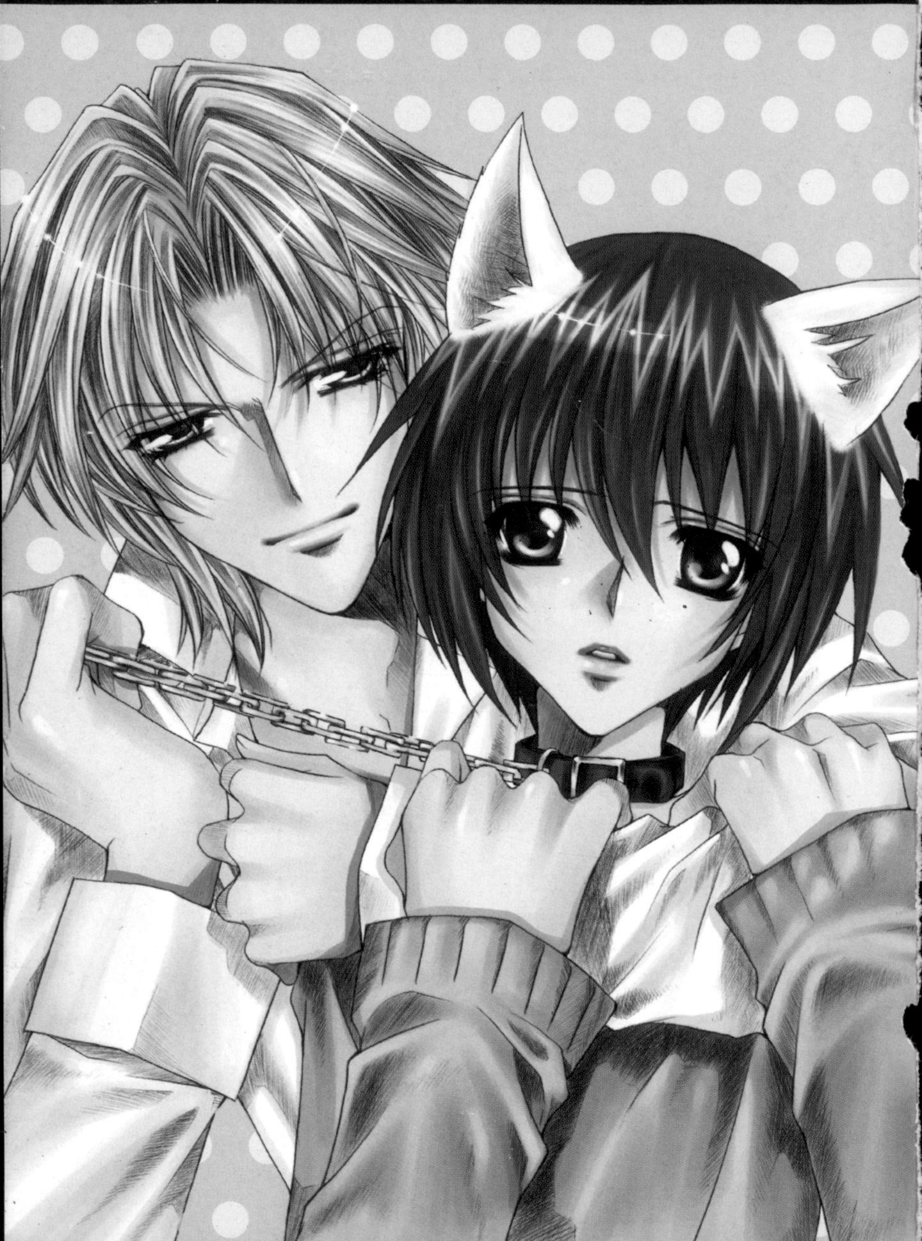

AI ORE! Love Me!

CONTENTS 3

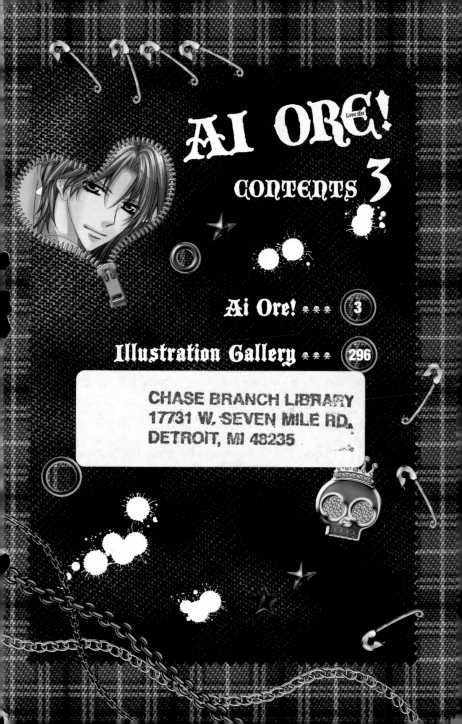

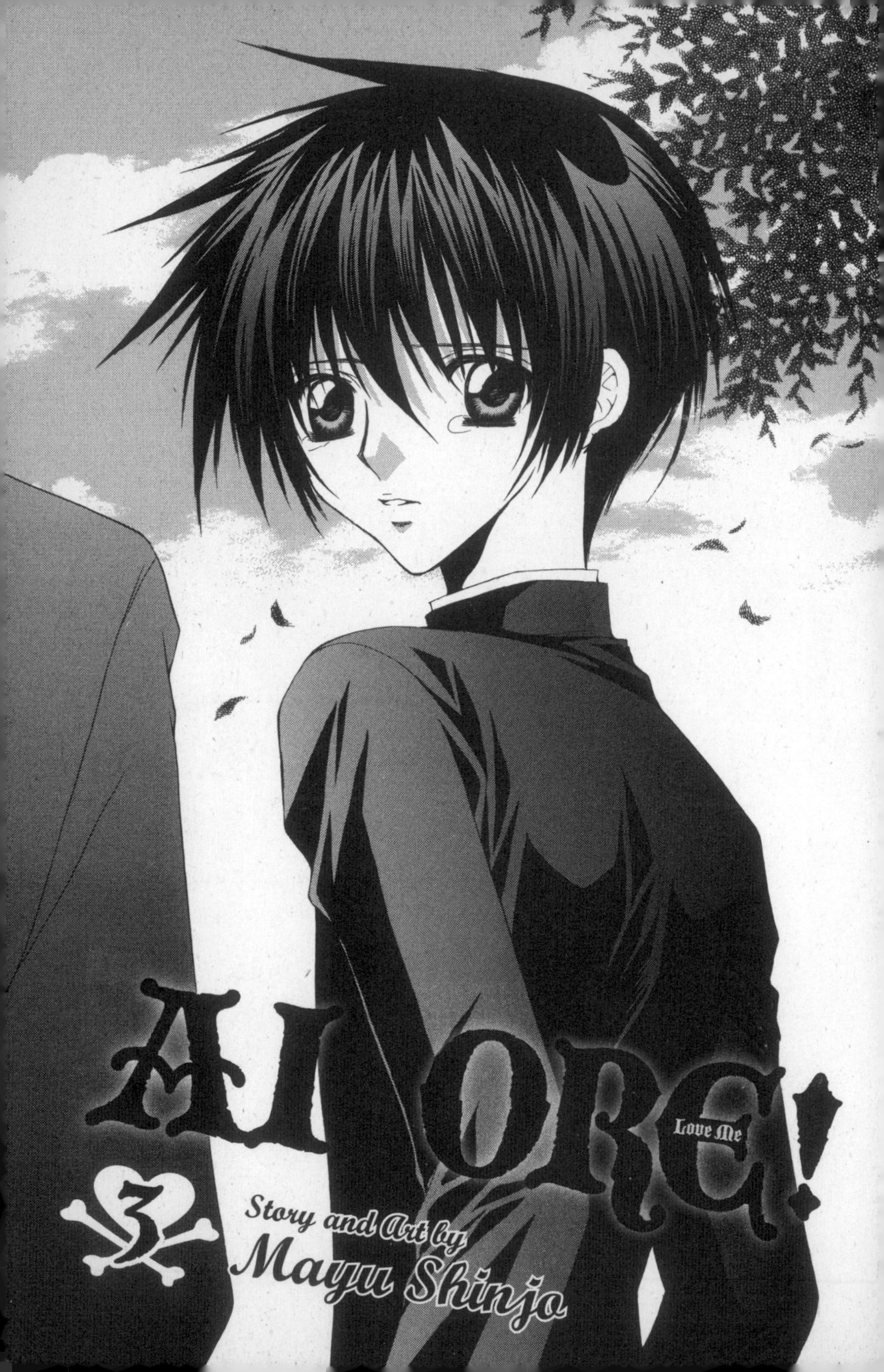
AI ORE!
Love Me
3
Story and Art by
Mayu Shinjo

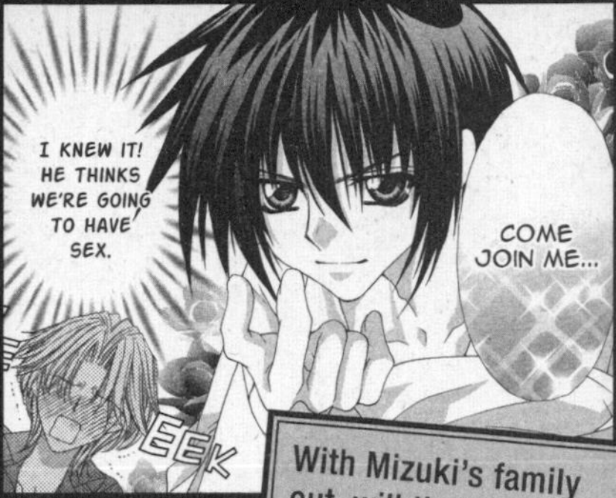
COME JOIN ME...
I KNEW IT! HE THINKS WE'RE GOING TO HAVE SEX.
EEK

With Mizuki's family out, will the two finally do XXX in her room?!

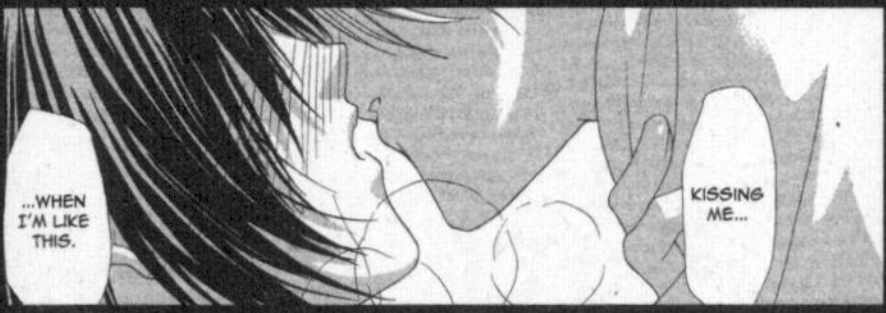
KISSING ME...
...WHEN I'M LIKE THIS.

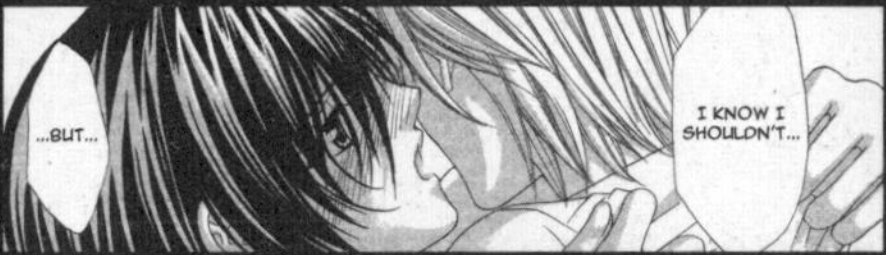
I KNOW I SHOULDN'T...
...BUT...

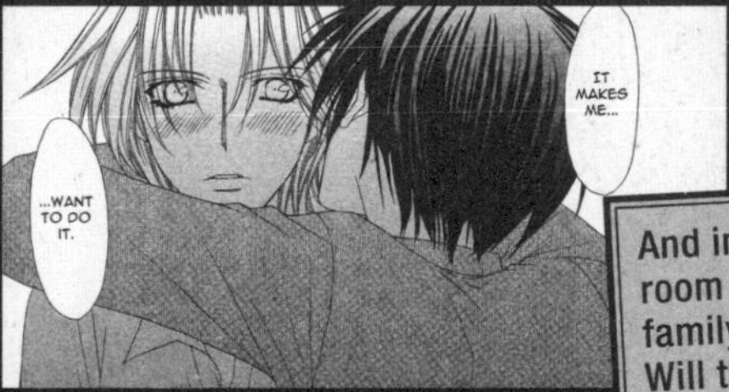
IT MAKES ME...
...WANT TO DO IT.

AI ORE! Love Me

And in Akira's room too (when his family is home)... Will they finally go through with it?!

Story Thus Far

☠ Mizuki Sakurazaka, the lead guitarist of indie girl band Blaue Rosen, is an extremely handsome girl. She is treated like a "prince" at St. Nobara Girls Academy. Her boyfriend, Akira Shiraishi, is an extremely cute boy who is considered to be the "princess" of Dankaisan Boys School.

☠ At first Mizuki rejects Akira's frequent sexual advances, but later decides to have XXX with him. However, Shinnosuke, a college student with a crush on Mizuki, intrudes and interrupts them at the last minute. But when Akira comes down with a fever, Mizuki nurses him back to health, and the couple grows even closer.

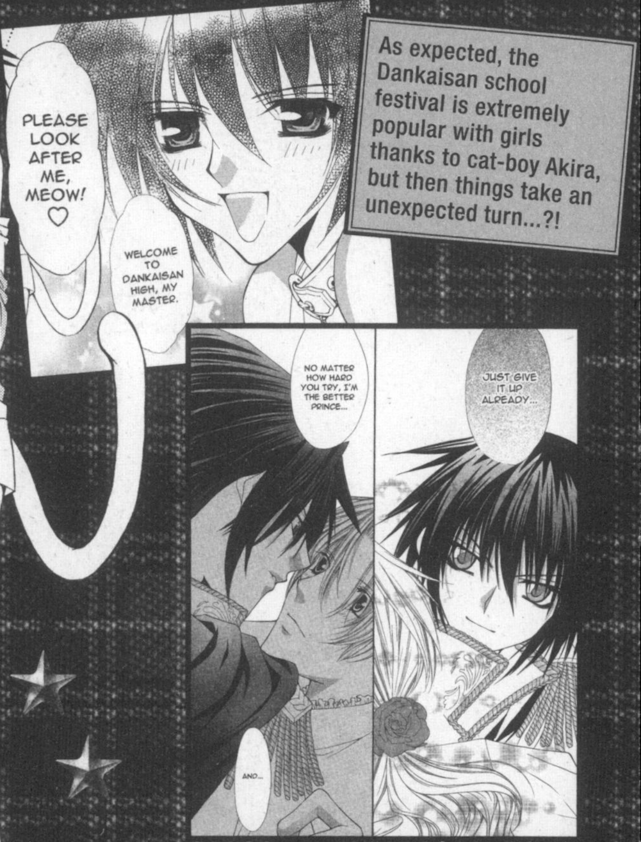
As expected, the Dankaisan school festival is extremely popular with girls thanks to cat-boy Akira, but then things take an unexpected turn...?!
PLEASE LOOK AFTER ME, MEOW! ♡
WELCOME TO DANKAISAN HIGH, MY MASTER.
JUST GIVE IT UP ALREADY...
NO MATTER HOW HARD YOU TRY, I'M THE BETTER PRINCE...
AND...

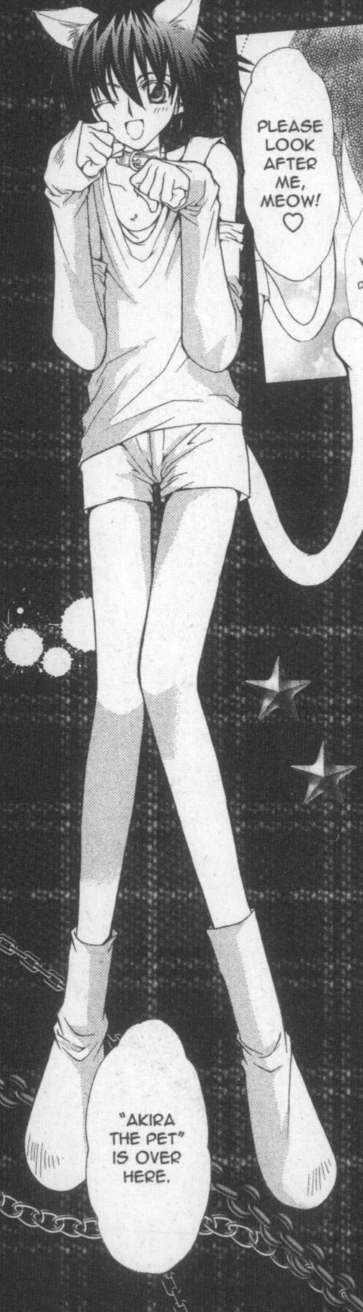
"AKIRA THE PET" IS OVER HERE.

Akira is forced to do a pet cosplay (wearing cat ears ♥) at the Dankaisan school festival as a way to get more females to visit the school, but Mizuki is really turned on by Akira and pounces on him as Dark Mizuki... Later, Akira dresses up as a prince at the St. Nobara school festival and dances with Mizuki (who is dressed as a princess) in a very manly manner! The two gradually get to know each other's various sides and continue to nurture their love...

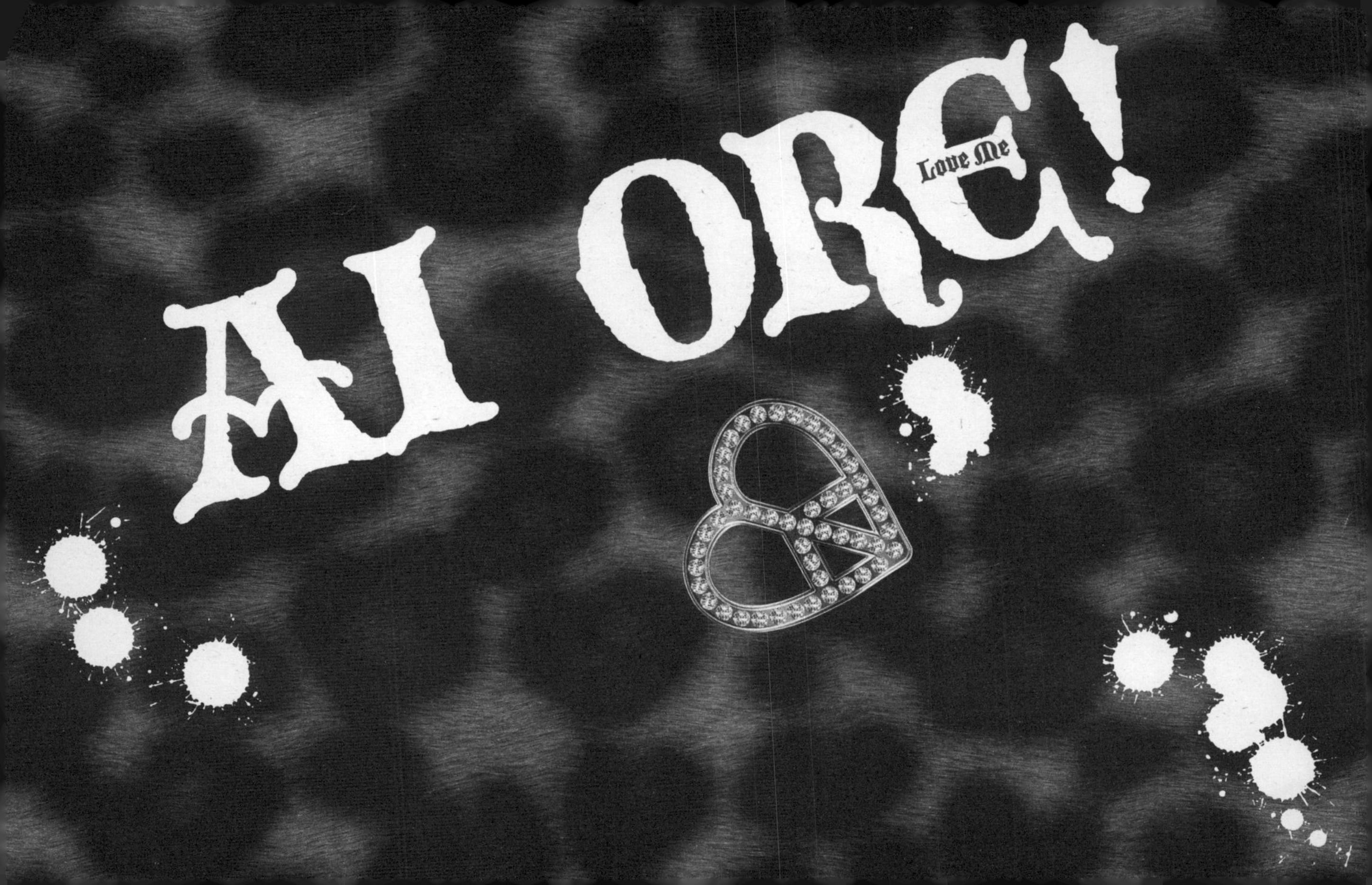
AI ORE!
Love Me

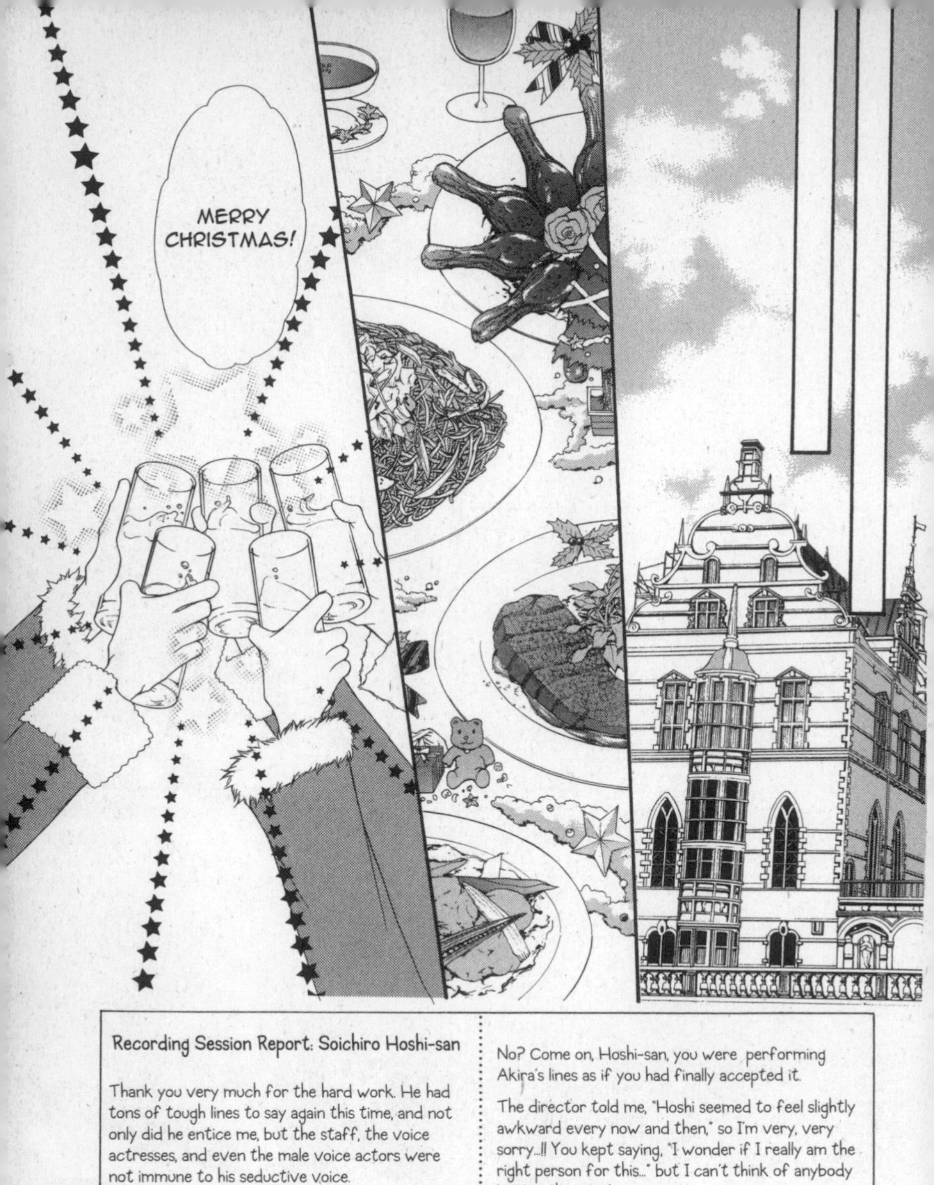
MERRY CHRISTMAS!

Recording Session Report: Soichiro Hoshi-san

Thank you very much for the hard work. He had tons of tough lines to say again this time, and not only did he entice me, but the staff, the voice actresses, and even the male voice actors were not immune to his seductive voice.

Akira's moe scenes have increased a lot compared to the first CD!! Isn't it about time for the embarrassment to slowly start turning to ecstasy... What? No? Come on, Hoshi-san, you were performing Akira's lines as if you had finally accepted it.

The director told me, "Hoshi seemed to feel slightly awkward every now and then," so I'm very, very sorry...!! You kept saying, "I wonder if I really am the right person for this..." but I can't think of anybody better than you!

So, Shinjo's choice of moe phrase by Akira is...

Thanks. GRIN ♡

It's such a great line...

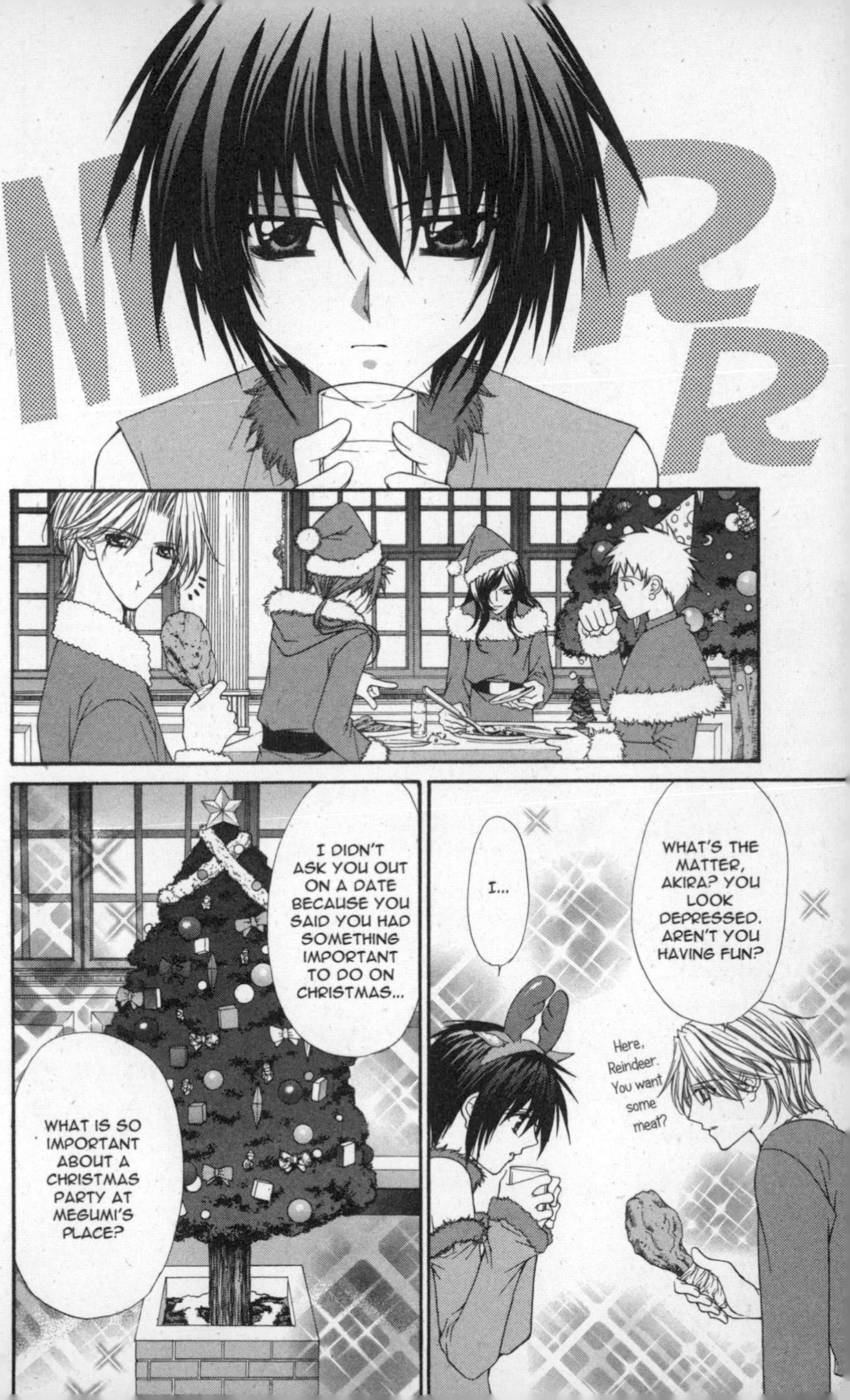
MRR
WHAT'S THE MATTER, AKIRA? YOU LOOK DEPRESSED. AREN'T YOU HAVING FUN?
I...
Here, Reindeer. You want some meat?
I DIDN'T ASK YOU OUT ON A DATE BECAUSE YOU SAID YOU HAD SOMETHING IMPORTANT TO DO ON CHRISTMAS...
WHAT IS SO IMPORTANT ABOUT A CHRISTMAS PARTY AT MEGUMI'S PLACE?

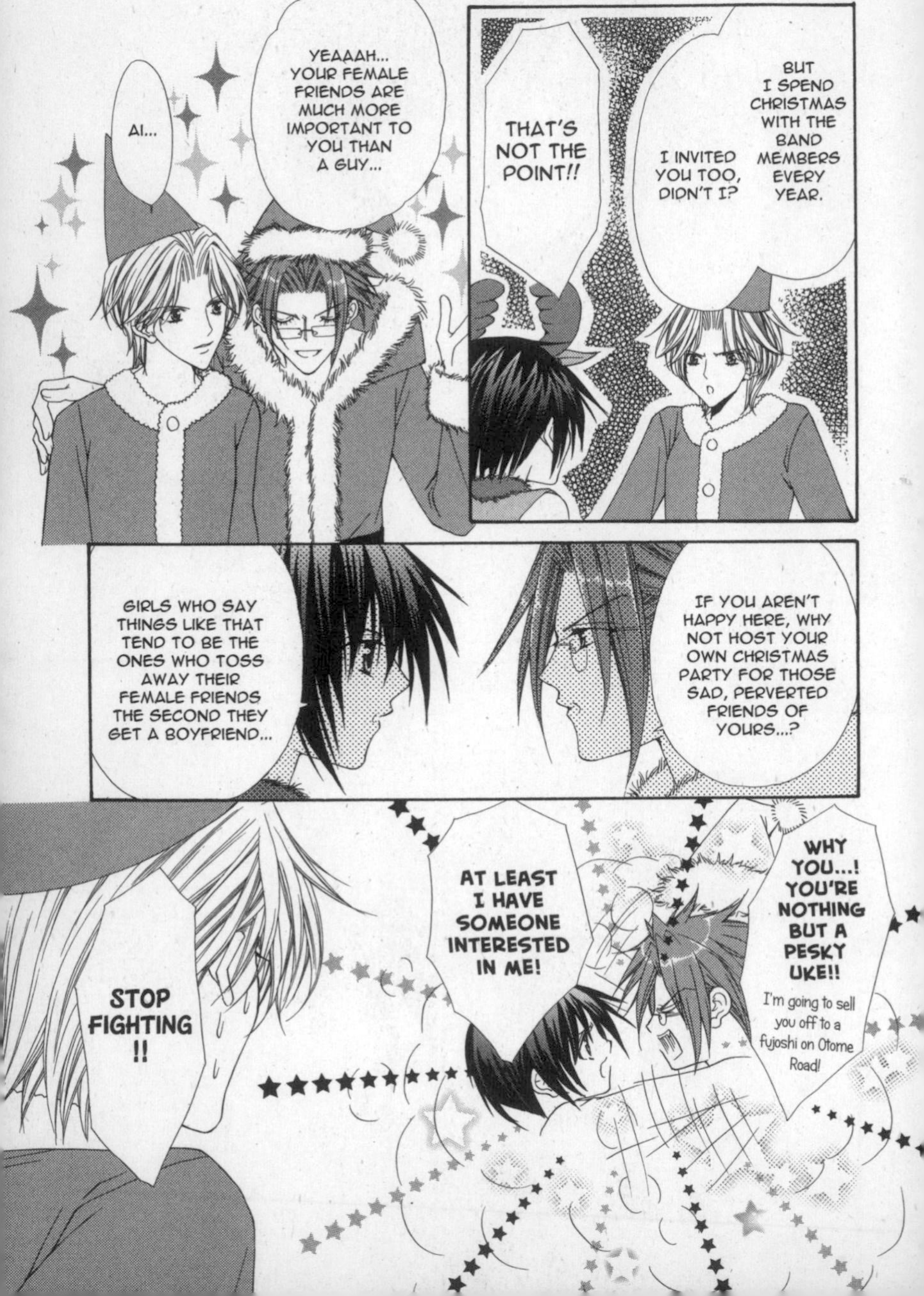
BUT I SPEND CHRISTMAS WITH THE BAND MEMBERS EVERY YEAR.
I INVITED YOU TOO, DIDN'T I?
THAT'S NOT THE POINT!!
YEAAAH... YOUR FEMALE FRIENDS ARE MUCH MORE IMPORTANT TO YOU THAN A GUY...
AI...
IF YOU AREN'T HAPPY HERE, WHY NOT HOST YOUR OWN CHRISTMAS PARTY FOR THOSE SAD, PERVERTED FRIENDS OF YOURS...?
GIRLS WHO SAY THINGS LIKE THAT TEND TO BE THE ONES WHO TOSS AWAY THEIR FEMALE FRIENDS THE SECOND THEY GET A BOYFRIEND...
WHY YOU...! YOU'RE NOTHING BUT A PESKY UKE!!
I'm going to sell you off to a fujoshi on Otome Road!
AT LEAST I HAVE SOMEONE INTERESTED IN ME!
STOP FIGHTING!!

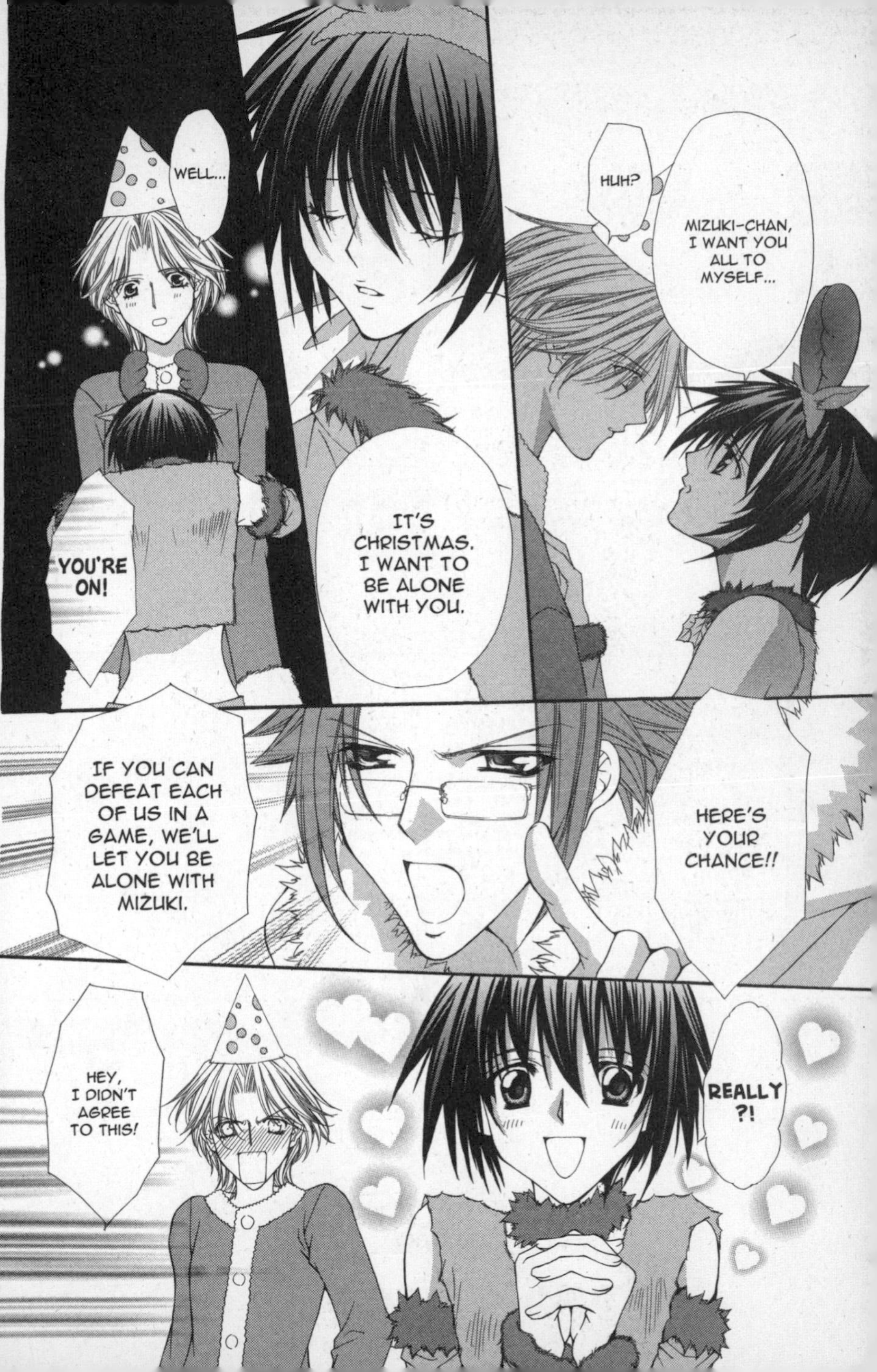
MIZUKI-CHAN, I WANT YOU ALL TO MYSELF...
HUH?
IT'S CHRISTMAS. I WANT TO BE ALONE WITH YOU.
WELL...
YOU'RE ON!
HERE'S YOUR CHANCE!!
IF YOU CAN DEFEAT EACH OF US IN A GAME, WE'LL LET YOU BE ALONE WITH MIZUKI.
REALLY?!
HEY, I DIDN'T AGREE TO THIS!

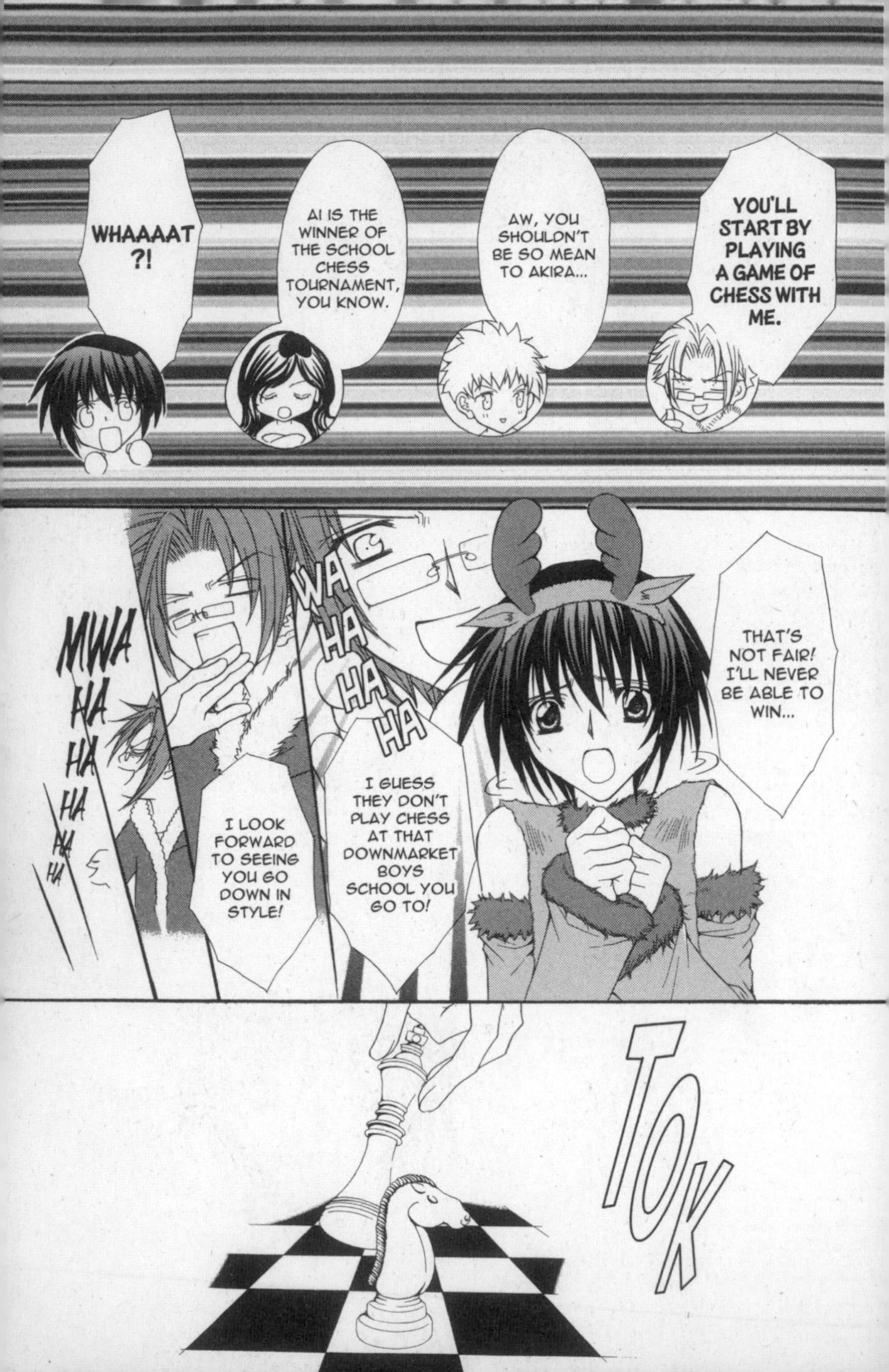
YOU'LL START BY PLAYING A GAME OF CHESS WITH ME.
AW, YOU SHOULDN'T BE SO MEAN TO AKIRA...
AI IS THE WINNER OF THE SCHOOL CHESS TOURNAMENT, YOU KNOW.
WHAAAAT?!
THAT'S NOT FAIR! I'LL NEVER BE ABLE TO WIN...
WA HA HA HA HA
I GUESS THEY DON'T PLAY CHESS AT THAT DOWNMARKET BOYS SCHOOL YOU GO TO!
I LOOK FORWARD TO SEEING YOU GO DOWN IN STYLE!
MWA HA HA HA HA HA
TOK

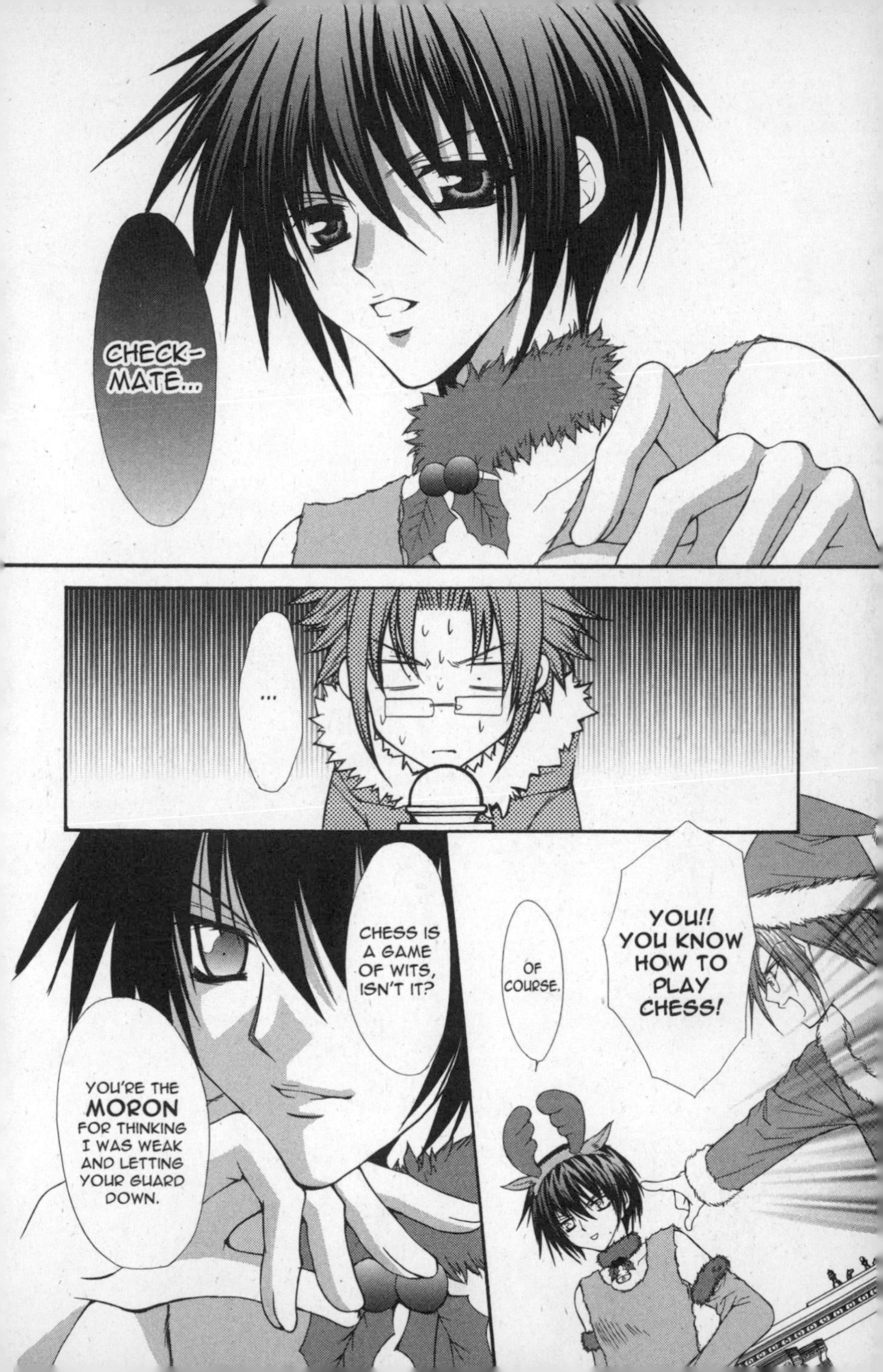
CHECK-MATE...
...
YOU!! YOU KNOW HOW TO PLAY CHESS!
OF COURSE.
CHESS IS A GAME OF WITS, ISN'T IT?
YOU'RE THE MORON FOR THINKING I WAS WEAK AND LETTING YOUR GUARD DOWN.

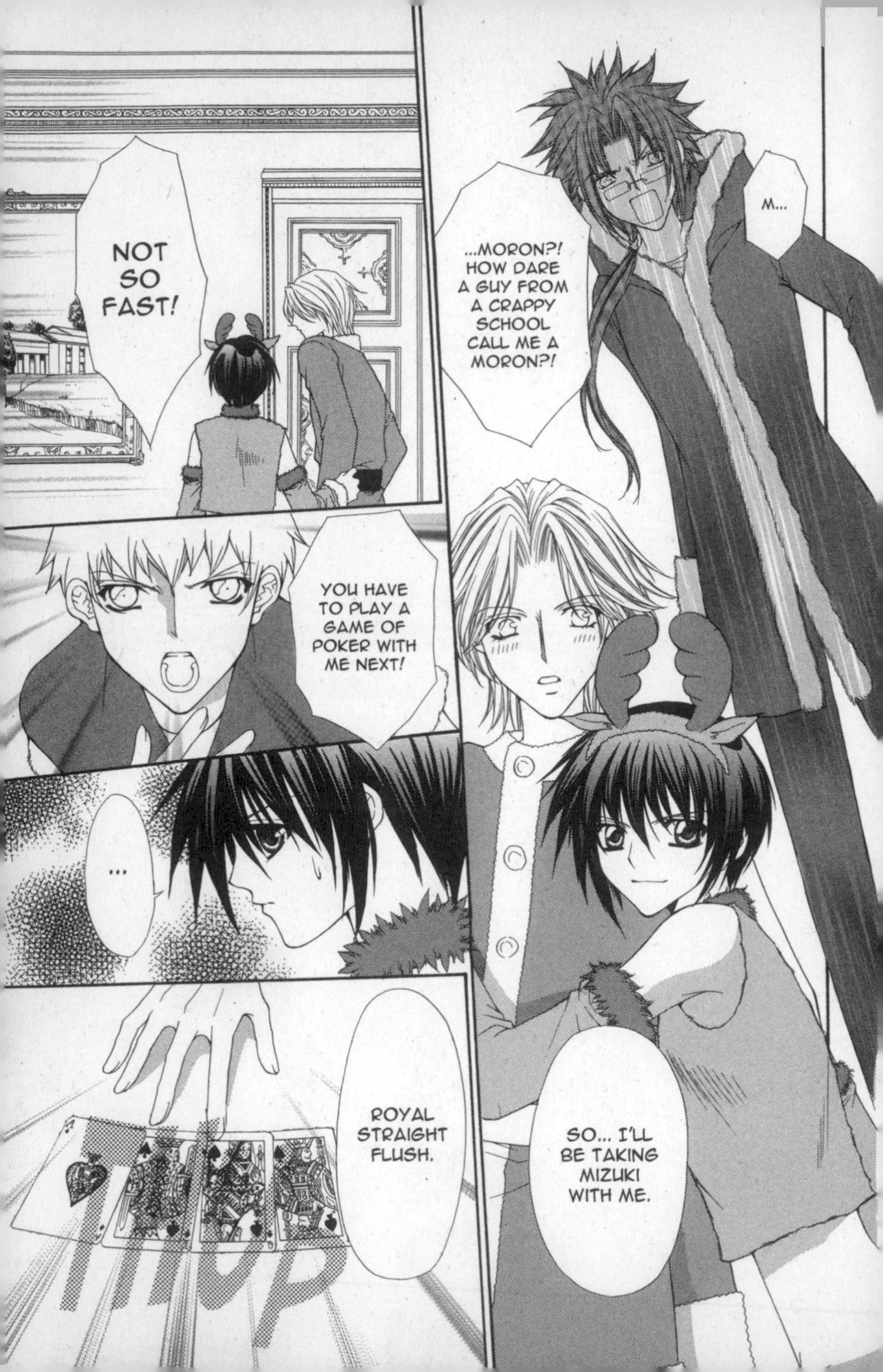
M...
...MORON?! HOW DARE A GUY FROM A CRAPPY SCHOOL CALL ME A MORON?!
NOT SO FAST!
YOU HAVE TO PLAY A GAME OF POKER WITH ME NEXT!
...
ROYAL STRAIGHT FLUSH.
SO... I'LL BE TAKING MIZUKI WITH ME.

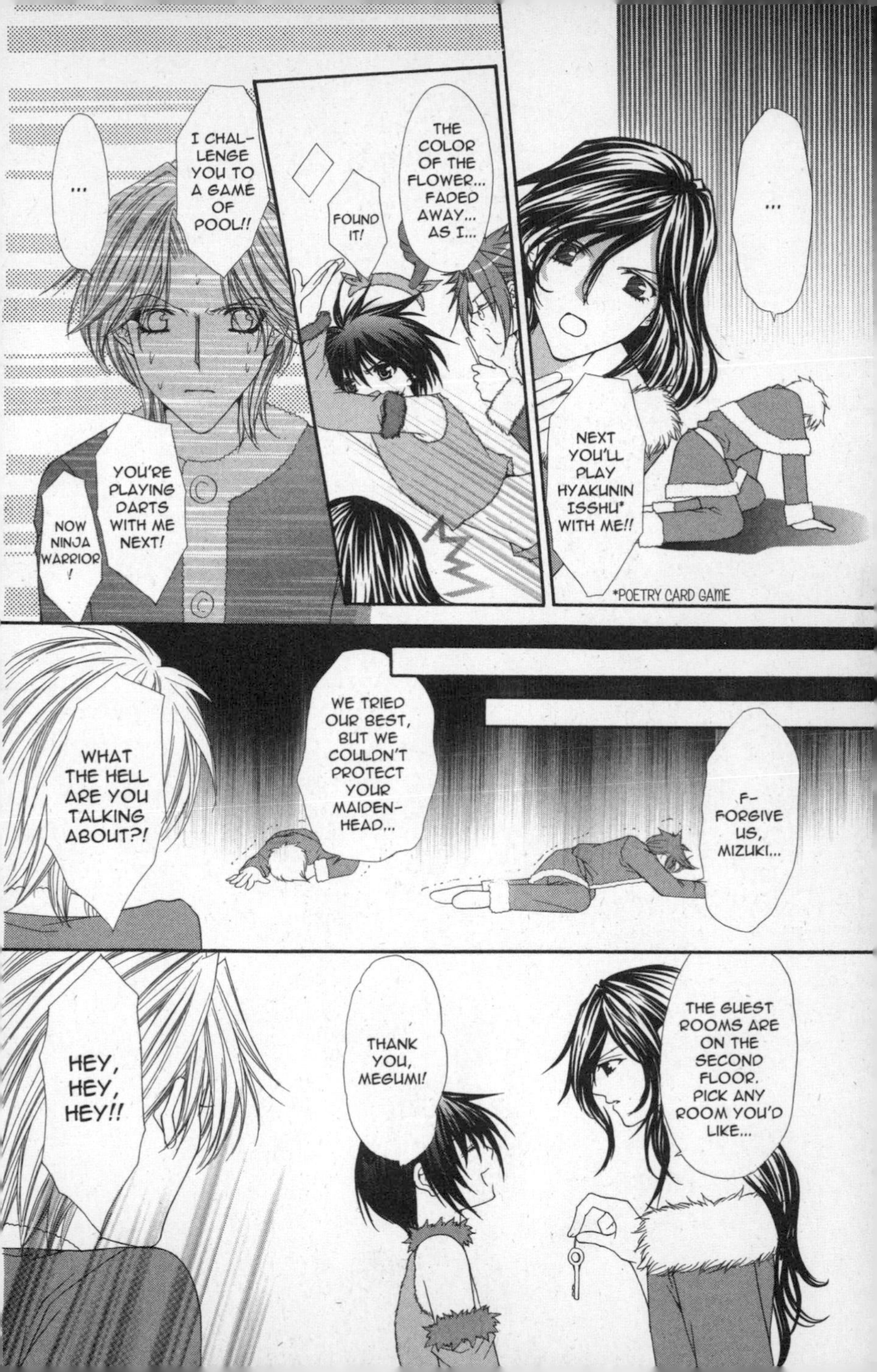
...
NEXT YOU'LL PLAY HYAKUNIN ISSHU* WITH ME!!
*POETRY CARD GAME
THE COLOR OF THE FLOWER... FADED AWAY... AS I...
FOUND IT!
I CHALLENGE YOU TO A GAME OF POOL!!
...
YOU'RE PLAYING DARTS WITH ME NEXT!
NOW NINJA WARRIOR!
F-FORGIVE US, MIZUKI...
WE TRIED OUR BEST, BUT WE COULDN'T PROTECT YOUR MAIDENHEAD...
WHAT THE HELL ARE YOU TALKING ABOUT?!
THE GUEST ROOMS ARE ON THE SECOND FLOOR. PICK ANY ROOM YOU'D LIKE...
THANK YOU, MEGUMI!
HEY, HEY, HEY!!

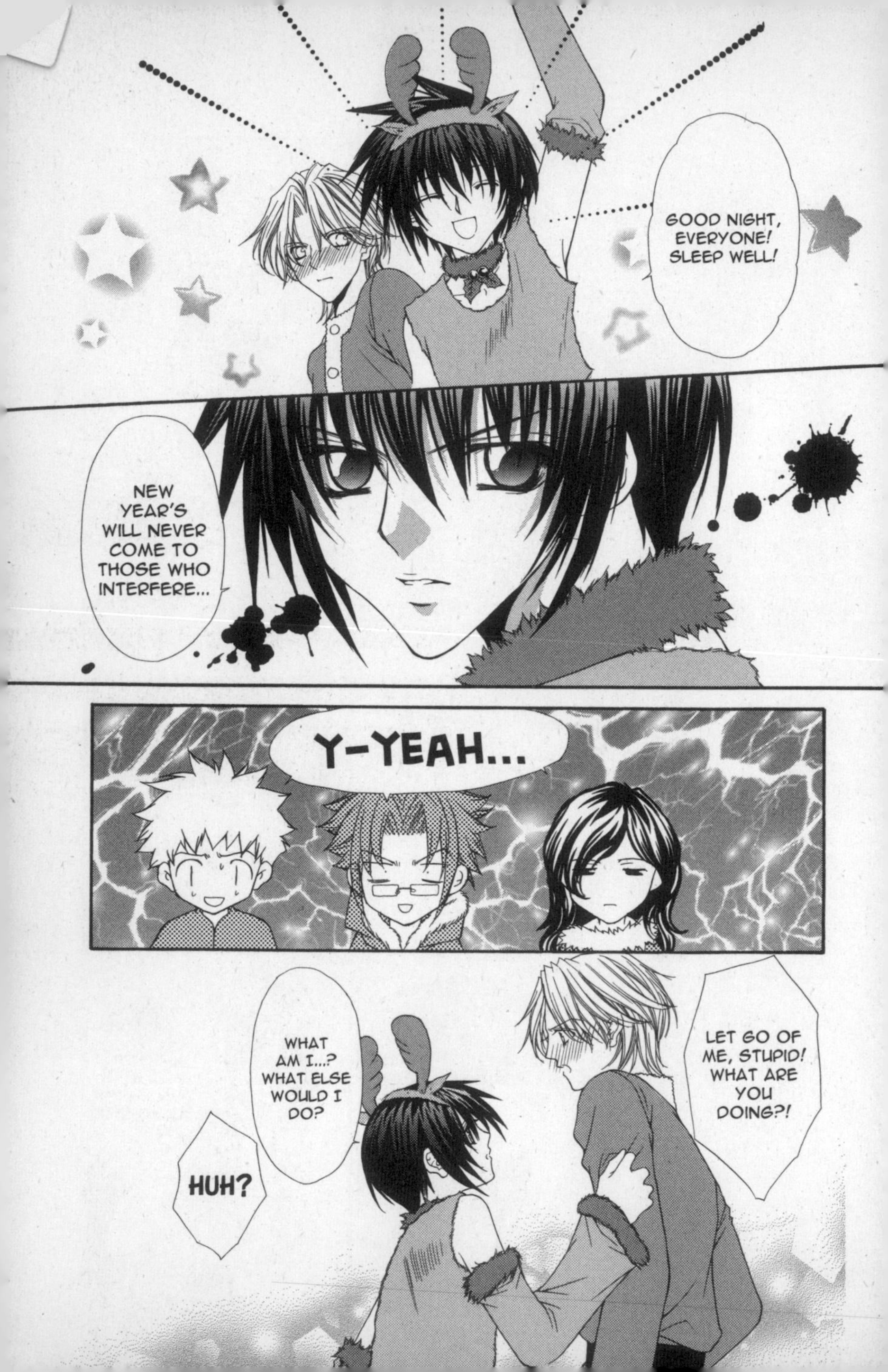
GOOD NIGHT, EVERYONE! SLEEP WELL!
NEW YEAR'S WILL NEVER COME TO THOSE WHO INTERFERE...
Y-YEAH...
LET GO OF ME, STUPID! WHAT ARE YOU DOING?!
WHAT AM I...? WHAT ELSE WOULD I DO?
HUH?

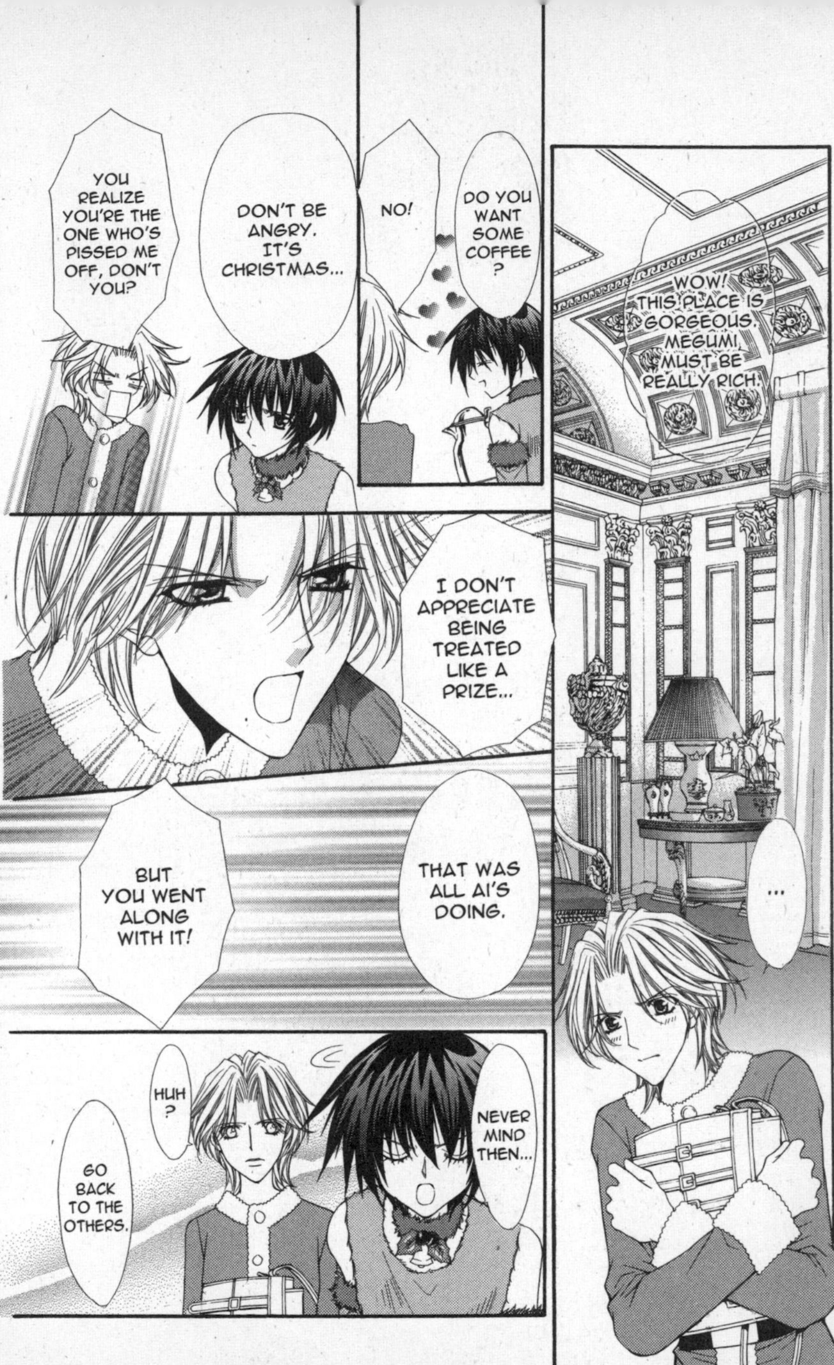
WOW! THIS PLACE IS GORGEOUS. MEGUMI MUST BE REALLY RICH.
...
DO YOU WANT SOME COFFEE?
NO!
DON'T BE ANGRY. IT'S CHRISTMAS...
YOU REALIZE YOU'RE THE ONE WHO'S PISSED ME OFF, DON'T YOU?
I DON'T APPRECIATE BEING TREATED LIKE A PRIZE...
THAT WAS ALL AI'S DOING.
BUT YOU WENT ALONG WITH IT!
NEVER MIND THEN...
HUH?
GO BACK TO THE OTHERS.

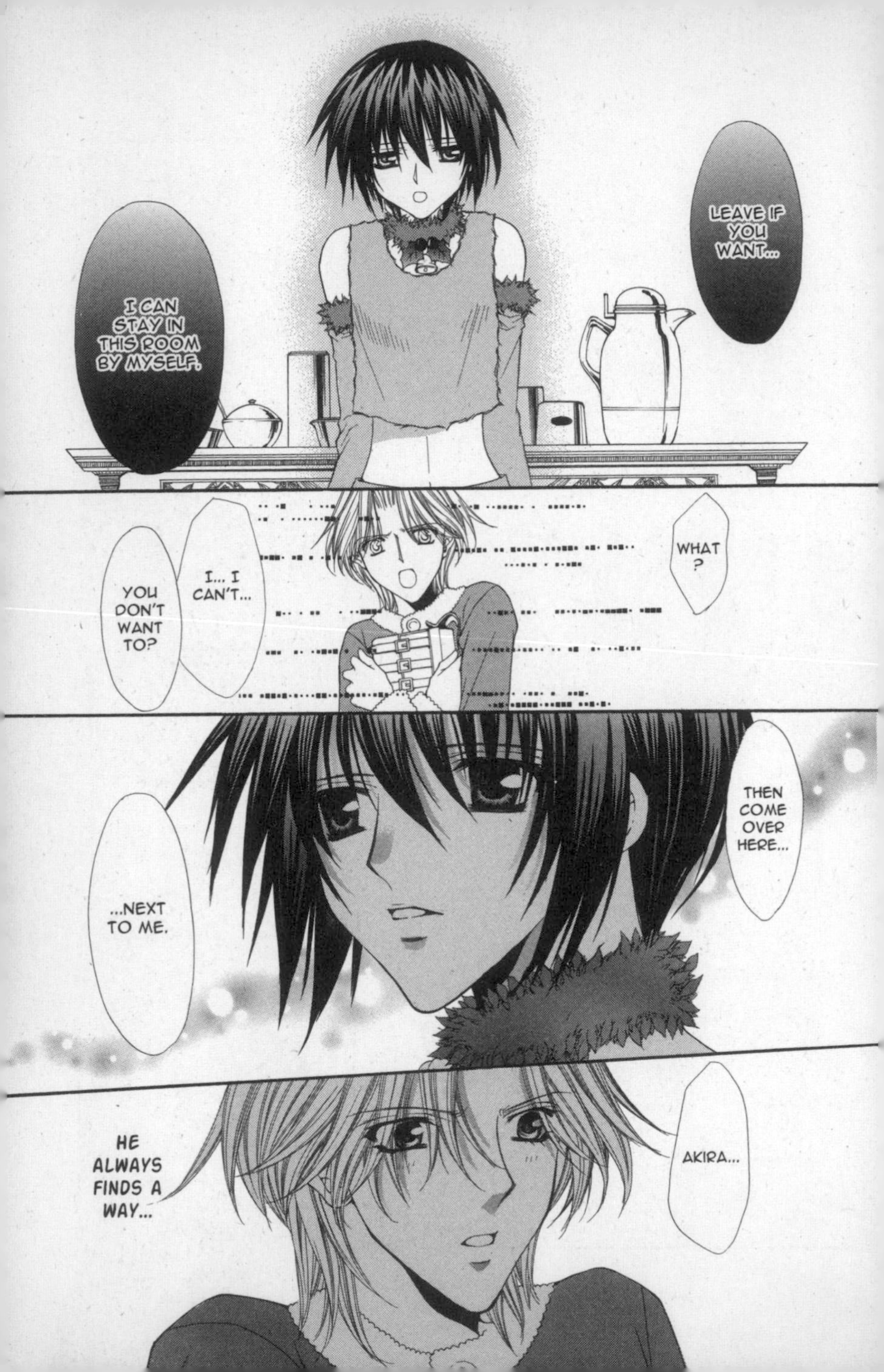
LEAVE IF YOU WANT...
I CAN STAY IN THIS ROOM BY MYSELF.
WHAT?
I... I CAN'T...
YOU DON'T WANT TO?
THEN COME OVER HERE...
...NEXT TO ME.
AKIRA...
HE ALWAYS FINDS A WAY...

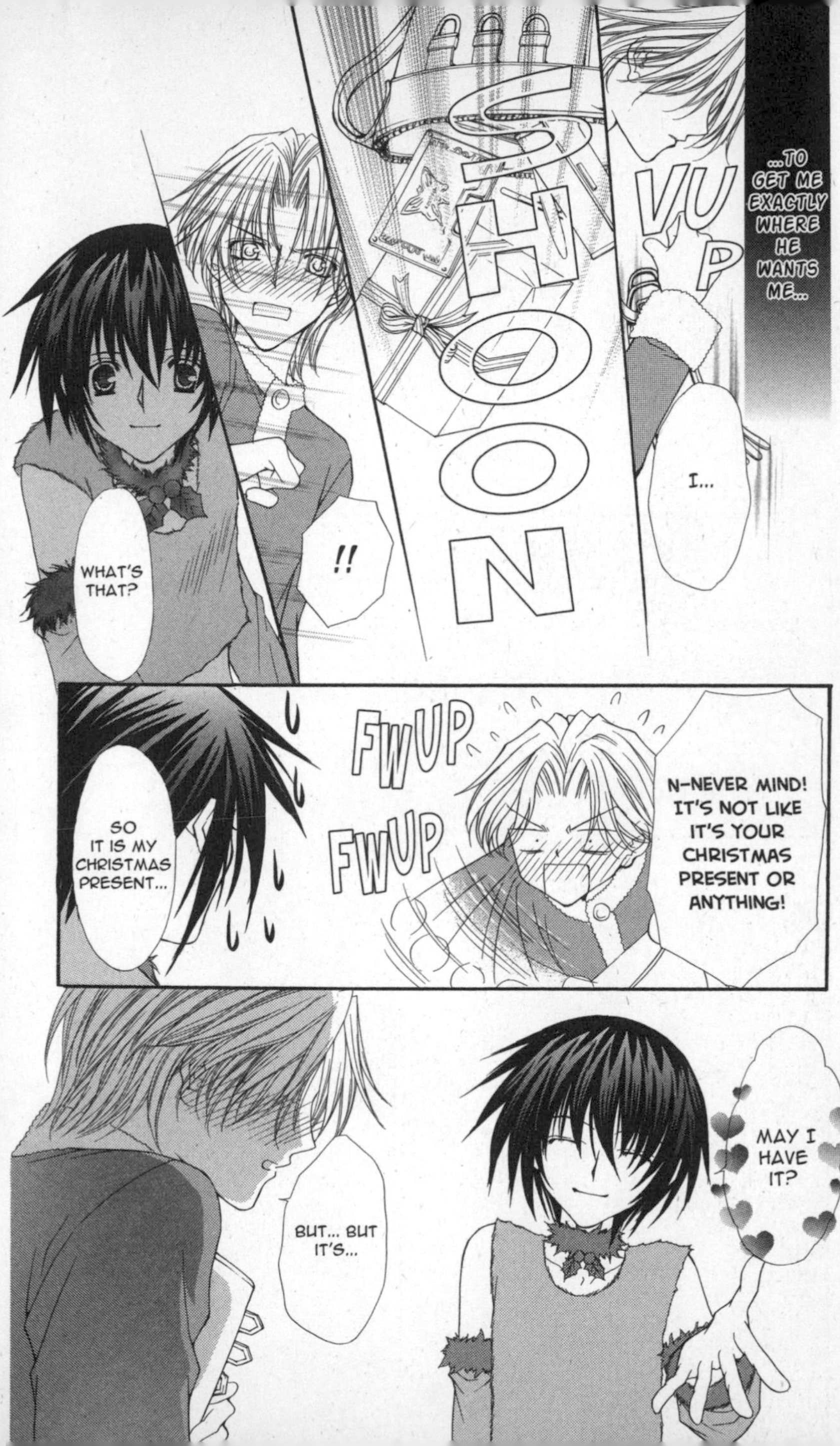
...TO GET ME EXACTLY WHERE HE WANTS ME...
VUP
I...
SHOOON
!!
WHAT'S THAT?
N-NEVER MIND! IT'S NOT LIKE IT'S YOUR CHRISTMAS PRESENT OR ANYTHING!
FWUP FWUP
SO IT IS MY CHRISTMAS PRESENT...
MAY I HAVE IT?
BUT... BUT IT'S...

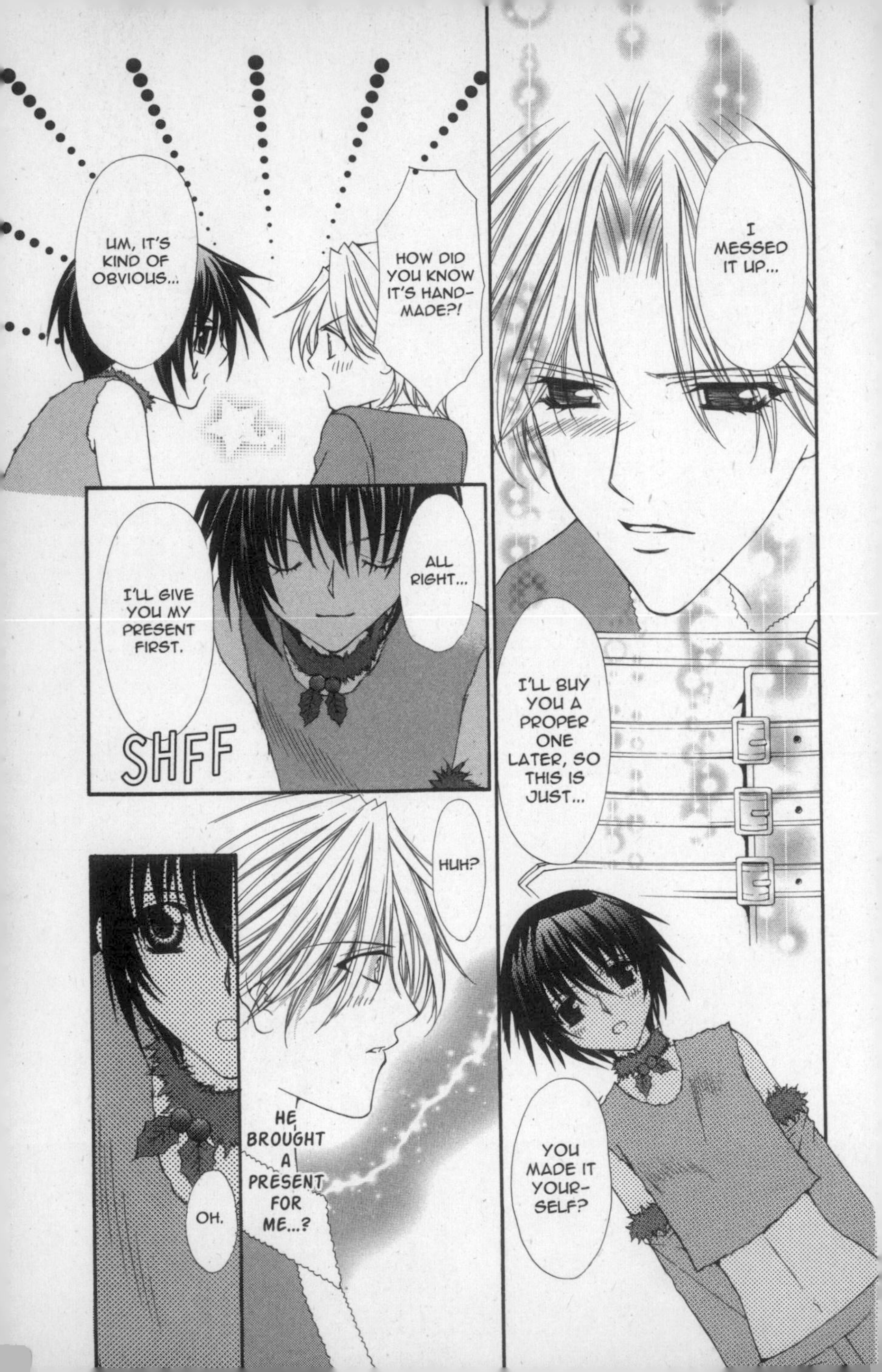
I MESSED IT UP...
I'LL BUY YOU A PROPER ONE LATER, SO THIS IS JUST...
YOU MADE IT YOURSELF?
HOW DID YOU KNOW IT'S HANDMADE?!
UM, IT'S KIND OF OBVIOUS...
ALL RIGHT...
I'LL GIVE YOU MY PRESENT FIRST.
SHFF
HUH?
HE BROUGHT A PRESENT FOR ME...?
OH.

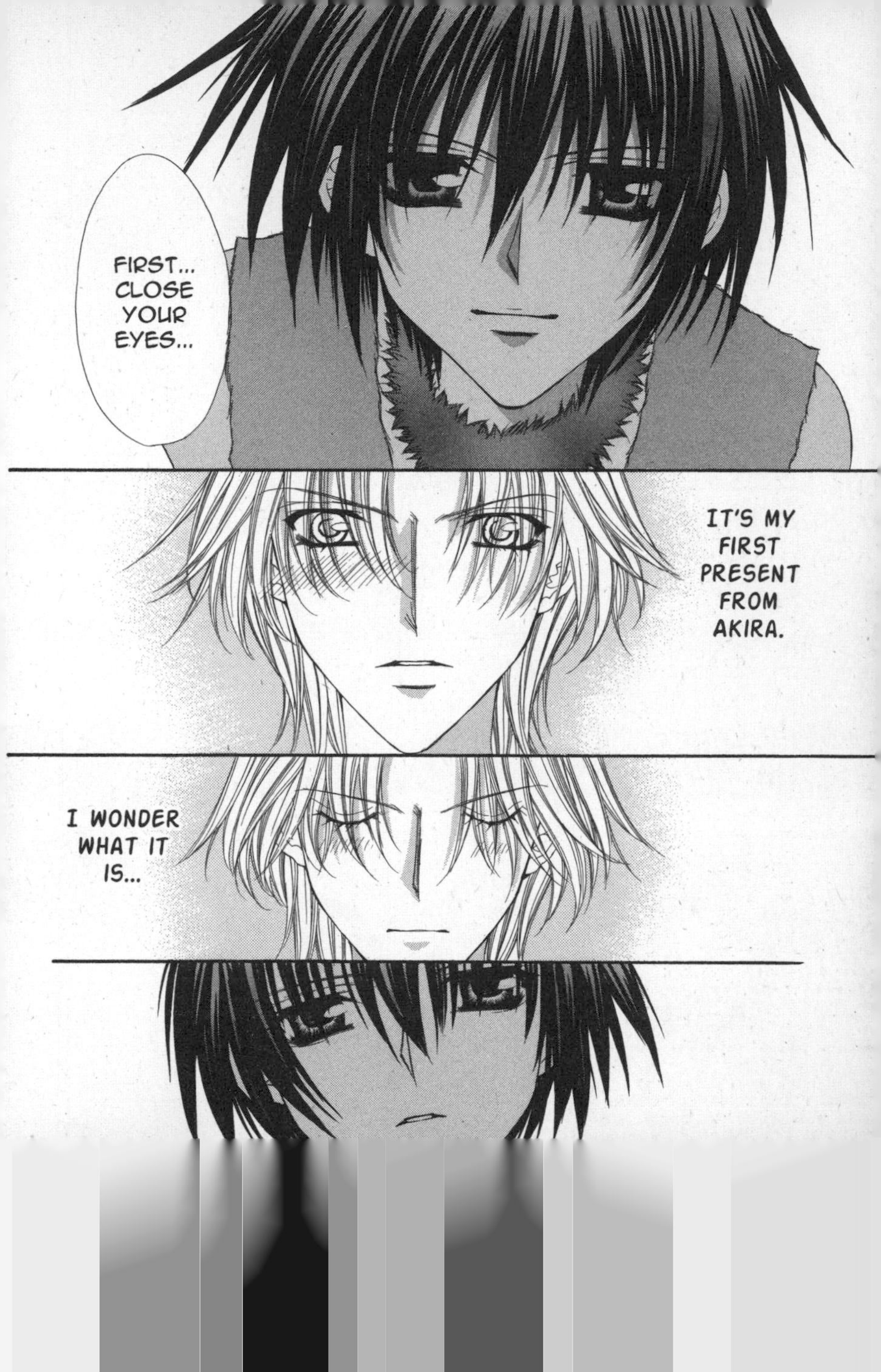
FIRST... CLOSE YOUR EYES...
IT'S MY FIRST PRESENT FROM AKIRA.
I WONDER WHAT IT IS...

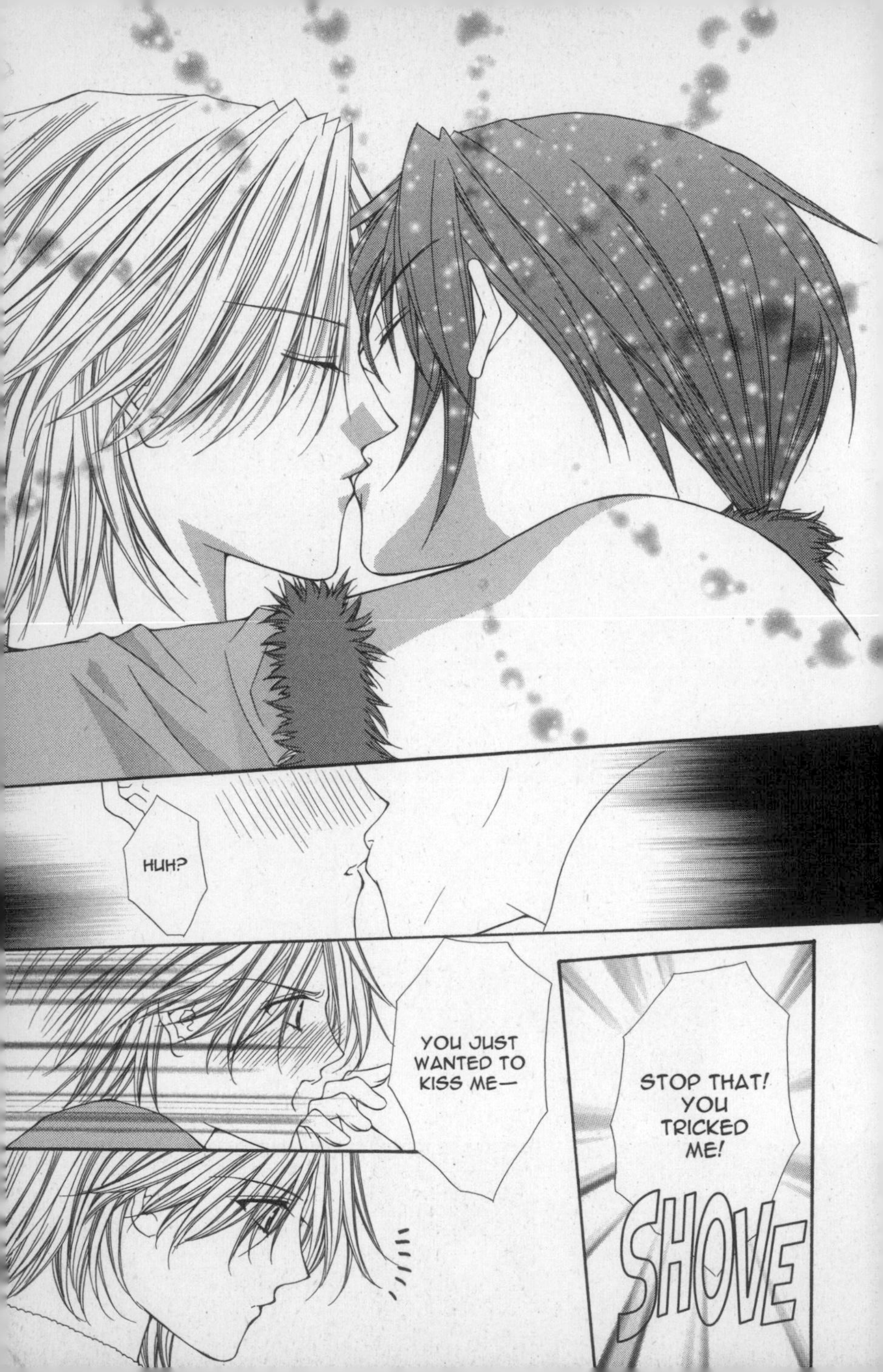
HUH?
STOP THAT! YOU TRICKED ME!
SHOVE
YOU JUST WANTED TO KISS ME—

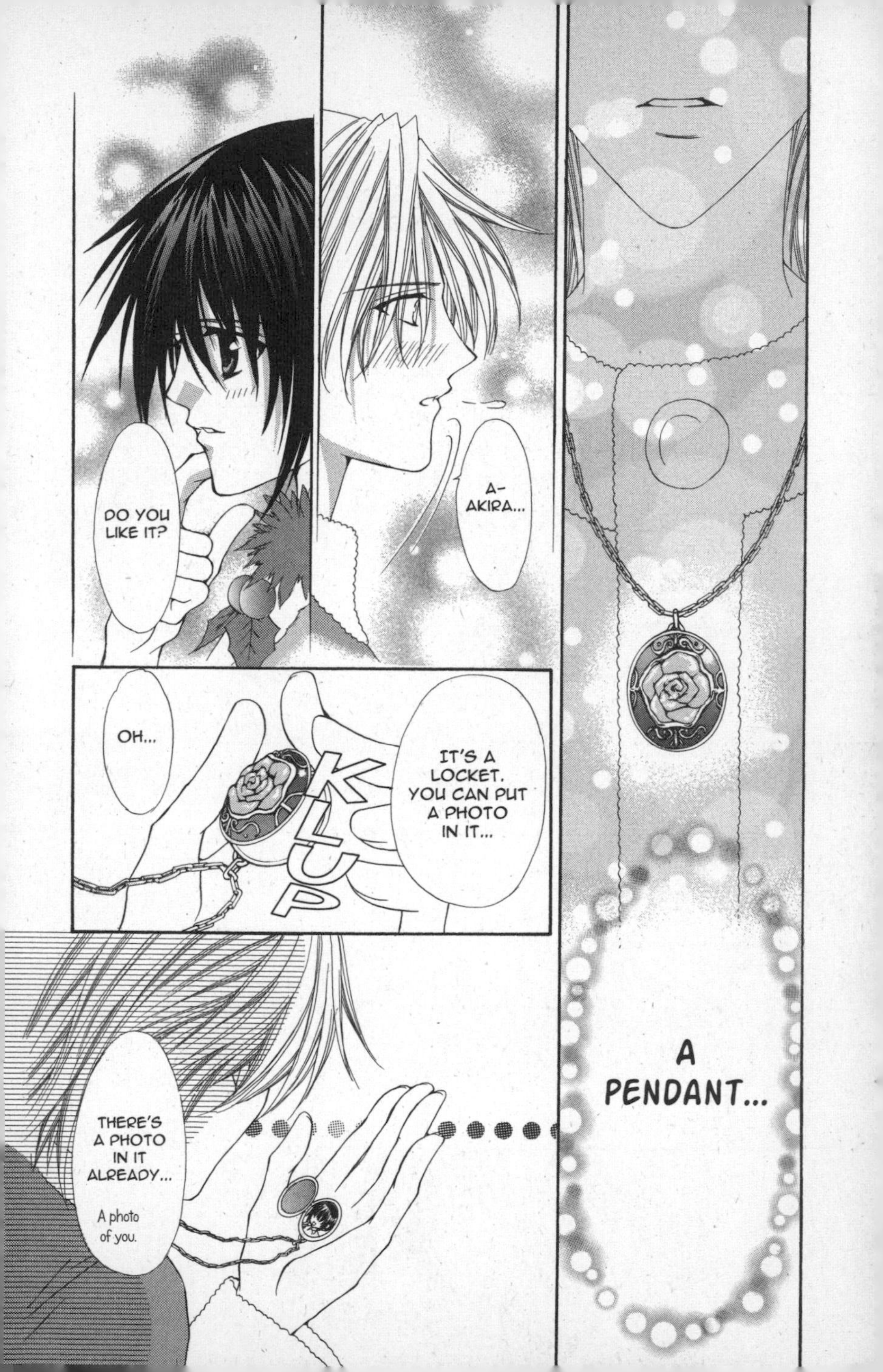
A PENDANT...
A-AKIRA...
DO YOU LIKE IT?
IT'S A LOCKET. YOU CAN PUT A PHOTO IN IT...
KLUP
OH...
THERE'S A PHOTO IN IT ALREADY...
A photo of you.

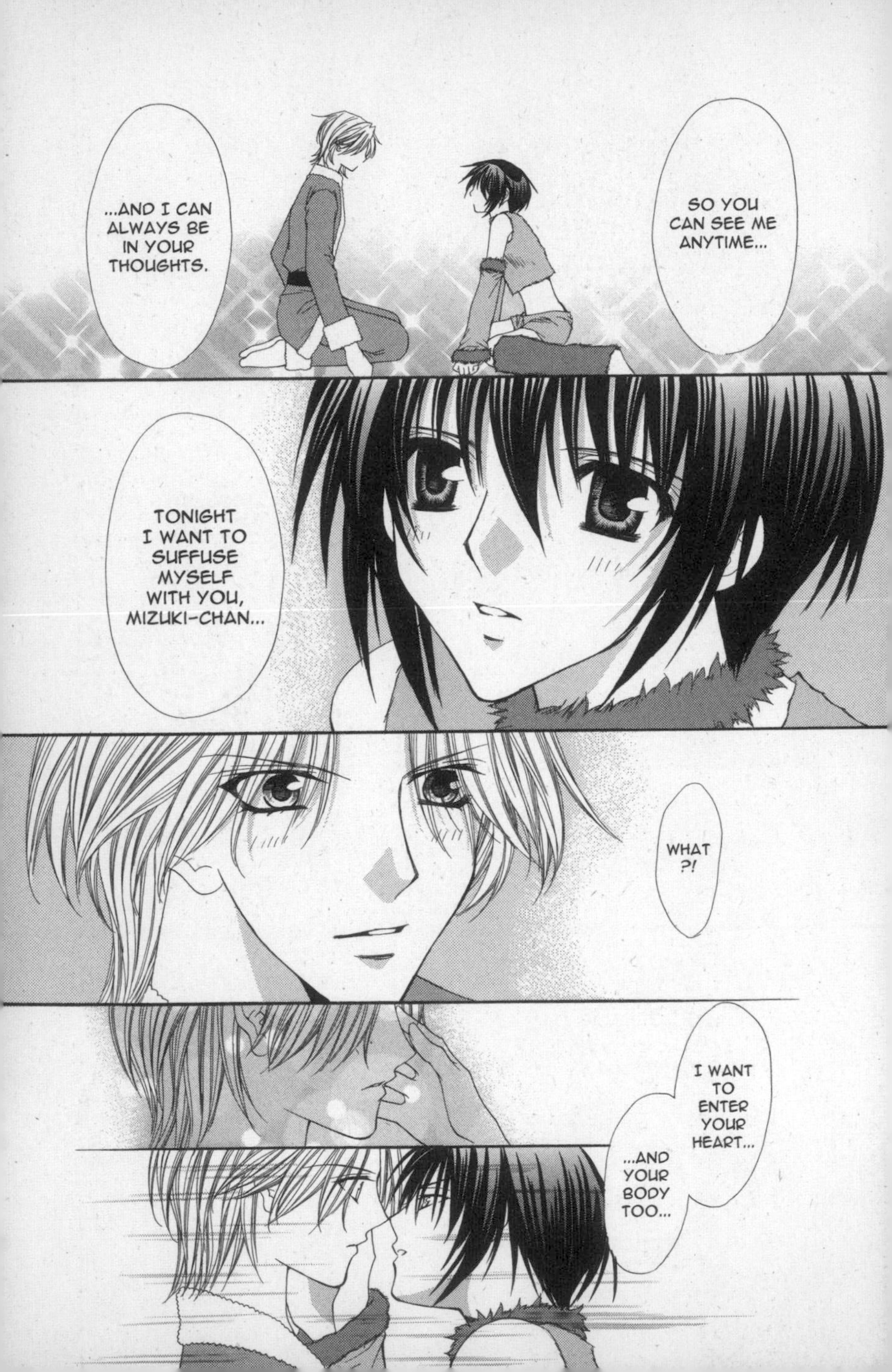
SO YOU CAN SEE ME ANYTIME...
...AND I CAN ALWAYS BE IN YOUR THOUGHTS.
TONIGHT I WANT TO SUFFUSE MYSELF WITH YOU, MIZUKI-CHAN...
WHAT?!
I WANT TO ENTER YOUR HEART...
...AND YOUR BODY TOO...

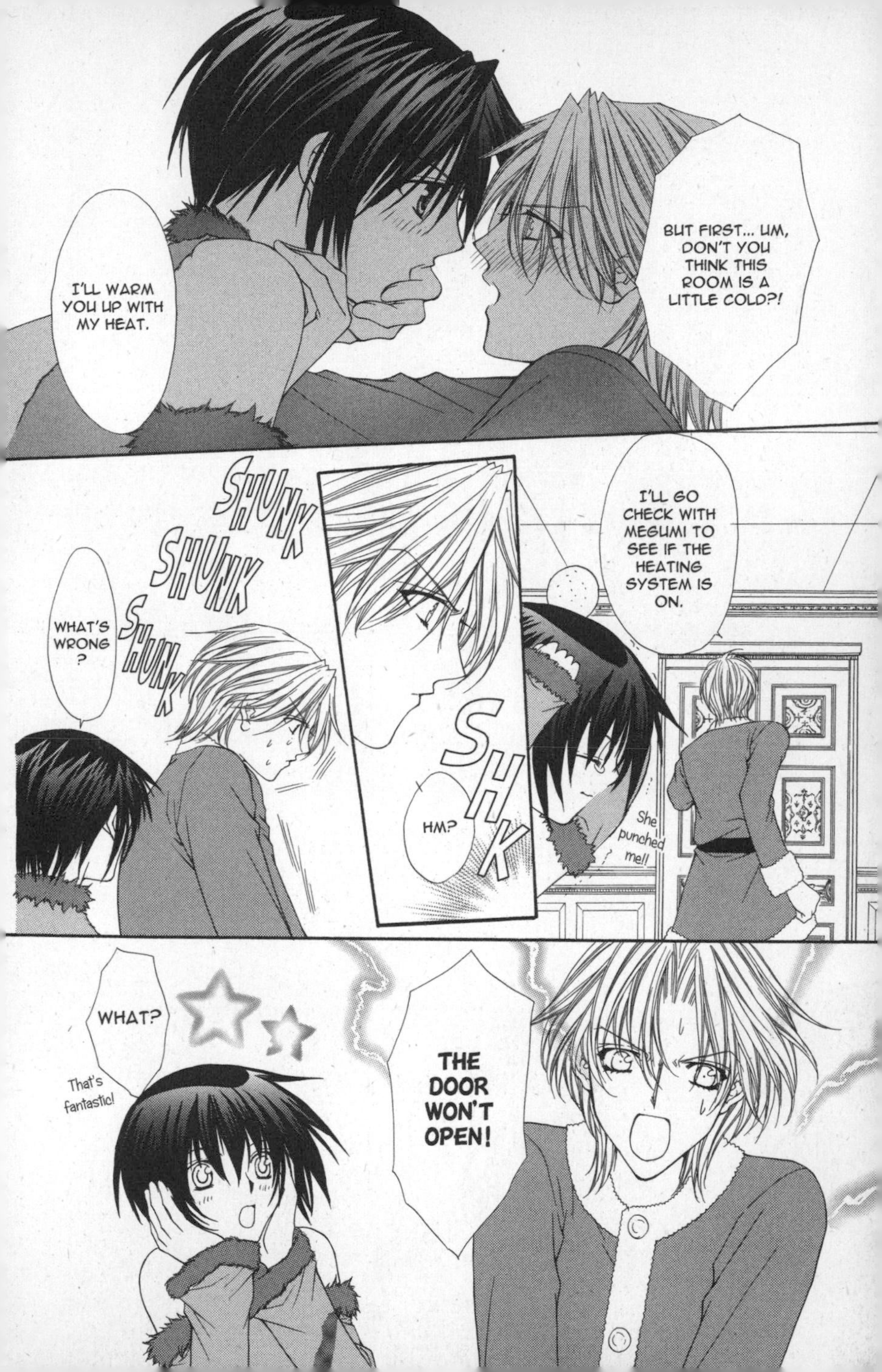
BUT FIRST... UM, DON'T YOU THINK THIS ROOM IS A LITTLE COLD?!
I'LL WARM YOU UP WITH MY HEAT.
I'LL GO CHECK WITH MEGUMI TO SEE IF THE HEATING SYSTEM IS ON.
She punched me!!
SHK
HM?
SHUNK SHUNK SHUNK
WHAT'S WRONG?
THE DOOR WON'T OPEN!
WHAT?
That's fantastic!

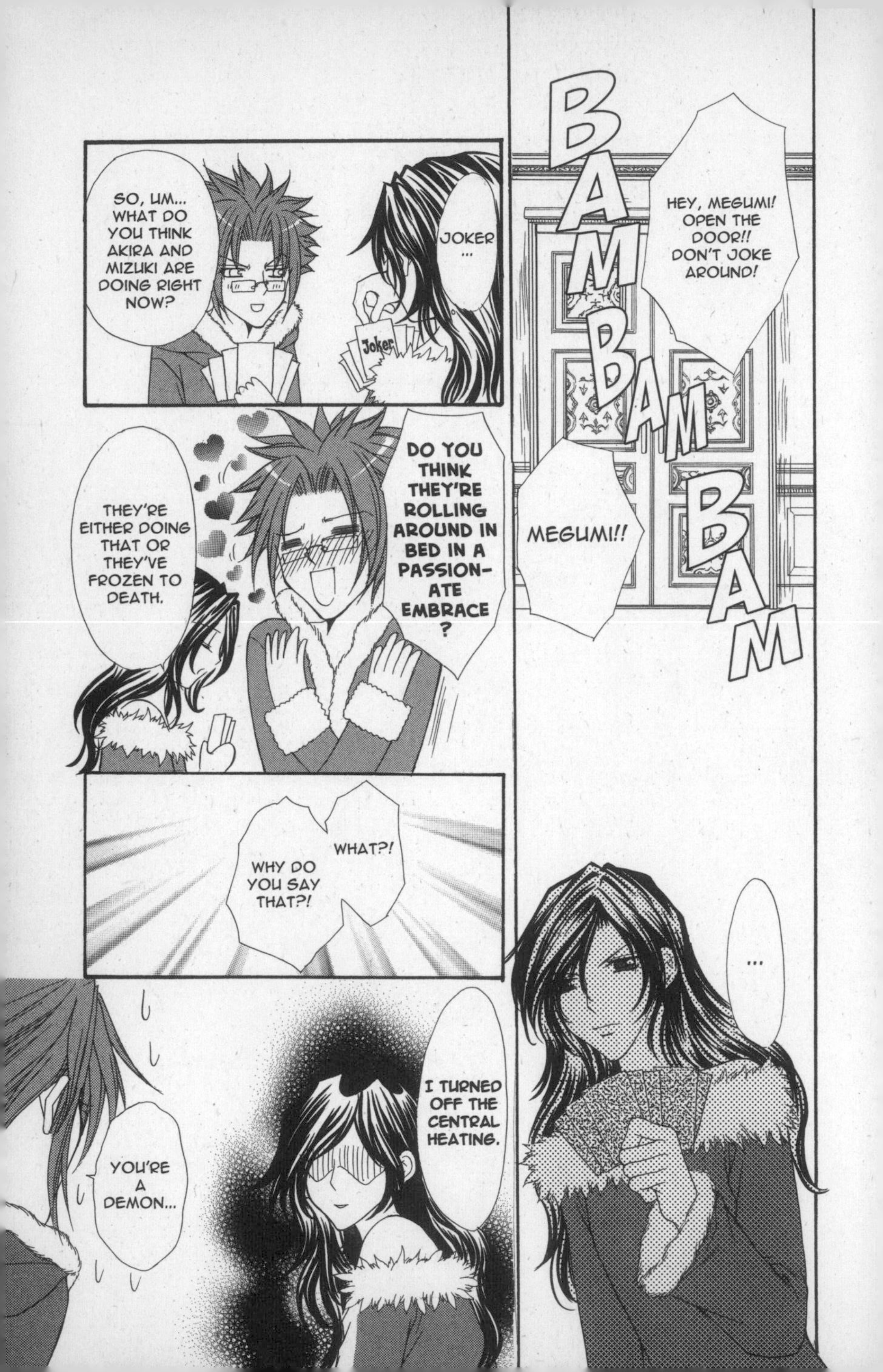
HEY, MEGUMI! OPEN THE DOOR!! DON'T JOKE AROUND!
BAM BAM BAM BAM
MEGUMI!!
...
JOKER ...
SO, UM... WHAT DO YOU THINK AKIRA AND MIZUKI ARE DOING RIGHT NOW?
DO YOU THINK THEY'RE ROLLING AROUND IN BED IN A PASSION-ATE EMBRACE ?
THEY'RE EITHER DOING THAT OR THEY'VE FROZEN TO DEATH.
WHAT?!
WHY DO YOU SAY THAT?!
I TURNED OFF THE CENTRAL HEATING.
YOU'RE A DEMON...

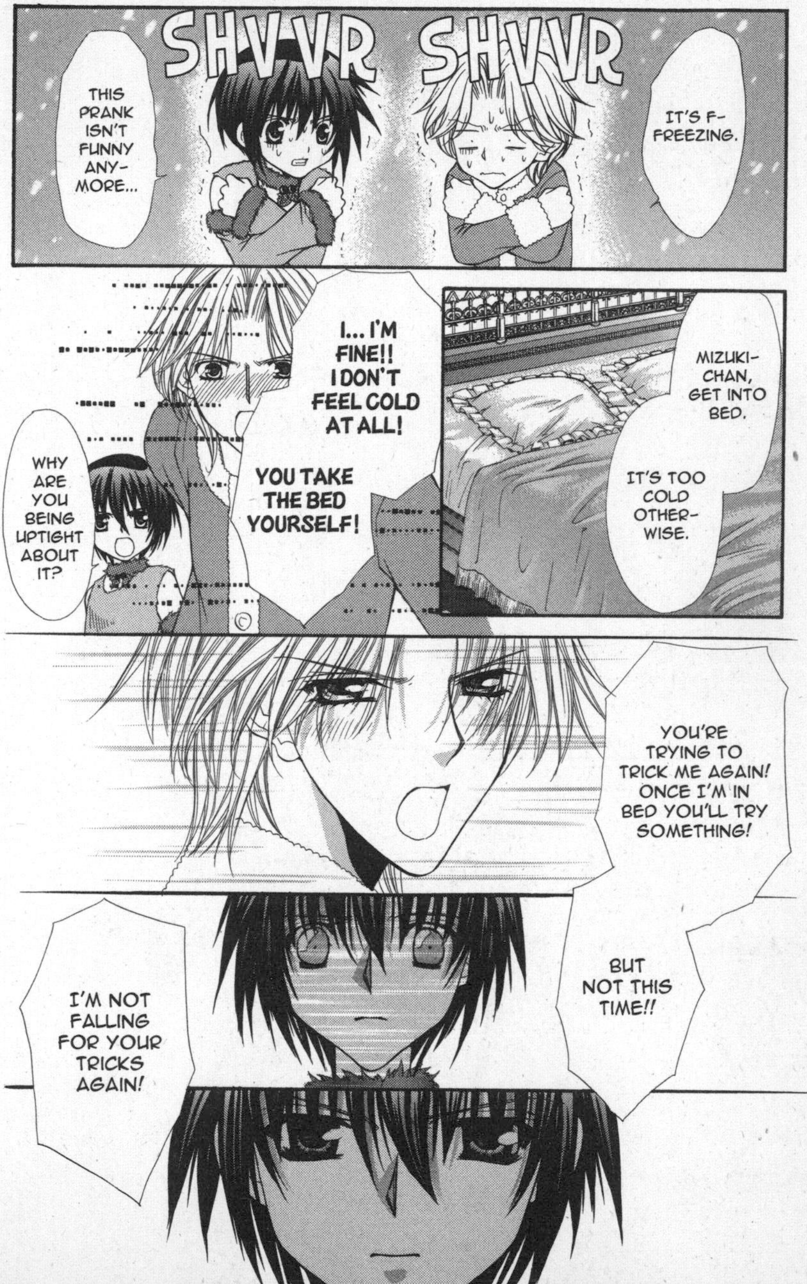
SHVVR SHVVR
IT'S F-FREEZING.
THIS PRANK ISN'T FUNNY ANYMORE...
MIZUKI-CHAN, GET INTO BED.
IT'S TOO COLD OTHERWISE.
I... I'M FINE!! I DON'T FEEL COLD AT ALL!
YOU TAKE THE BED YOURSELF!
WHY ARE YOU BEING UPTIGHT ABOUT IT?
YOU'RE TRYING TO TRICK ME AGAIN! ONCE I'M IN BED YOU'LL TRY SOMETHING!
BUT NOT THIS TIME!!
I'M NOT FALLING FOR YOUR TRICKS AGAIN!

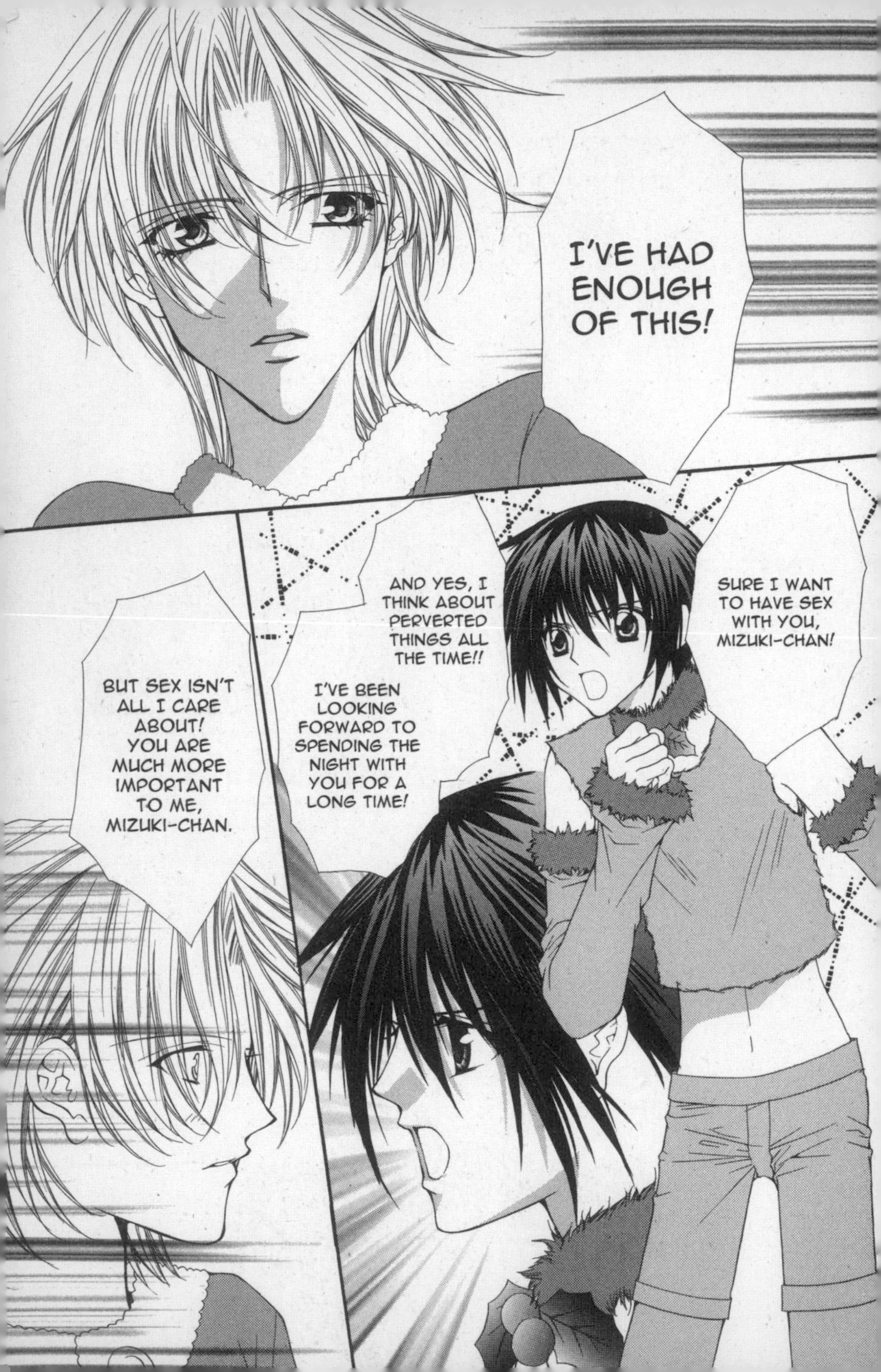
I'VE HAD ENOUGH OF THIS!
SURE I WANT TO HAVE SEX WITH YOU, MIZUKI-CHAN!
AND YES, I THINK ABOUT PERVERTED THINGS ALL THE TIME!!
I'VE BEEN LOOKING FORWARD TO SPENDING THE NIGHT WITH YOU FOR A LONG TIME!
BUT SEX ISN'T ALL I CARE ABOUT! YOU ARE MUCH MORE IMPORTANT TO ME, MIZUKI-CHAN.

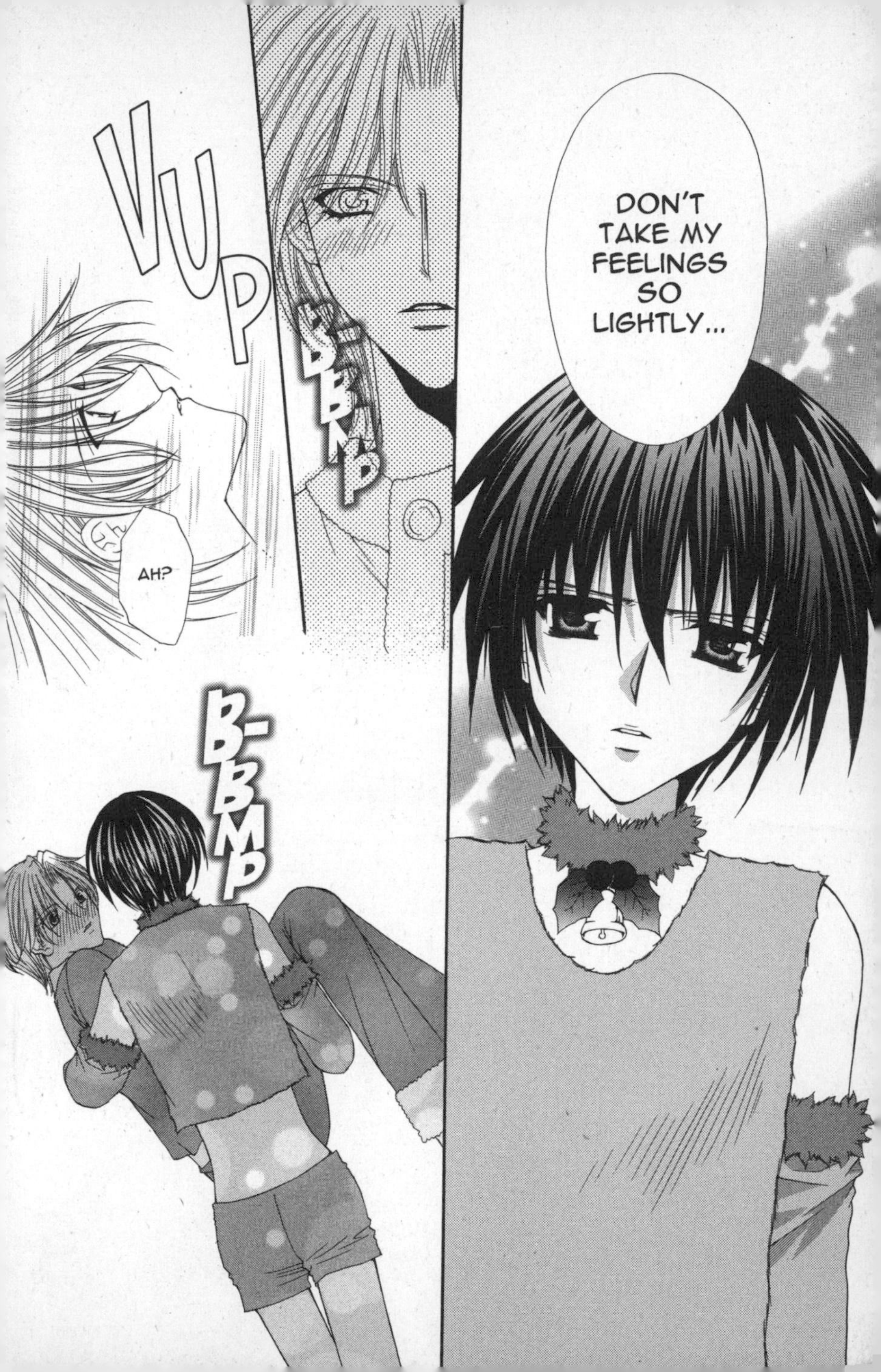
DON'T TAKE MY FEELINGS SO LIGHTLY...
B-BUMP
VUP
AH?
B-BUMP

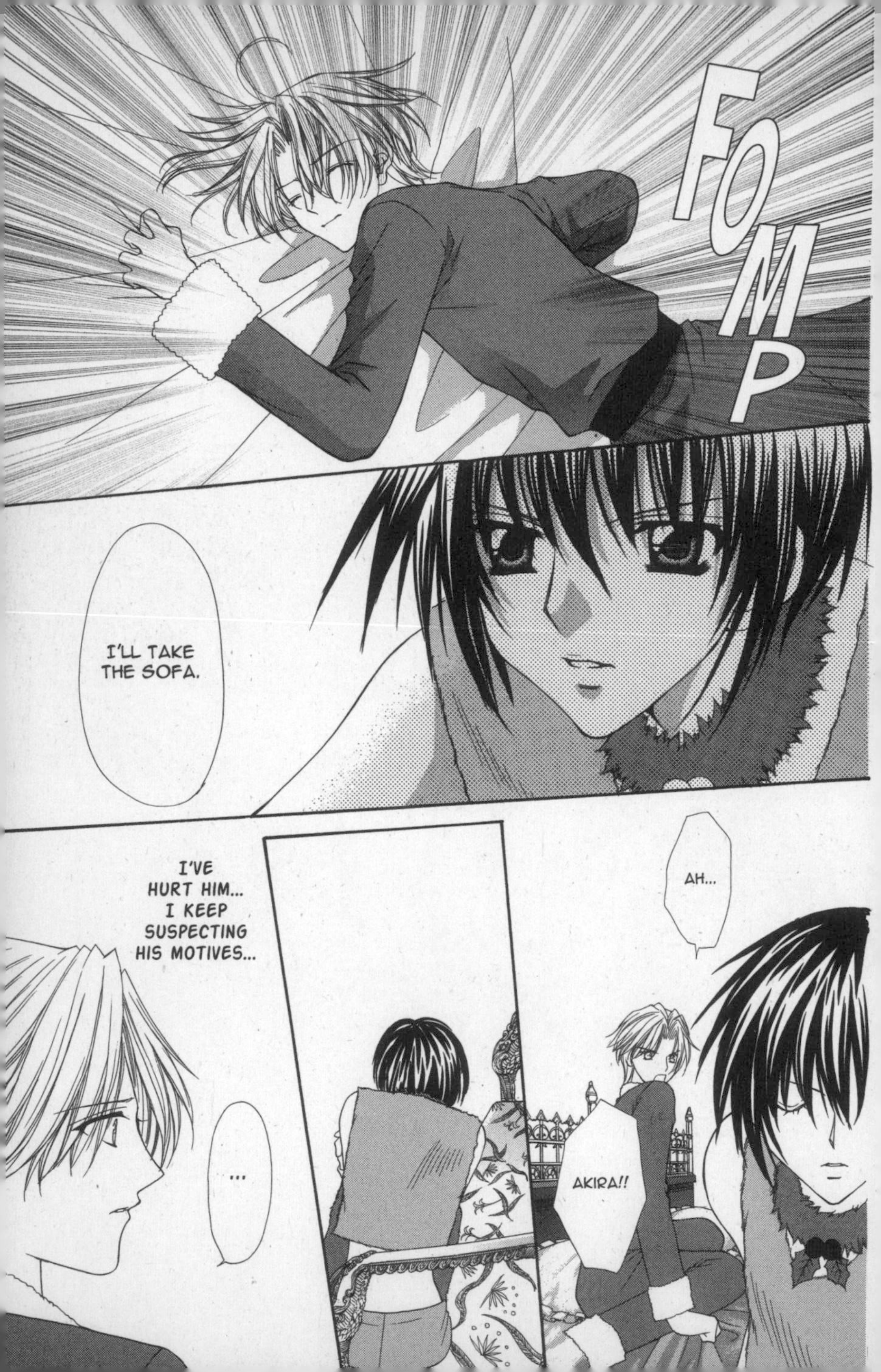
FOMP
I'LL TAKE THE SOFA.
AH...
AKIRA!!
I'VE HURT HIM... I KEEP SUSPECTING HIS MOTIVES...
...

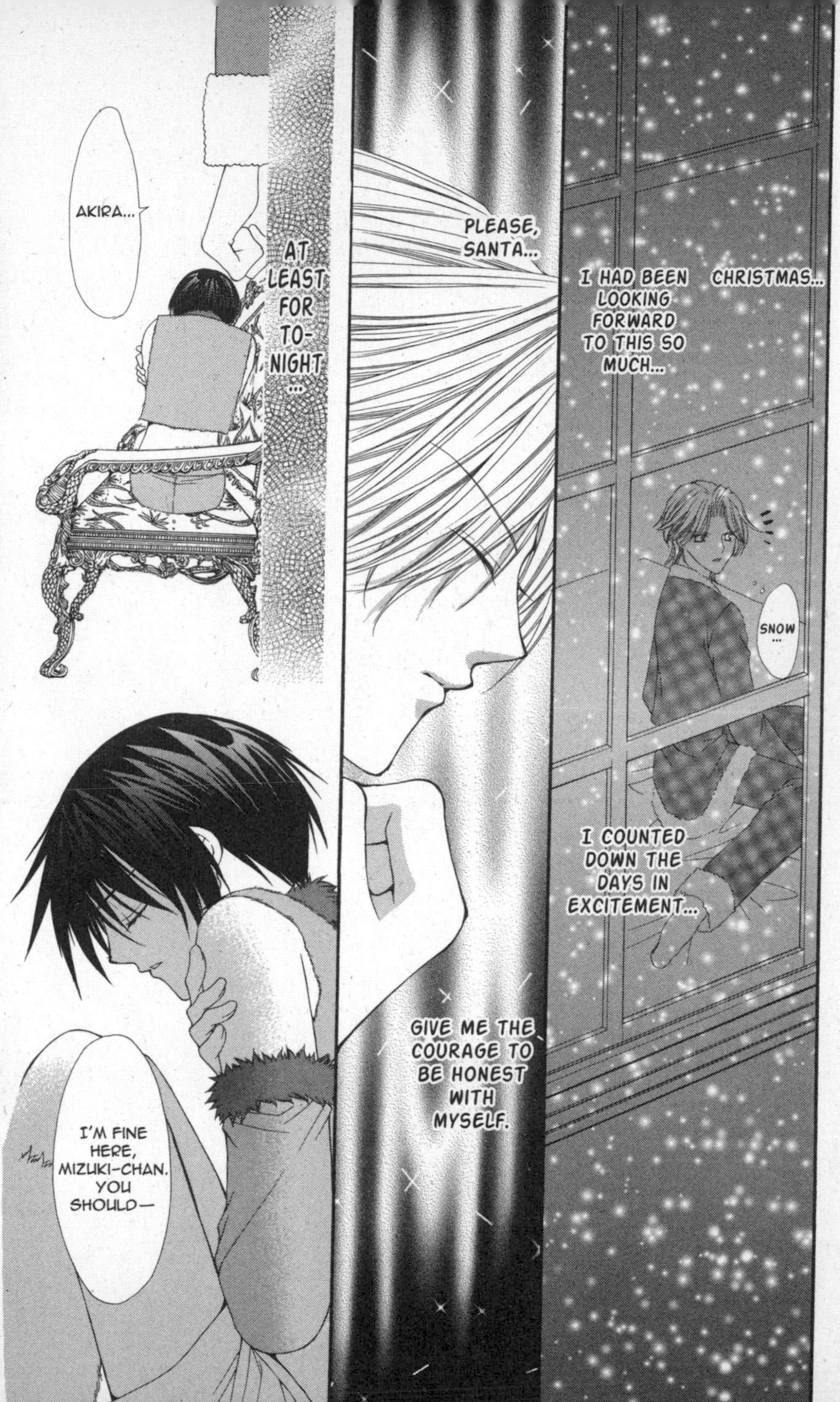
CHRISTMAS...
I HAD BEEN LOOKING FORWARD TO THIS SO MUCH...
SNOW...
I COUNTED DOWN THE DAYS IN EXCITEMENT...
PLEASE, SANTA...
GIVE ME THE COURAGE TO BE HONEST WITH MYSELF.
AT LEAST FOR TO-NIGHT...
AKIRA...
I'M FINE HERE, MIZUKI-CHAN. YOU SHOULD—

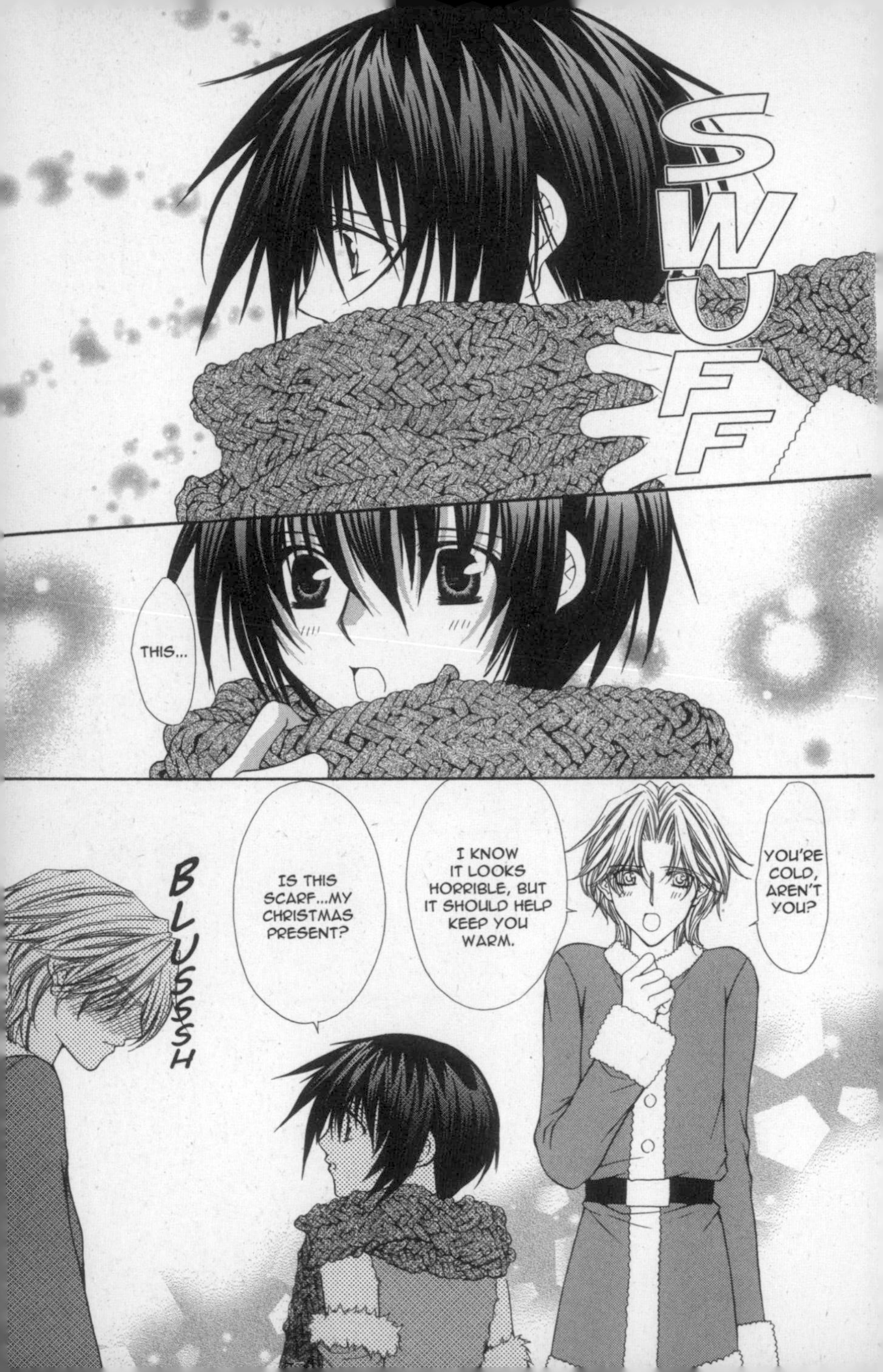
SWUFF
THIS...
YOU'RE COLD, AREN'T YOU?
I KNOW IT LOOKS HORRIBLE, BUT IT SHOULD HELP KEEP YOU WARM.
IS THIS SCARF...MY CHRISTMAS PRESENT?
BLUSSSH

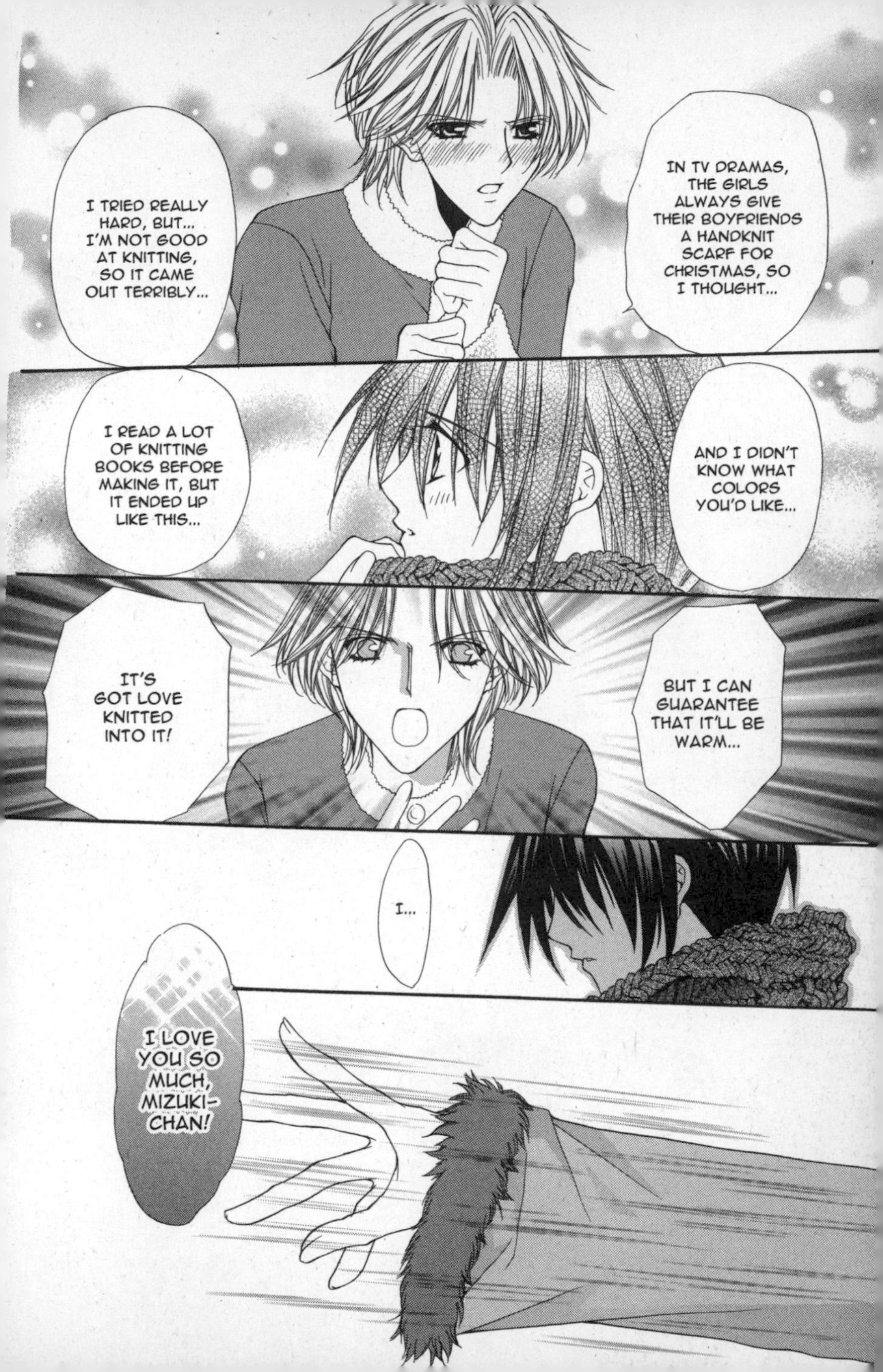
IN TV DRAMAS, THE GIRLS ALWAYS GIVE THEIR BOYFRIENDS A HANDKNIT SCARF FOR CHRISTMAS, SO I THOUGHT...
I TRIED REALLY HARD, BUT... I'M NOT GOOD AT KNITTING, SO IT CAME OUT TERRIBLY...
AND I DIDN'T KNOW WHAT COLORS YOU'D LIKE...
I READ A LOT OF KNITTING BOOKS BEFORE MAKING IT, BUT IT ENDED UP LIKE THIS...
BUT I CAN GUARANTEE THAT IT'LL BE WARM...
IT'S GOT LOVE KNITTED INTO IT!
I...
I LOVE YOU SO MUCH, MIZUKI-CHAN!

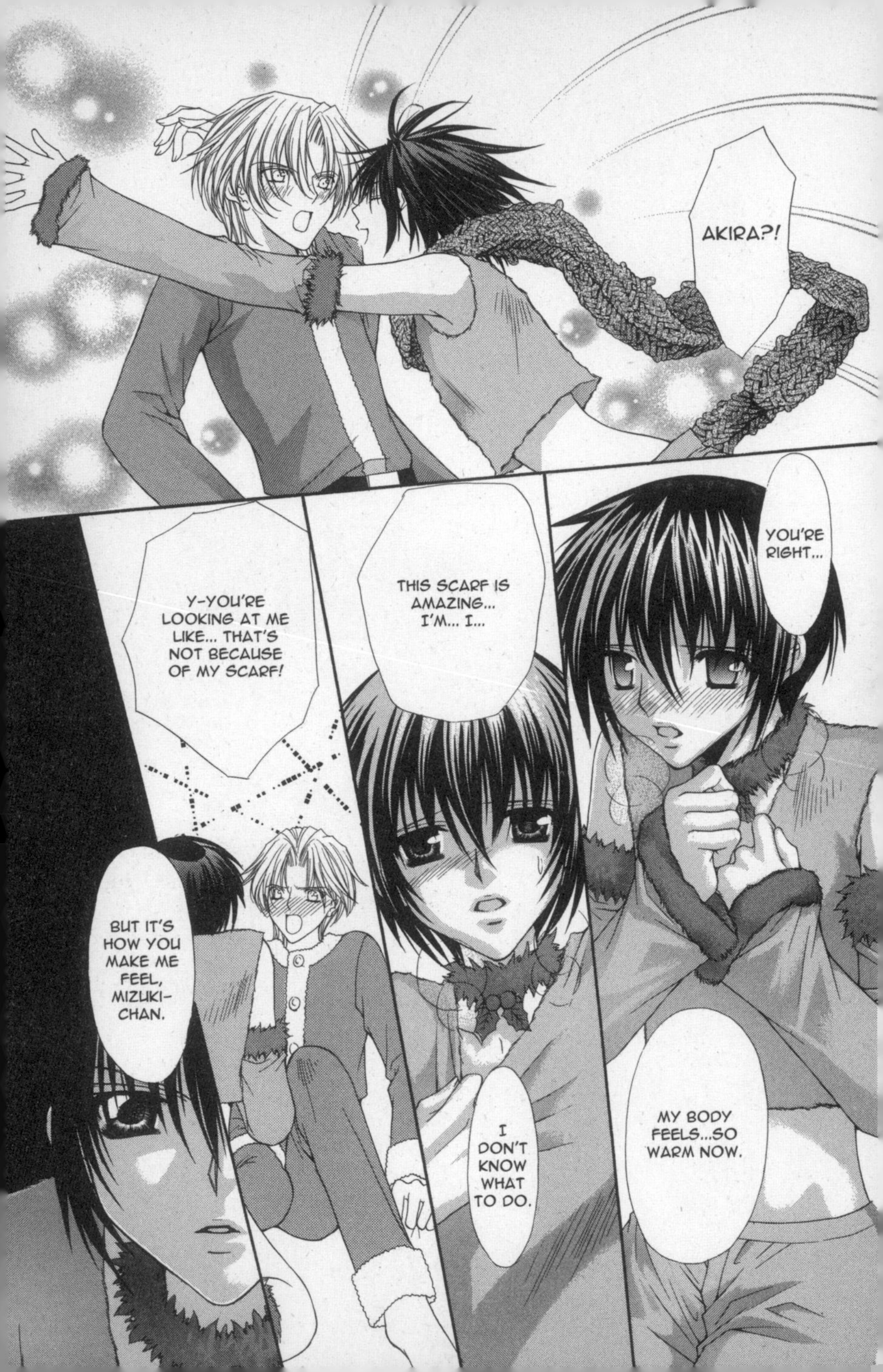
AKIRA?!
YOU'RE RIGHT...
MY BODY FEELS...SO WARM NOW.
THIS SCARF IS AMAZING... I'M... I...
I DON'T KNOW WHAT TO DO.
Y-YOU'RE LOOKING AT ME LIKE... THAT'S NOT BECAUSE OF MY SCARF!
BUT IT'S HOW YOU MAKE ME FEEL, MIZUKI-CHAN.

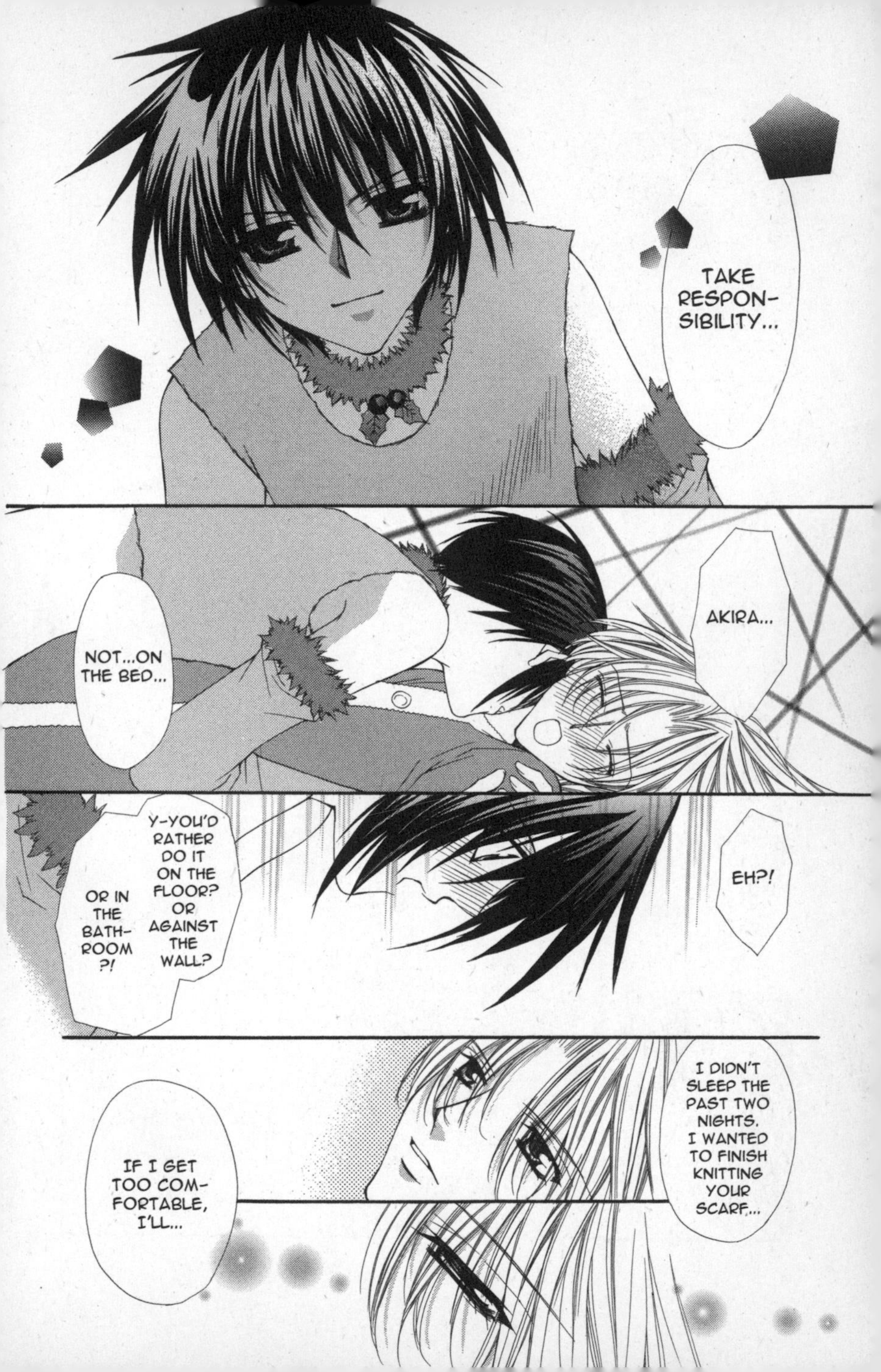
TAKE RESPON-SIBILITY...
AKIRA...
NOT...ON THE BED...
EH?!
Y-YOU'D RATHER DO IT ON THE FLOOR? OR AGAINST THE WALL?
OR IN THE BATH-ROOM?!
I DIDN'T SLEEP THE PAST TWO NIGHTS. I WANTED TO FINISH KNITTING YOUR SCARF,...
IF I GET TOO COM-FORTABLE, I'LL...

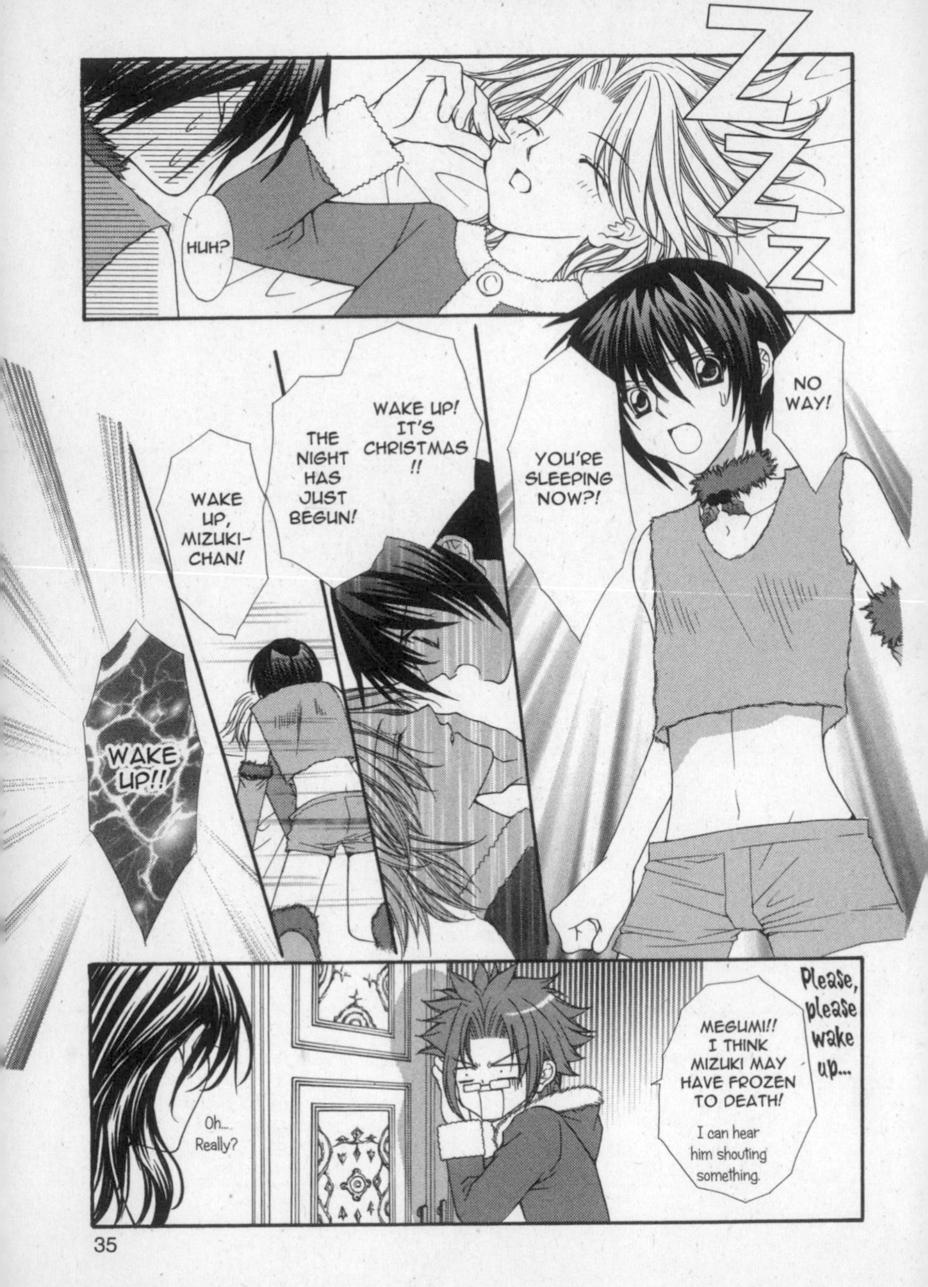
ZZZ
HUH?
NO WAY!
YOU'RE SLEEPING NOW?!
WAKE UP! IT'S CHRISTMAS!!
THE NIGHT HAS JUST BEGUN!
WAKE UP, MIZUKI-CHAN!
WAKE UP!!
Please, please wake up...
MEGUMI!! I THINK MIZUKI MAY HAVE FROZEN TO DEATH!
I can hear him shouting something.
Oh... Really?

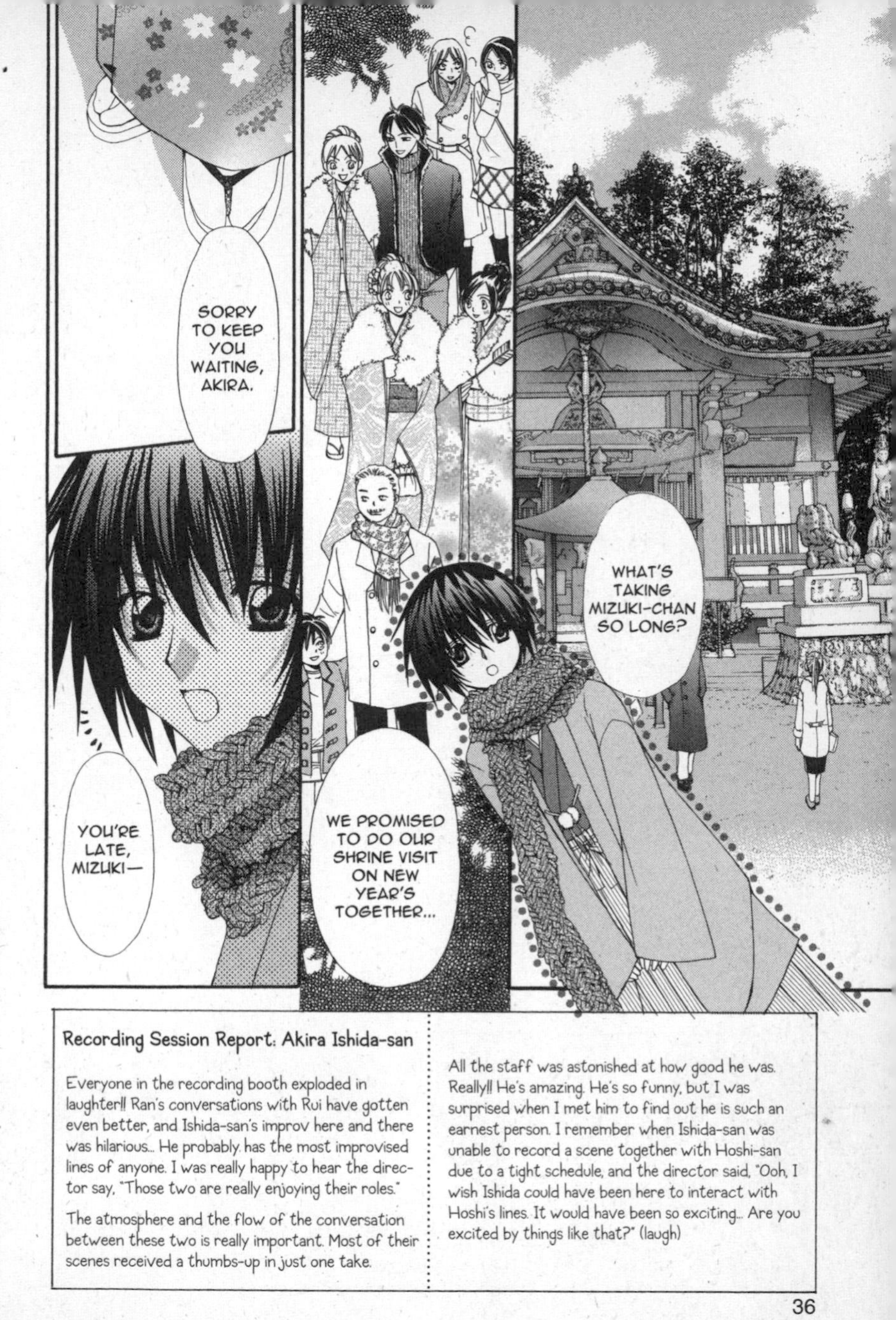
WHAT'S TAKING MIZUKI-CHAN SO LONG?
WE PROMISED TO DO OUR SHRINE VISIT ON NEW YEAR'S TOGETHER...
SORRY TO KEEP YOU WAITING, AKIRA.
YOU'RE LATE, MIZUKI—

Recording Session Report: Akira Ishida-san

Everyone in the recording booth exploded in laughter!! Ran's conversations with Rui have gotten even better, and Ishida-san's improv here and there was hilarious... He probably has the most improvised lines of anyone. I was really happy to hear the director say, "Those two are really enjoying their roles."

The atmosphere and the flow of the conversation between these two is really important. Most of their scenes received a thumbs-up in just one take.

All the staff was astonished at how good he was. Really!! He's amazing. He's so funny, but I was surprised when I met him to find out he is such an earnest person. I remember when Ishida-san was unable to record a scene together with Hoshi-san due to a tight schedule, and the director said, "Ooh, I wish Ishida could have been here to interact with Hoshi's lines. It would have been so exciting... Are you excited by things like that?" (laugh)

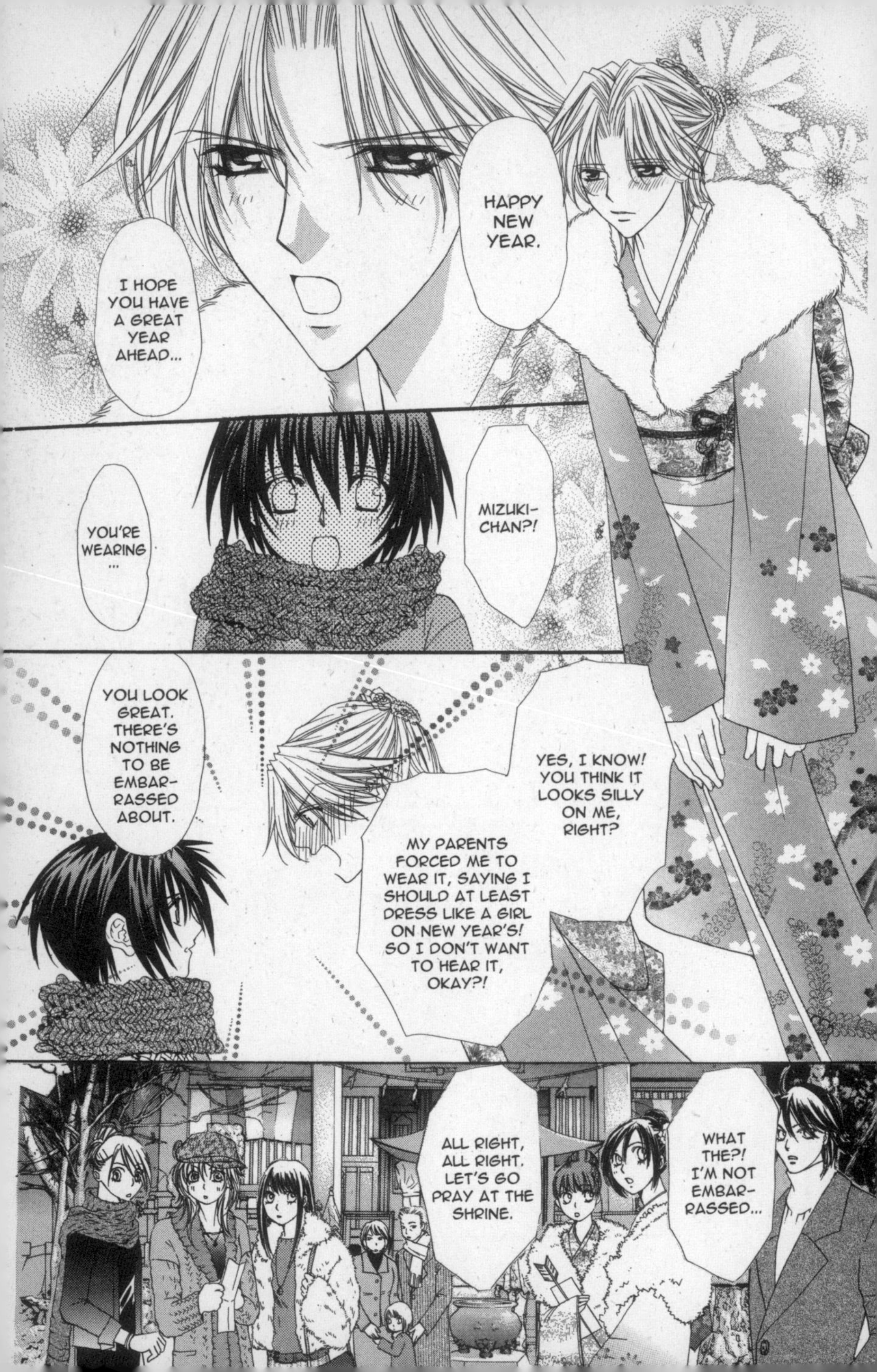
HAPPY NEW YEAR.
I HOPE YOU HAVE A GREAT YEAR AHEAD...
MIZUKI-CHAN?!
YOU'RE WEARING...
YES, I KNOW! YOU THINK IT LOOKS SILLY ON ME, RIGHT?
MY PARENTS FORCED ME TO WEAR IT, SAYING I SHOULD AT LEAST DRESS LIKE A GIRL ON NEW YEAR'S! SO I DON'T WANT TO HEAR IT, OKAY?!
YOU LOOK GREAT. THERE'S NOTHING TO BE EMBARRASSED ABOUT.
WHAT THE?! I'M NOT EMBARRASSED...
ALL RIGHT, ALL RIGHT. LET'S GO PRAY AT THE SHRINE.

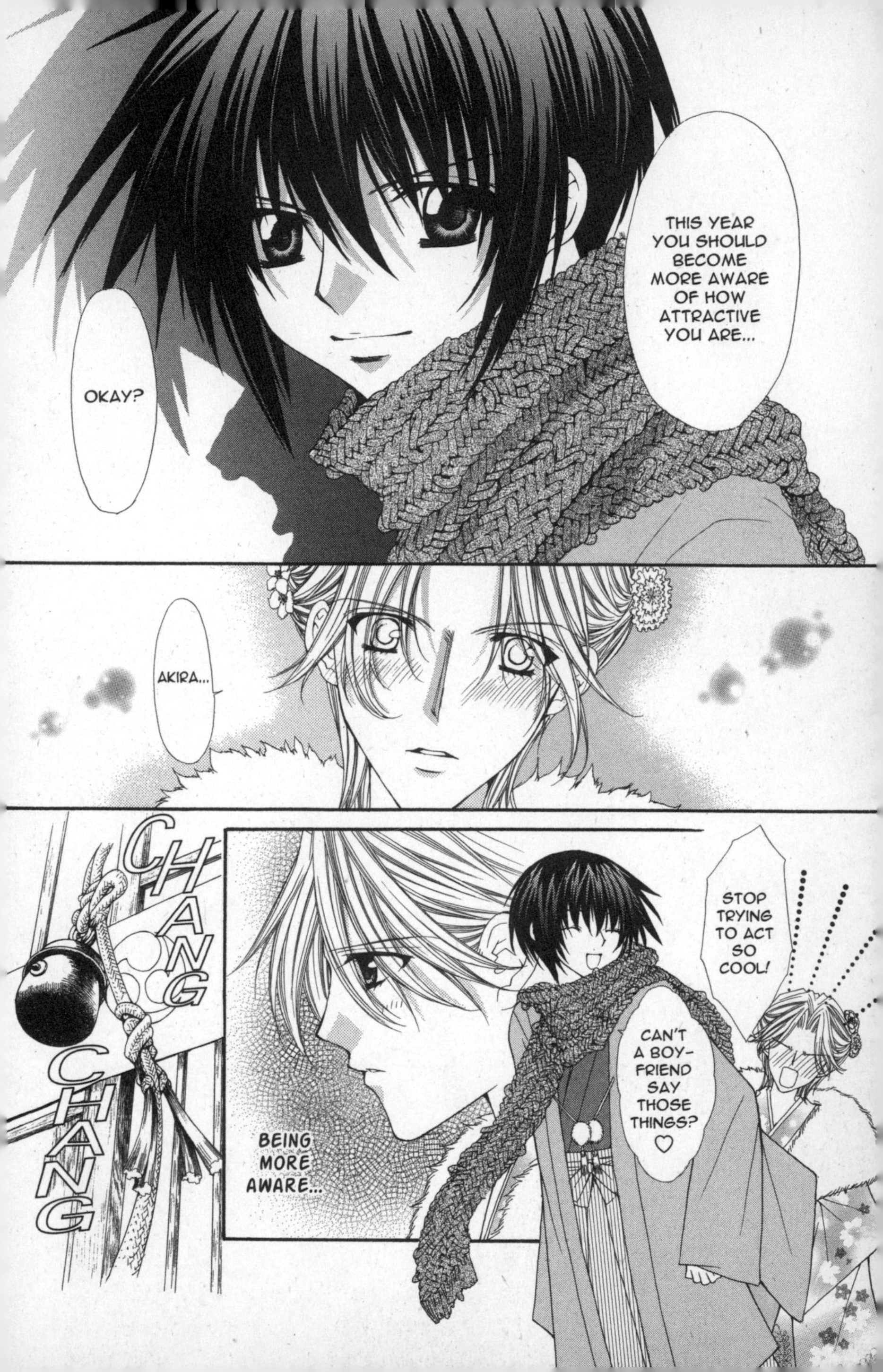
THIS YEAR YOU SHOULD BECOME MORE AWARE OF HOW ATTRACTIVE YOU ARE...
OKAY?
AKIRA...
STOP TRYING TO ACT SO COOL!
CAN'T A BOY-FRIEND SAY THOSE THINGS? ♡
BEING MORE AWARE...
CHANG
CHANG

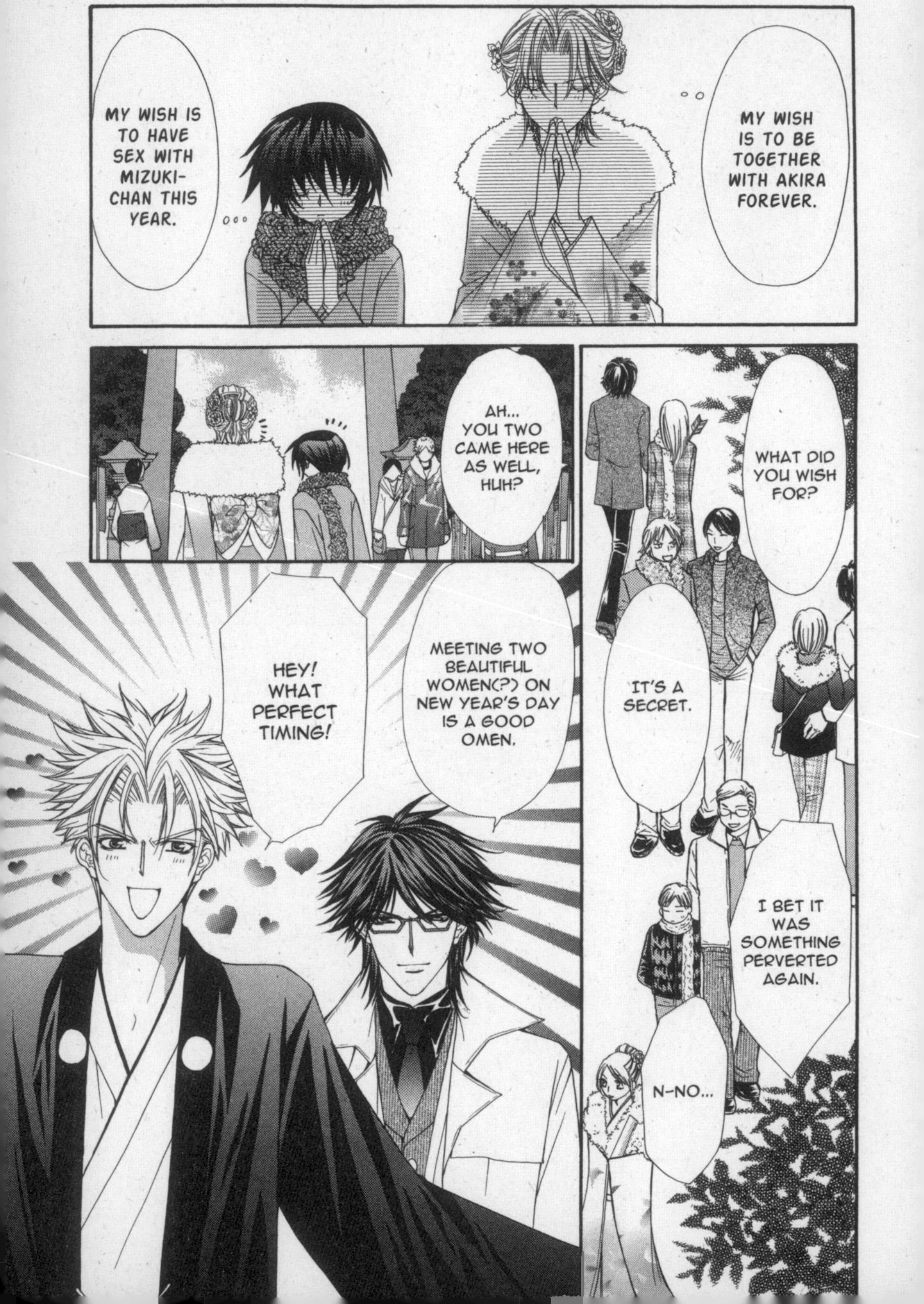
MY WISH IS TO BE TOGETHER WITH AKIRA FOREVER.
MY WISH IS TO HAVE SEX WITH MIZUKI-CHAN THIS YEAR.
WHAT DID YOU WISH FOR?
IT'S A SECRET.
I BET IT WAS SOMETHING PERVERTED AGAIN.
N-NO...
AH... YOU TWO CAME HERE AS WELL, HUH?
MEETING TWO BEAUTIFUL WOMEN(?) ON NEW YEAR'S DAY IS A GOOD OMEN.
HEY! WHAT PERFECT TIMING!

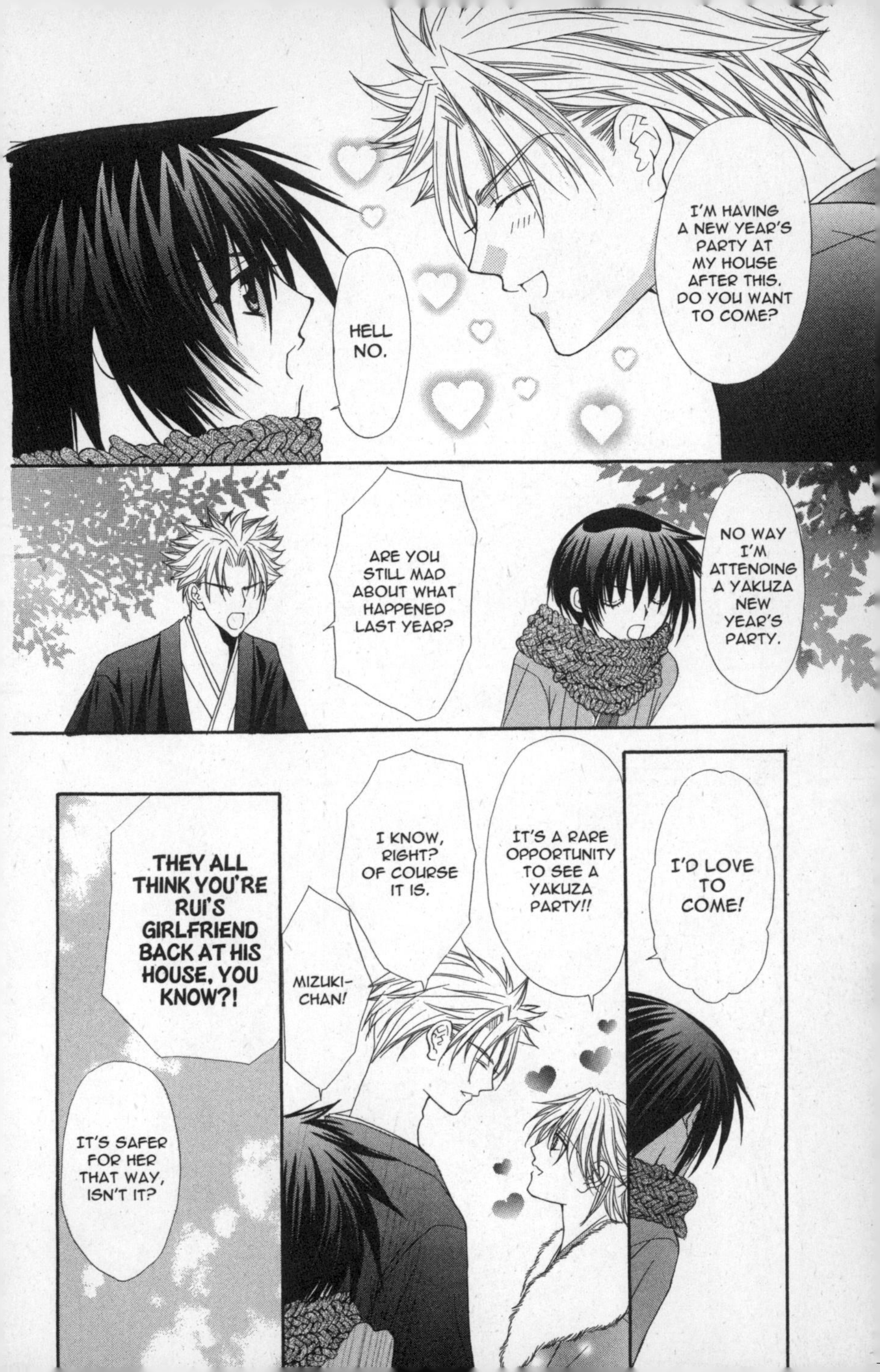
I'M HAVING A NEW YEAR'S PARTY AT MY HOUSE AFTER THIS. DO YOU WANT TO COME?
HELL NO.
NO WAY I'M ATTENDING A YAKUZA NEW YEAR'S PARTY.
ARE YOU STILL MAD ABOUT WHAT HAPPENED LAST YEAR?
I'D LOVE TO COME!
IT'S A RARE OPPORTUNITY TO SEE A YAKUZA PARTY!!
I KNOW, RIGHT? OF COURSE IT IS.
MIZUKI-CHAN!
THEY ALL THINK YOU'RE RUI'S GIRLFRIEND BACK AT HIS HOUSE, YOU KNOW?!
IT'S SAFER FOR HER THAT WAY, ISN'T IT?

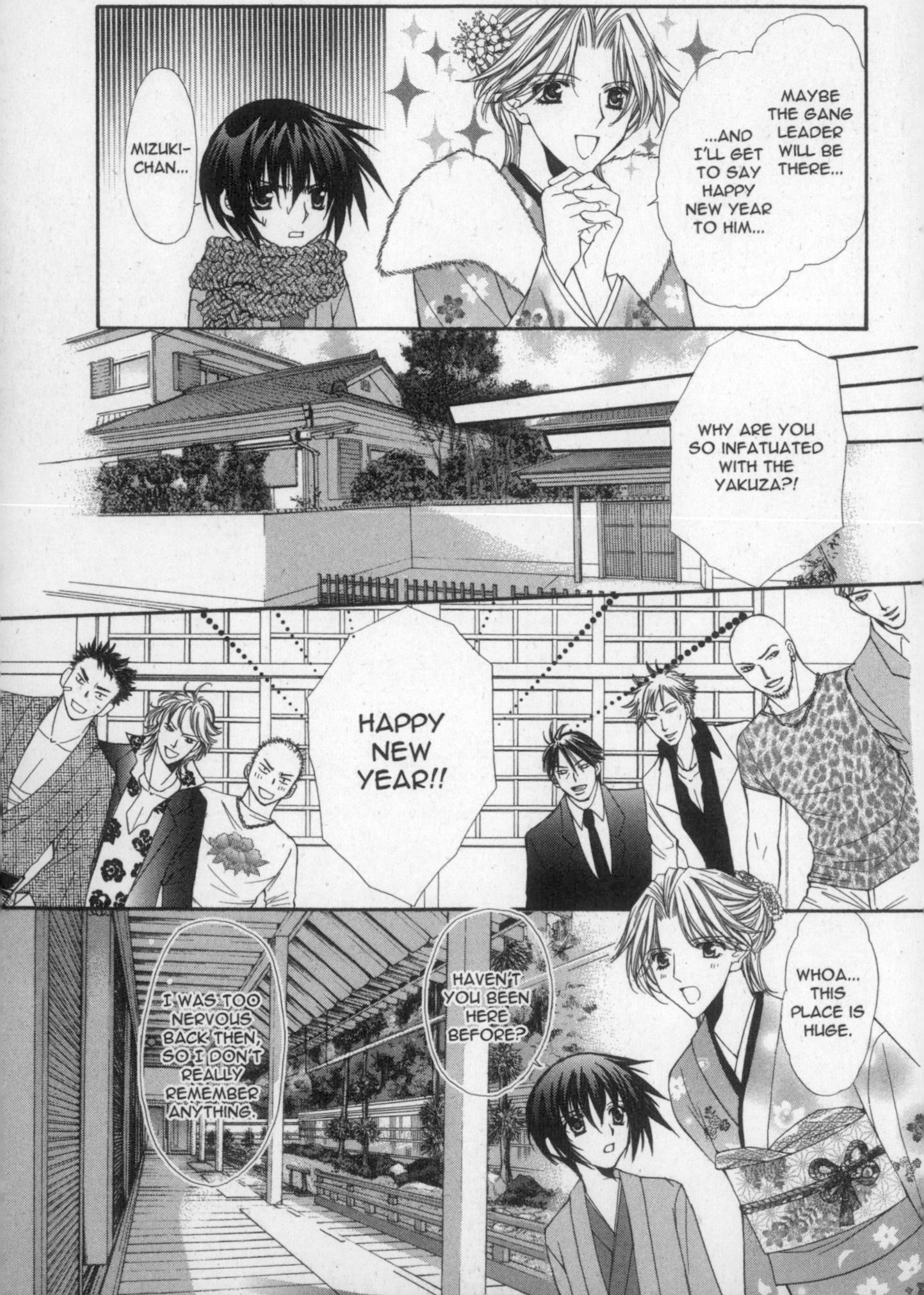
MAYBE THE GANG LEADER WILL BE THERE...
...AND I'LL GET TO SAY HAPPY NEW YEAR TO HIM...
MIZUKI-CHAN...
WHY ARE YOU SO INFATUATED WITH THE YAKUZA?!
HAPPY NEW YEAR!!
WHOA... THIS PLACE IS HUGE.
HAVEN'T YOU BEEN HERE BEFORE?
I WAS TOO NERVOUS BACK THEN, SO I DON'T REALLY REMEMBER ANYTHING.

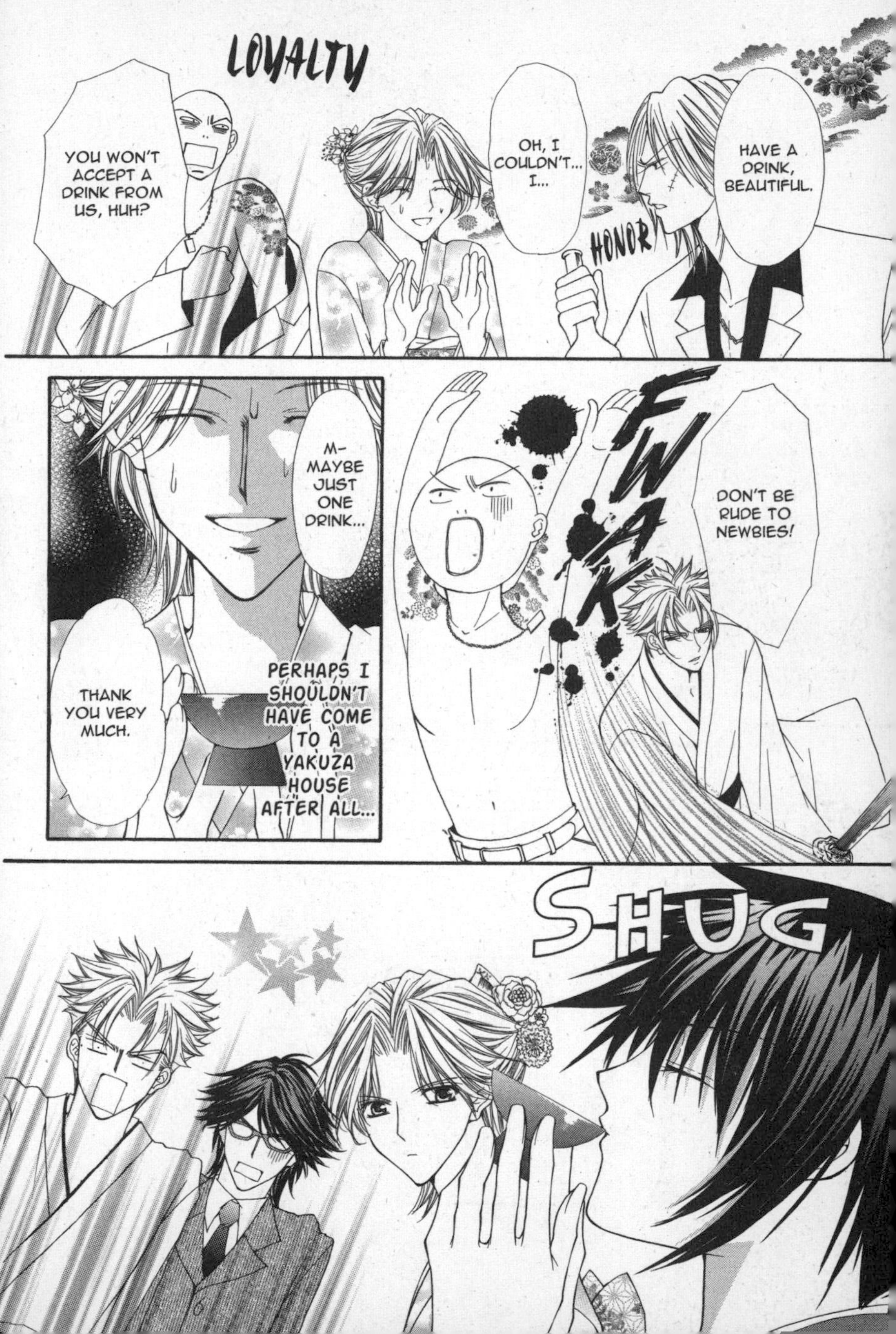
HAVE A DRINK, BEAUTIFUL.
HONOR
OH, I COULDN'T... I...
LOYALTY
YOU WON'T ACCEPT A DRINK FROM US, HUH?
DON'T BE RUDE TO NEWBIES!
FWAK
M-MAYBE JUST ONE DRINK...
PERHAPS I SHOULDN'T HAVE COME TO A YAKUZA HOUSE AFTER ALL...
THANK YOU VERY MUCH.
SHUG

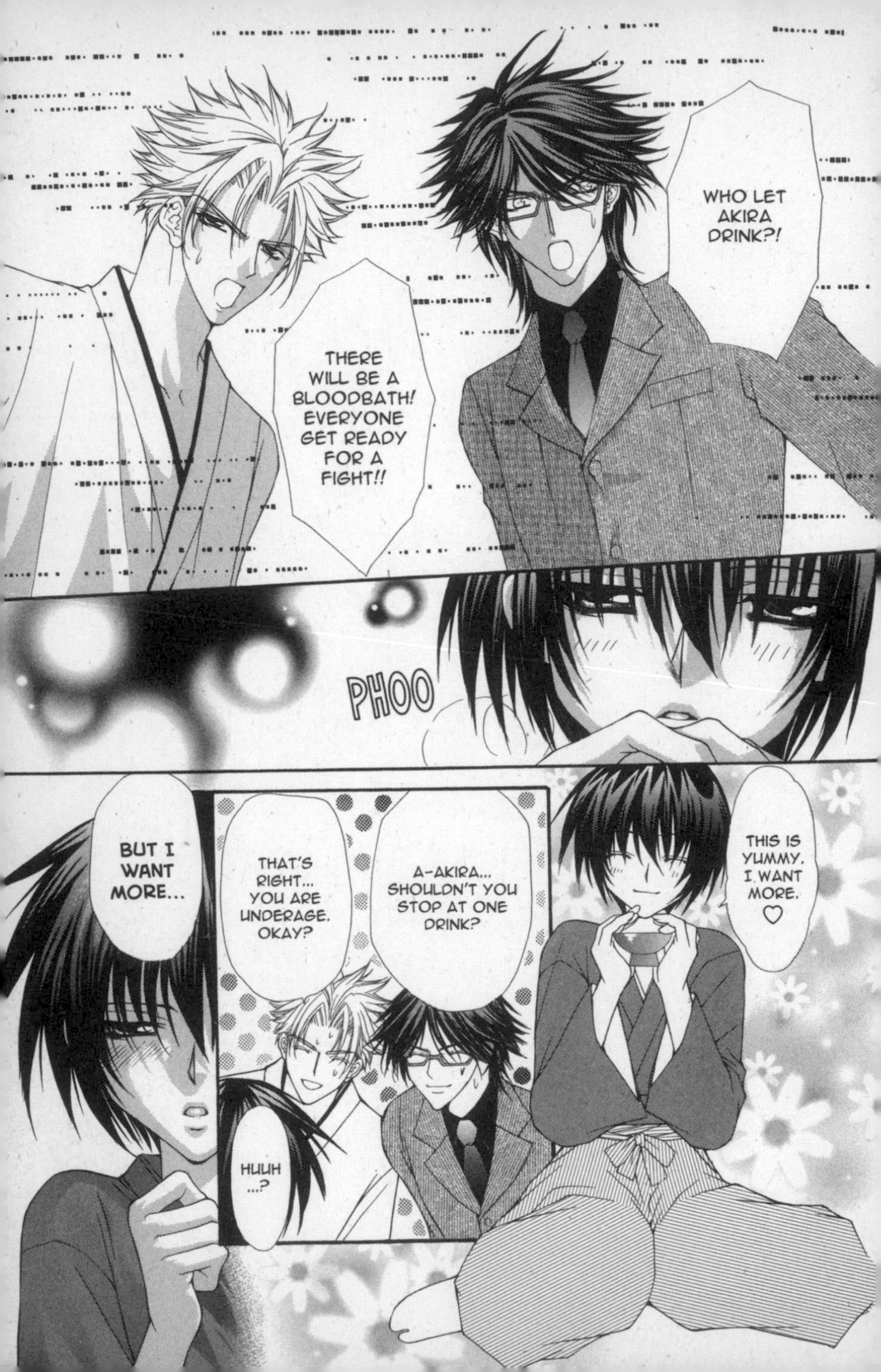
WHO LET AKIRA DRINK?!
THERE WILL BE A BLOODBATH! EVERYONE GET READY FOR A FIGHT!!
PHOO
THIS IS YUMMY. I WANT MORE. ♡
A-AKIRA... SHOULDN'T YOU STOP AT ONE DRINK?
THAT'S RIGHT... YOU ARE UNDERAGE. OKAY?
HUUH ...?
BUT I WANT MORE...

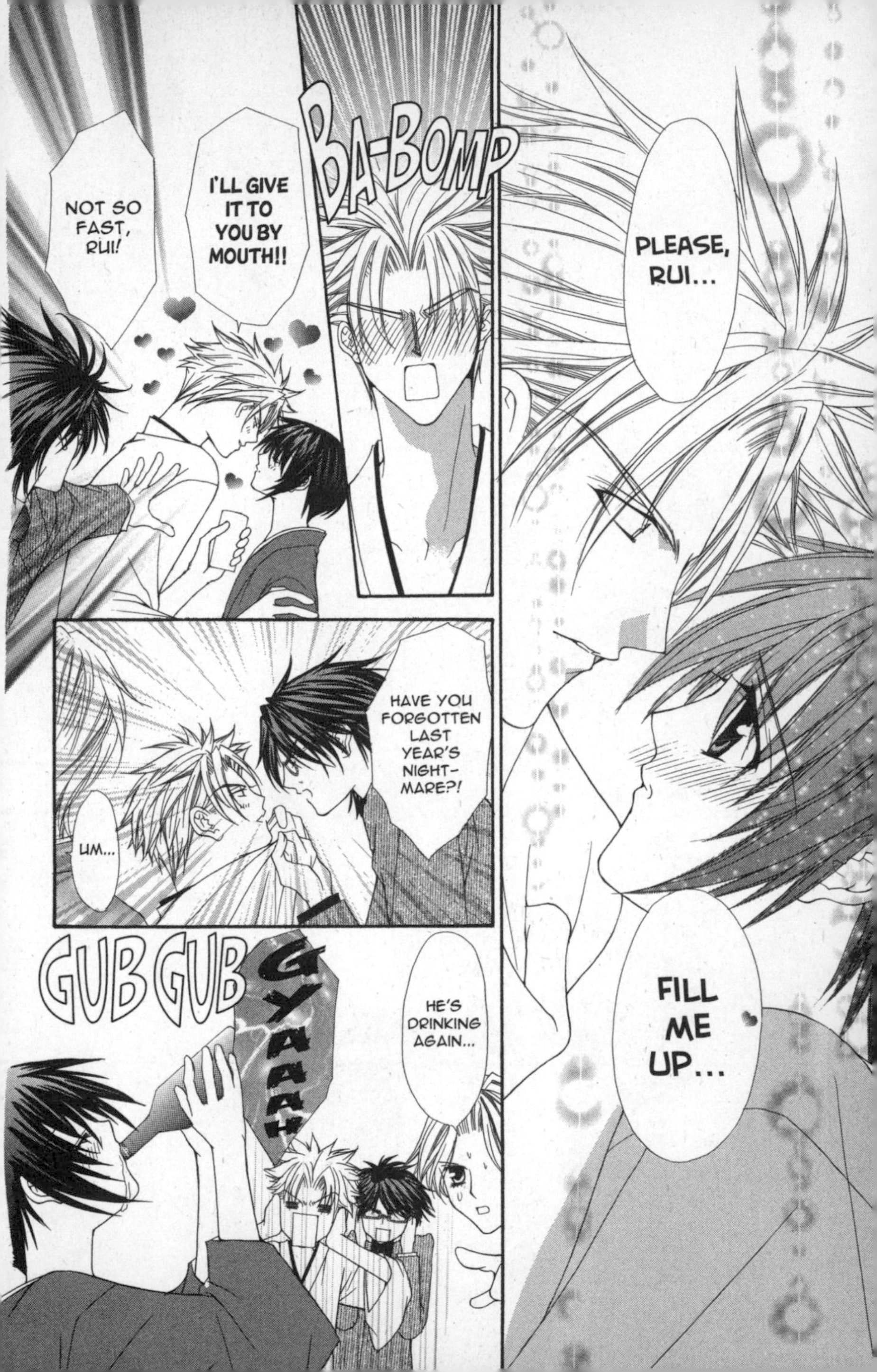
PLEASE, RUI...
FILL ME UP...
BA-BOMP
I'LL GIVE IT TO YOU BY MOUTH!!
NOT SO FAST, RUI!
HAVE YOU FORGOTTEN LAST YEAR'S NIGHT-MARE?!
UM...
HE'S DRINKING AGAIN...
GYAAAAH
GUB GUB

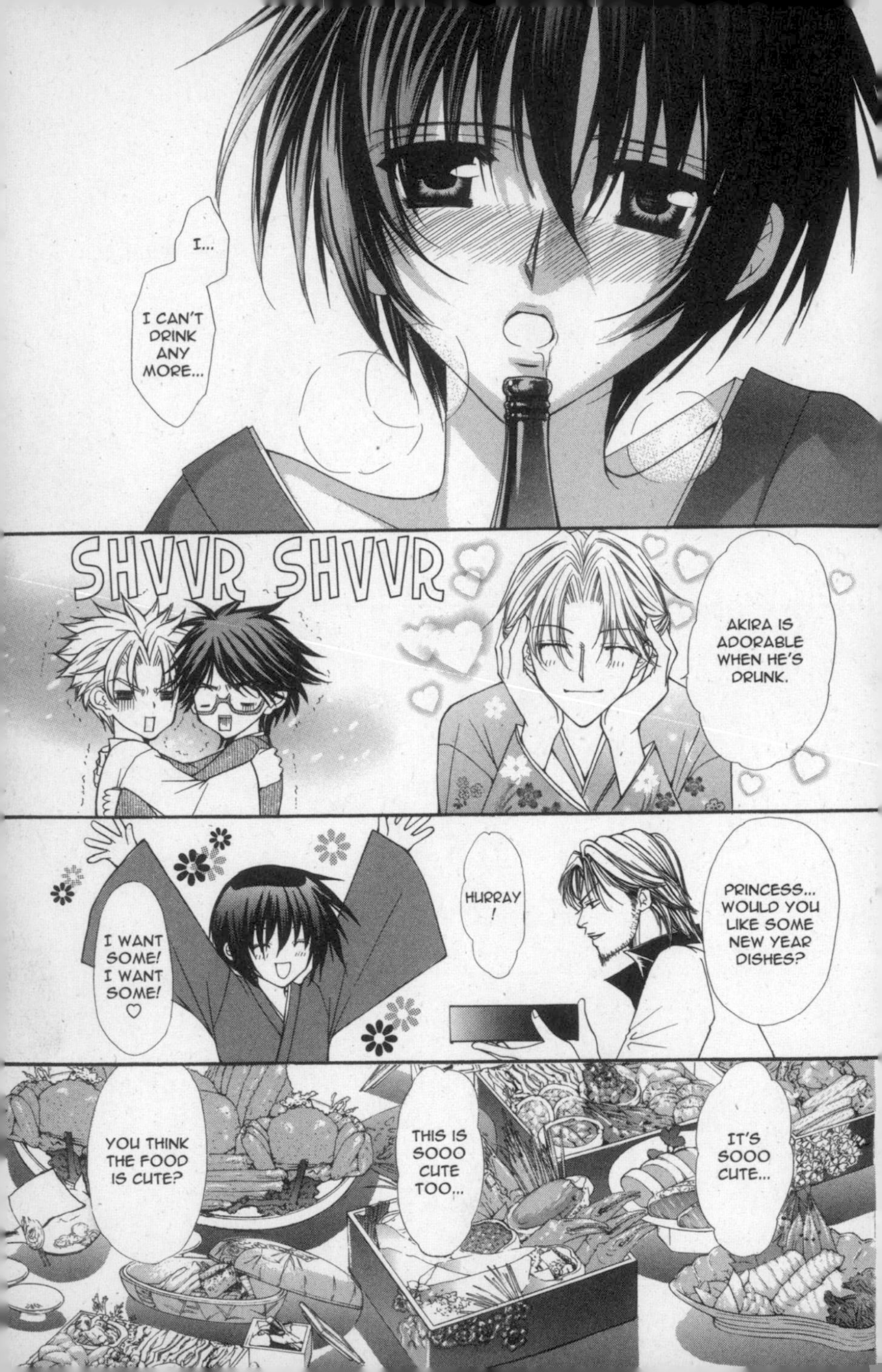
I...
I CAN'T DRINK ANY MORE...
AKIRA IS ADORABLE WHEN HE'S DRUNK.
SHVVR SHVVR
PRINCESS... WOULD YOU LIKE SOME NEW YEAR DISHES?
HURRAY!
I WANT SOME! I WANT SOME! ♡
IT'S SOOO CUTE...
THIS IS SOOO CUTE TOO...
YOU THINK THE FOOD IS CUTE?

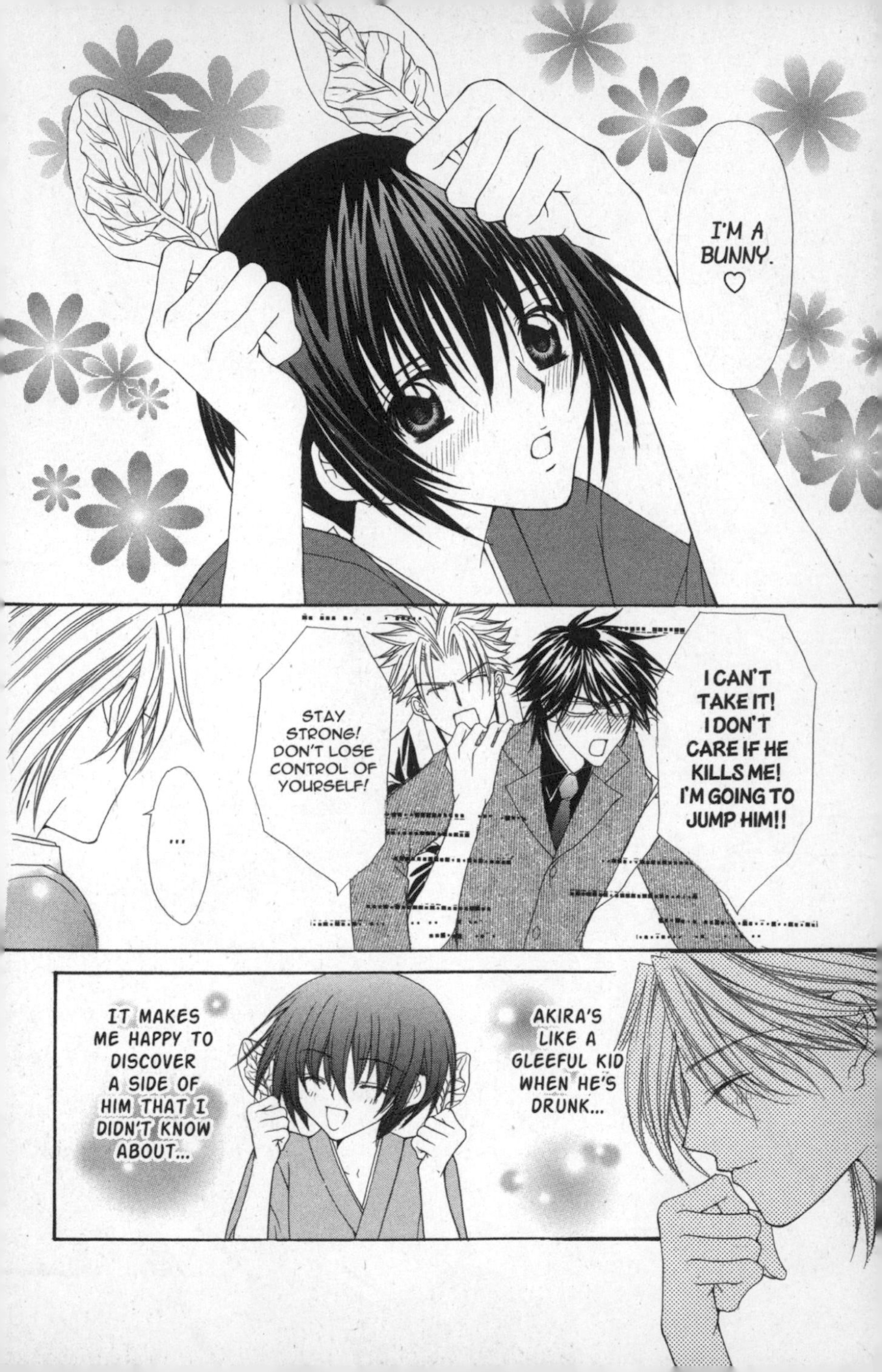
I'M A BUNNY. ♡
I CAN'T TAKE IT! I DON'T CARE IF HE KILLS ME! I'M GOING TO JUMP HIM!!
STAY STRONG! DON'T LOSE CONTROL OF YOURSELF!
...
AKIRA'S LIKE A GLEEFUL KID WHEN HE'S DRUNK...
IT MAKES ME HAPPY TO DISCOVER A SIDE OF HIM THAT I DIDN'T KNOW ABOUT...

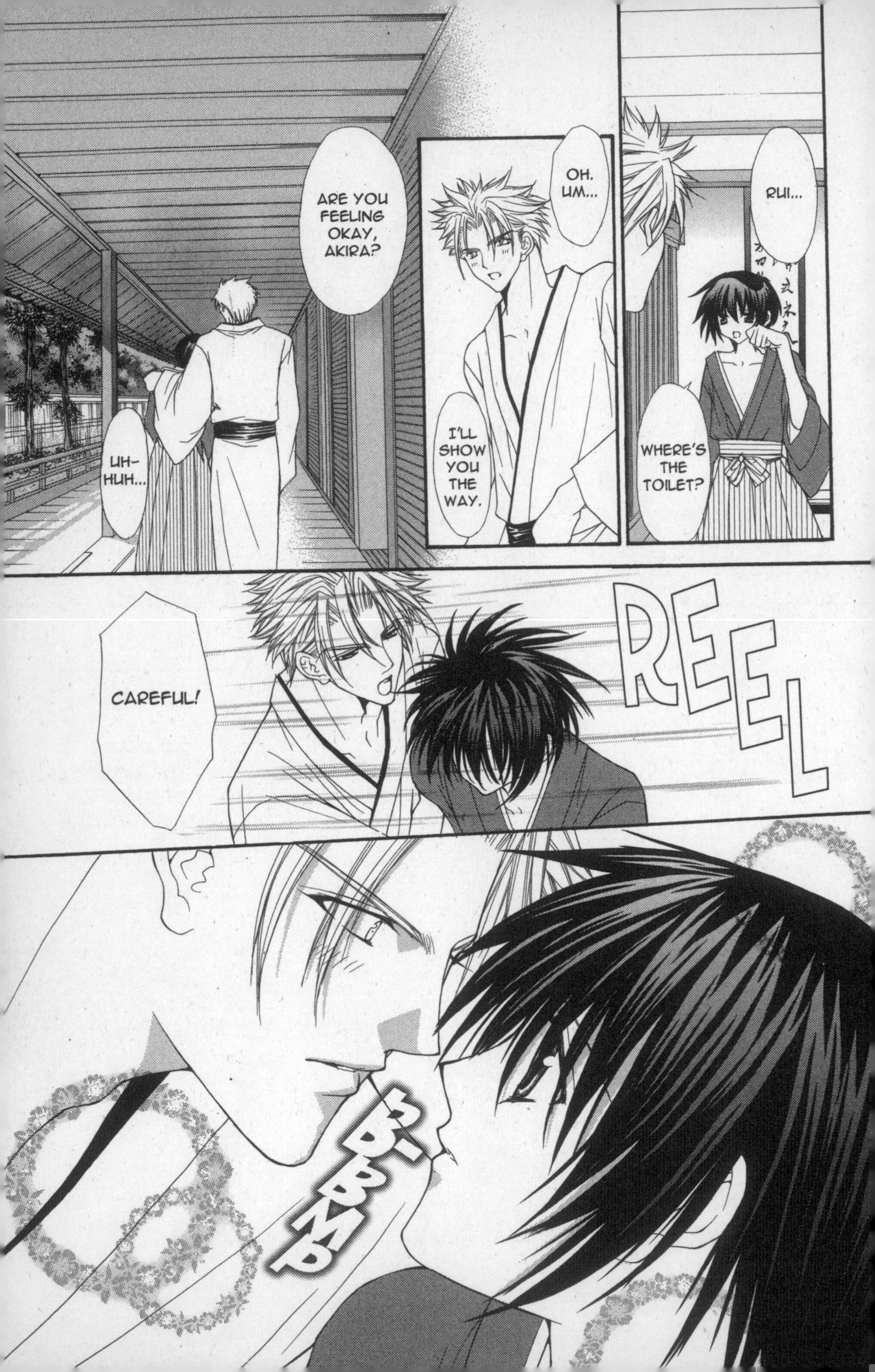
RUI...
WHERE'S THE TOILET?
OH. UM...
I'LL SHOW YOU THE WAY.
ARE YOU FEELING OKAY, AKIRA?
UH-HUH...
REEL
CAREFUL!
B-BMP

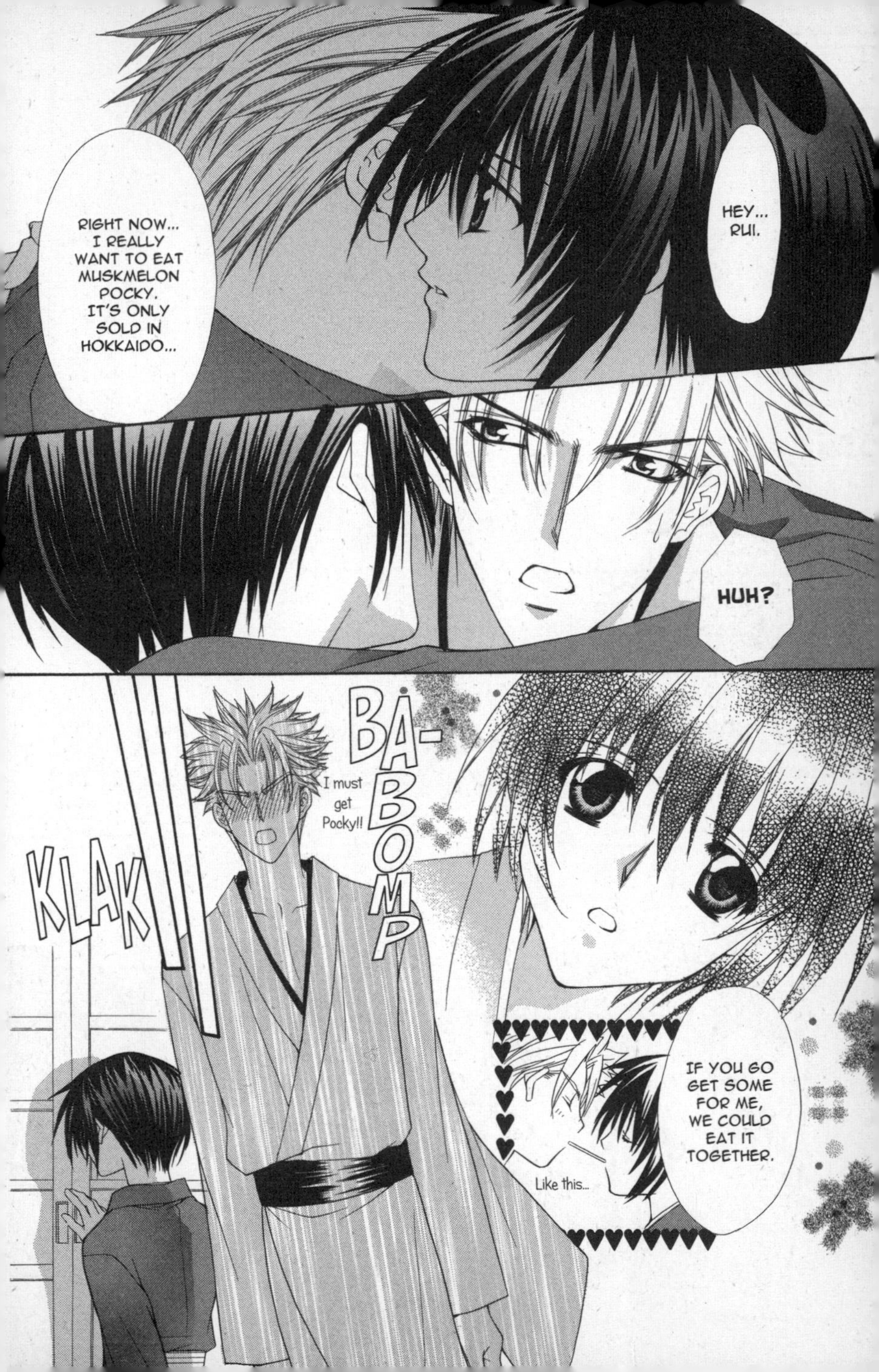
HEY... RUI.
RIGHT NOW... I REALLY WANT TO EAT MUSKMELON POCKY. IT'S ONLY SOLD IN HOKKAIDO...
HUH?
IF YOU GO GET SOME FOR ME, WE COULD EAT IT TOGETHER.
Like this...
BA-BOMP
I must get Pocky!!
KLAK

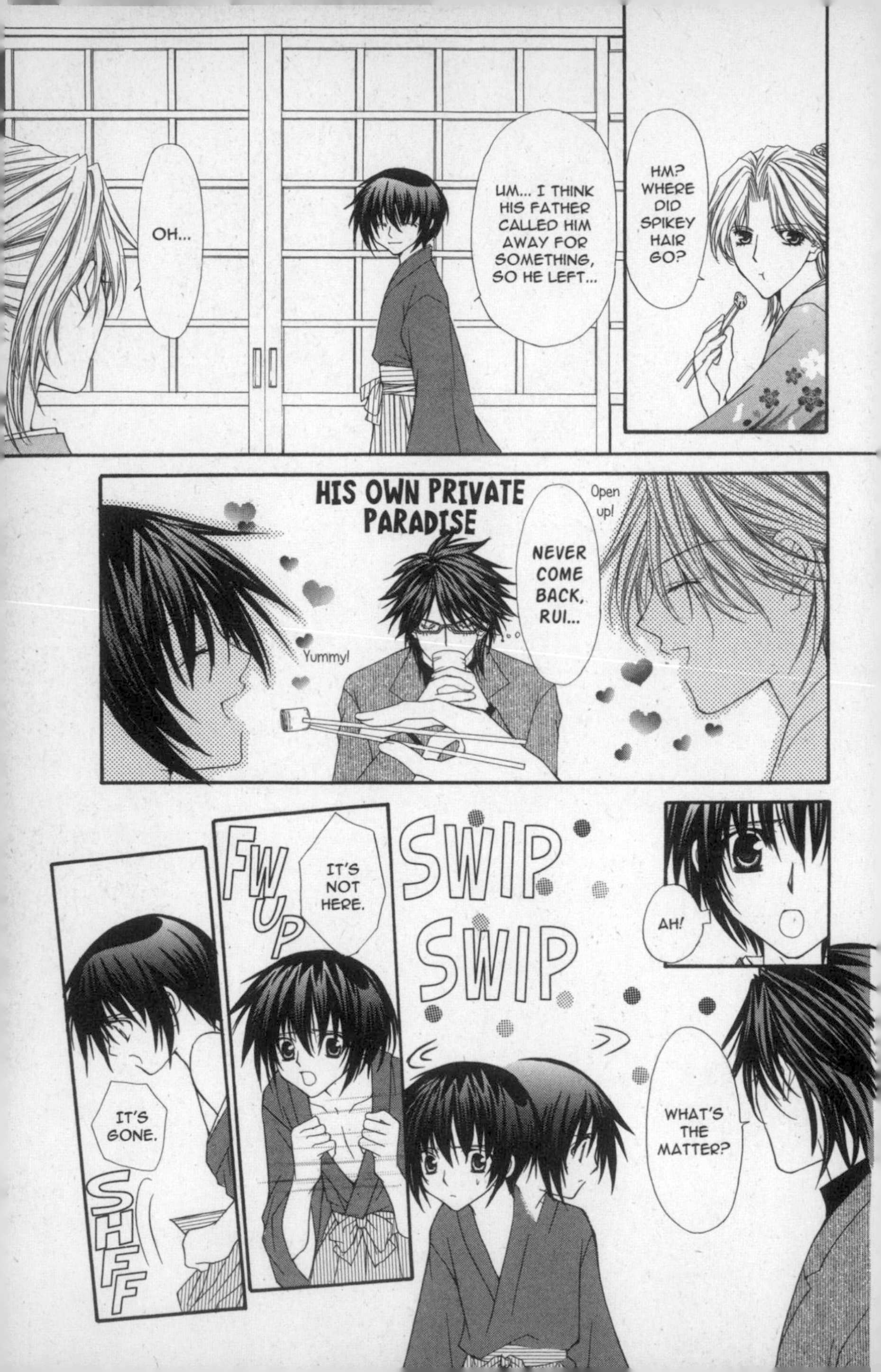
HM? WHERE DID SPIKEY HAIR GO?
UM... I THINK HIS FATHER CALLED HIM AWAY FOR SOMETHING, SO HE LEFT...
OH...
Open up!
NEVER COME BACK, RUI...
HIS OWN PRIVATE PARADISE
Yummy!
AH!
SWIP SWIP
WHAT'S THE MATTER?
FWUP
IT'S NOT HERE.
IT'S GONE.
SHFF

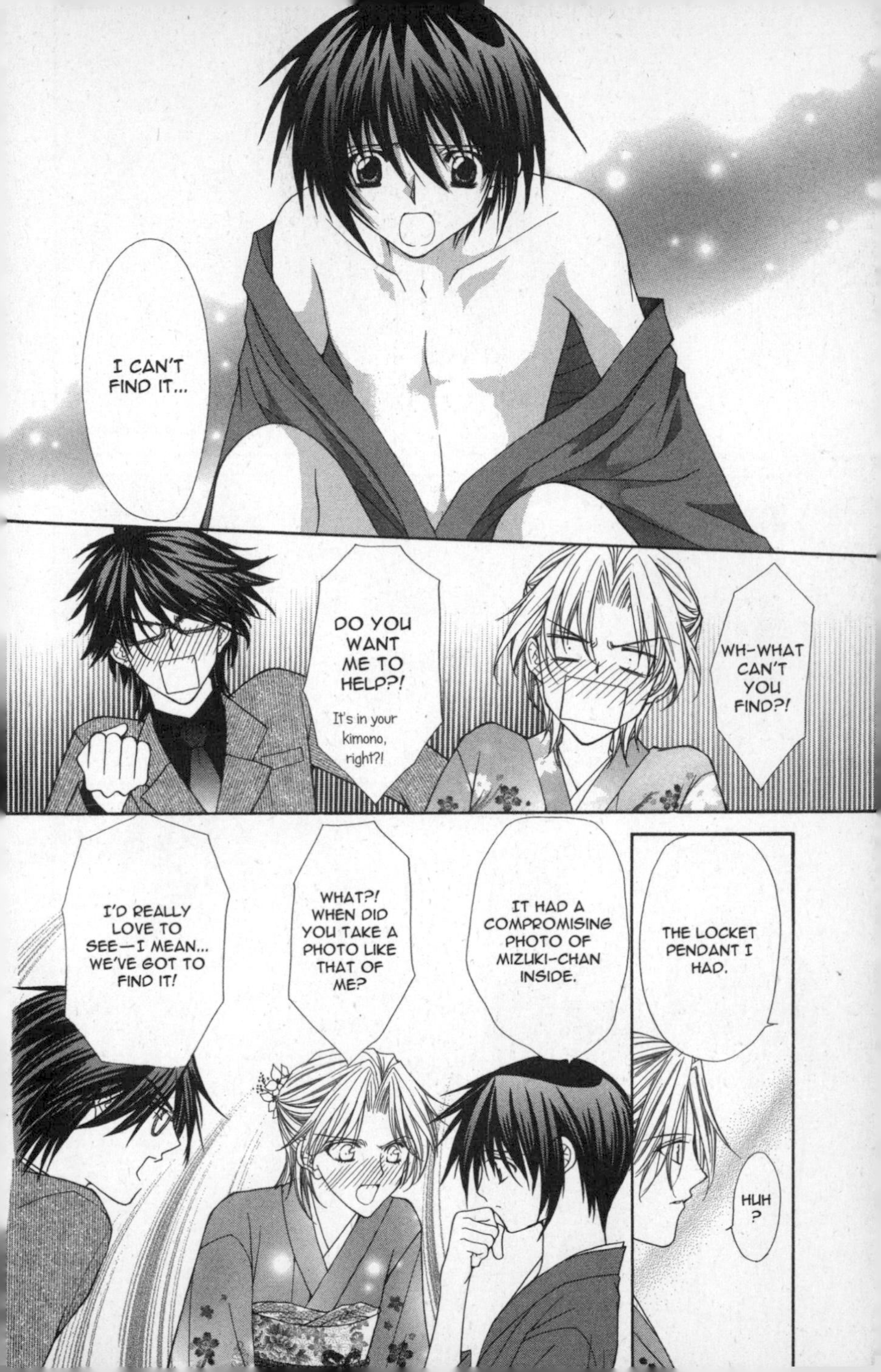
I CAN'T FIND IT...
WH-WHAT CAN'T YOU FIND?!
DO YOU WANT ME TO HELP?!
It's in your kimono, right?!
THE LOCKET PENDANT I HAD.
HUH?
IT HAD A COMPROMISING PHOTO OF MIZUKI-CHAN INSIDE.
WHAT?! WHEN DID YOU TAKE A PHOTO LIKE THAT OF ME?
I'D REALLY LOVE TO SEE—I MEAN... WE'VE GOT TO FIND IT!

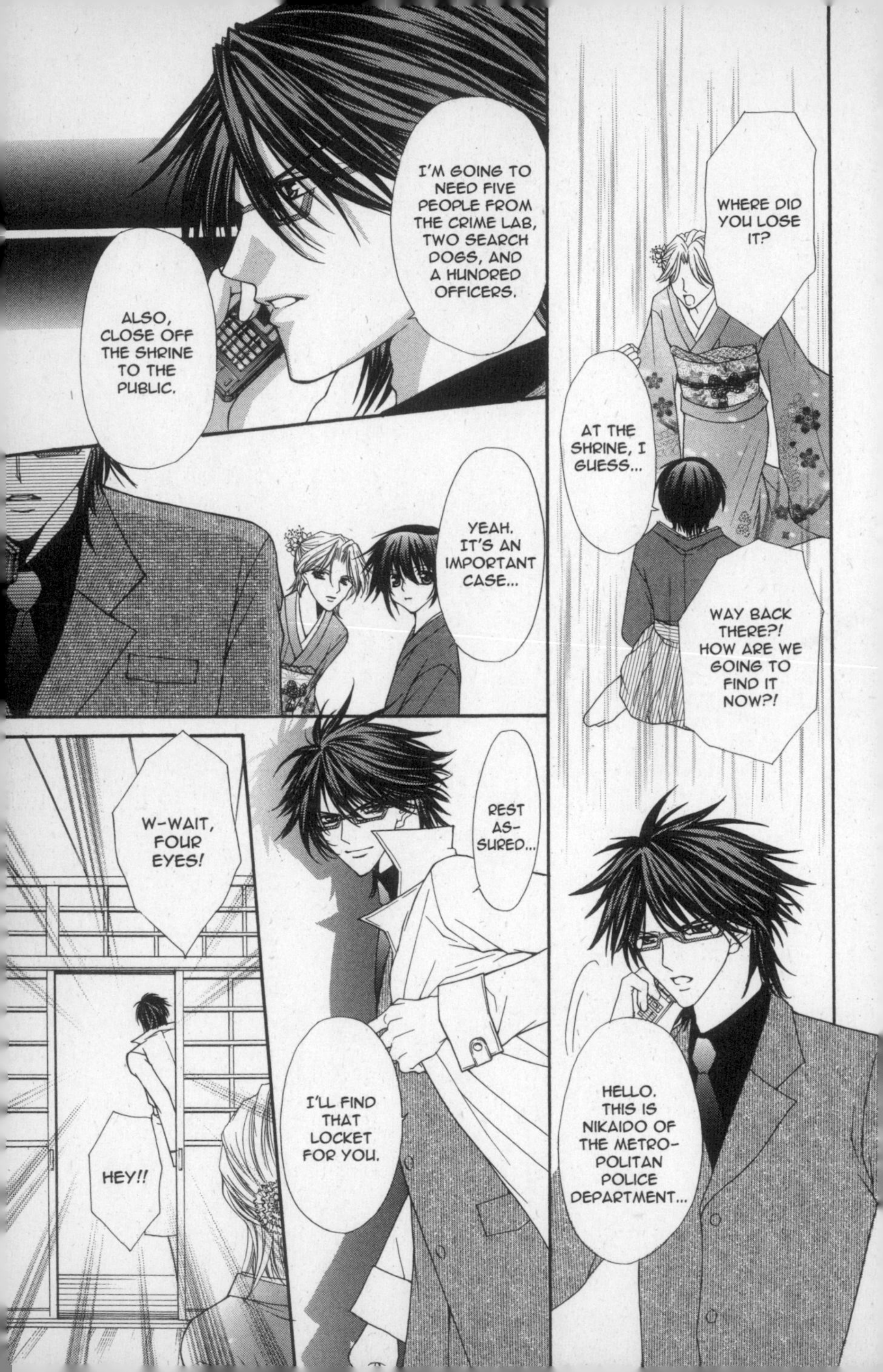
WHERE DID YOU LOSE IT?
AT THE SHRINE, I GUESS...
WAY BACK THERE?! HOW ARE WE GOING TO FIND IT NOW?!
HELLO. THIS IS NIKAIDO OF THE METRO-POLITAN POLICE DEPARTMENT...
I'M GOING TO NEED FIVE PEOPLE FROM THE CRIME LAB, TWO SEARCH DOGS, AND A HUNDRED OFFICERS.
ALSO, CLOSE OFF THE SHRINE TO THE PUBLIC.
YEAH. IT'S AN IMPORTANT CASE...
REST AS-SURED...
I'LL FIND THAT LOCKET FOR YOU.
W-WAIT, FOUR EYES!
HEY!!

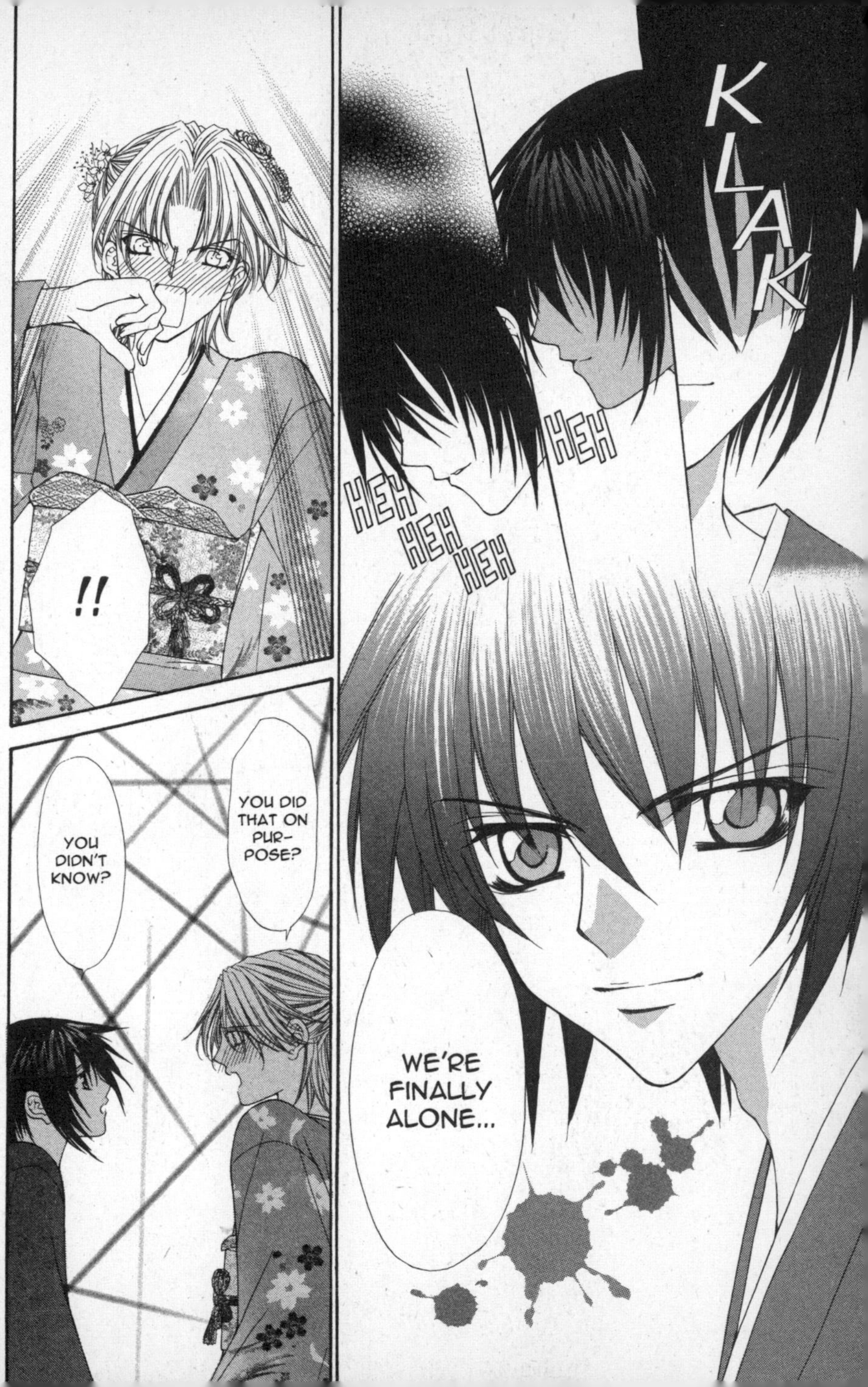
KLAK
HEH
HEH HEH HEH
WE'RE FINALLY ALONE...
!!
YOU DID THAT ON PUR-POSE?
YOU DIDN'T KNOW?

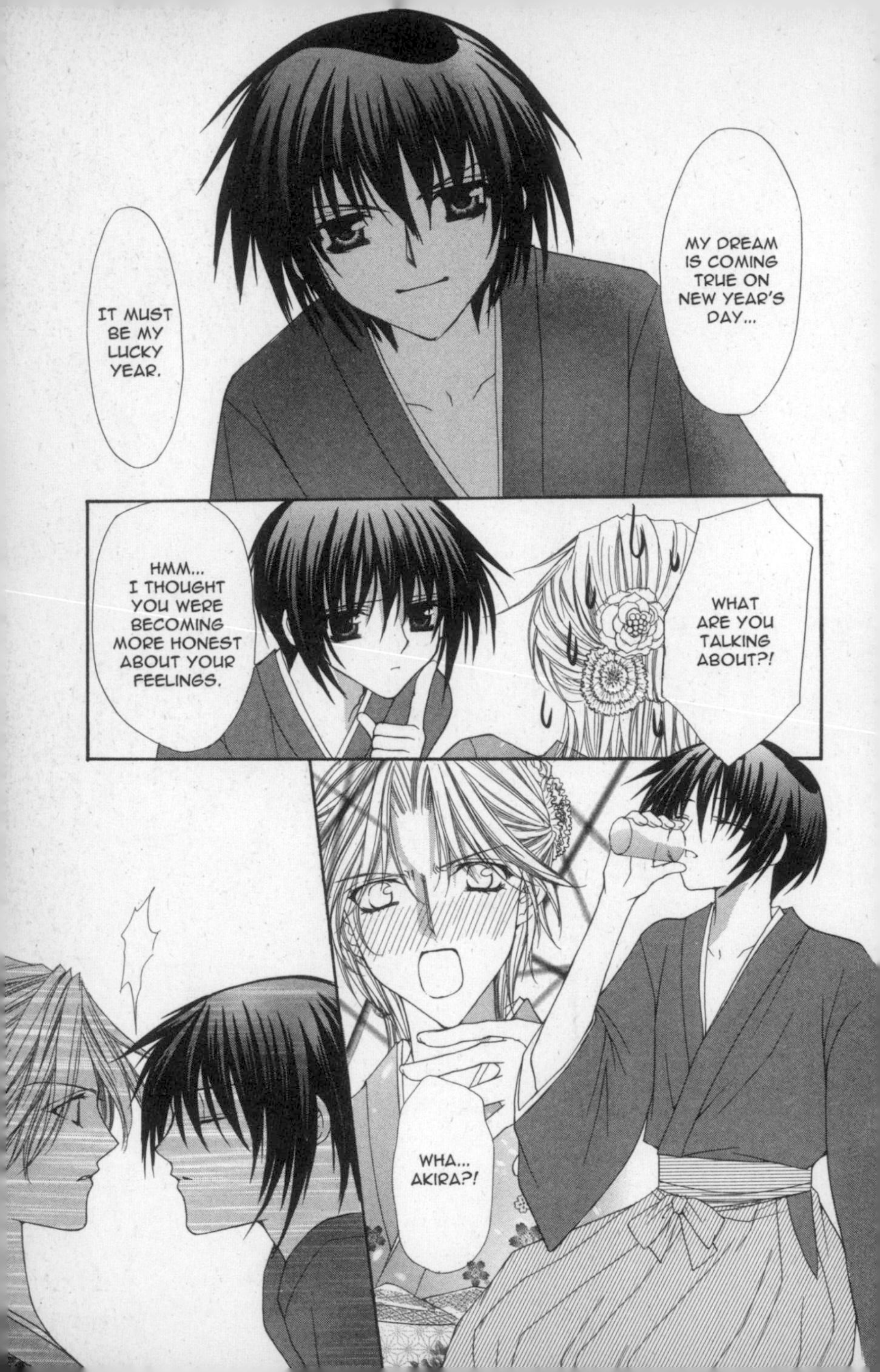
MY DREAM IS COMING TRUE ON NEW YEAR'S DAY...
IT MUST BE MY LUCKY YEAR.
WHAT ARE YOU TALKING ABOUT?!
HMM... I THOUGHT YOU WERE BECOMING MORE HONEST ABOUT YOUR FEELINGS.
WHA... AKIRA?!

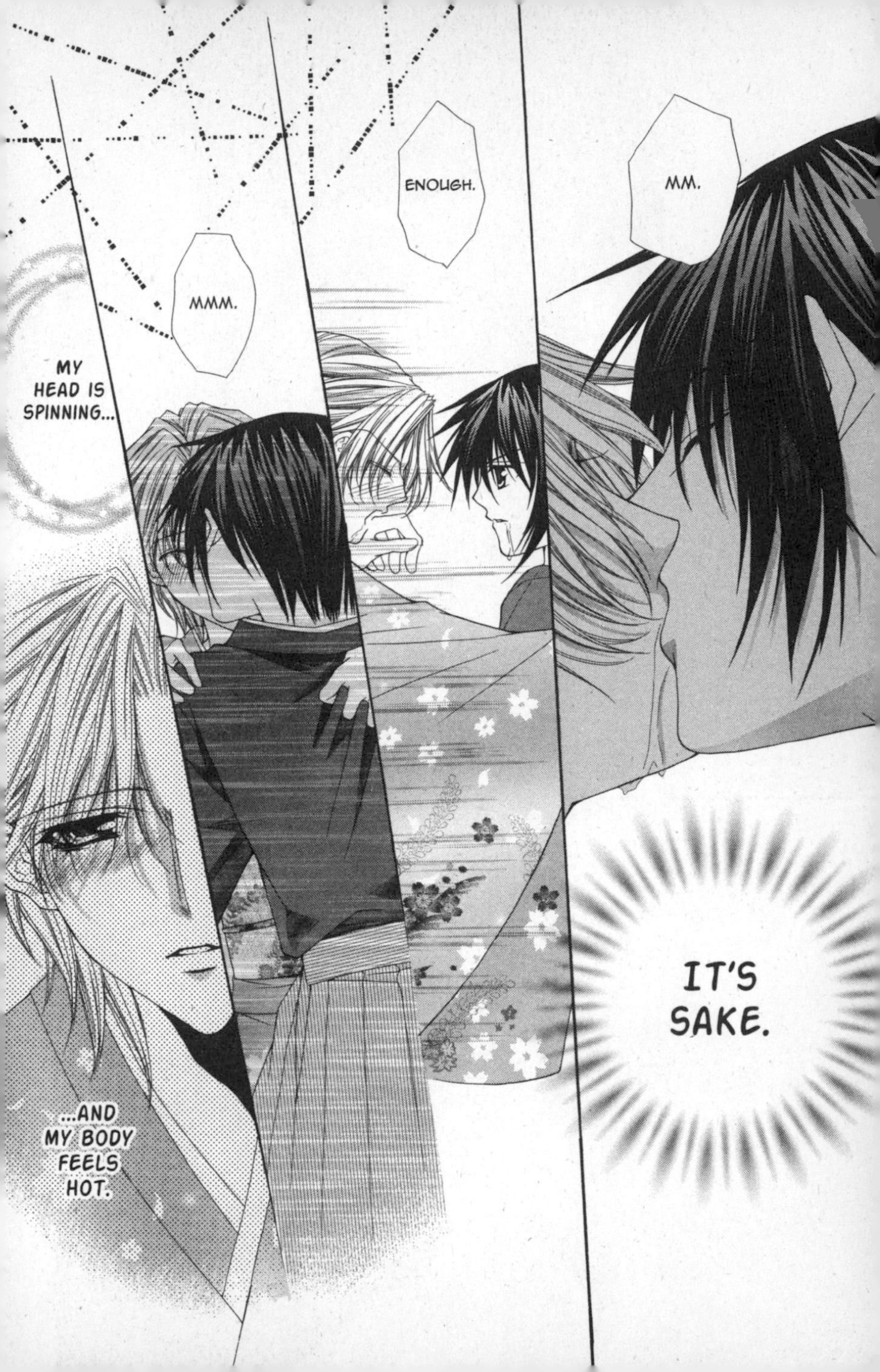
MM.
IT'S SAKE.
ENOUGH.
MMM.
MY HEAD IS SPINNING...
...AND MY BODY FEELS HOT.

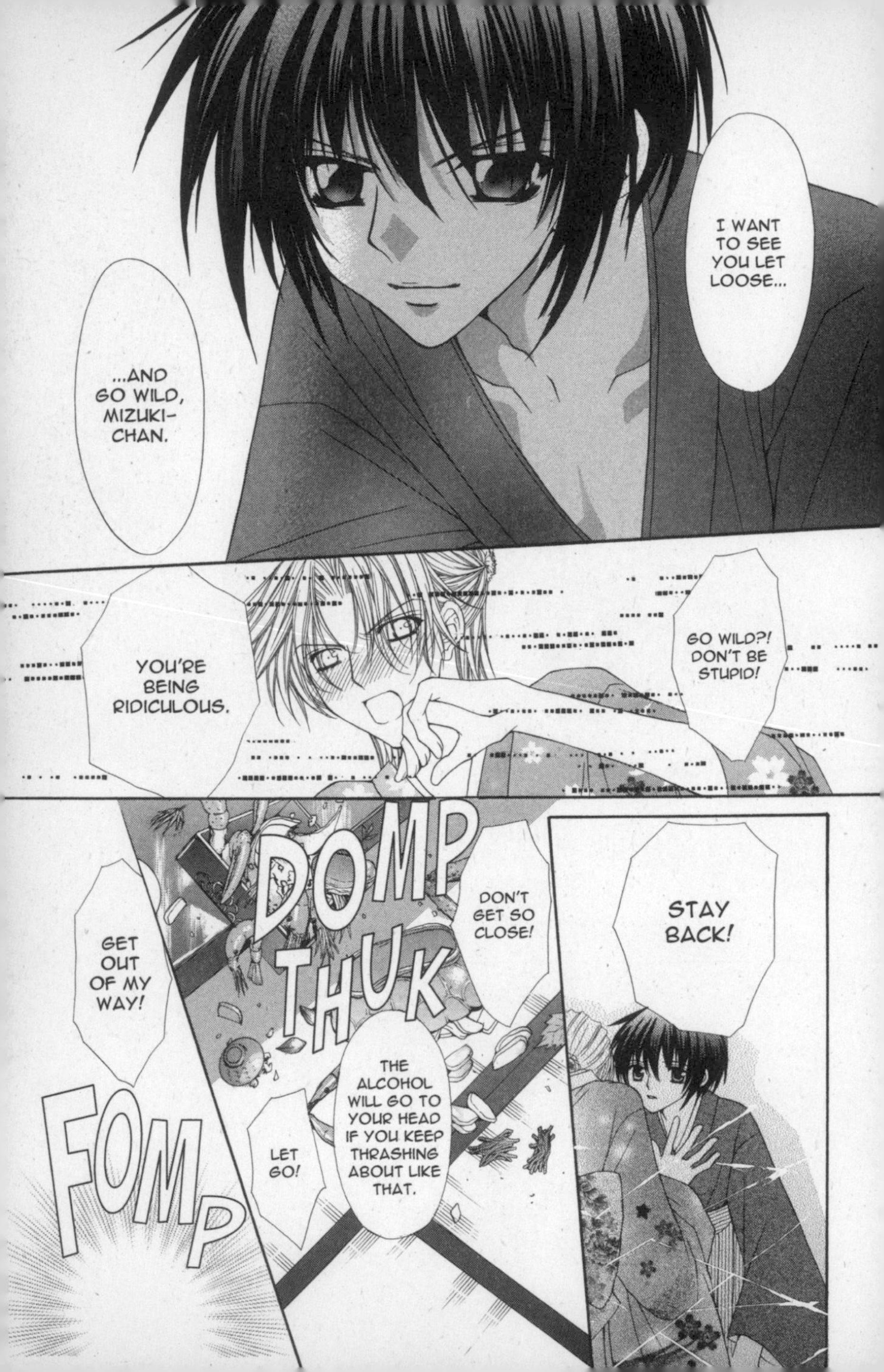
I WANT TO SEE YOU LET LOOSE...
...AND GO WILD, MIZUKI-CHAN.
GO WILD?! DON'T BE STUPID!
YOU'RE BEING RIDICULOUS.
STAY BACK!
DON'T GET SO CLOSE!
DOMP
THUK
GET OUT OF MY WAY!
THE ALCOHOL WILL GO TO YOUR HEAD IF YOU KEEP THRASHING ABOUT LIKE THAT.
LET GO!
FOMP

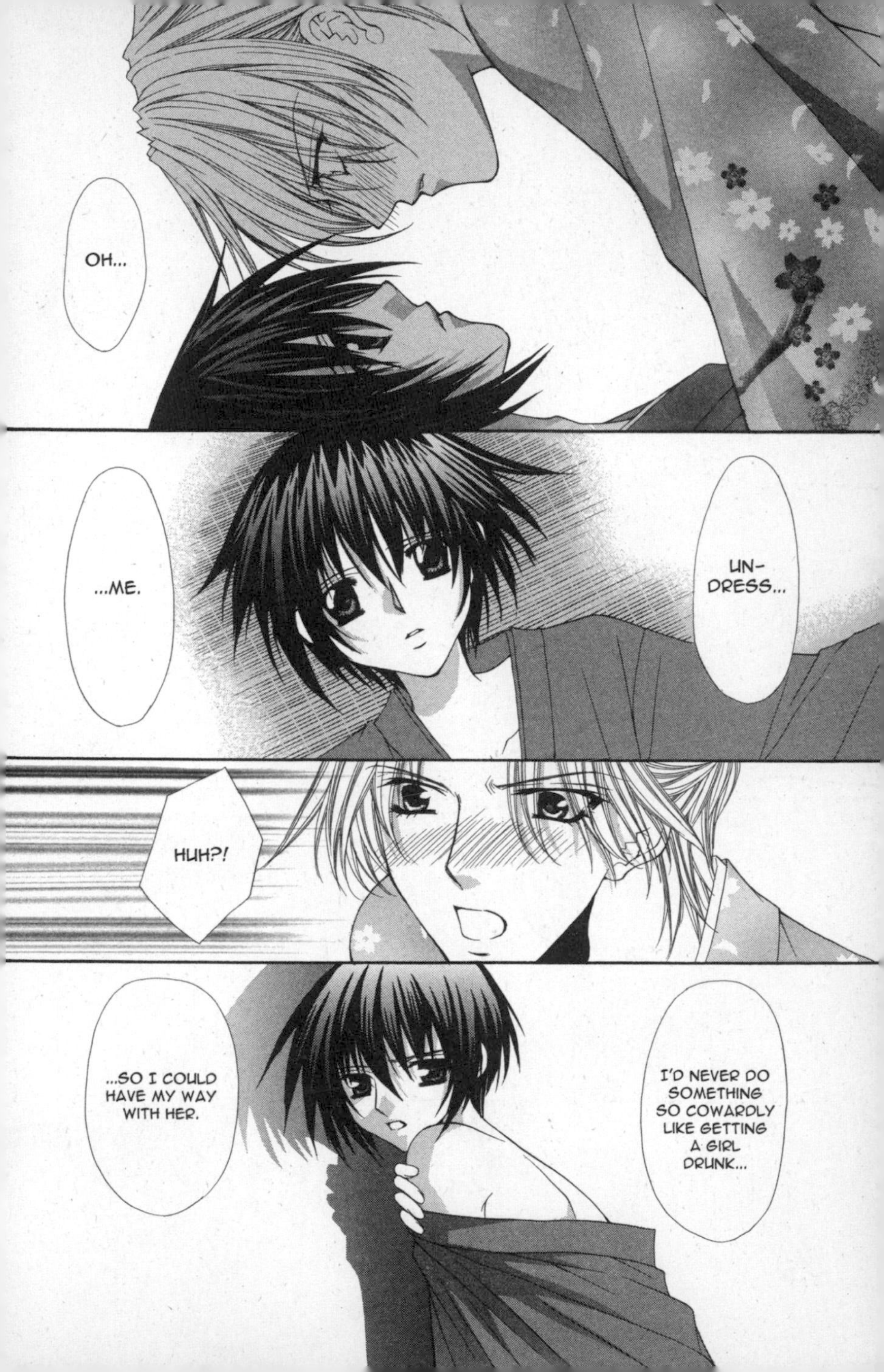
OH...
UN-DRESS...
...ME.
HUH?!
I'D NEVER DO SOMETHING SO COWARDLY LIKE GETTING A GIRL DRUNK...
...SO I COULD HAVE MY WAY WITH HER.

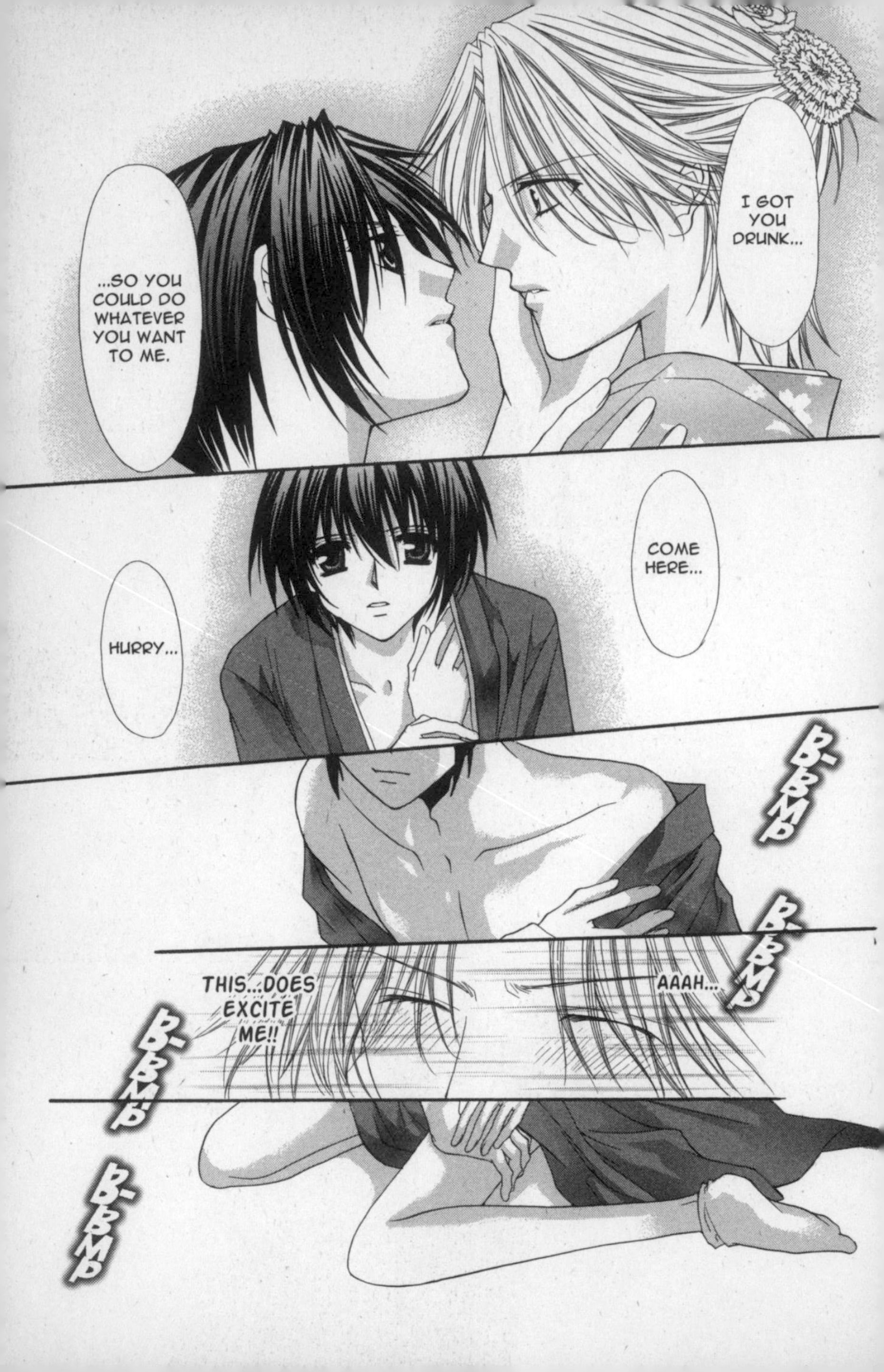
I GOT YOU DRUNK...
...SO YOU COULD DO WHATEVER YOU WANT TO ME.
COME HERE...
HURRY...
B-BMP
B-BMP
AAAH...
THIS...DOES EXCITE ME!!
B-BMP
B-BMP

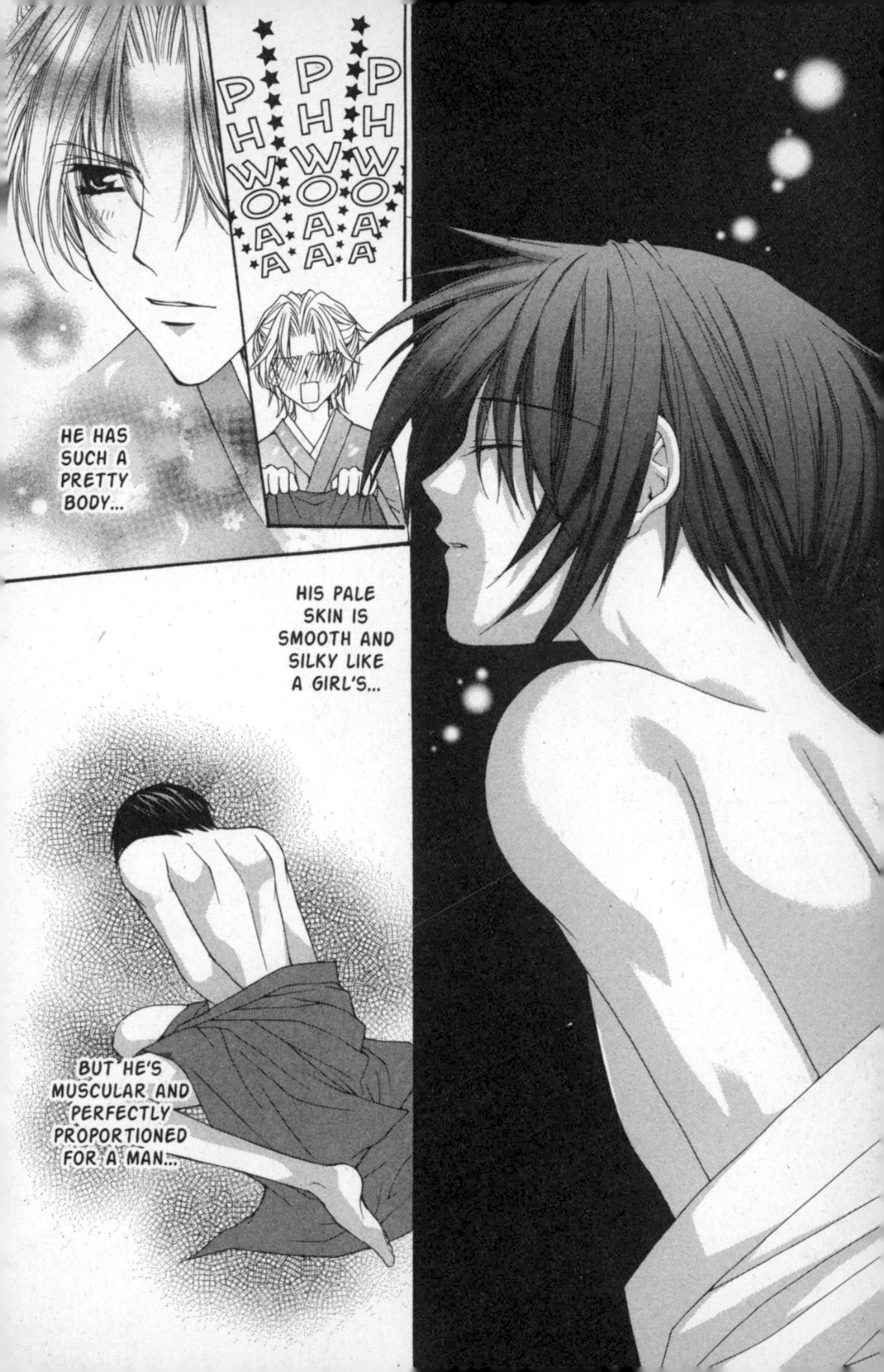
PHWOAA
PHWOAA
PHWOAA
HE HAS SUCH A PRETTY BODY...
HIS PALE SKIN IS SMOOTH AND SILKY LIKE A GIRL'S...
BUT HE'S MUSCULAR AND PERFECTLY PROPORTIONED FOR A MAN...

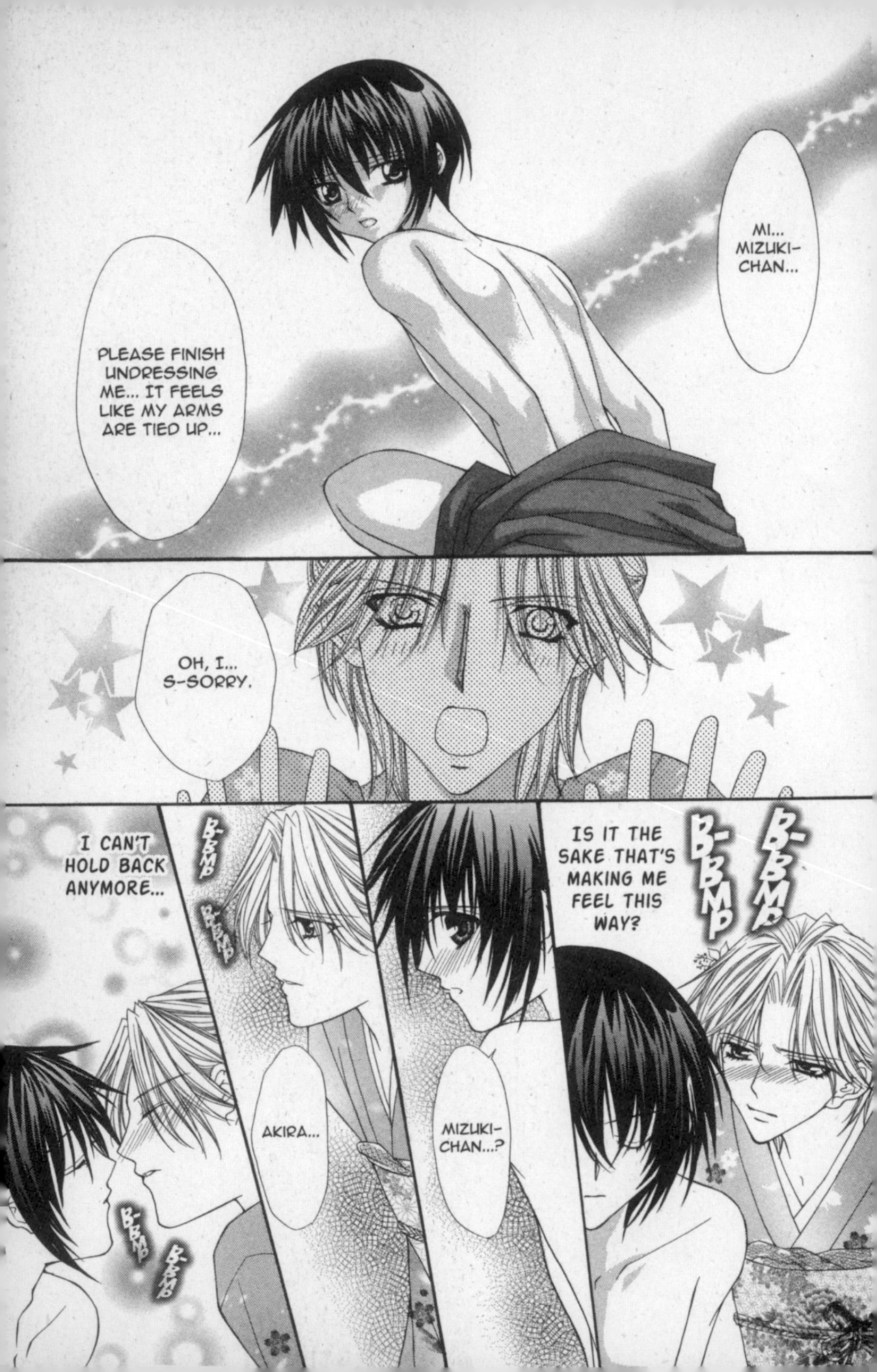
MI... MIZUKI-CHAN...
PLEASE FINISH UNDRESSING ME... IT FEELS LIKE MY ARMS ARE TIED UP...
OH, I... S-SORRY.
B-BMP
B-BMP
IS IT THE SAKE THAT'S MAKING ME FEEL THIS WAY?
MIZUKI-CHAN...?
AKIRA...
B-BMP
B-BMP
I CAN'T HOLD BACK ANYMORE...
B-BMP
B-BMP

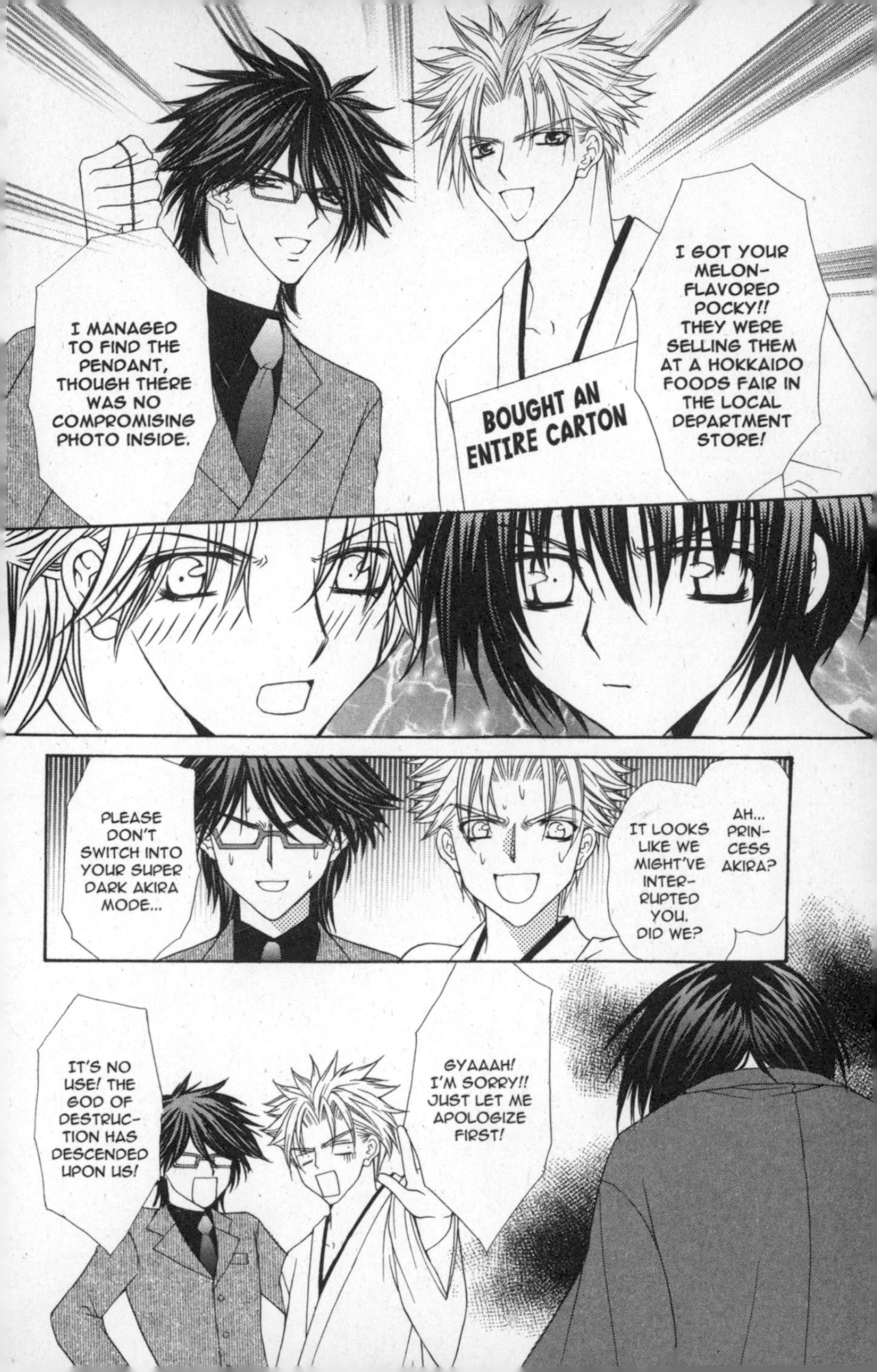
I GOT YOUR MELON-FLAVORED POCKY!! THEY WERE SELLING THEM AT A HOKKAIDO FOODS FAIR IN THE LOCAL DEPARTMENT STORE!
BOUGHT AN ENTIRE CARTON
I MANAGED TO FIND THE PENDANT, THOUGH THERE WAS NO COMPROMISING PHOTO INSIDE.
AH... PRIN-CESS AKIRA?
IT LOOKS LIKE WE MIGHT'VE INTER-RUPTED YOU, DID WE?
PLEASE DON'T SWITCH INTO YOUR SUPER DARK AKIRA MODE...
GYAAAH! I'M SORRY!! JUST LET ME APOLOGIZE FIRST!
IT'S NO USE! THE GOD OF DESTRUC-TION HAS DESCENDED UPON US!

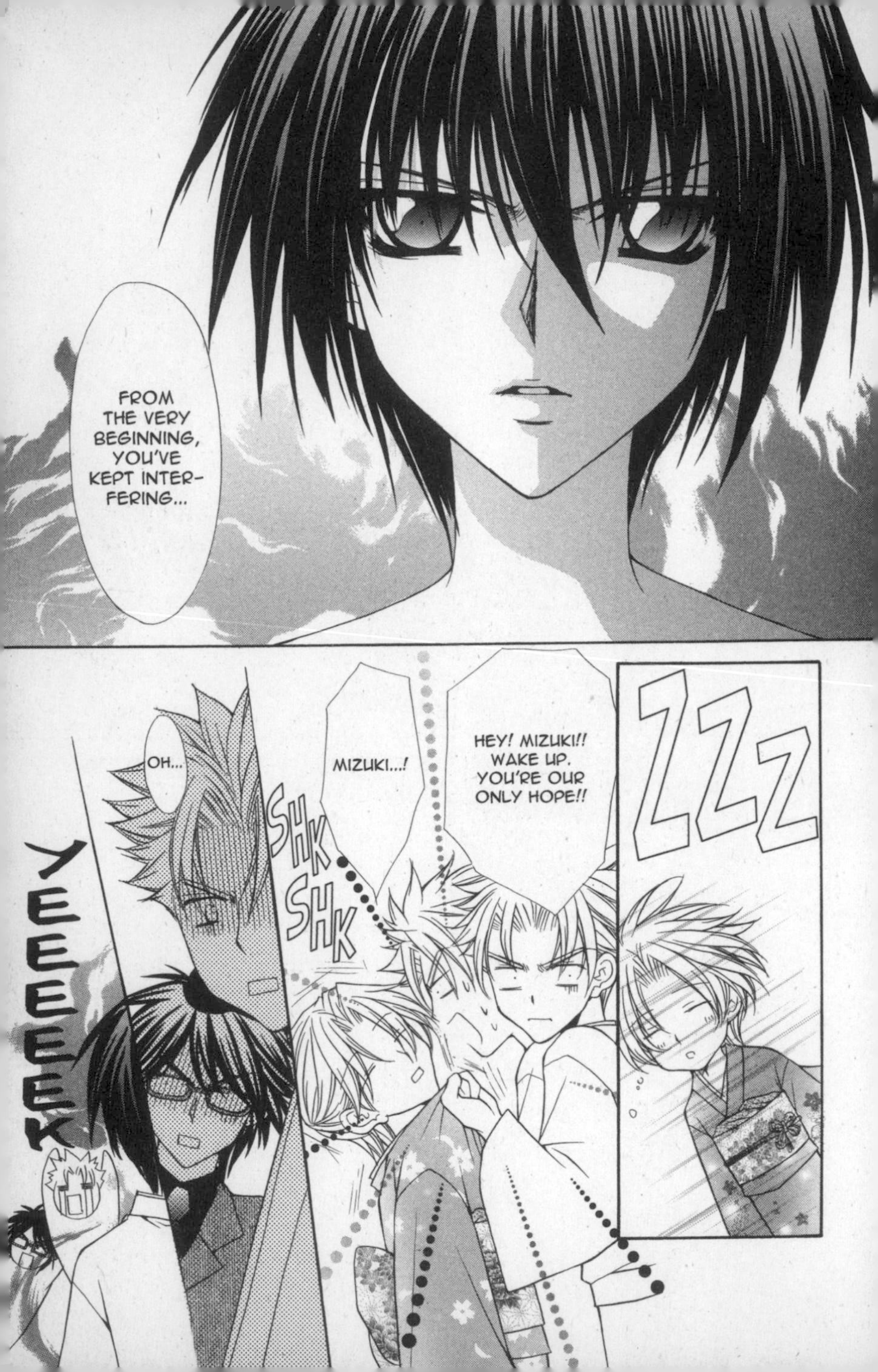
FROM THE VERY BEGINNING, YOU'VE KEPT INTER-FERING...
ZZZ
HEY! MIZUKI!! WAKE UP. YOU'RE OUR ONLY HOPE!!
MIZUKI...!
SHK SHK
OH...
YEEEEEEK

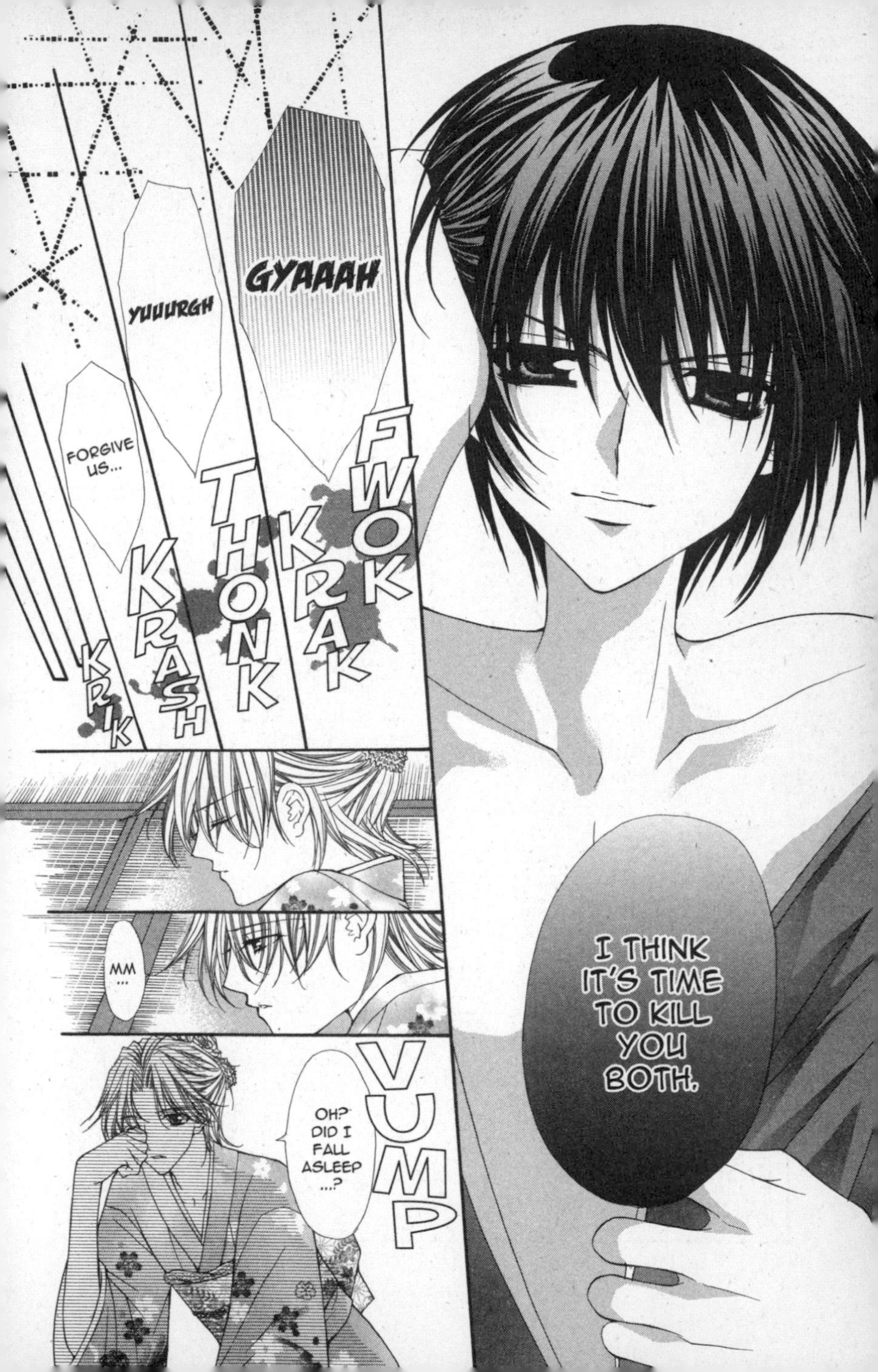
I THINK IT'S TIME TO KILL YOU BOTH.
GYAAAH
YUUURGH
FORGIVE US...
FWOK
KRAK
THONK
KRASH
KRIK
MM ...
VUMP
OH? DID I FALL ASLEEP ...?

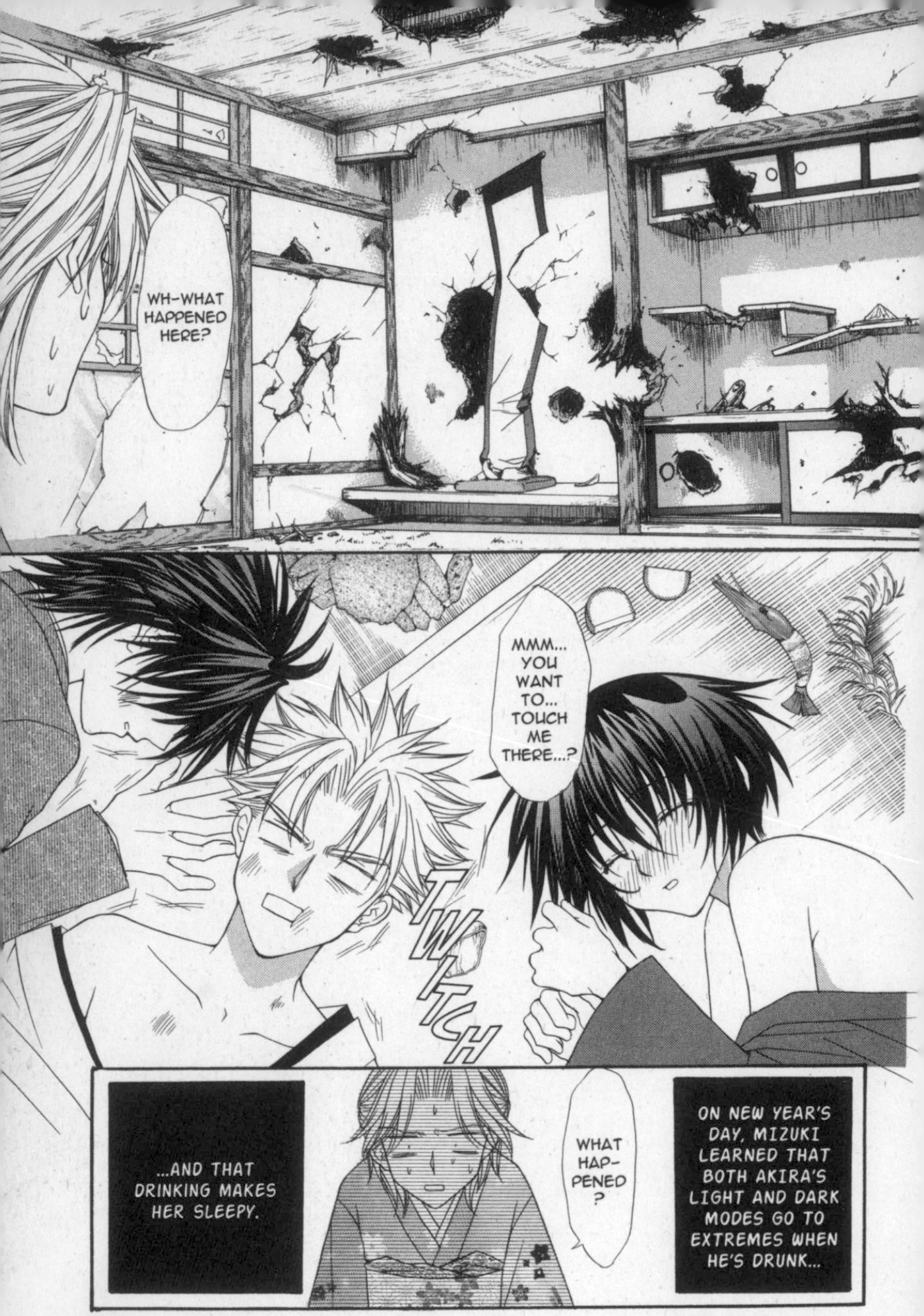
WH-WHAT HAPPENED HERE?
MMM... YOU WANT TO... TOUCH ME THERE...?
TWITCH
ON NEW YEAR'S DAY, MIZUKI LEARNED THAT BOTH AKIRA'S LIGHT AND DARK MODES GO TO EXTREMES WHEN HE'S DRUNK...
WHAT HAP-PENED?
...AND THAT DRINKING MAKES HER SLEEPY.

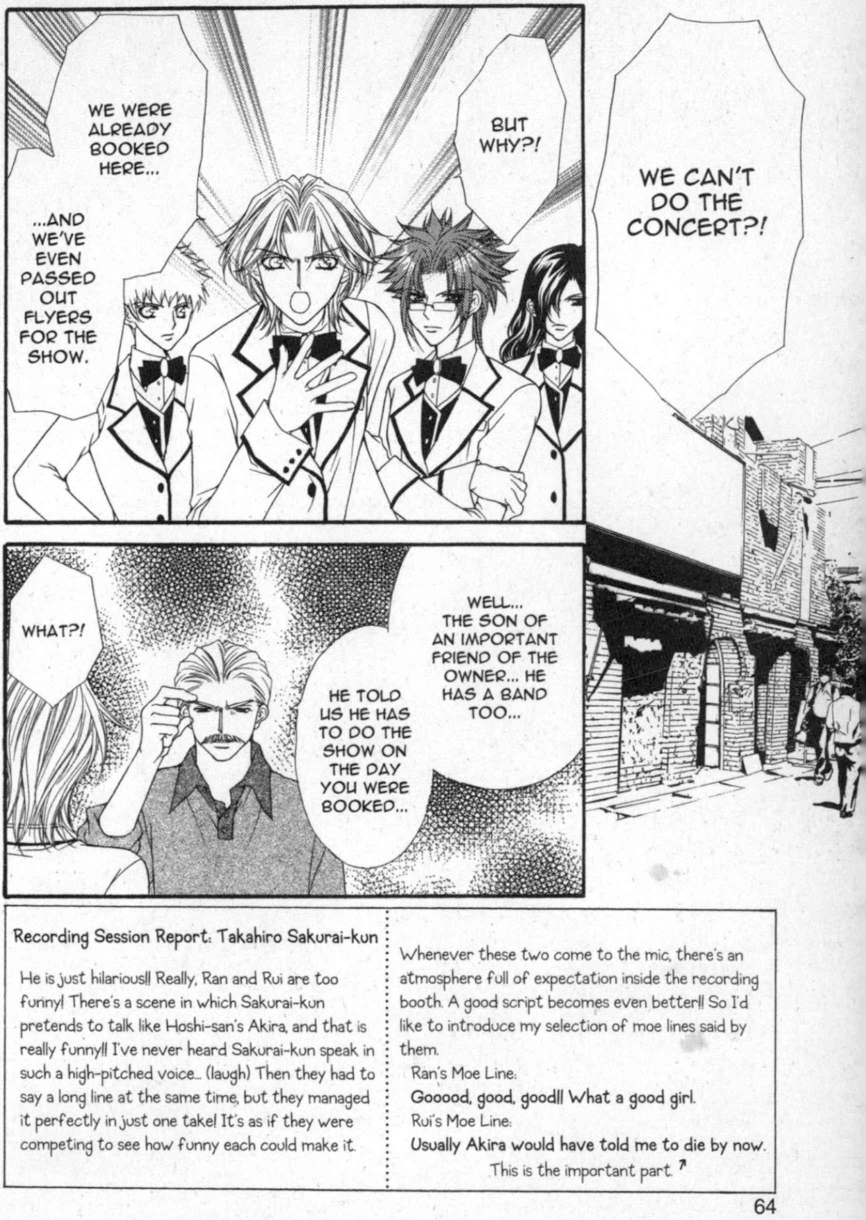
WE CAN'T DO THE CONCERT?!
BUT WHY?!
WE WERE ALREADY BOOKED HERE...
...AND WE'VE EVEN PASSED OUT FLYERS FOR THE SHOW.
WELL... THE SON OF AN IMPORTANT FRIEND OF THE OWNER... HE HAS A BAND TOO...
HE TOLD US HE HAS TO DO THE SHOW ON THE DAY YOU WERE BOOKED...
WHAT?!

Recording Session Report: Takahiro Sakurai-kun

He is just hilarious!! Really, Ran and Rui are too funny! There's a scene in which Sakurai-kun pretends to talk like Hoshi-san's Akira, and that is really funny!! I've never heard Sakurai-kun speak in such a high-pitched voice... (laugh) Then they had to say a long line at the same time, but they managed it perfectly in just one take! It's as if they were competing to see how funny each could make it.

Whenever these two come to the mic, there's an atmosphere full of expectation inside the recording booth. A good script becomes even better!! So I'd like to introduce my selection of moe lines said by them.

Ran's Moe Line:

Gooood, good, good!! What a good girl.

Rui's Moe Line:

Usually Akira would have told me to die by now.

This is the important part. ↗

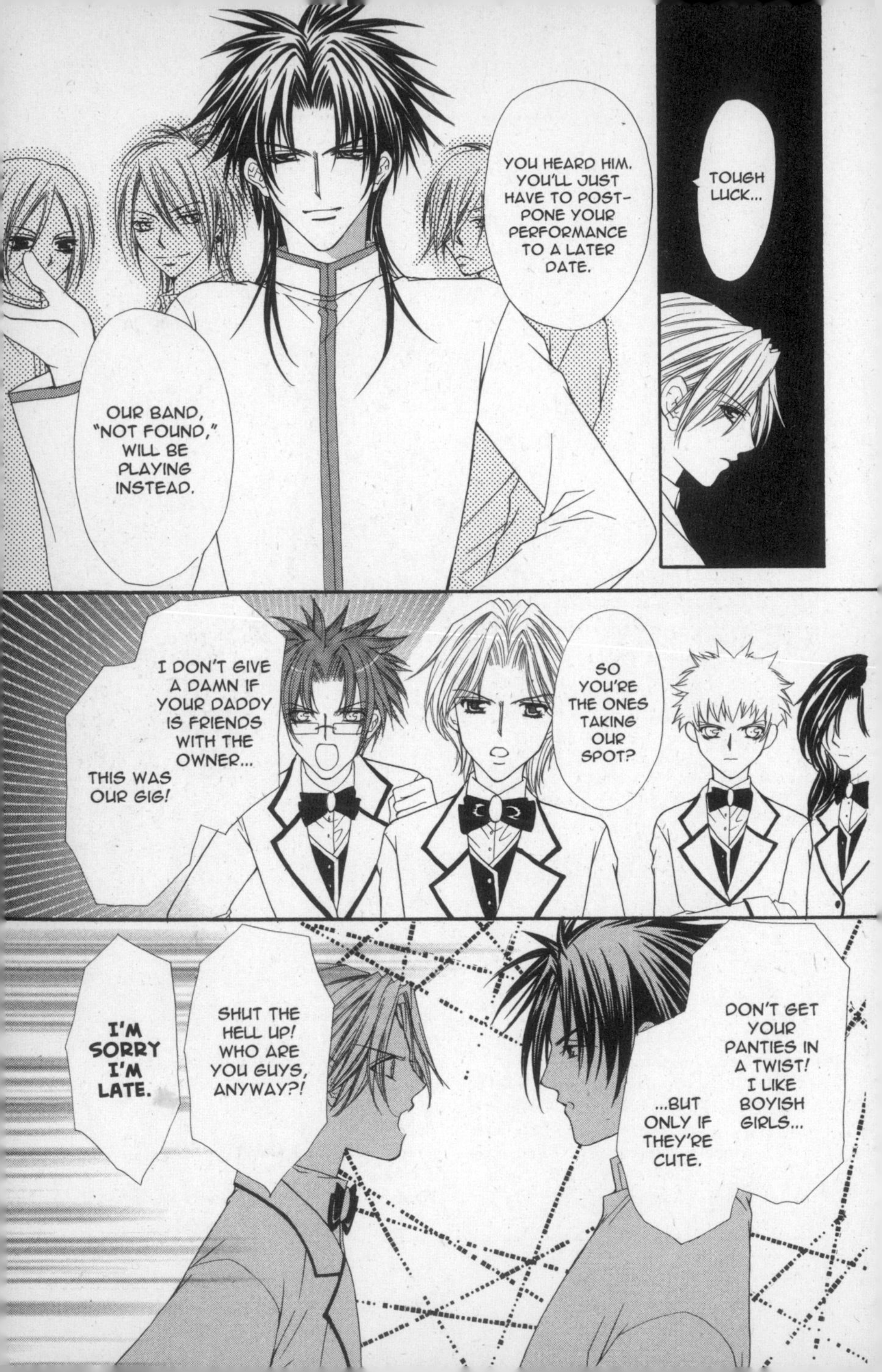
TOUGH LUCK...
YOU HEARD HIM. YOU'LL JUST HAVE TO POST-PONE YOUR PERFORMANCE TO A LATER DATE.
OUR BAND, "NOT FOUND," WILL BE PLAYING INSTEAD.
SO YOU'RE THE ONES TAKING OUR SPOT?
I DON'T GIVE A DAMN IF YOUR DADDY IS FRIENDS WITH THE OWNER...
THIS WAS OUR GIG!
DON'T GET YOUR PANTIES IN A TWIST! I LIKE BOYISH GIRLS...
...BUT ONLY IF THEY'RE CUTE.
SHUT THE HELL UP! WHO ARE YOU GUYS, ANYWAY?!
I'M SORRY I'M LATE.

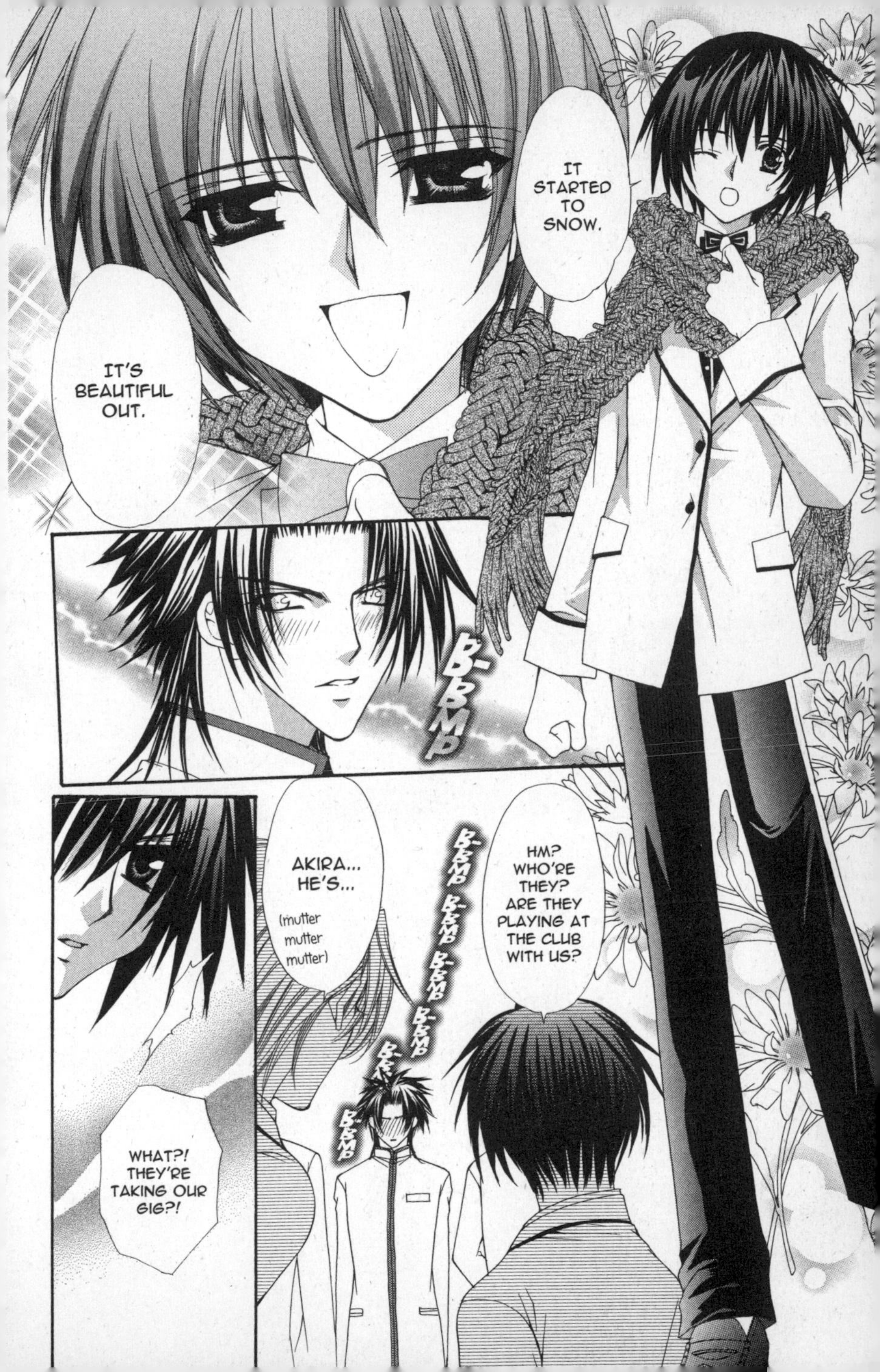
IT STARTED TO SNOW.
IT'S BEAUTIFUL OUT.
B-B-BMP
HM? WHO'RE THEY? ARE THEY PLAYING AT THE CLUB WITH US?
AKIRA... HE'S...
(mutter mutter mutter)
B-BMP B-BMP B-BMP B-BMP B-BMP B-BMP
WHAT?! THEY'RE TAKING OUR GIG?!

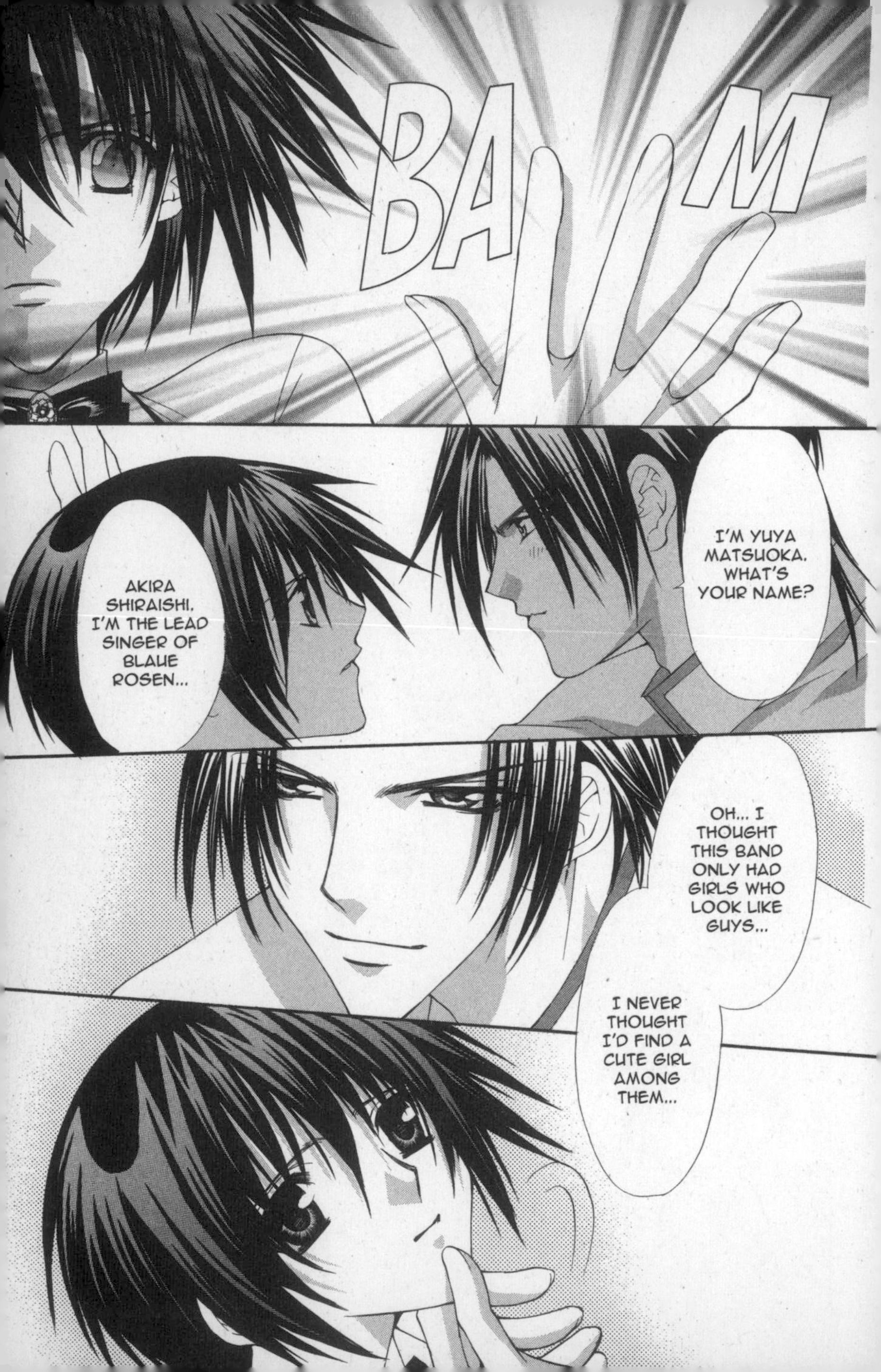
BAM
I'M YUYA MATSUOKA. WHAT'S YOUR NAME?
AKIRA SHIRAISHI. I'M THE LEAD SINGER OF BLAUE ROSEN...
OH... I THOUGHT THIS BAND ONLY HAD GIRLS WHO LOOK LIKE GUYS...
I NEVER THOUGHT I'D FIND A CUTE GIRL AMONG THEM...

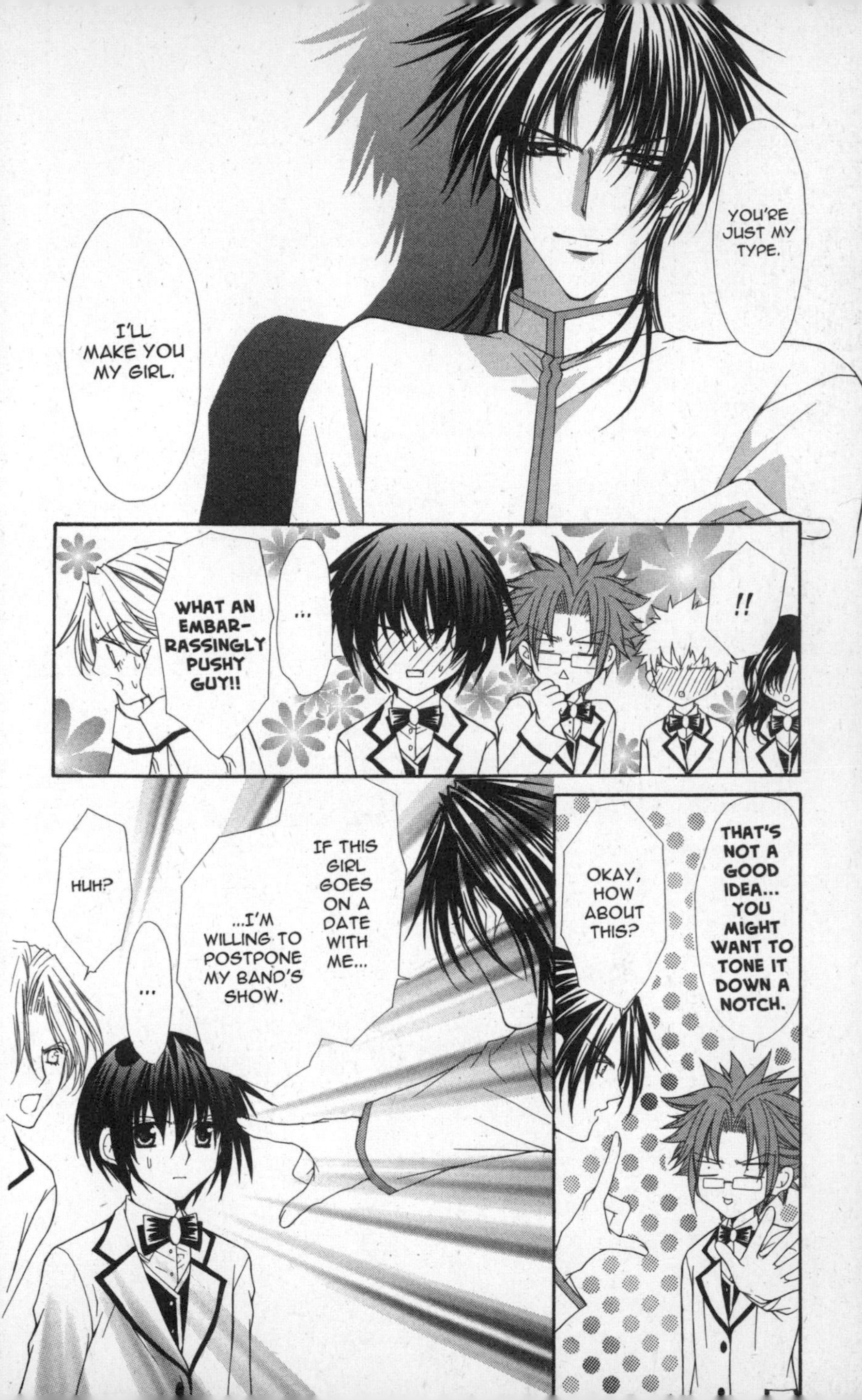
YOU'RE JUST MY TYPE.
I'LL MAKE YOU MY GIRL.
!!
...
WHAT AN EMBAR-RASSINGLY PUSHY GUY!!
THAT'S NOT A GOOD IDEA... YOU MIGHT WANT TO TONE IT DOWN A NOTCH.
OKAY, HOW ABOUT THIS?
IF THIS GIRL GOES ON A DATE WITH ME...
...I'M WILLING TO POSTPONE MY BAND'S SHOW.
HUH?
...

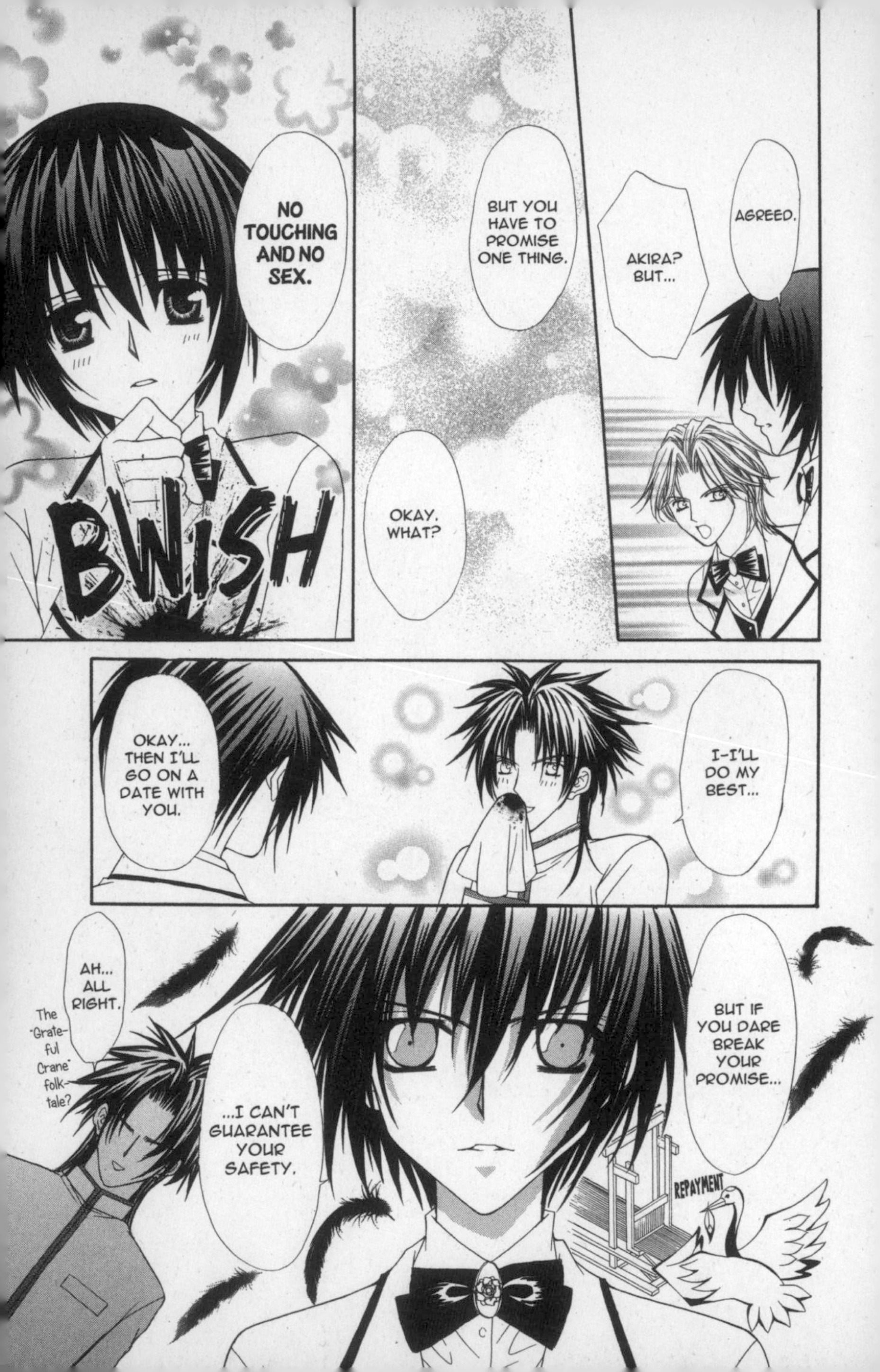
AGREED.
AKIRA? BUT...
BUT YOU HAVE TO PROMISE ONE THING.
OKAY. WHAT?
NO TOUCHING AND NO SEX.
BWISH
I-I'LL DO MY BEST...
OKAY... THEN I'LL GO ON A DATE WITH YOU.
BUT IF YOU DARE BREAK YOUR PROMISE...
REPAYMENT
...I CAN'T GUARANTEE YOUR SAFETY.
AH... ALL RIGHT.
The "Grateful Crane" folktale?

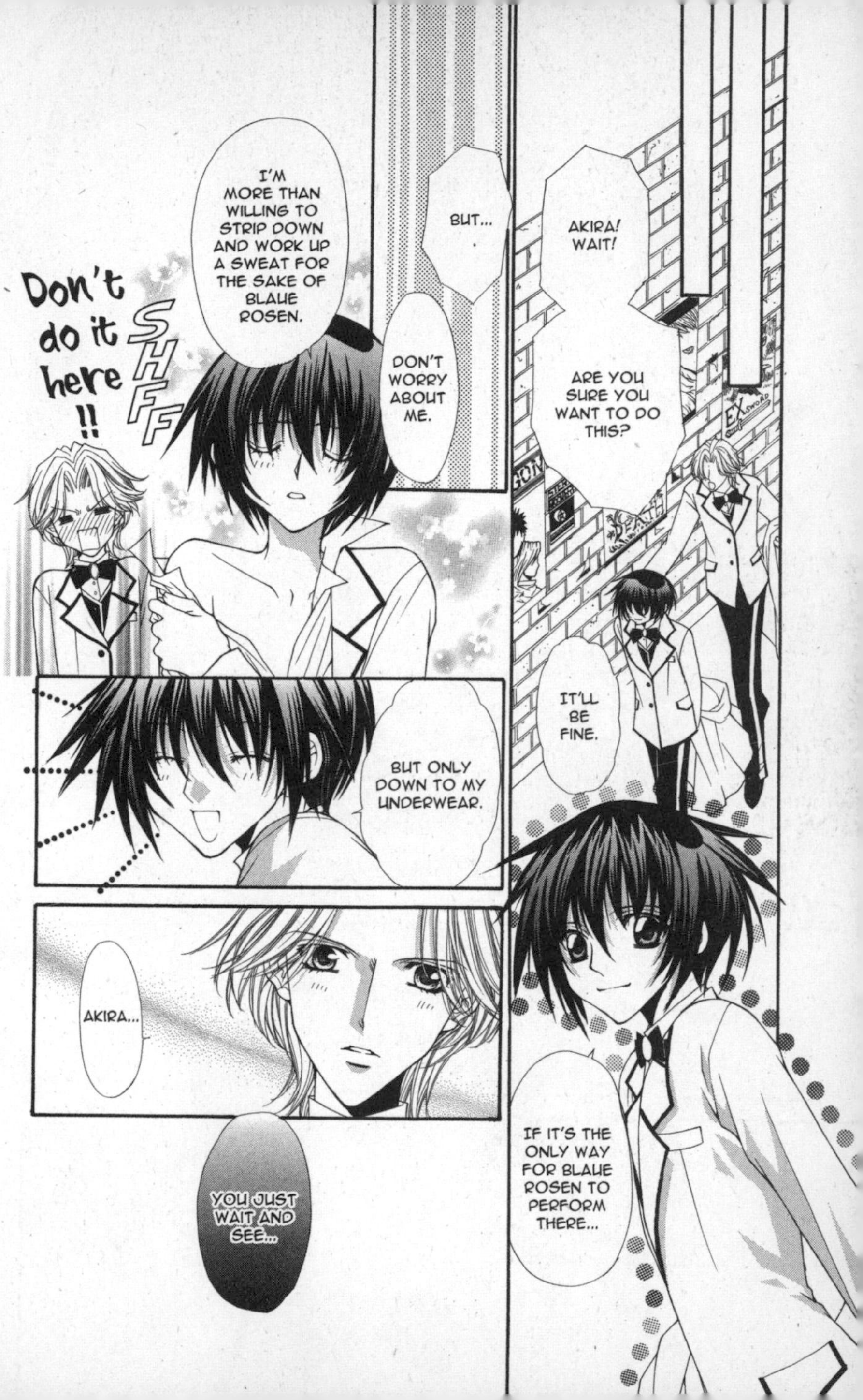
AKIRA! WAIT!
ARE YOU SURE YOU WANT TO DO THIS?
IT'LL BE FINE.
IF IT'S THE ONLY WAY FOR BLAUE ROSEN TO PERFORM THERE...
BUT...
DON'T WORRY ABOUT ME.
I'M MORE THAN WILLING TO STRIP DOWN AND WORK UP A SWEAT FOR THE SAKE OF BLAUE ROSEN.
SHFF
Don't do it here!!
BUT ONLY DOWN TO MY UNDERWEAR.
AKIRA...
YOU JUST WAIT AND SEE...

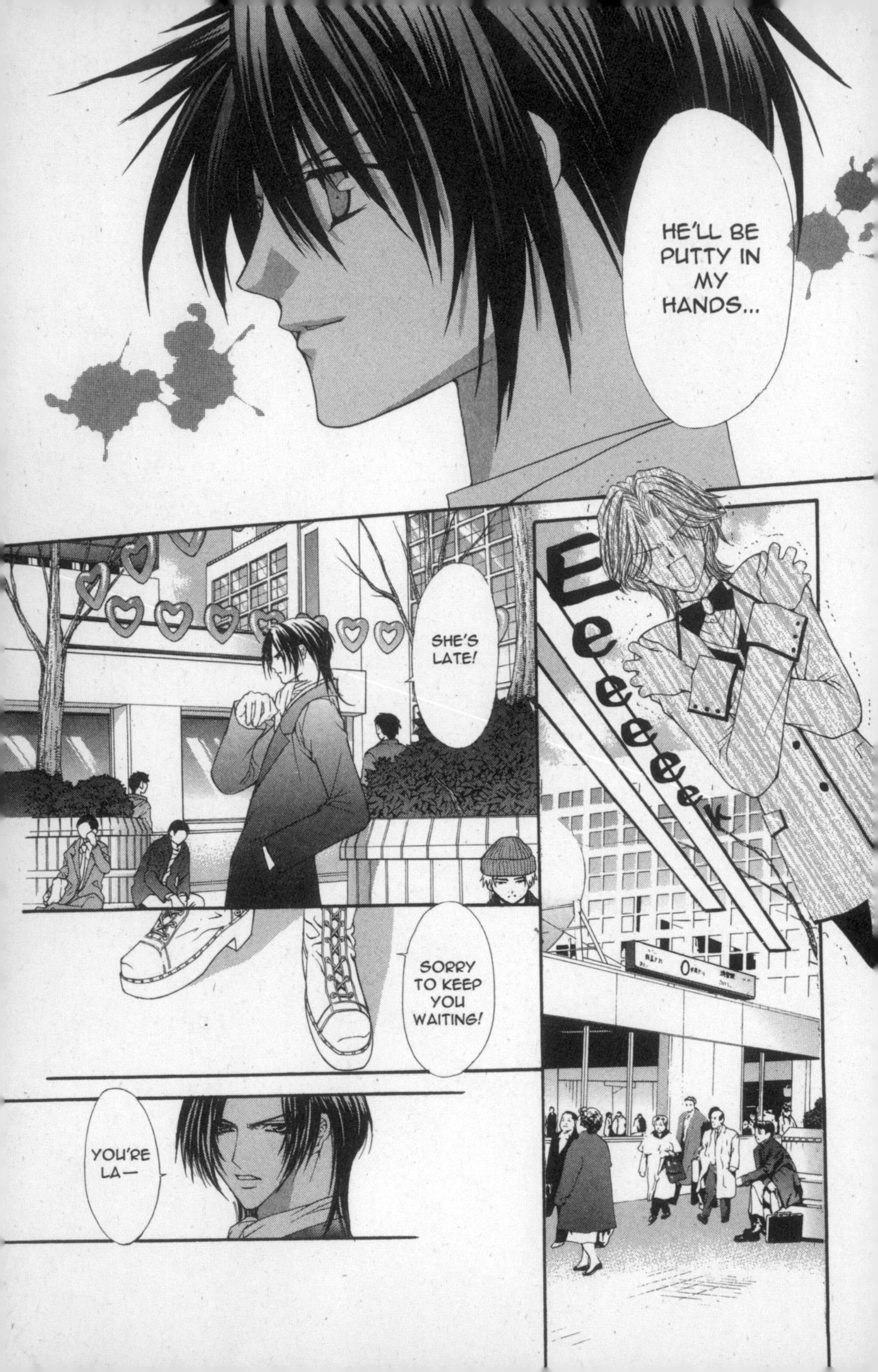
HE'LL BE PUTTY IN MY HANDS...
Eeeeeek
SHE'S LATE!
SORRY TO KEEP YOU WAITING!
YOU'RE LA—

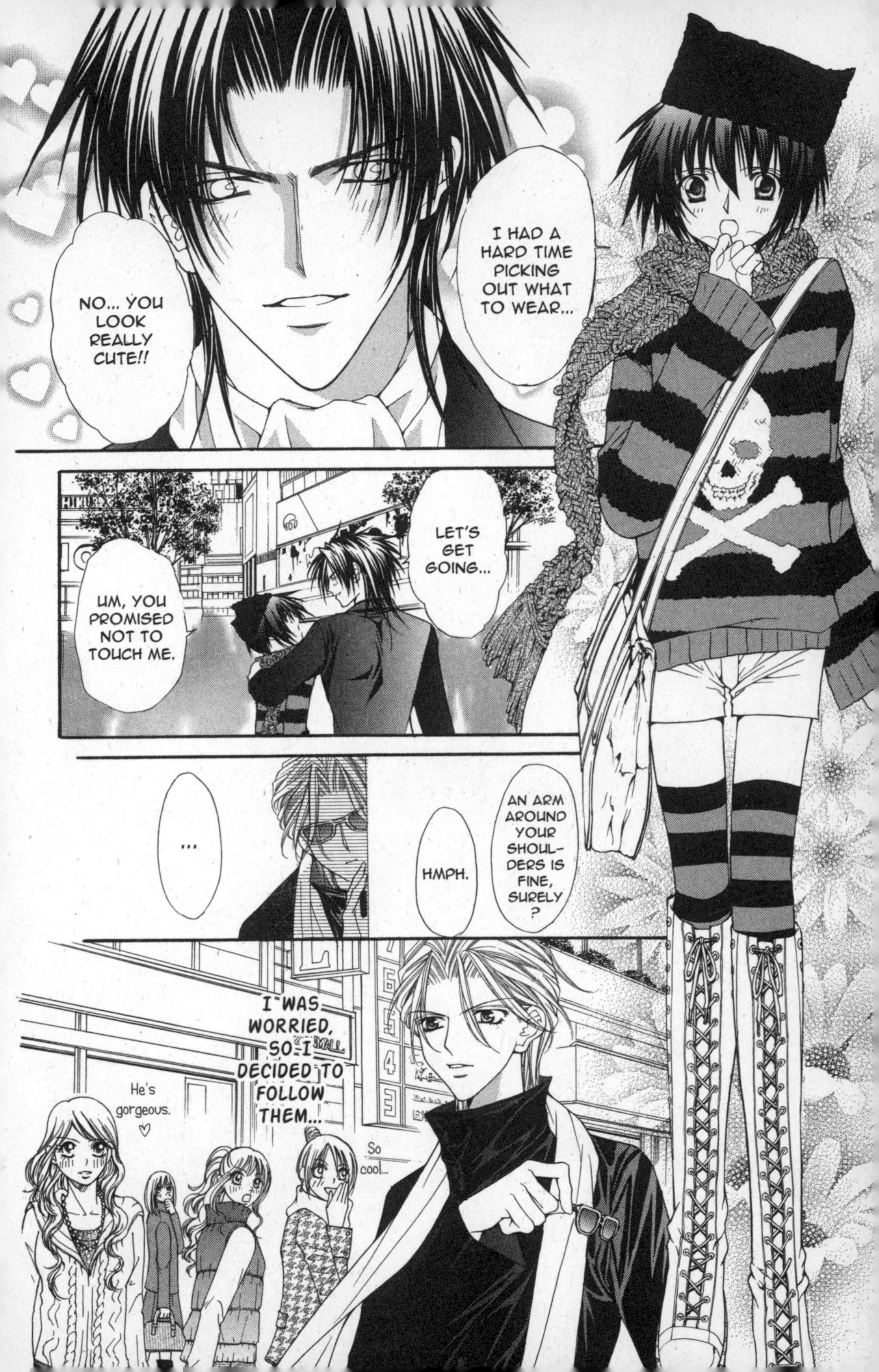
I HAD A HARD TIME PICKING OUT WHAT TO WEAR...
NO... YOU LOOK REALLY CUTE!!
LET'S GET GOING...
UM, YOU PROMISED NOT TO TOUCH ME.
AN ARM AROUND YOUR SHOULDERS IS FINE, SURELY?
HMPH.
...
I WAS WORRIED, SO I DECIDED TO FOLLOW THEM...
So cool...
He's gorgeous. ♡

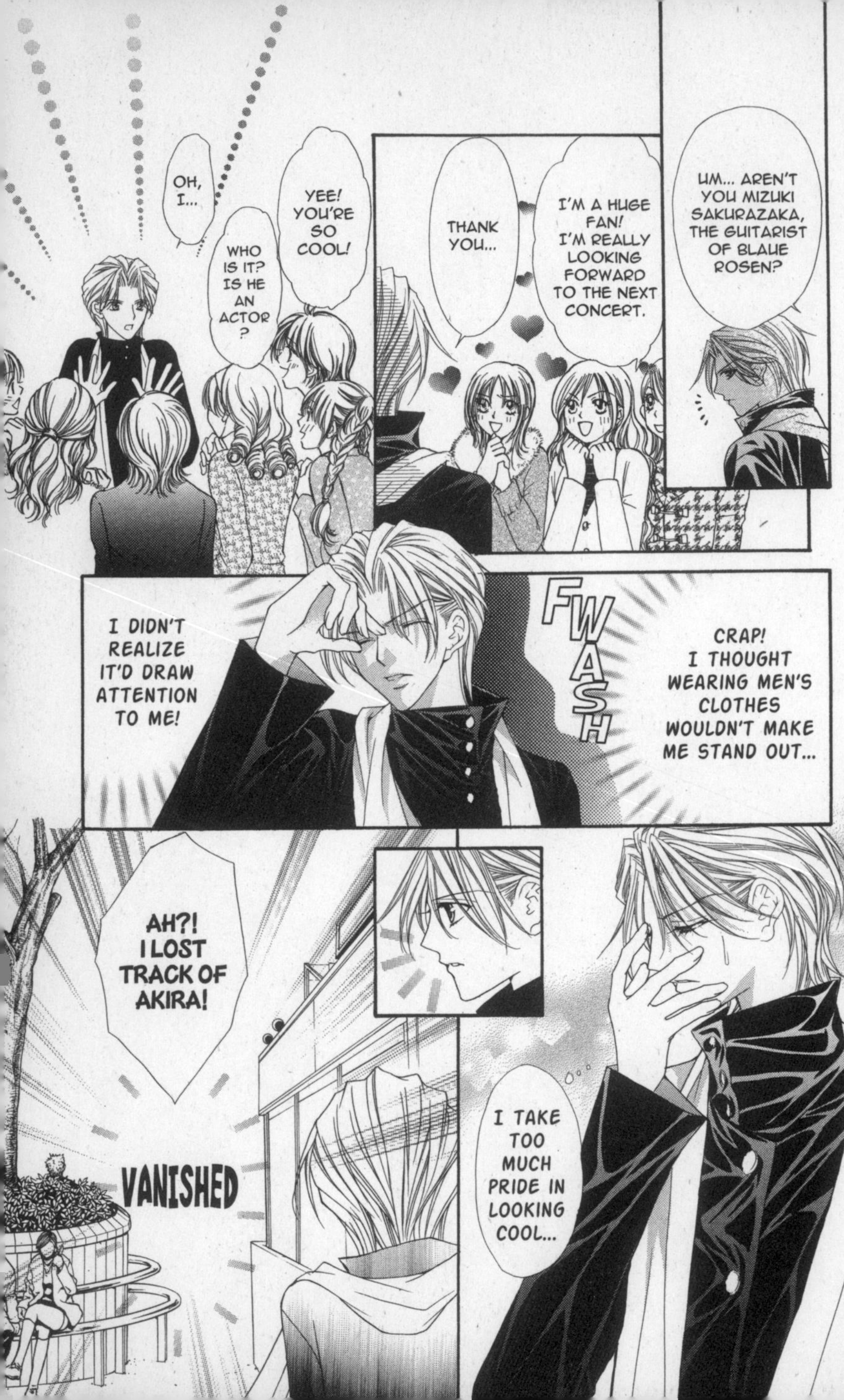
UM... AREN'T YOU MIZUKI SAKURAZAKA, THE GUITARIST OF BLAUE ROSEN?
I'M A HUGE FAN! I'M REALLY LOOKING FORWARD TO THE NEXT CONCERT.
THANK YOU...
YEE! YOU'RE SO COOL!
OH, I...
WHO IS IT? IS HE AN ACTOR?
CRAP! I THOUGHT WEARING MEN'S CLOTHES WOULDN'T MAKE ME STAND OUT...
FWASH
I DIDN'T REALIZE IT'D DRAW ATTENTION TO ME!
I TAKE TOO MUCH PRIDE IN LOOKING COOL...
AH?! I LOST TRACK OF AKIRA!
VANISHED

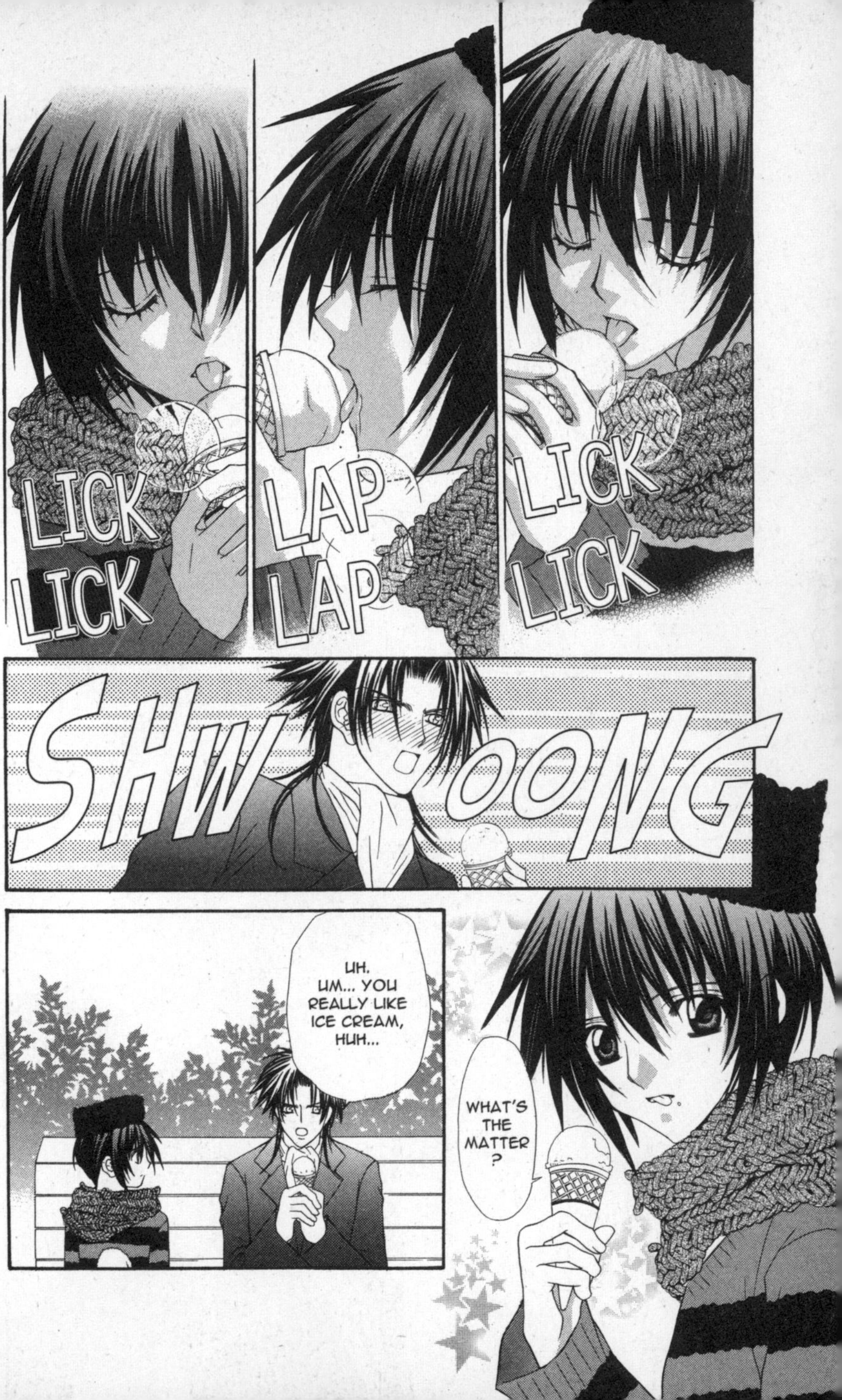
LICK LICK
LAP LAP
LICK LICK
SHWOONG
WHAT'S THE MATTER?
UH. UM... YOU REALLY LIKE ICE CREAM, HUH...

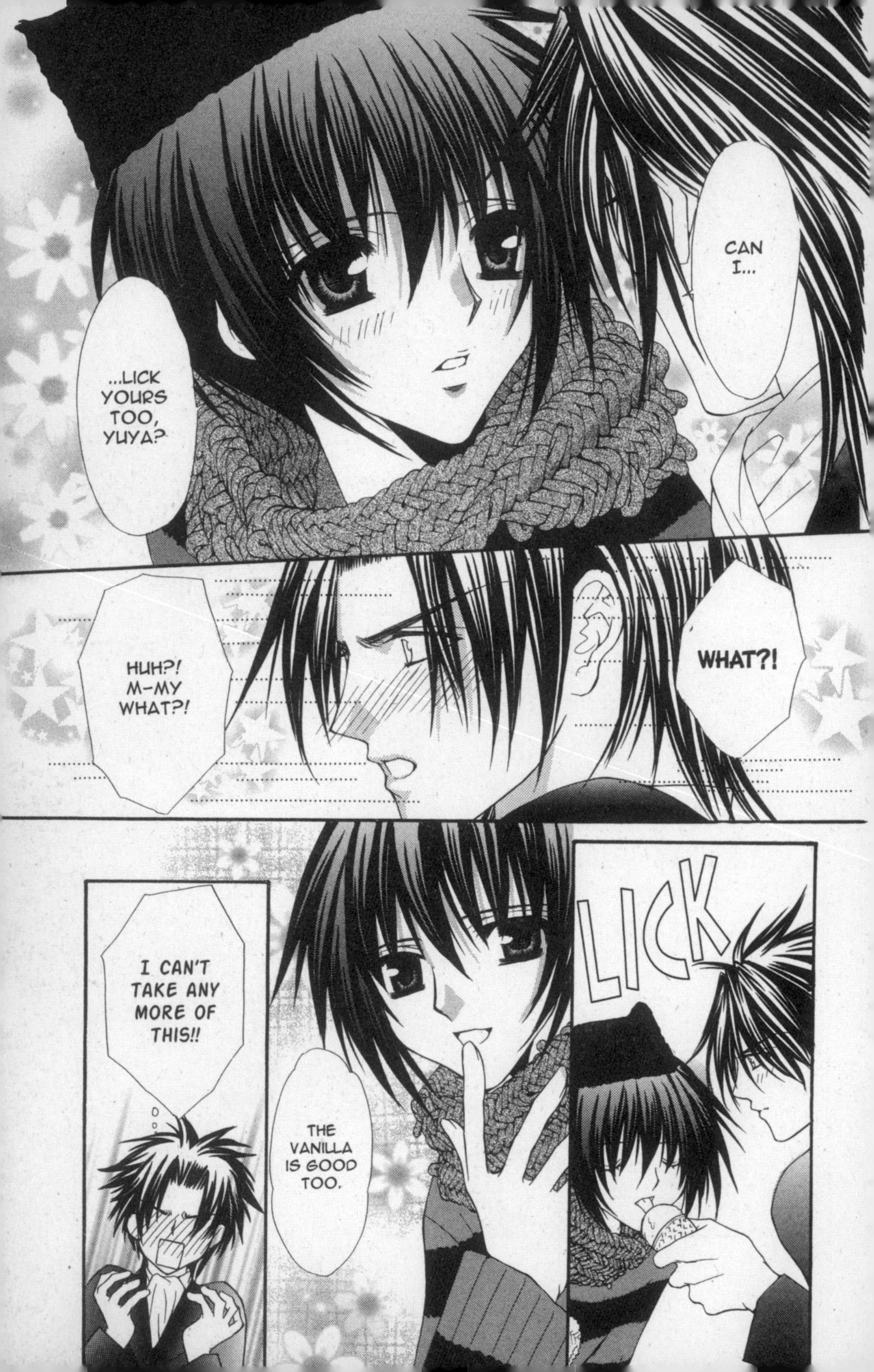
CAN I...
...LICK YOURS TOO, YUYA?
WHAT?!
HUH?! M-MY WHAT?!
LICK
THE VANILLA IS GOOD TOO.
I CAN'T TAKE ANY MORE OF THIS!!

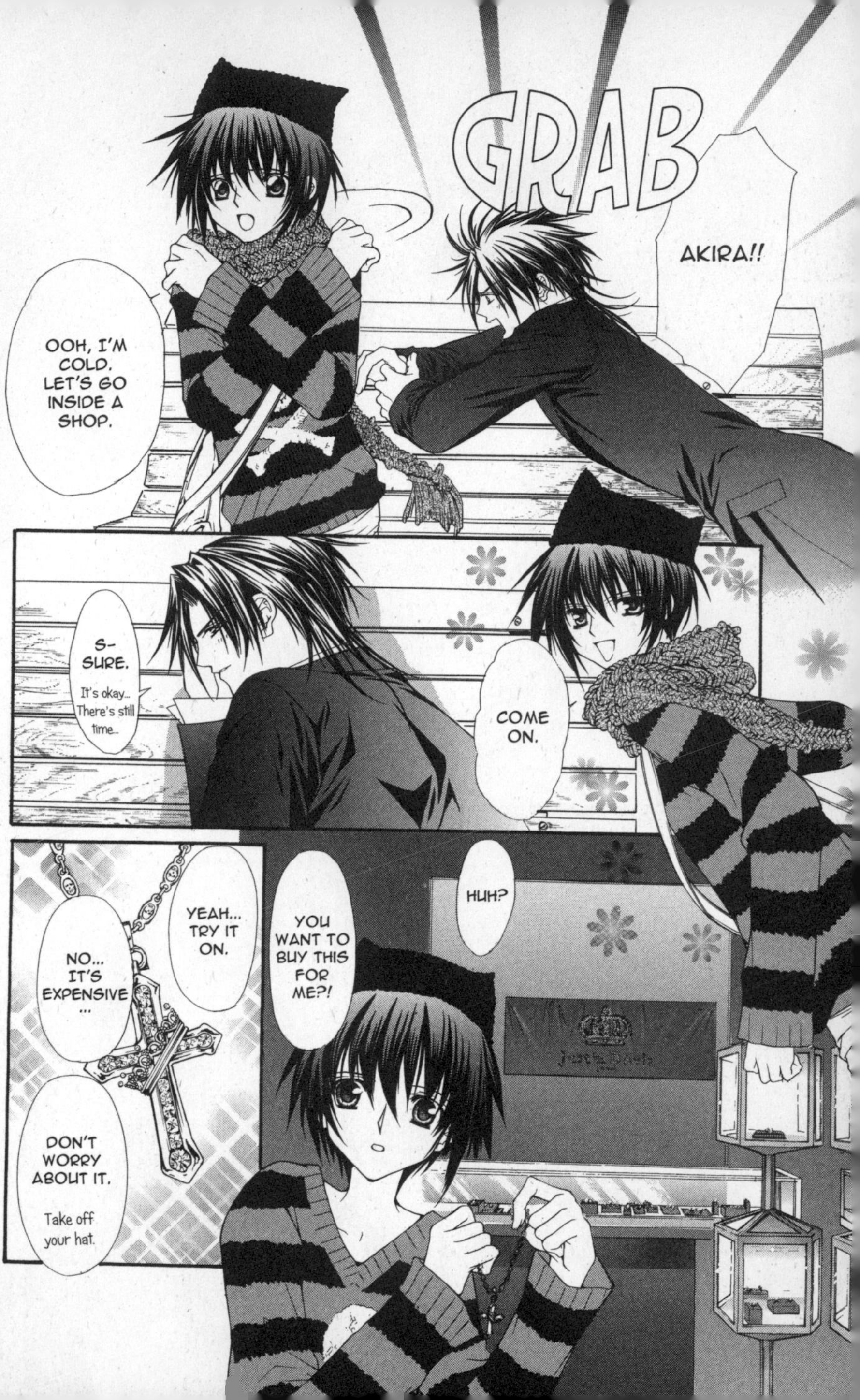
GRAB
AKIRA!!
OOH, I'M COLD. LET'S GO INSIDE A SHOP.
COME ON.
S-SURE.
It's okay... There's still time...
HUH?
YOU WANT TO BUY THIS FOR ME?!
YEAH... TRY IT ON.
NO... IT'S EXPENSIVE...
DON'T WORRY ABOUT IT.
Take off your hat.

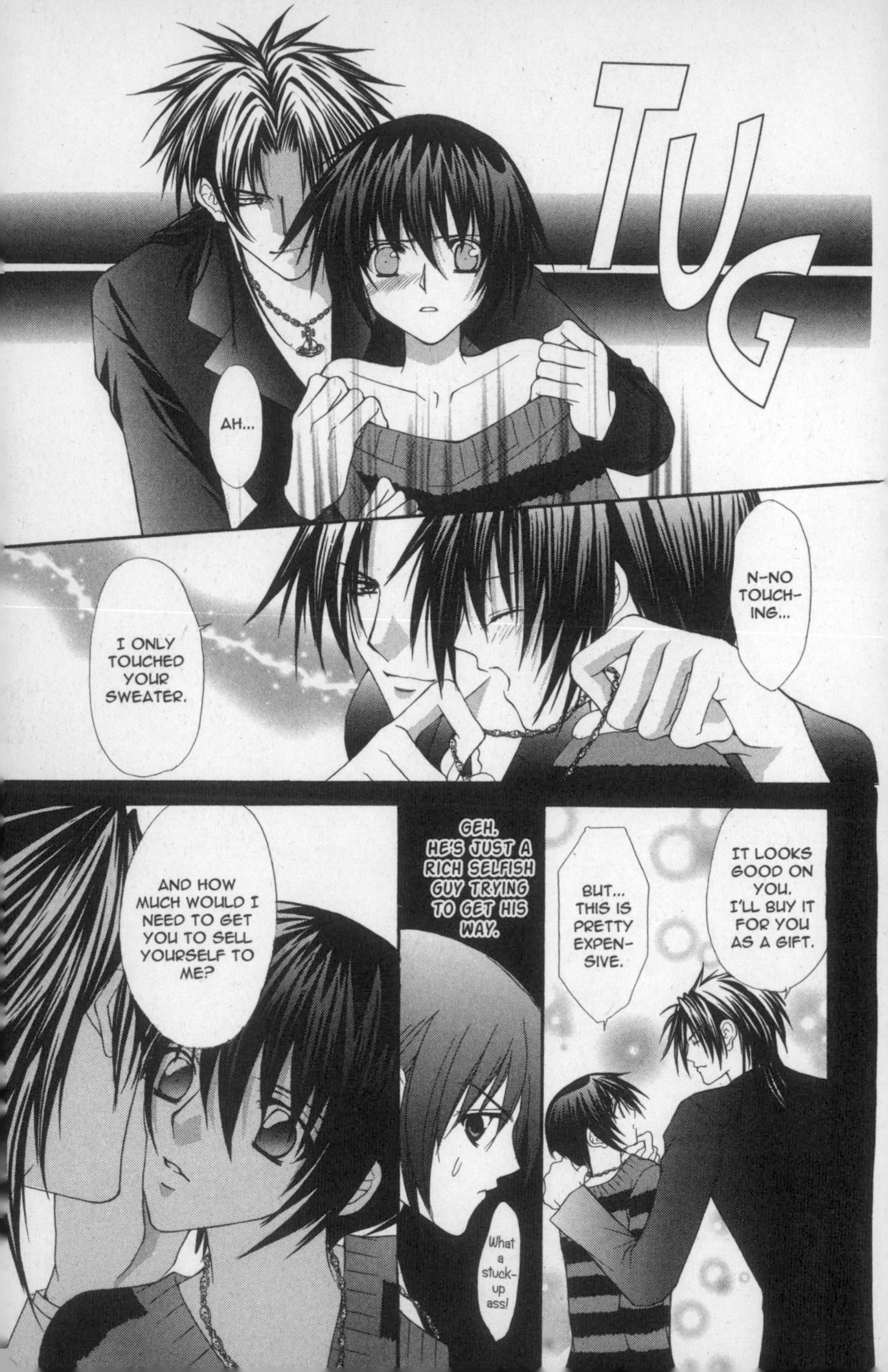
TUG
AH...
N-NO TOUCHING...
I ONLY TOUCHED YOUR SWEATER.
IT LOOKS GOOD ON YOU. I'LL BUY IT FOR YOU AS A GIFT.
BUT... THIS IS PRETTY EXPENSIVE.
GEH. HE'S JUST A RICH SELFISH GUY TRYING TO GET HIS WAY.
What a stuck-up ass!
AND HOW MUCH WOULD I NEED TO GET YOU TO SELL YOURSELF TO ME?

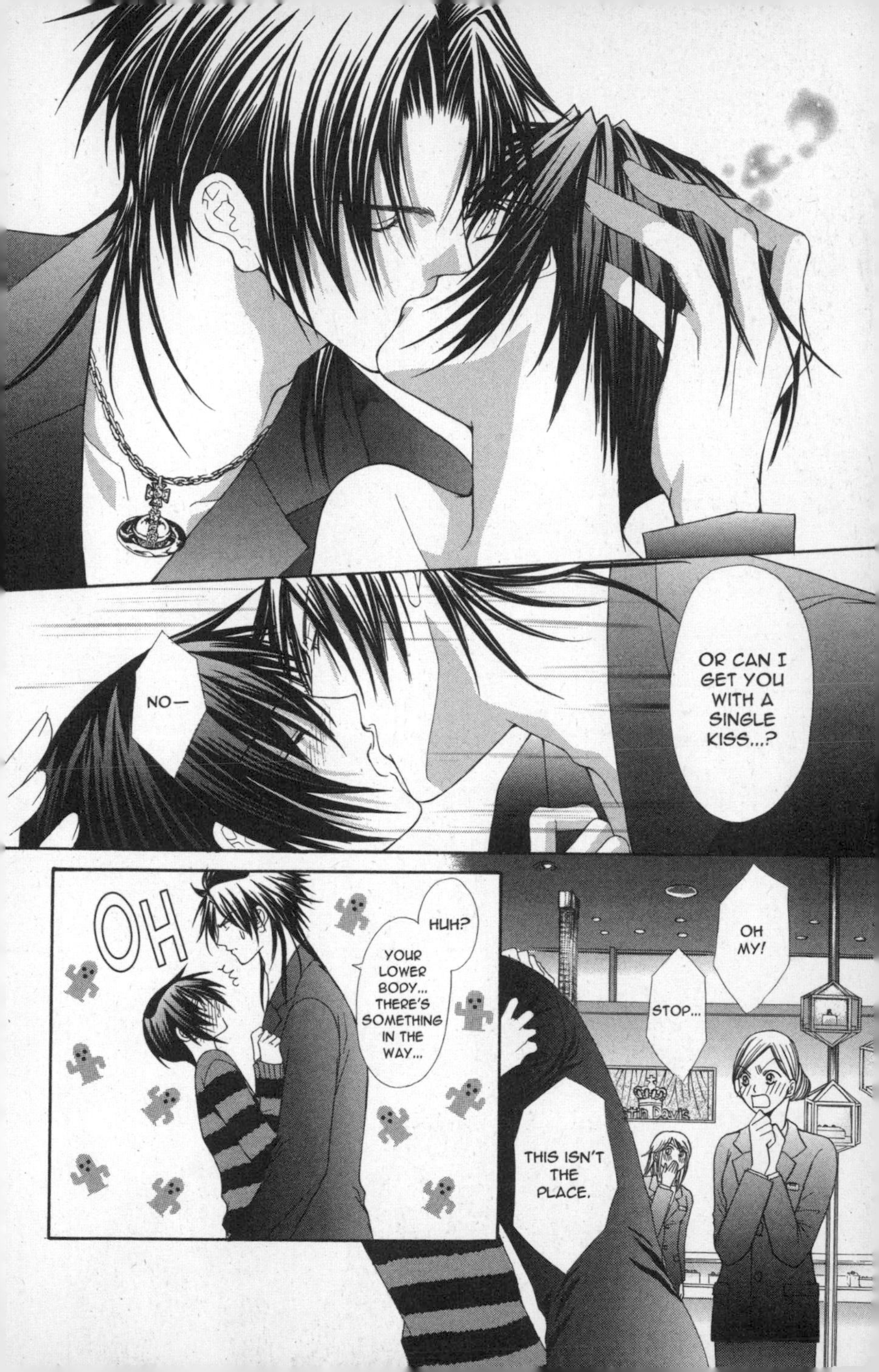

OR CAN I GET YOU WITH A SINGLE KISS...?
NO—
OH MY!
STOP...
THIS ISN'T THE PLACE.
HUH?
YOUR LOWER BODY... THERE'S SOMETHING IN THE WAY...
OH

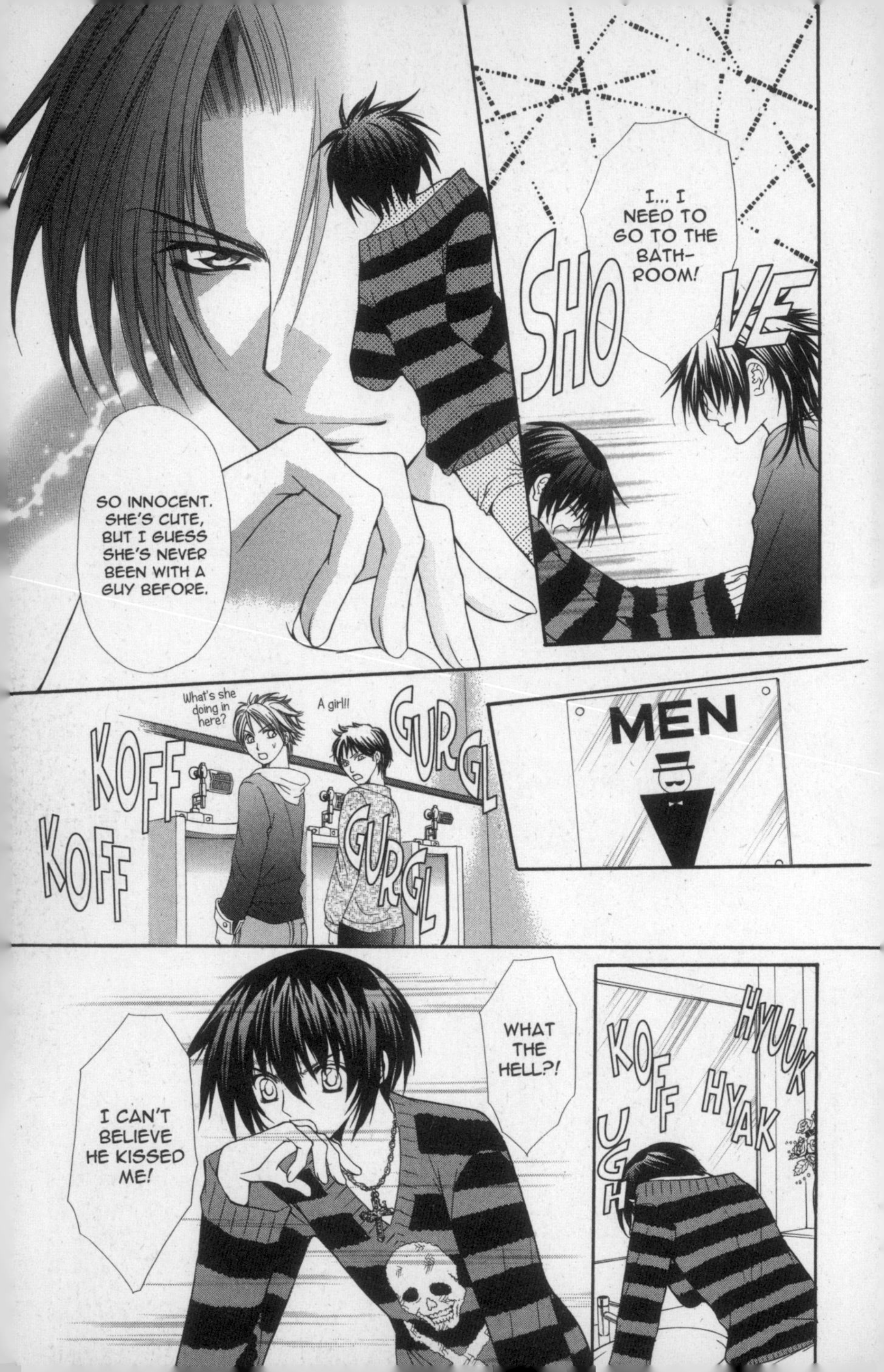

I... I NEED TO GO TO THE BATH-ROOM!
SHOVE
SO INNOCENT. SHE'S CUTE, BUT I GUESS SHE'S NEVER BEEN WITH A GUY BEFORE.
MEN
GURGL
A girl!!
What's she doing in here?
KOFF
KOFF
GURGL
HYUUK
KOFF
HYAK
UGH
WHAT THE HELL?!
I CAN'T BELIEVE HE KISSED ME!

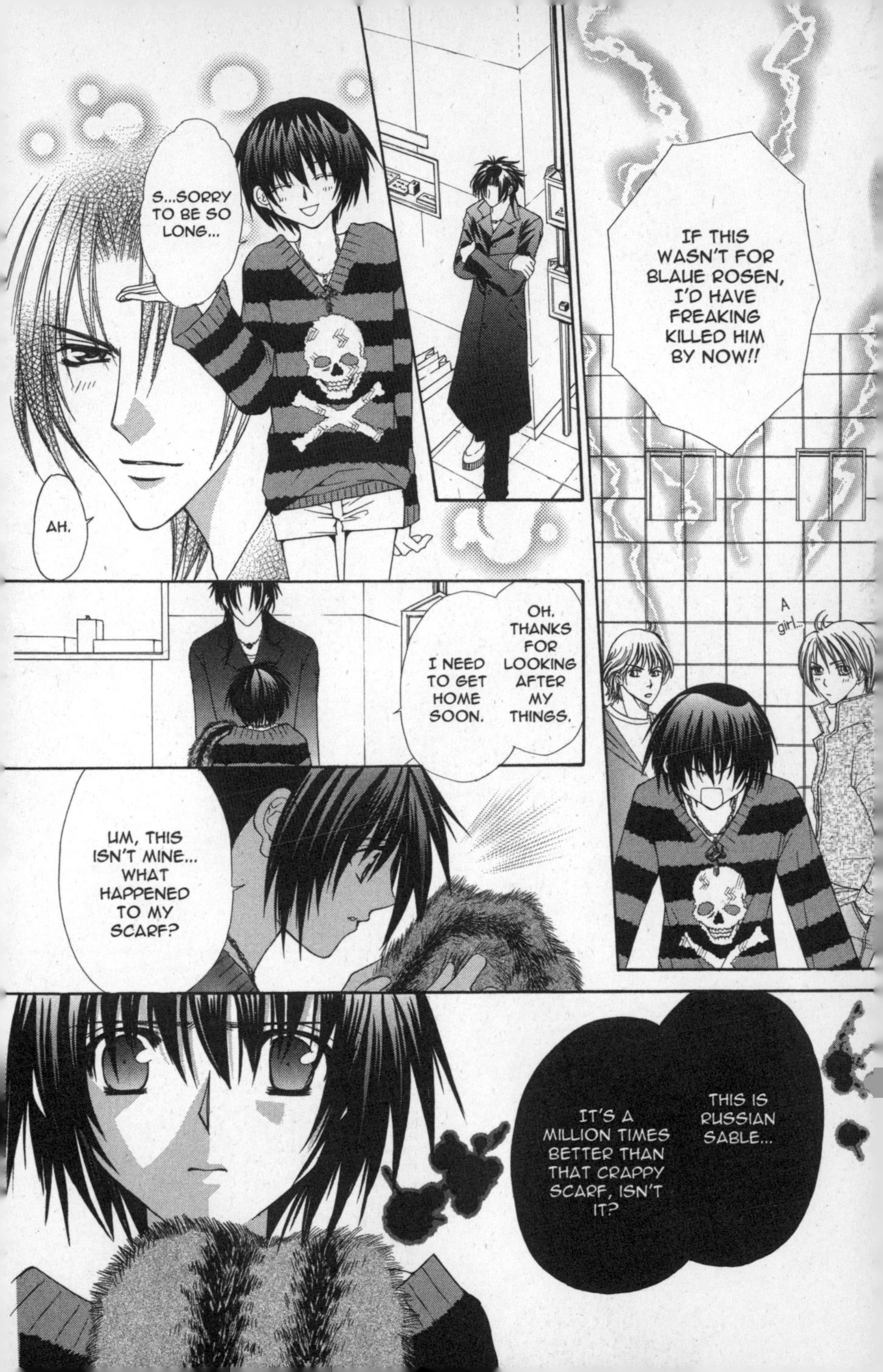
IF THIS WASN'T FOR BLAUE ROSEN, I'D HAVE FREAKING KILLED HIM BY NOW!!
A girl...
S...SORRY TO BE SO LONG...
AH.
OH. THANKS FOR LOOKING AFTER MY THINGS.
I NEED TO GET HOME SOON.
UM, THIS ISN'T MINE... WHAT HAPPENED TO MY SCARF?
THIS IS RUSSIAN SABLE...
IT'S A MILLION TIMES BETTER THAN THAT CRAPPY SCARF, ISN'T IT?

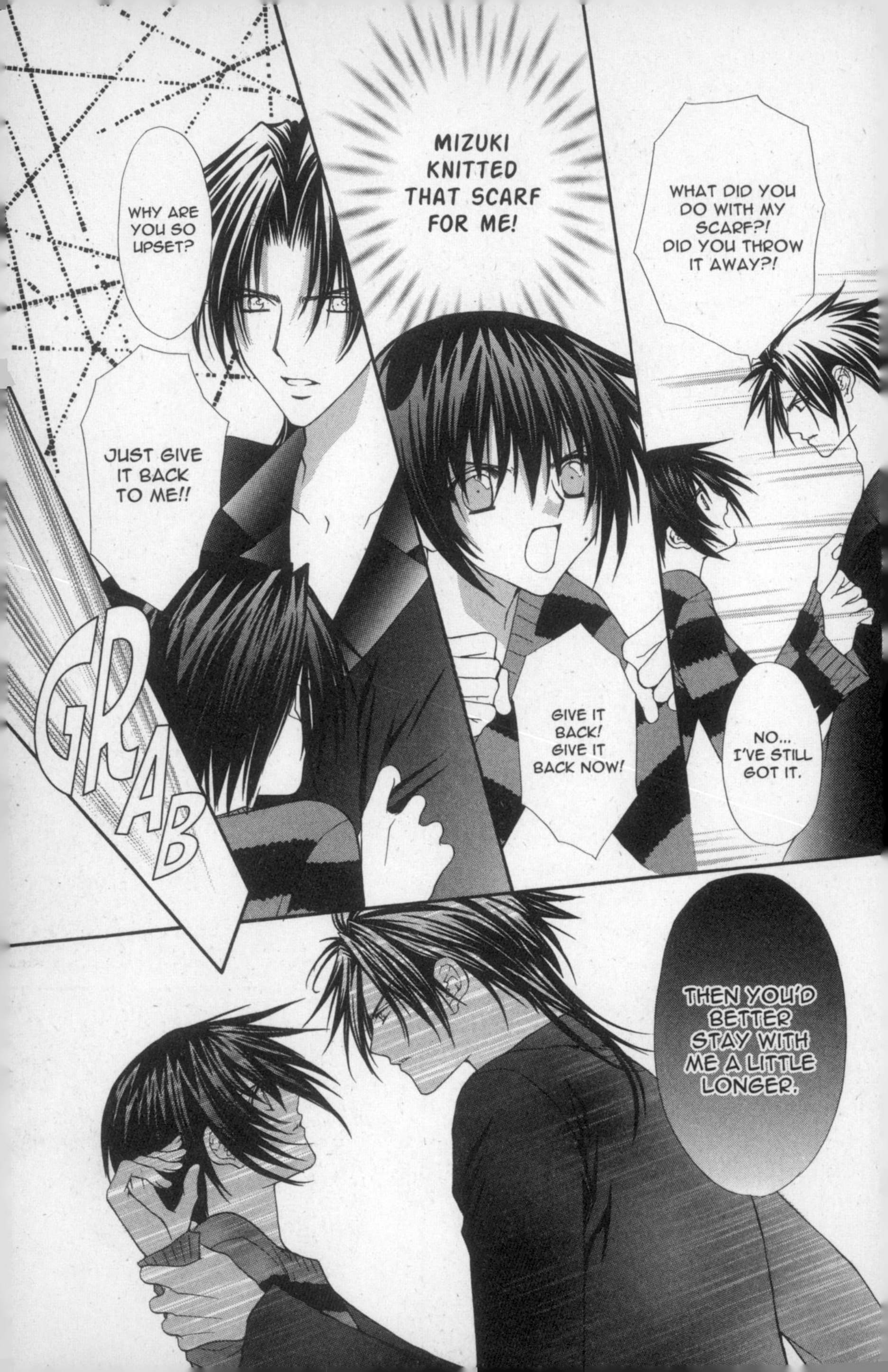
WHAT DID YOU DO WITH MY SCARF?! DID YOU THROW IT AWAY?!
NO... I'VE STILL GOT IT.
MIZUKI KNITTED THAT SCARF FOR ME!
GIVE IT BACK! GIVE IT BACK NOW!
WHY ARE YOU SO UPSET?
JUST GIVE IT BACK TO ME!!
GRAB
THEN YOU'D BETTER STAY WITH ME A LITTLE LONGER.

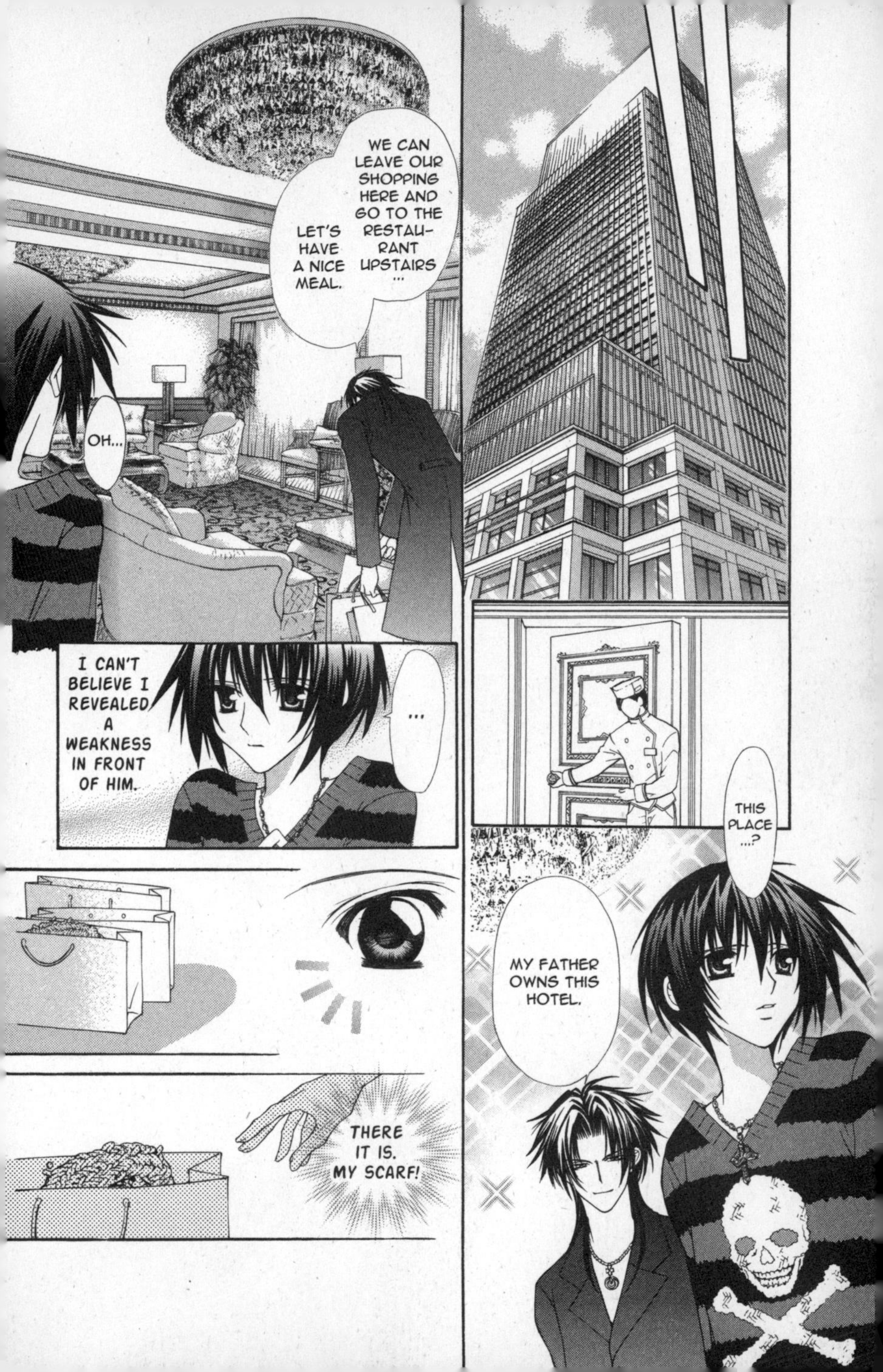
THIS PLACE ...?
MY FATHER OWNS THIS HOTEL.
WE CAN LEAVE OUR SHOPPING HERE AND GO TO THE RESTAU-RANT UPSTAIRS ...
LET'S HAVE A NICE MEAL.
OH...
...
I CAN'T BELIEVE I REVEALED A WEAKNESS IN FRONT OF HIM.
THERE IT IS. MY SCARF!

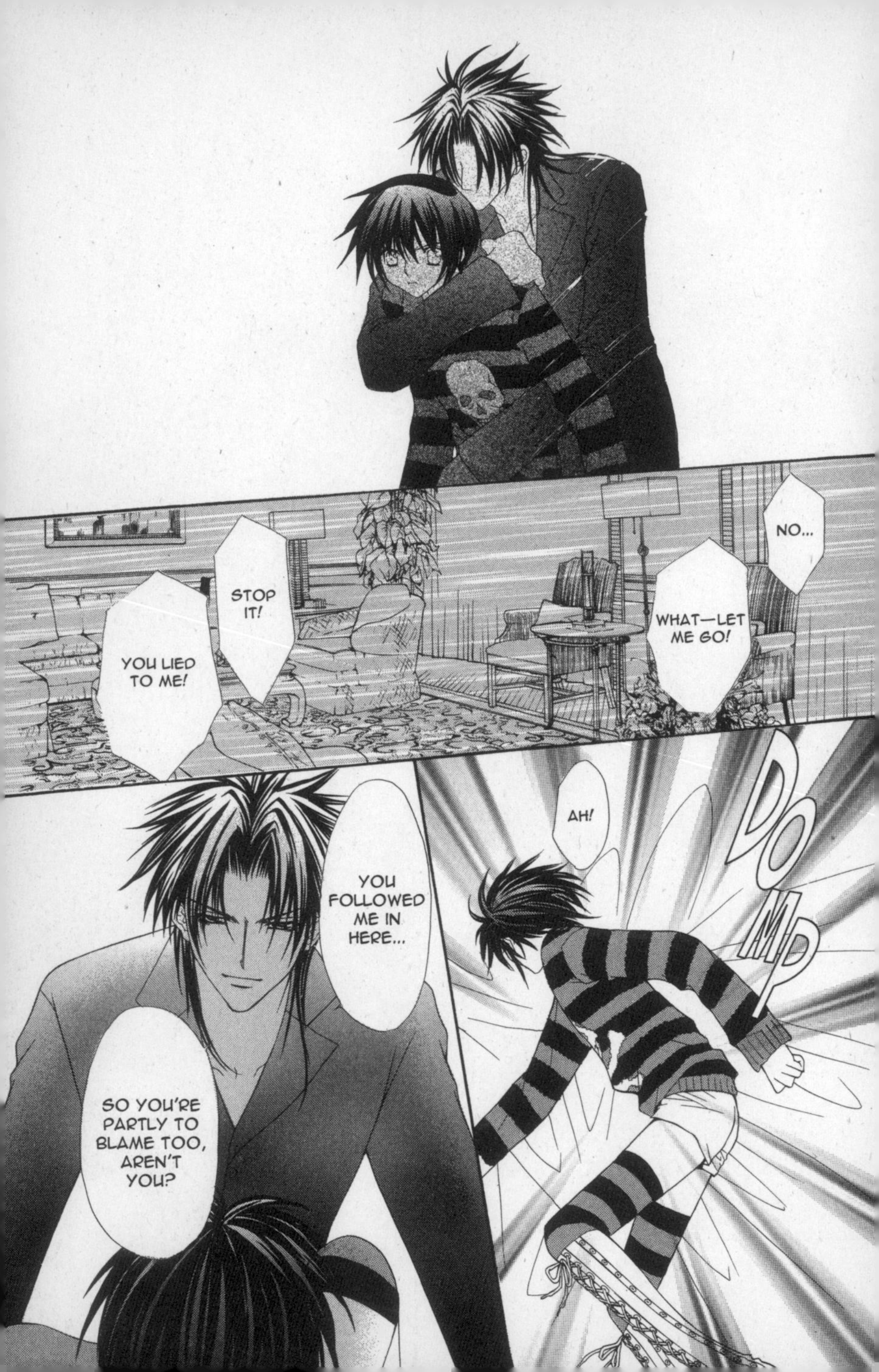
NO...
WHAT—LET ME GO!
STOP IT!
YOU LIED TO ME!
DOMP
AH!
YOU FOLLOWED ME IN HERE...
SO YOU'RE PARTLY TO BLAME TOO, AREN'T YOU?

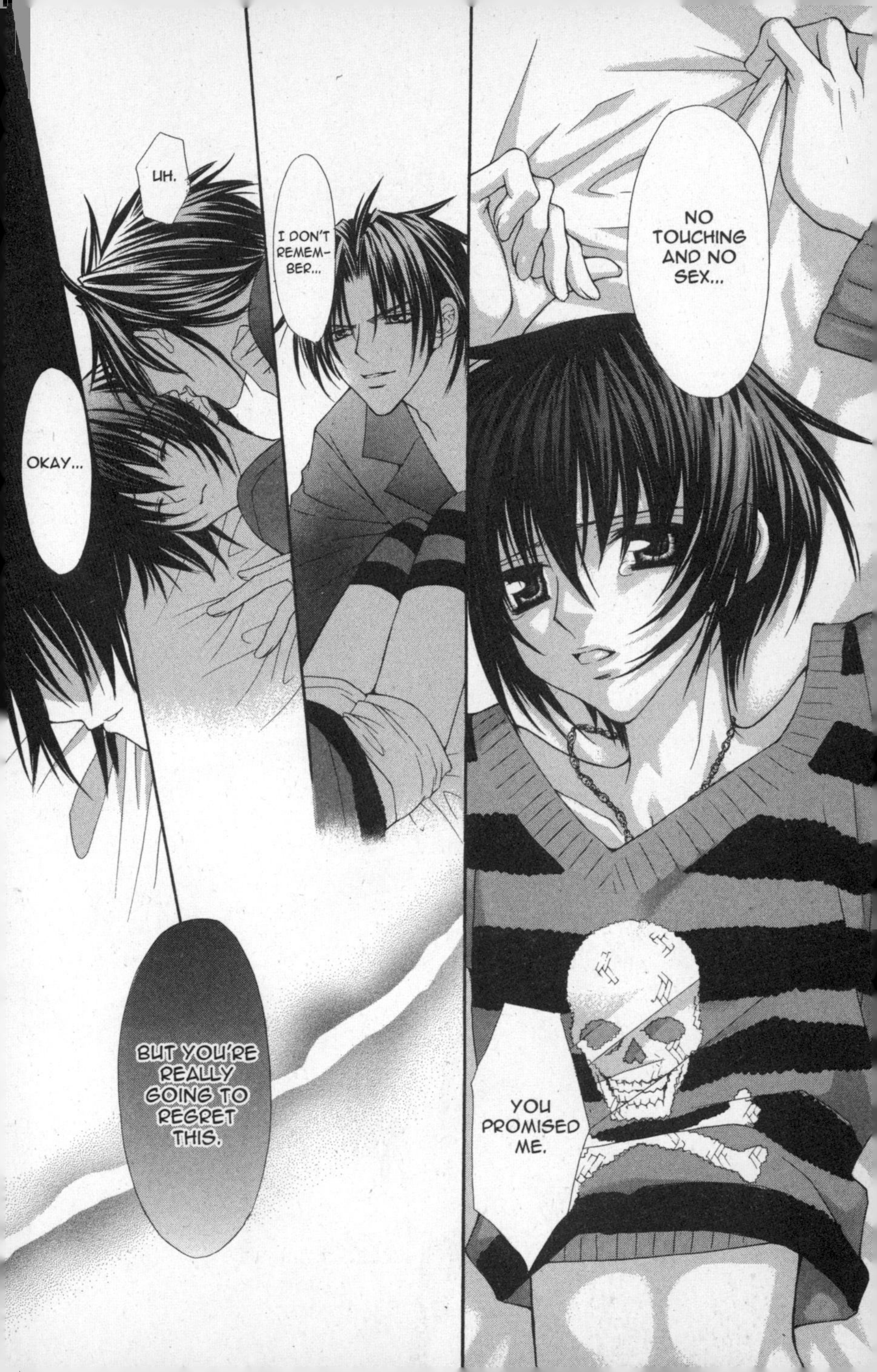
NO TOUCHING AND NO SEX...
YOU PROMISED ME.
I DON'T REMEMBER...
UH.
OKAY...
BUT YOU'RE REALLY GOING TO REGRET THIS.

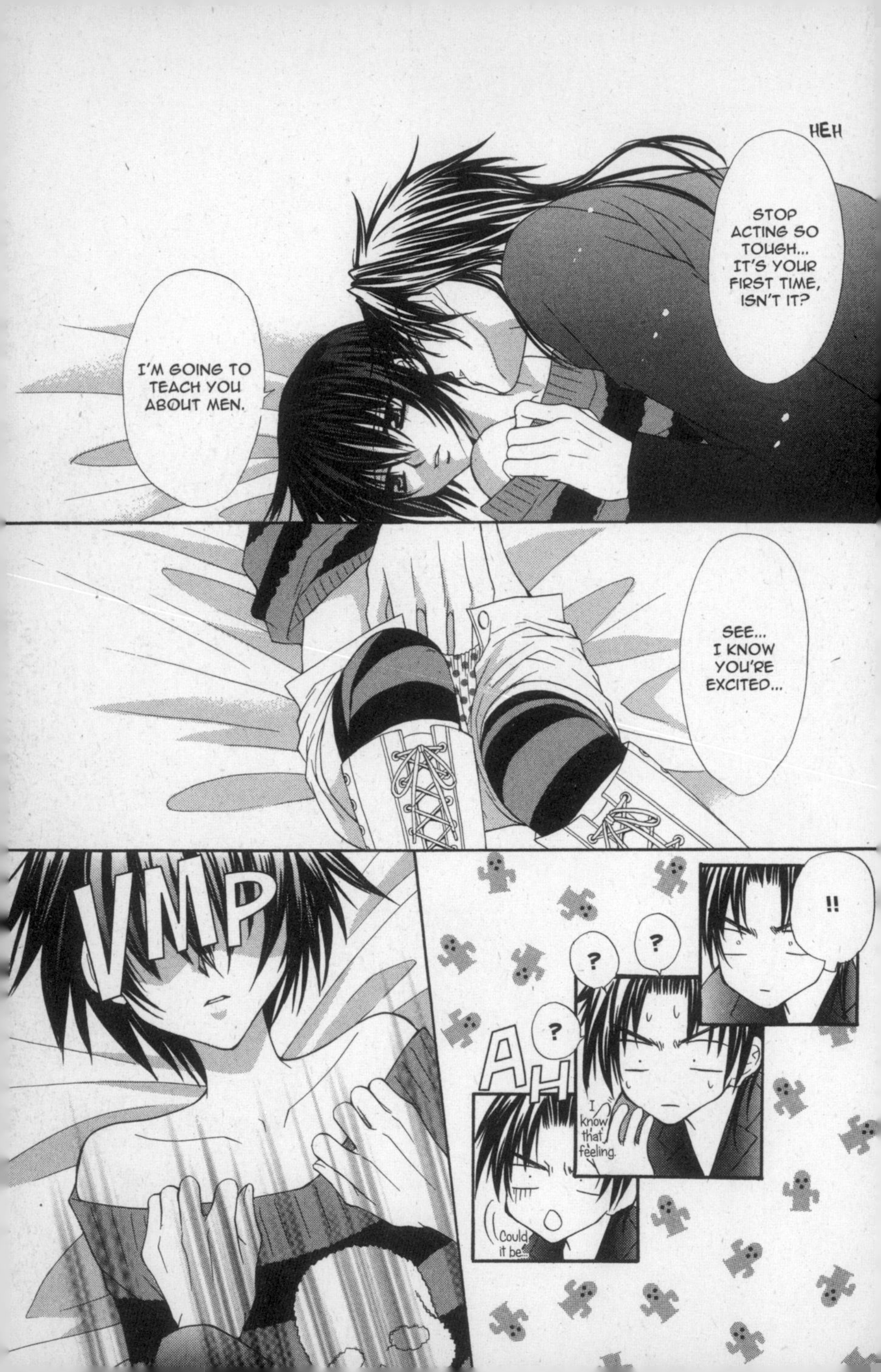
HEH
STOP ACTING SO TOUGH... IT'S YOUR FIRST TIME, ISN'T IT?
I'M GOING TO TEACH YOU ABOUT MEN.
SEE... I KNOW YOU'RE EXCITED...
!!
?
?
?
AH
I know that feeling.
Could it be...
VMP

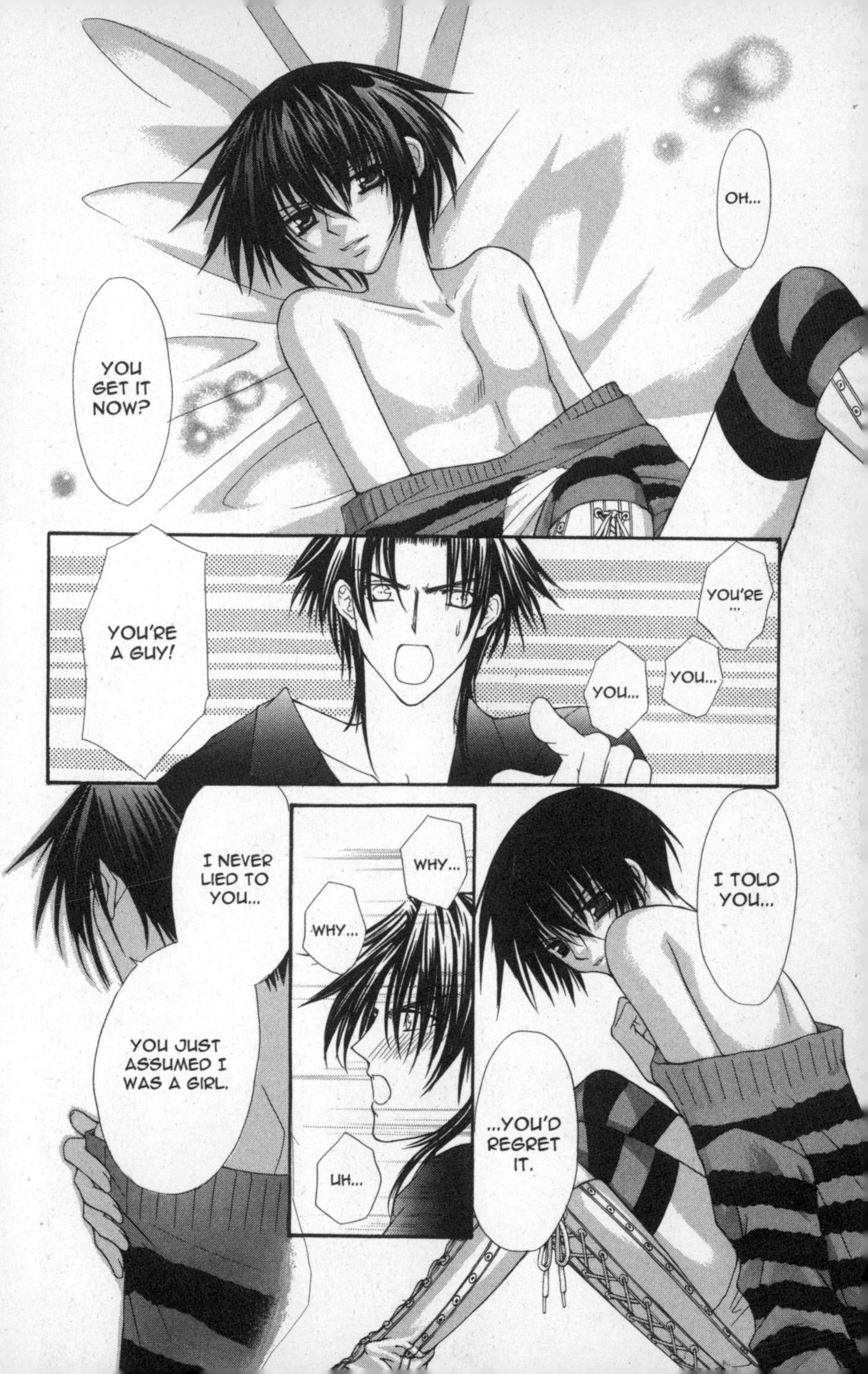
OH...
YOU GET IT NOW?
YOU'RE ...
YOU...
YOU...
YOU'RE A GUY!
I TOLD YOU...
...YOU'D REGRET IT.
WHY...
WHY...
UH...
I NEVER LIED TO YOU...
YOU JUST ASSUMED I WAS A GIRL.

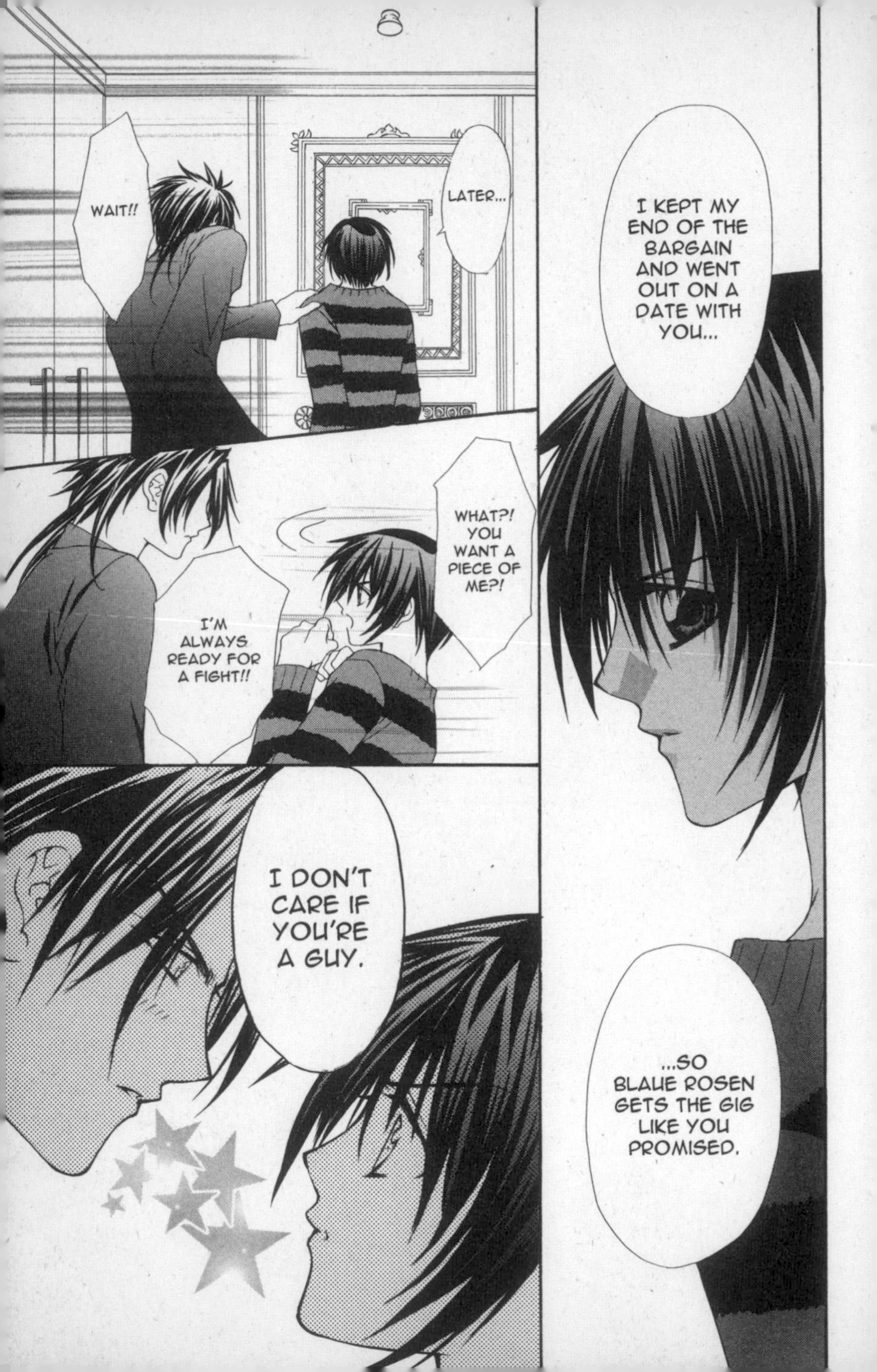
I KEPT MY END OF THE BARGAIN AND WENT OUT ON A DATE WITH YOU...
...SO BLAUE ROSEN GETS THE GIG LIKE YOU PROMISED.
LATER...
WAIT!!
WHAT?! YOU WANT A PIECE OF ME?!
I'M ALWAYS READY FOR A FIGHT!!
I DON'T CARE IF YOU'RE A GUY.

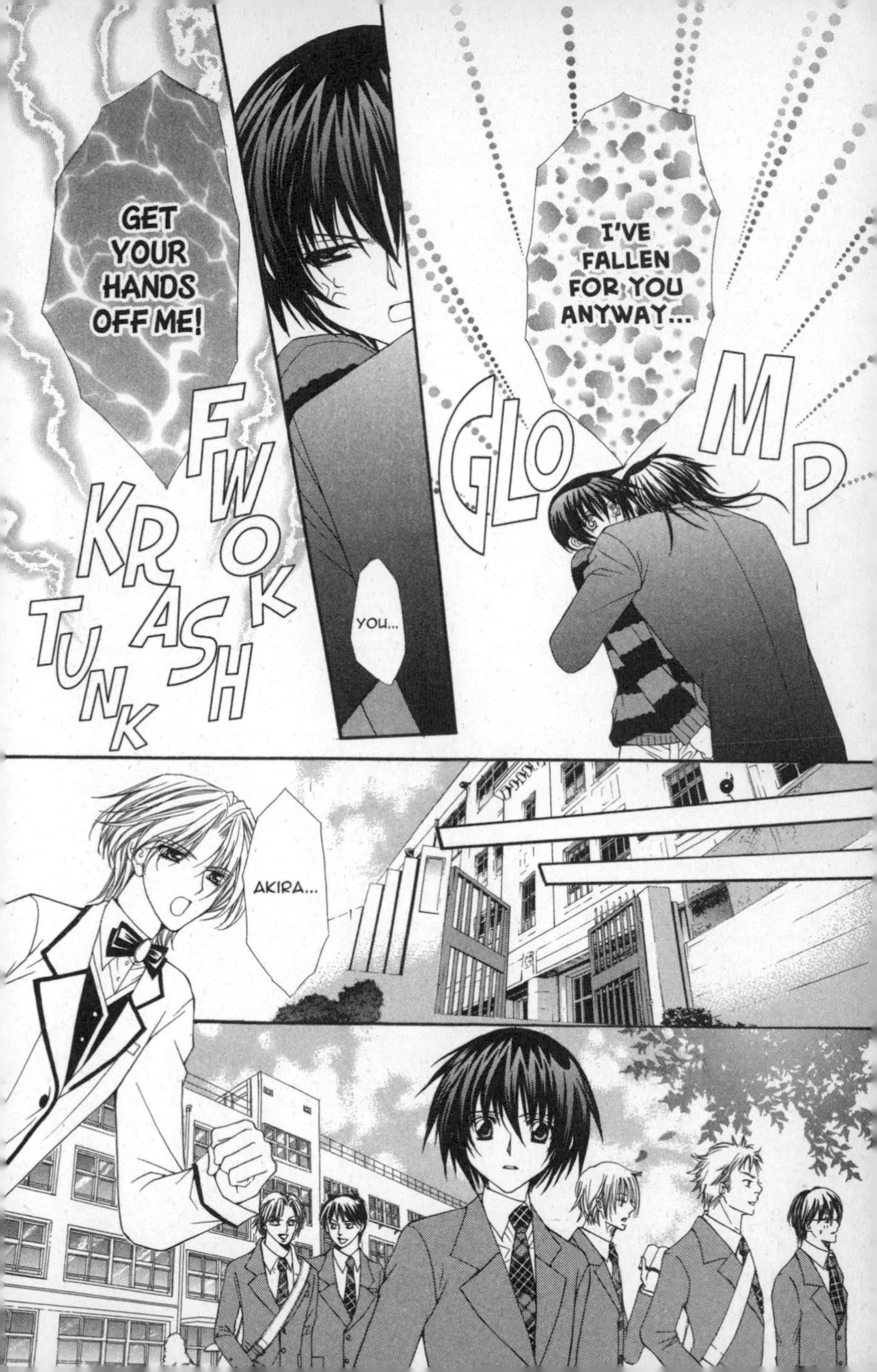
I'VE FALLEN FOR YOU ANYWAY...
GLOMP
YOU...
GET YOUR HANDS OFF ME!
FWOK
KRASH
TUNK
AKIRA...

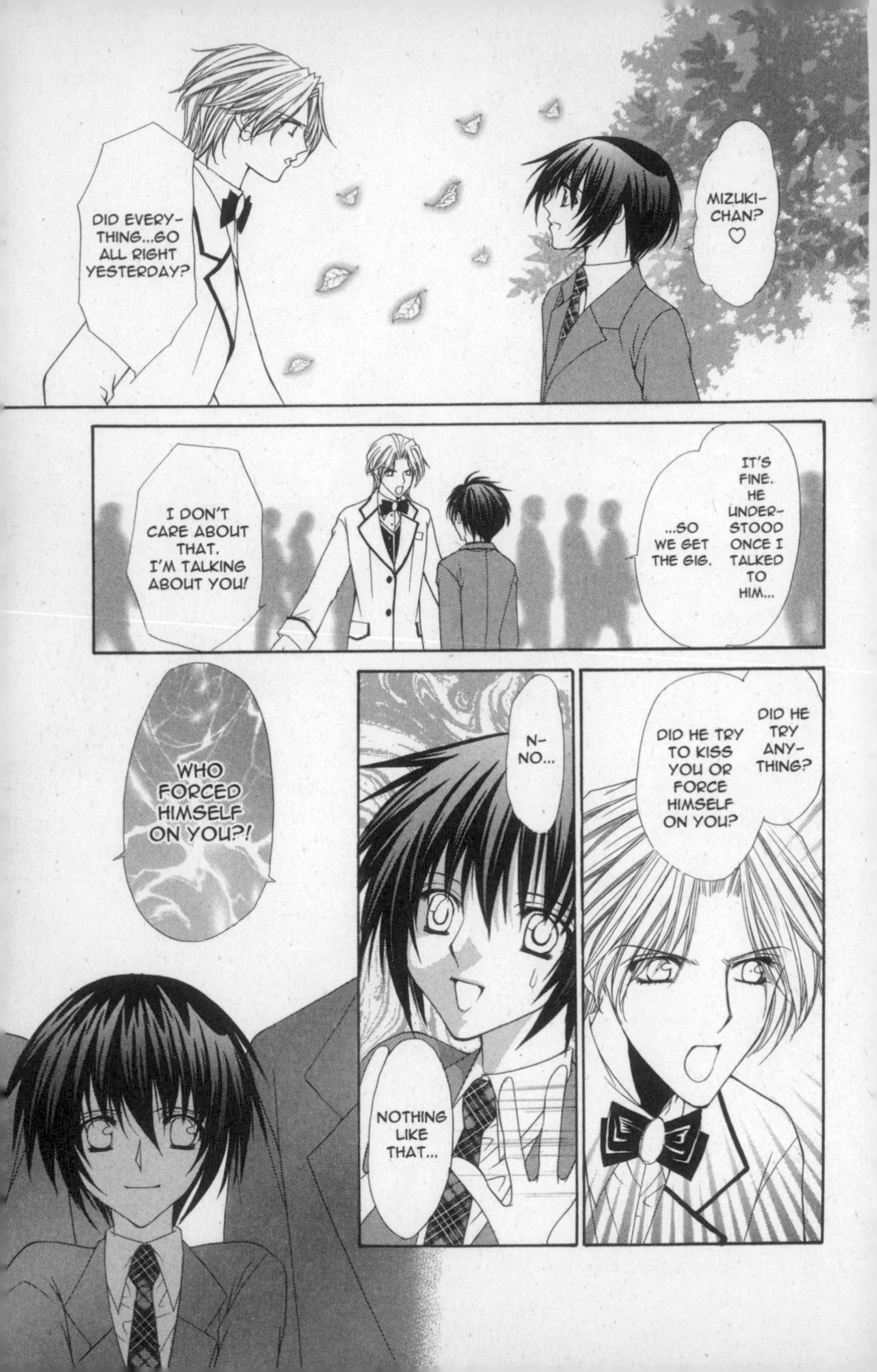

MIZUKI-CHAN? ♡
DID EVERY-THING...GO ALL RIGHT YESTERDAY?
IT'S FINE. HE UNDER-STOOD ONCE I TALKED TO HIM...
...SO WE GET THE GIG.
I DON'T CARE ABOUT THAT. I'M TALKING ABOUT YOU!
DID HE TRY ANY-THING?
DID HE TRY TO KISS YOU OR FORCE HIMSELF ON YOU?
N-NO...
NOTHING LIKE THAT...
WHO FORCED HIMSELF ON YOU?!

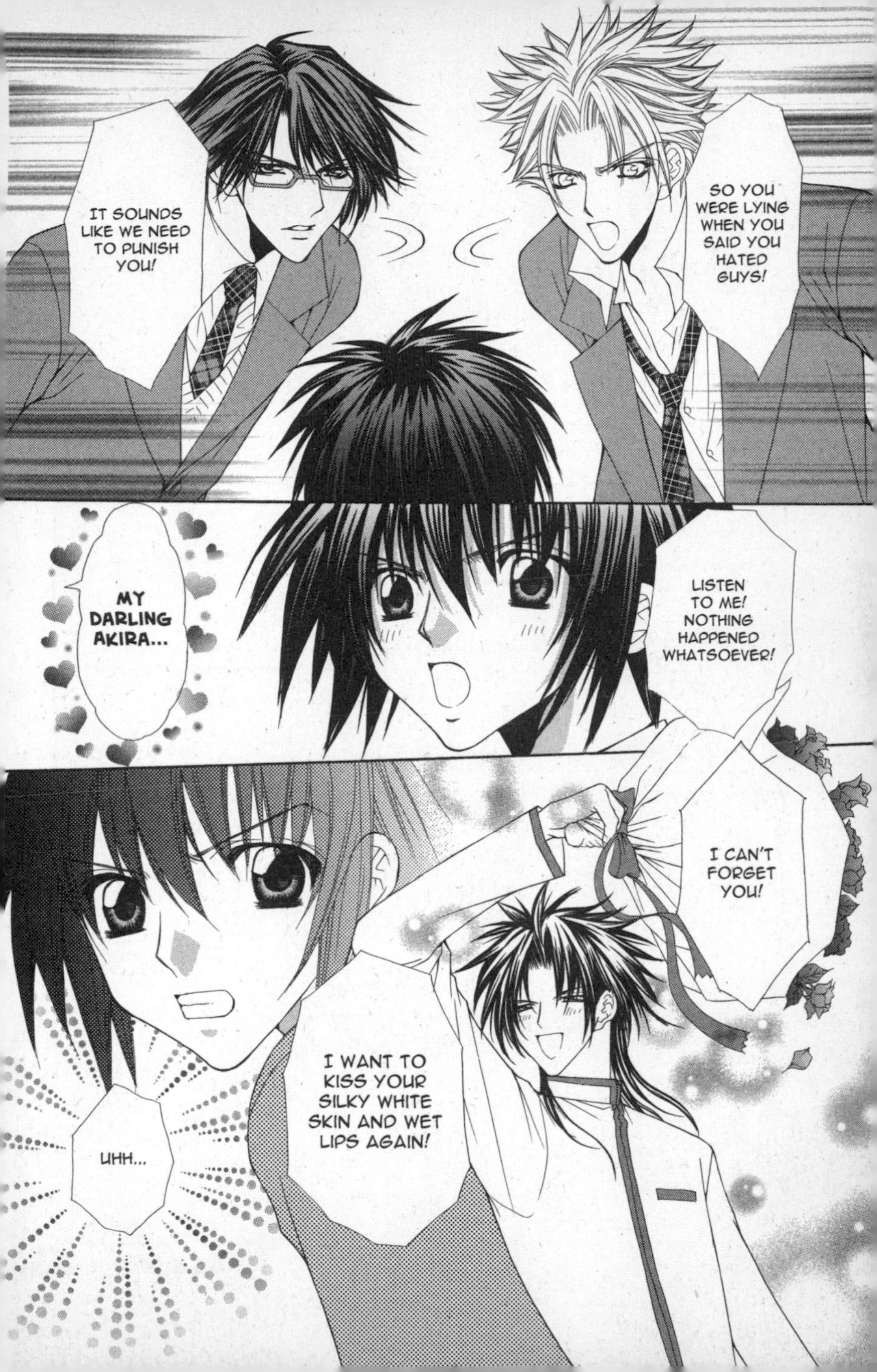
SO YOU WERE LYING WHEN YOU SAID YOU HATED GUYS!
IT SOUNDS LIKE WE NEED TO PUNISH YOU!
LISTEN TO ME! NOTHING HAPPENED WHATSOEVER!
MY DARLING AKIRA...
I CAN'T FORGET YOU!
I WANT TO KISS YOUR SILKY WHITE SKIN AND WET LIPS AGAIN!
UHH...

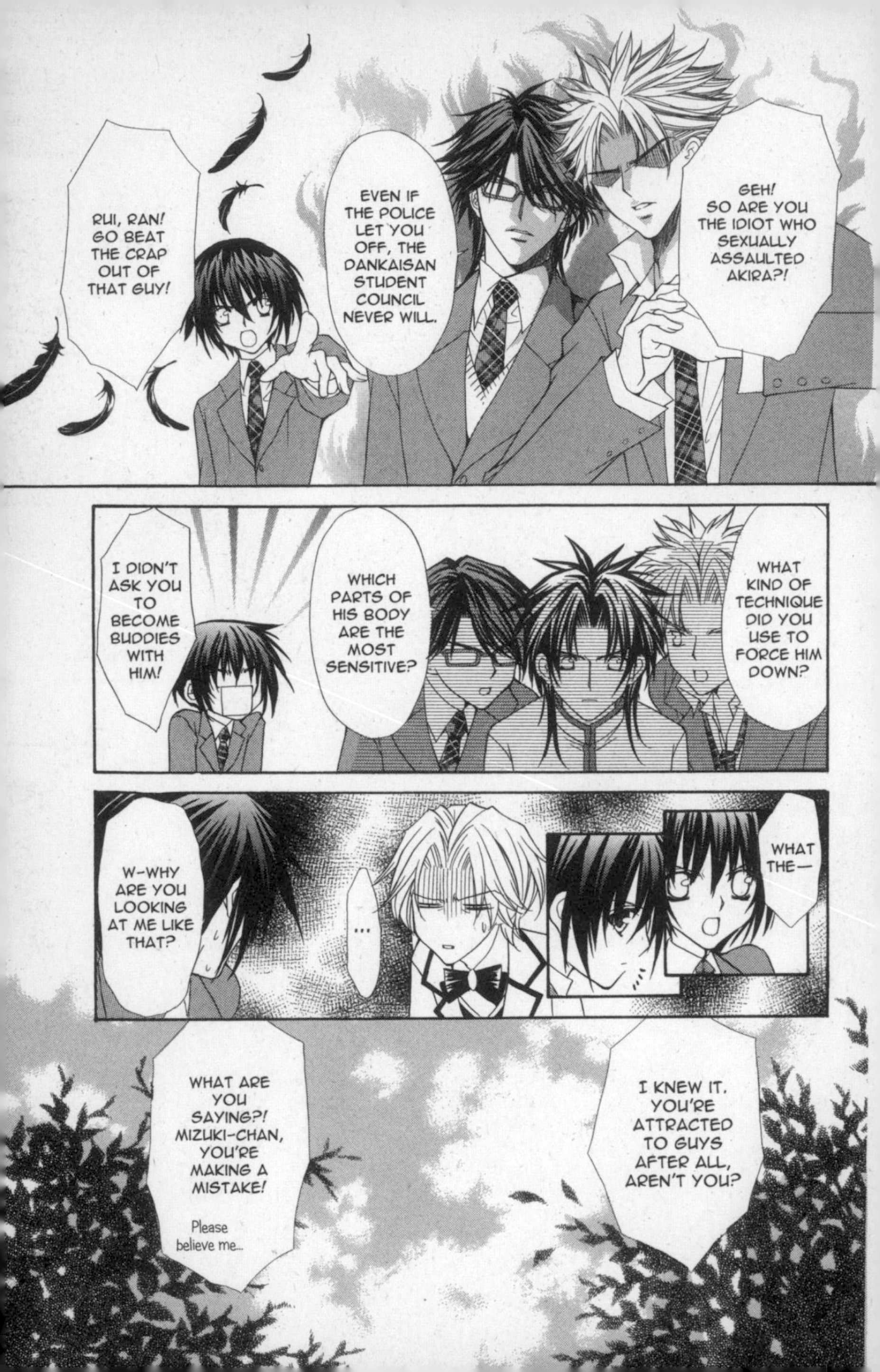
GEH! SO ARE YOU THE IDIOT WHO SEXUALLY ASSAULTED AKIRA?!
EVEN IF THE POLICE LET YOU OFF, THE DANKAISAN STUDENT COUNCIL NEVER WILL.
RUI, RAN! GO BEAT THE CRAP OUT OF THAT GUY!
WHAT KIND OF TECHNIQUE DID YOU USE TO FORCE HIM DOWN?
WHICH PARTS OF HIS BODY ARE THE MOST SENSITIVE?
I DIDN'T ASK YOU TO BECOME BUDDIES WITH HIM!
WHAT THE—
...
W-WHY ARE YOU LOOKING AT ME LIKE THAT?
I KNEW IT. YOU'RE ATTRACTED TO GUYS AFTER ALL, AREN'T YOU?
WHAT ARE YOU SAYING?! MIZUKI-CHAN, YOU'RE MAKING A MISTAKE!
Please believe me...

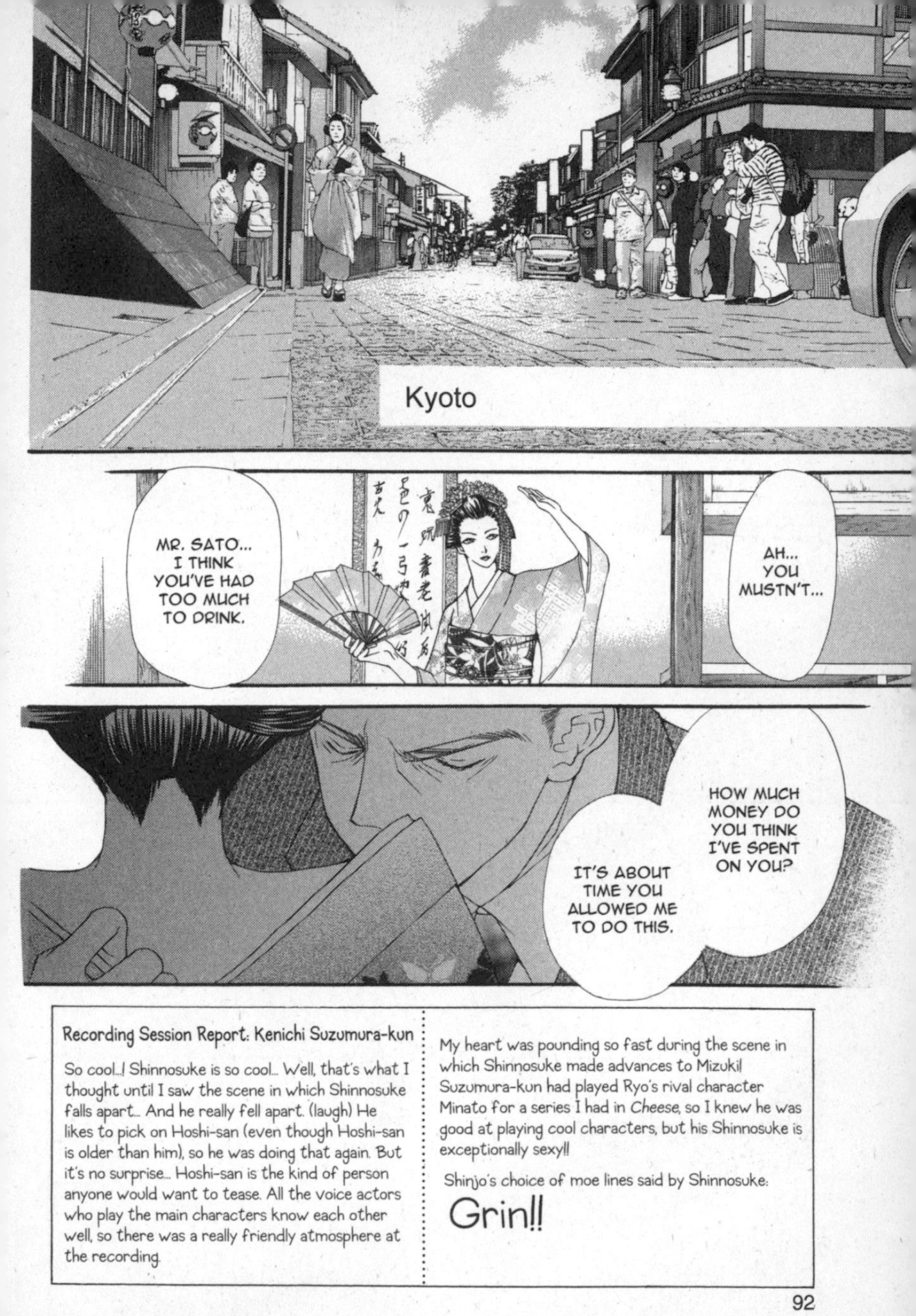
Kyoto
AH... YOU MUSTN'T...
MR. SATO... I THINK YOU'VE HAD TOO MUCH TO DRINK.
HOW MUCH MONEY DO YOU THINK I'VE SPENT ON YOU?
IT'S ABOUT TIME YOU ALLOWED ME TO DO THIS.

Recording Session Report: Kenichi Suzumura-kun

So cool...! Shinnosuke is so cool... Well, that's what I thought until I saw the scene in which Shinnosuke falls apart... And he really fell apart. (laugh) He likes to pick on Hoshi-san (even though Hoshi-san is older than him), so he was doing that again. But it's no surprise... Hoshi-san is the kind of person anyone would want to tease. All the voice actors who play the main characters know each other well, so there was a really friendly atmosphere at the recording.

My heart was pounding so fast during the scene in which Shinnosuke made advances to Mizuki! Suzumura-kun had played Ryo's rival character Minato for a series I had in *Cheese*, so I knew he was good at playing cool characters, but his Shinnosuke is exceptionally sexy!!

Shinjo's choice of moe lines said by Shinnosuke:

Grin!!

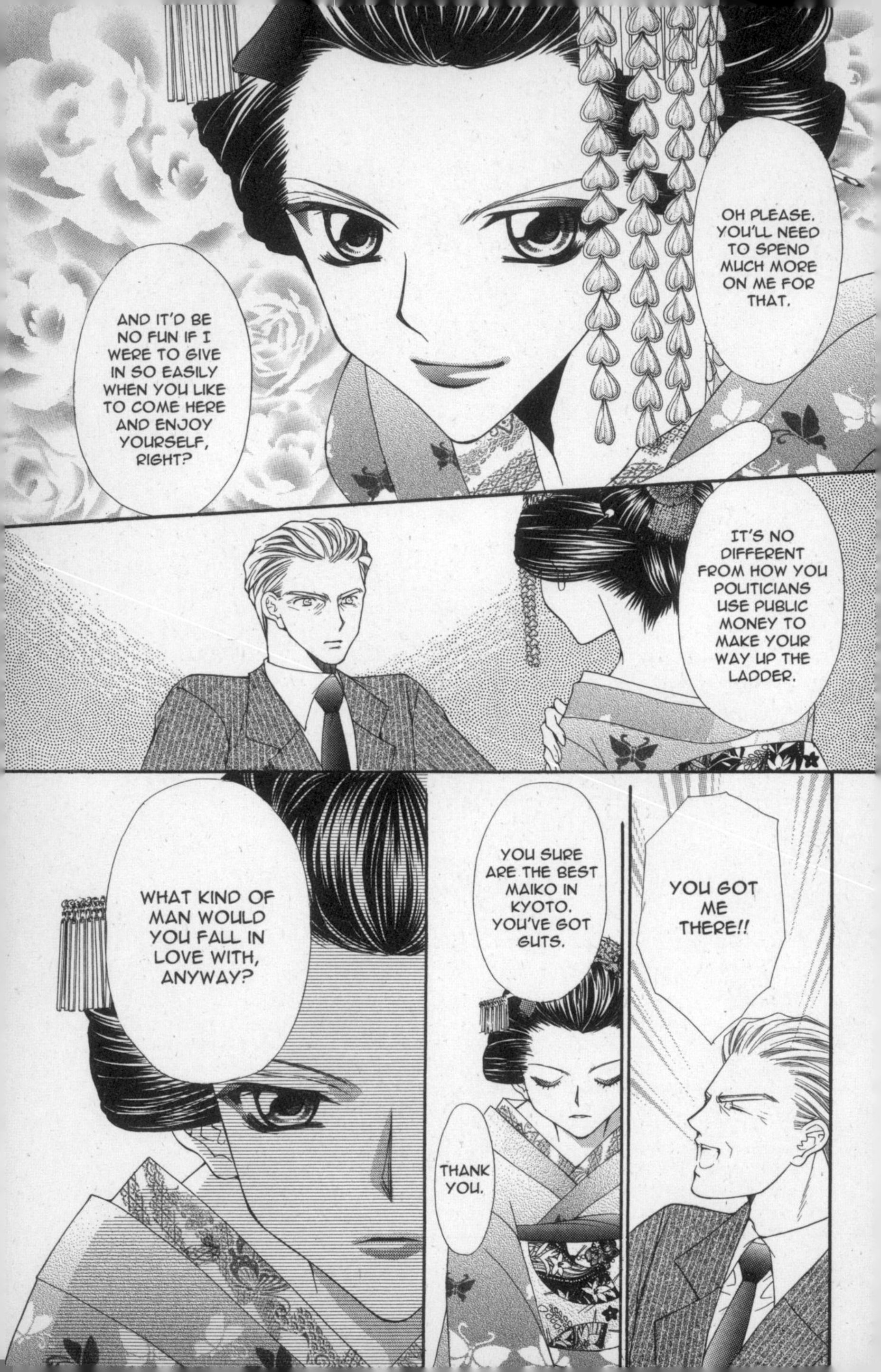
OH PLEASE. YOU'LL NEED TO SPEND MUCH MORE ON ME FOR THAT.
AND IT'D BE NO FUN IF I WERE TO GIVE IN SO EASILY WHEN YOU LIKE TO COME HERE AND ENJOY YOURSELF, RIGHT?
IT'S NO DIFFERENT FROM HOW YOU POLITICIANS USE PUBLIC MONEY TO MAKE YOUR WAY UP THE LADDER.
YOU GOT ME THERE!!
YOU SURE ARE THE BEST MAIKO IN KYOTO. YOU'VE GOT GUTS.
THANK YOU.
WHAT KIND OF MAN WOULD YOU FALL IN LOVE WITH, ANYWAY?

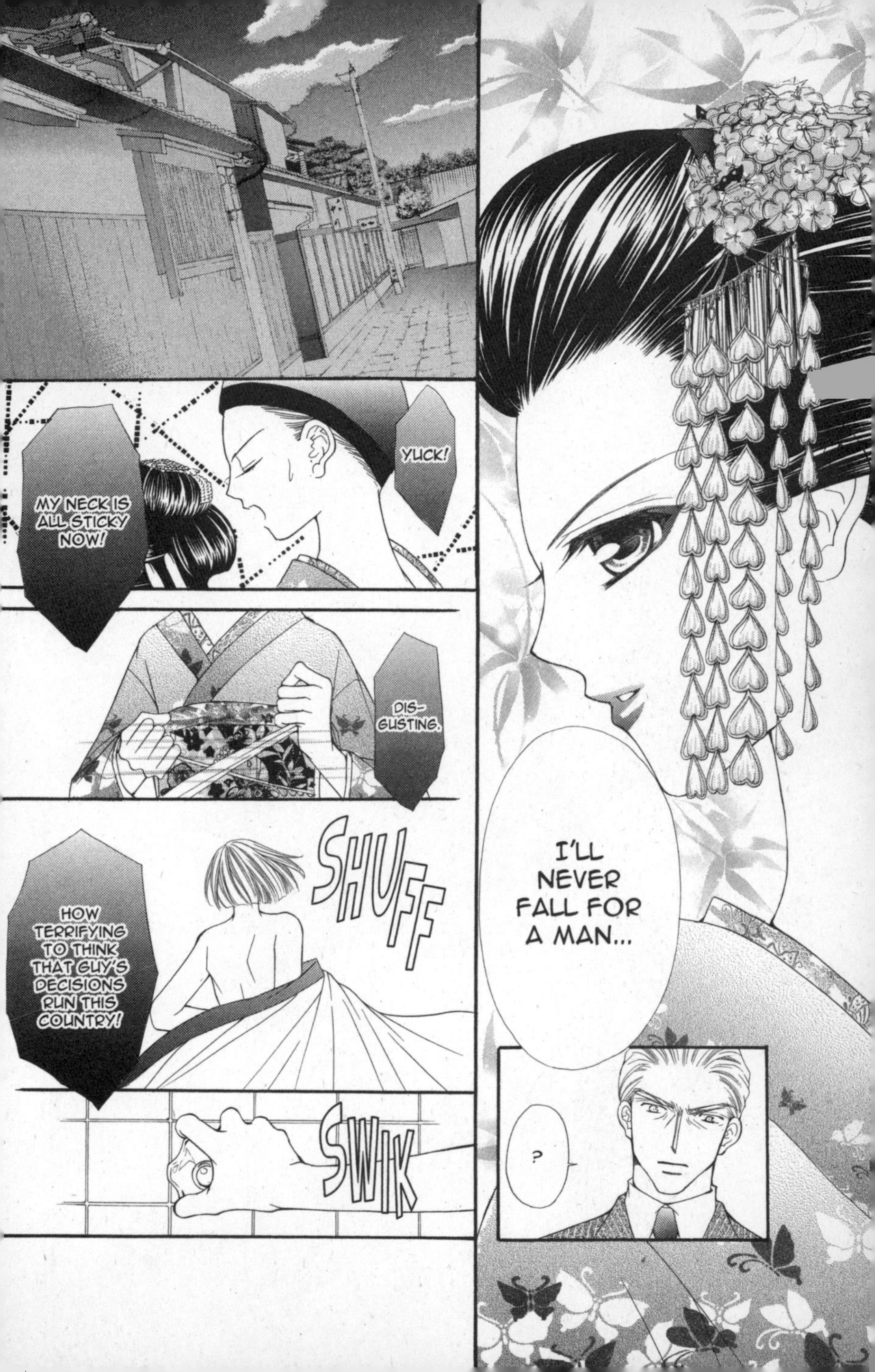

I'LL NEVER FALL FOR A MAN...
?
YUCK!
MY NECK IS ALL STICKY NOW!
DIS-GUSTING.
SHUFF
HOW TERRIFYING TO THINK THAT GUY'S DECISIONS RUN THIS COUNTRY!
SWIK

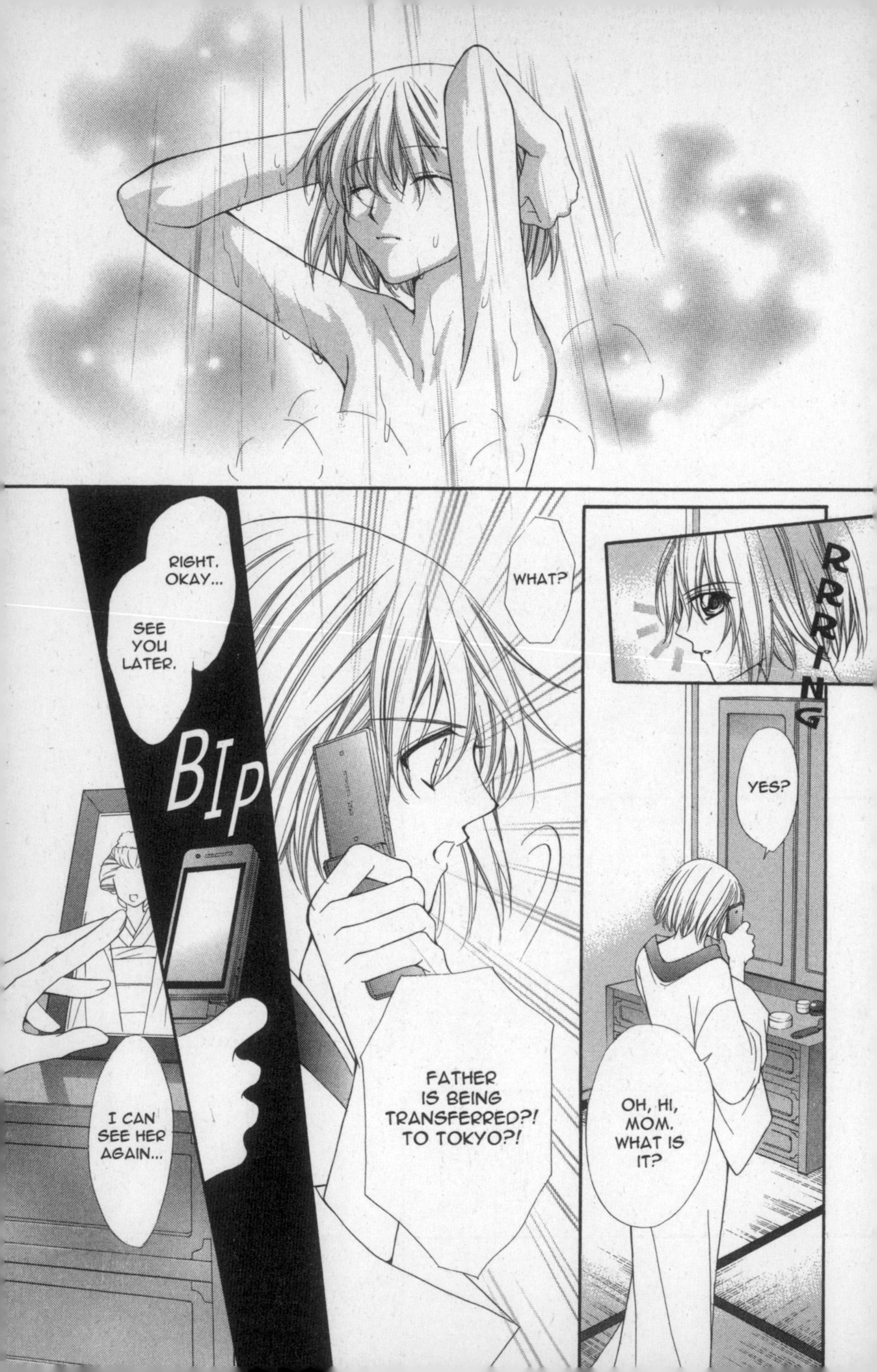
RRRING
YES?
OH, HI, MOM. WHAT IS IT?
WHAT?
FATHER IS BEING TRANSFERRED?! TO TOKYO?!
RIGHT. OKAY...
SEE YOU LATER.
BIP
I CAN SEE HER AGAIN...

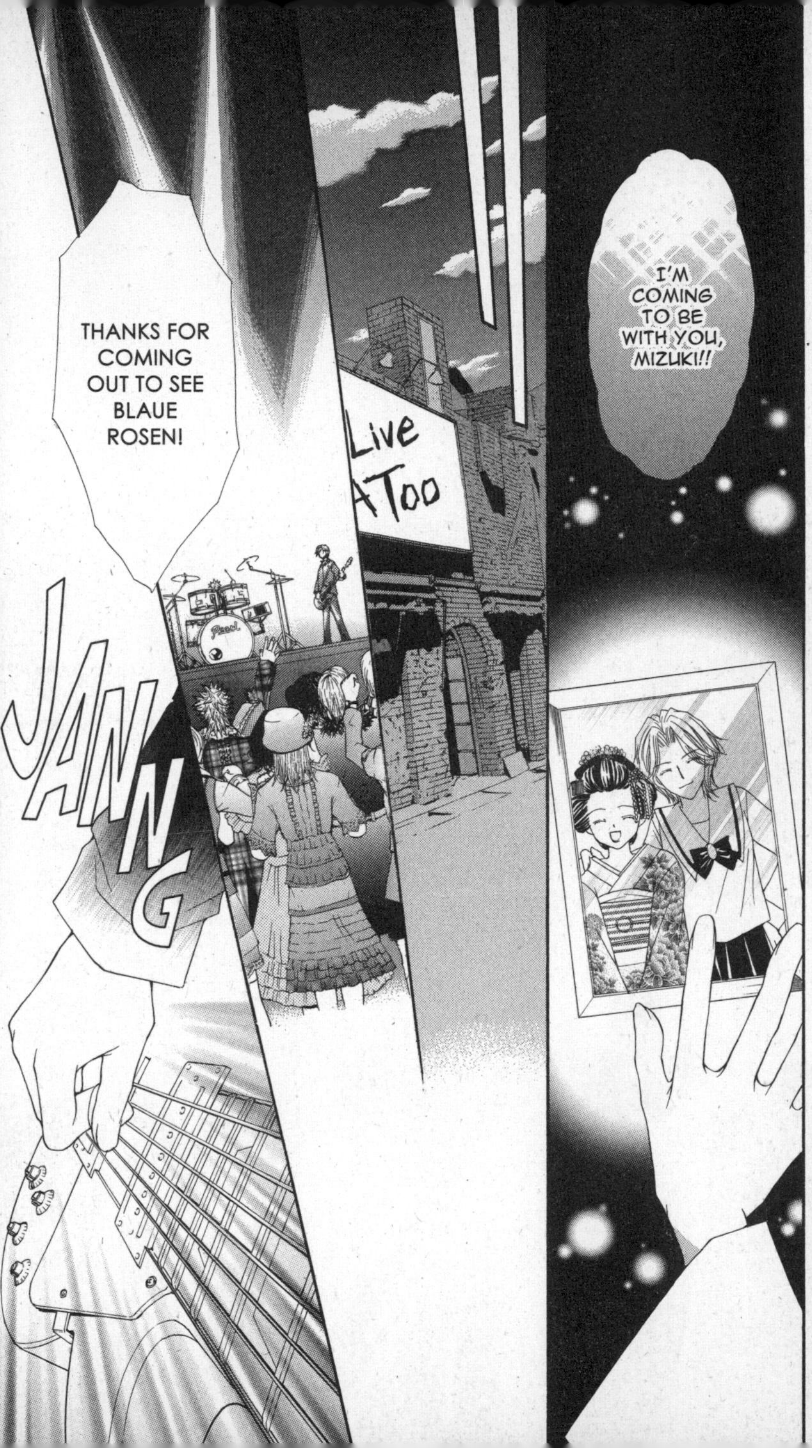
I'M COMING TO BE WITH YOU, MIZUKI!!
Live
THANKS FOR COMING OUT TO SEE BLAUE ROSEN!
JANNG

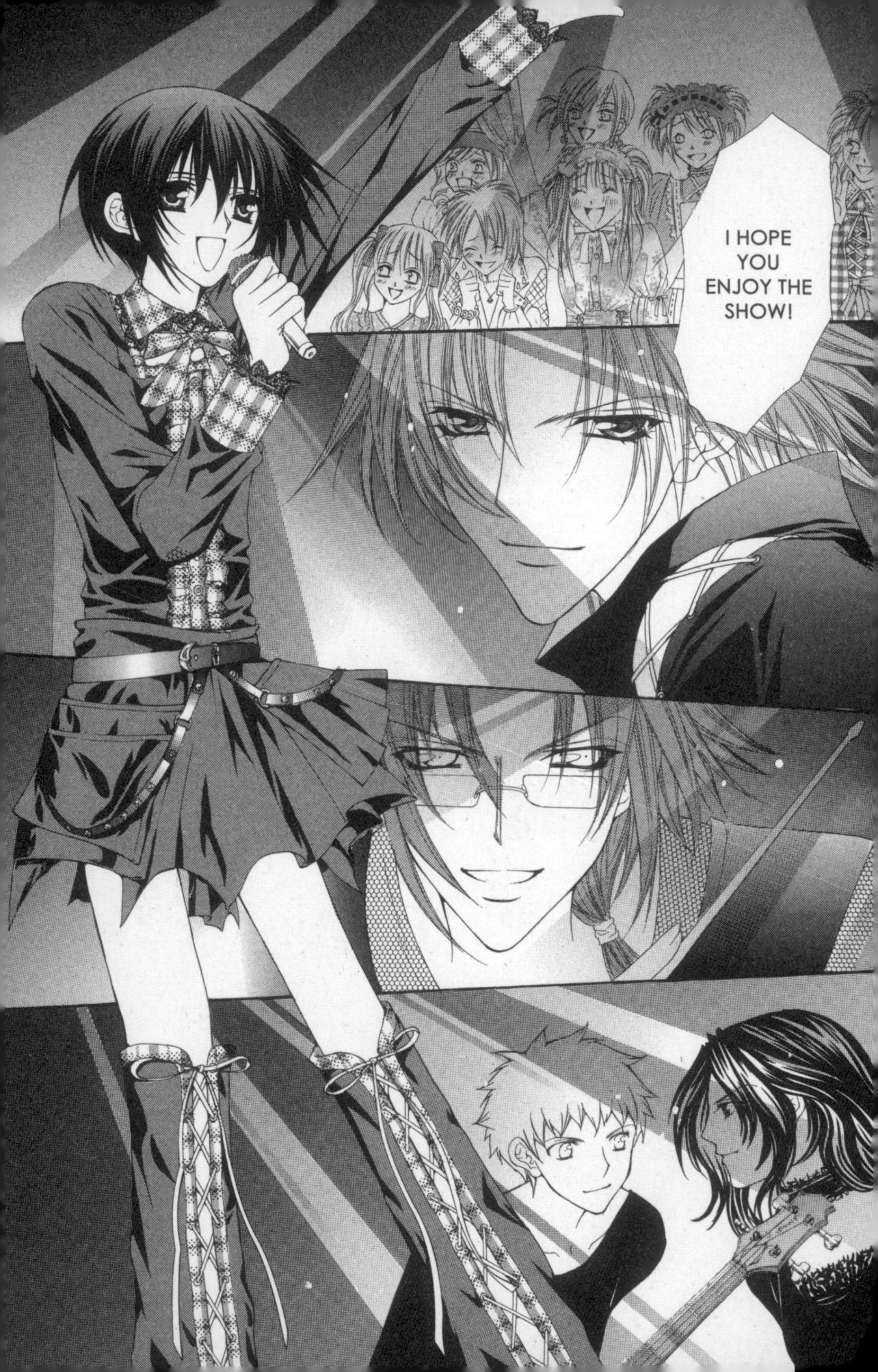
I HOPE YOU ENJOY THE SHOW!

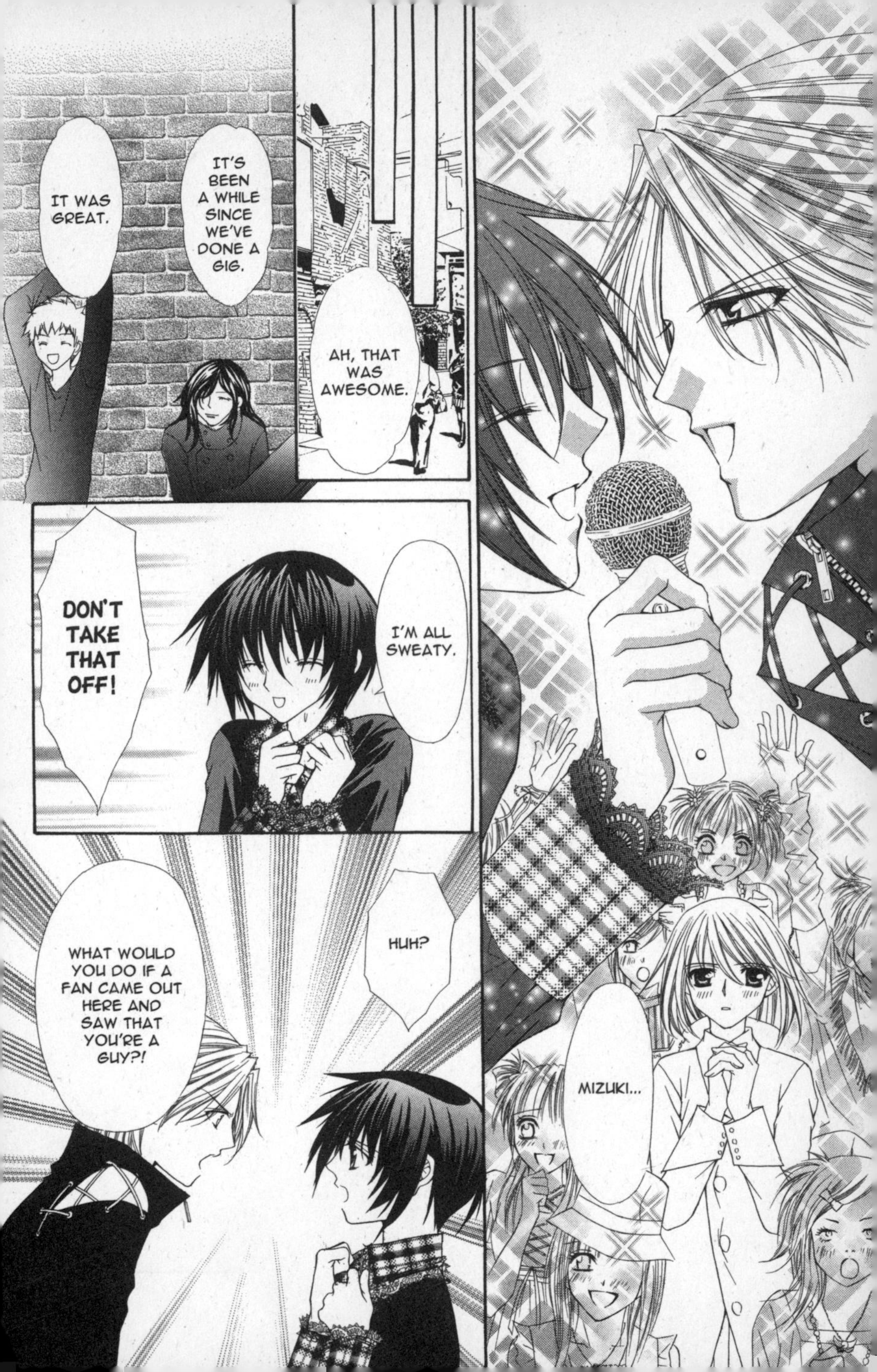
MIZUKI...
AH, THAT WAS AWESOME.
IT'S BEEN A WHILE SINCE WE'VE DONE A GIG.
IT WAS GREAT.
I'M ALL SWEATY.
DON'T TAKE THAT OFF!
HUH?
WHAT WOULD YOU DO IF A FAN CAME OUT HERE AND SAW THAT YOU'RE A GUY?!

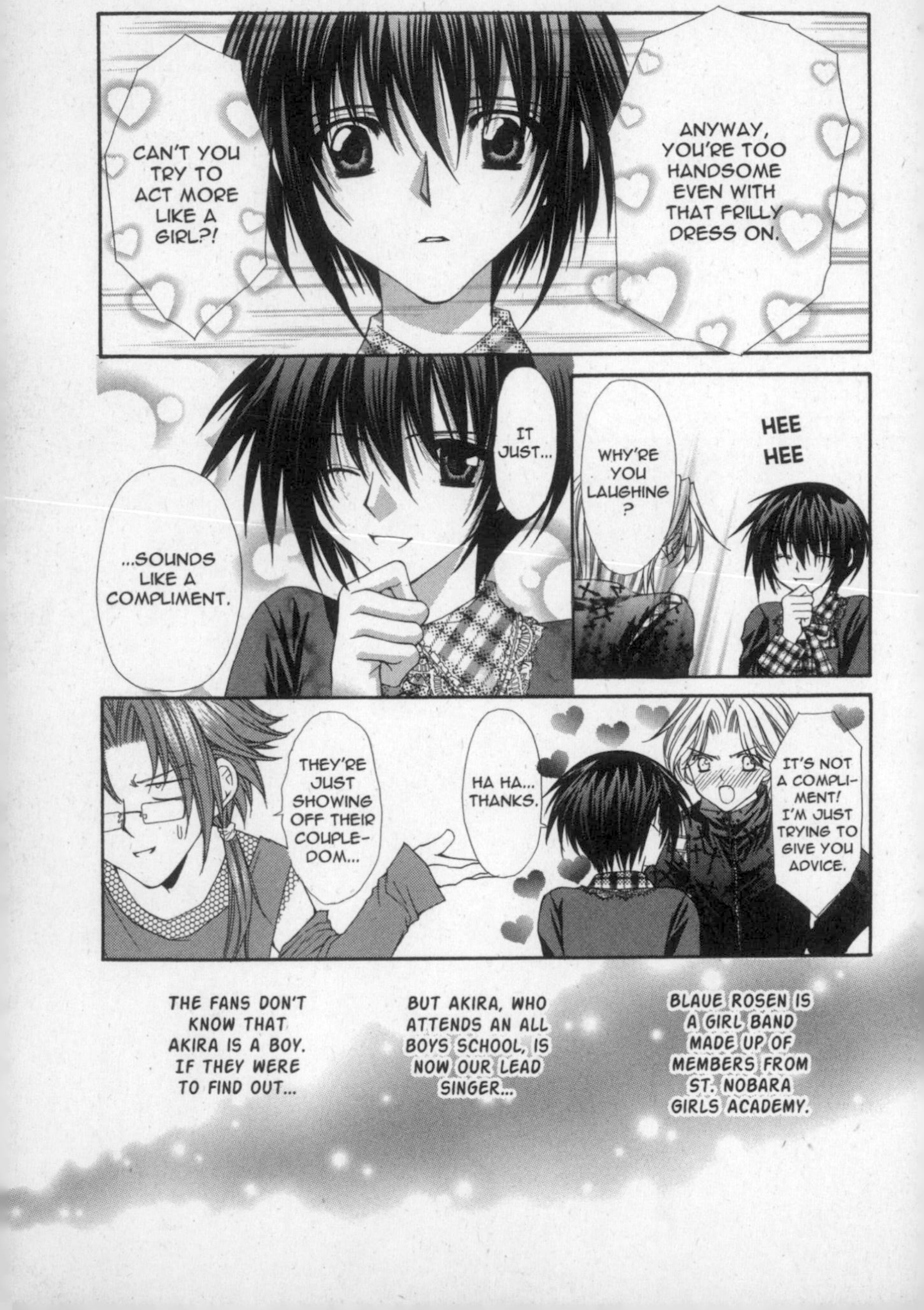
ANYWAY, YOU'RE TOO HANDSOME EVEN WITH THAT FRILLY DRESS ON.
CAN'T YOU TRY TO ACT MORE LIKE A GIRL?!
HEE HEE
WHY'RE YOU LAUGHING?
IT JUST...
...SOUNDS LIKE A COMPLIMENT.
IT'S NOT A COMPLIMENT! I'M JUST TRYING TO GIVE YOU ADVICE.
HA HA... THANKS.
THEY'RE JUST SHOWING OFF THEIR COUPLEDOM...
BLAUE ROSEN IS A GIRL BAND MADE UP OF MEMBERS FROM ST. NOBARA GIRLS ACADEMY.
BUT AKIRA, WHO ATTENDS AN ALL BOYS SCHOOL, IS NOW OUR LEAD SINGER...
THE FANS DON'T KNOW THAT AKIRA IS A BOY. IF THEY WERE TO FIND OUT...

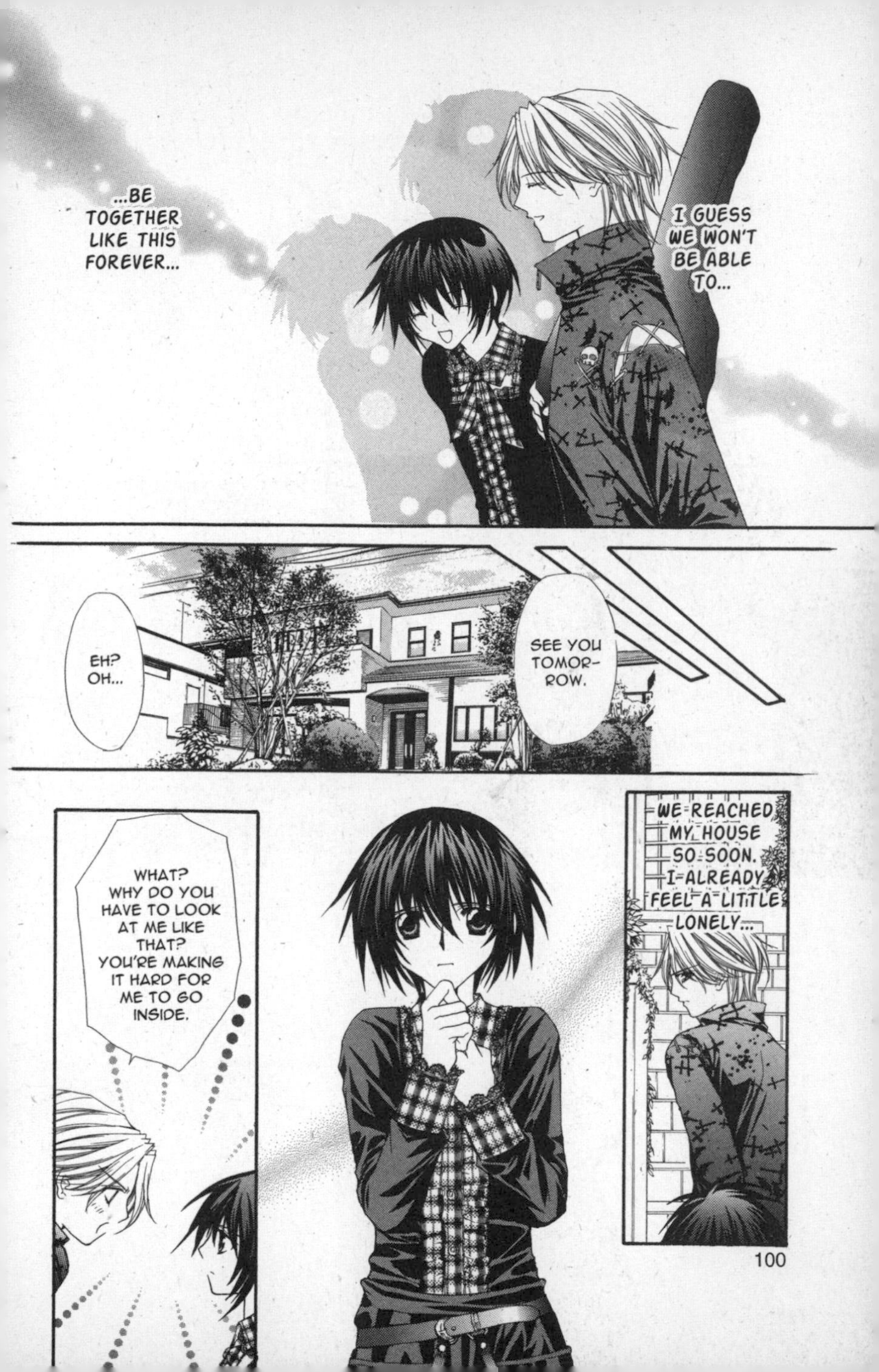
I GUESS WE WON'T BE ABLE TO...
...BE TOGETHER LIKE THIS FOREVER...
SEE YOU TOMOR-ROW.
EH? OH...
WE REACHED MY HOUSE SO SOON. I ALREADY FEEL A LITTLE LONELY...
WHAT? WHY DO YOU HAVE TO LOOK AT ME LIKE THAT? YOU'RE MAKING IT HARD FOR ME TO GO INSIDE.

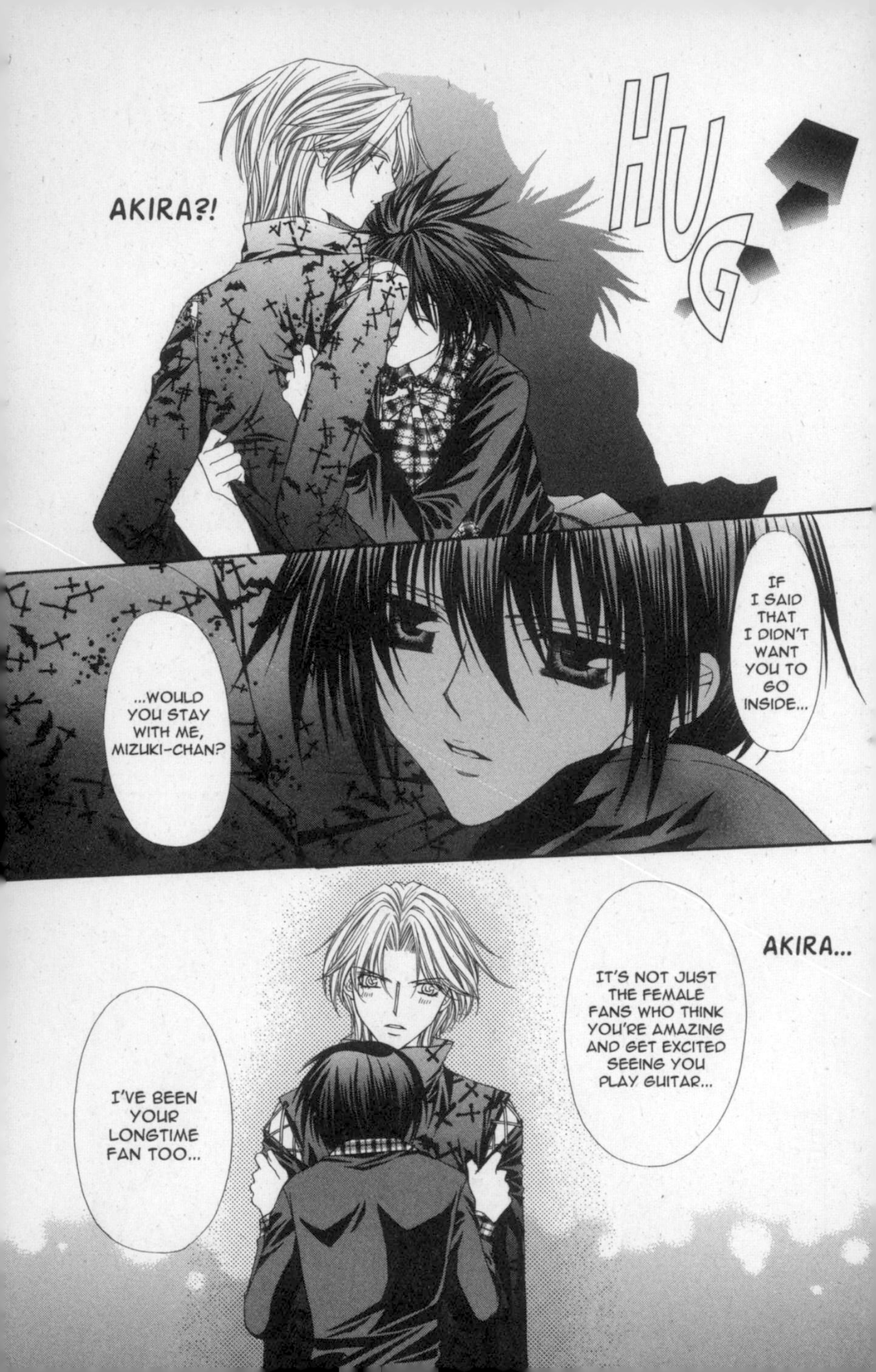
HUG
AKIRA?!
IF I SAID THAT I DIDN'T WANT YOU TO GO INSIDE...
...WOULD YOU STAY WITH ME, MIZUKI-CHAN?
AKIRA...
IT'S NOT JUST THE FEMALE FANS WHO THINK YOU'RE AMAZING AND GET EXCITED SEEING YOU PLAY GUITAR...
I'VE BEEN YOUR LONGTIME FAN TOO...

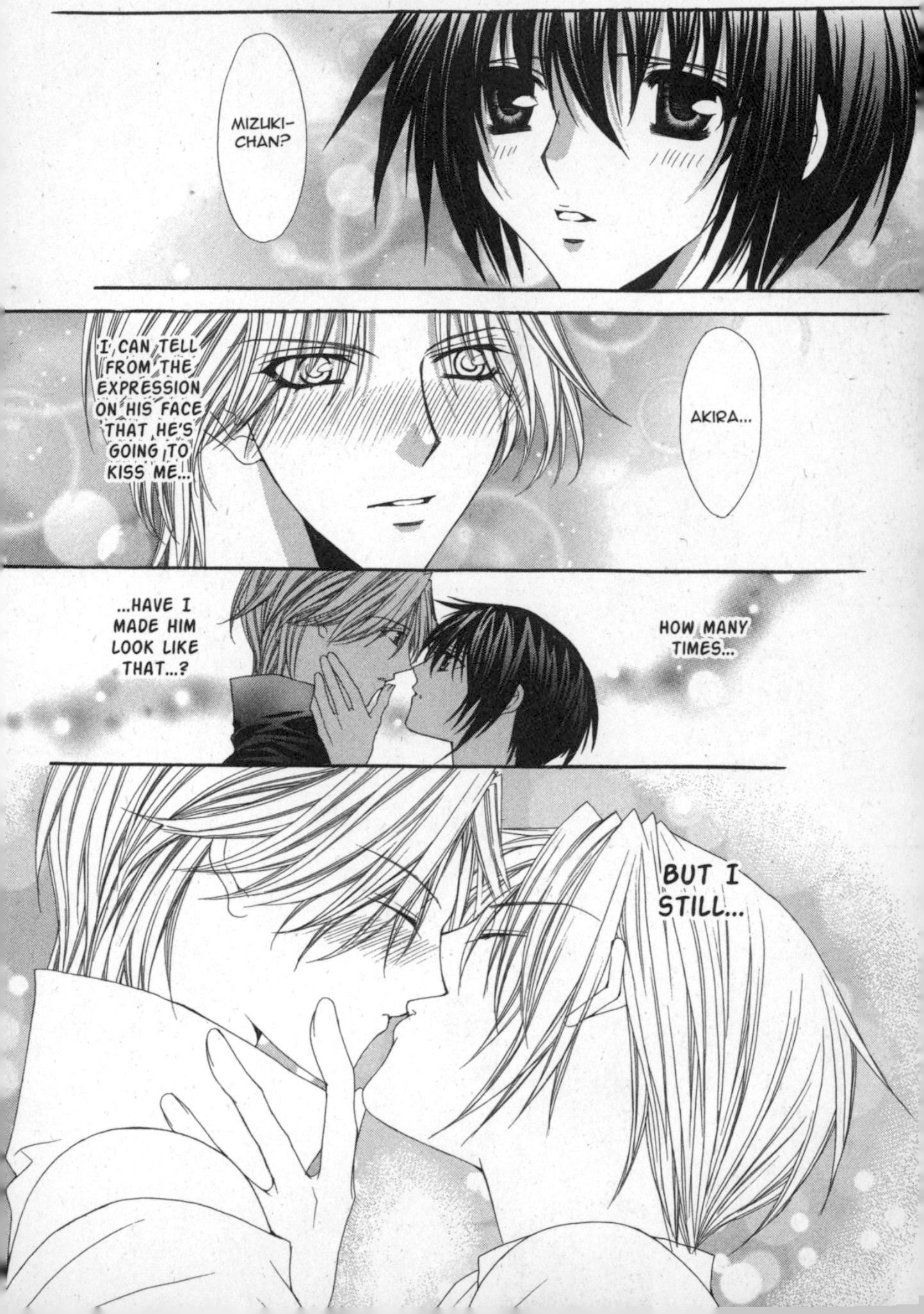
MIZUKI-CHAN?
AKIRA...
I CAN TELL FROM THE EXPRESSION ON HIS FACE THAT HE'S GOING TO KISS ME...
HOW MANY TIMES...
...HAVE I MADE HIM LOOK LIKE THAT...?
BUT I STILL...

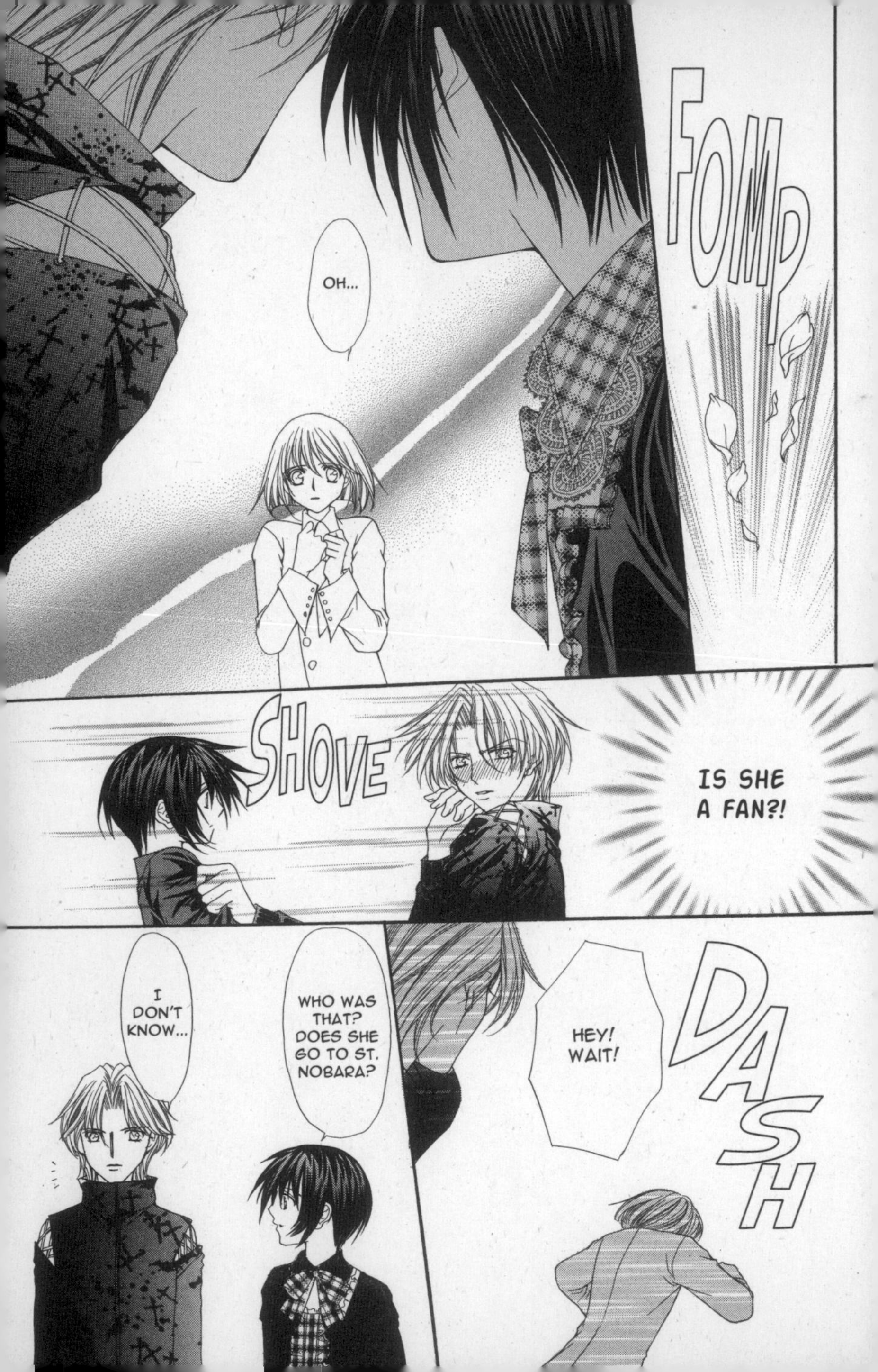
FOMP
OH...
IS SHE A FAN?!
SHOVE
DASH
HEY! WAIT!
WHO WAS THAT? DOES SHE GO TO ST. NOBARA?
I DON'T KNOW...

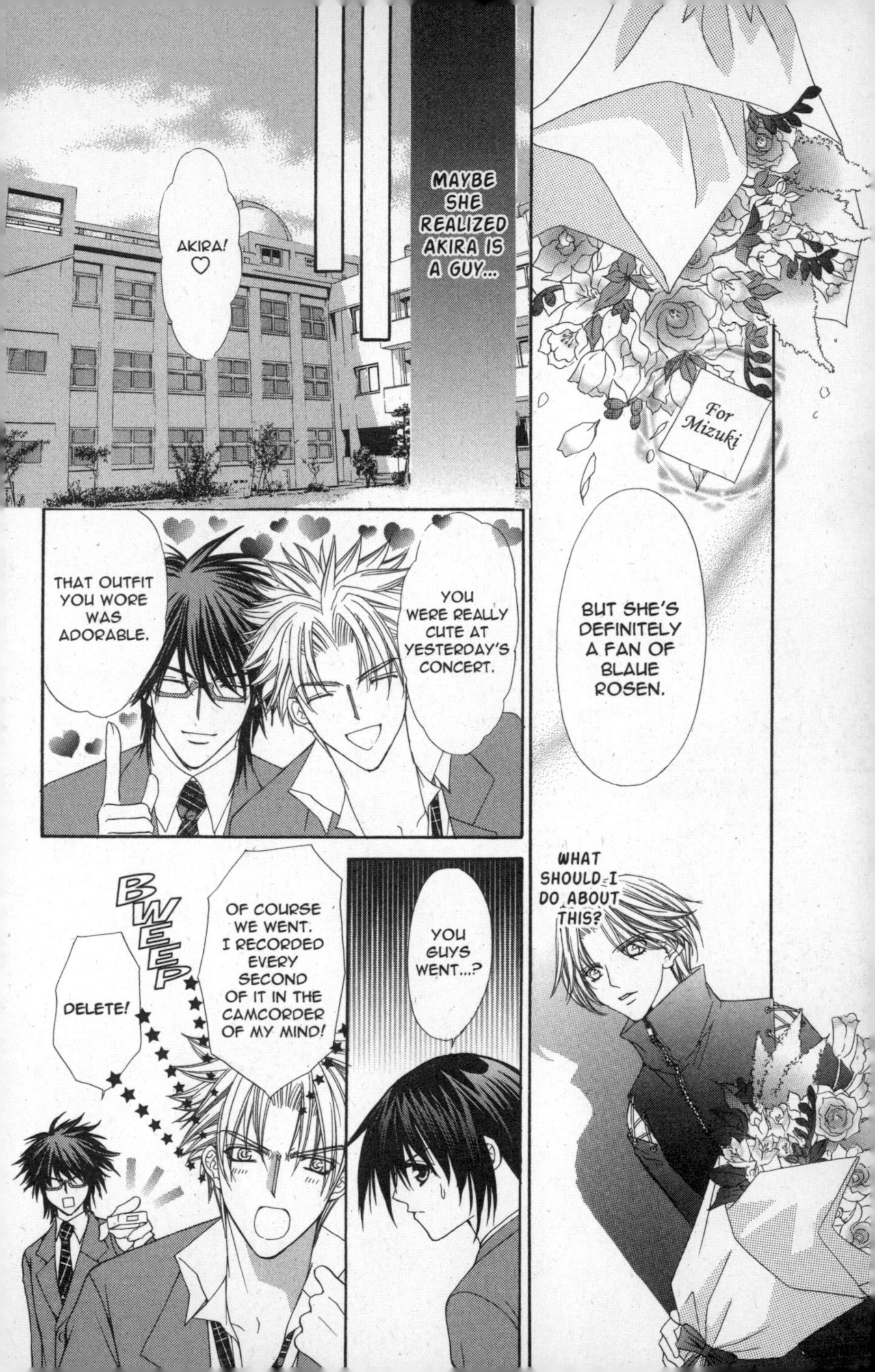
For Mizuki
BUT SHE'S DEFINITELY A FAN OF BLAUE ROSEN.
WHAT SHOULD I DO ABOUT THIS?
MAYBE SHE REALIZED AKIRA IS A GUY...
AKIRA! ♡
YOU WERE REALLY CUTE AT YESTERDAY'S CONCERT.
THAT OUTFIT YOU WORE WAS ADORABLE.
YOU GUYS WENT...?
OF COURSE WE WENT. I RECORDED EVERY SECOND OF IT IN THE CAMCORDER OF MY MIND!
BWEEP
DELETE!

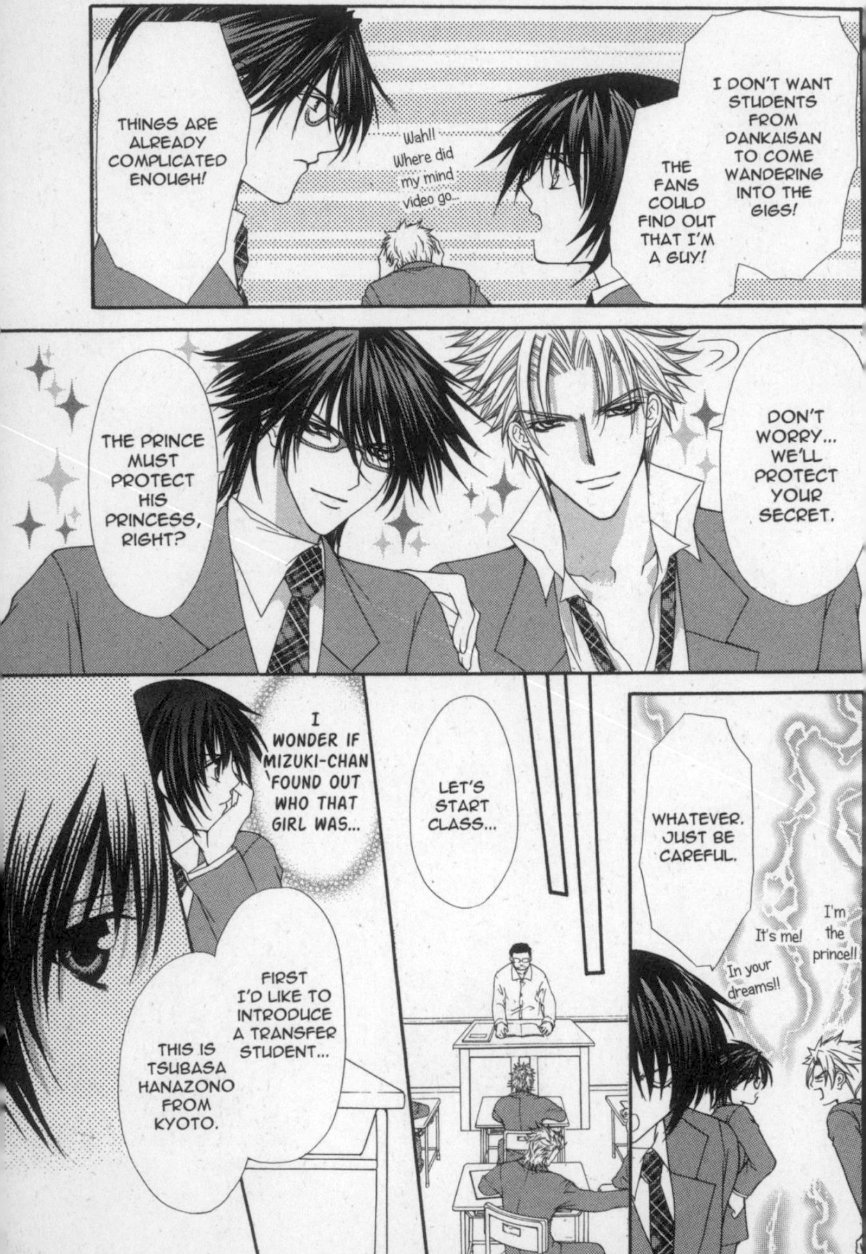
I DON'T WANT STUDENTS FROM DANKAISAN TO COME WANDERING INTO THE GIGS!
THE FANS COULD FIND OUT THAT I'M A GUY!
Wah!! Where did my mind video go...
THINGS ARE ALREADY COMPLICATED ENOUGH!
DON'T WORRY... WE'LL PROTECT YOUR SECRET.
THE PRINCE MUST PROTECT HIS PRINCESS, RIGHT?
WHATEVER. JUST BE CAREFUL.
I'm the prince!!
It's me!
In your dreams!!
LET'S START CLASS...
I WONDER IF MIZUKI-CHAN FOUND OUT WHO THAT GIRL WAS...
FIRST I'D LIKE TO INTRODUCE A TRANSFER STUDENT...
THIS IS TSUBASA HANAZONO FROM KYOTO.

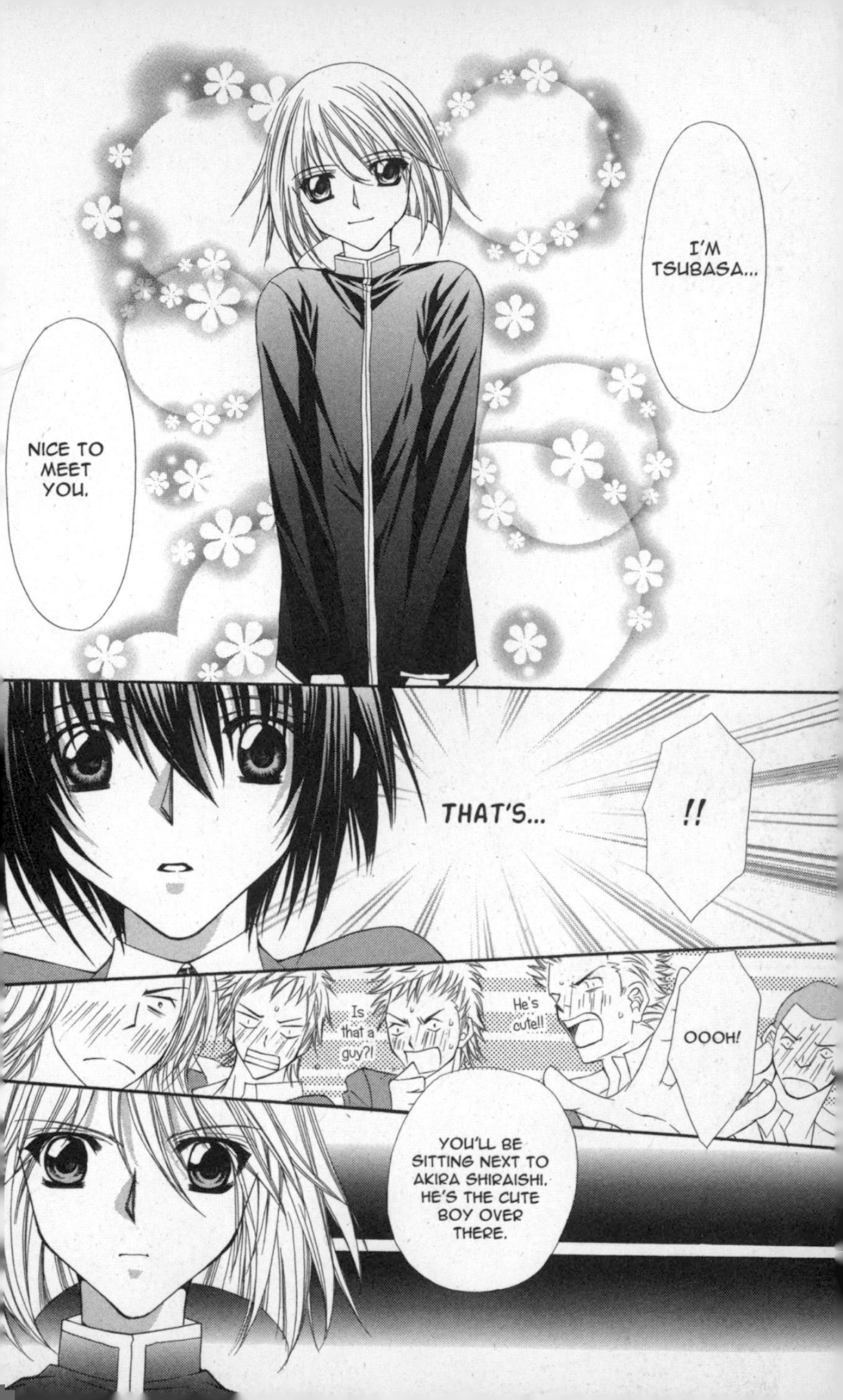
I'M TSUBASA...
NICE TO MEET YOU.
!!
THAT'S...
OOOH!
He's cute!!
Is that a guy?!
YOU'LL BE SITTING NEXT TO AKIRA SHIRAISHI. HE'S THE CUTE BOY OVER THERE.

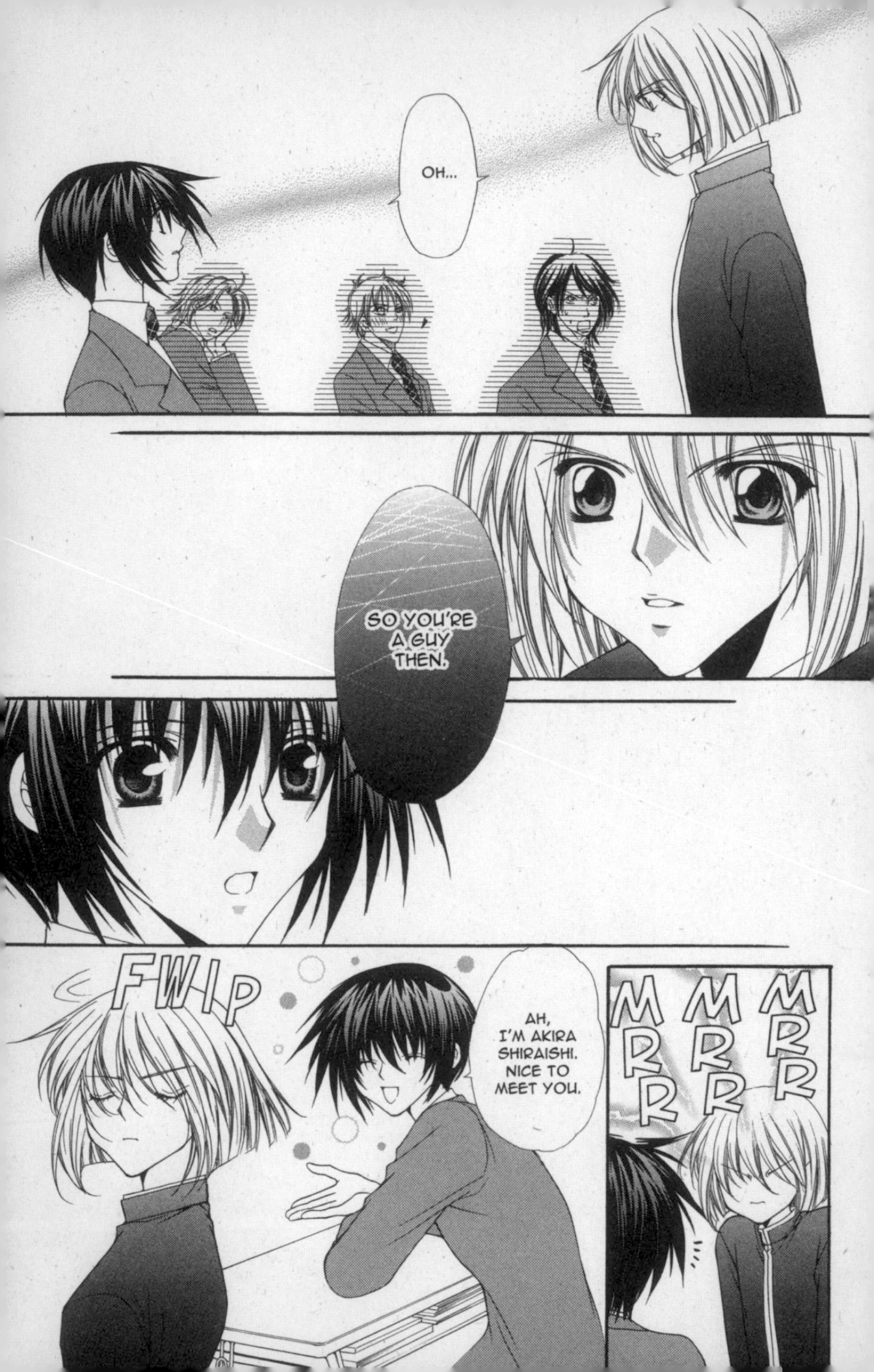
OH...
SO YOU'RE A GUY THEN.
MRR MRR MRR
AH, I'M AKIRA SHIRAISHI. NICE TO MEET YOU.
FWIP

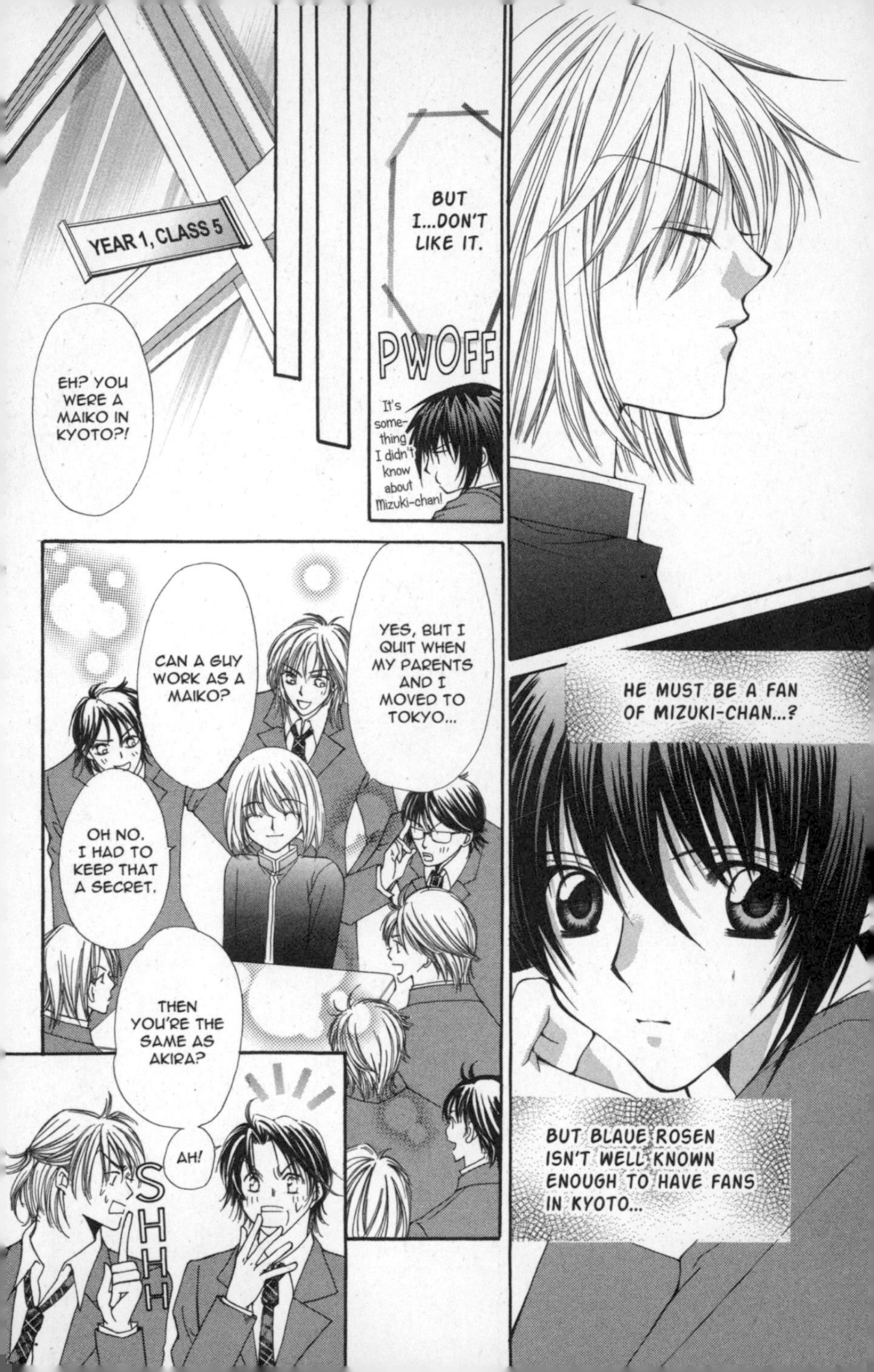
BUT I...DON'T LIKE IT.
PWOFF
It's something I didn't know about Mizuki-chan!
YEAR 1, CLASS 5
EH? YOU WERE A MAIKO IN KYOTO?!
HE MUST BE A FAN OF MIZUKI-CHAN...?
BUT BLAUE ROSEN ISN'T WELL KNOWN ENOUGH TO HAVE FANS IN KYOTO...
YES, BUT I QUIT WHEN MY PARENTS AND I MOVED TO TOKYO...
CAN A GUY WORK AS A MAIKO?
OH NO. I HAD TO KEEP THAT A SECRET.
THEN YOU'RE THE SAME AS AKIRA?
AH!
SHHH

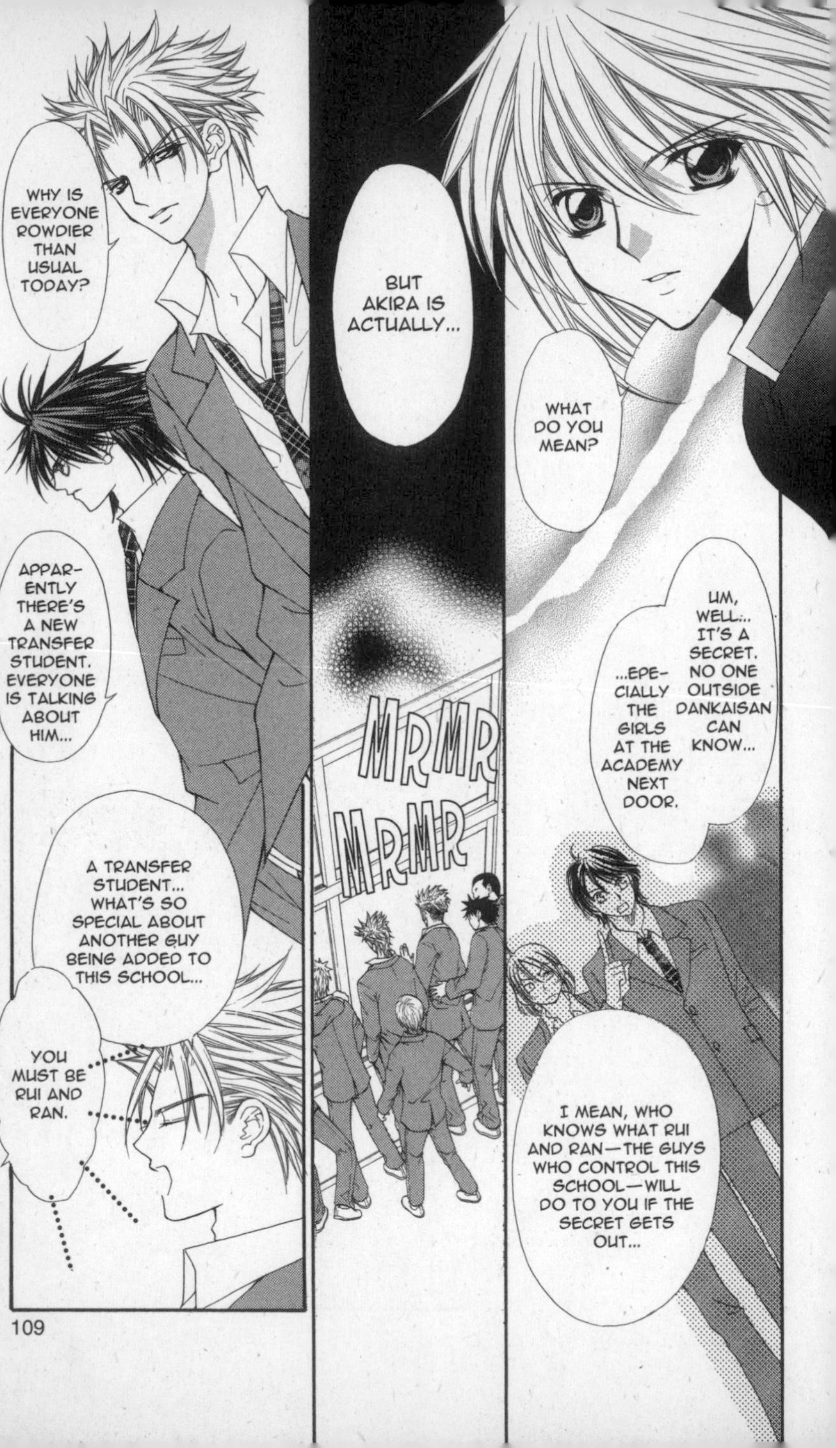
WHAT DO YOU MEAN?
UM, WELL... IT'S A SECRET. NO ONE OUTSIDE DANKAISAN CAN KNOW...
...EPECIALLY THE GIRLS AT THE ACADEMY NEXT DOOR.
I MEAN, WHO KNOWS WHAT RUI AND RAN—THE GUYS WHO CONTROL THIS SCHOOL—WILL DO TO YOU IF THE SECRET GETS OUT...
BUT AKIRA IS ACTUALLY...
MRMR
MRMR
WHY IS EVERYONE ROWDIER THAN USUAL TODAY?
APPARENTLY THERE'S A NEW TRANSFER STUDENT. EVERYONE IS TALKING ABOUT HIM...
A TRANSFER STUDENT... WHAT'S SO SPECIAL ABOUT ANOTHER GUY BEING ADDED TO THIS SCHOOL...
YOU MUST BE RUI AND RAN.

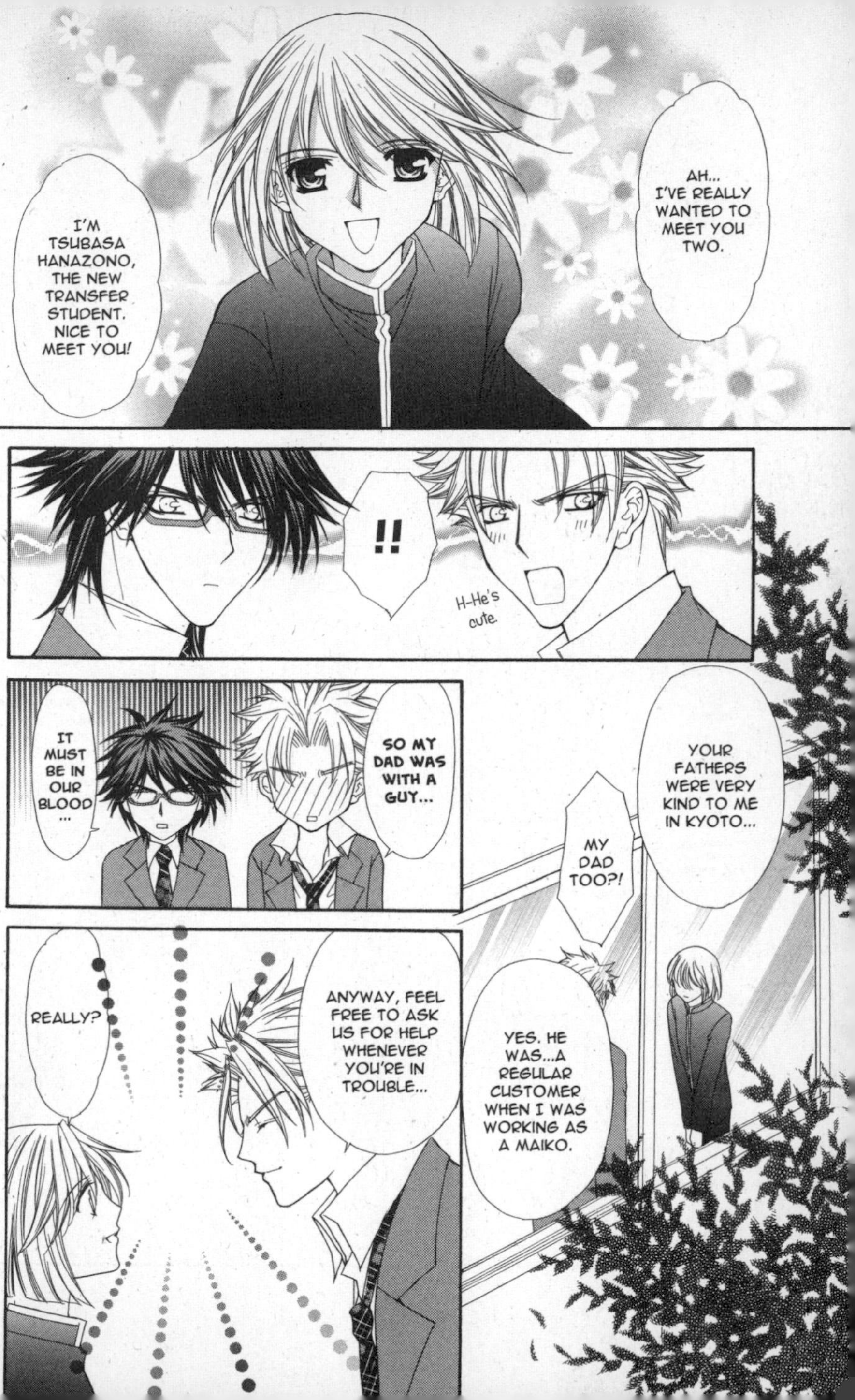
AH... I'VE REALLY WANTED TO MEET YOU TWO.
I'M TSUBASA HANAZONO, THE NEW TRANSFER STUDENT. NICE TO MEET YOU!
!!
H-He's cute.
YOUR FATHERS WERE VERY KIND TO ME IN KYOTO...
MY DAD TOO?!
YES. HE WAS...A REGULAR CUSTOMER WHEN I WAS WORKING AS A MAIKO.
SO MY DAD WAS WITH A GUY...
IT MUST BE IN OUR BLOOD...
ANYWAY, FEEL FREE TO ASK US FOR HELP WHENEVER YOU'RE IN TROUBLE...
REALLY?

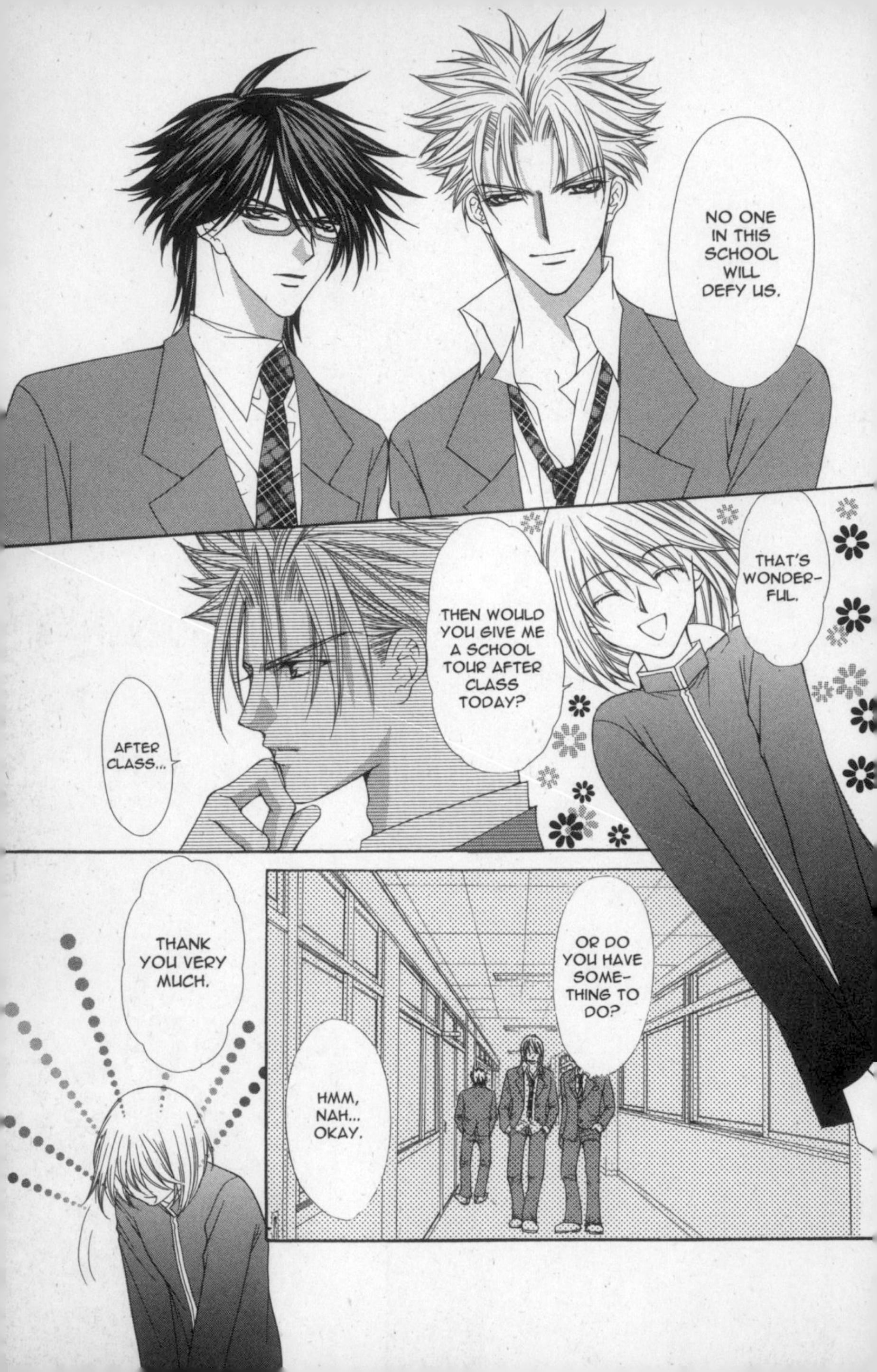
NO ONE IN THIS SCHOOL WILL DEFY US.
THAT'S WONDER-FUL.
THEN WOULD YOU GIVE ME A SCHOOL TOUR AFTER CLASS TODAY?
AFTER CLASS...
OR DO YOU HAVE SOME-THING TO DO?
HMM, NAH... OKAY.
THANK YOU VERY MUCH.

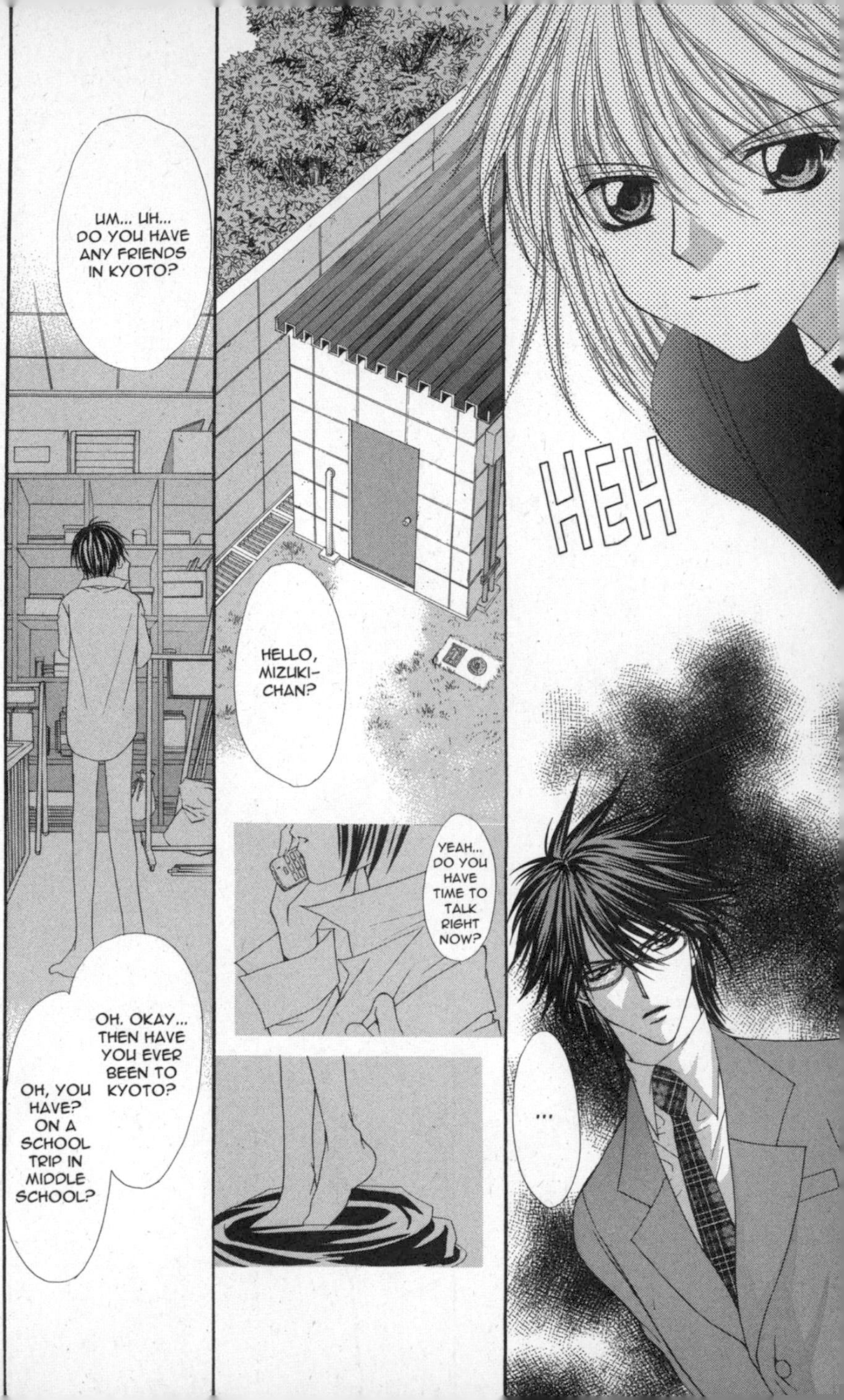
HEH
...
HELLO, MIZUKI-CHAN?
YEAH... DO YOU HAVE TIME TO TALK RIGHT NOW?
UM... UH... DO YOU HAVE ANY FRIENDS IN KYOTO?
OH. OKAY... THEN HAVE YOU EVER BEEN TO KYOTO?
OH, YOU HAVE? ON A SCHOOL TRIP IN MIDDLE SCHOOL?

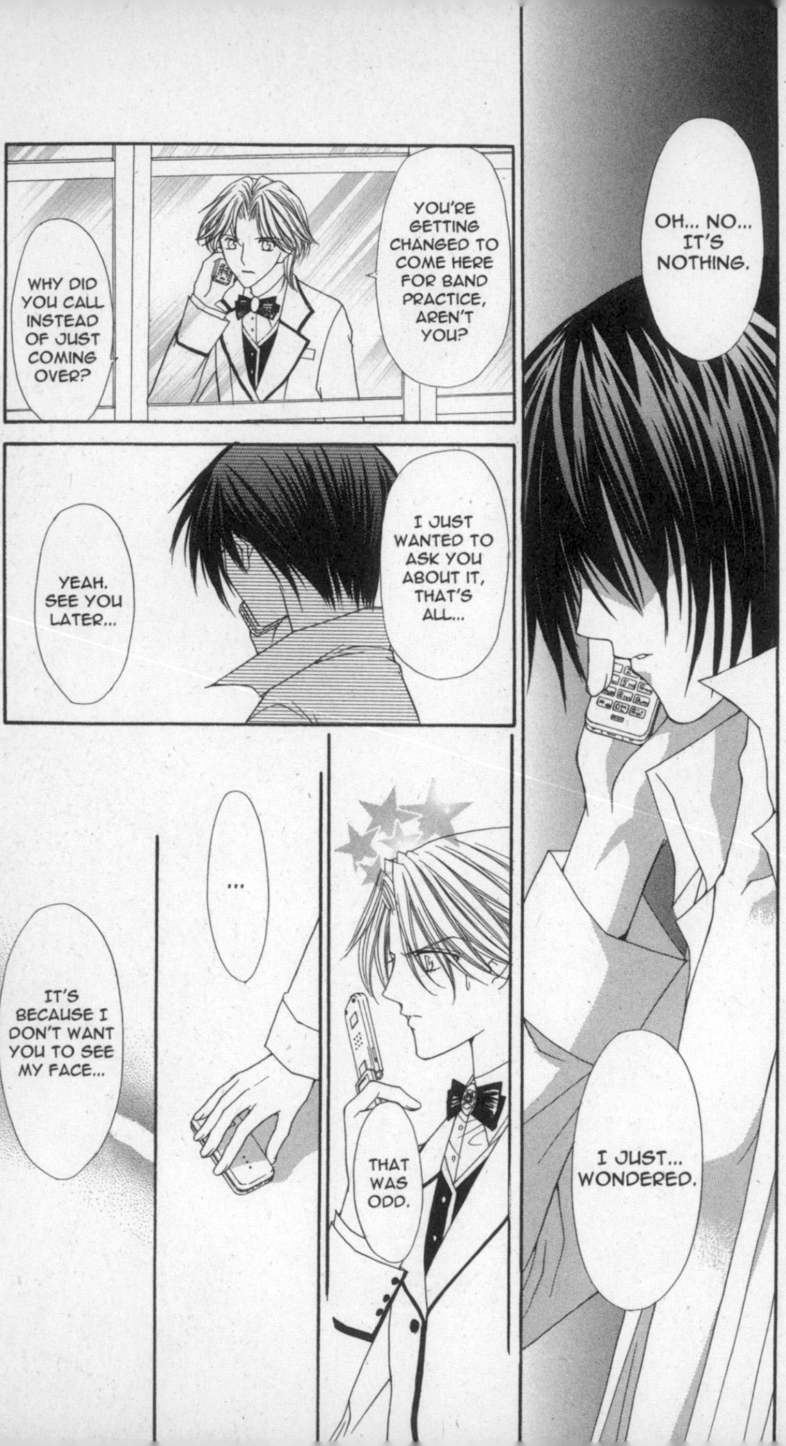
OH... NO... IT'S NOTHING.
I JUST... WONDERED.
YOU'RE GETTING CHANGED TO COME HERE FOR BAND PRACTICE, AREN'T YOU?
WHY DID YOU CALL INSTEAD OF JUST COMING OVER?
I JUST WANTED TO ASK YOU ABOUT IT, THAT'S ALL...
YEAH. SEE YOU LATER...
THAT WAS ODD.
...
IT'S BECAUSE I DON'T WANT YOU TO SEE MY FACE...

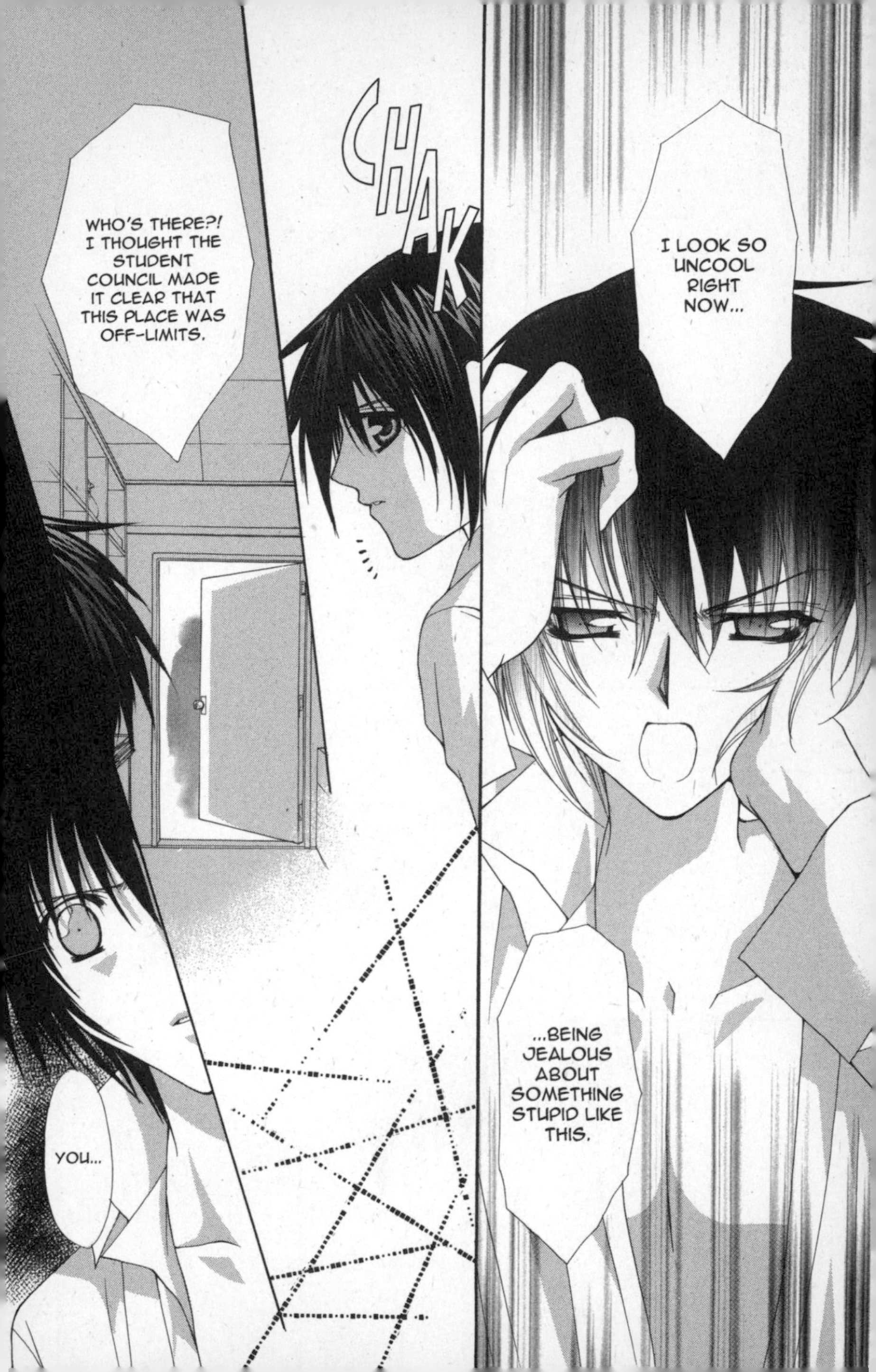
I LOOK SO UNCOOL RIGHT NOW...
...BEING JEALOUS ABOUT SOMETHING STUPID LIKE THIS.
CHAK
WHO'S THERE?! I THOUGHT THE STUDENT COUNCIL MADE IT CLEAR THAT THIS PLACE WAS OFF-LIMITS.
YOU...

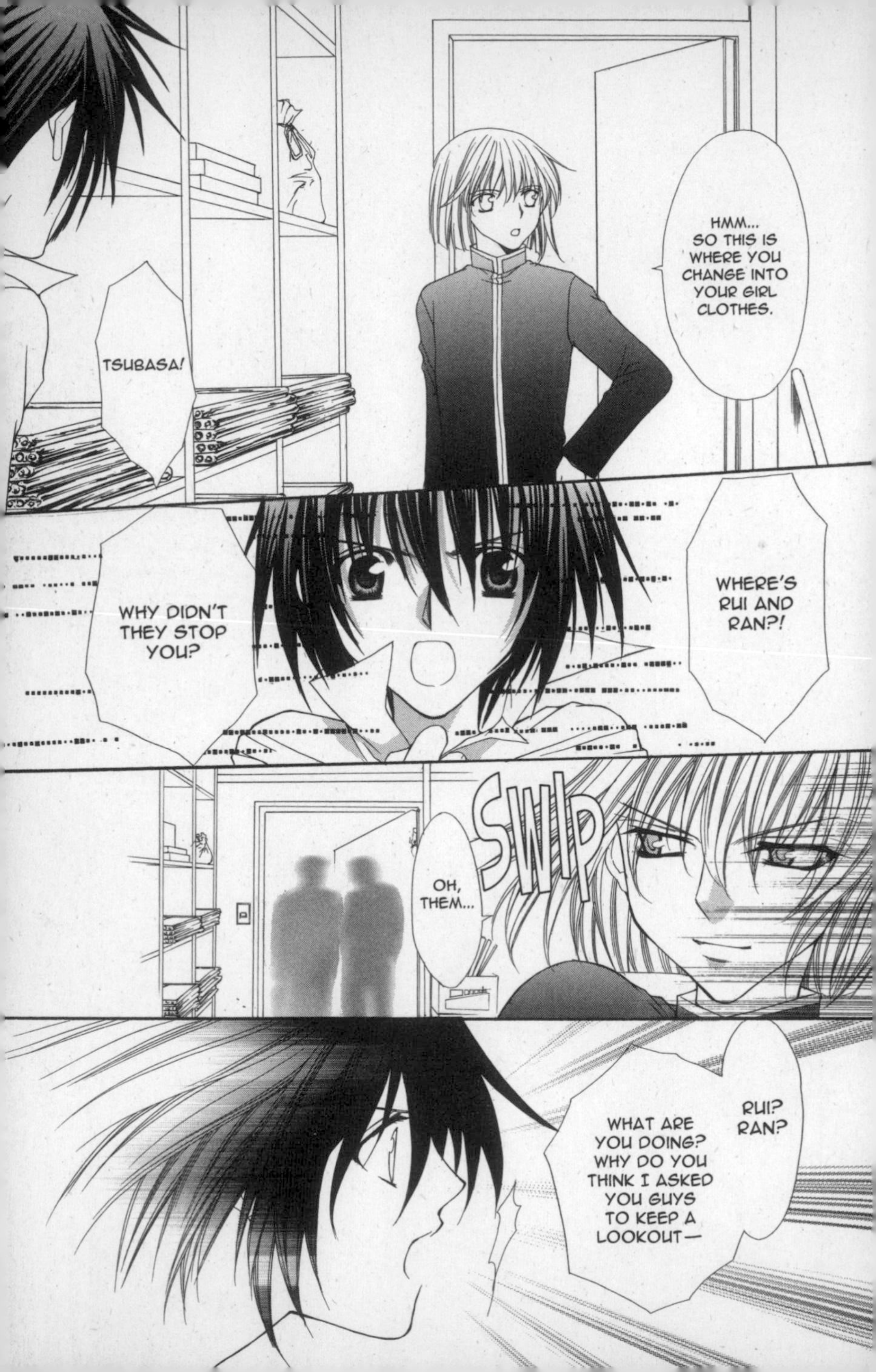
HMM... SO THIS IS WHERE YOU CHANGE INTO YOUR GIRL CLOTHES.
TSUBASA!
WHERE'S RUI AND RAN?!
WHY DIDN'T THEY STOP YOU?
SWIP
OH, THEM...
RUI? RAN?
WHAT ARE YOU DOING? WHY DO YOU THINK I ASKED YOU GUYS TO KEEP A LOOKOUT—

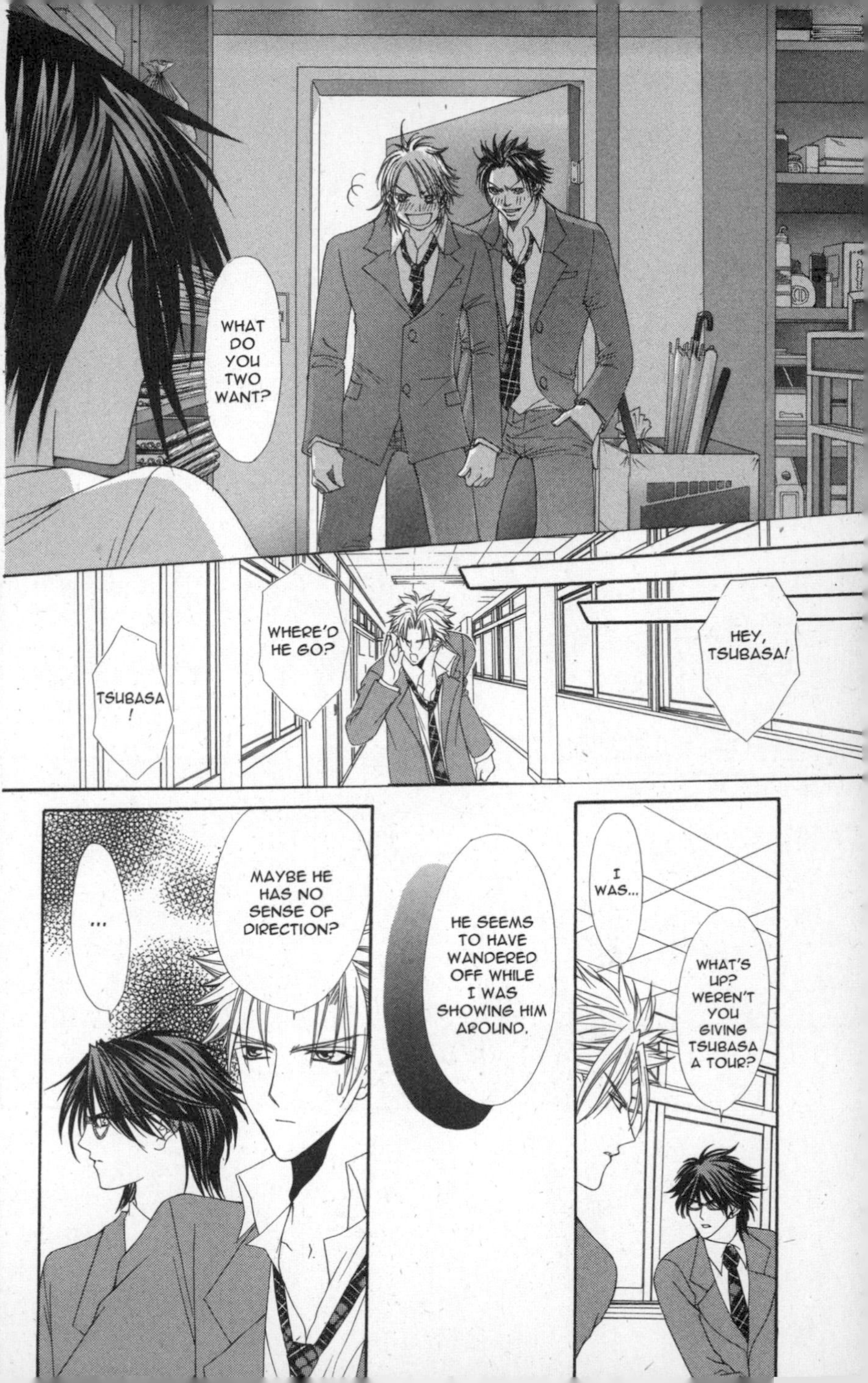
WHAT DO YOU TWO WANT?
HEY, TSUBASA!
WHERE'D HE GO?
TSUBASA!
WHAT'S UP? WEREN'T YOU GIVING TSUBASA A TOUR?
I WAS...
HE SEEMS TO HAVE WANDERED OFF WHILE I WAS SHOWING HIM AROUND.
MAYBE HE HAS NO SENSE OF DIRECTION?
...

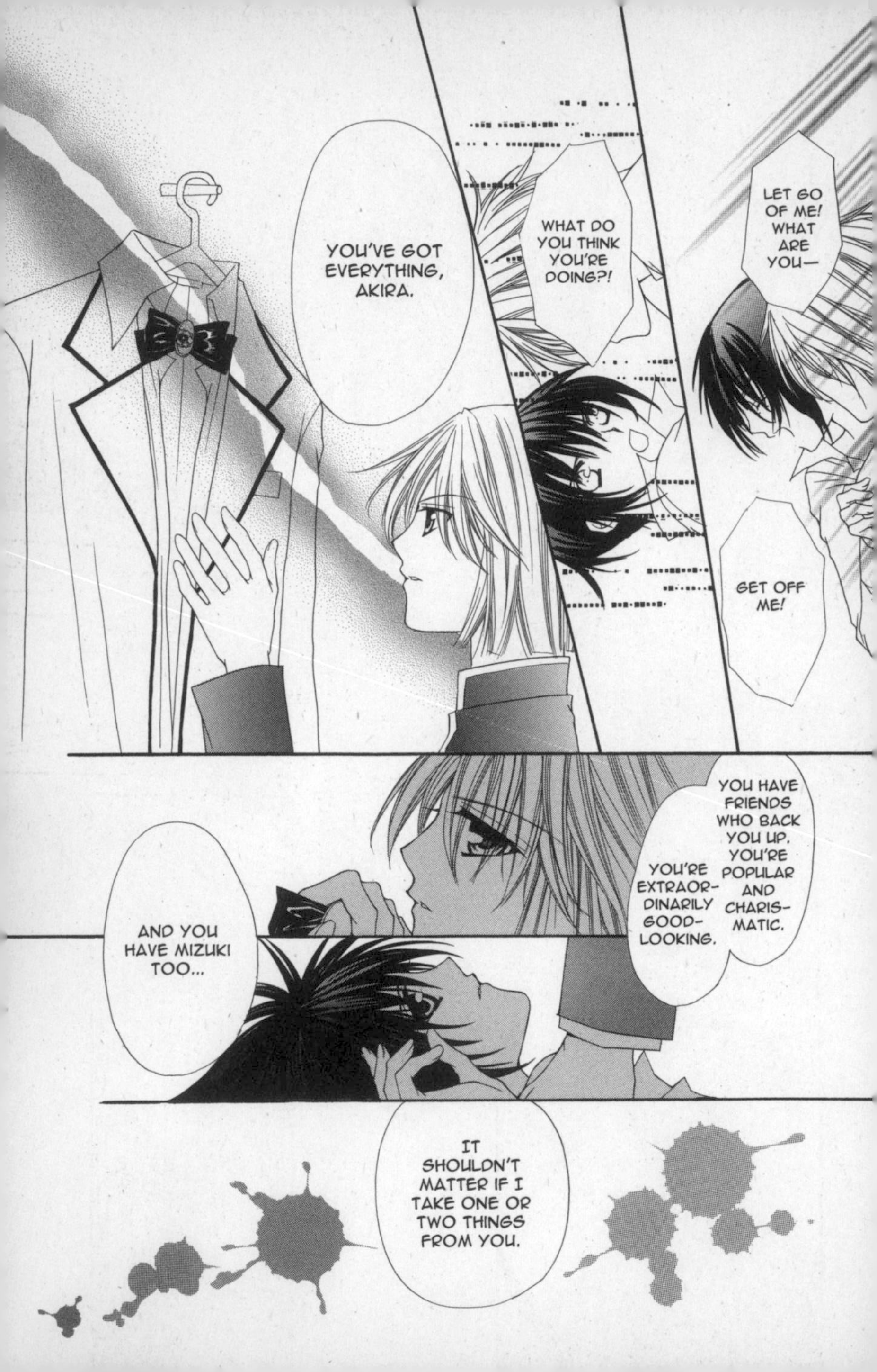
LET GO OF ME! WHAT ARE YOU—
GET OFF ME!
WHAT DO YOU THINK YOU'RE DOING?!
YOU'VE GOT EVERYTHING, AKIRA.
YOU HAVE FRIENDS WHO BACK YOU UP. YOU'RE POPULAR AND CHARISMATIC.
YOU'RE EXTRAORDINARILY GOOD-LOOKING.
AND YOU HAVE MIZUKI TOO...
IT SHOULDN'T MATTER IF I TAKE ONE OR TWO THINGS FROM YOU.

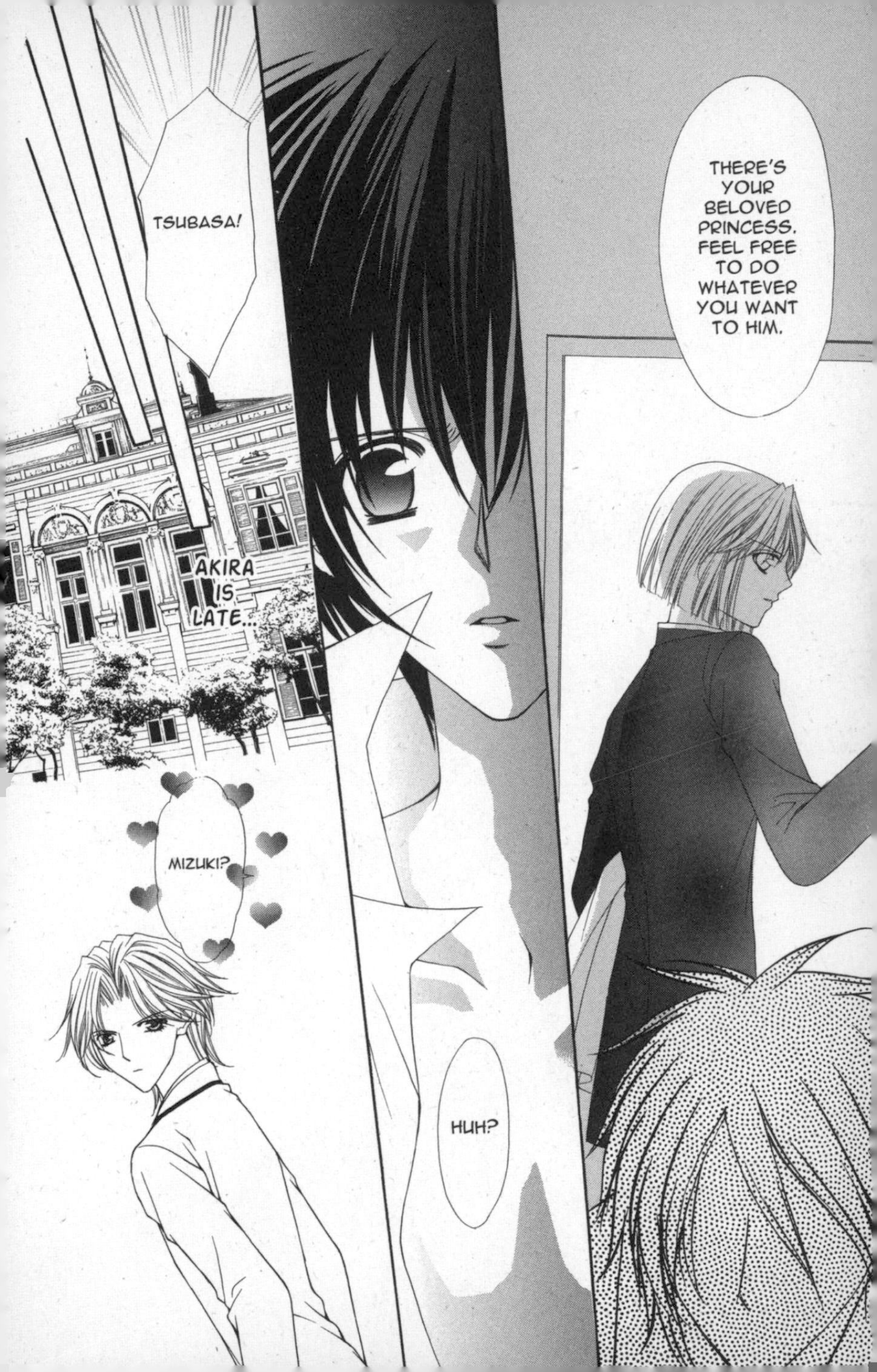
THERE'S YOUR BELOVED PRINCESS. FEEL FREE TO DO WHATEVER YOU WANT TO HIM.
HUH?
TSUBASA!
AKIRA IS LATE...
MIZUKI?

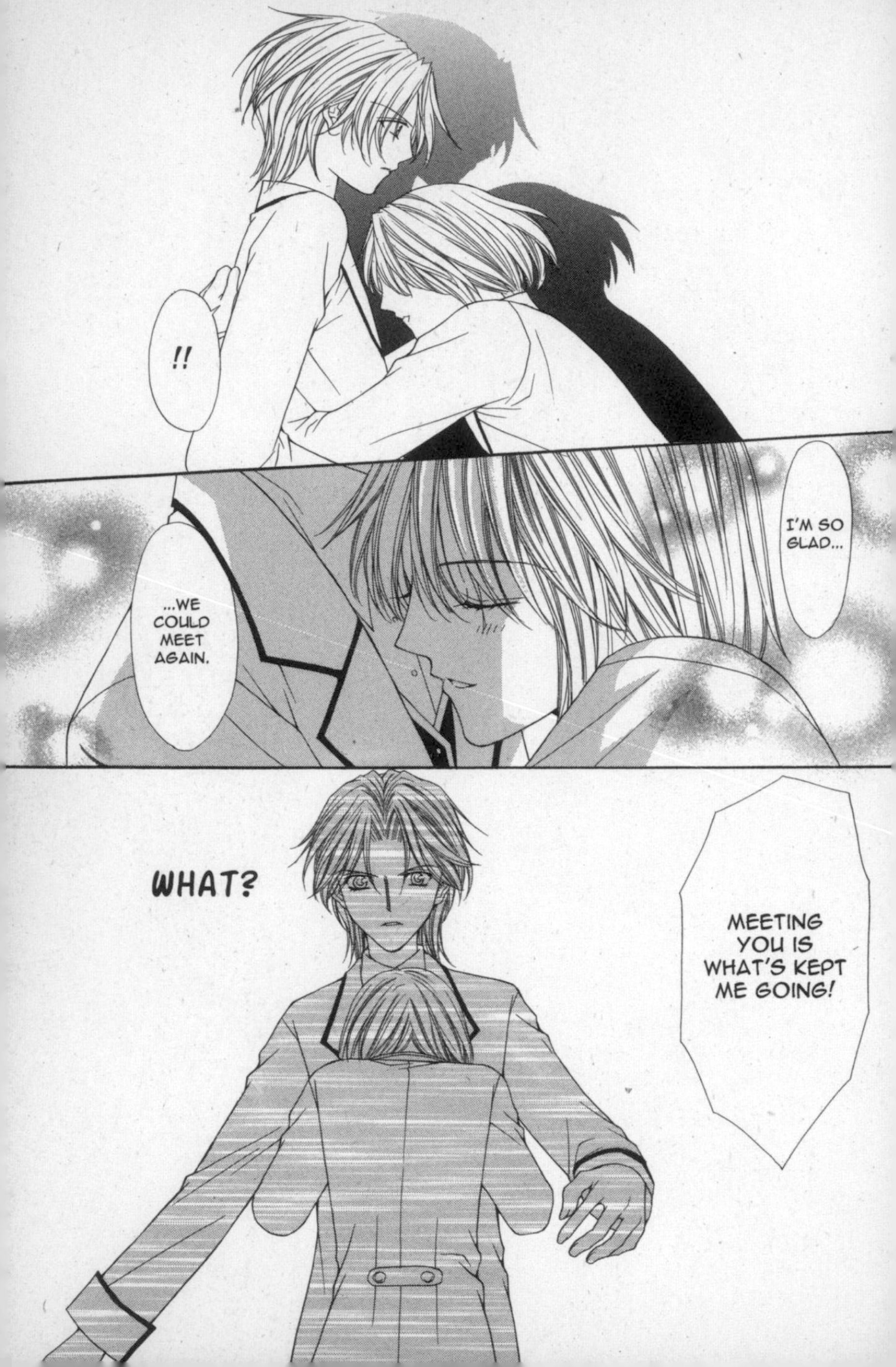
!!
I'M SO GLAD...
...WE COULD MEET AGAIN.
MEETING YOU IS WHAT'S KEPT ME GOING!
WHAT?

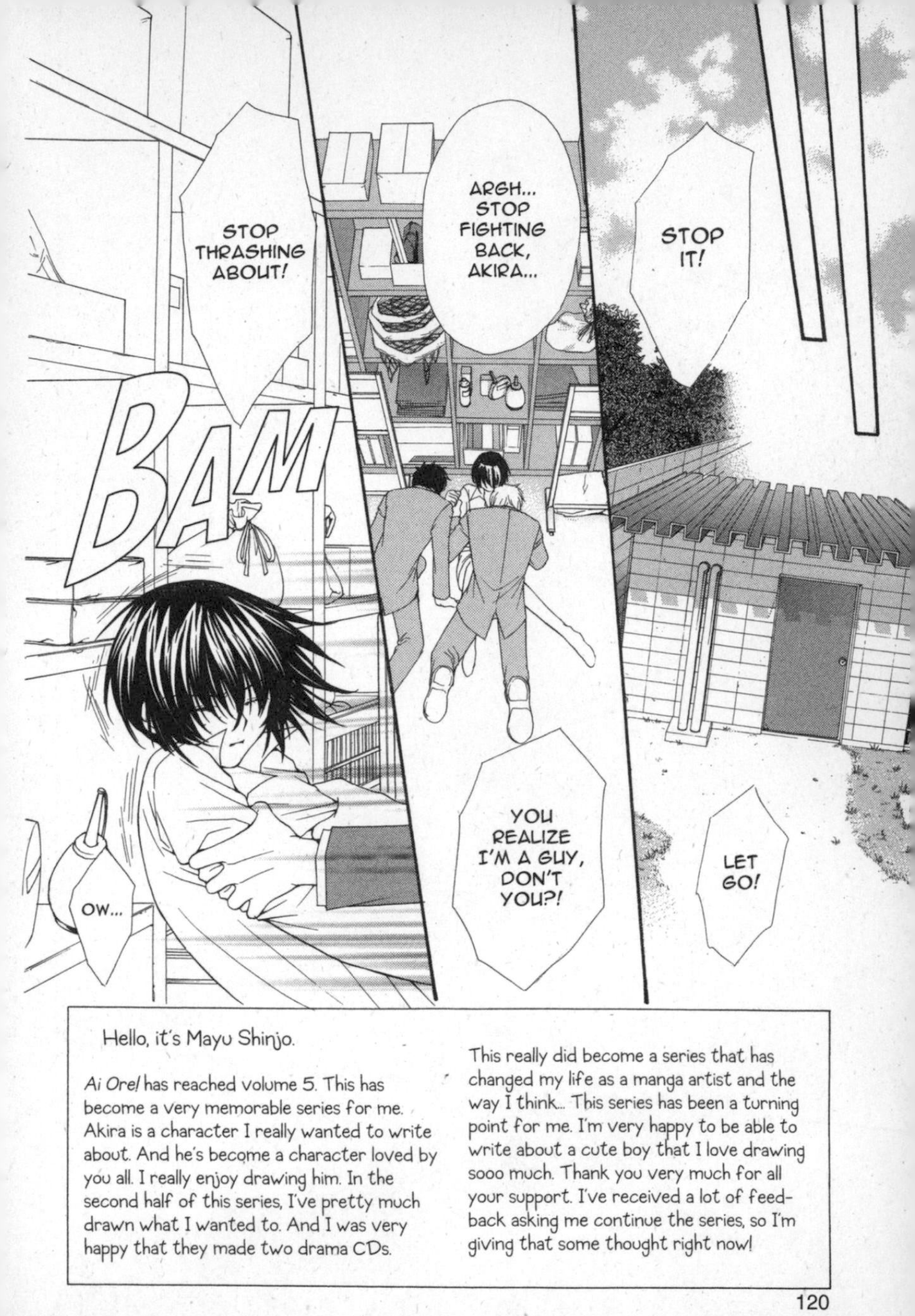
STOP IT!
LET GO!
ARGH... STOP FIGHTING BACK, AKIRA...
YOU REALIZE I'M A GUY, DON'T YOU?!
STOP THRASHING ABOUT!
BAM
OW...

Hello, it's Mayu Shinjo.

Ai Ore! has reached volume 5. This has become a very memorable series for me. Akira is a character I really wanted to write about. And he's become a character loved by you all. I really enjoy drawing him. In the second half of this series, I've pretty much drawn what I wanted to. And I was very happy that they made two drama CDs.

This really did become a series that has changed my life as a manga artist and the way I think... This series has been a turning point for me. I'm very happy to be able to write about a cute boy that I love drawing sooo much. Thank you very much for all your support. I've received a lot of feed-back asking me continue the series, so I'm giving that some thought right now!

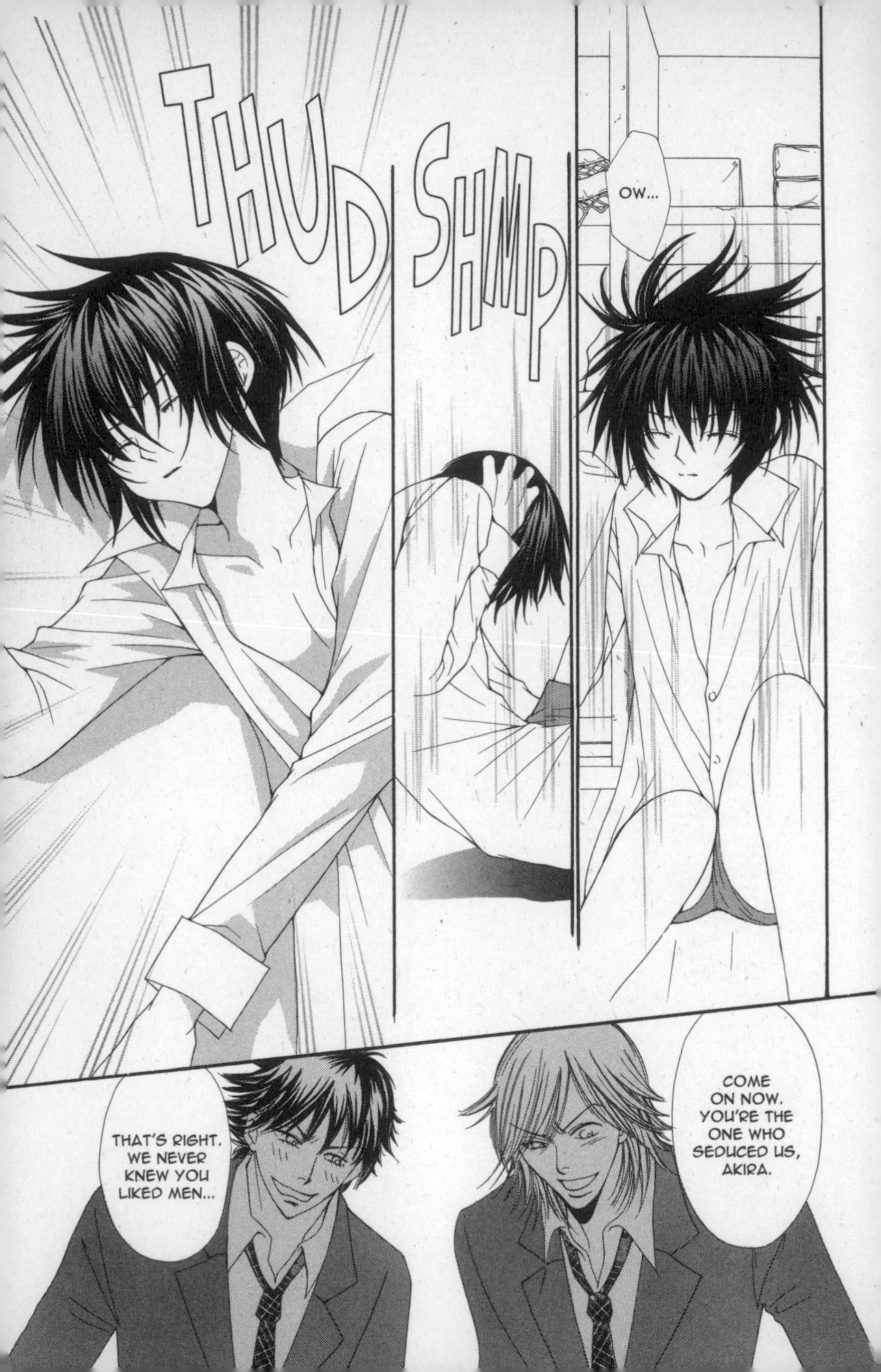
OW...
SHMP
THUD
COME ON NOW. YOU'RE THE ONE WHO SEDUCED US, AKIRA.
THAT'S RIGHT. WE NEVER KNEW YOU LIKED MEN...

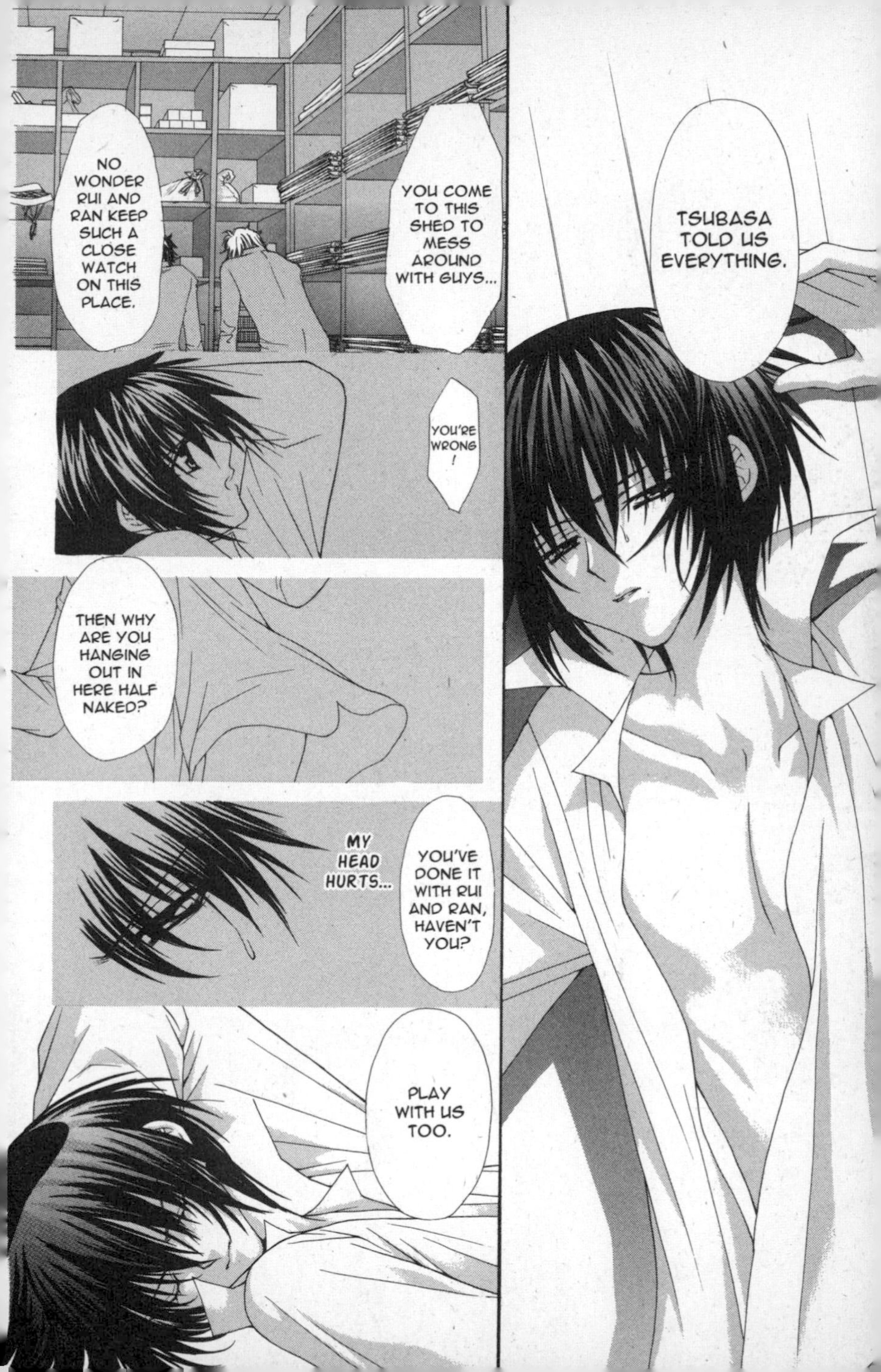
TSUBASA TOLD US EVERYTHING.
YOU COME TO THIS SHED TO MESS AROUND WITH GUYS...
NO WONDER RUI AND RAN KEEP SUCH A CLOSE WATCH ON THIS PLACE.
YOU'RE WRONG!
THEN WHY ARE YOU HANGING OUT IN HERE HALF NAKED?
YOU'VE DONE IT WITH RUI AND RAN, HAVEN'T YOU?
MY HEAD HURTS...
PLAY WITH US TOO.

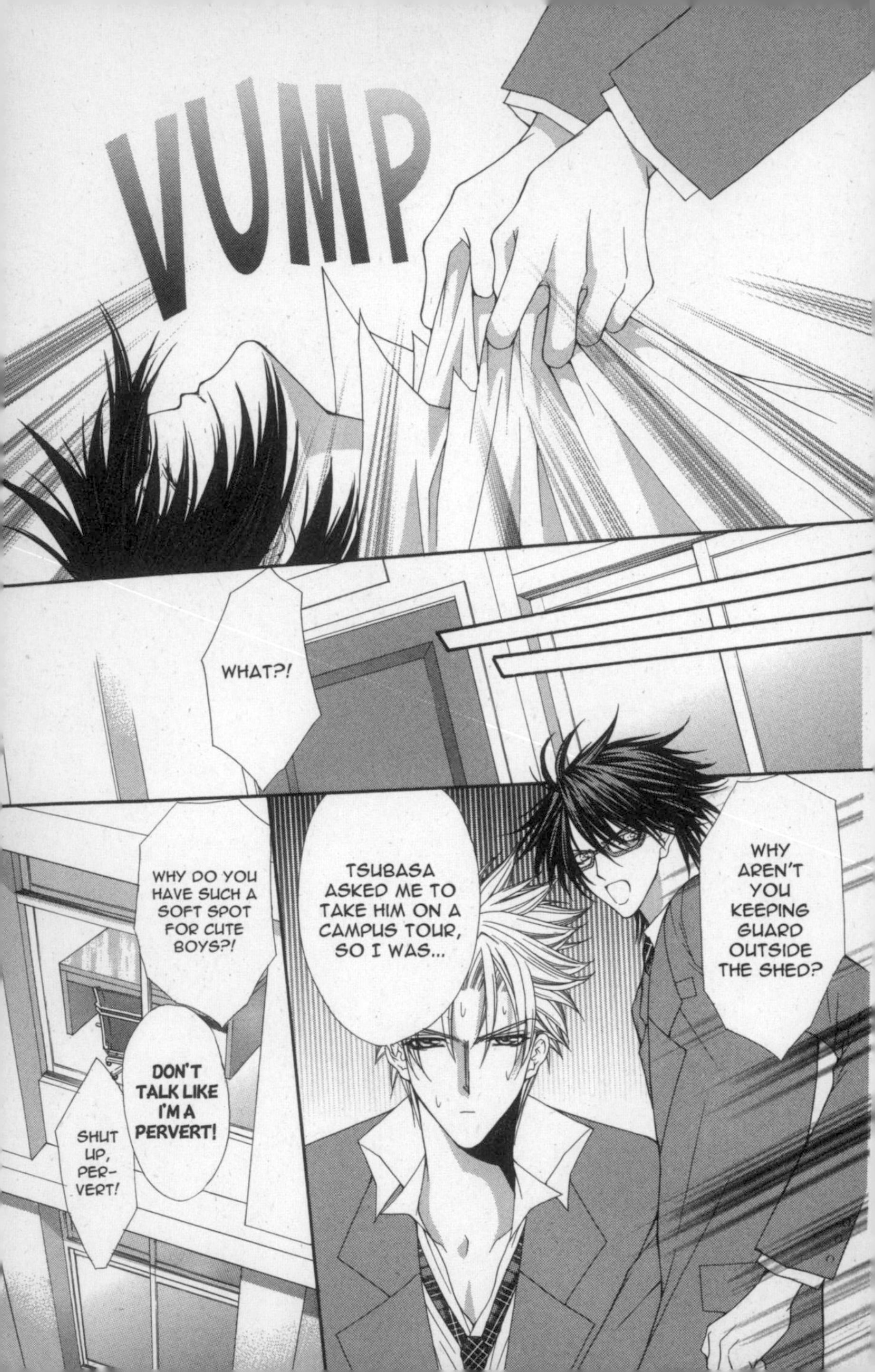
VUMP
WHAT?!
WHY AREN'T YOU KEEPING GUARD OUTSIDE THE SHED?
TSUBASA ASKED ME TO TAKE HIM ON A CAMPUS TOUR, SO I WAS...
WHY DO YOU HAVE SUCH A SOFT SPOT FOR CUTE BOYS?!
DON'T TALK LIKE I'M A PERVERT!
SHUT UP, PER-VERT!

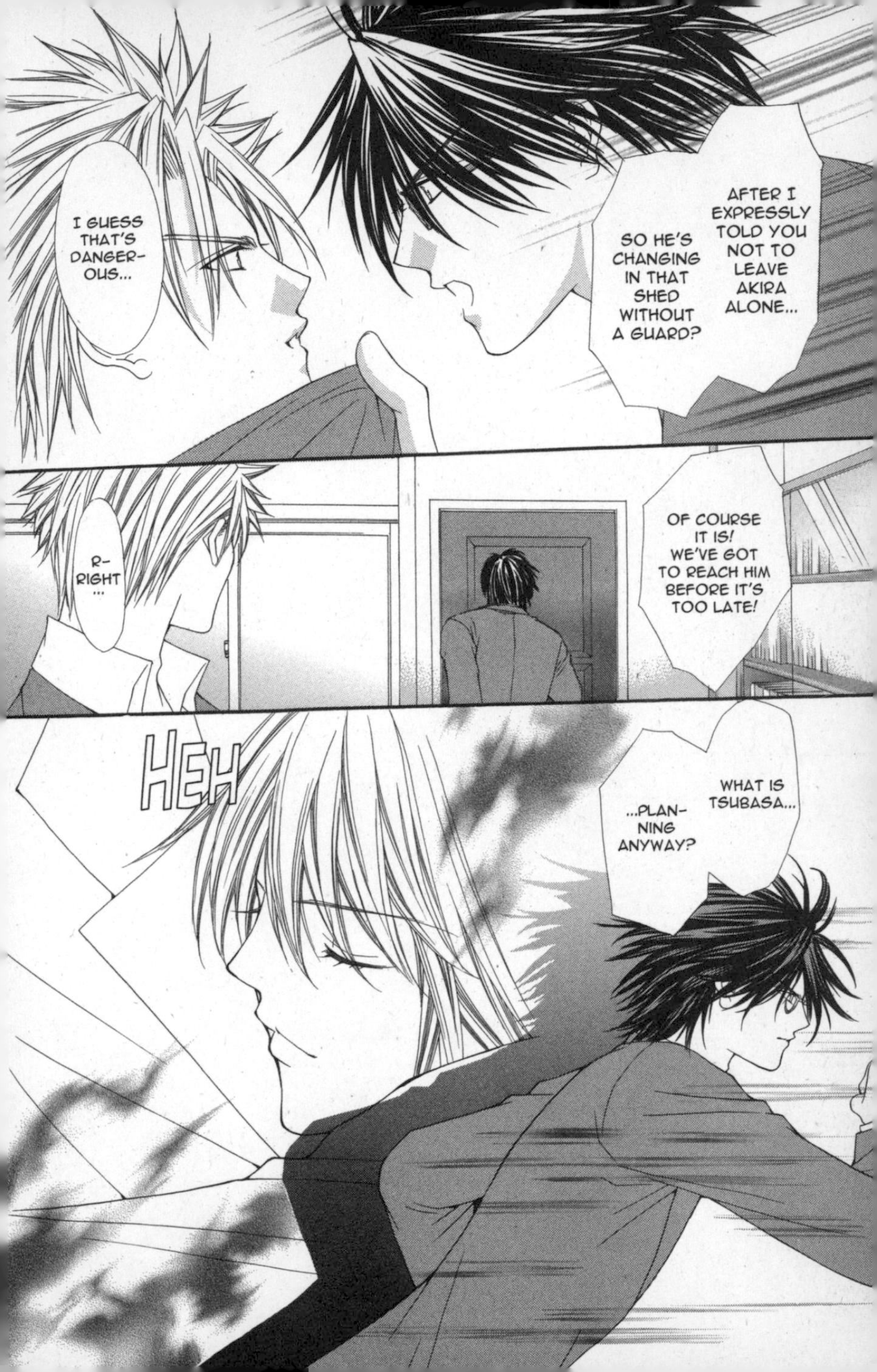
AFTER I EXPRESSLY TOLD YOU NOT TO LEAVE AKIRA ALONE...
SO HE'S CHANGING IN THAT SHED WITHOUT A GUARD?
I GUESS THAT'S DANGER-OUS...
OF COURSE IT IS! WE'VE GOT TO REACH HIM BEFORE IT'S TOO LATE!
R-RIGHT...
WHAT IS TSUBASA...
...PLAN-NING ANYWAY?
HEH

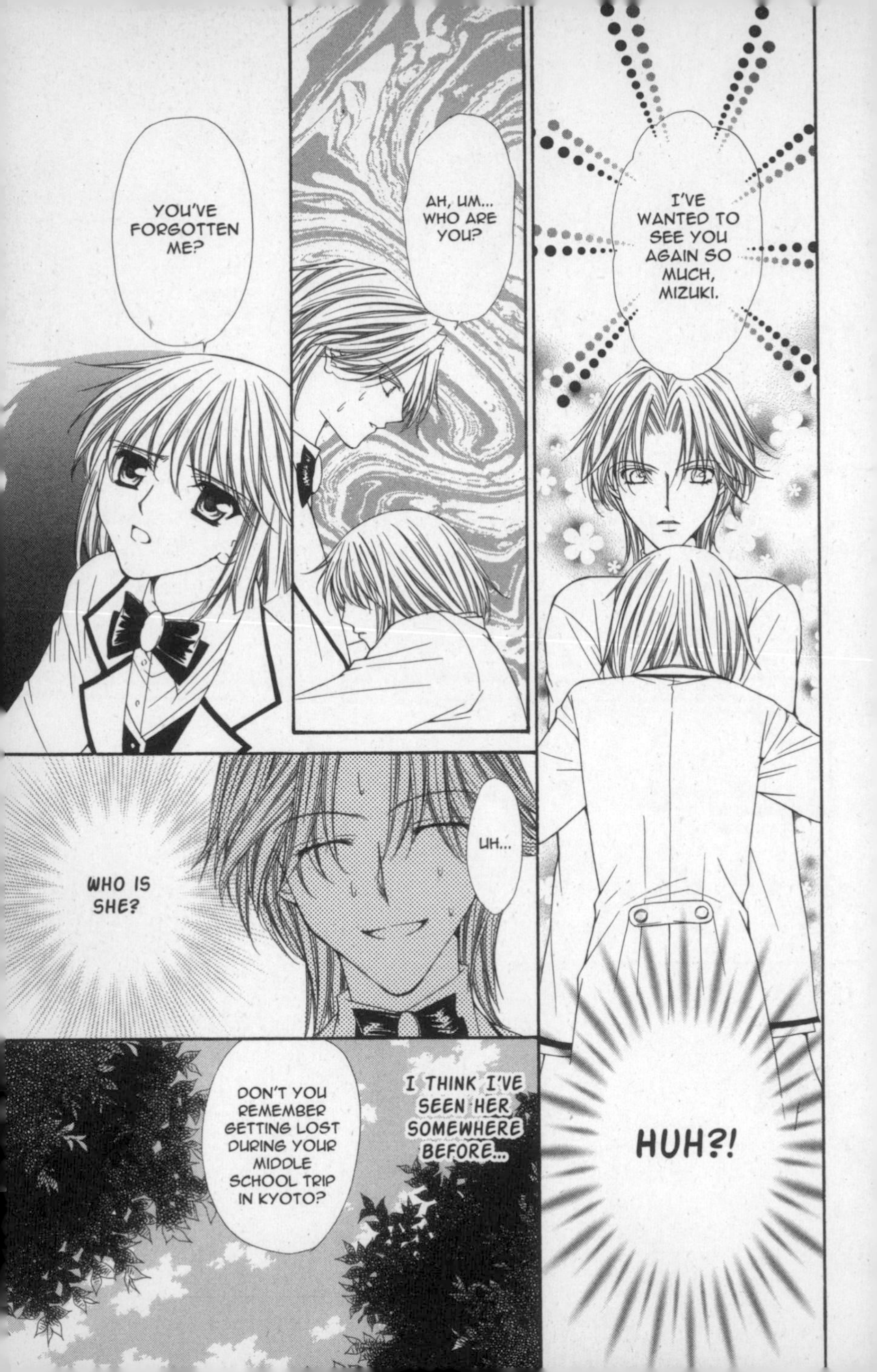
I'VE WANTED TO SEE YOU AGAIN SO MUCH, MIZUKI.
HUH?!
AH, UM... WHO ARE YOU?
YOU'VE FORGOTTEN ME?
UH...
WHO IS SHE?
I THINK I'VE SEEN HER SOMEWHERE BEFORE...
DON'T YOU REMEMBER GETTING LOST DURING YOUR MIDDLE SCHOOL TRIP IN KYOTO?

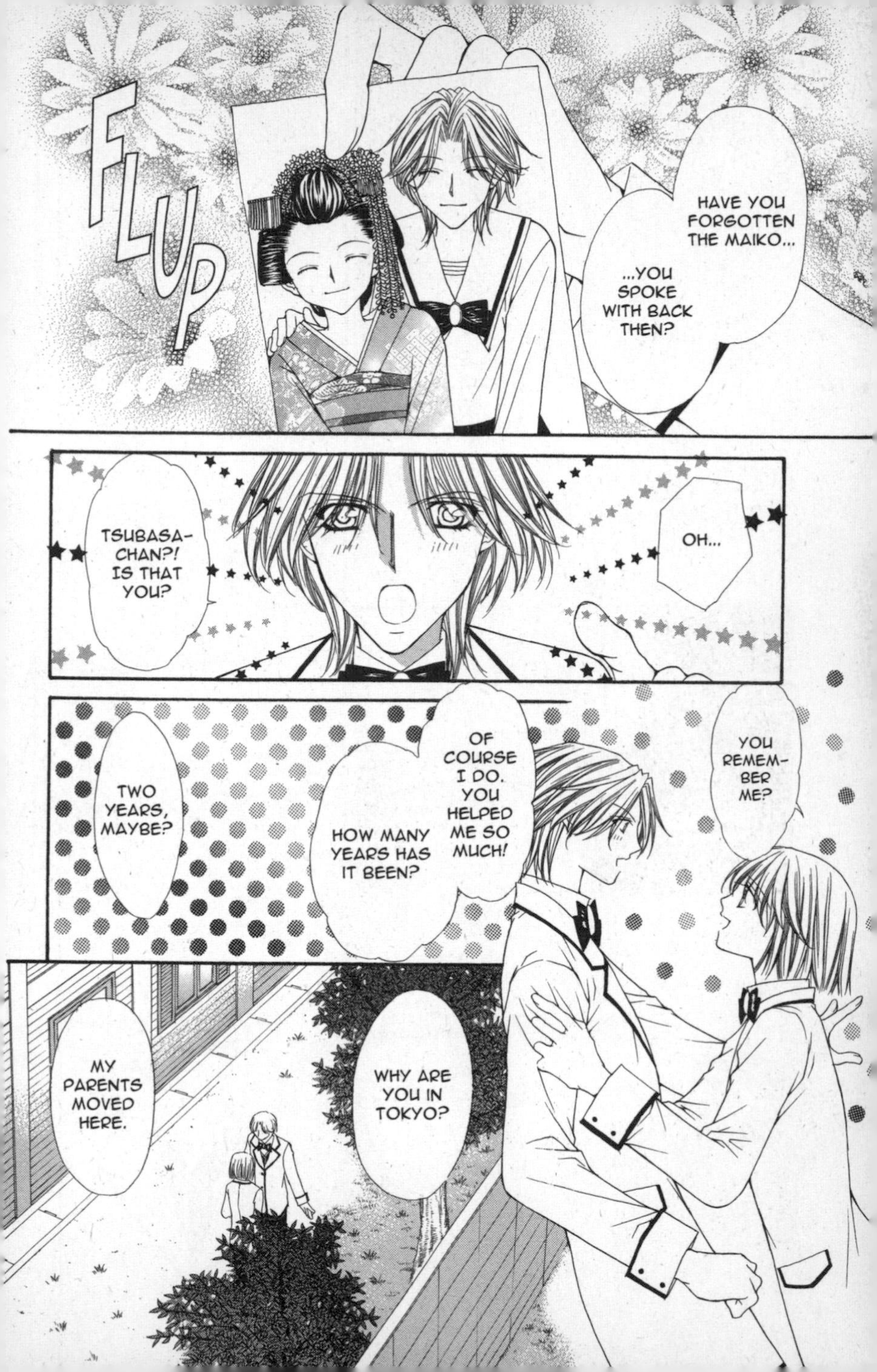
HAVE YOU FORGOTTEN THE MAIKO...
...YOU SPOKE WITH BACK THEN?
FLUP
OH...
TSUBASA-CHAN?! IS THAT YOU?
YOU REMEM-BER ME?
OF COURSE I DO. YOU HELPED ME SO MUCH!
HOW MANY YEARS HAS IT BEEN?
TWO YEARS, MAYBE?
WHY ARE YOU IN TOKYO?
MY PARENTS MOVED HERE.

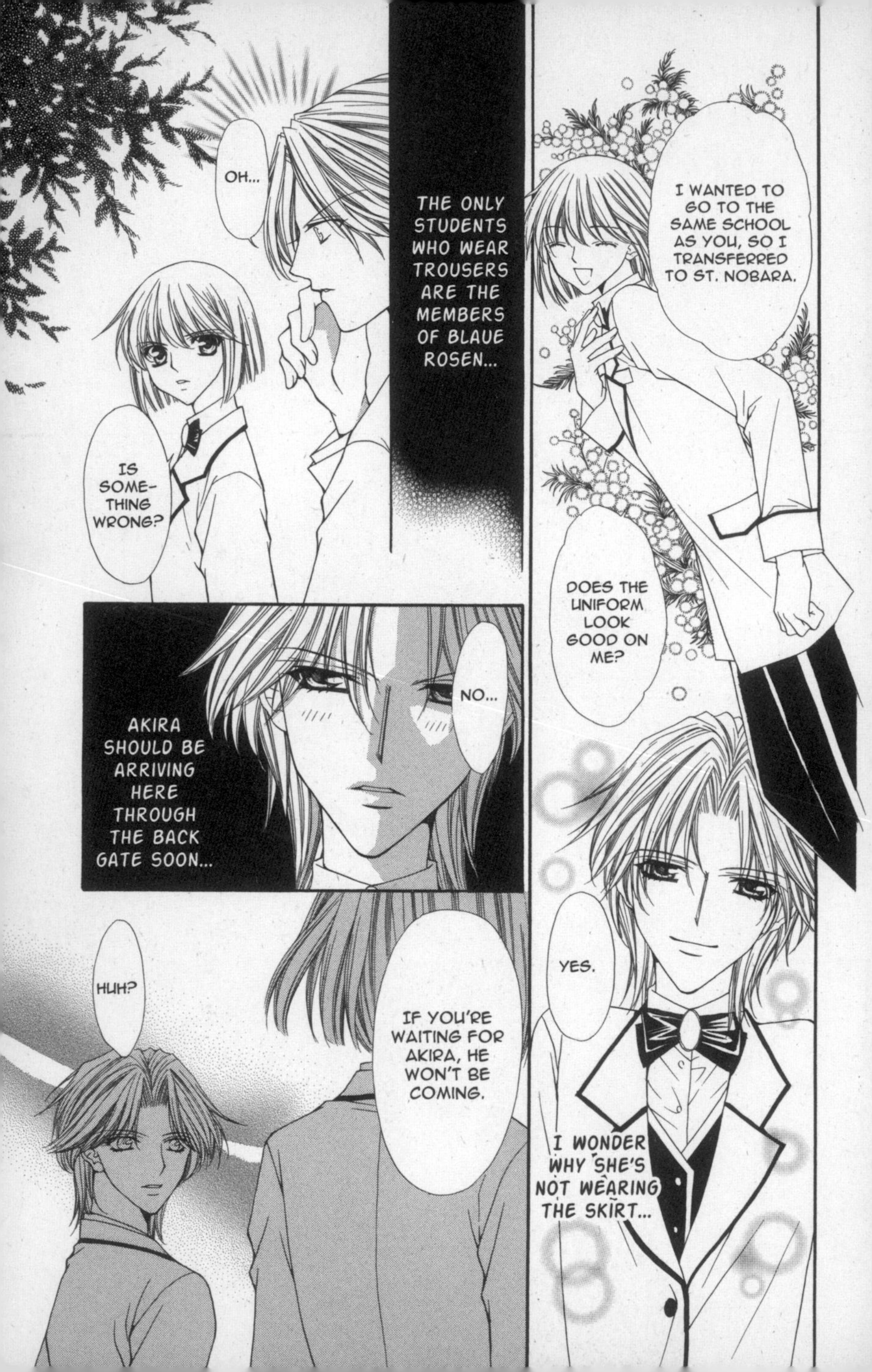
I WANTED TO GO TO THE SAME SCHOOL AS YOU, SO I TRANSFERRED TO ST. NOBARA.
DOES THE UNIFORM LOOK GOOD ON ME?
YES.
I WONDER WHY SHE'S NOT WEARING THE SKIRT...
THE ONLY STUDENTS WHO WEAR TROUSERS ARE THE MEMBERS OF BLAUE ROSEN...
OH...
IS SOME-THING WRONG?
NO...
AKIRA SHOULD BE ARRIVING HERE THROUGH THE BACK GATE SOON...
IF YOU'RE WAITING FOR AKIRA, HE WON'T BE COMING.
HUH?

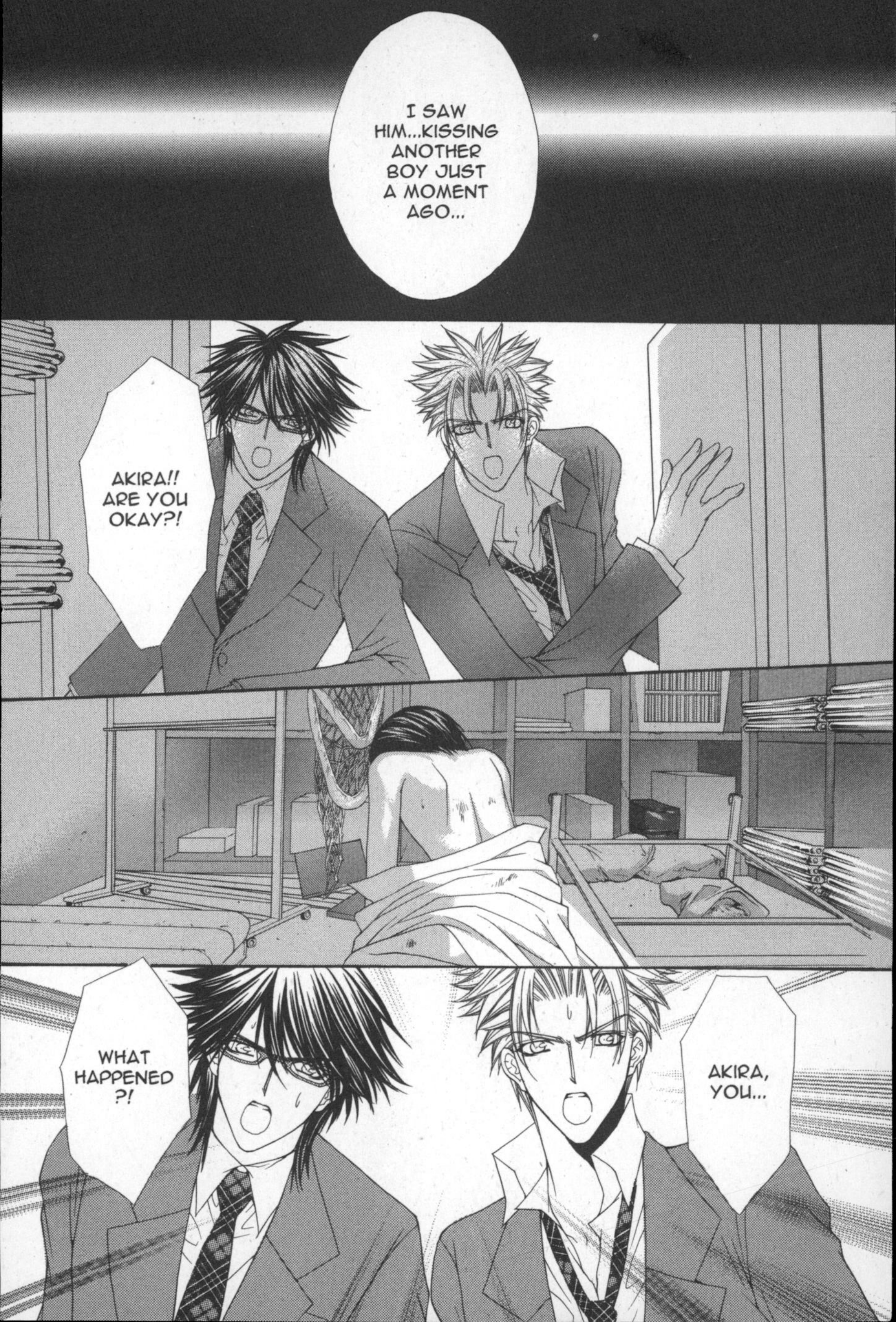
I SAW HIM...KISSING ANOTHER BOY JUST A MOMENT AGO...
AKIRA!! ARE YOU OKAY?!
AKIRA, YOU...
WHAT HAPPENED ?!

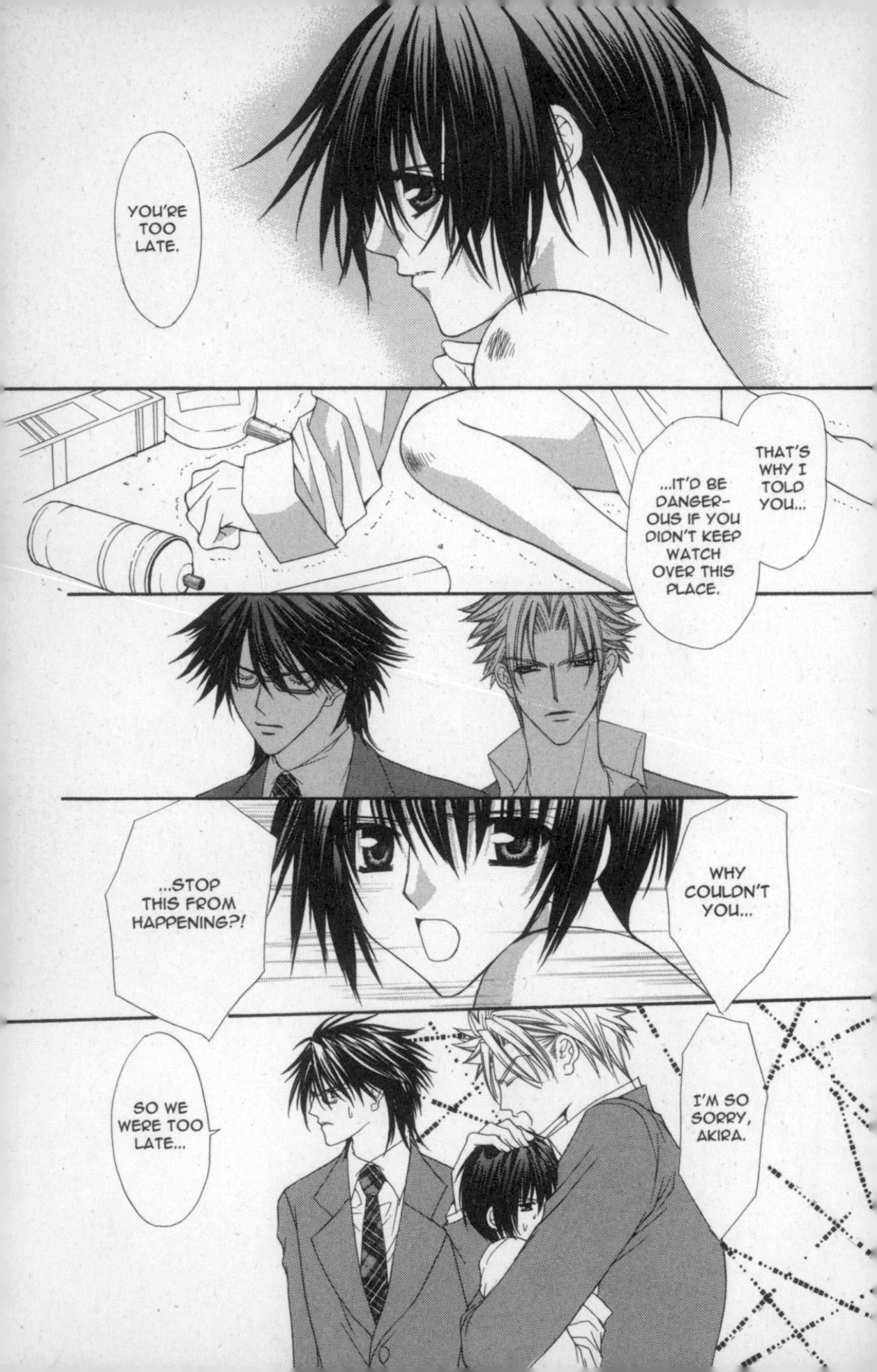
YOU'RE TOO LATE.
THAT'S WHY I TOLD YOU...
...IT'D BE DANGEROUS IF YOU DIDN'T KEEP WATCH OVER THIS PLACE.
WHY COULDN'T YOU...
...STOP THIS FROM HAPPENING?!
I'M SO SORRY, AKIRA.
SO WE WERE TOO LATE...

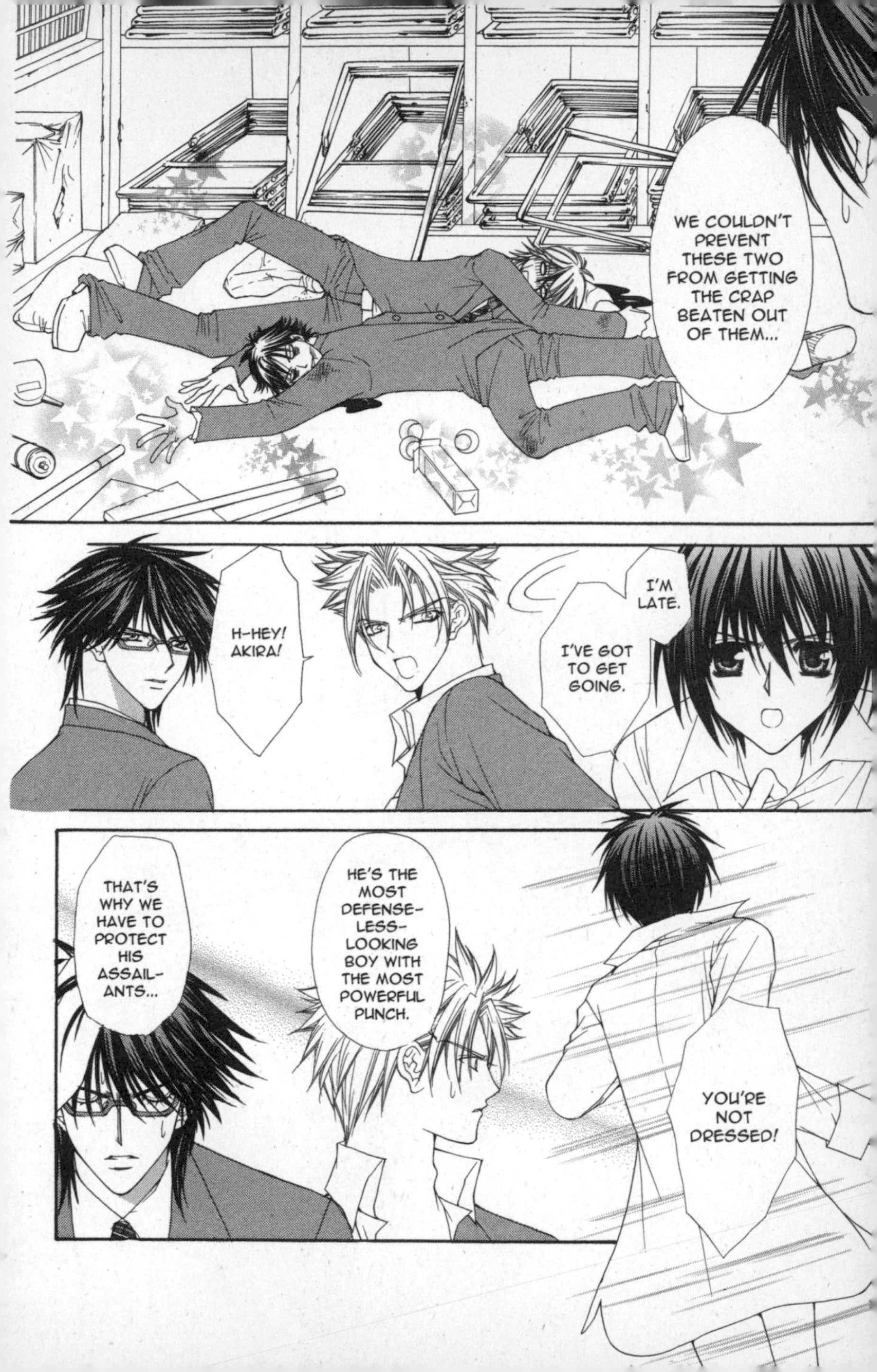
WE COULDN'T PREVENT THESE TWO FROM GETTING THE CRAP BEATEN OUT OF THEM...
I'M LATE.
I'VE GOT TO GET GOING.
H-HEY! AKIRA!
YOU'RE NOT DRESSED!
HE'S THE MOST DEFENSELESS-LOOKING BOY WITH THE MOST POWERFUL PUNCH.
THAT'S WHY WE HAVE TO PROTECT HIS ASSAILANTS...

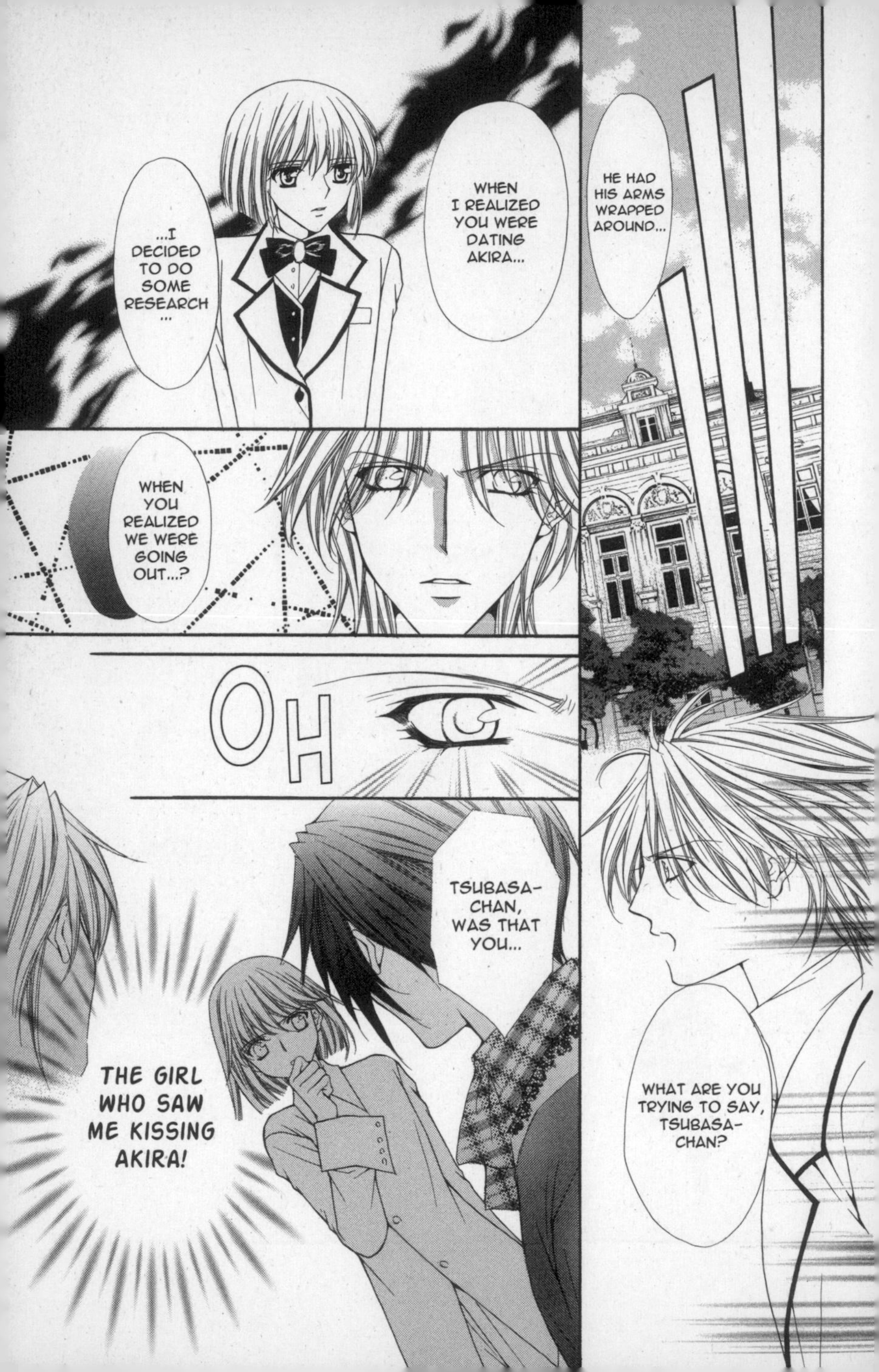
HE HAD HIS ARMS WRAPPED AROUND...
WHAT ARE YOU TRYING TO SAY, TSUBASA-CHAN?
WHEN I REALIZED YOU WERE DATING AKIRA...
...I DECIDED TO DO SOME RESEARCH...
WHEN YOU REALIZED WE WERE GOING OUT...?
OH
TSUBASA-CHAN, WAS THAT YOU...
THE GIRL WHO SAW ME KISSING AKIRA!

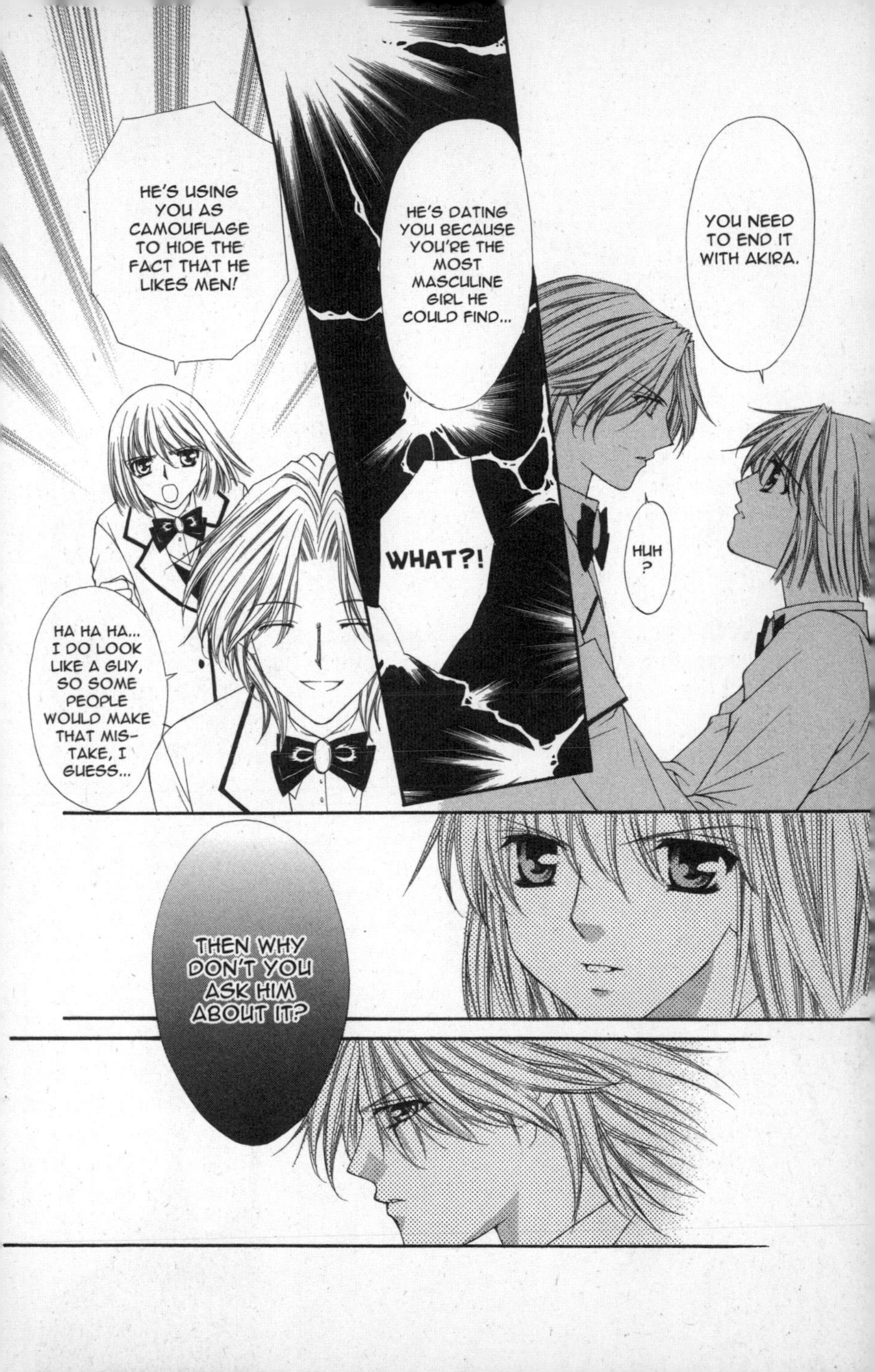
YOU NEED TO END IT WITH AKIRA.
HUH?
HE'S DATING YOU BECAUSE YOU'RE THE MOST MASCULINE GIRL HE COULD FIND...
WHAT?!
HE'S USING YOU AS CAMOUFLAGE TO HIDE THE FACT THAT HE LIKES MEN!
HA HA HA... I DO LOOK LIKE A GUY, SO SOME PEOPLE WOULD MAKE THAT MIS-TAKE, I GUESS...
THEN WHY DON'T YOU ASK HIM ABOUT IT?

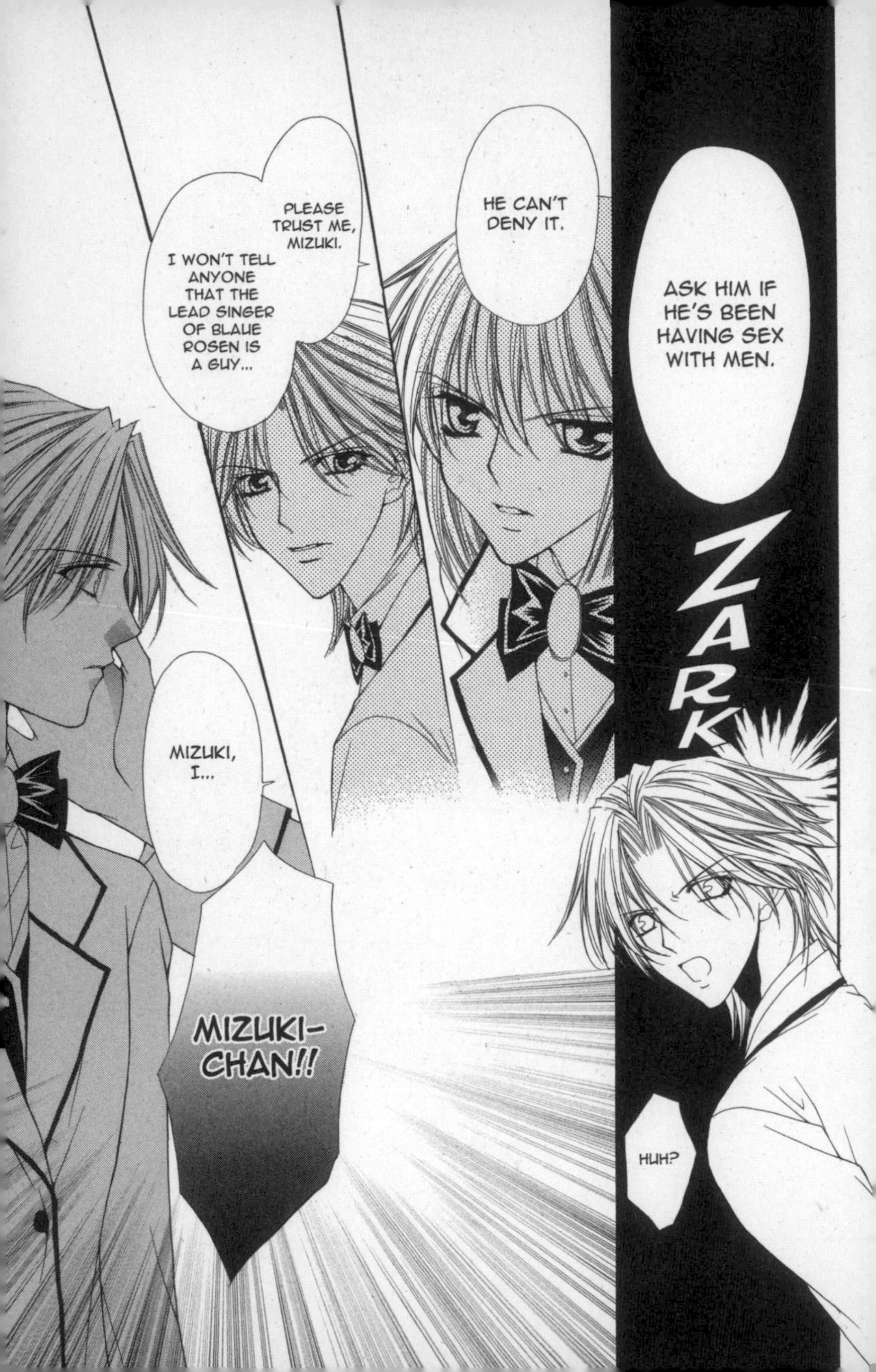
ASK HIM IF HE'S BEEN HAVING SEX WITH MEN.
ZARK
HUH?
HE CAN'T DENY IT.
PLEASE TRUST ME, MIZUKI.
I WON'T TELL ANYONE THAT THE LEAD SINGER OF BLAUE ROSEN IS A GUY...
MIZUKI, I...
MIZUKI-CHAN!!

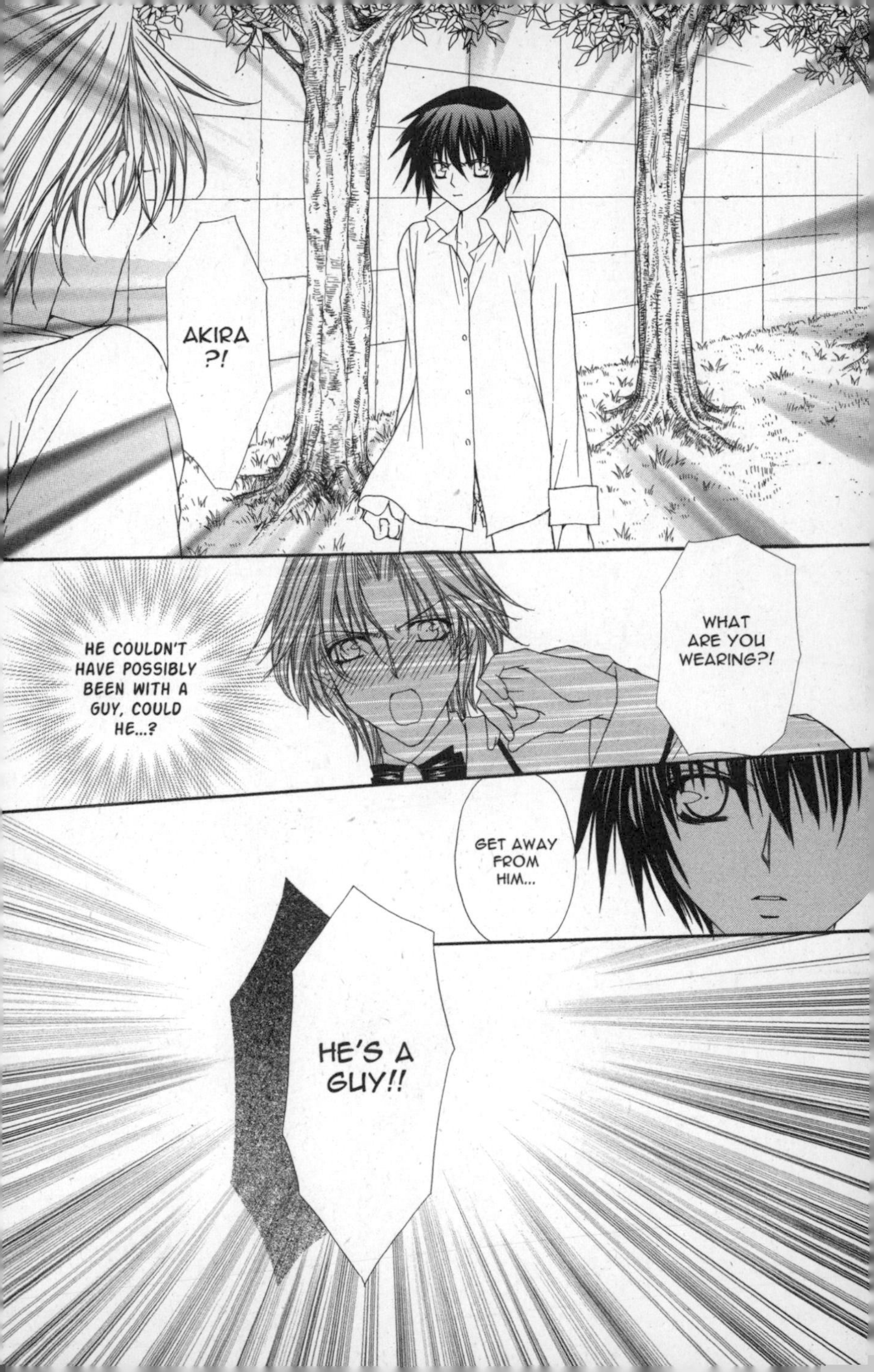
AKIRA ?!
WHAT ARE YOU WEARING?!
HE COULDN'T HAVE POSSIBLY BEEN WITH A GUY, COULD HE...?
GET AWAY FROM HIM...
HE'S A GUY!!

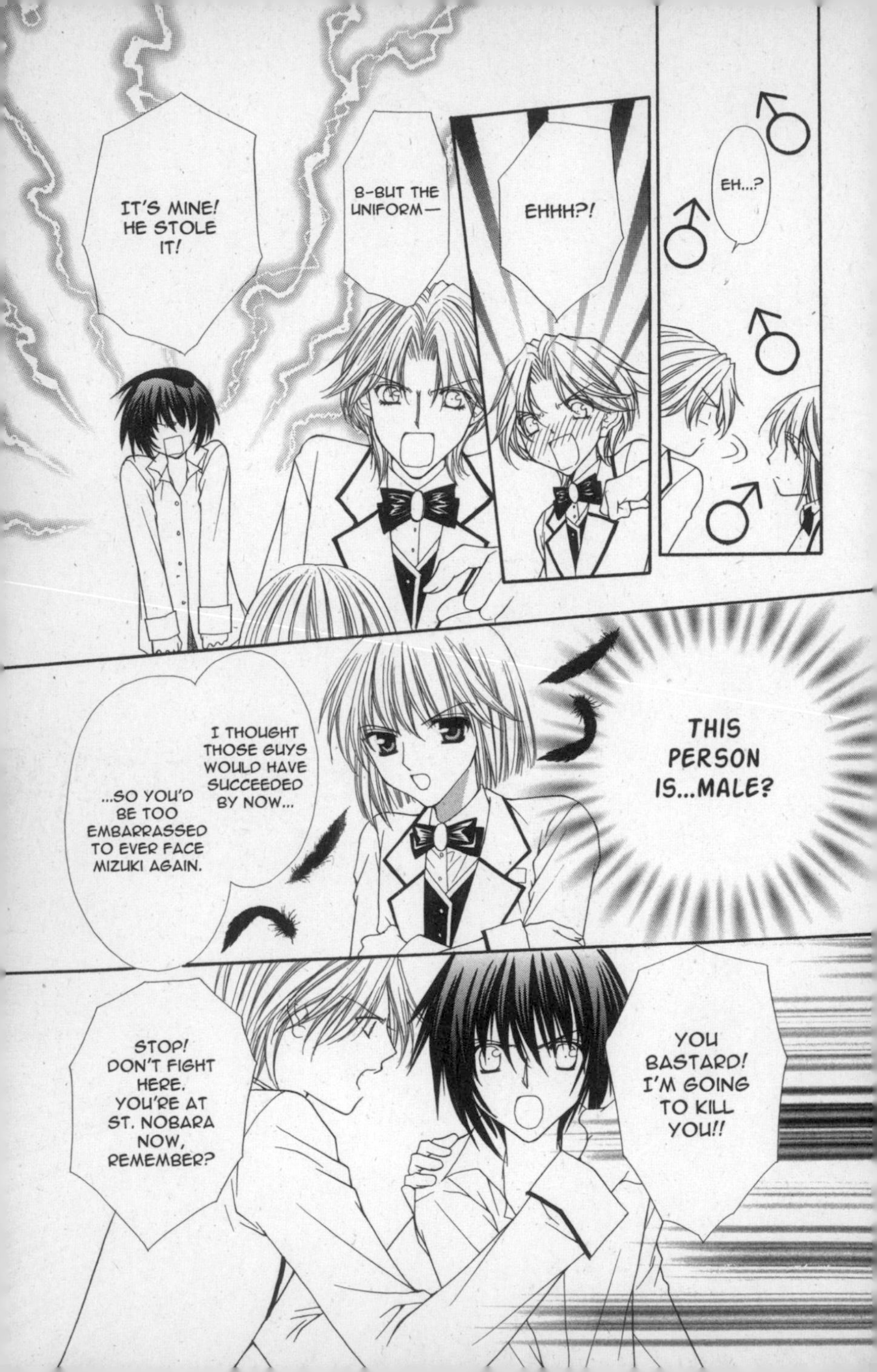
EH...?
EHHH?!
B-BUT THE UNIFORM—
IT'S MINE! HE STOLE IT!
THIS PERSON IS...MALE?
I THOUGHT THOSE GUYS WOULD HAVE SUCCEEDED BY NOW...
...SO YOU'D BE TOO EMBARRASSED TO EVER FACE MIZUKI AGAIN.
YOU BASTARD! I'M GOING TO KILL YOU!!
STOP! DON'T FIGHT HERE. YOU'RE AT ST. NOBARA NOW, REMEMBER?

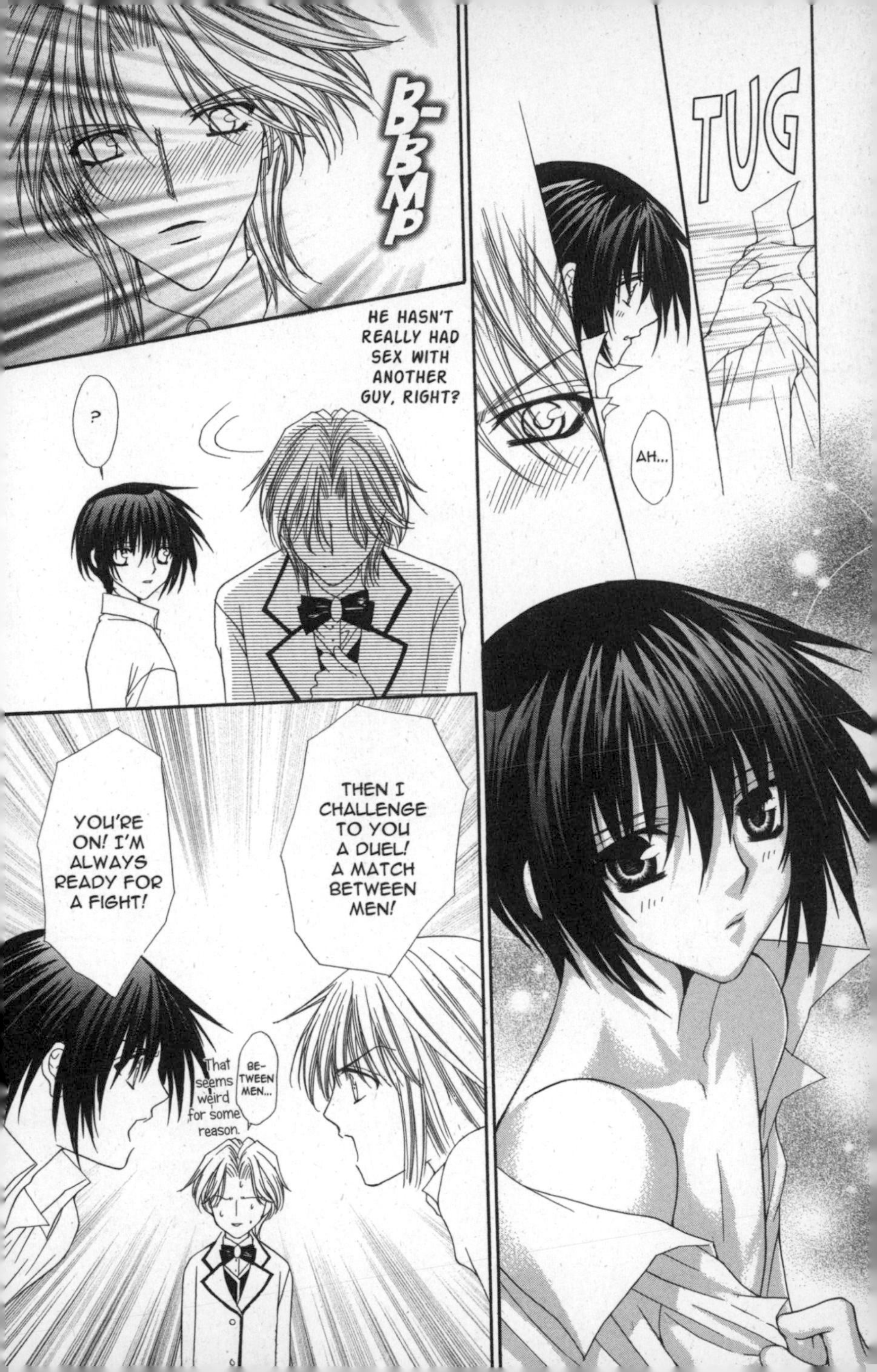
TUG
AH...
B-BUMP
HE HASN'T REALLY HAD SEX WITH ANOTHER GUY, RIGHT?
?
THEN I CHALLENGE TO YOU A DUEL! A MATCH BETWEEN MEN!
YOU'RE ON! I'M ALWAYS READY FOR A FIGHT!
BE-TWEEN MEN...
That seems weird for some reason.

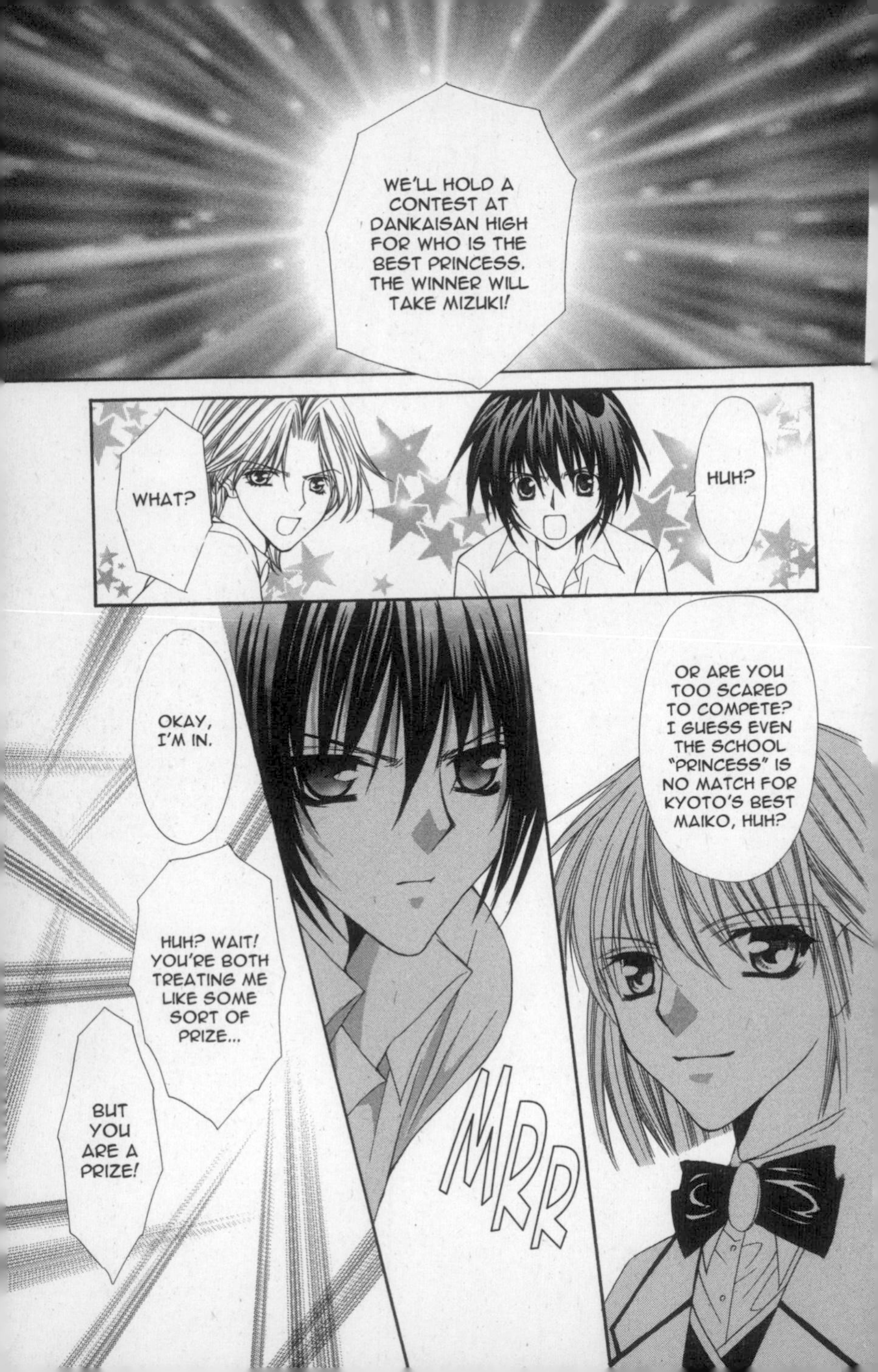
WE'LL HOLD A CONTEST AT DANKAISAN HIGH FOR WHO IS THE BEST PRINCESS. THE WINNER WILL TAKE MIZUKI!
HUH?
WHAT?
OR ARE YOU TOO SCARED TO COMPETE? I GUESS EVEN THE SCHOOL "PRINCESS" IS NO MATCH FOR KYOTO'S BEST MAIKO, HUH?
OKAY, I'M IN.
HUH? WAIT! YOU'RE BOTH TREATING ME LIKE SOME SORT OF PRIZE...
MRR
BUT YOU ARE A PRIZE!

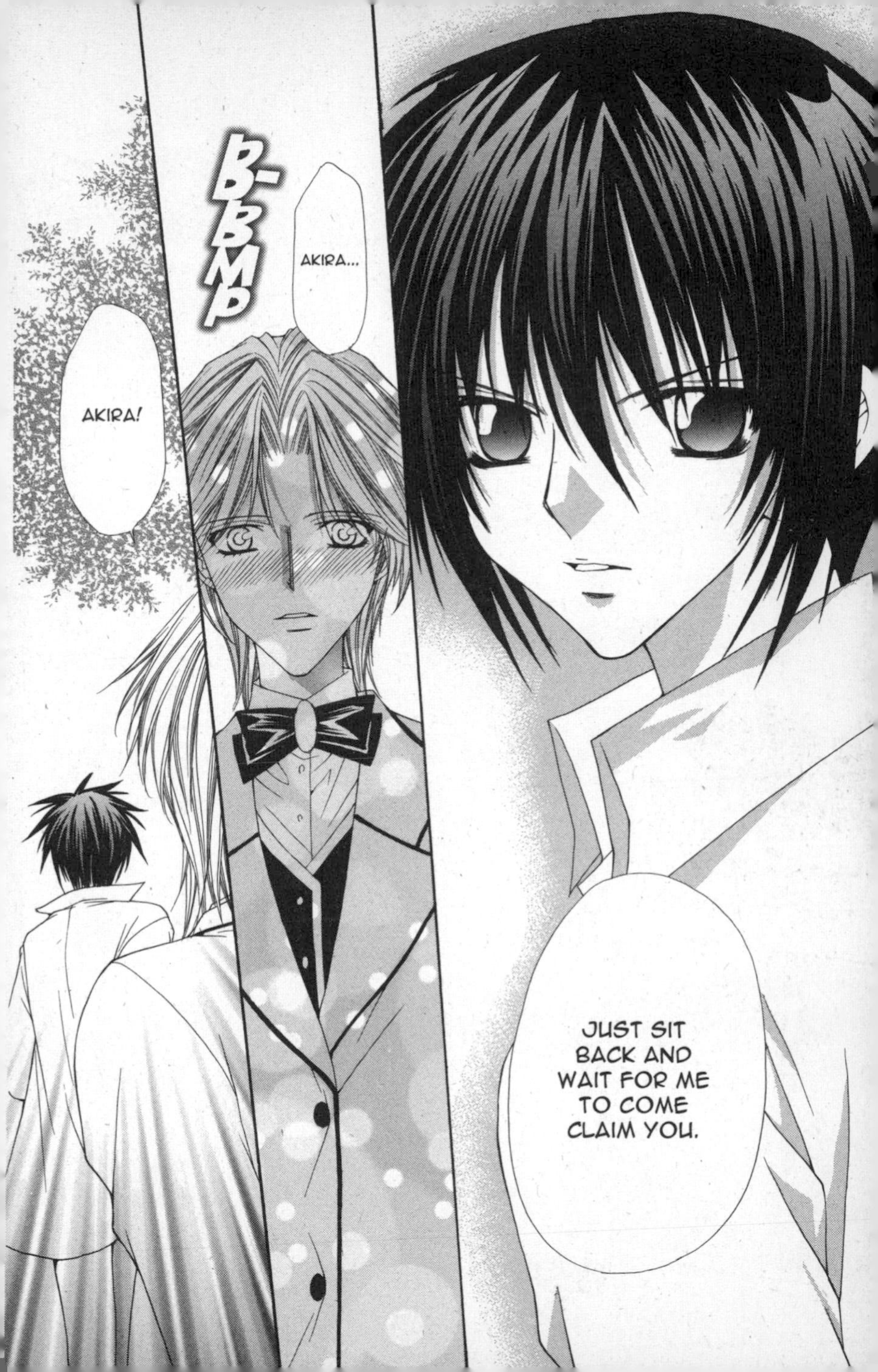
JUST SIT BACK AND WAIT FOR ME TO COME CLAIM YOU.
AKIRA...
B-BMP
AKIRA!

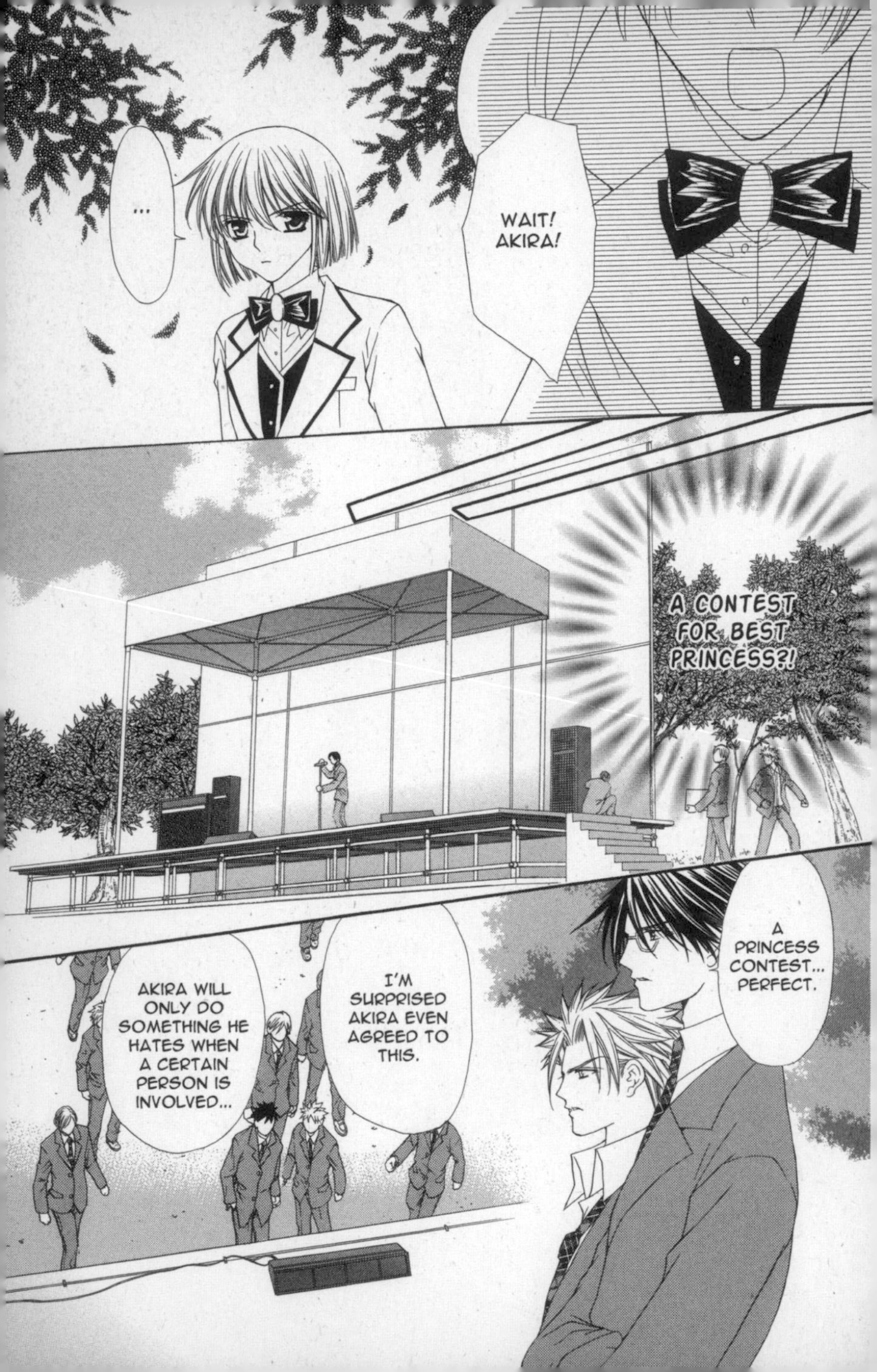
WAIT! AKIRA!
...
A CONTEST FOR BEST PRINCESS?!
A PRINCESS CONTEST... PERFECT.
I'M SURPRISED AKIRA EVEN AGREED TO THIS.
AKIRA WILL ONLY DO SOMETHING HE HATES WHEN A CERTAIN PERSON IS INVOLVED...

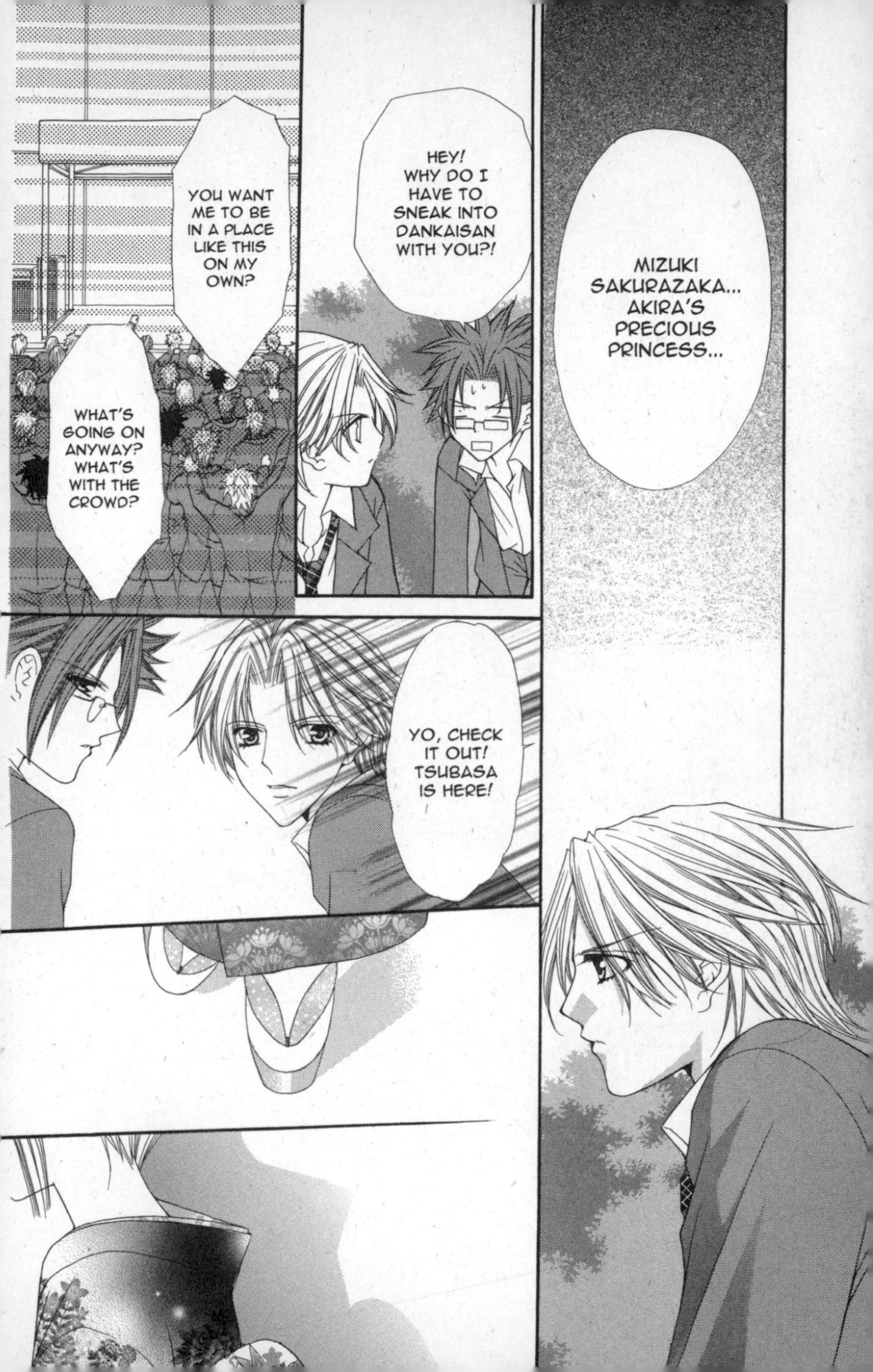
MIZUKI SAKURAZAKA... AKIRA'S PRECIOUS PRINCESS...
HEY! WHY DO I HAVE TO SNEAK INTO DANKAISAN WITH YOU?!
YOU WANT ME TO BE IN A PLACE LIKE THIS ON MY OWN?
WHAT'S GOING ON ANYWAY? WHAT'S WITH THE CROWD?
YO, CHECK IT OUT! TSUBASA IS HERE!

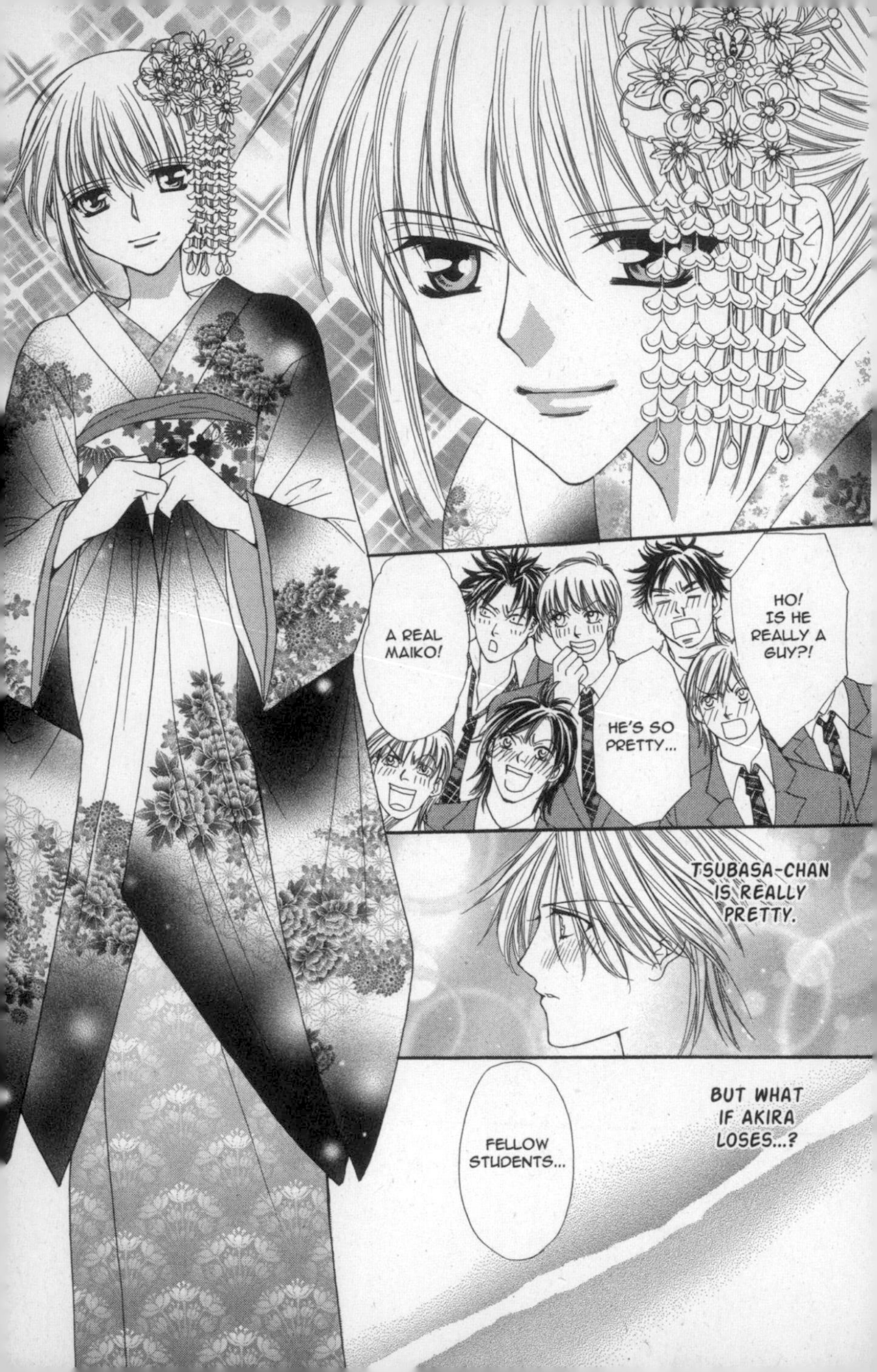
HO! IS HE REALLY A GUY?!
HE'S SO PRETTY...
A REAL MAIKO!
TSUBASA-CHAN IS REALLY PRETTY.
BUT WHAT IF AKIRA LOSES...?
FELLOW STUDENTS...

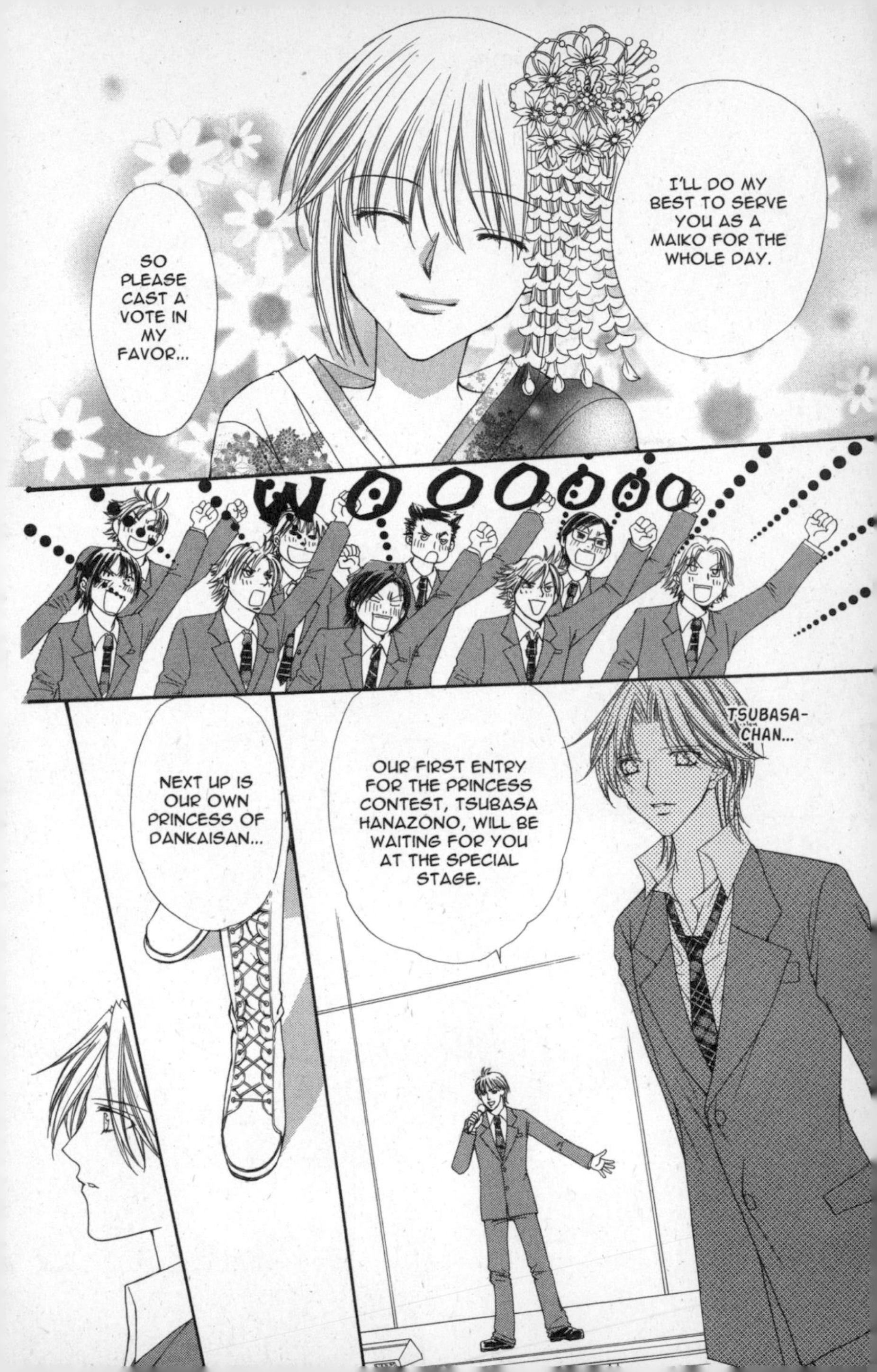
I'LL DO MY BEST TO SERVE YOU AS A MAIKO FOR THE WHOLE DAY.
SO PLEASE CAST A VOTE IN MY FAVOR...
WOOOOOO
TSUBASA-CHAN...
OUR FIRST ENTRY FOR THE PRINCESS CONTEST, TSUBASA HANAZONO, WILL BE WAITING FOR YOU AT THE SPECIAL STAGE.
NEXT UP IS OUR OWN PRINCESS OF DANKAISAN...

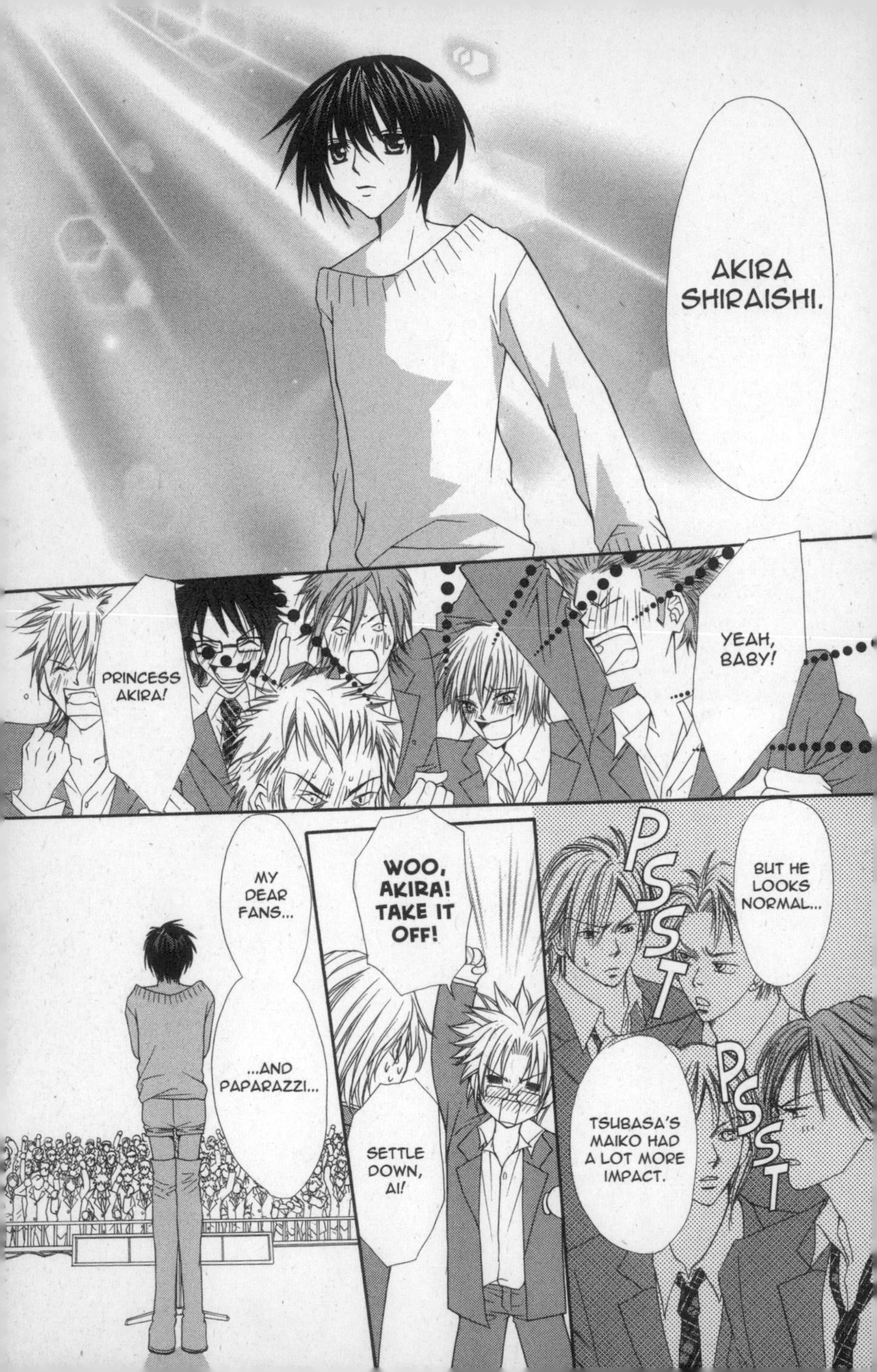
AKIRA SHIRAISHI.
YEAH, BABY!
PRINCESS AKIRA!
BUT HE LOOKS NORMAL...
PSST
PSST
TSUBASA'S MAIKO HAD A LOT MORE IMPACT.
WOO, AKIRA! TAKE IT OFF!
SETTLE DOWN, AI!
MY DEAR FANS...
...AND PAPARAZZI...

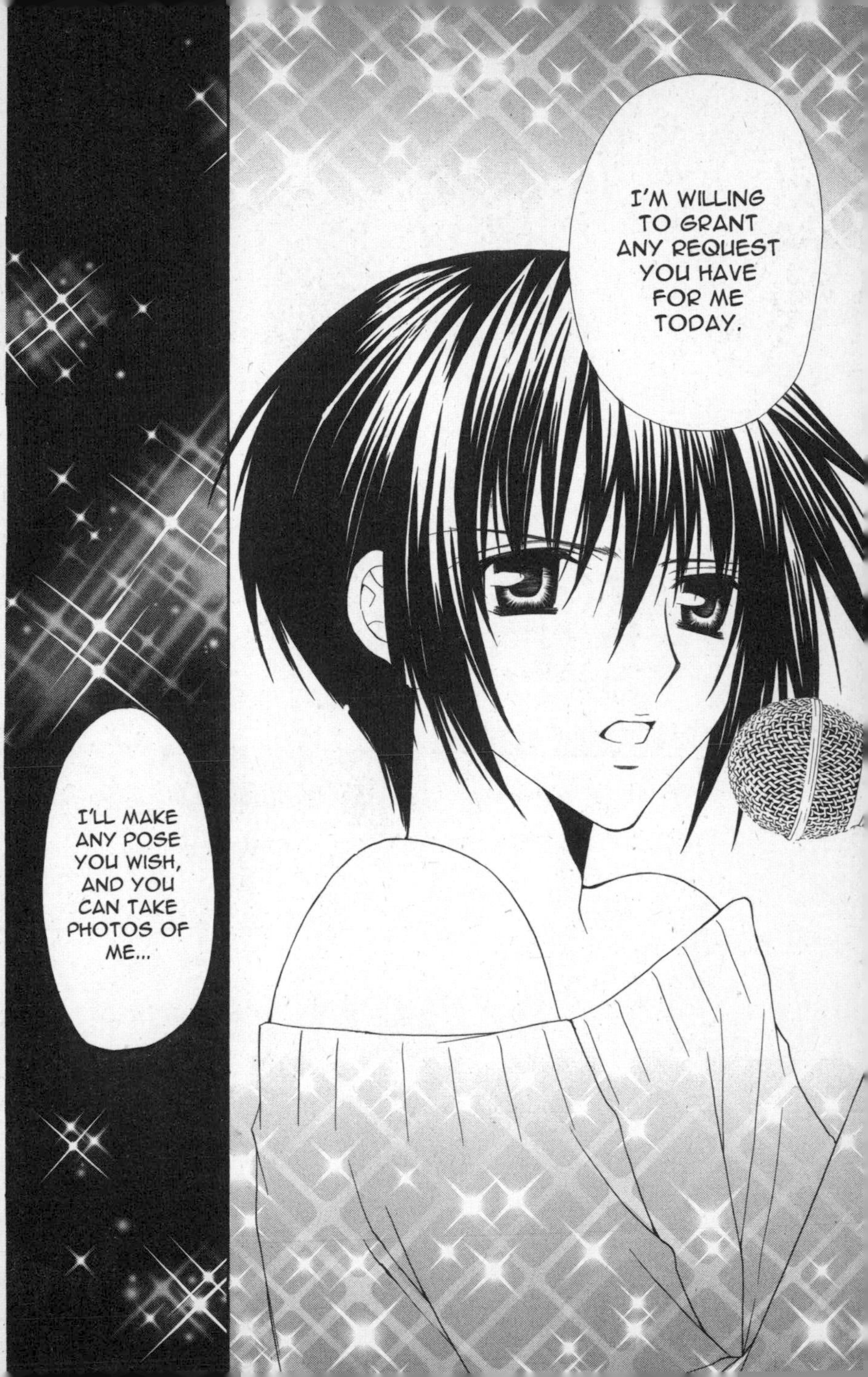
I'M WILLING TO GRANT ANY REQUEST YOU HAVE FOR ME TODAY.
I'LL MAKE ANY POSE YOU WISH, AND YOU CAN TAKE PHOTOS OF ME...

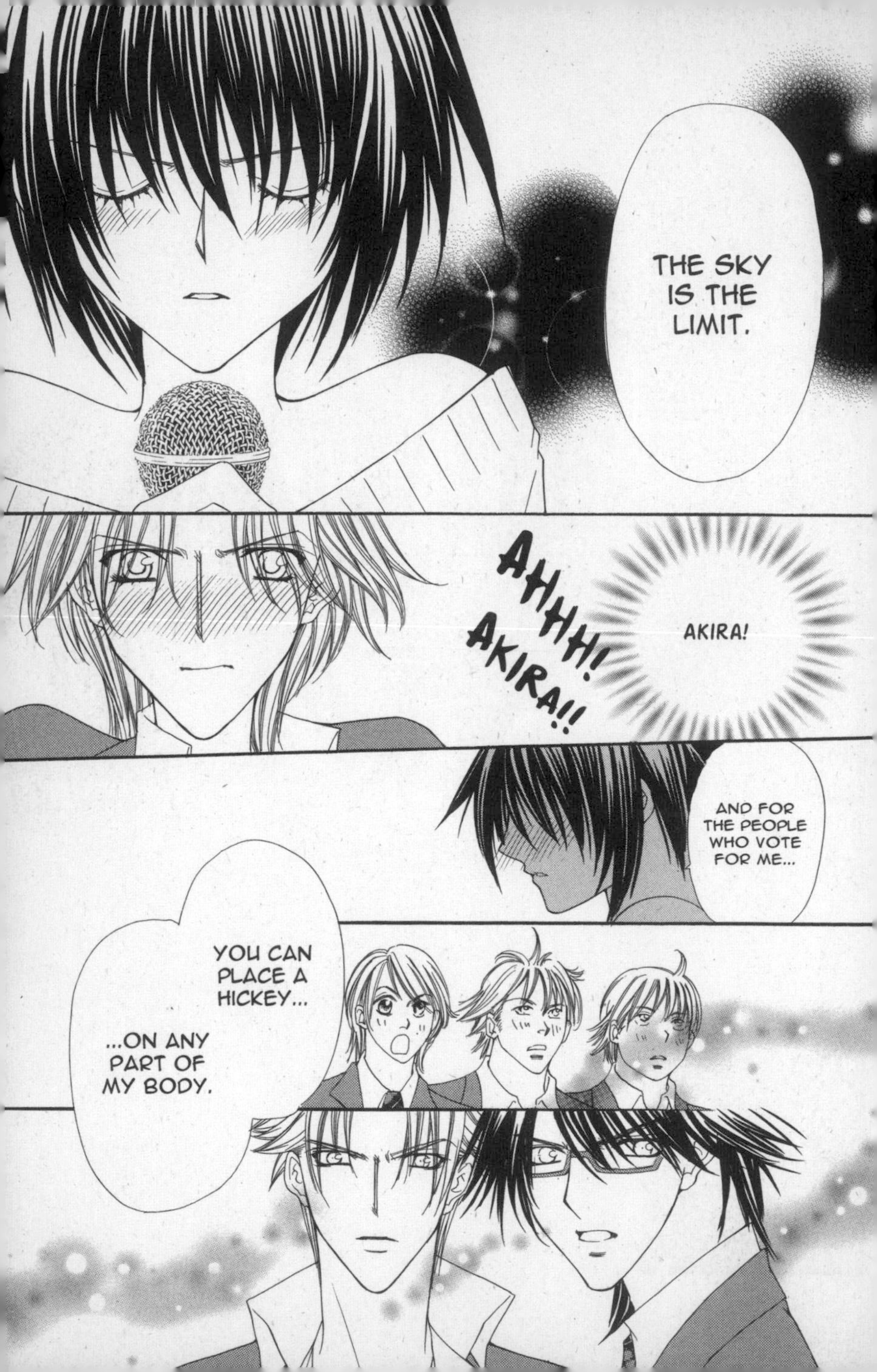
THE SKY IS THE LIMIT.
AKIRA!
AHHHH! AKIRA!!
AND FOR THE PEOPLE WHO VOTE FOR ME...
YOU CAN PLACE A HICKEY...
...ON ANY PART OF MY BODY.

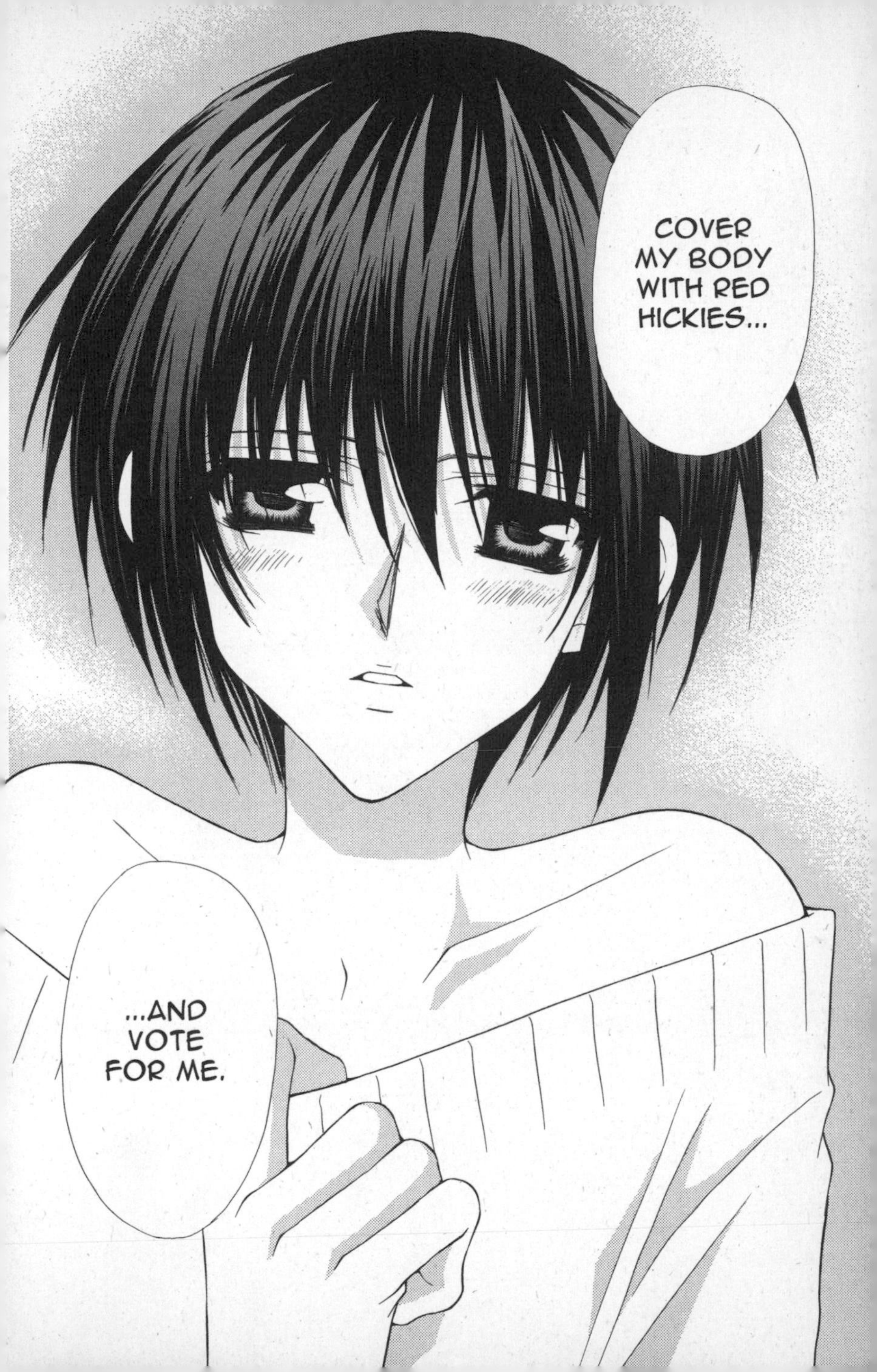
COVER MY BODY WITH RED HICKIES...
...AND VOTE FOR ME.

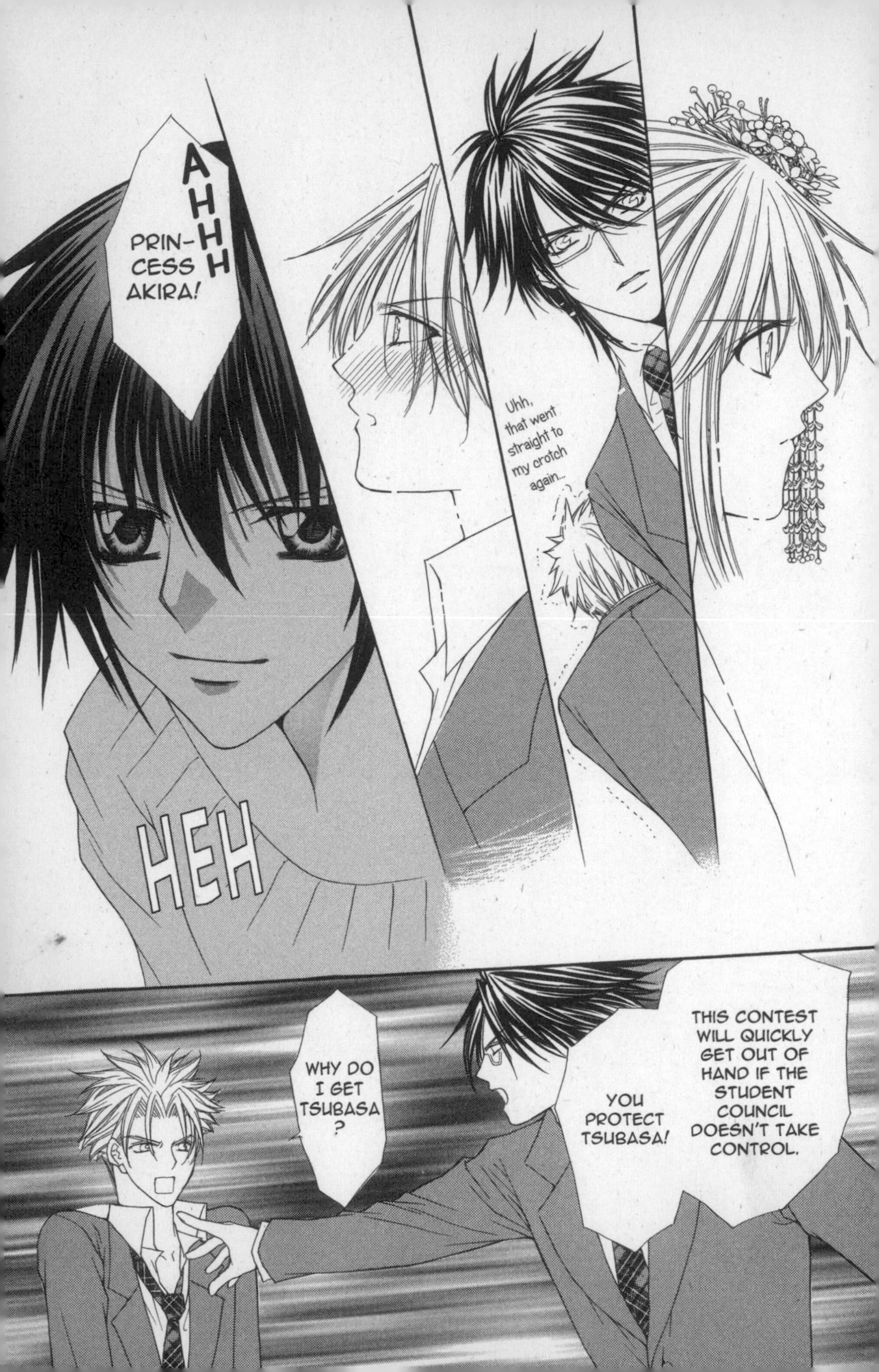
Uhh, that went straight to my crotch again...
AHHH
PRIN-CESS AKIRA!
HEH
THIS CONTEST WILL QUICKLY GET OUT OF HAND IF THE STUDENT COUNCIL DOESN'T TAKE CONTROL.
YOU PROTECT TSUBASA!
WHY DO I GET TSUBASA?

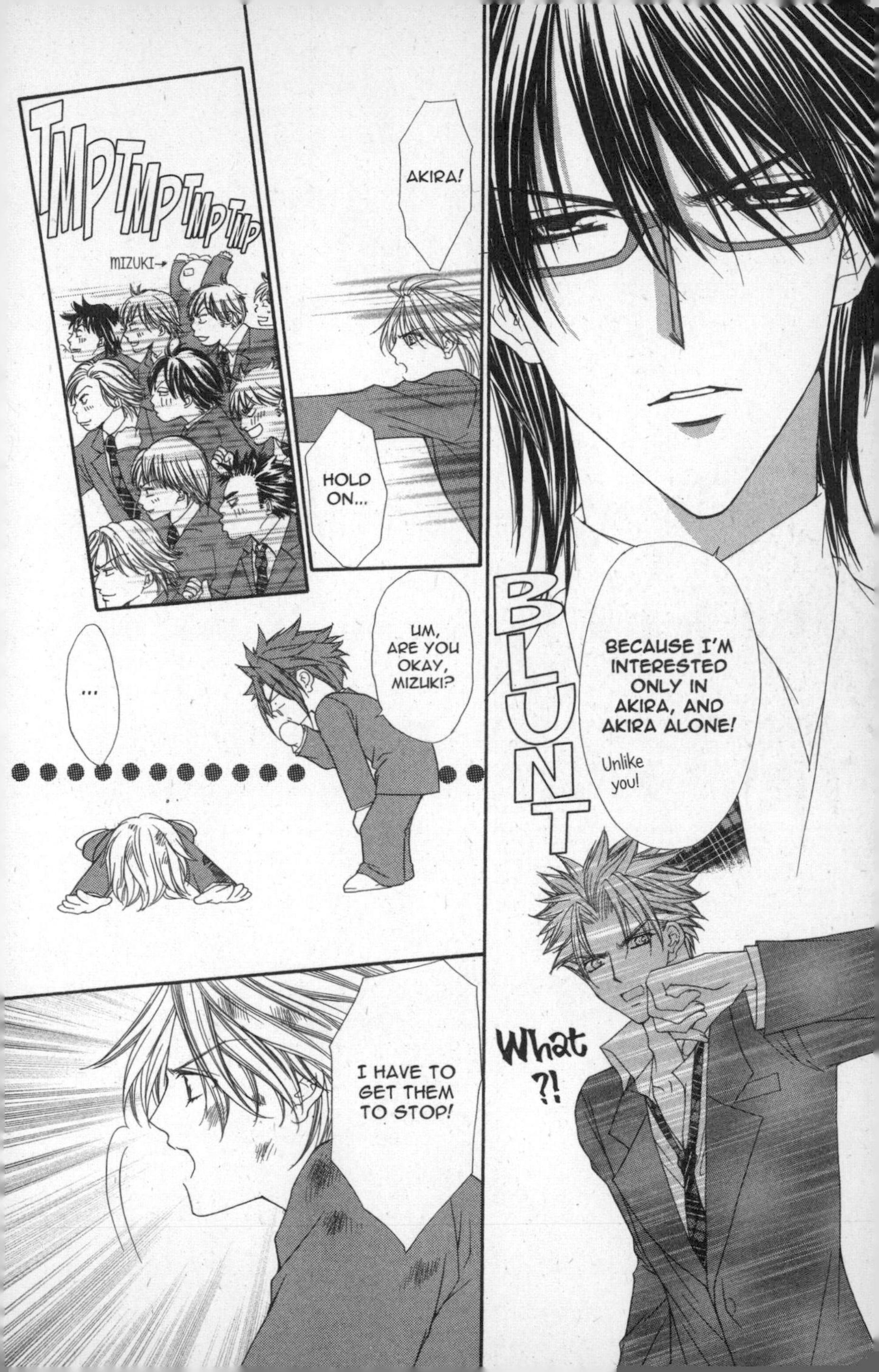

BECAUSE I'M INTERESTED ONLY IN AKIRA, AND AKIRA ALONE!
Unlike you!
BLUNT
What?!
AKIRA!
HOLD ON...
TMPTMPTMPTMP
MIZUKI→
UM, ARE YOU OKAY, MIZUKI?
...
I HAVE TO GET THEM TO STOP!

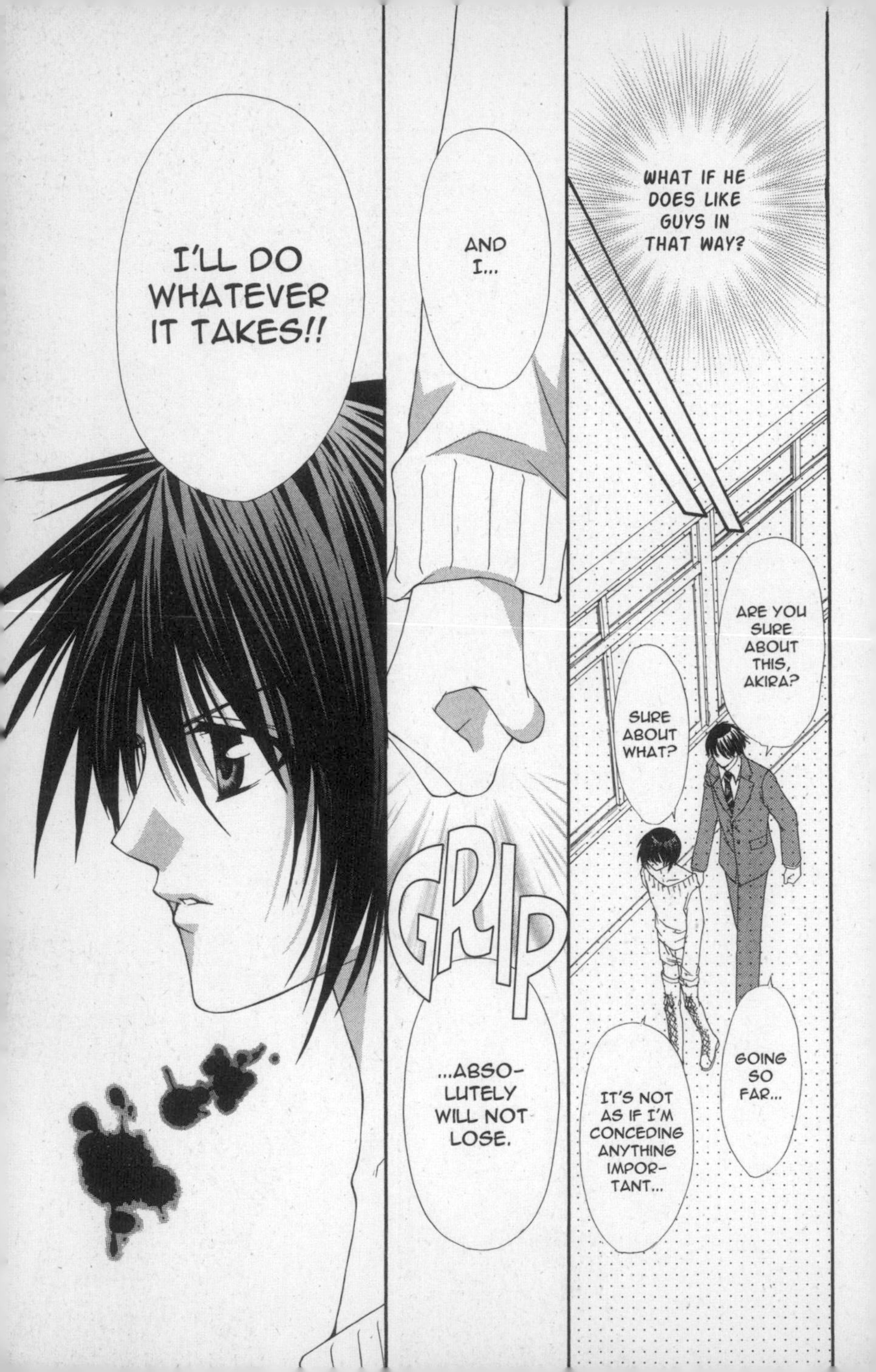
WHAT IF HE DOES LIKE GUYS IN THAT WAY?
ARE YOU SURE ABOUT THIS, AKIRA?
SURE ABOUT WHAT?
GOING SO FAR...
IT'S NOT AS IF I'M CONCEDING ANYTHING IMPOR-TANT...
AND I...
GRIP
...ABSO-LUTELY WILL NOT LOSE.
I'LL DO WHATEVER IT TAKES!!

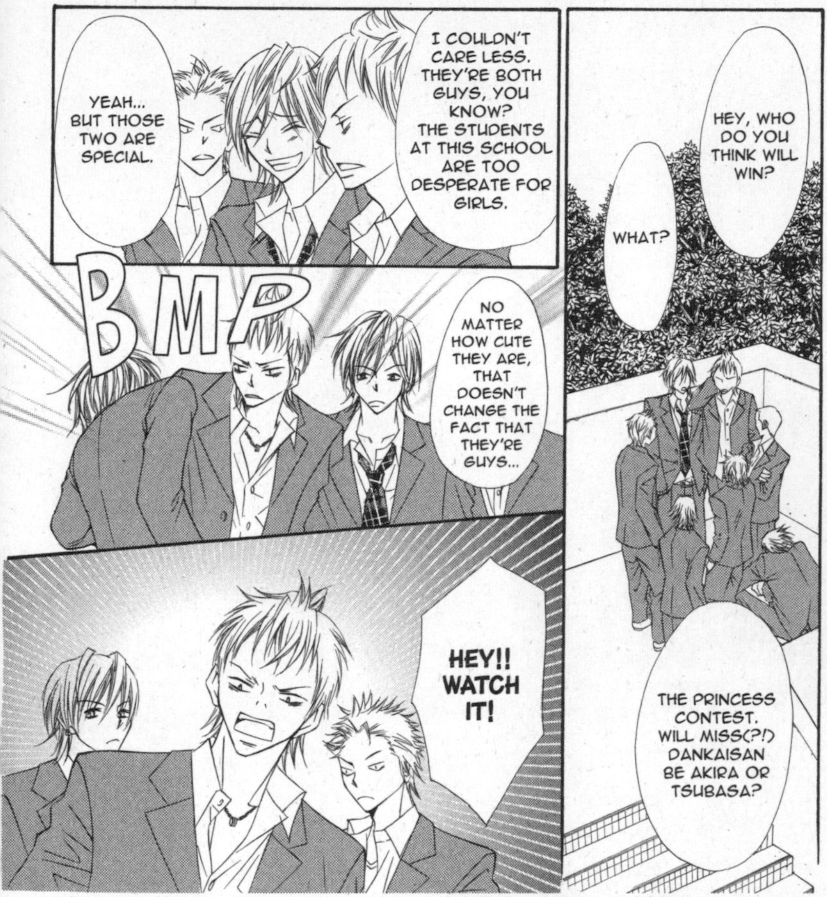
HEY, WHO DO YOU THINK WILL WIN?
WHAT?
THE PRINCESS CONTEST. WILL MISS(?!) DANKAISAN BE AKIRA OR TSUBASA?
I COULDN'T CARE LESS. THEY'RE BOTH GUYS, YOU KNOW? THE STUDENTS AT THIS SCHOOL ARE TOO DESPERATE FOR GIRLS.
YEAH... BUT THOSE TWO ARE SPECIAL.
NO MATTER HOW CUTE THEY ARE, THAT DOESN'T CHANGE THE FACT THAT THEY'RE GUYS...
BMP
HEY!! WATCH IT!

I want to see this kind of Akira!!

Akira shedding tears of frustration. He hardly ever loses... Well, he's never lost yet, so something major must have happened for him to cry like this.

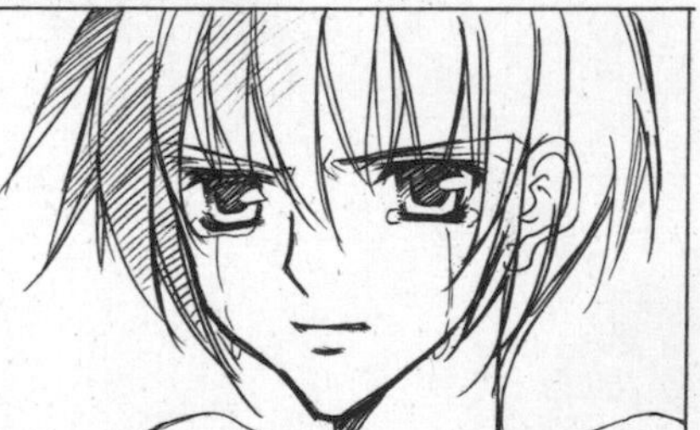

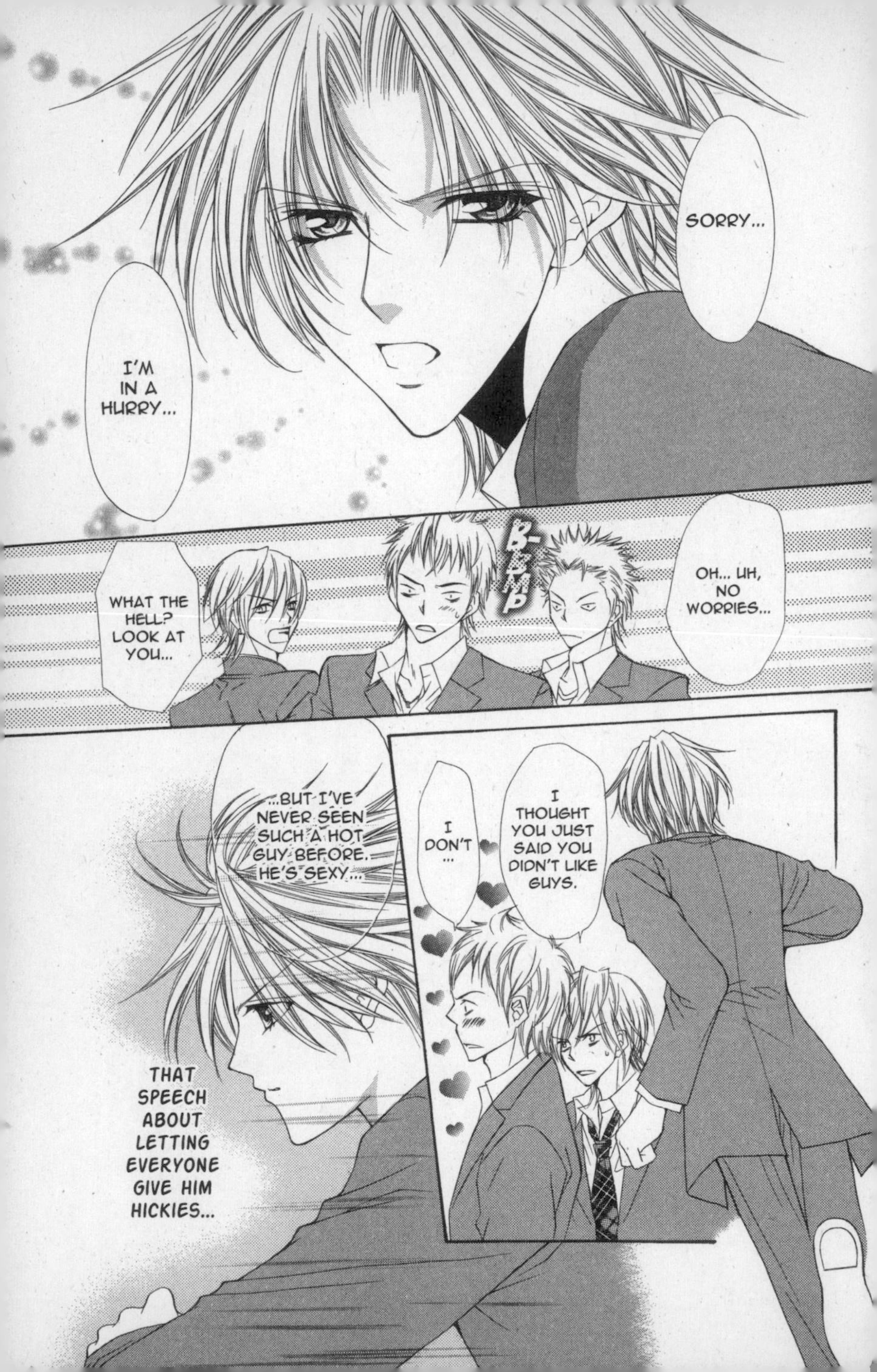
SORRY...
I'M IN A HURRY...
OH... UH, NO WORRIES...
B-BUMP
WHAT THE HELL? LOOK AT YOU...
I THOUGHT YOU JUST SAID YOU DIDN'T LIKE GUYS.
I DON'T ...
...BUT I'VE NEVER SEEN SUCH A HOT GUY BEFORE. HE'S SEXY...
THAT SPEECH ABOUT LETTING EVERYONE GIVE HIM HICKIES...

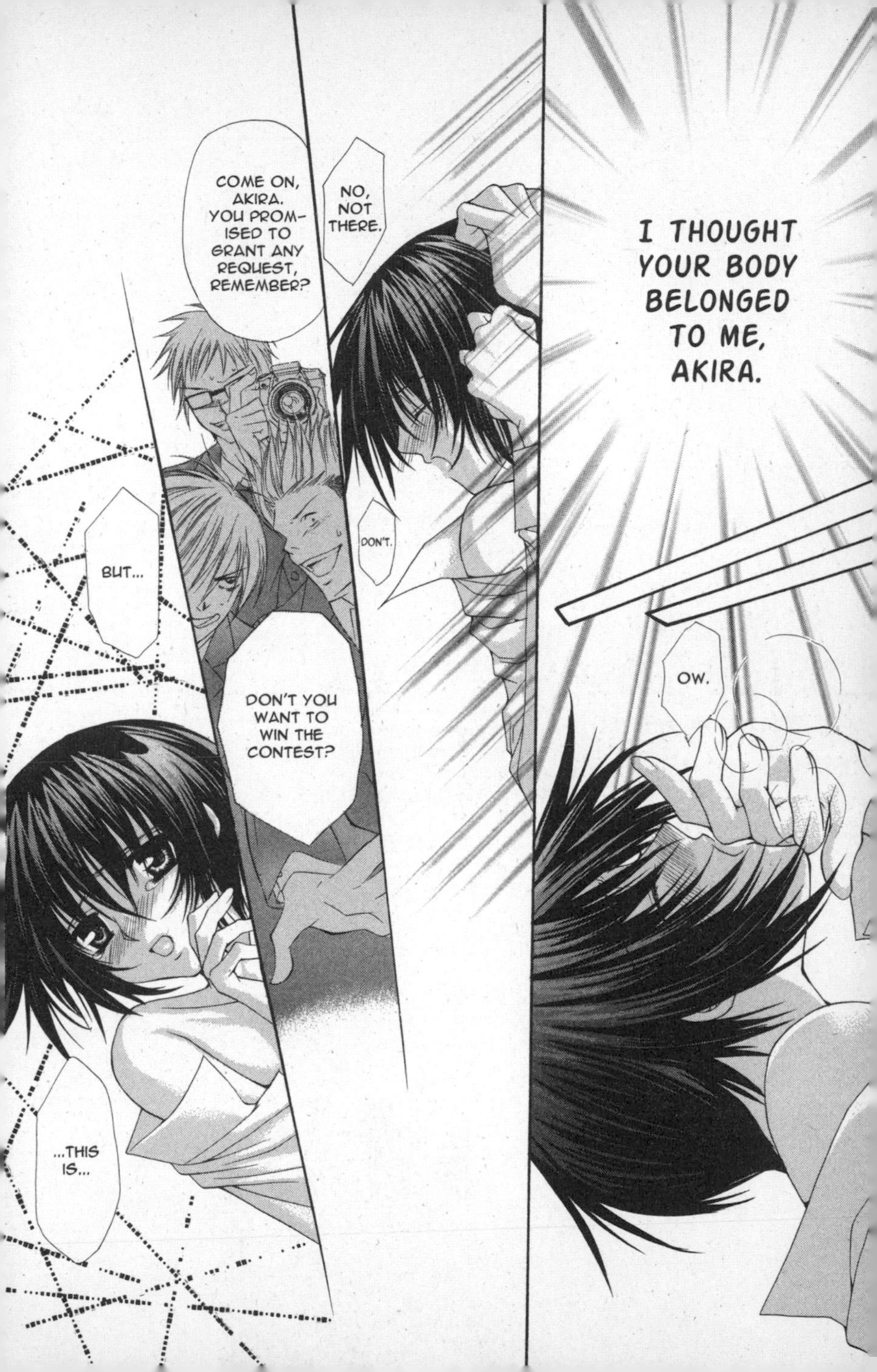
I THOUGHT YOUR BODY BELONGED TO ME, AKIRA.
OW.
NO, NOT THERE.
DON'T.
COME ON, AKIRA. YOU PROMISED TO GRANT ANY REQUEST, REMEMBER?
DON'T YOU WANT TO WIN THE CONTEST?
BUT...
...THIS IS...

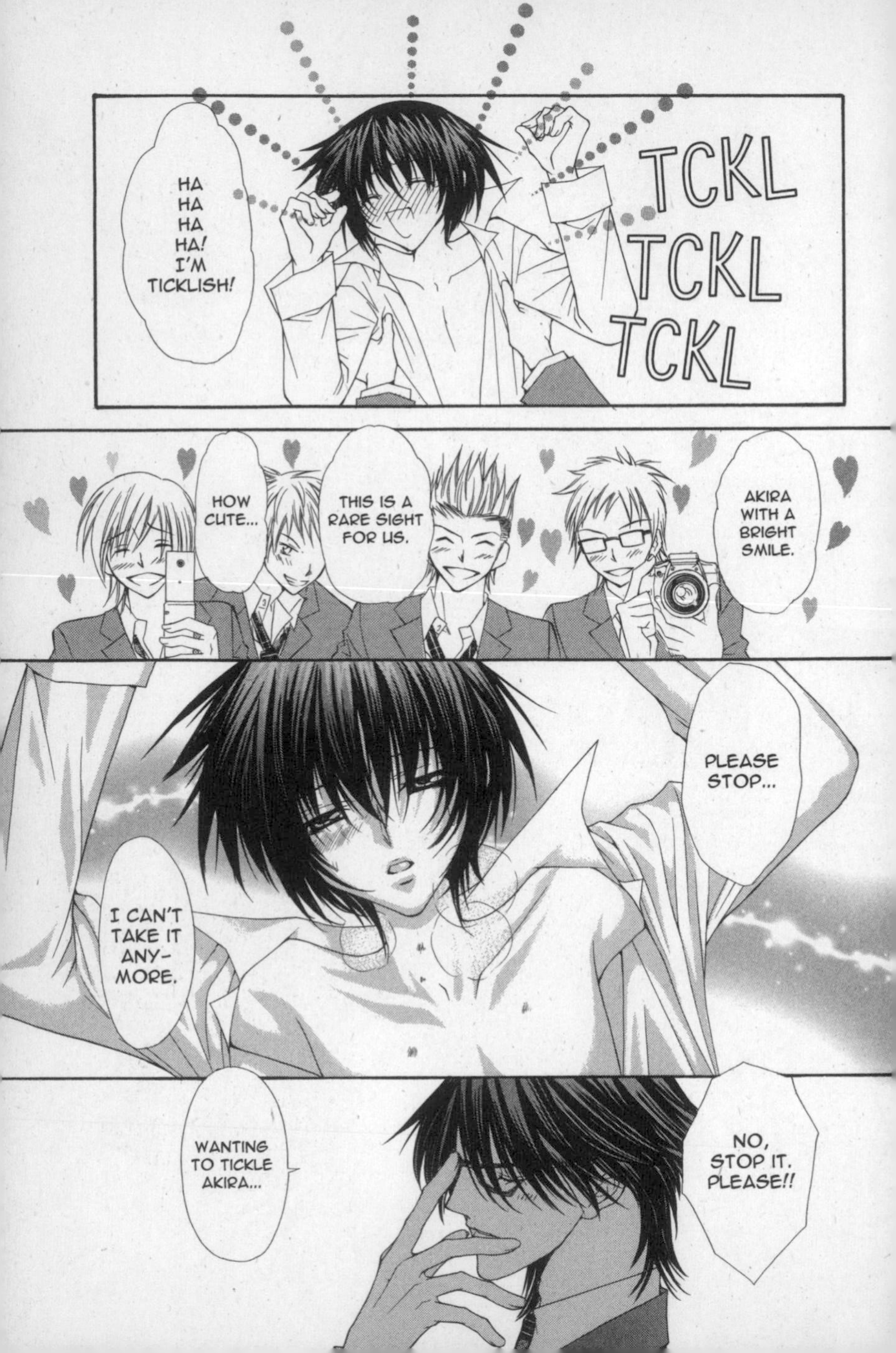
TCKL TCKL TCKL
HA HA HA HA! I'M TICKLISH!
AKIRA WITH A BRIGHT SMILE.
THIS IS A RARE SIGHT FOR US.
HOW CUTE...
PLEASE STOP...
I CAN'T TAKE IT ANY-MORE.
NO, STOP IT. PLEASE!!
WANTING TO TICKLE AKIRA...

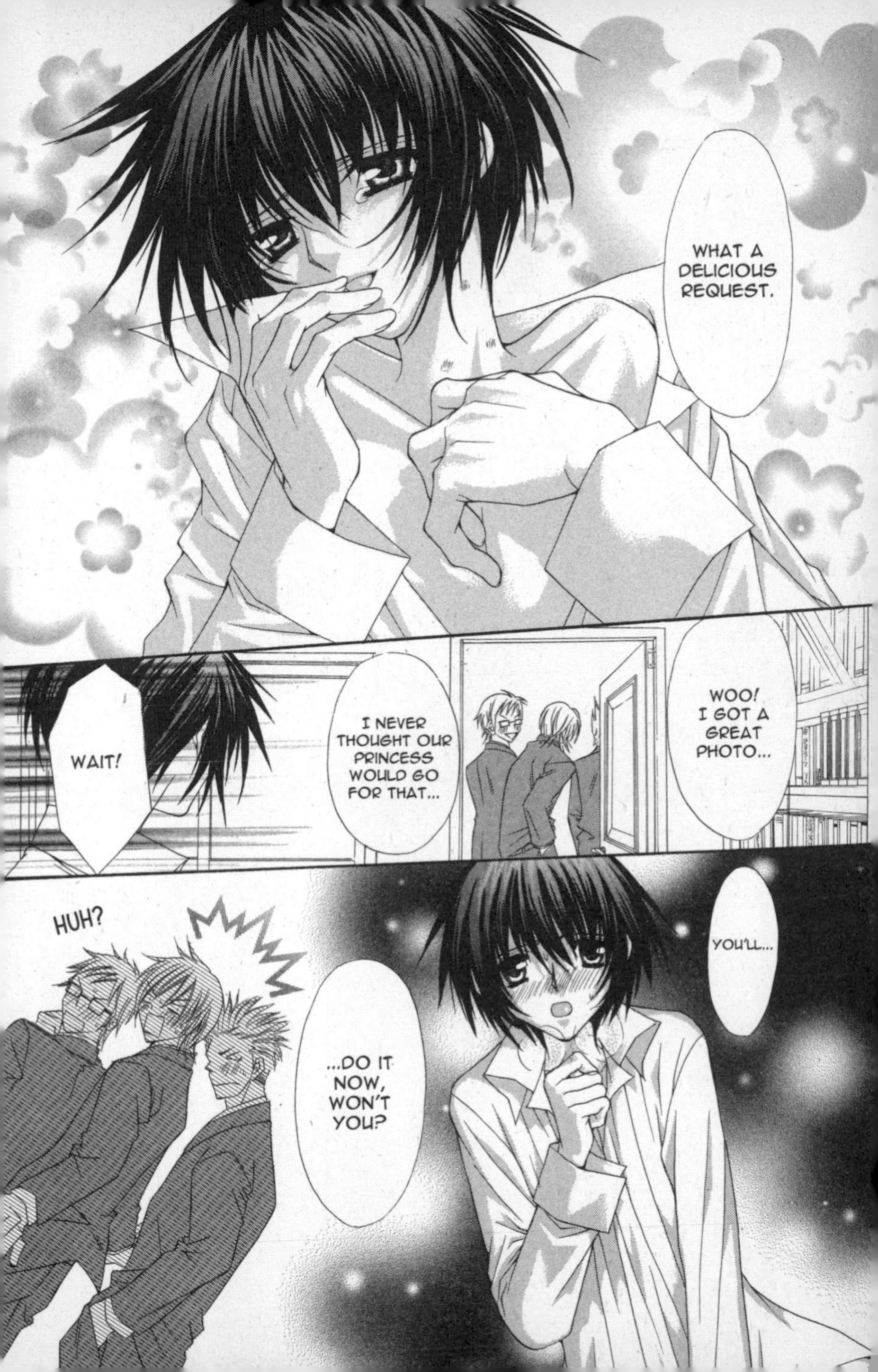
WHAT A DELICIOUS REQUEST.
WOO! I GOT A GREAT PHOTO...
I NEVER THOUGHT OUR PRINCESS WOULD GO FOR THAT...
WAIT!
YOU'LL...
...DO IT NOW, WON'T YOU?
HUH?

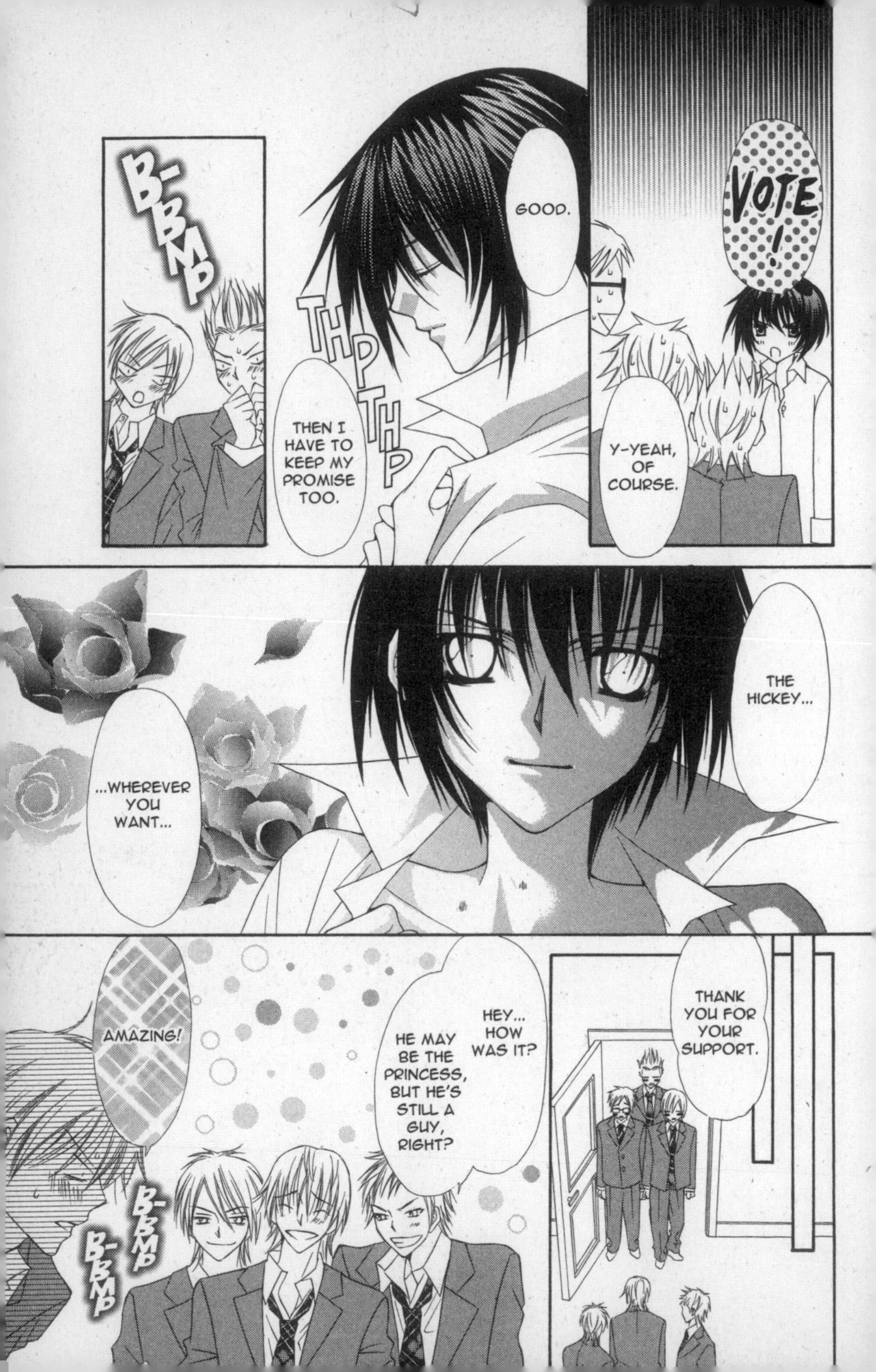
VOTE!
Y-YEAH, OF COURSE.
GOOD.
THEN I HAVE TO KEEP MY PROMISE TOO.
THP THP
B-BMP
THE HICKEY...
...WHEREVER YOU WANT...
THANK YOU FOR YOUR SUPPORT.
HEY... HOW WAS IT?
HE MAY BE THE PRINCESS, BUT HE'S STILL A GUY, RIGHT?
AMAZING!
B-BMP
B-BMP

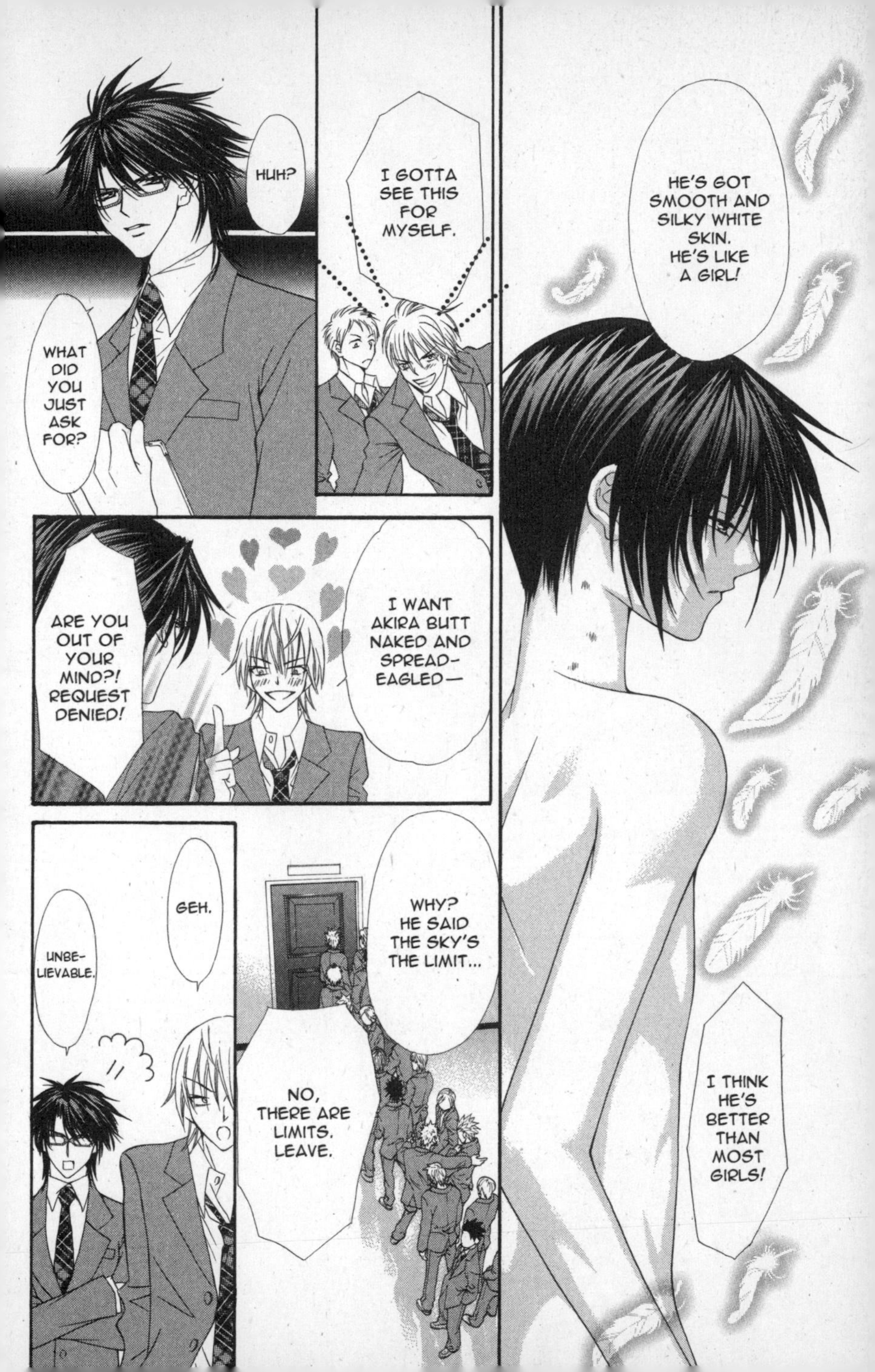
HE'S GOT SMOOTH AND SILKY WHITE SKIN. HE'S LIKE A GIRL!
I THINK HE'S BETTER THAN MOST GIRLS!
I GOTTA SEE THIS FOR MYSELF.
HUH?
WHAT DID YOU JUST ASK FOR?
I WANT AKIRA BUTT NAKED AND SPREAD-EAGLED—
ARE YOU OUT OF YOUR MIND?! REQUEST DENIED!
WHY? HE SAID THE SKY'S THE LIMIT...
NO, THERE ARE LIMITS. LEAVE.
GEH.
UNBE-LIEVABLE.

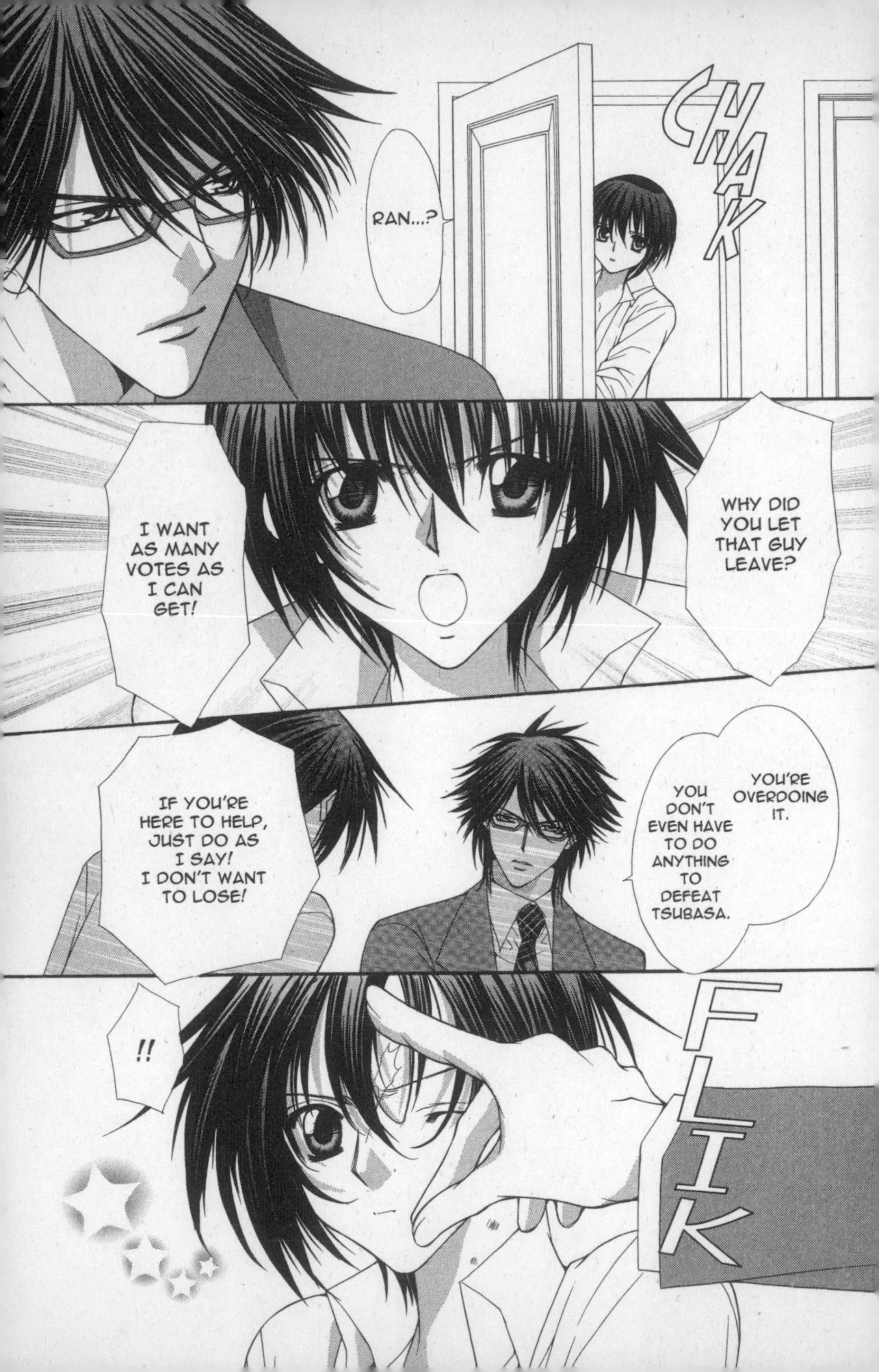
CHAK
RAN...?
WHY DID YOU LET THAT GUY LEAVE?
I WANT AS MANY VOTES AS I CAN GET!
YOU'RE OVERDOING IT.
YOU DON'T EVEN HAVE TO DO ANYTHING TO DEFEAT TSUBASA.
IF YOU'RE HERE TO HELP, JUST DO AS I SAY! I DON'T WANT TO LOSE!
FLIK
!!

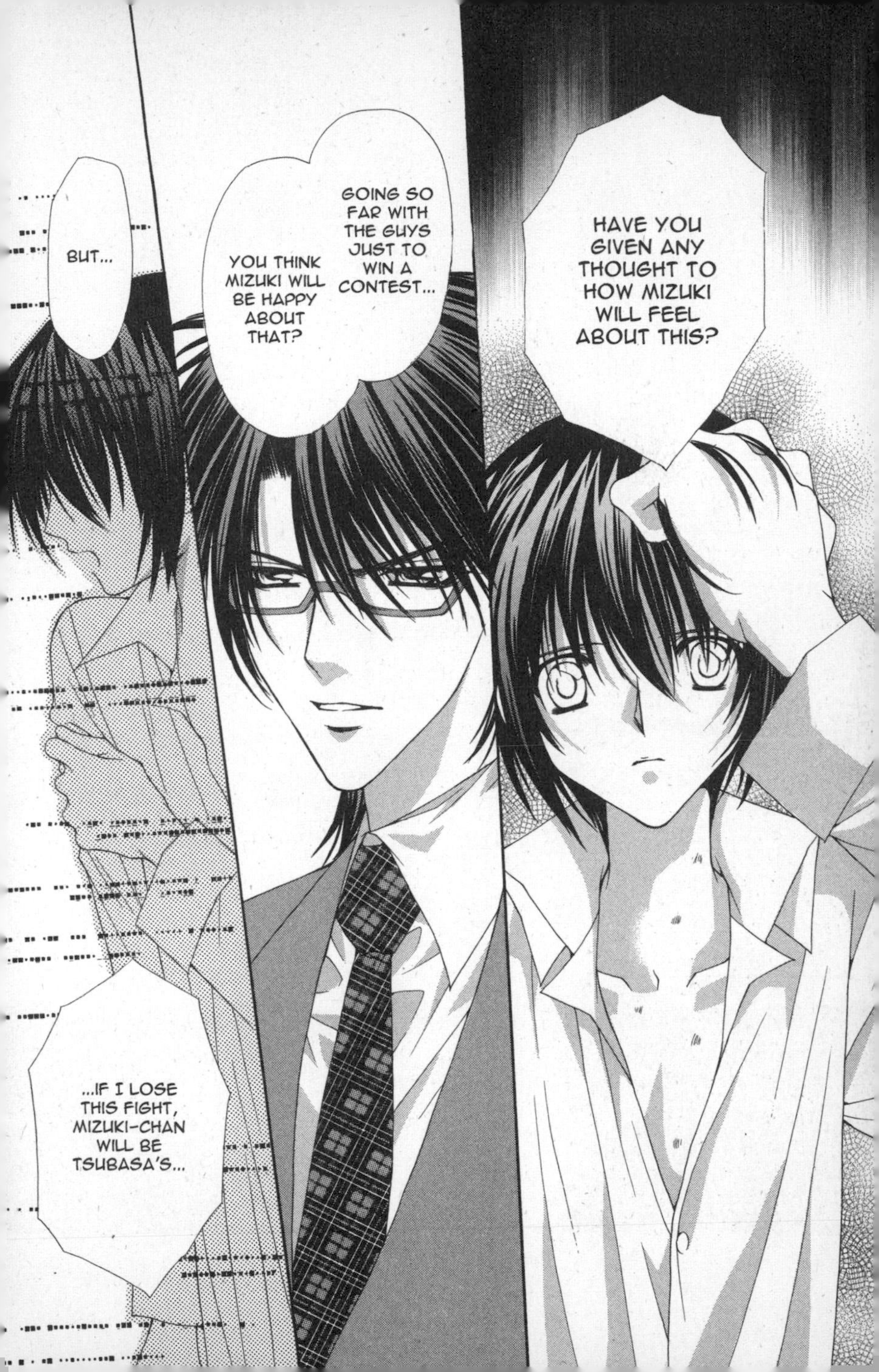
HAVE YOU GIVEN ANY THOUGHT TO HOW MIZUKI WILL FEEL ABOUT THIS?
GOING SO FAR WITH THE GUYS JUST TO WIN A CONTEST... YOU THINK MIZUKI WILL BE HAPPY ABOUT THAT?
BUT...
...IF I LOSE THIS FIGHT, MIZUKI-CHAN WILL BE TSUBASA'S...

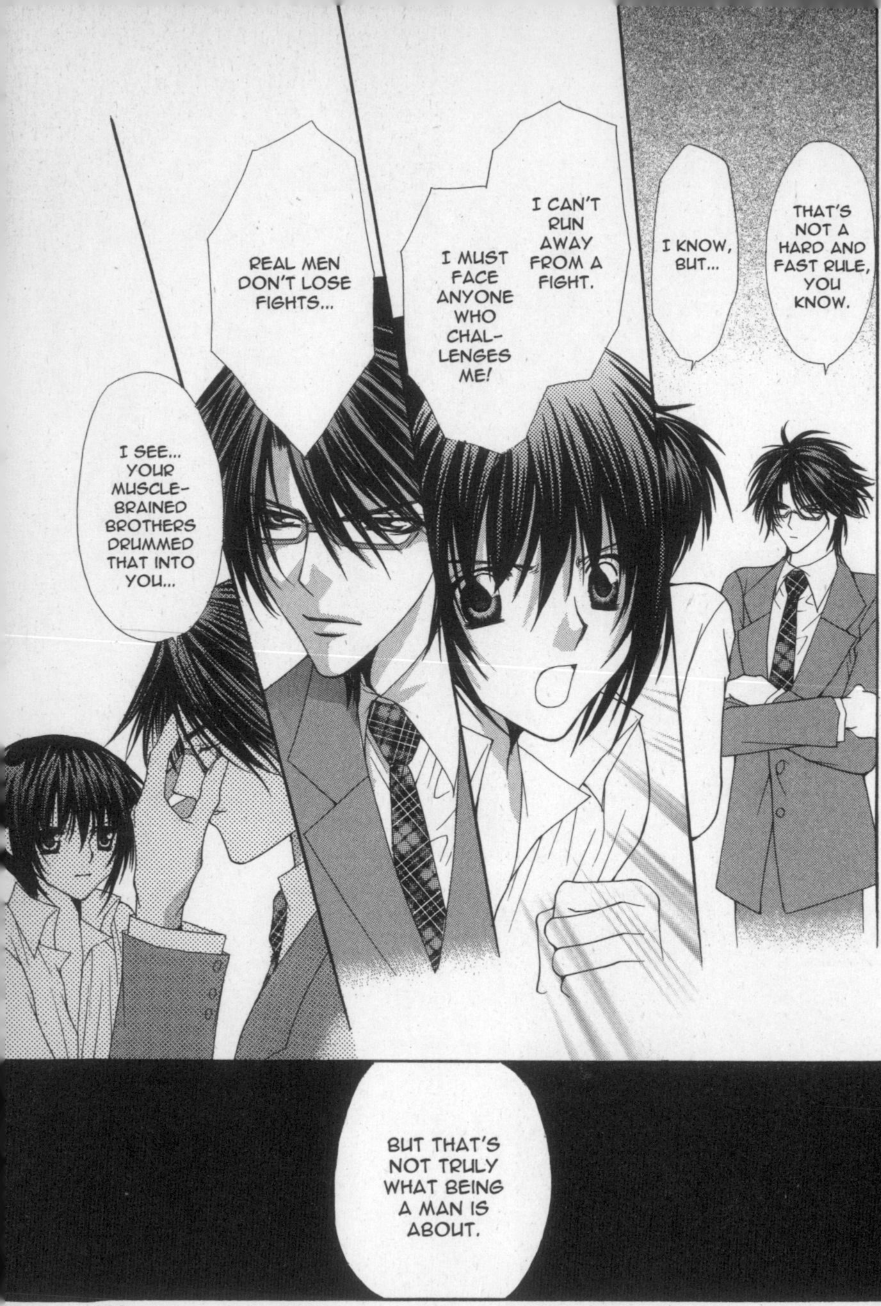
THAT'S NOT A HARD AND FAST RULE, YOU KNOW.
I KNOW, BUT...
I CAN'T RUN AWAY FROM A FIGHT.
I MUST FACE ANYONE WHO CHAL-LENGES ME!
REAL MEN DON'T LOSE FIGHTS...
I SEE... YOUR MUSCLE-BRAINED BROTHERS DRUMMED THAT INTO YOU...
BUT THAT'S NOT TRULY WHAT BEING A MAN IS ABOUT.

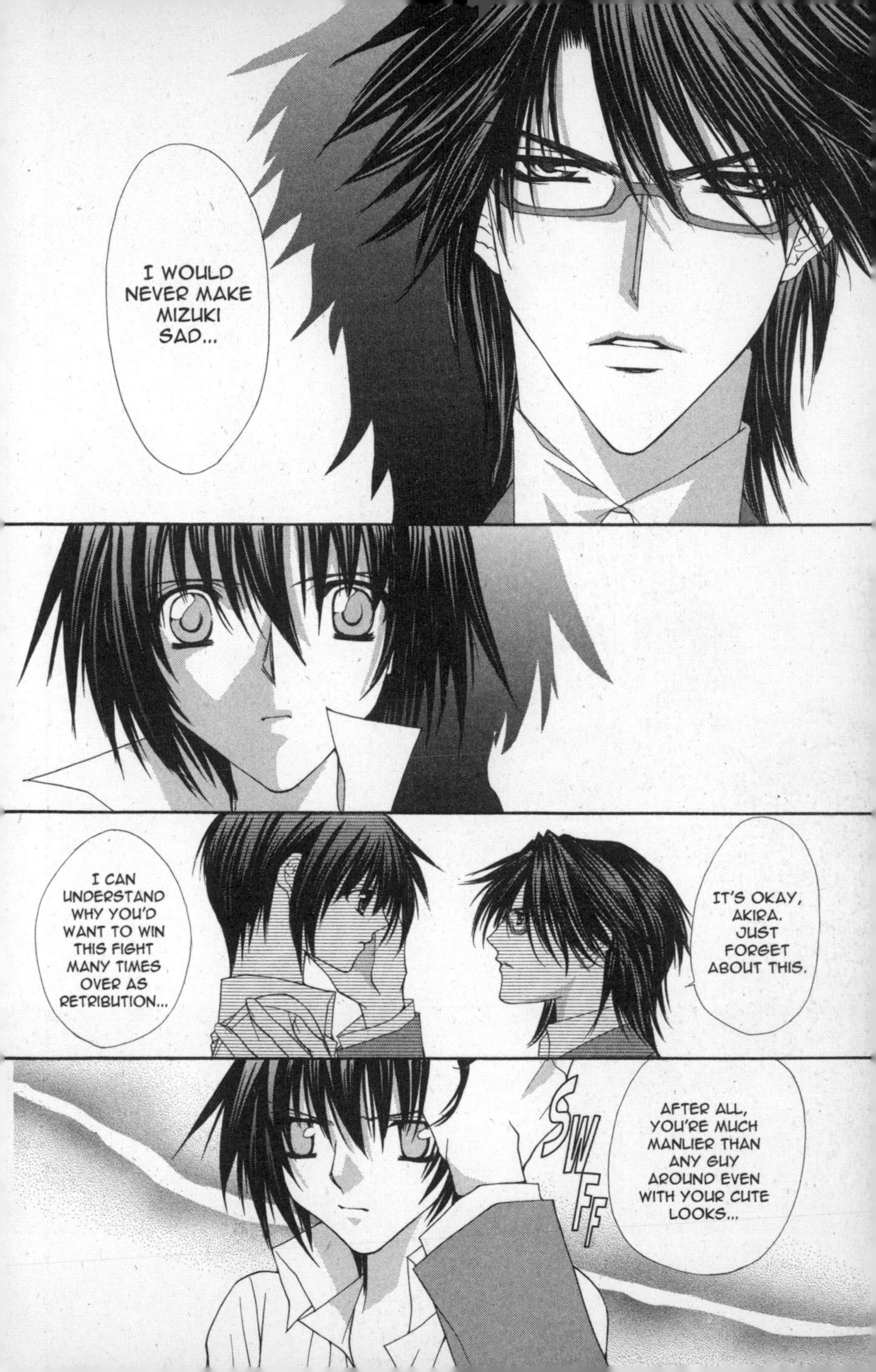
I WOULD NEVER MAKE MIZUKI SAD...
IT'S OKAY, AKIRA. JUST FORGET ABOUT THIS.
I CAN UNDERSTAND WHY YOU'D WANT TO WIN THIS FIGHT MANY TIMES OVER AS RETRIBUTION...
AFTER ALL, YOU'RE MUCH MANLIER THAN ANY GUY AROUND EVEN WITH YOUR CUTE LOOKS...
SWFF

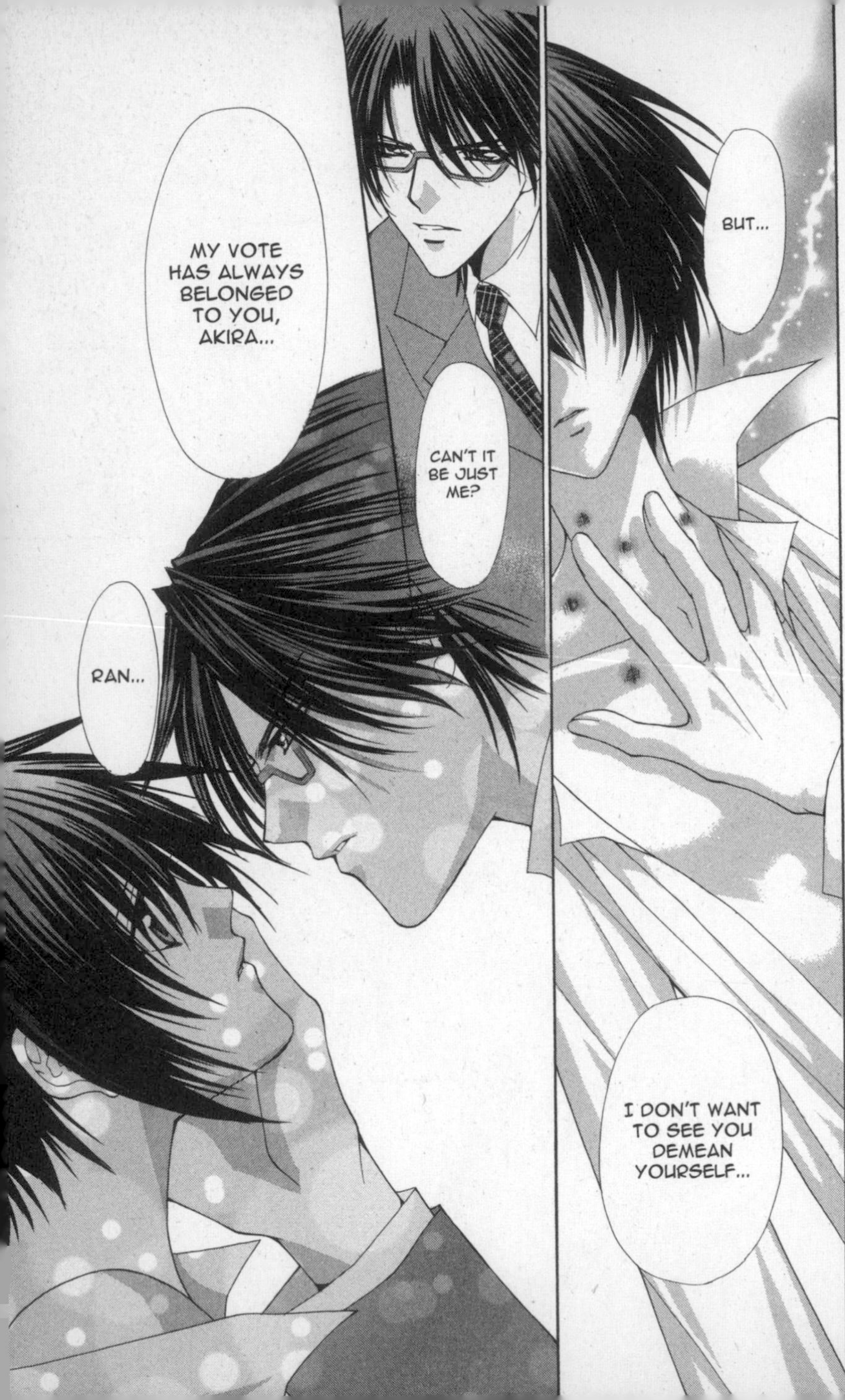
BUT...
I DON'T WANT TO SEE YOU DEMEAN YOURSELF...
CAN'T IT BE JUST ME?
MY VOTE HAS ALWAYS BELONGED TO YOU, AKIRA...
RAN...

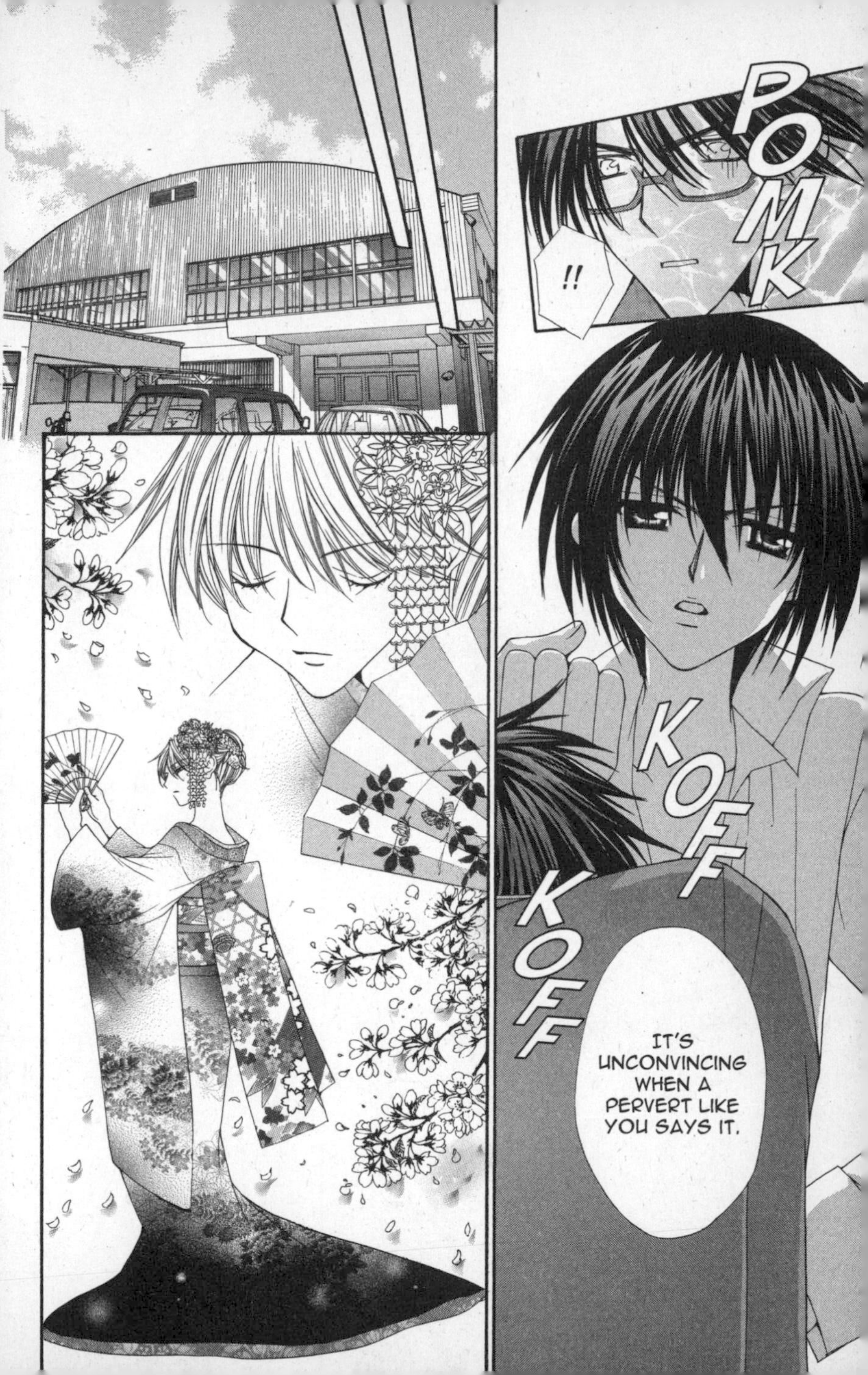
POMK
!!
KOFF KOFF
IT'S UNCONVINCING WHEN A PERVERT LIKE YOU SAYS IT.

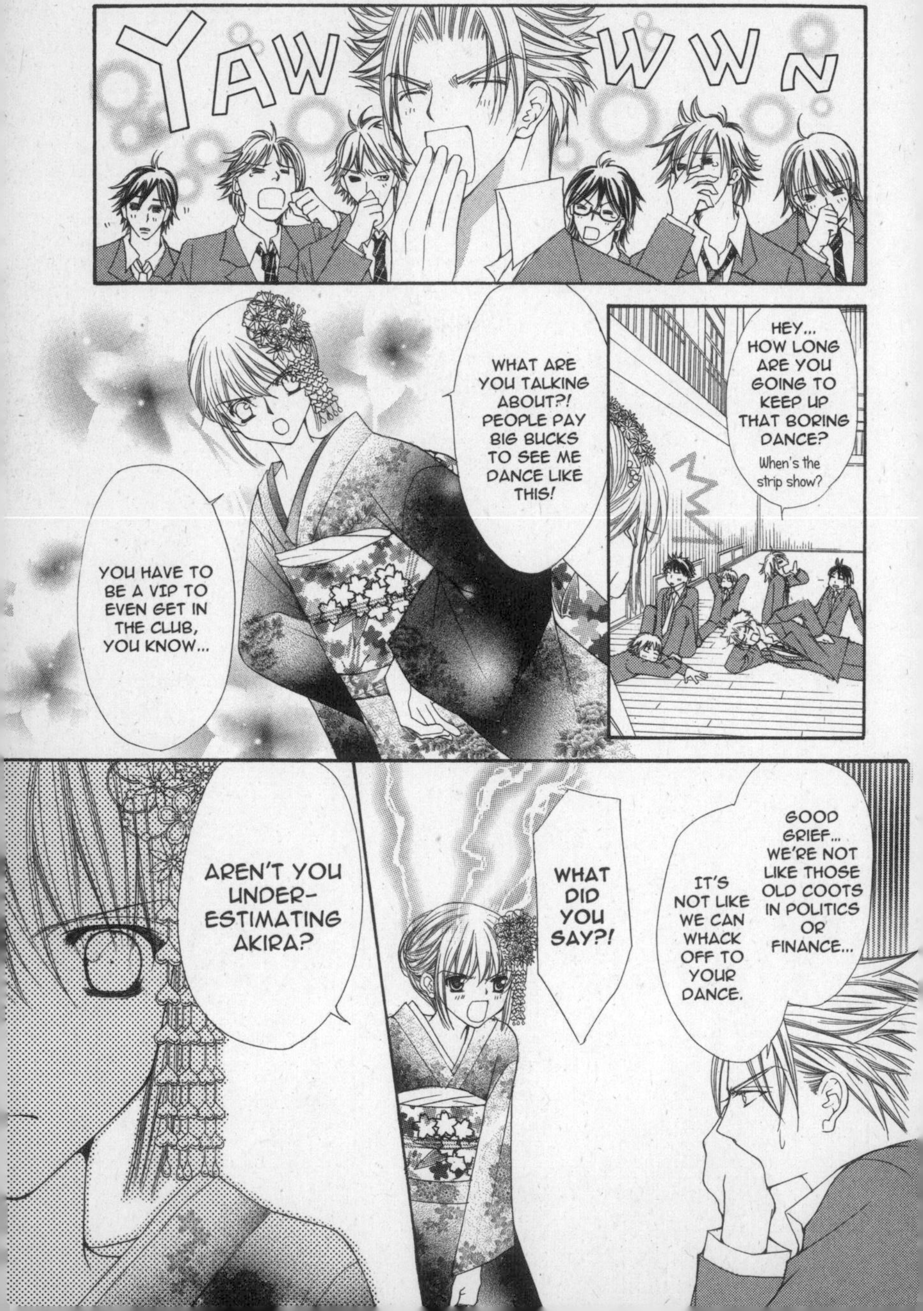
YAWWWN
HEY... HOW LONG ARE YOU GOING TO KEEP UP THAT BORING DANCE?
When's the strip show?
WHAT ARE YOU TALKING ABOUT?! PEOPLE PAY BIG BUCKS TO SEE ME DANCE LIKE THIS!
YOU HAVE TO BE A VIP TO EVEN GET IN THE CLUB, YOU KNOW...
GOOD GRIEF... WE'RE NOT LIKE THOSE OLD COOTS IN POLITICS OR FINANCE...
IT'S NOT LIKE WE CAN WHACK OFF TO YOUR DANCE.
WHAT DID YOU SAY?!
AREN'T YOU UNDER-ESTIMATING AKIRA?

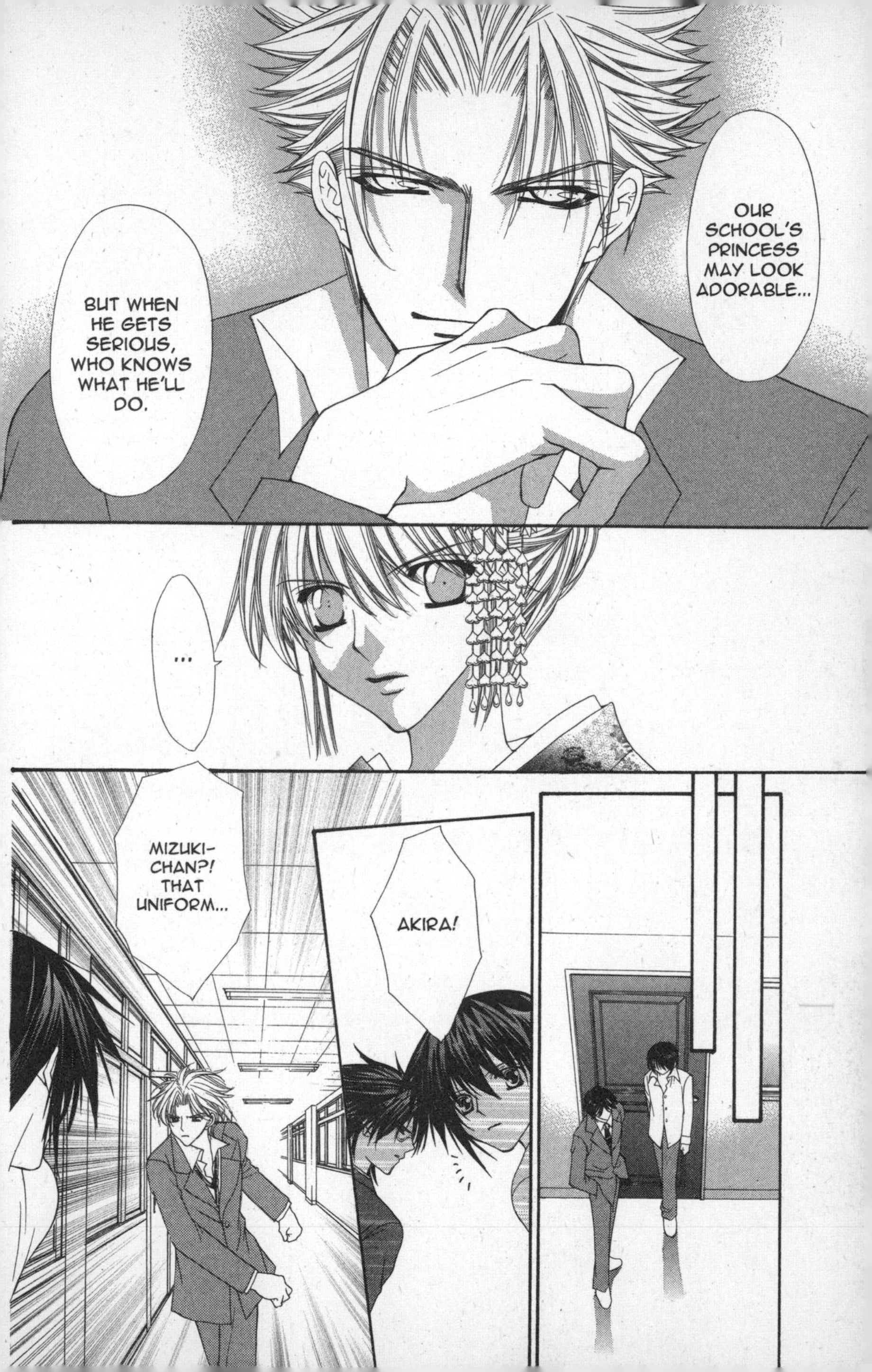
OUR SCHOOL'S PRINCESS MAY LOOK ADORABLE...
BUT WHEN HE GETS SERIOUS, WHO KNOWS WHAT HE'LL DO.
...
AKIRA!
MIZUKI-CHAN?! THAT UNIFORM...

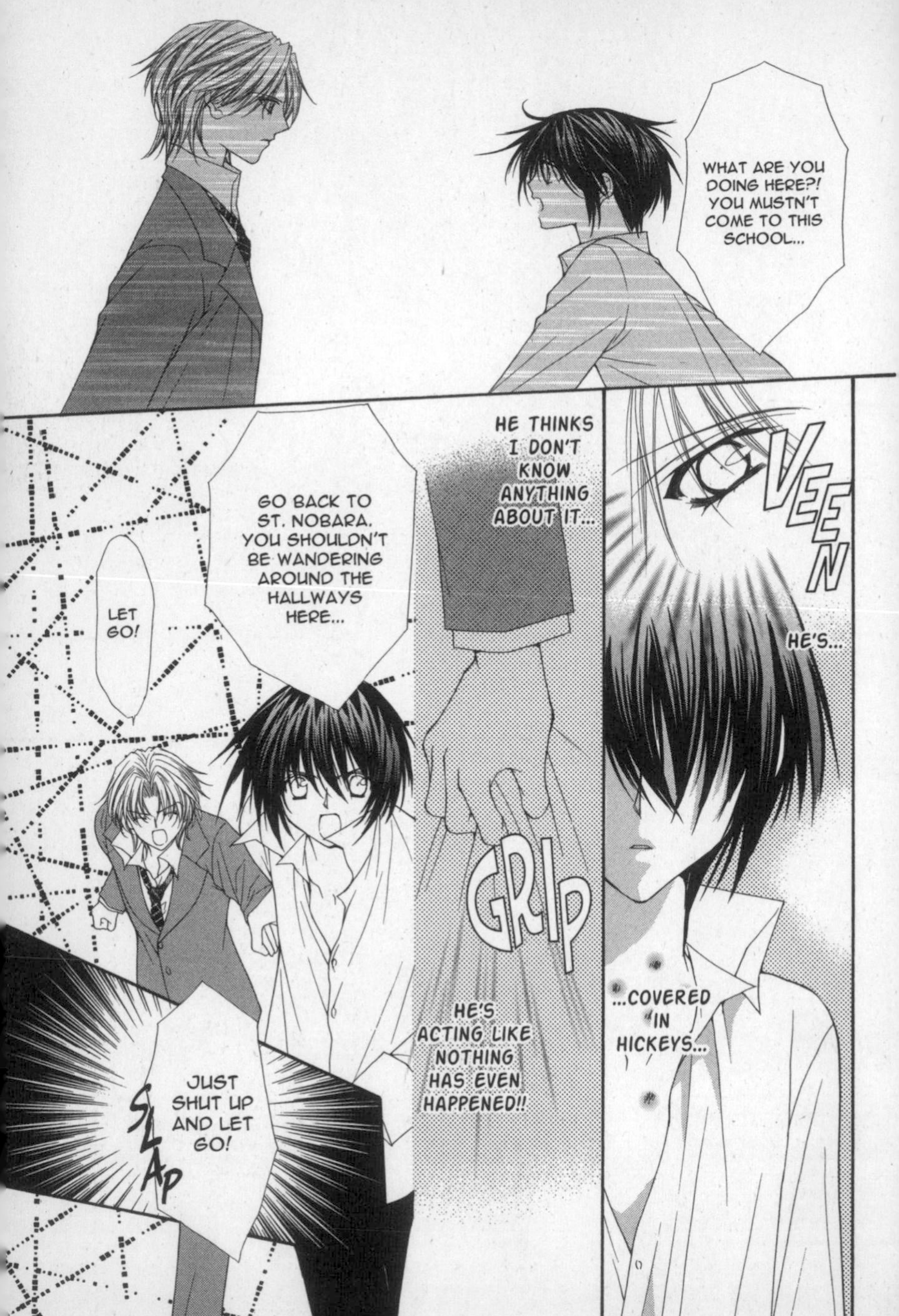
WHAT ARE YOU DOING HERE?! YOU MUSTN'T COME TO THIS SCHOOL...
VEEN
HE'S...
...COVERED IN HICKEYS...
HE THINKS I DON'T KNOW ANYTHING ABOUT IT...
GRIP
HE'S ACTING LIKE NOTHING HAS EVEN HAPPENED!!
GO BACK TO ST. NOBARA. YOU SHOULDN'T BE WANDERING AROUND THE HALLWAYS HERE...
LET GO!
JUST SHUT UP AND LET GO!
SLAP

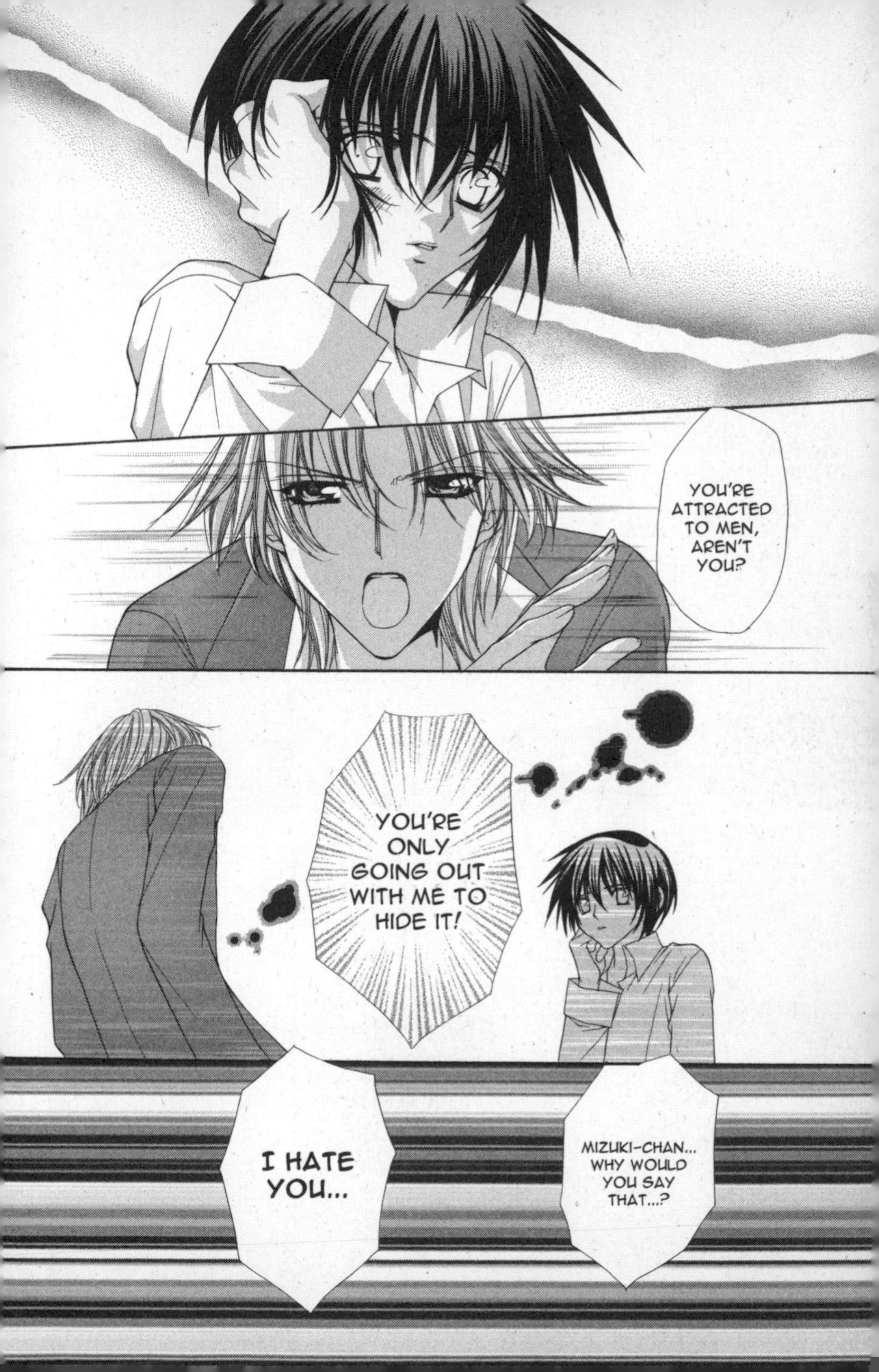
YOU'RE ATTRACTED TO MEN, AREN'T YOU?
YOU'RE ONLY GOING OUT WITH ME TO HIDE IT!
MIZUKI-CHAN... WHY WOULD YOU SAY THAT...?
I HATE YOU...

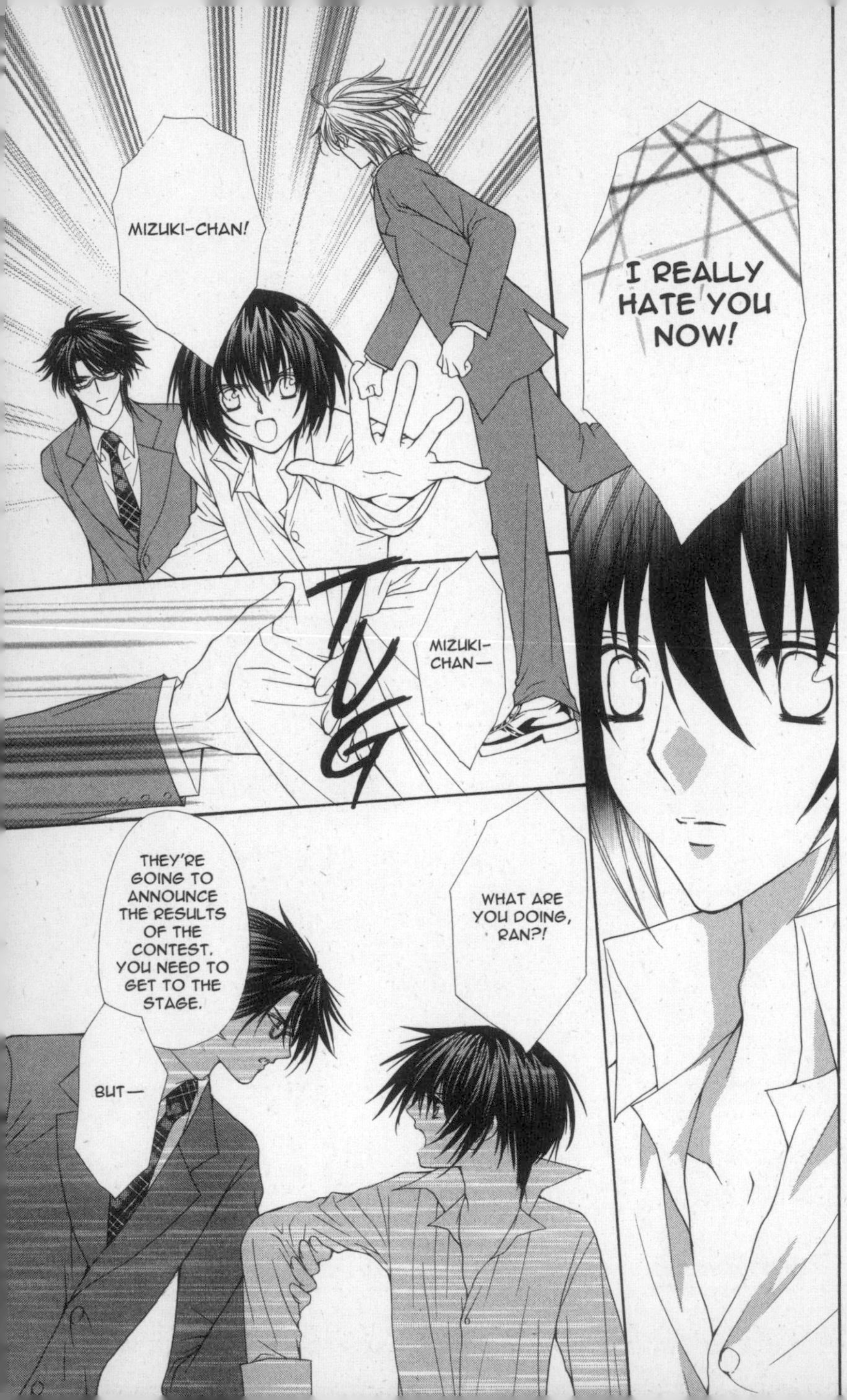
I REALLY HATE YOU NOW!
MIZUKI-CHAN!
MIZUKI-CHAN—
TUG
WHAT ARE YOU DOING, RAN?!
THEY'RE GOING TO ANNOUNCE THE RESULTS OF THE CONTEST. YOU NEED TO GET TO THE STAGE.
BUT—

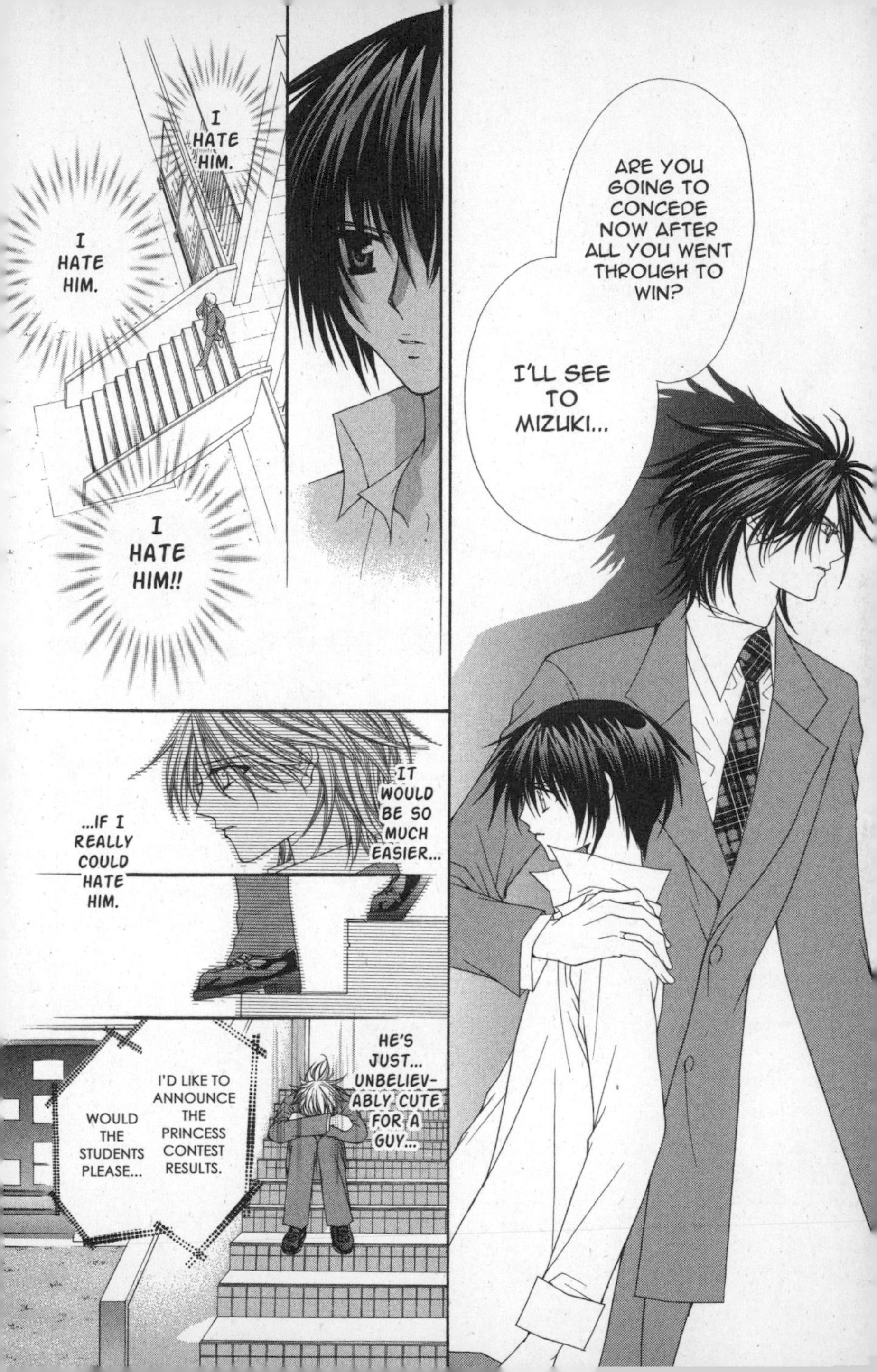
ARE YOU GOING TO CONCEDE NOW AFTER ALL YOU WENT THROUGH TO WIN?
I'LL SEE TO MIZUKI...
I HATE HIM.
I HATE HIM.
I HATE HIM!!
IT WOULD BE SO MUCH EASIER...
...IF I REALLY COULD HATE HIM.
HE'S JUST... UNBELIEV-ABLY CUTE FOR A GUY...
I'D LIKE TO ANNOUNCE THE PRINCESS CONTEST RESULTS.
WOULD THE STUDENTS PLEASE...

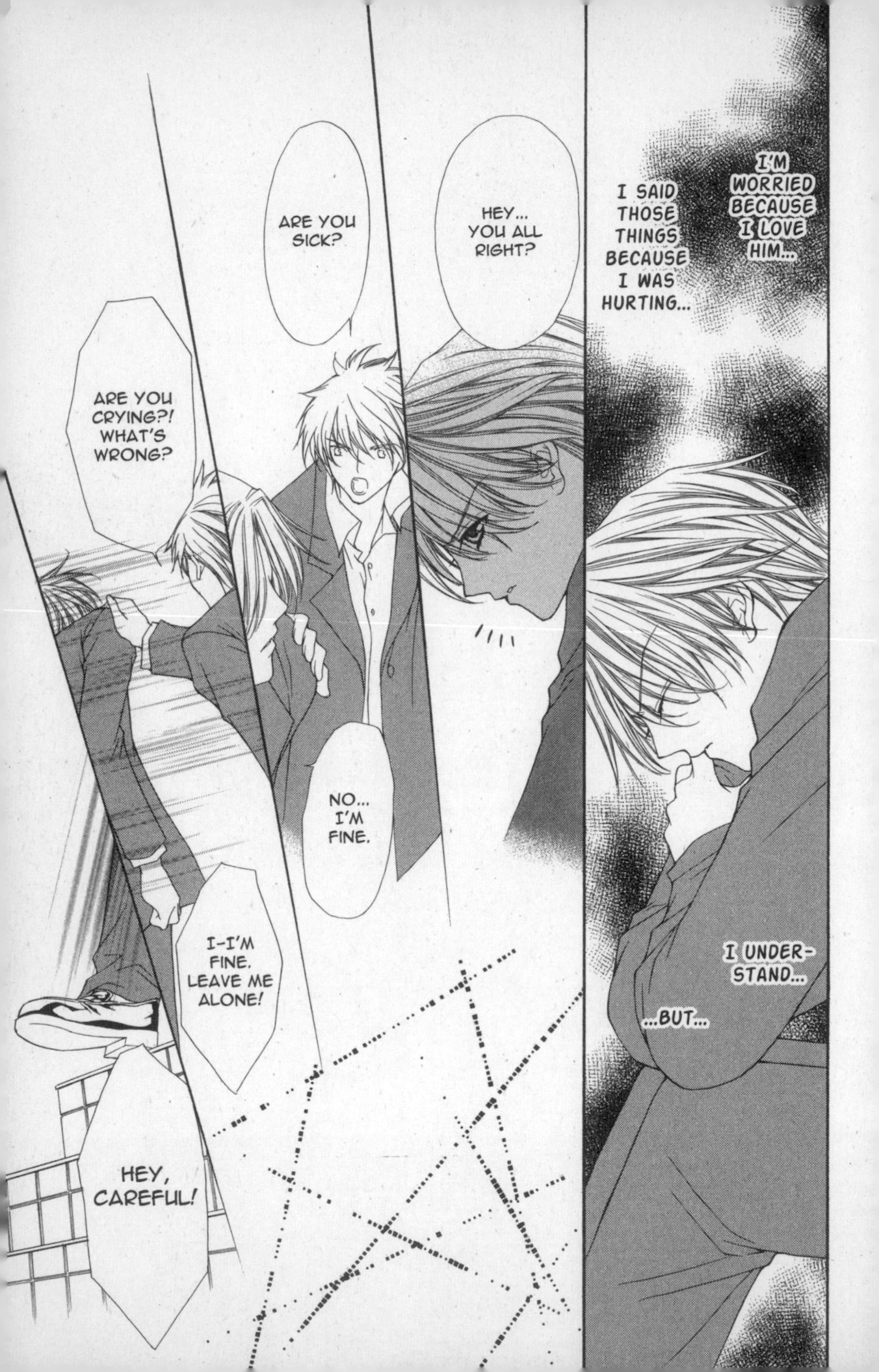
I'M WORRIED BECAUSE I LOVE HIM...
I SAID THOSE THINGS BECAUSE I WAS HURTING...
I UNDER-STAND...
...BUT...
HEY... YOU ALL RIGHT?
ARE YOU SICK?
NO... I'M FINE.
ARE YOU CRYING?! WHAT'S WRONG?
I-I'M FINE. LEAVE ME ALONE!
HEY, CAREFUL!

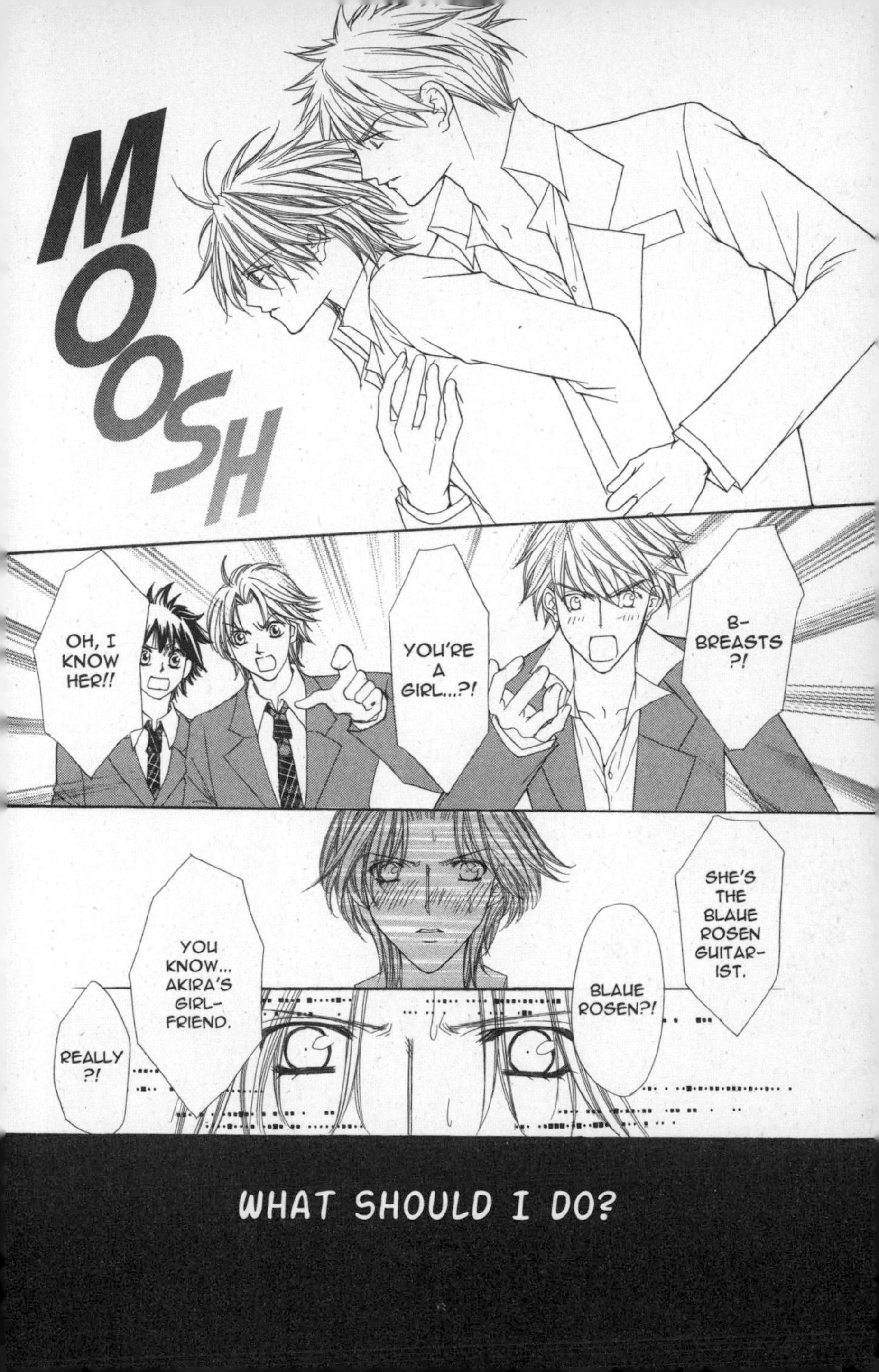
MOOSH
B-BREASTS?!
YOU'RE A GIRL...?!
OH, I KNOW HER!!
SHE'S THE BLAUE ROSEN GUITAR-IST.
BLAUE ROSEN?!
YOU KNOW... AKIRA'S GIRL-FRIEND.
REALLY?!
WHAT SHOULD I DO?

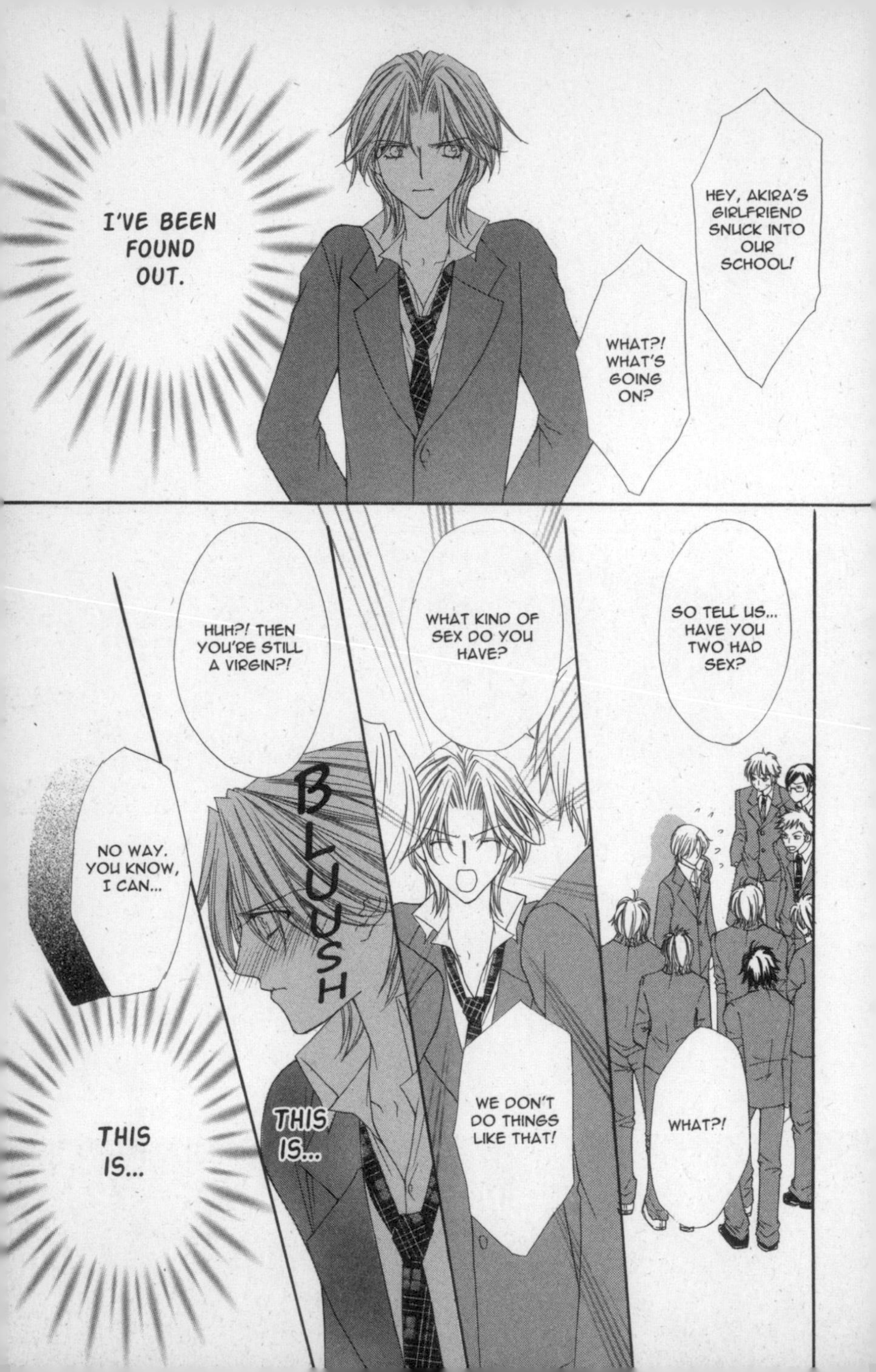
HEY, AKIRA'S GIRLFRIEND SNUCK INTO OUR SCHOOL!
WHAT?! WHAT'S GOING ON?
I'VE BEEN FOUND OUT.
SO TELL US... HAVE YOU TWO HAD SEX?
WHAT?!
WHAT KIND OF SEX DO YOU HAVE?
WE DON'T DO THINGS LIKE THAT!
HUH?! THEN YOU'RE STILL A VIRGIN?!
BLUUSH
NO WAY. YOU KNOW, I CAN...
THIS IS...
THIS IS...

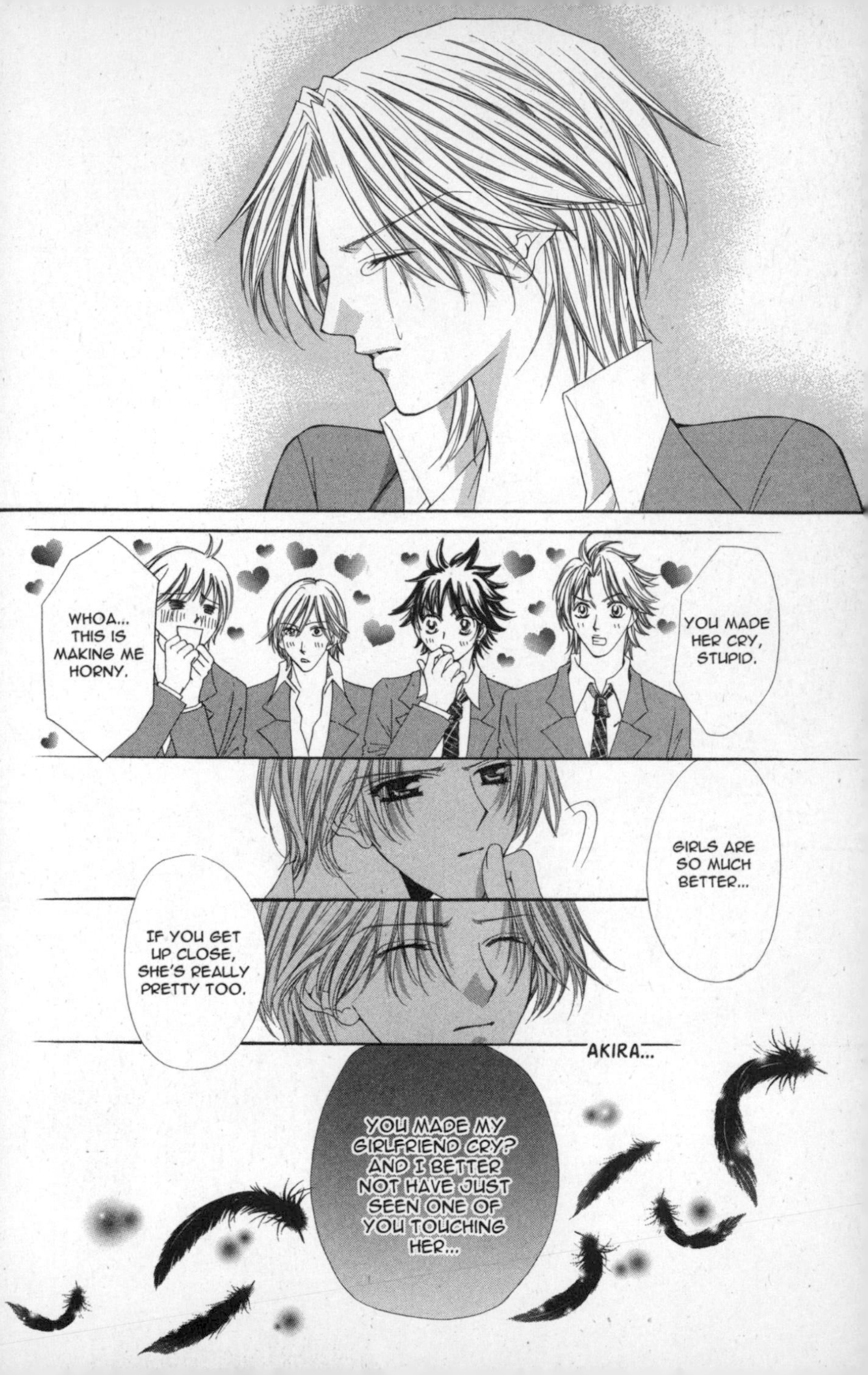
YOU MADE HER CRY, STUPID.
WHOA... THIS IS MAKING ME HORNY.
GIRLS ARE SO MUCH BETTER...
IF YOU GET UP CLOSE, SHE'S REALLY PRETTY TOO.
AKIRA...
YOU MADE MY GIRLFRIEND CRY? AND I BETTER NOT HAVE JUST SEEN ONE OF YOU TOUCHING HER...

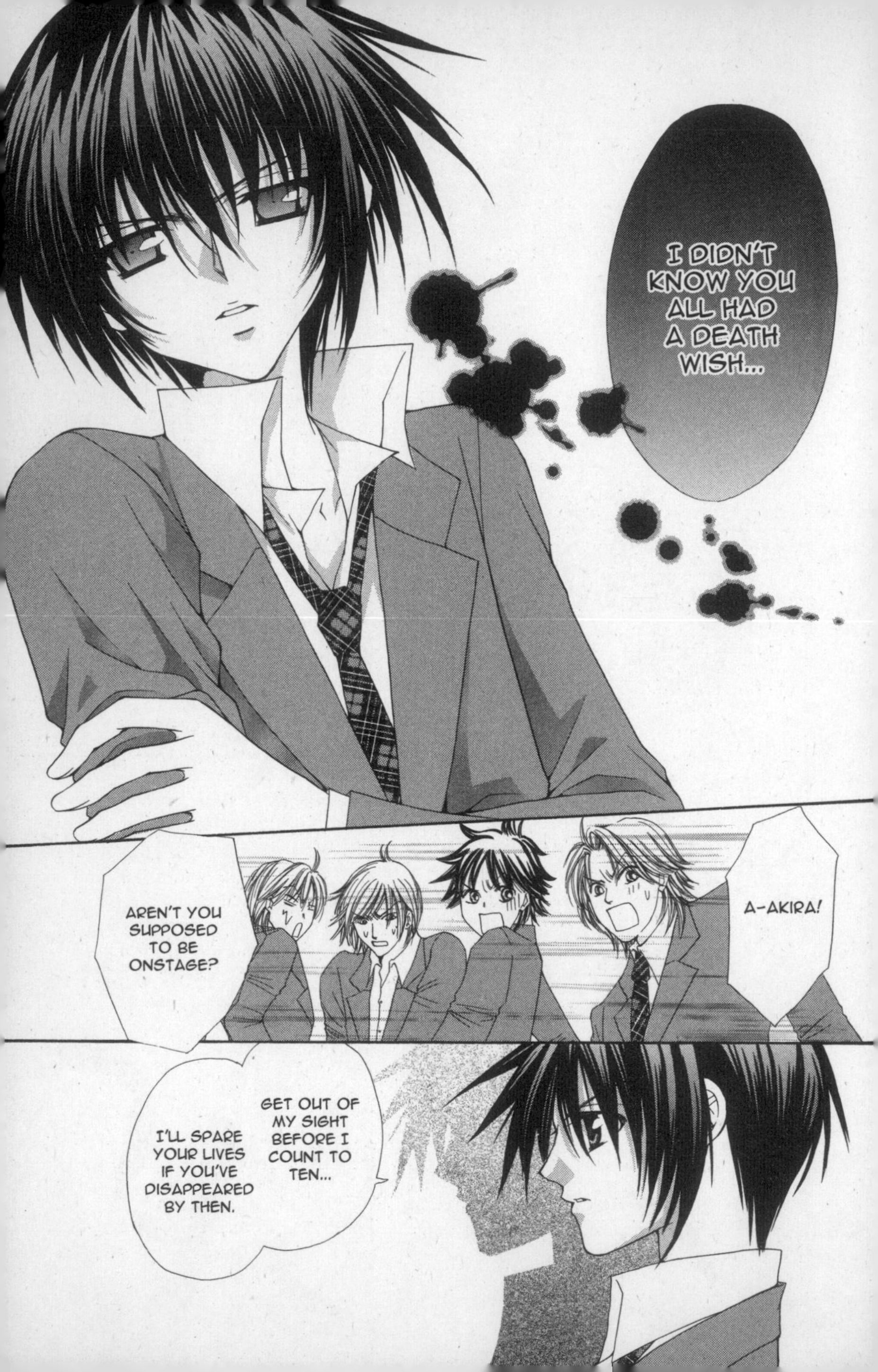
I DIDN'T KNOW YOU ALL HAD A DEATH WISH...
A-AKIRA!
AREN'T YOU SUPPOSED TO BE ONSTAGE?
GET OUT OF MY SIGHT BEFORE I COUNT TO TEN...
I'LL SPARE YOUR LIVES IF YOU'VE DISAPPEARED BY THEN.

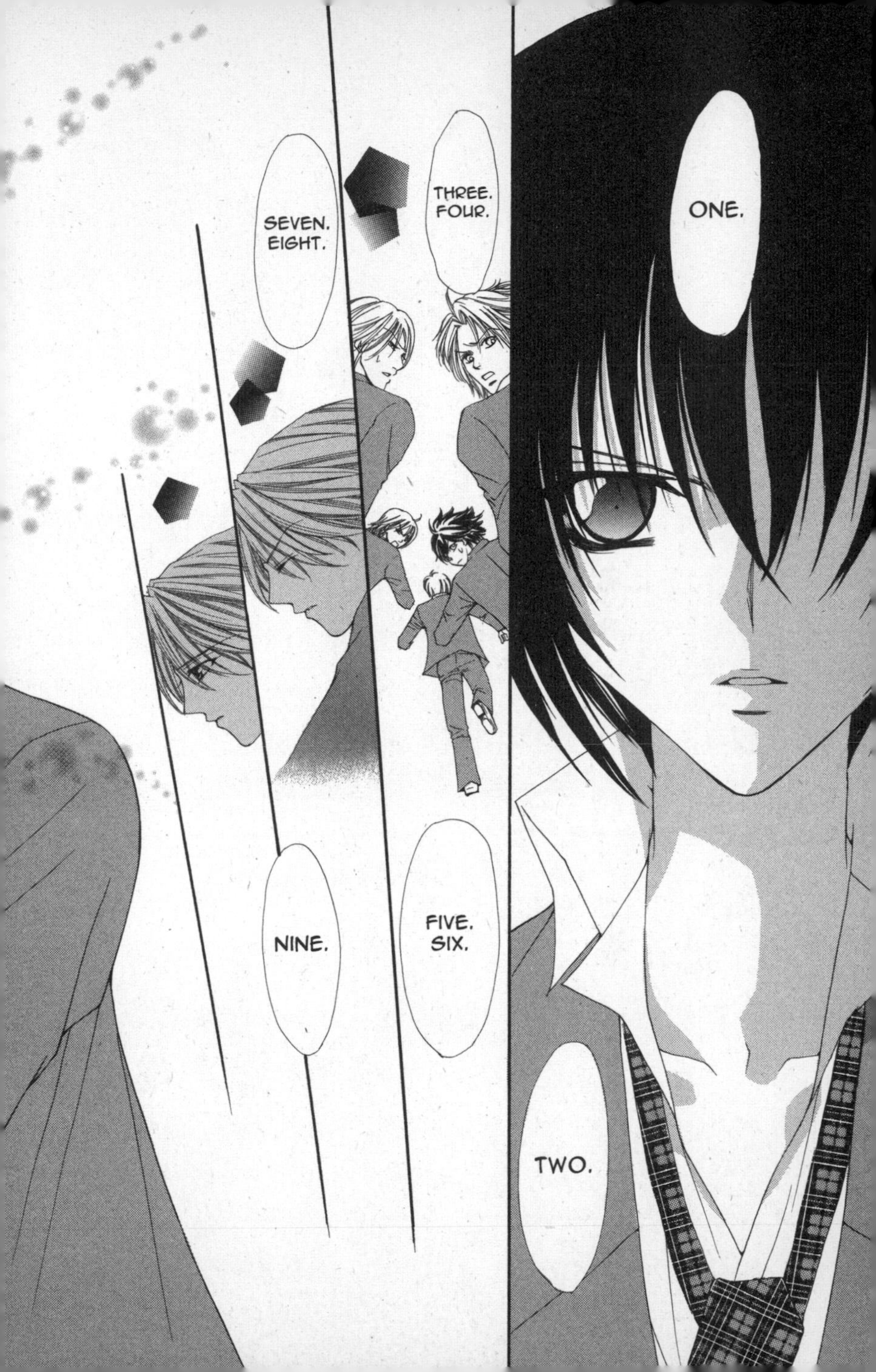
ONE.
TWO.
THREE. FOUR.
FIVE. SIX.
SEVEN. EIGHT.
NINE.

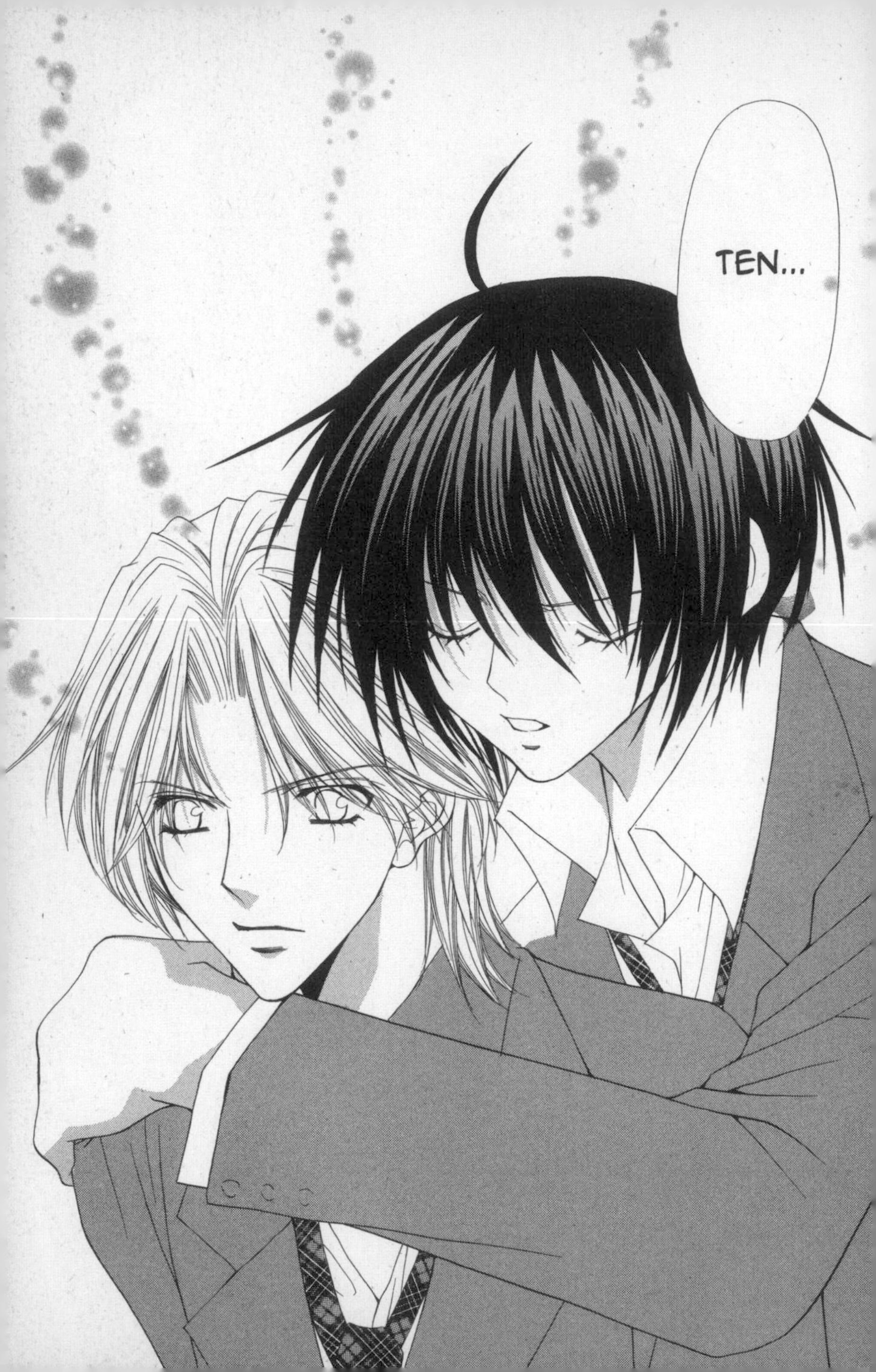
TEN...

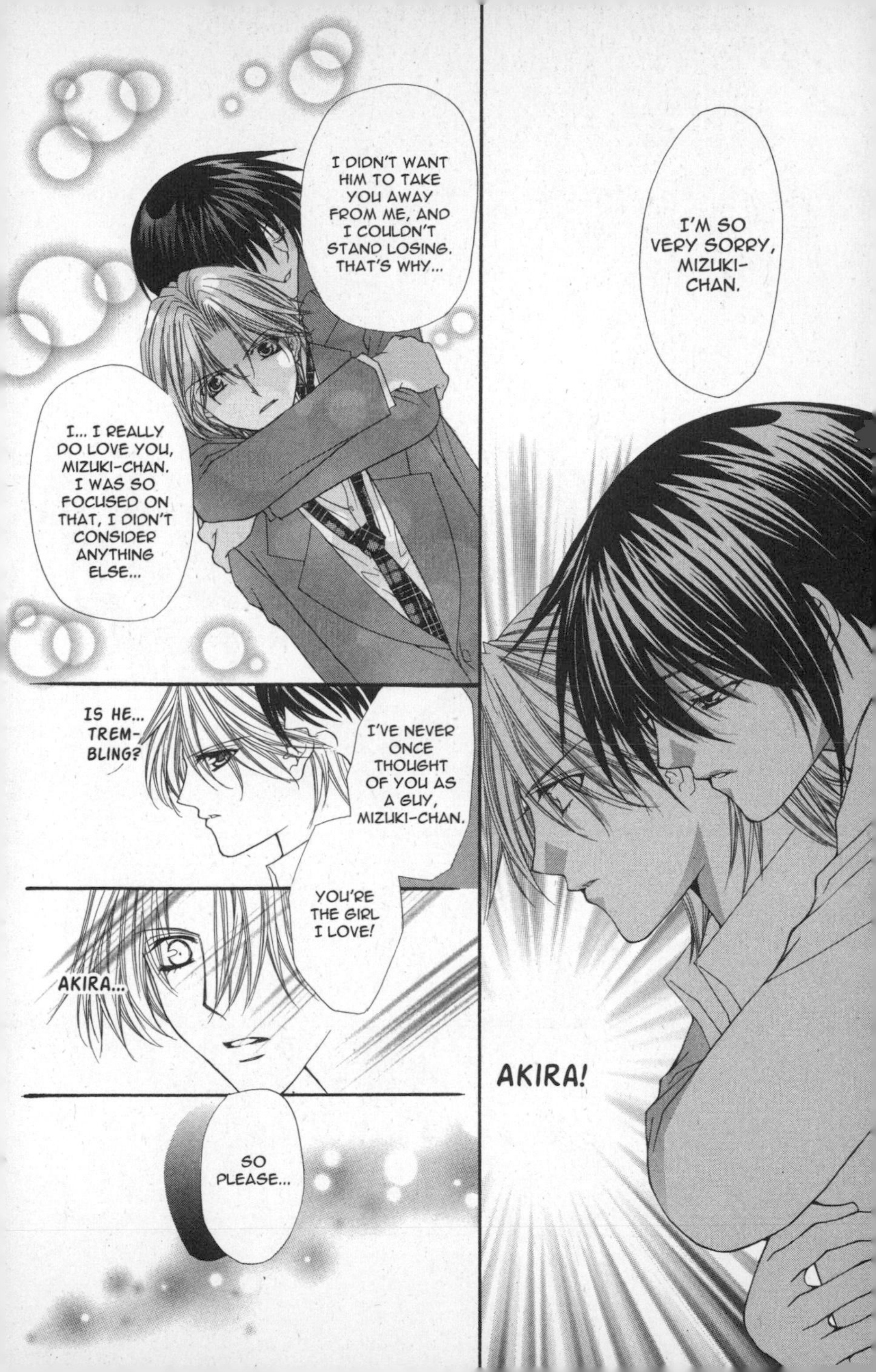
I'M SO VERY SORRY, MIZUKI-CHAN.
AKIRA!
I DIDN'T WANT HIM TO TAKE YOU AWAY FROM ME, AND I COULDN'T STAND LOSING. THAT'S WHY...
I... I REALLY DO LOVE YOU, MIZUKI-CHAN. I WAS SO FOCUSED ON THAT, I DIDN'T CONSIDER ANYTHING ELSE...
I'VE NEVER ONCE THOUGHT OF YOU AS A GUY, MIZUKI-CHAN.
IS HE... TREMBLING?
YOU'RE THE GIRL I LOVE!
AKIRA...
SO PLEASE...

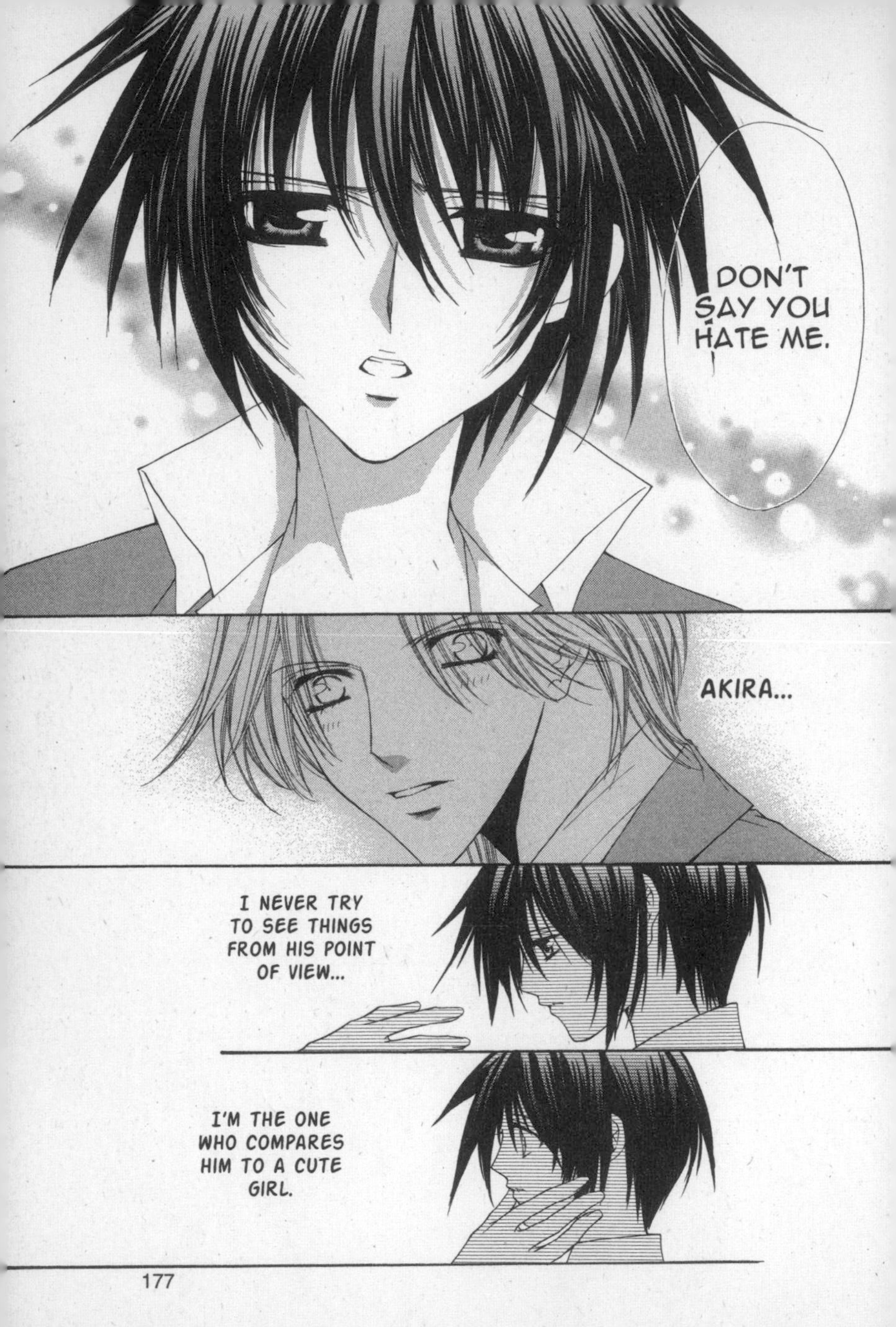
DON'T SAY YOU HATE ME.
AKIRA...
I NEVER TRY TO SEE THINGS FROM HIS POINT OF VIEW...
I'M THE ONE WHO COMPARES HIM TO A CUTE GIRL.

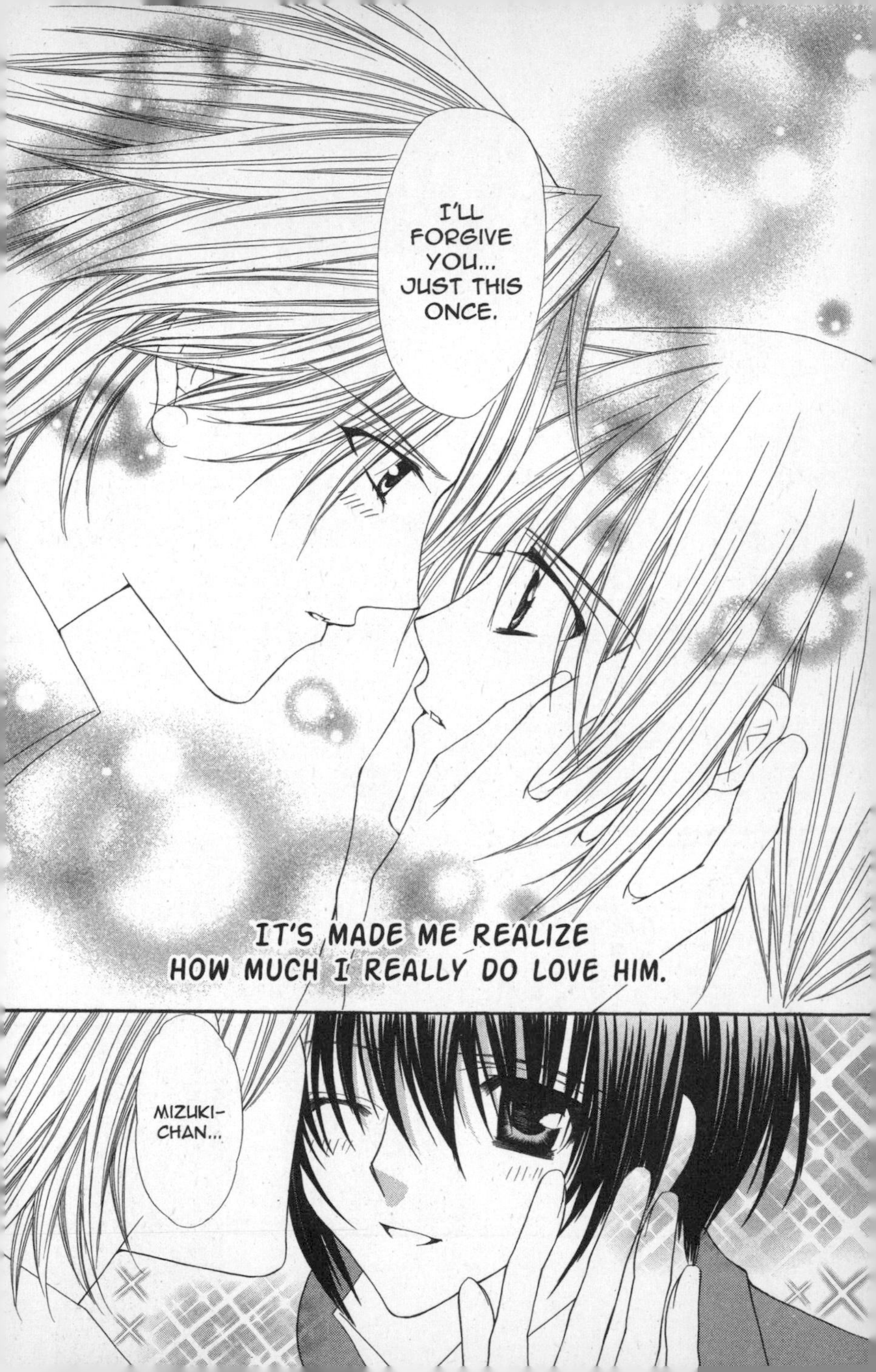
I'LL FORGIVE YOU... JUST THIS ONCE.
IT'S MADE ME REALIZE HOW MUCH I REALLY DO LOVE HIM.
MIZUKI-CHAN...

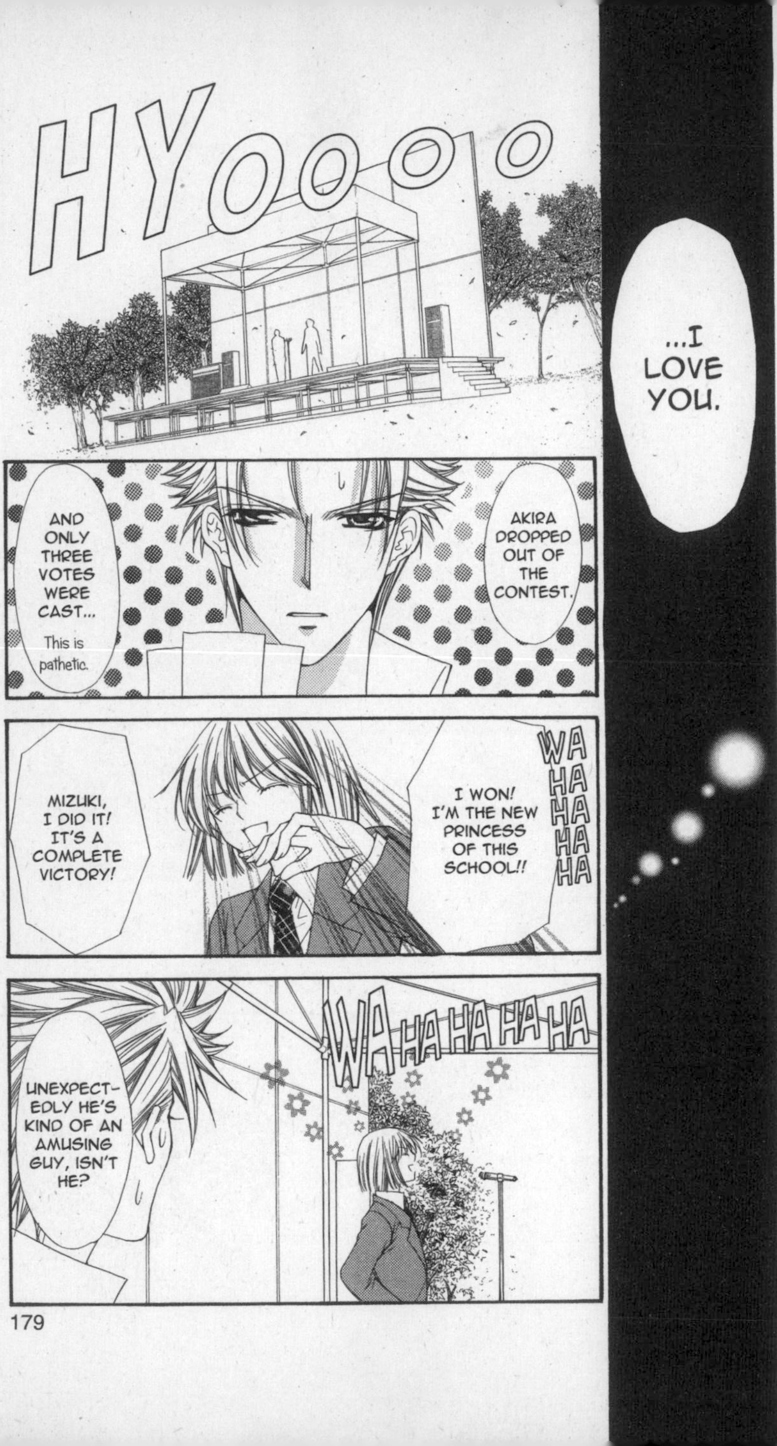
...I LOVE YOU.
HYOOOO
AKIRA DROPPED OUT OF THE CONTEST.
AND ONLY THREE VOTES WERE CAST...
This is pathetic.
WAHAHAHAHA
I WON! I'M THE NEW PRINCESS OF THIS SCHOOL!!
MIZUKI, I DID IT! IT'S A COMPLETE VICTORY!
WAHAHAHAHA
UNEXPECT-EDLY HE'S KIND OF AN AMUSING GUY, ISN'T HE?

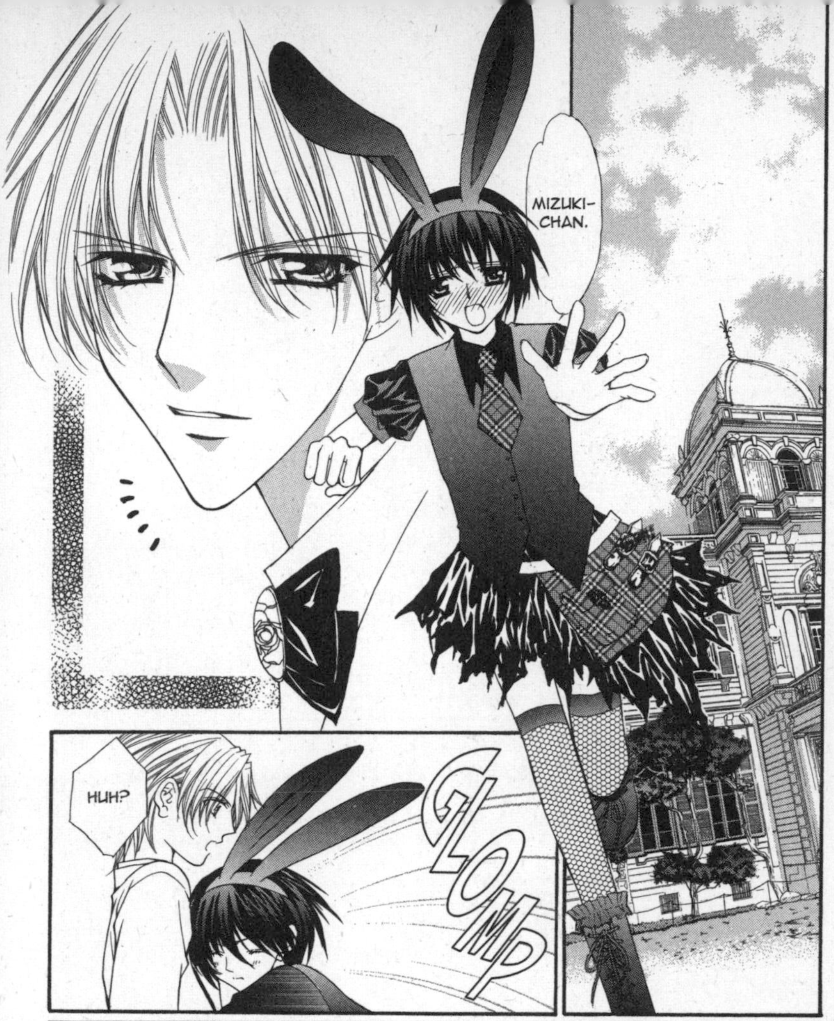
MIZUKI-
CHAN.
GLOMP
HUH?

I want to see this kind of Akira!!

Akira in a bunny hoodie.
I actually wanted to dress him in more cosplay. Making him wear something cute isn't very difficult, but I wanted him in something cool like military uniforms and military uniforms and military... (That's it?!)

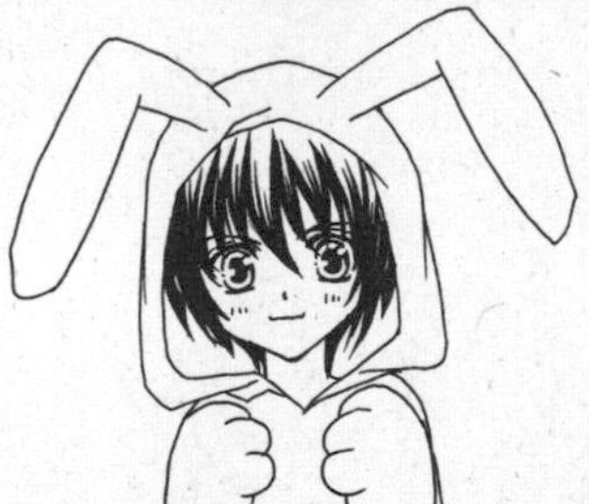

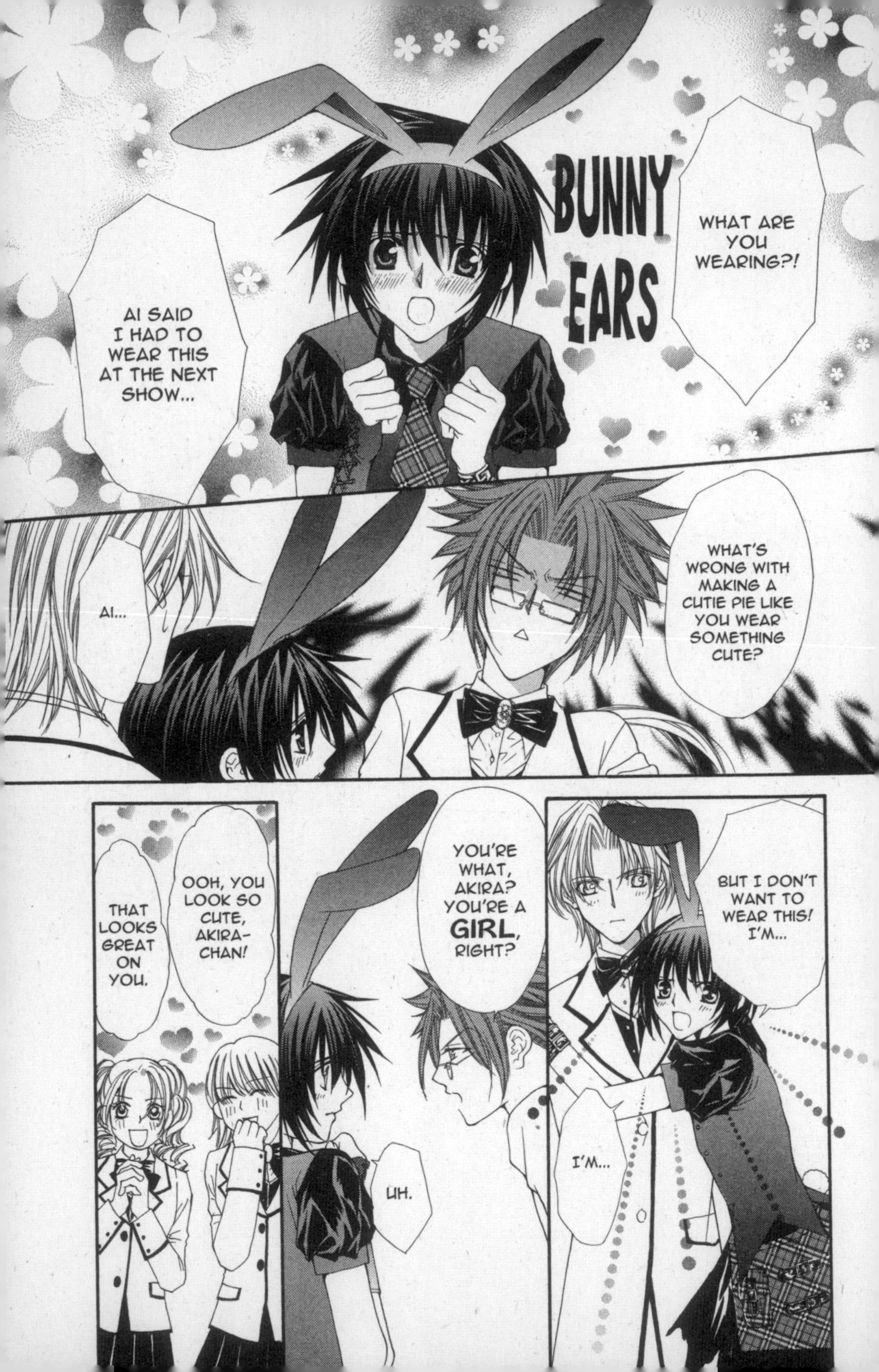
WHAT ARE YOU WEARING?!
BUNNY EARS
AI SAID I HAD TO WEAR THIS AT THE NEXT SHOW...
WHAT'S WRONG WITH MAKING A CUTIE PIE LIKE YOU WEAR SOMETHING CUTE?
AI...
BUT I DON'T WANT TO WEAR THIS! I'M...
I'M...
YOU'RE WHAT, AKIRA? YOU'RE A GIRL, RIGHT?
UH.
OOH, YOU LOOK SO CUTE, AKIRA-CHAN!
THAT LOOKS GREAT ON YOU.

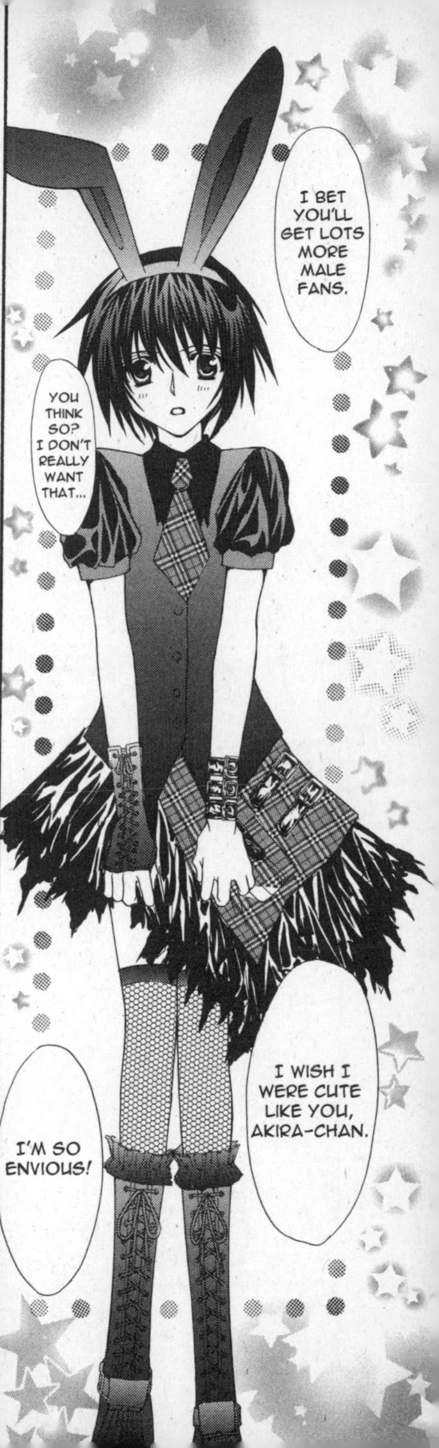
I BET YOU'LL GET LOTS MORE MALE FANS.
YOU THINK SO? I DON'T REALLY WANT THAT...
I WISH I WERE CUTE LIKE YOU, AKIRA-CHAN.
I'M SO ENVIOUS!

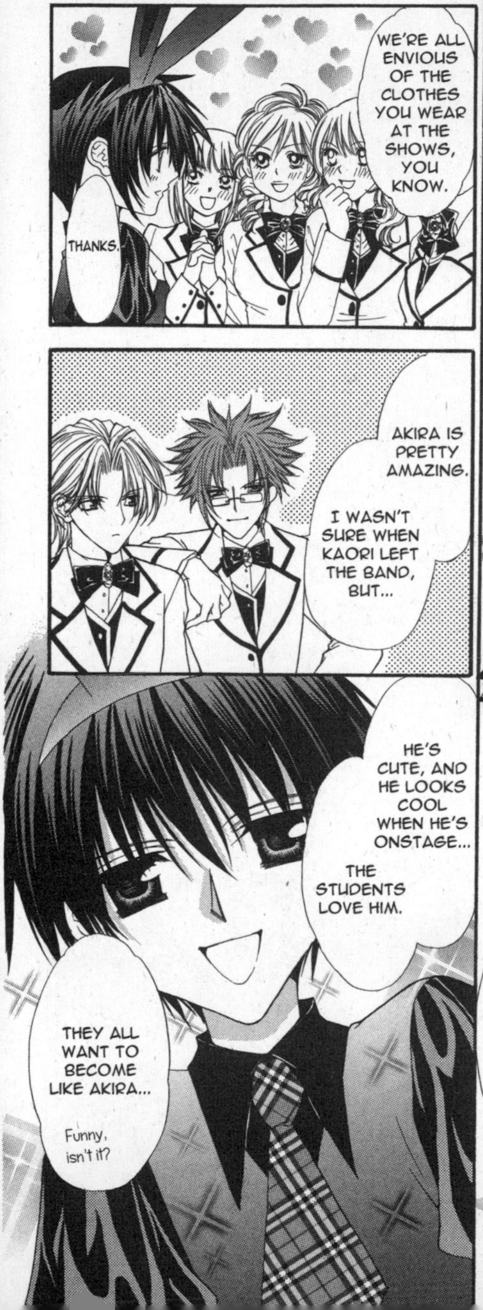
WE'RE ALL ENVIOUS OF THE CLOTHES YOU WEAR AT THE SHOWS, YOU KNOW.
THANKS.
AKIRA IS PRETTY AMAZING.
I WASN'T SURE WHEN KAORI LEFT THE BAND, BUT...
HE'S CUTE, AND HE LOOKS COOL WHEN HE'S ONSTAGE...
THE STUDENTS LOVE HIM.
THEY ALL WANT TO BECOME LIKE AKIRA...
Funny, isn't it?

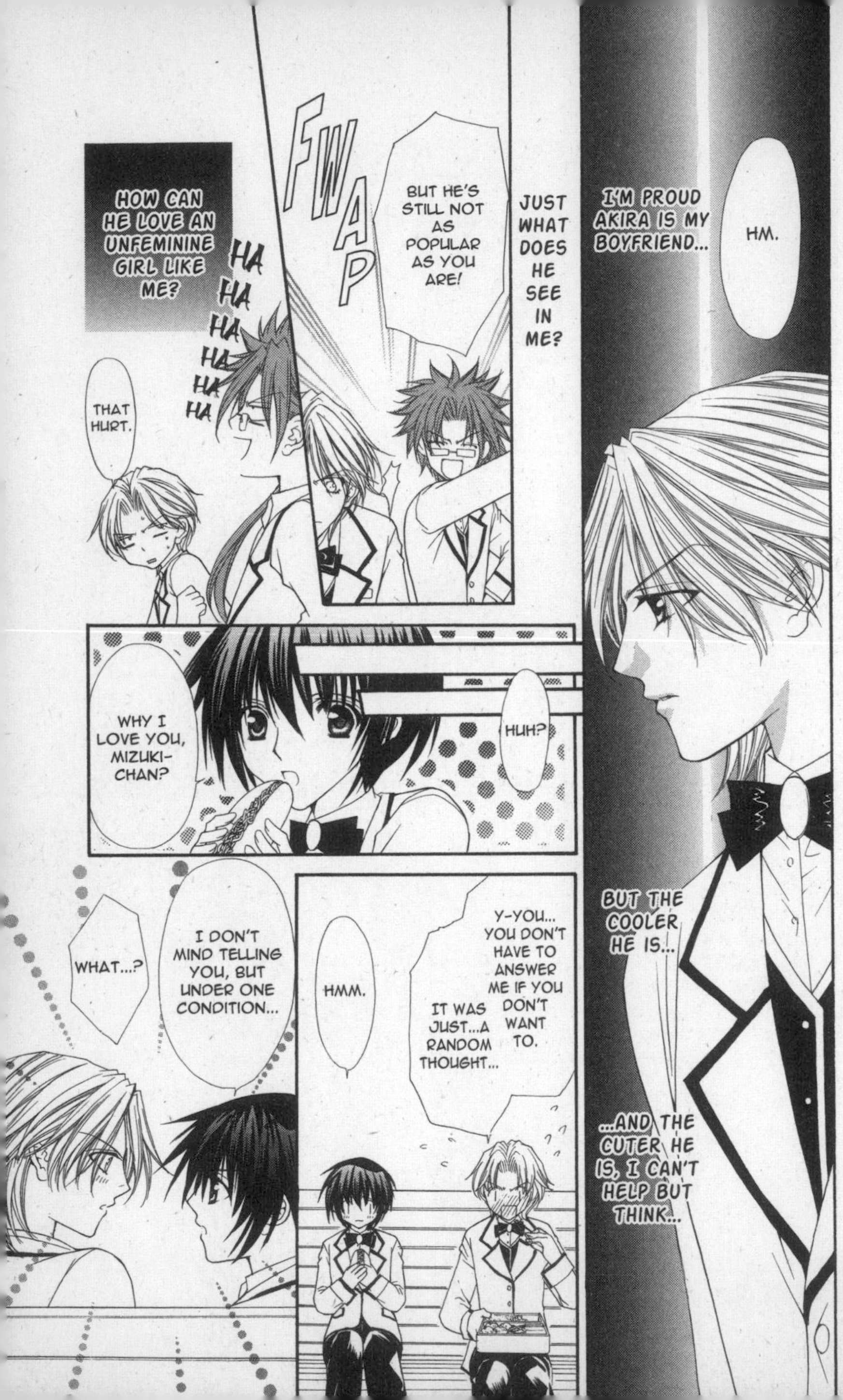
HM.
I'M PROUD AKIRA IS MY BOYFRIEND...
BUT THE COOLER HE IS...
...AND THE CUTER HE IS, I CAN'T HELP BUT THINK...
JUST WHAT DOES HE SEE IN ME?
BUT HE'S STILL NOT AS POPULAR AS YOU ARE!
FWAP
HOW CAN HE LOVE AN UNFEMININE GIRL LIKE ME?
HA HA HA HA HA HA
THAT HURT.
HUH?
WHY I LOVE YOU, MIZUKI-CHAN?
Y-YOU... YOU DON'T HAVE TO ANSWER ME IF YOU DON'T WANT TO.
IT WAS JUST...A RANDOM THOUGHT...
HMM.
I DON'T MIND TELLING YOU, BUT UNDER ONE CONDITION...
WHAT...?

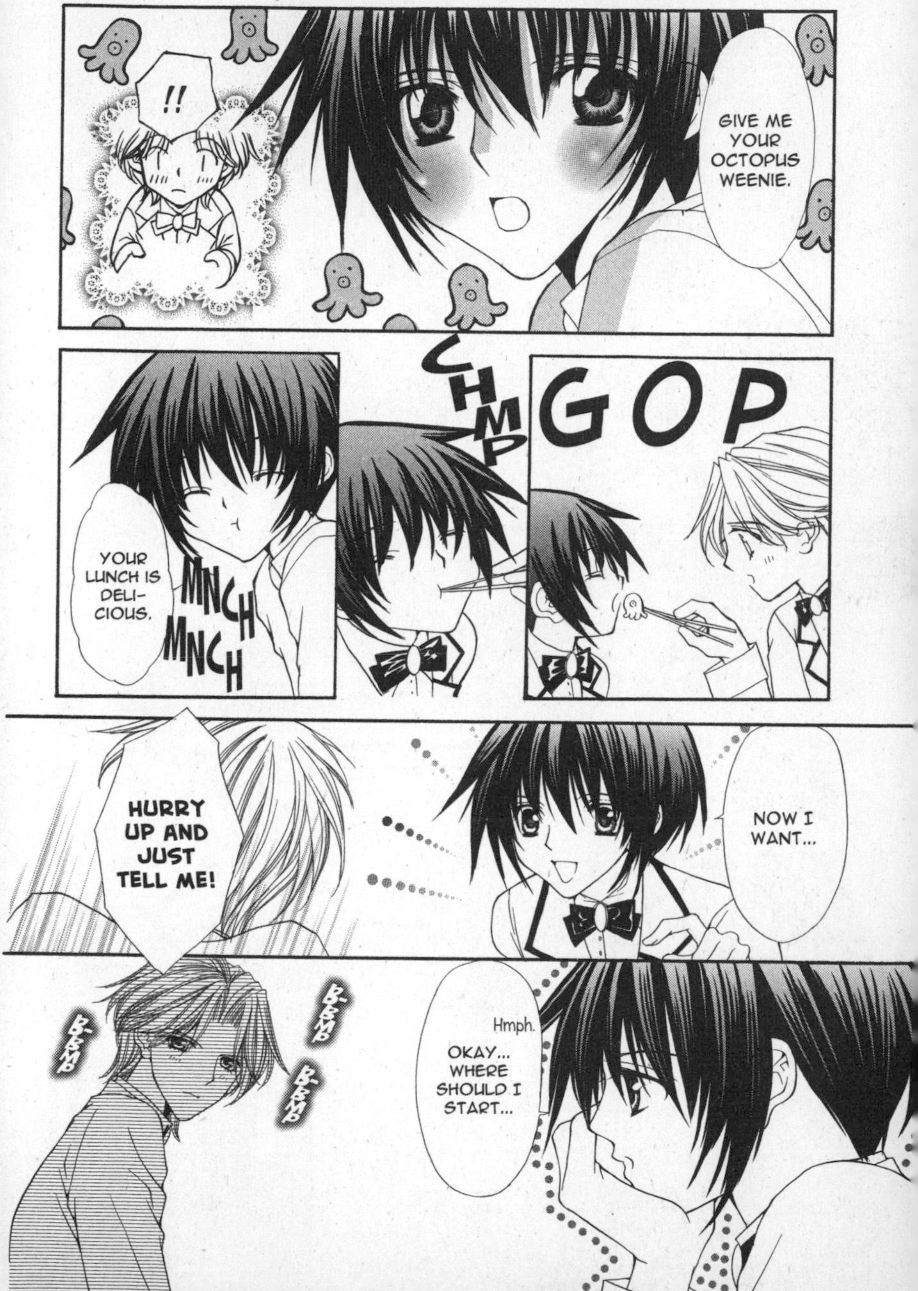
GIVE ME YOUR OCTOPUS WEENIE.
!!
GOP
CHMP
YOUR LUNCH IS DELICIOUS.
MNCH MNCH
NOW I WANT...
HURRY UP AND JUST TELL ME!
Hmph.
OKAY... WHERE SHOULD I START...
B-BMP
B-BMP
B-BMP

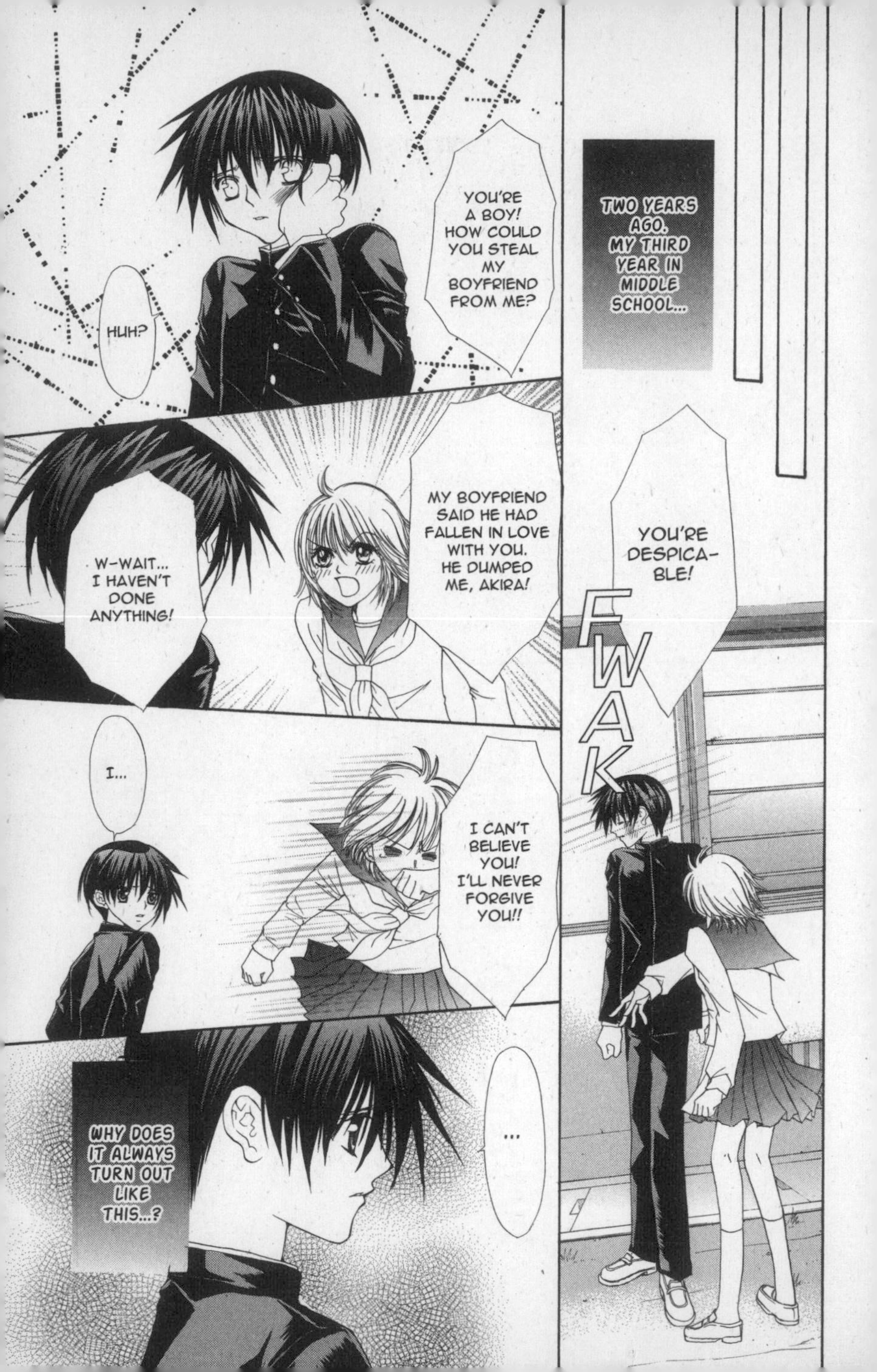
TWO YEARS AGO. MY THIRD YEAR IN MIDDLE SCHOOL...
YOU'RE DESPICABLE!
FWAK
YOU'RE A BOY! HOW COULD YOU STEAL MY BOYFRIEND FROM ME?
HUH?
MY BOYFRIEND SAID HE HAD FALLEN IN LOVE WITH YOU. HE DUMPED ME, AKIRA!
W-WAIT... I HAVEN'T DONE ANYTHING!
I CAN'T BELIEVE YOU! I'LL NEVER FORGIVE YOU!!
I...
...
WHY DOES IT ALWAYS TURN OUT LIKE THIS...?

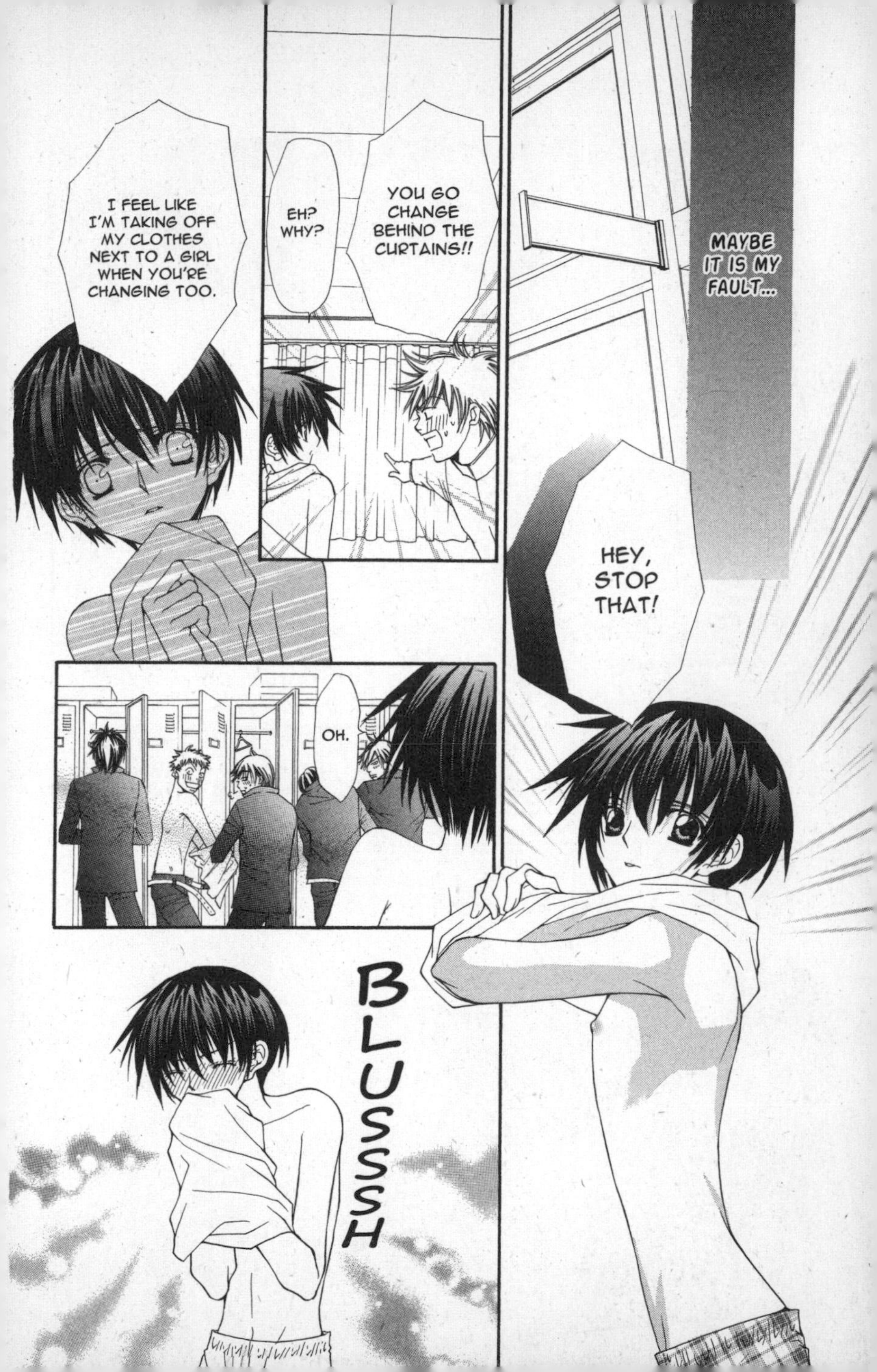
MAYBE IT IS MY FAULT...
HEY, STOP THAT!
YOU GO CHANGE BEHIND THE CURTAINS!!
EH? WHY?
I FEEL LIKE I'M TAKING OFF MY CLOTHES NEXT TO A GIRL WHEN YOU'RE CHANGING TOO.
OH.
BLUSSSH

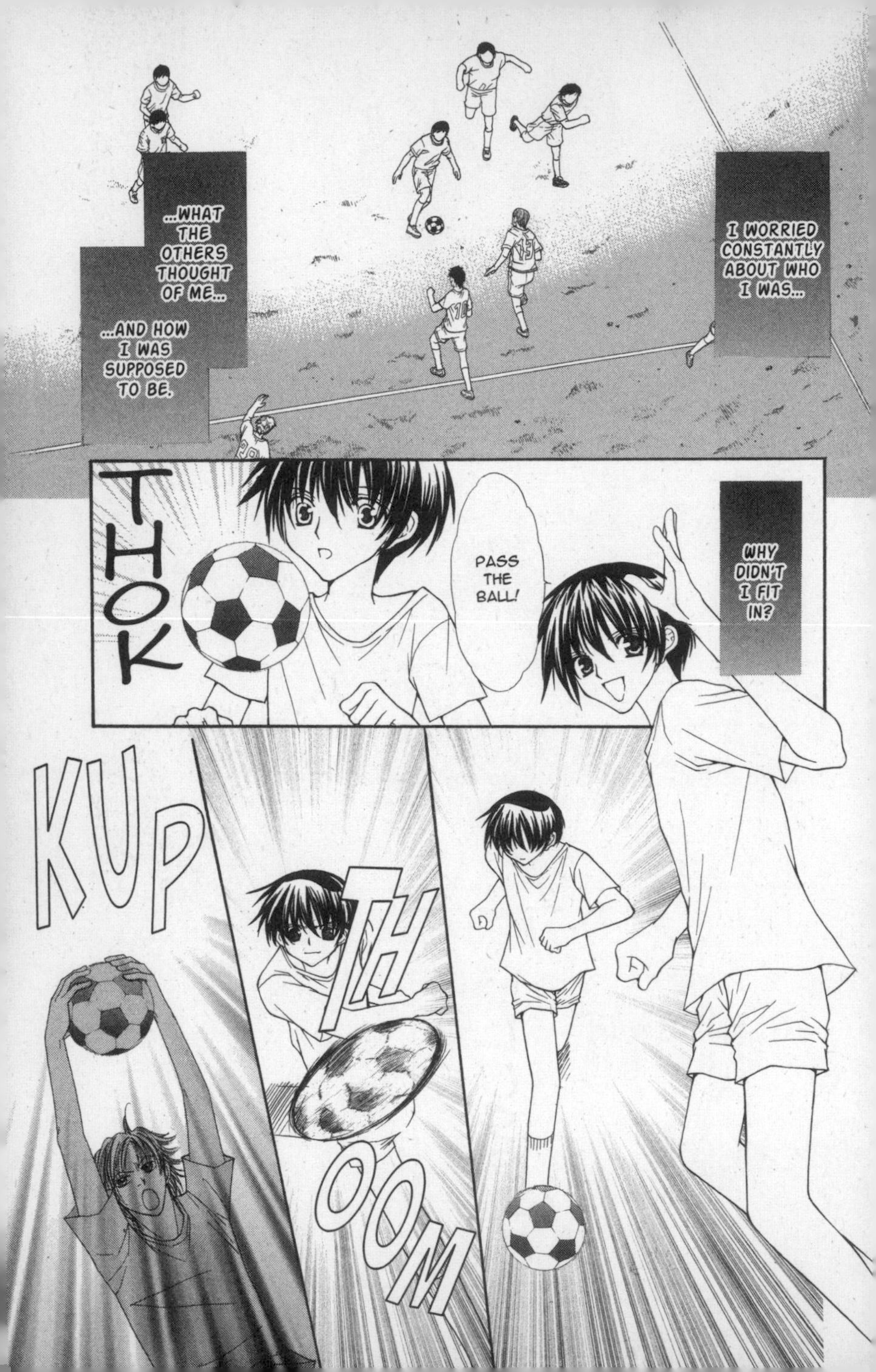
I WORRIED CONSTANTLY ABOUT WHO I WAS...
...WHAT THE OTHERS THOUGHT OF ME...
...AND HOW I WAS SUPPOSED TO BE.
WHY DIDN'T I FIT IN?
PASS THE BALL!
THOK
THOOM
KUP

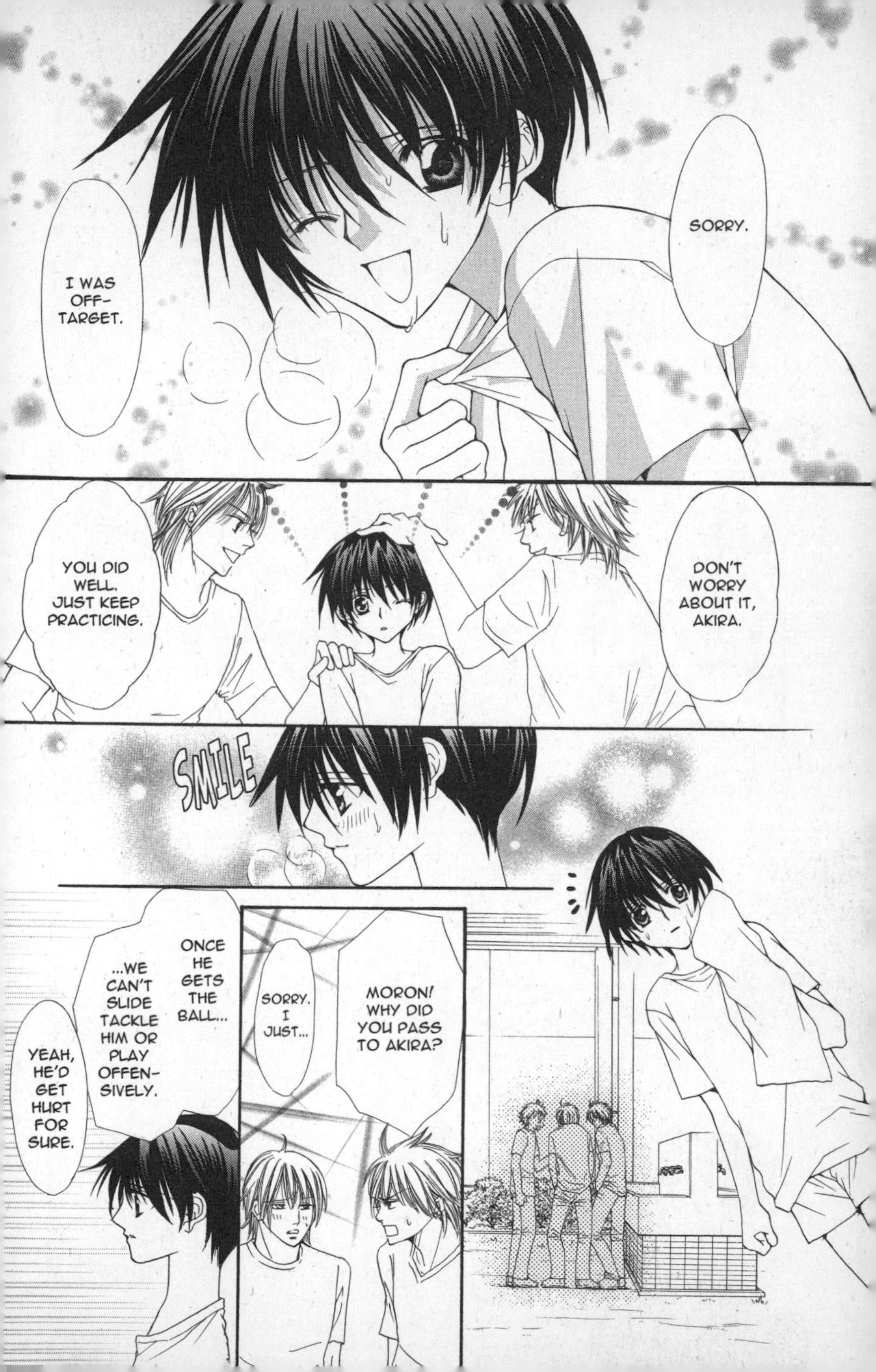
SORRY.
I WAS OFF-TARGET.
DON'T WORRY ABOUT IT, AKIRA.
YOU DID WELL. JUST KEEP PRACTICING.
SMILE
MORON! WHY DID YOU PASS TO AKIRA?
SORRY. I JUST...
ONCE HE GETS THE BALL...
...WE CAN'T SLIDE TACKLE HIM OR PLAY OFFENSIVELY.
YEAH, HE'D GET HURT FOR SURE.

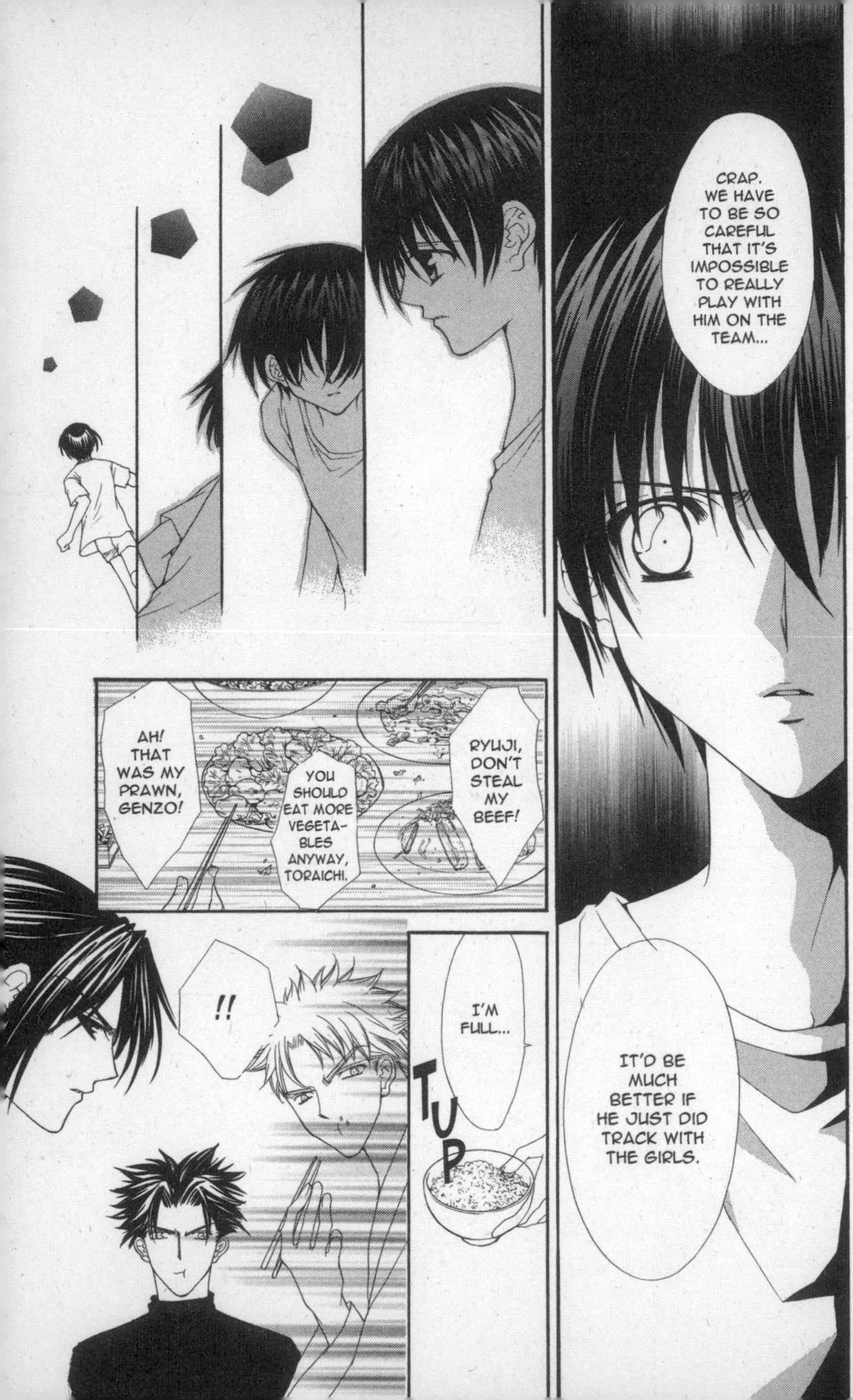
CRAP. WE HAVE TO BE SO CAREFUL THAT IT'S IMPOSSIBLE TO REALLY PLAY WITH HIM ON THE TEAM...
IT'D BE MUCH BETTER IF HE JUST DID TRACK WITH THE GIRLS.
RYUJI, DON'T STEAL MY BEEF!
YOU SHOULD EAT MORE VEGETA-BLES ANYWAY, TORAICHI.
AH! THAT WAS MY PRAWN, GENZO!
I'M FULL...
TUP
!!

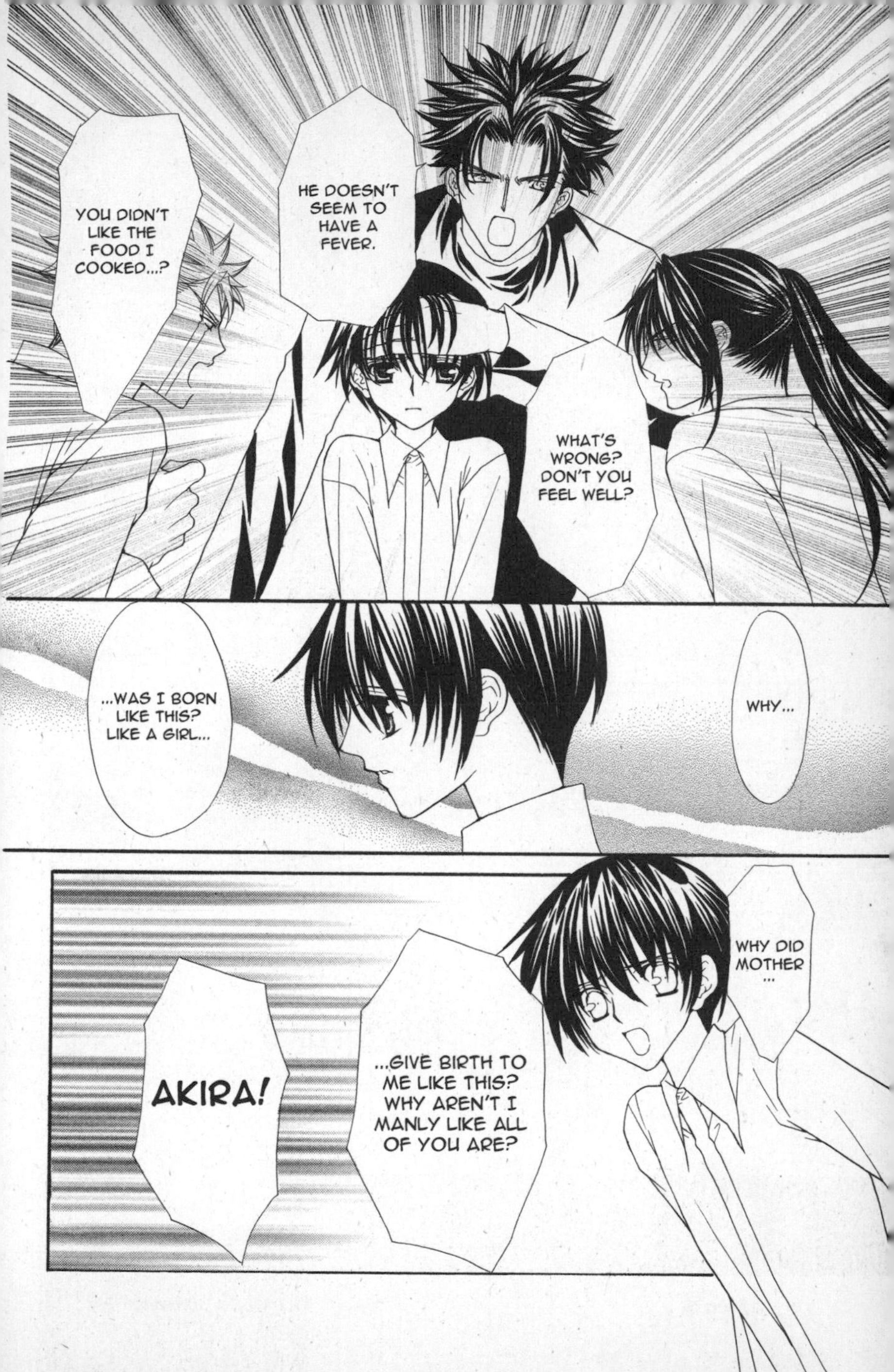
WHAT'S WRONG? DON'T YOU FEEL WELL?
HE DOESN'T SEEM TO HAVE A FEVER.
YOU DIDN'T LIKE THE FOOD I COOKED...?
WHY...
...WAS I BORN LIKE THIS? LIKE A GIRL...
WHY DID MOTHER ...
...GIVE BIRTH TO ME LIKE THIS? WHY AREN'T I MANLY LIKE ALL OF YOU ARE?
AKIRA!

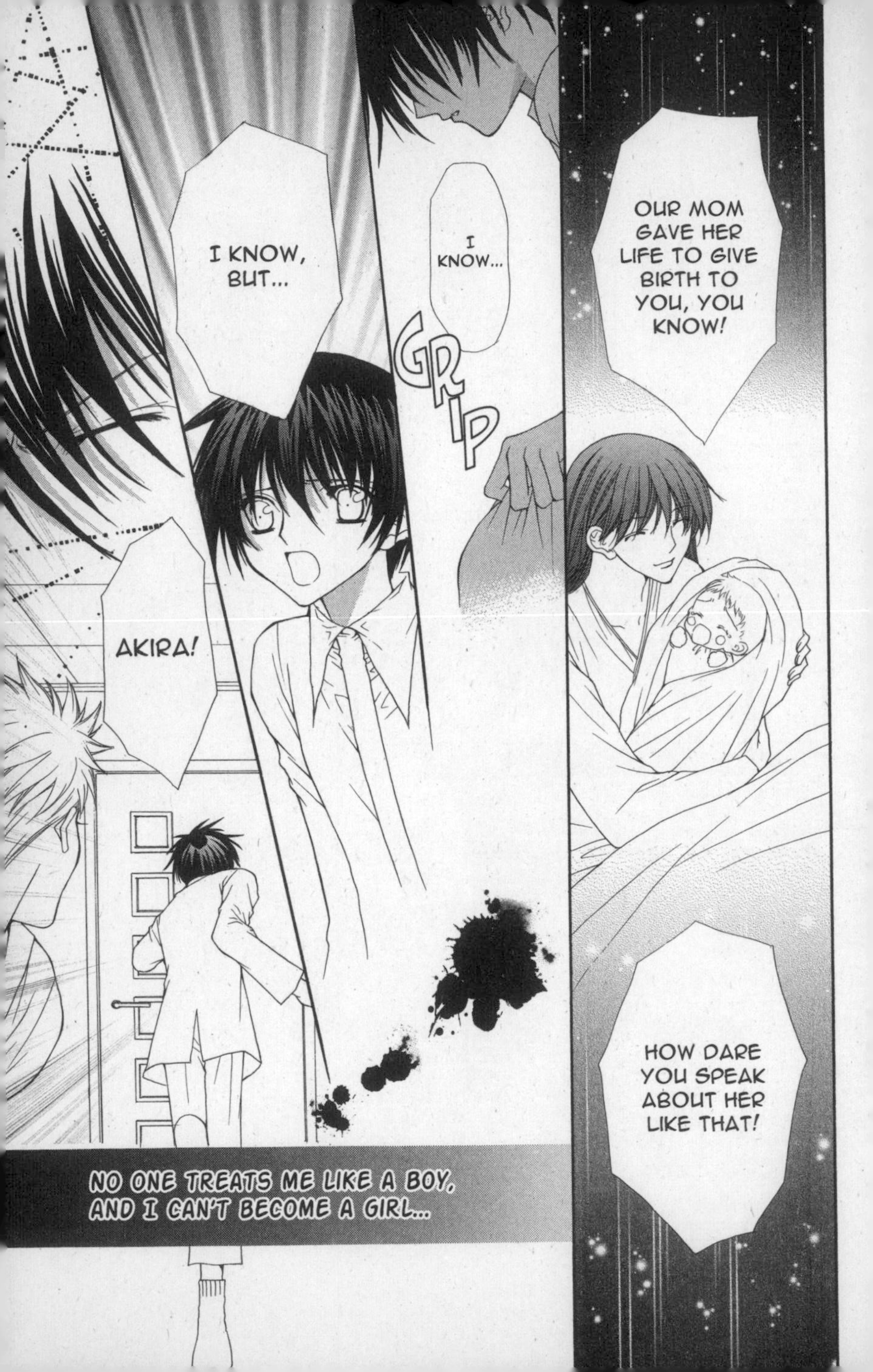
OUR MOM GAVE HER LIFE TO GIVE BIRTH TO YOU, YOU KNOW!
HOW DARE YOU SPEAK ABOUT HER LIKE THAT!
I KNOW...
GRIP
I KNOW, BUT...
AKIRA!
NO ONE TREATS ME LIKE A BOY, AND I CAN'T BECOME A GIRL...

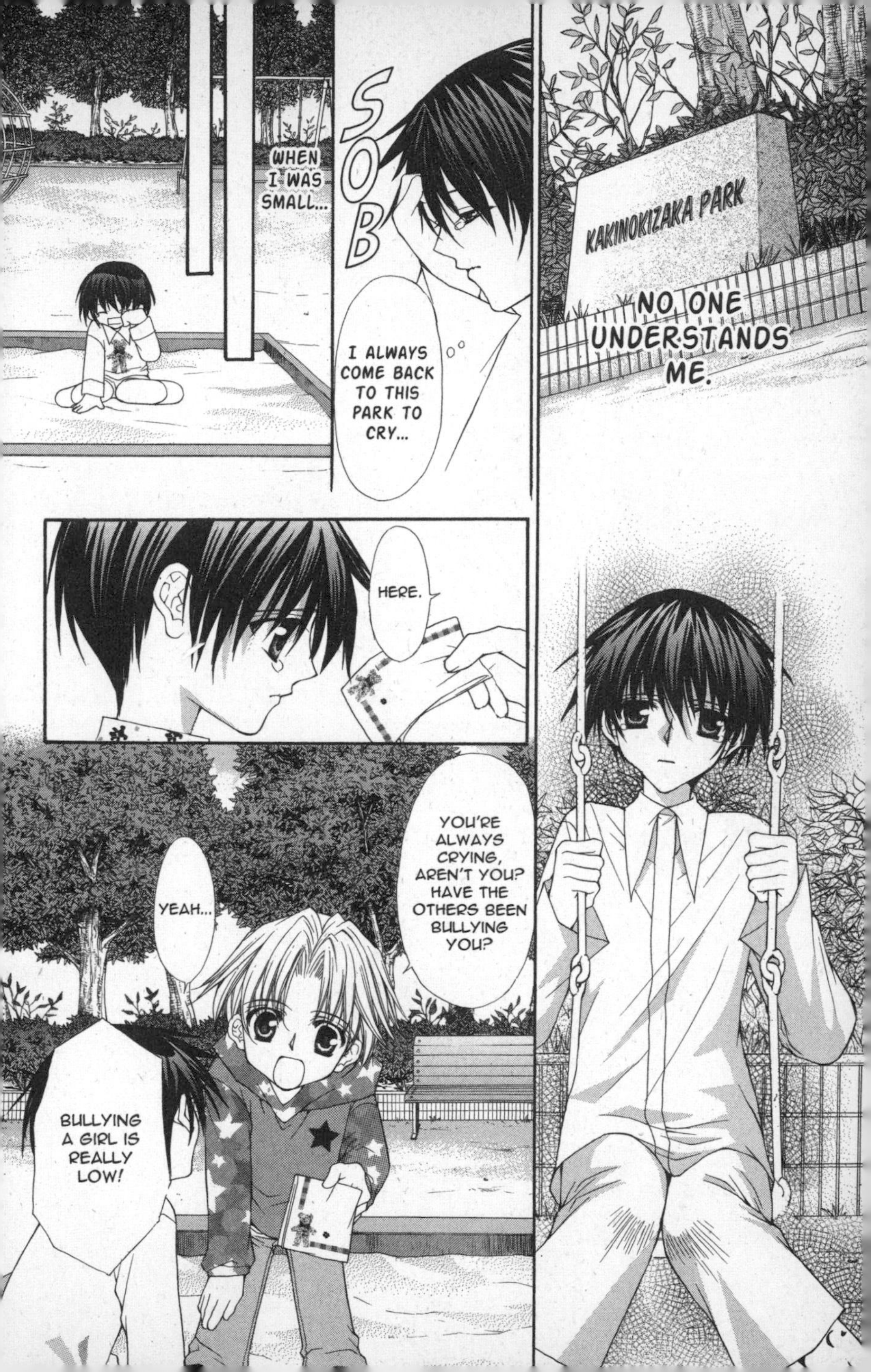
KAKINOKIZAKA PARK
NO ONE UNDERSTANDS ME.
SOB
I ALWAYS COME BACK TO THIS PARK TO CRY...
WHEN I WAS SMALL...
HERE.
YOU'RE ALWAYS CRYING, AREN'T YOU? HAVE THE OTHERS BEEN BULLYING YOU?
YEAH...
BULLYING A GIRL IS REALLY LOW!

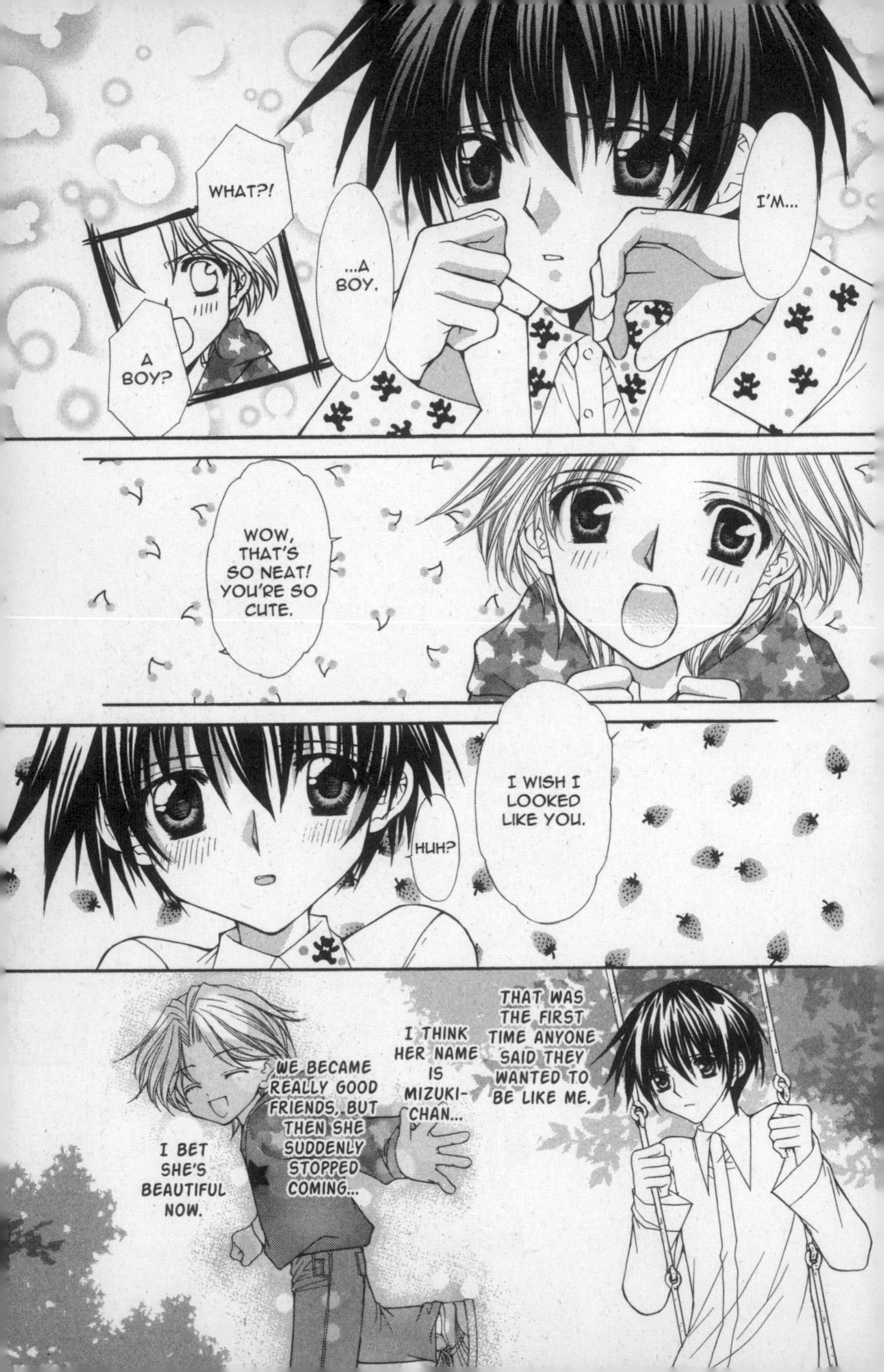
I'M...
...A BOY.
WHAT?!
A BOY?
WOW, THAT'S SO NEAT! YOU'RE SO CUTE.
I WISH I LOOKED LIKE YOU.
HUH?
THAT WAS THE FIRST TIME ANYONE SAID THEY WANTED TO BE LIKE ME.
I THINK HER NAME IS MIZUKI-CHAN...
WE BECAME REALLY GOOD FRIENDS, BUT THEN SHE SUDDENLY STOPPED COMING...
I BET SHE'S BEAUTIFUL NOW.

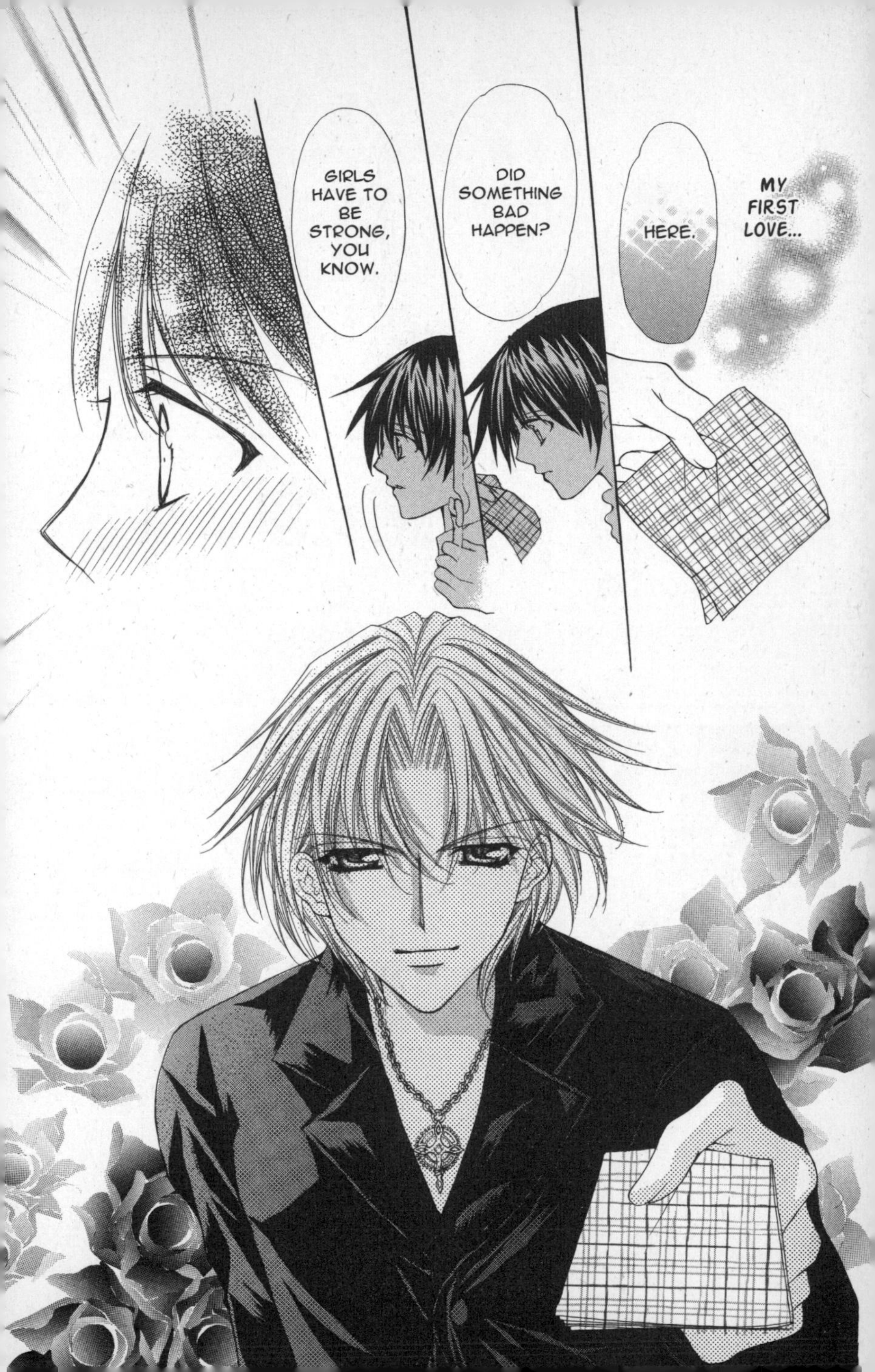
MY FIRST LOVE...
HERE.
DID SOMETHING BAD HAPPEN?
GIRLS HAVE TO BE STRONG, YOU KNOW.

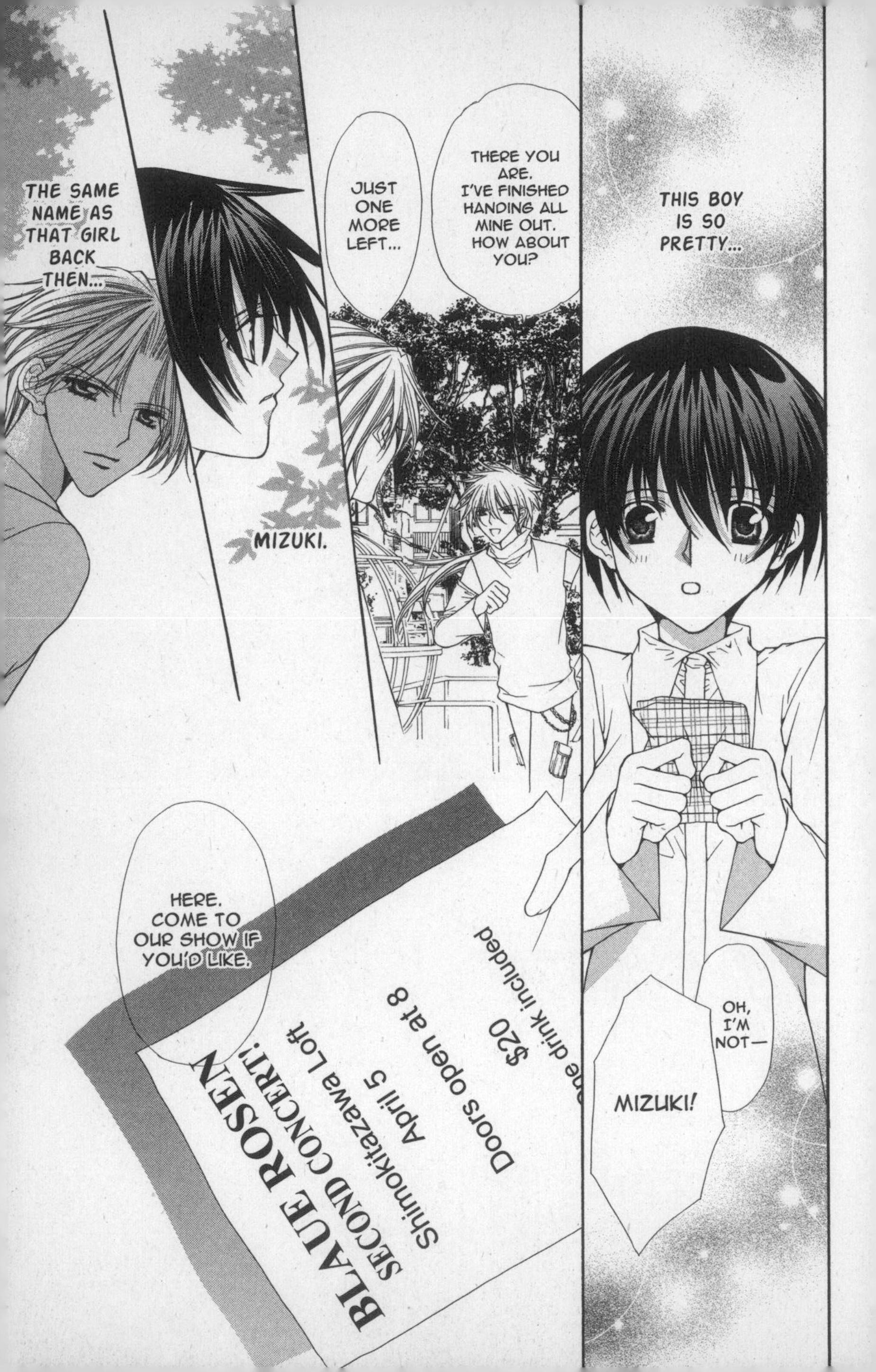
THIS BOY IS SO PRETTY...
OH, I'M NOT—
MIZUKI!
THERE YOU ARE. I'VE FINISHED HANDING ALL MINE OUT. HOW ABOUT YOU?
JUST ONE MORE LEFT...
THE SAME NAME AS THAT GIRL BACK THEN...
MIZUKI.
HERE. COME TO OUR SHOW IF YOU'D LIKE.
BLAUE ROSEN
SECOND CONCERT!
Shimokitazawa Loft
April 5
Doors open at 8
$20
ne drink included

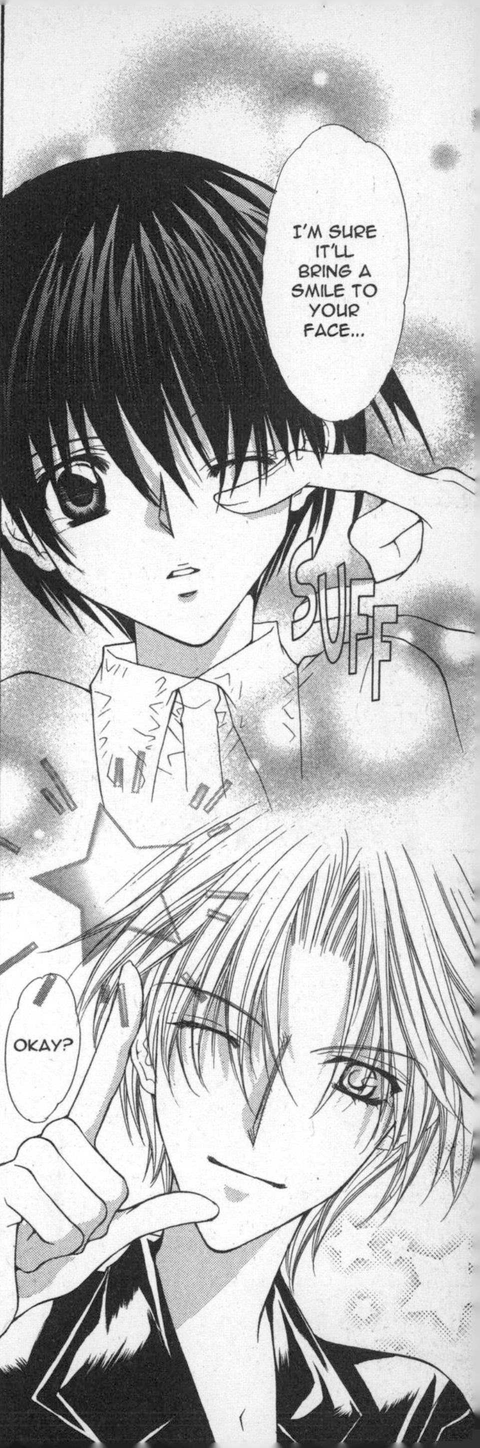
I'M SURE IT'LL BRING A SMILE TO YOUR FACE...
SUFF
OKAY?
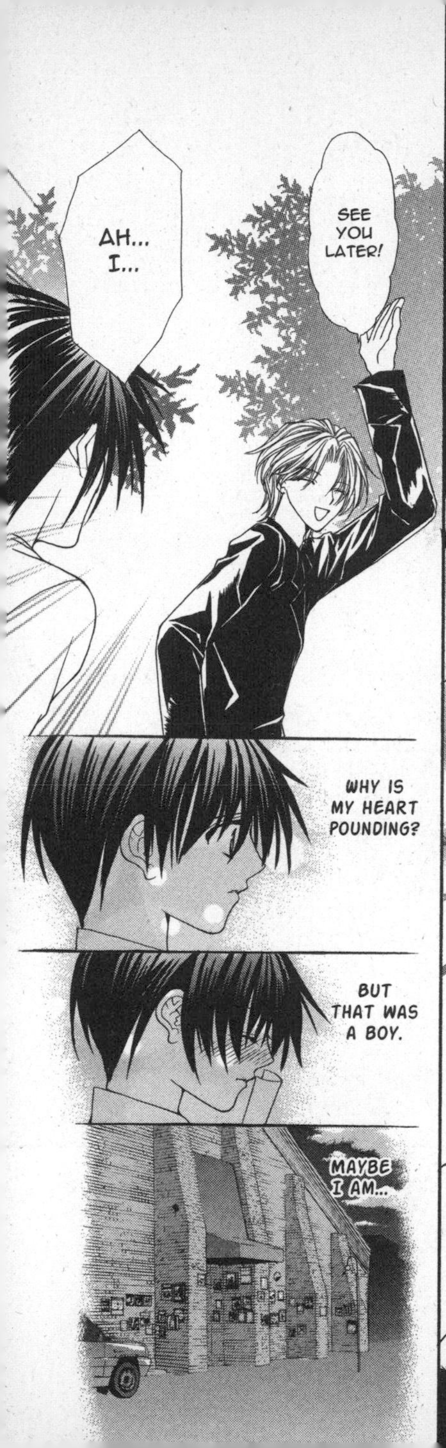
SEE YOU LATER!
AH... I...
WHY IS MY HEART POUNDING?
BUT THAT WAS A BOY.
MAYBE I AM...

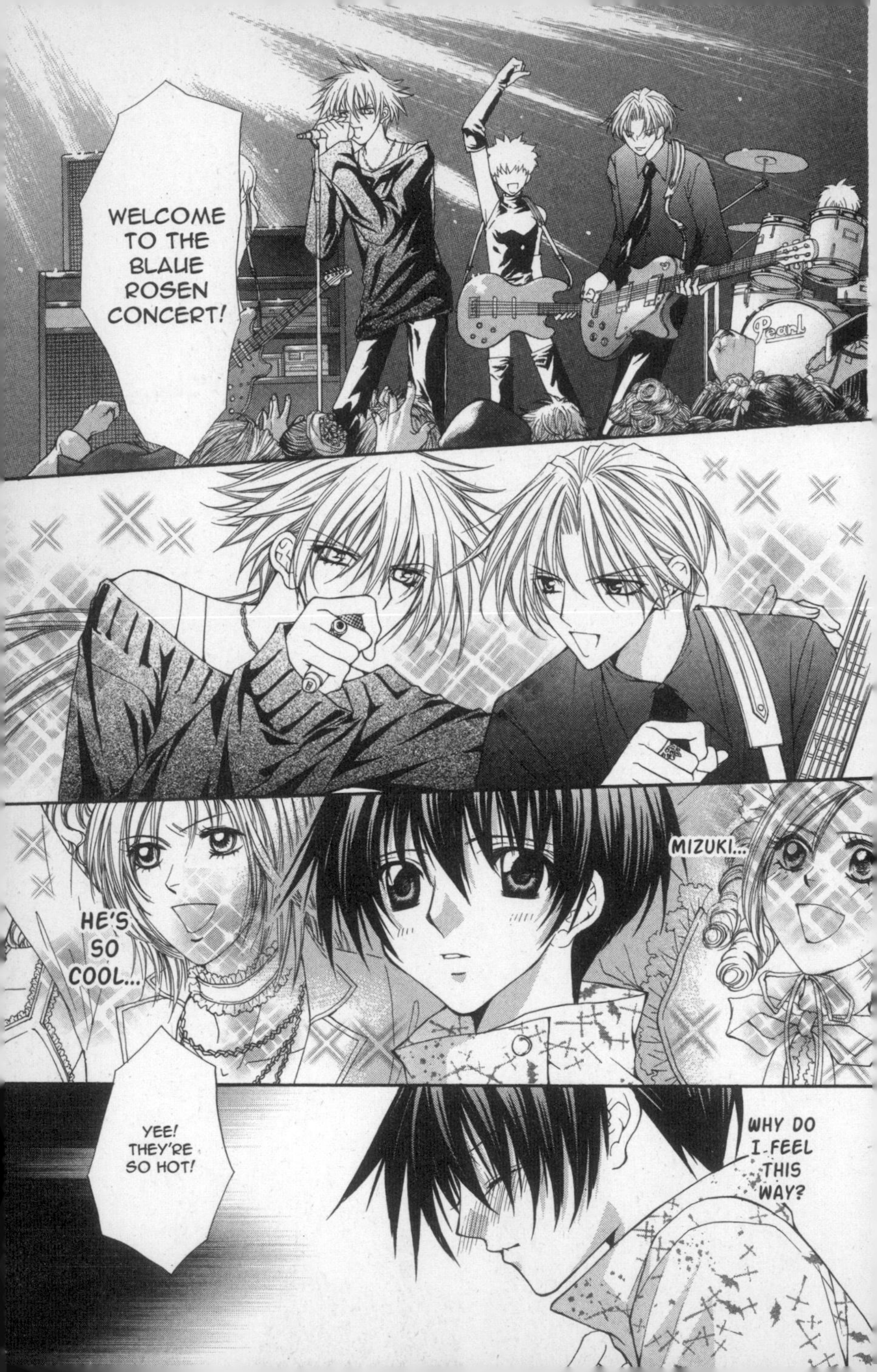
WELCOME TO THE BLAUE ROSEN CONCERT!
Pearl
MIZUKI...
HE'S SO COOL...
YEE! THEY'RE SO HOT!
WHY DO I FEEL THIS WAY?

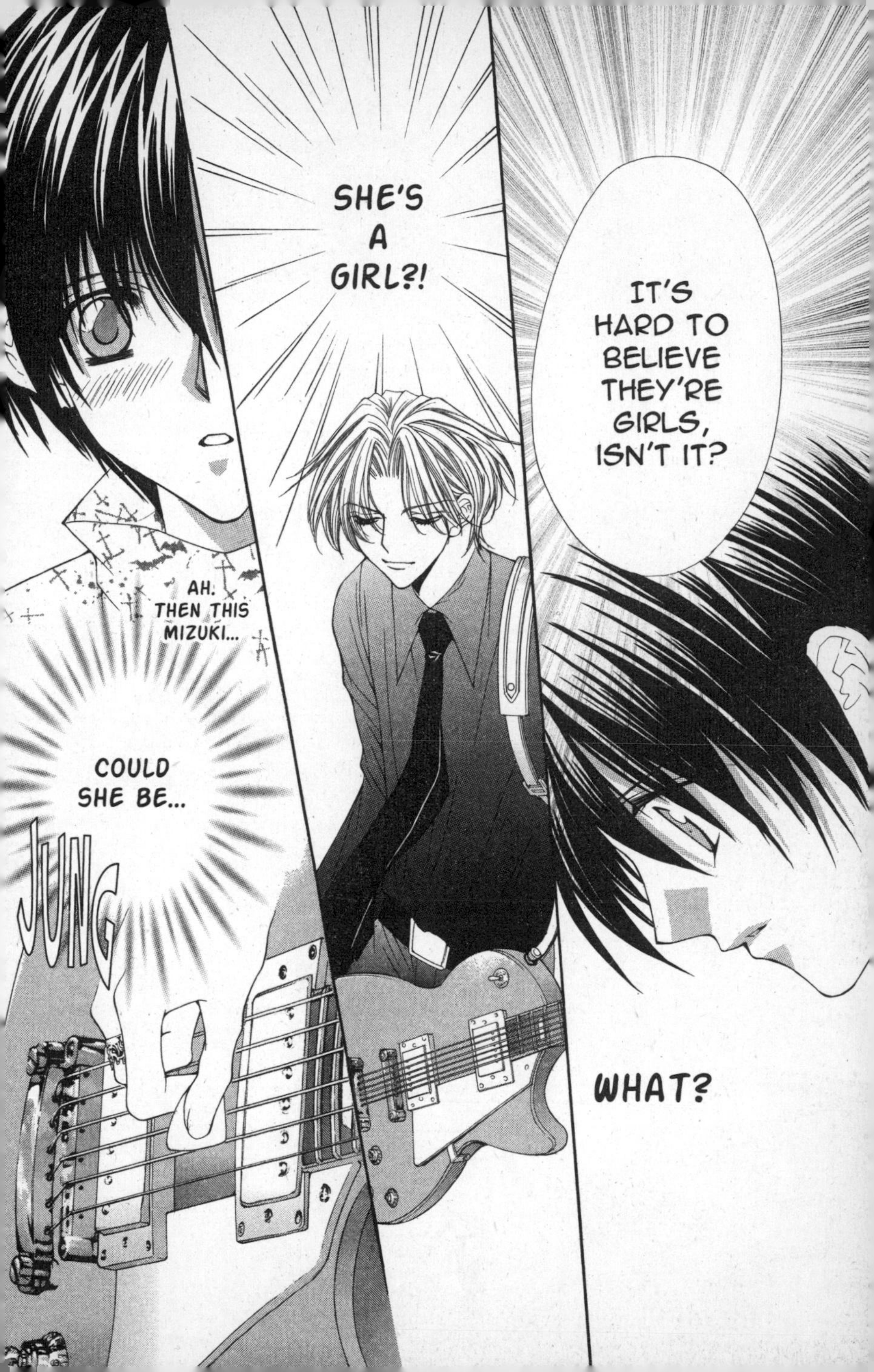
IT'S HARD TO BELIEVE THEY'RE GIRLS, ISN'T IT?
WHAT?
SHE'S A GIRL?!
AH. THEN THIS MIZUKI...
COULD SHE BE...
JUNG

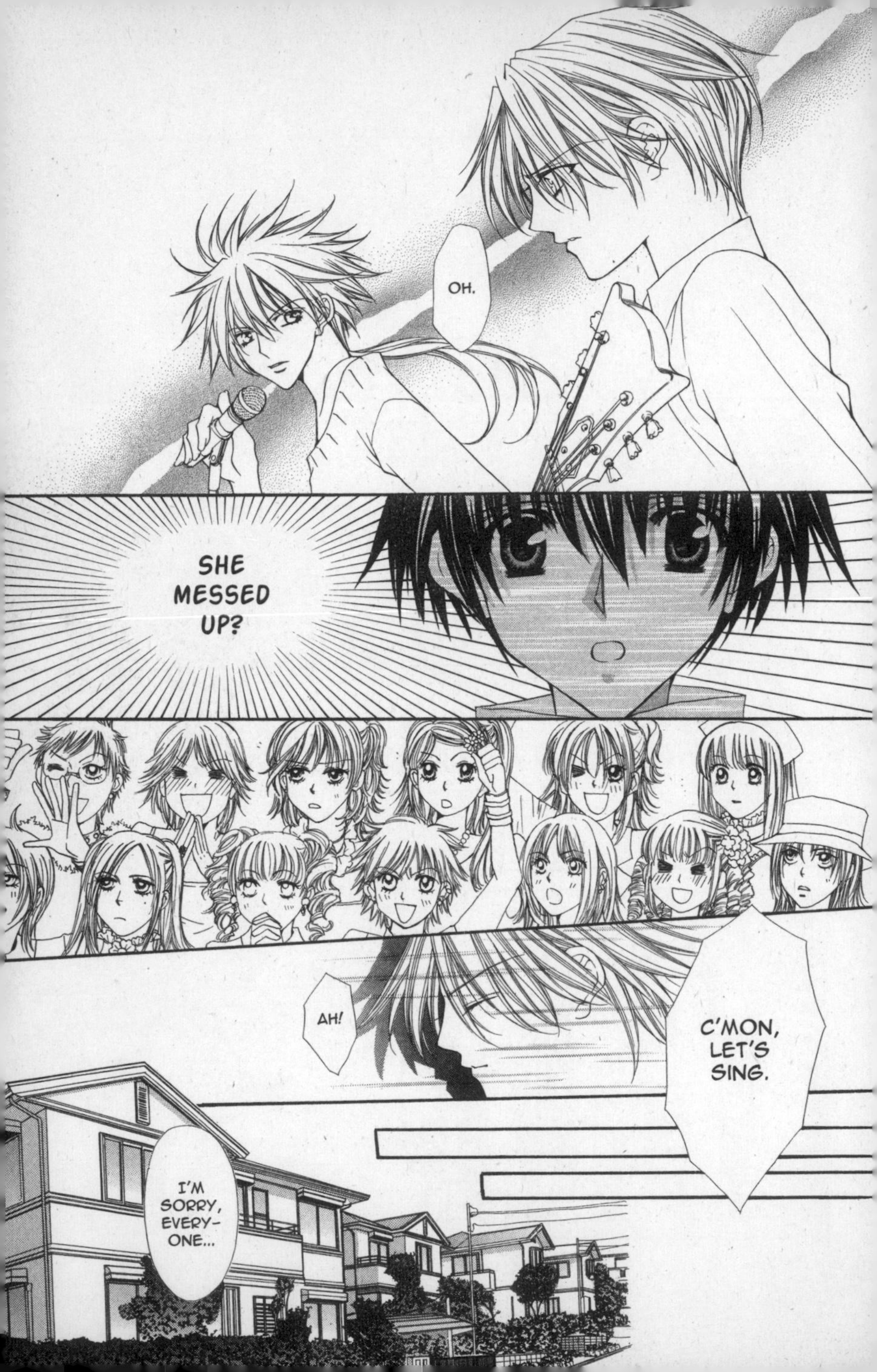
OH.
SHE MESSED UP?
C'MON, LET'S SING.
AH!
I'M SORRY, EVERY-ONE...

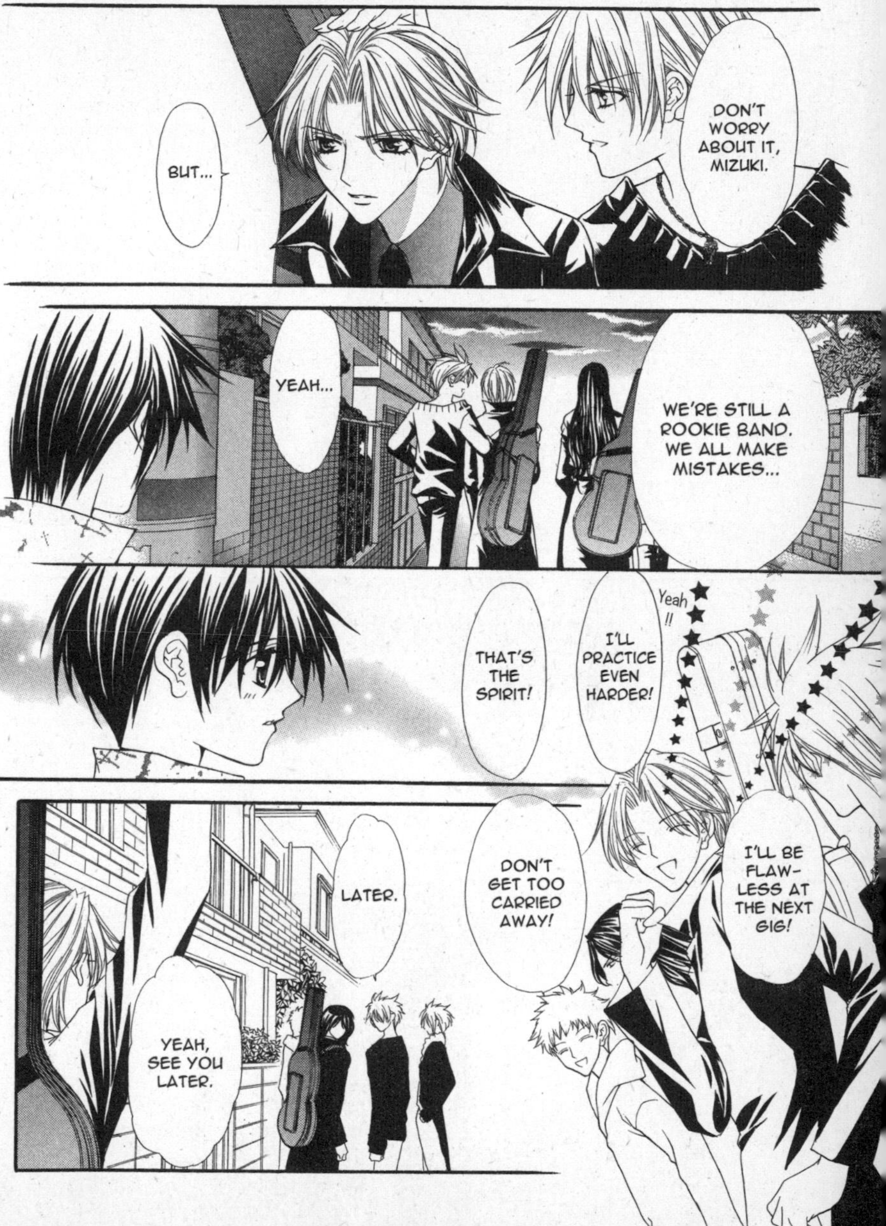
DON'T WORRY ABOUT IT, MIZUKI.
BUT...
WE'RE STILL A ROOKIE BAND. WE ALL MAKE MISTAKES...
YEAH...
Yeah !!
I'LL PRACTICE EVEN HARDER!
THAT'S THE SPIRIT!
I'LL BE FLAW-LESS AT THE NEXT GIG!
DON'T GET TOO CARRIED AWAY!
LATER.
YEAH, SEE YOU LATER.

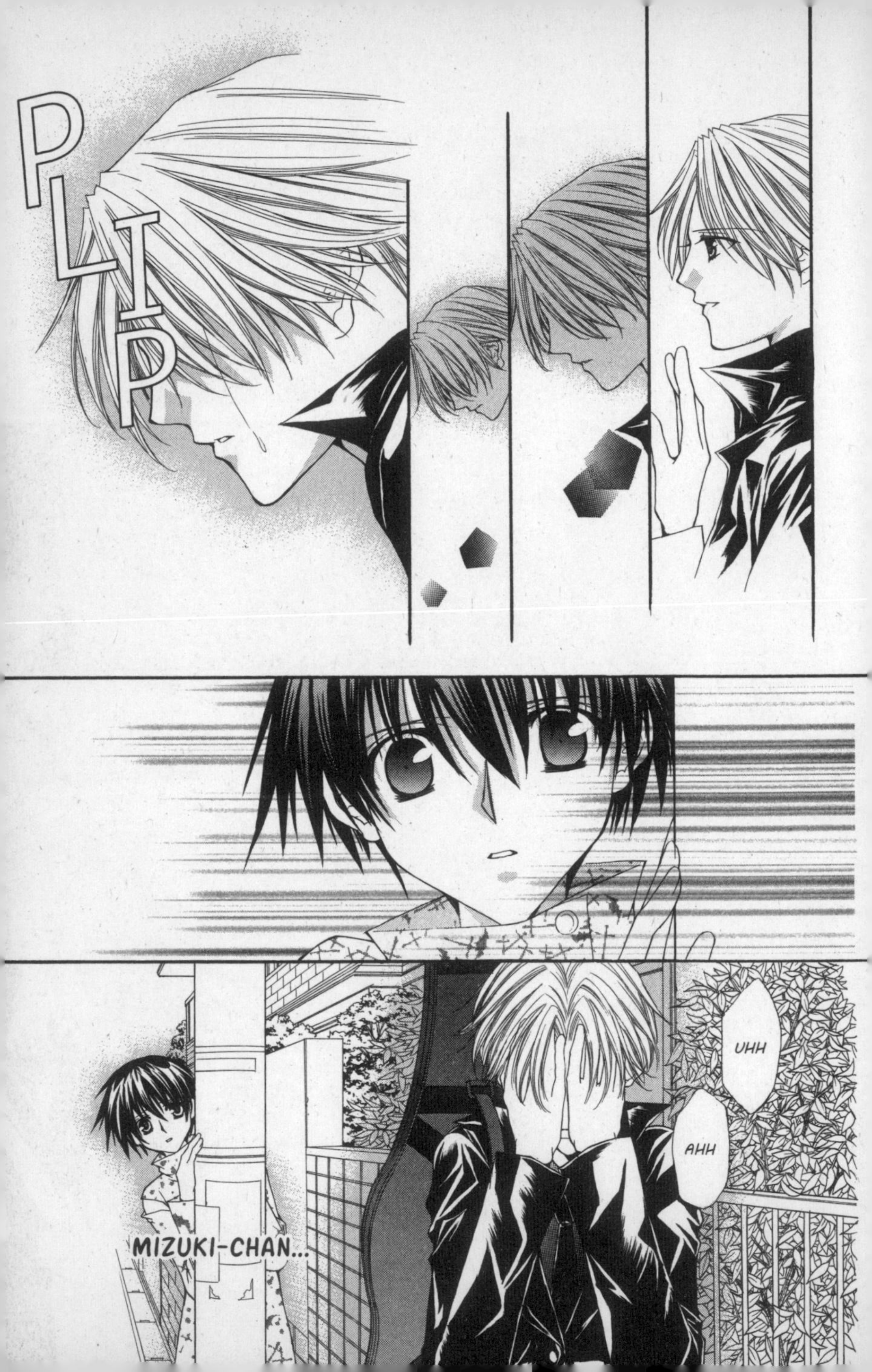
PLIP
UHH
AHH
MIZUKI-CHAN...

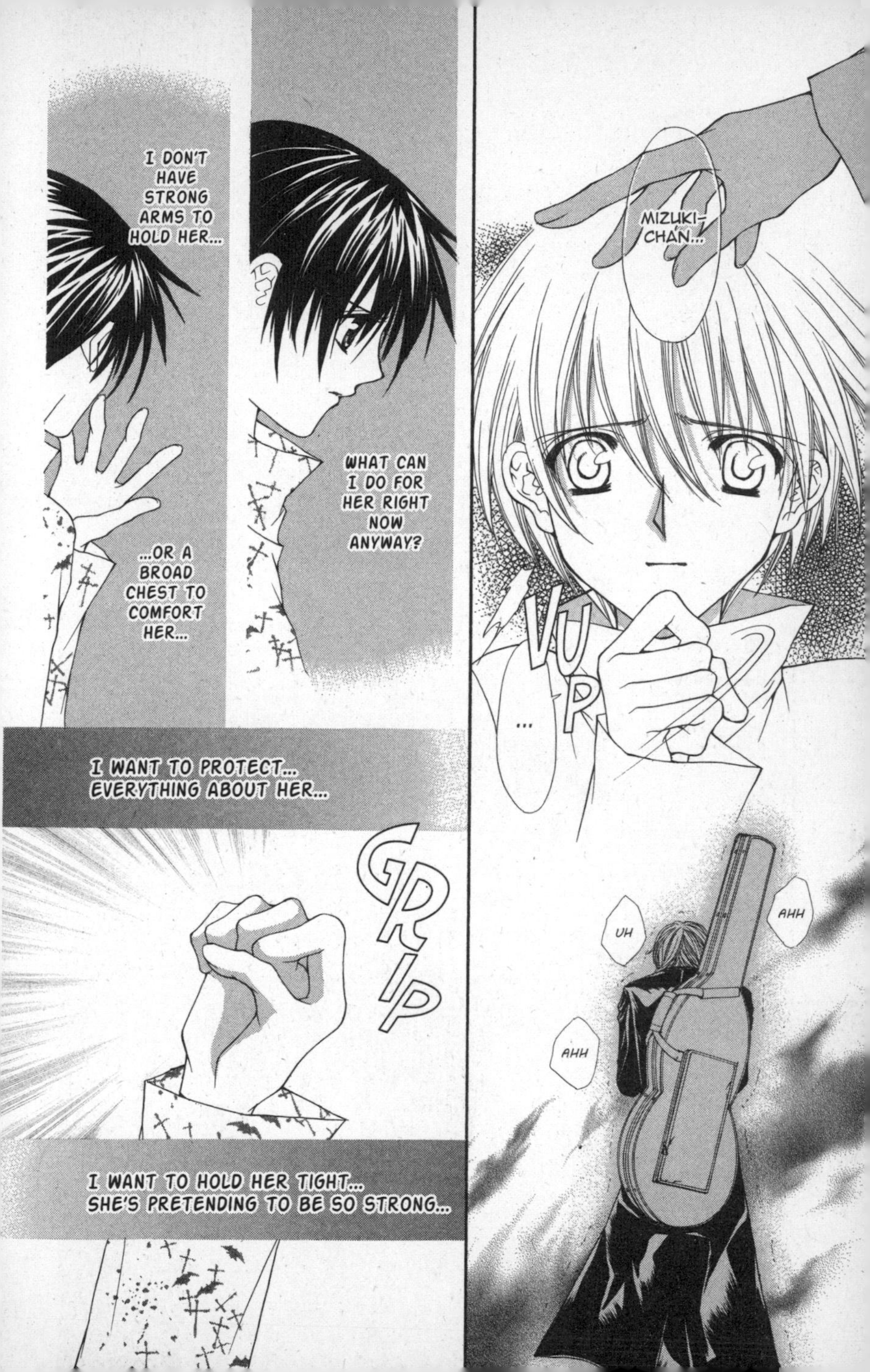
MIZUKI-CHAN...
VUP
...
AHH
UH
AHH
I DON'T HAVE STRONG ARMS TO HOLD HER...
...OR A BROAD CHEST TO COMFORT HER...
WHAT CAN I DO FOR HER RIGHT NOW ANYWAY?
I WANT TO PROTECT... EVERYTHING ABOUT HER...
GRIP
I WANT TO HOLD HER TIGHT... SHE'S PRETENDING TO BE SO STRONG...

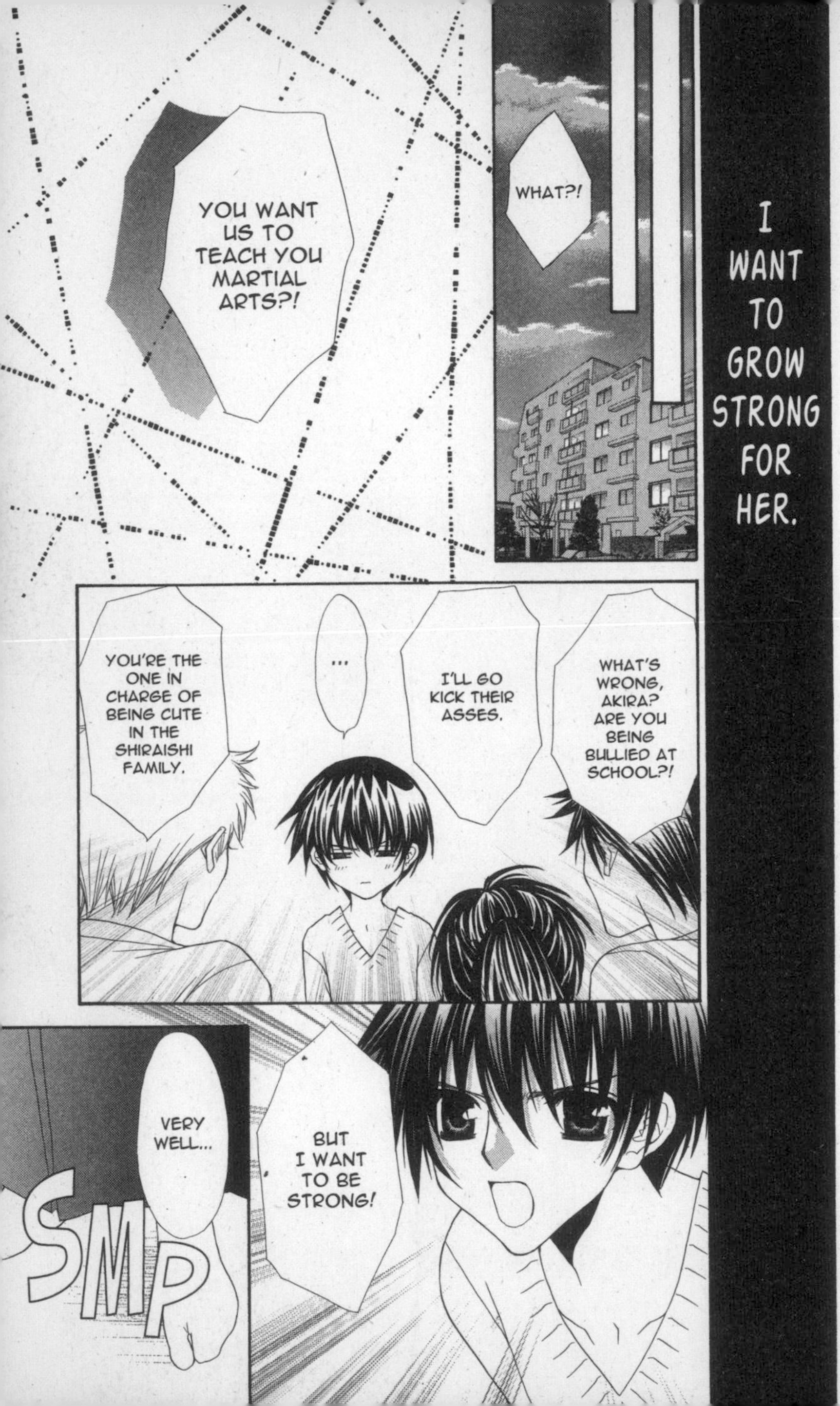
I WANT TO GROW STRONG FOR HER.
WHAT?!
YOU WANT US TO TEACH YOU MARTIAL ARTS?!
WHAT'S WRONG, AKIRA? ARE YOU BEING BULLIED AT SCHOOL?!
I'LL GO KICK THEIR ASSES.
...
YOU'RE THE ONE IN CHARGE OF BEING CUTE IN THE SHIRAISHI FAMILY.
BUT I WANT TO BE STRONG!
VERY WELL...
SMP

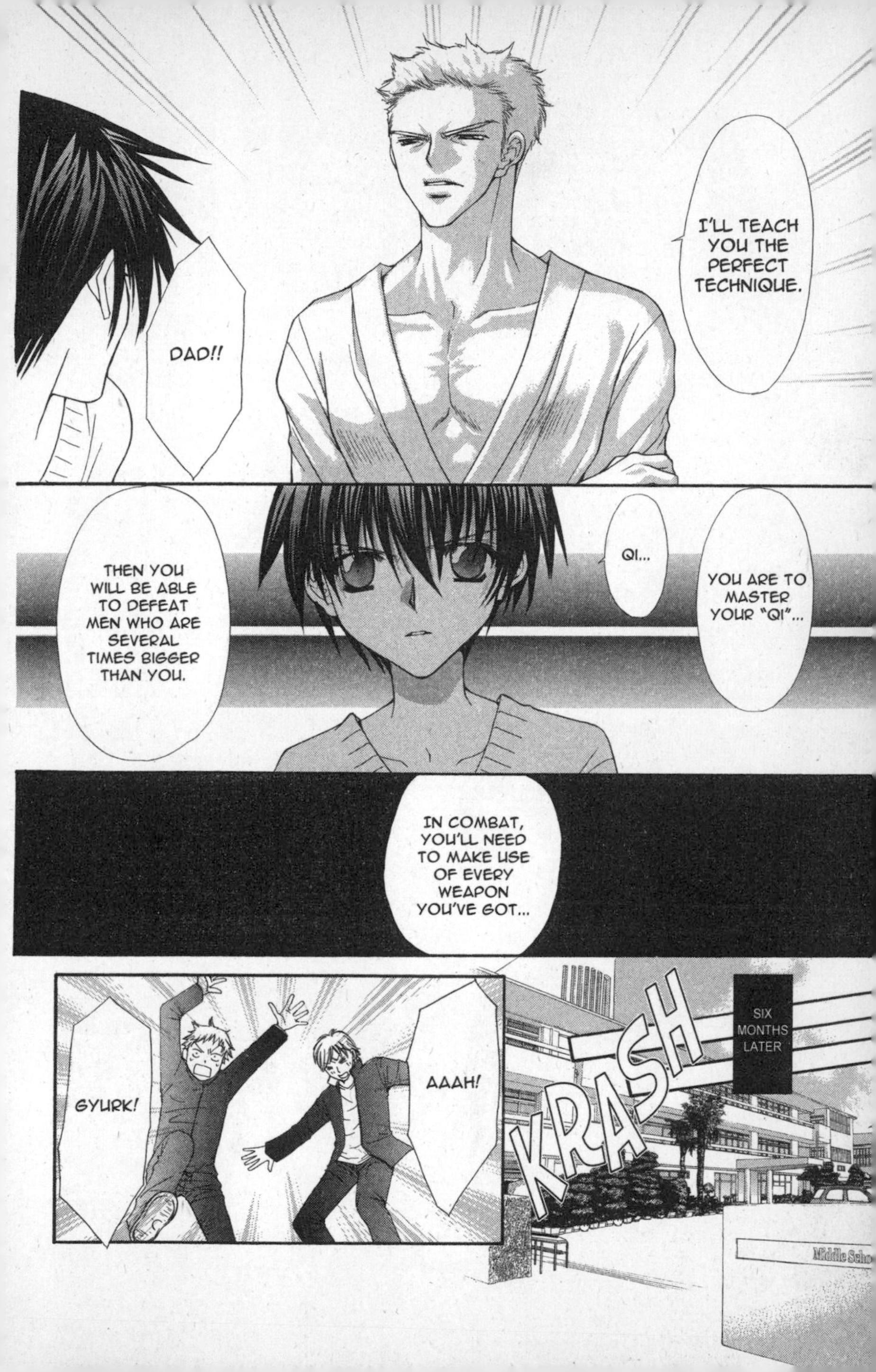
I'LL TEACH YOU THE PERFECT TECHNIQUE.
DAD!!
YOU ARE TO MASTER YOUR "QI"...
QI...
THEN YOU WILL BE ABLE TO DEFEAT MEN WHO ARE SEVERAL TIMES BIGGER THAN YOU.
IN COMBAT, YOU'LL NEED TO MAKE USE OF EVERY WEAPON YOU'VE GOT...
SIX MONTHS LATER
KRASH
Middle Scho
AAAH!
GYURK!

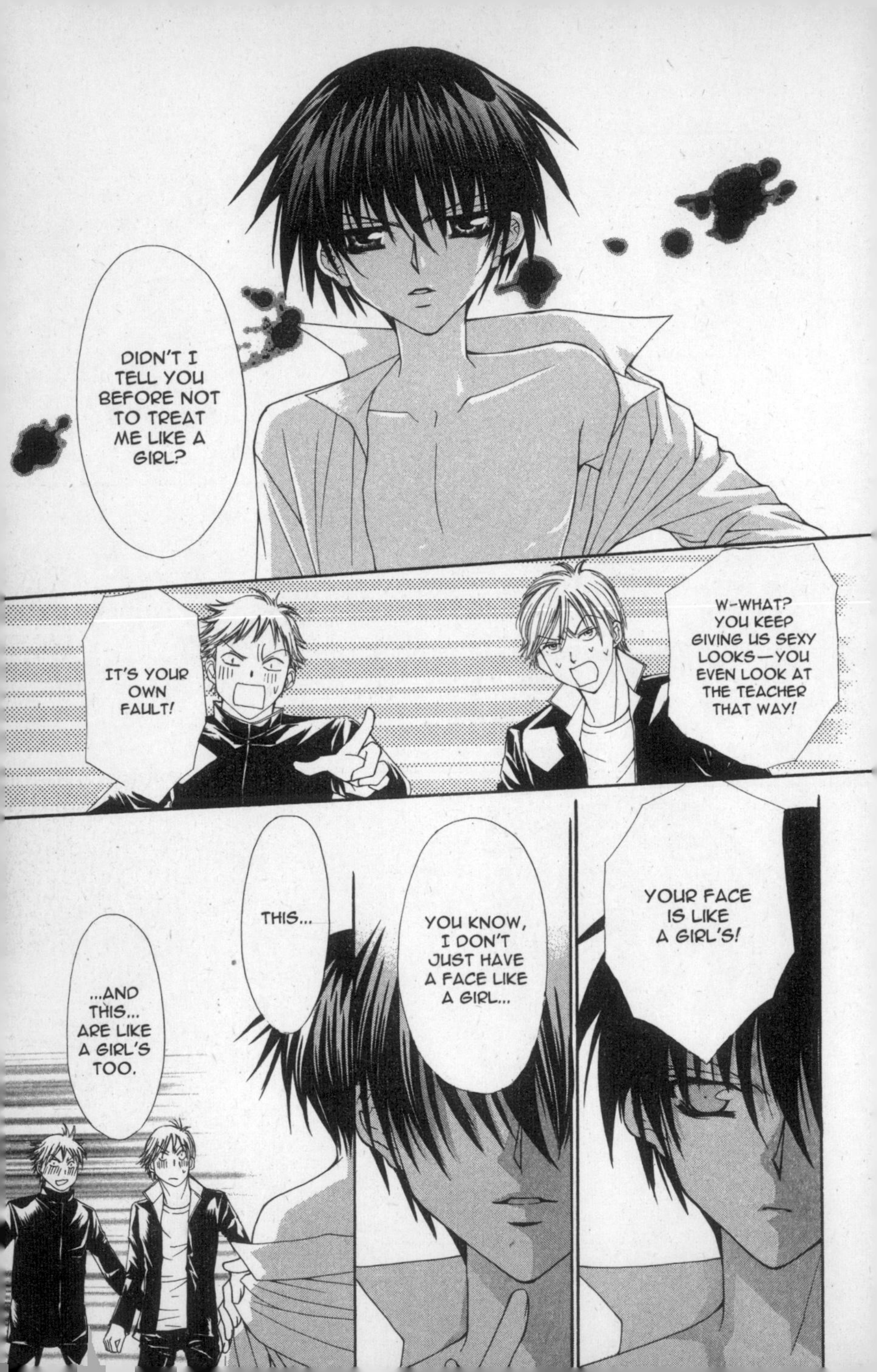
DIDN'T I TELL YOU BEFORE NOT TO TREAT ME LIKE A GIRL?
W-WHAT? YOU KEEP GIVING US SEXY LOOKS—YOU EVEN LOOK AT THE TEACHER THAT WAY!
IT'S YOUR OWN FAULT!
YOUR FACE IS LIKE A GIRL'S!
YOU KNOW, I DON'T JUST HAVE A FACE LIKE A GIRL...
THIS...
...AND THIS... ARE LIKE A GIRL'S TOO.

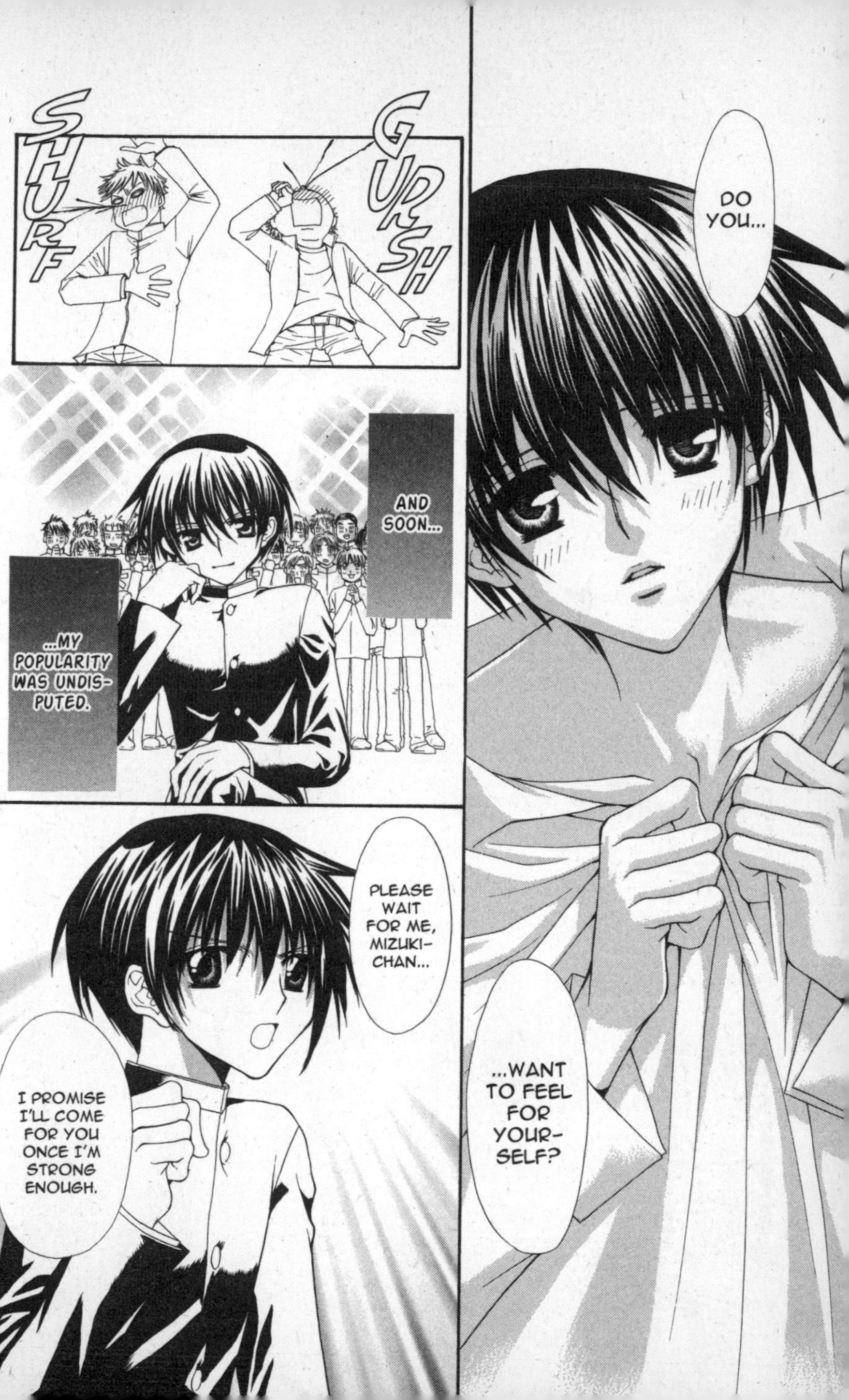
DO YOU...
...WANT TO FEEL FOR YOURSELF?
SHURF
GURSH
AND SOON...
...MY POPULARITY WAS UNDISPUTED.
PLEASE WAIT FOR ME, MIZUKI-CHAN...
I PROMISE I'LL COME FOR YOU ONCE I'M STRONG ENOUGH.

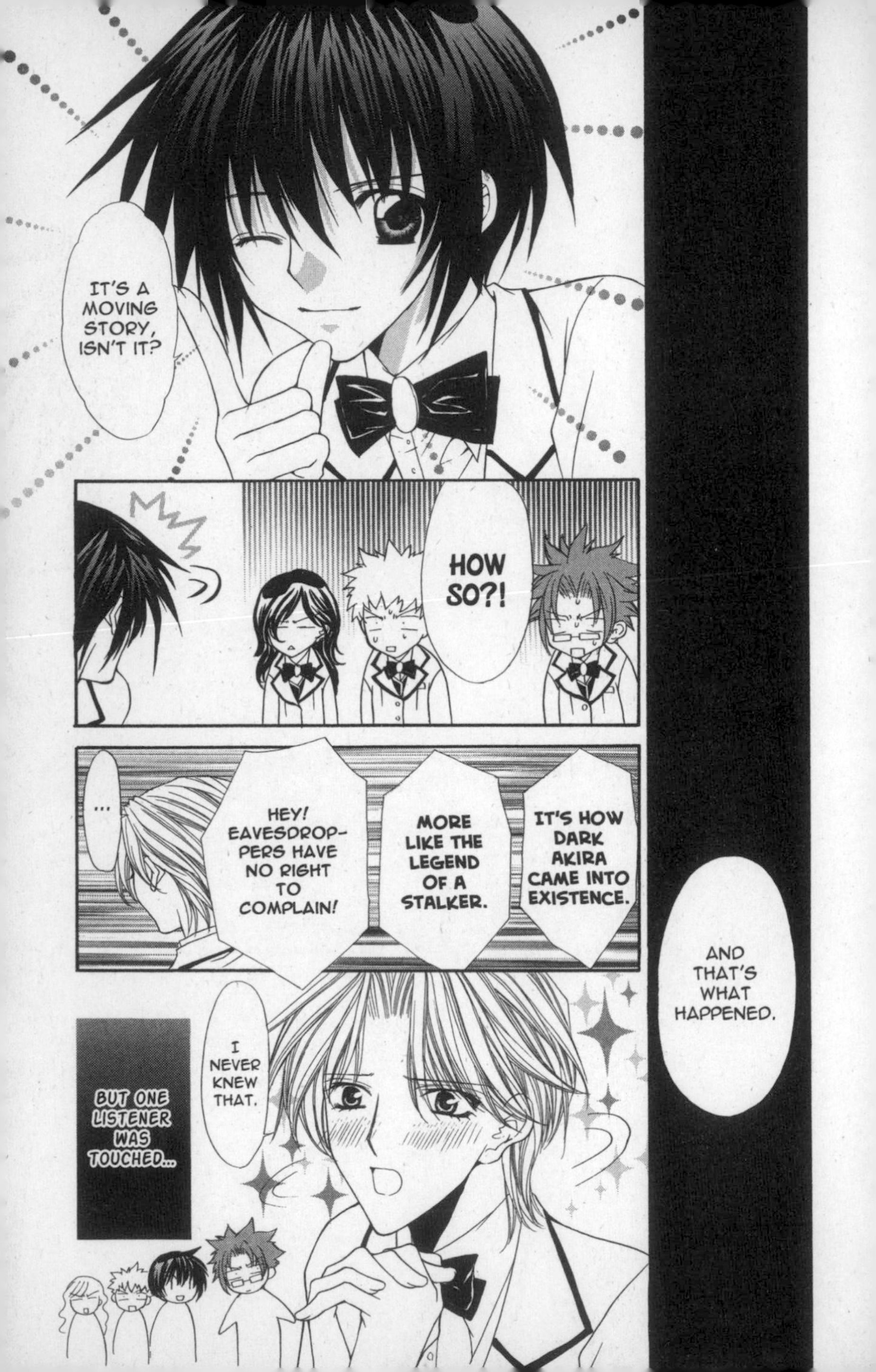
AND THAT'S WHAT HAPPENED.
IT'S A MOVING STORY, ISN'T IT?
HOW SO?!
IT'S HOW DARK AKIRA CAME INTO EXISTENCE.
MORE LIKE THE LEGEND OF A STALKER.
HEY! EAVESDROP-PERS HAVE NO RIGHT TO COMPLAIN!
...
I NEVER KNEW THAT.
BUT ONE LISTENER WAS TOUCHED...

BUT I LOVE YOU! I'M NOT INTERESTED IN OTHER MEN.
YOU MUSTN'T FALL IN LOVE WITH ME...
I'M SURE THERE'S A MUCH BETTER GUY FOR YOU OUT THERE.

Ai Ore! Talk

How did you like the second drama CD? I could feel how much the staff members loved *Ai Ore!* when we were creating the drama CD. I held a little party with the production crew the other day to celebrate the completion of the second CD, but we all ended up talking about what to do for the third. I came up with a very extreme extra track to include, and the storywriter took notes. (laugh) If a third CD is to come out, I can promise you that it will be even more over-the-top than the second. I hope we can make it... (laugh)

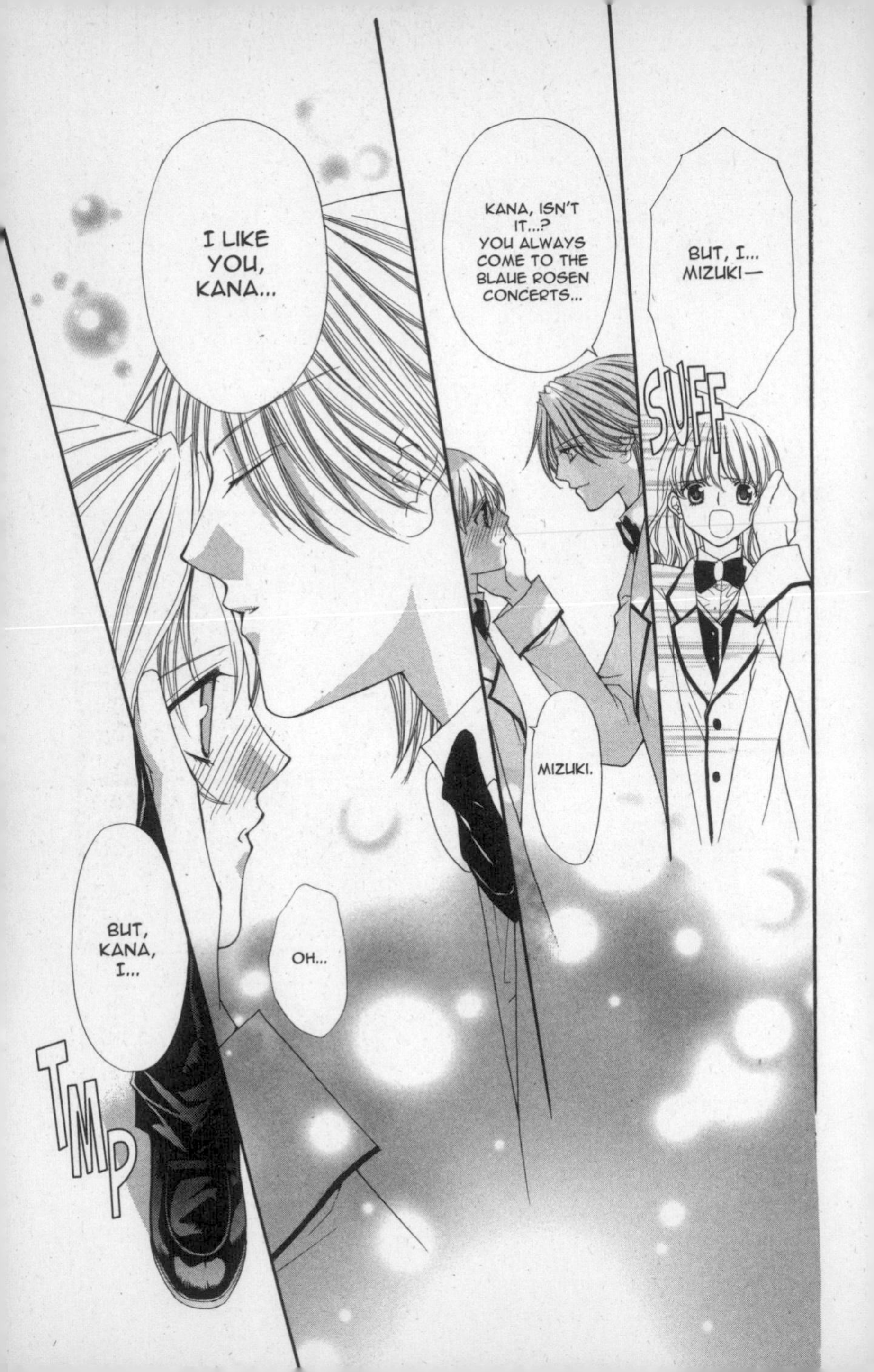
BUT, I... MIZUKI—
SUFF
KANA, ISN'T IT...? YOU ALWAYS COME TO THE BLAUE ROSEN CONCERTS...
MIZUKI.
I LIKE YOU, KANA...
OH...
BUT, KANA, I...
TMP

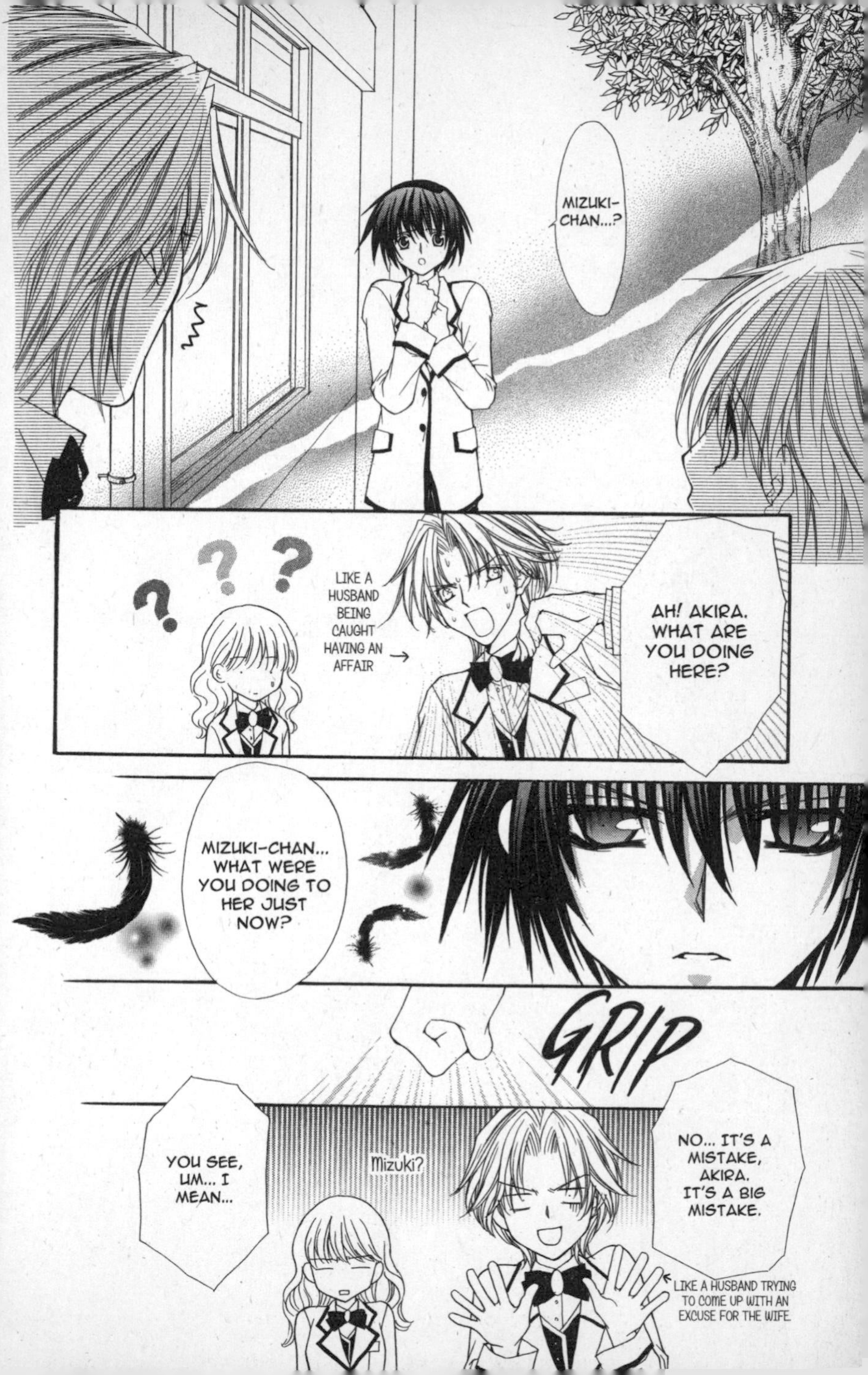
MIZUKI-CHAN...?
AH! AKIRA. WHAT ARE YOU DOING HERE?
LIKE A HUSBAND BEING CAUGHT HAVING AN AFFAIR
MIZUKI-CHAN... WHAT WERE YOU DOING TO HER JUST NOW?
GRIP
NO... IT'S A MISTAKE, AKIRA. IT'S A BIG MISTAKE.
LIKE A HUSBAND TRYING TO COME UP WITH AN EXCUSE FOR THE WIFE.
Mizuki?
YOU SEE, UM... I MEAN...

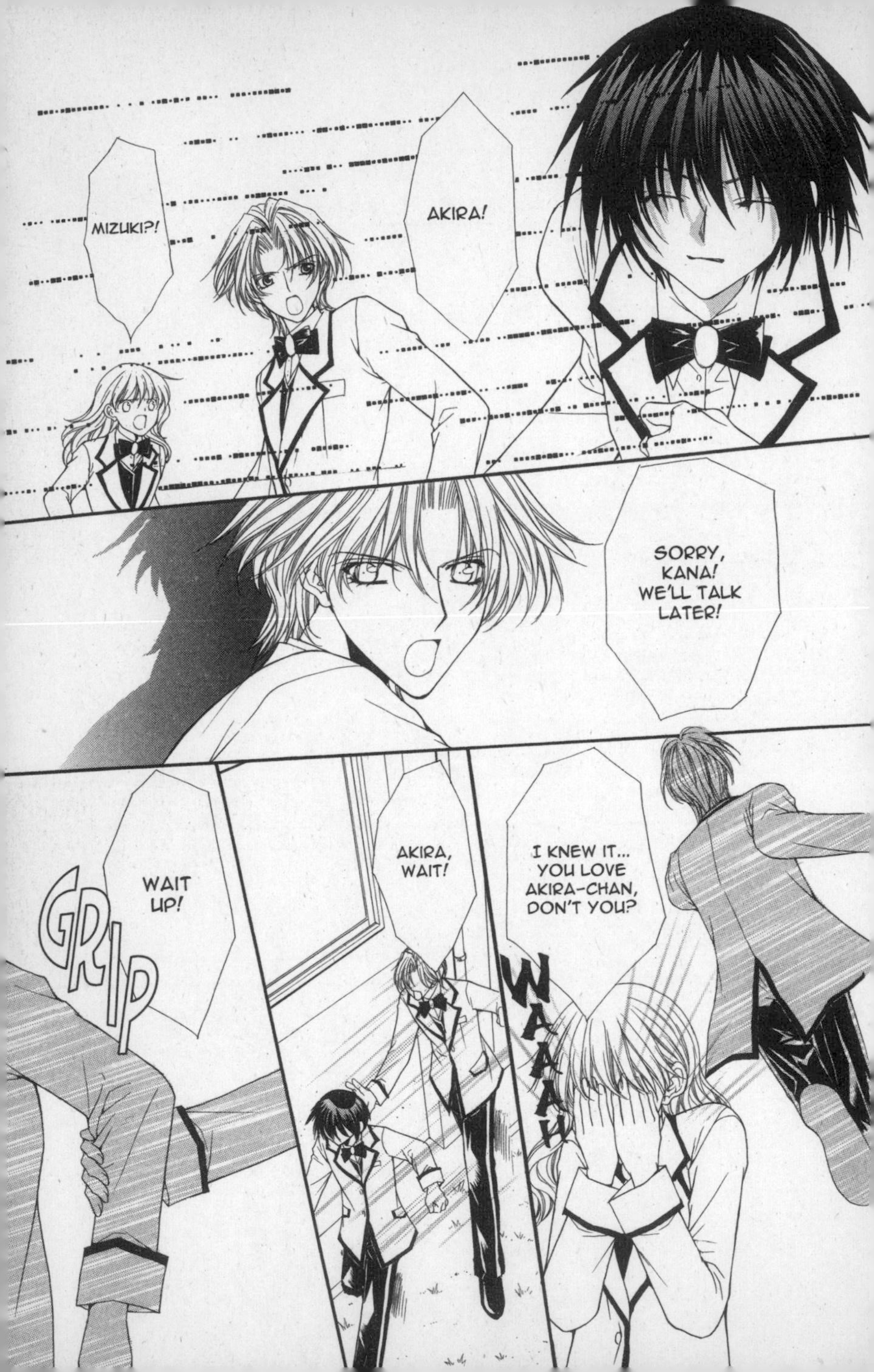
AKIRA!
MIZUKI?!
SORRY, KANA! WE'LL TALK LATER!
I KNEW IT... YOU LOVE AKIRA-CHAN, DON'T YOU?
WAAAAH
AKIRA, WAIT!
WAIT UP!
GRIP

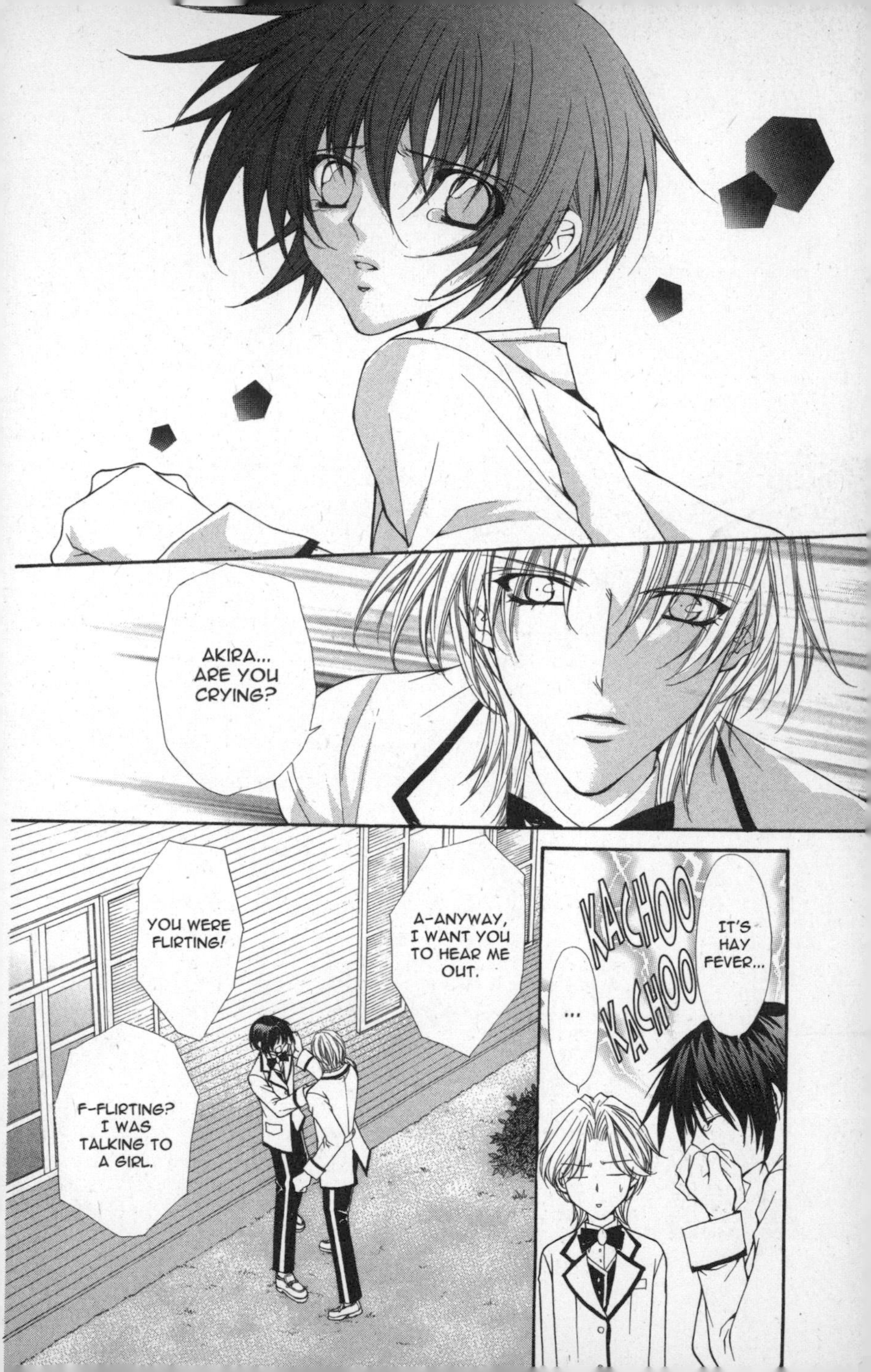
AKIRA... ARE YOU CRYING?
IT'S HAY FEVER...
KACHOO
KACHOO
...
A-ANYWAY, I WANT YOU TO HEAR ME OUT.
YOU WERE FLIRTING!
F-FLIRTING? I WAS TALKING TO A GIRL.

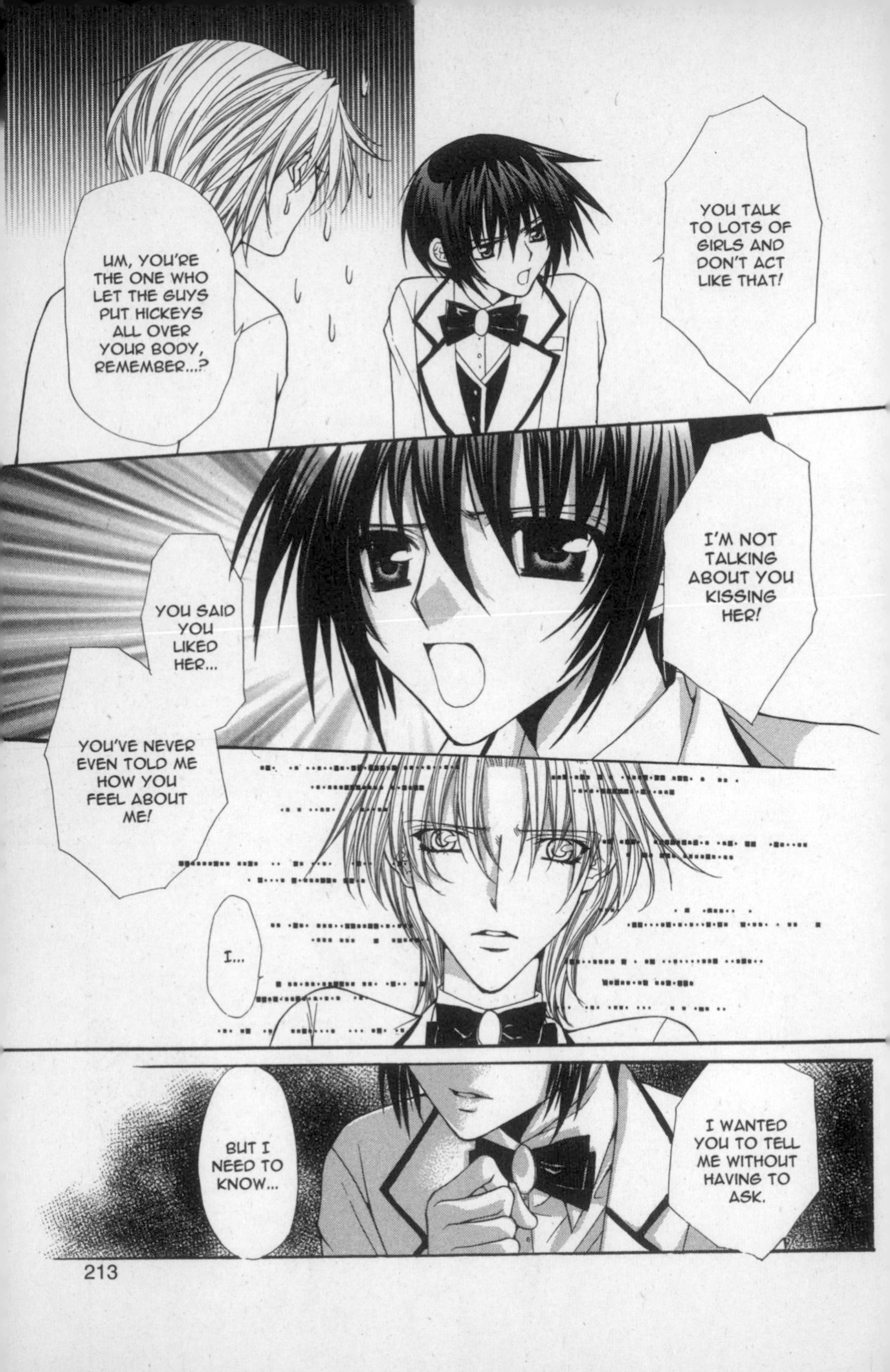
YOU TALK TO LOTS OF GIRLS AND DON'T ACT LIKE THAT!
UM, YOU'RE THE ONE WHO LET THE GUYS PUT HICKEYS ALL OVER YOUR BODY, REMEMBER...?
I'M NOT TALKING ABOUT YOU KISSING HER!
YOU SAID YOU LIKED HER...
YOU'VE NEVER EVEN TOLD ME HOW YOU FEEL ABOUT ME!
I...
I WANTED YOU TO TELL ME WITHOUT HAVING TO ASK.
BUT I NEED TO KNOW...

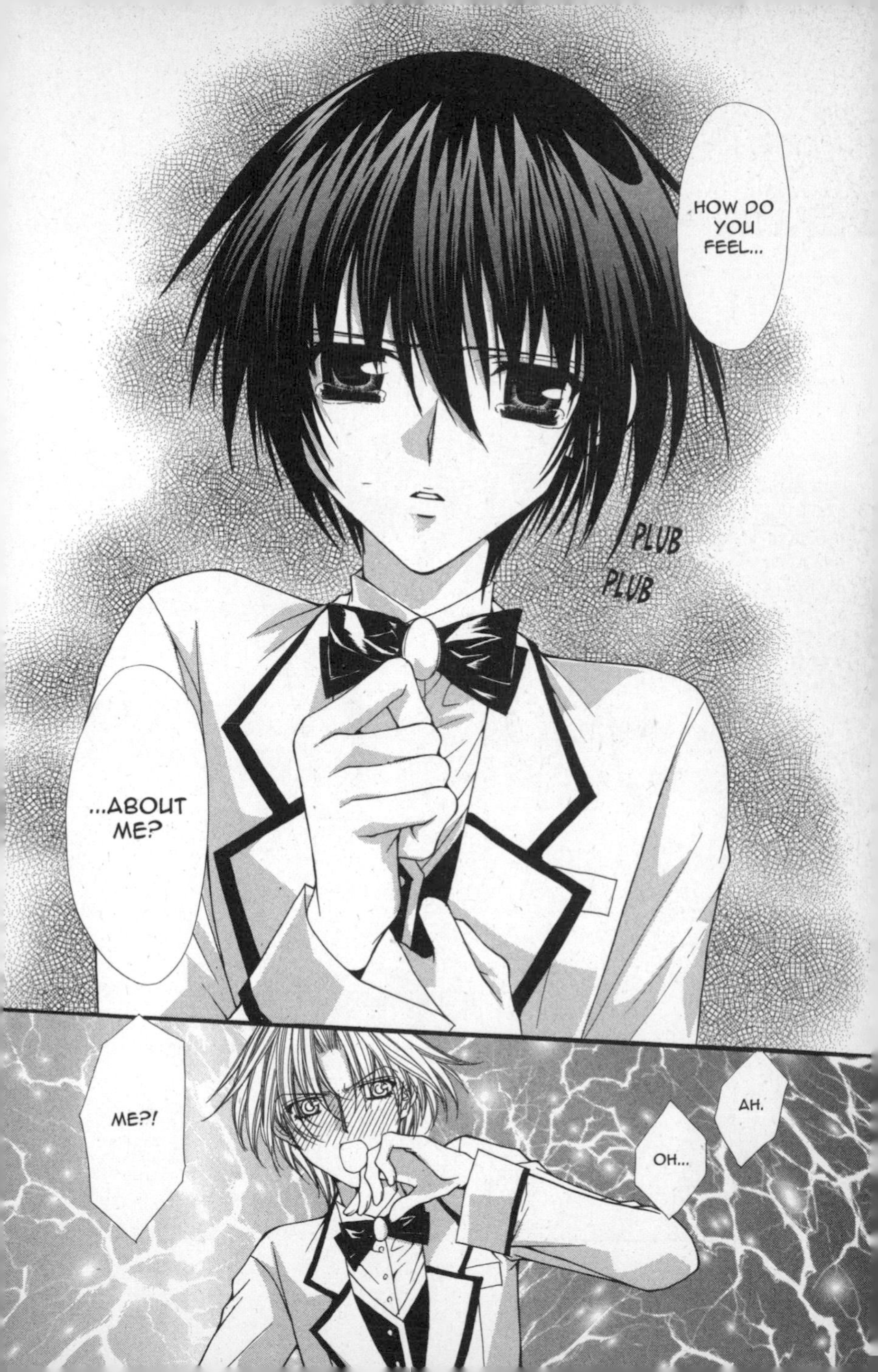

HOW DO YOU FEEL...
PLUB
PLUB
...ABOUT ME?
AH.
OH...
ME?!

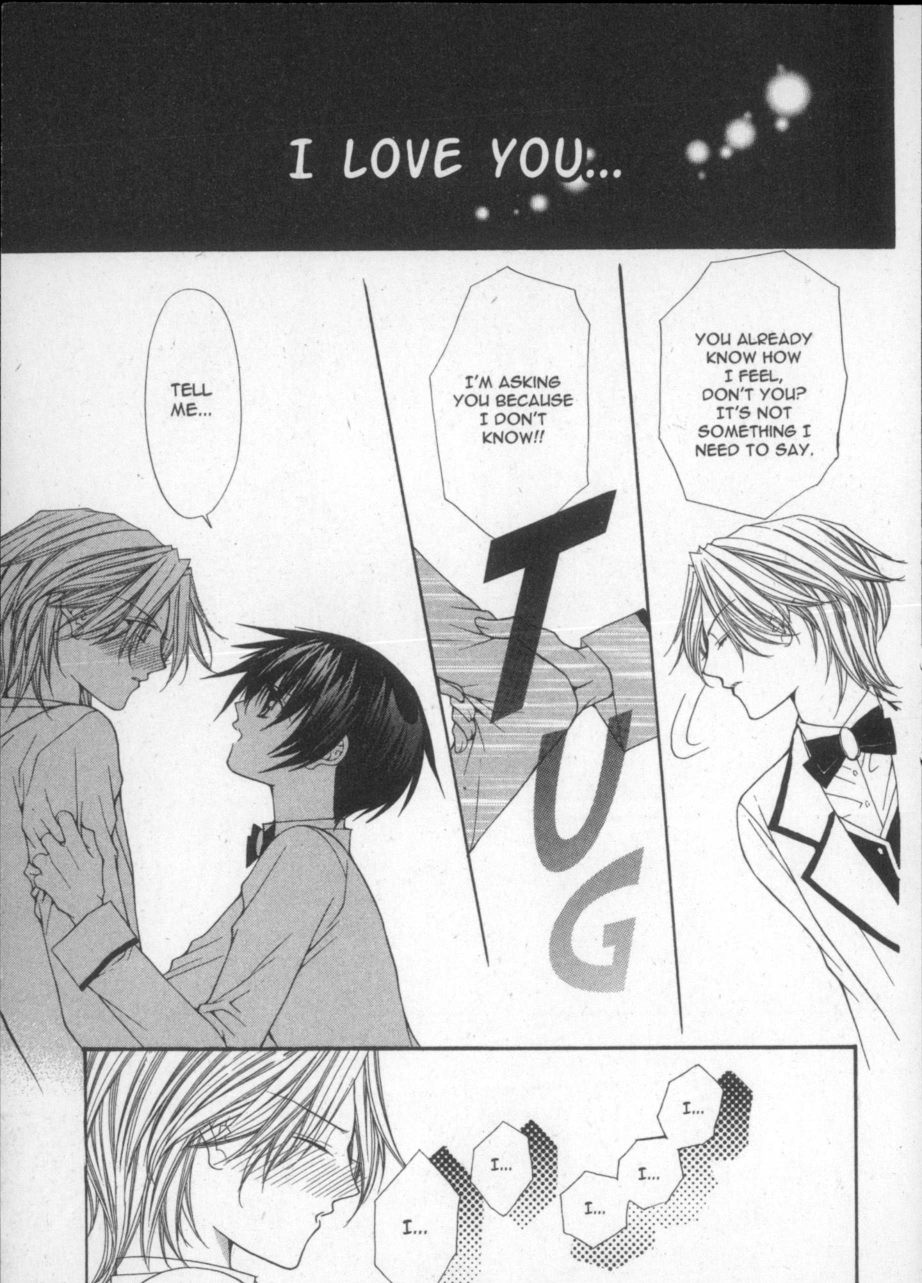
I LOVE YOU...
YOU ALREADY KNOW HOW I FEEL, DON'T YOU? IT'S NOT SOMETHING I NEED TO SAY.
I'M ASKING YOU BECAUSE I DON'T KNOW!!
TUG
TELL ME...
I...
I...
I...
I...
I...

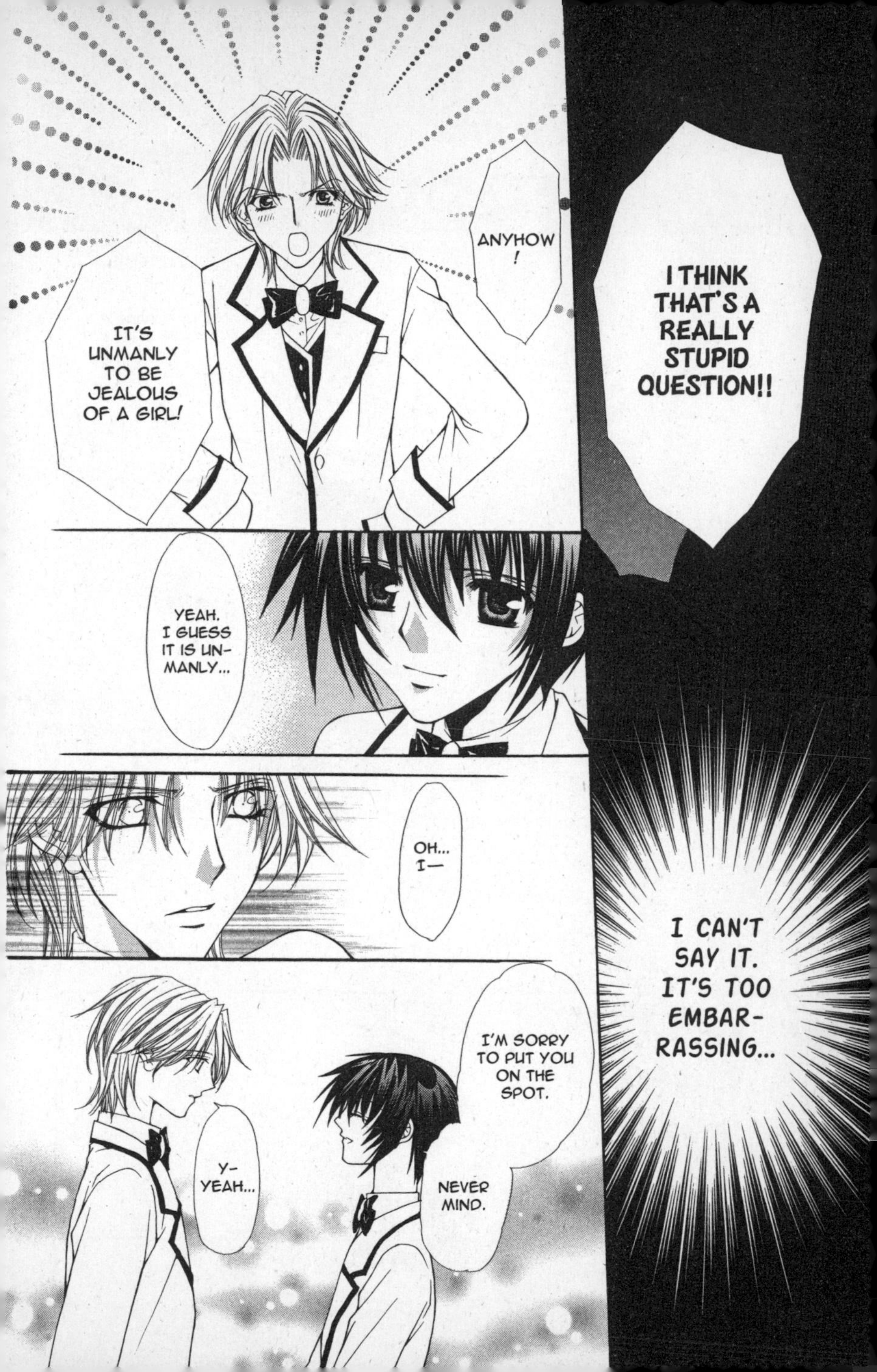
I THINK THAT'S A REALLY STUPID QUESTION!!
ANYHOW!
IT'S UNMANLY TO BE JEALOUS OF A GIRL!
YEAH. I GUESS IT IS UN-MANLY...
I CAN'T SAY IT. IT'S TOO EMBAR-RASSING...
OH... I—
I'M SORRY TO PUT YOU ON THE SPOT.
NEVER MIND.
Y-YEAH...

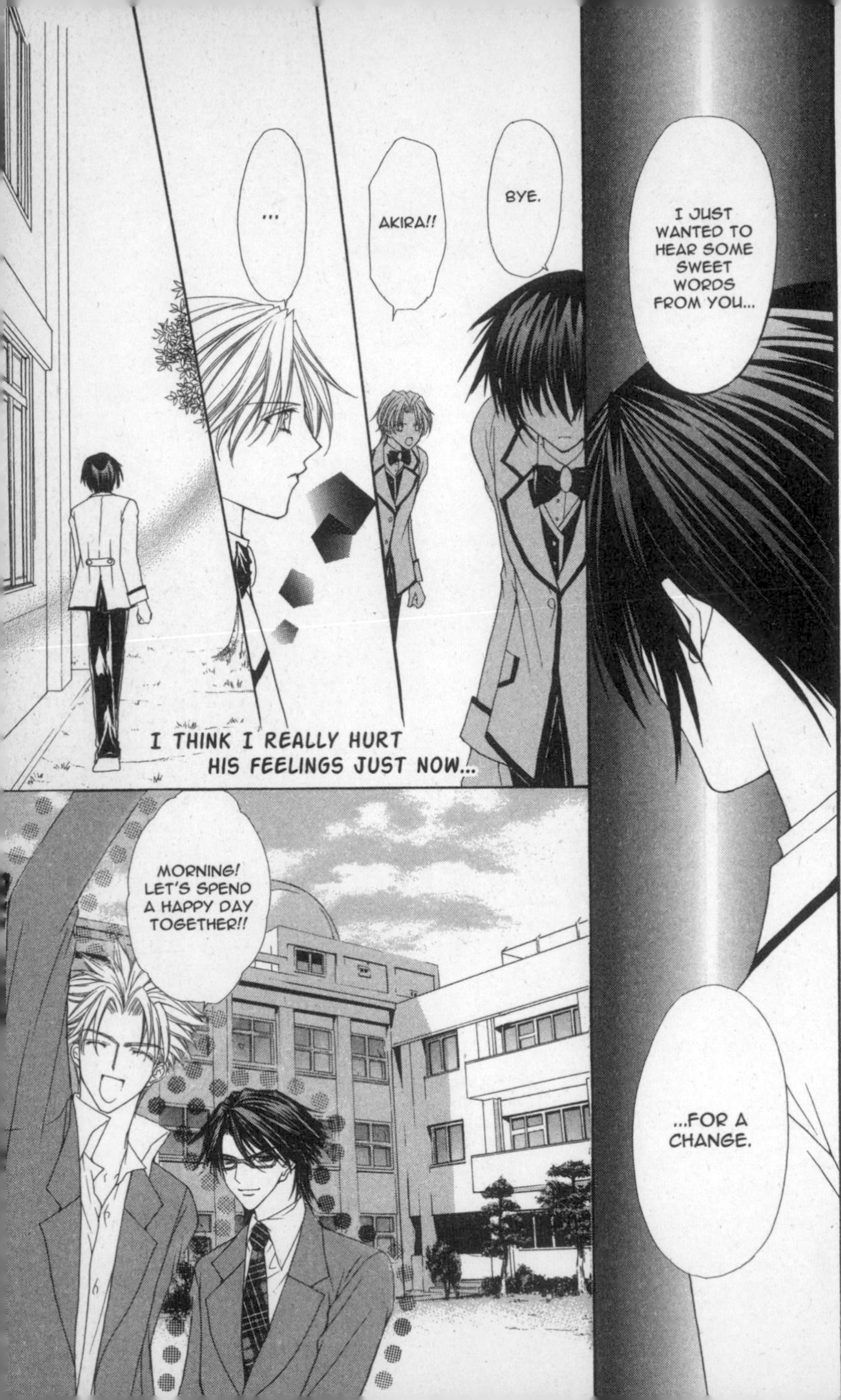
I JUST WANTED TO HEAR SOME SWEET WORDS FROM YOU...
...FOR A CHANGE.
BYE.
AKIRA!!
...
I THINK I REALLY HURT HIS FEELINGS JUST NOW...
MORNING! LET'S SPEND A HAPPY DAY TOGETHER!!

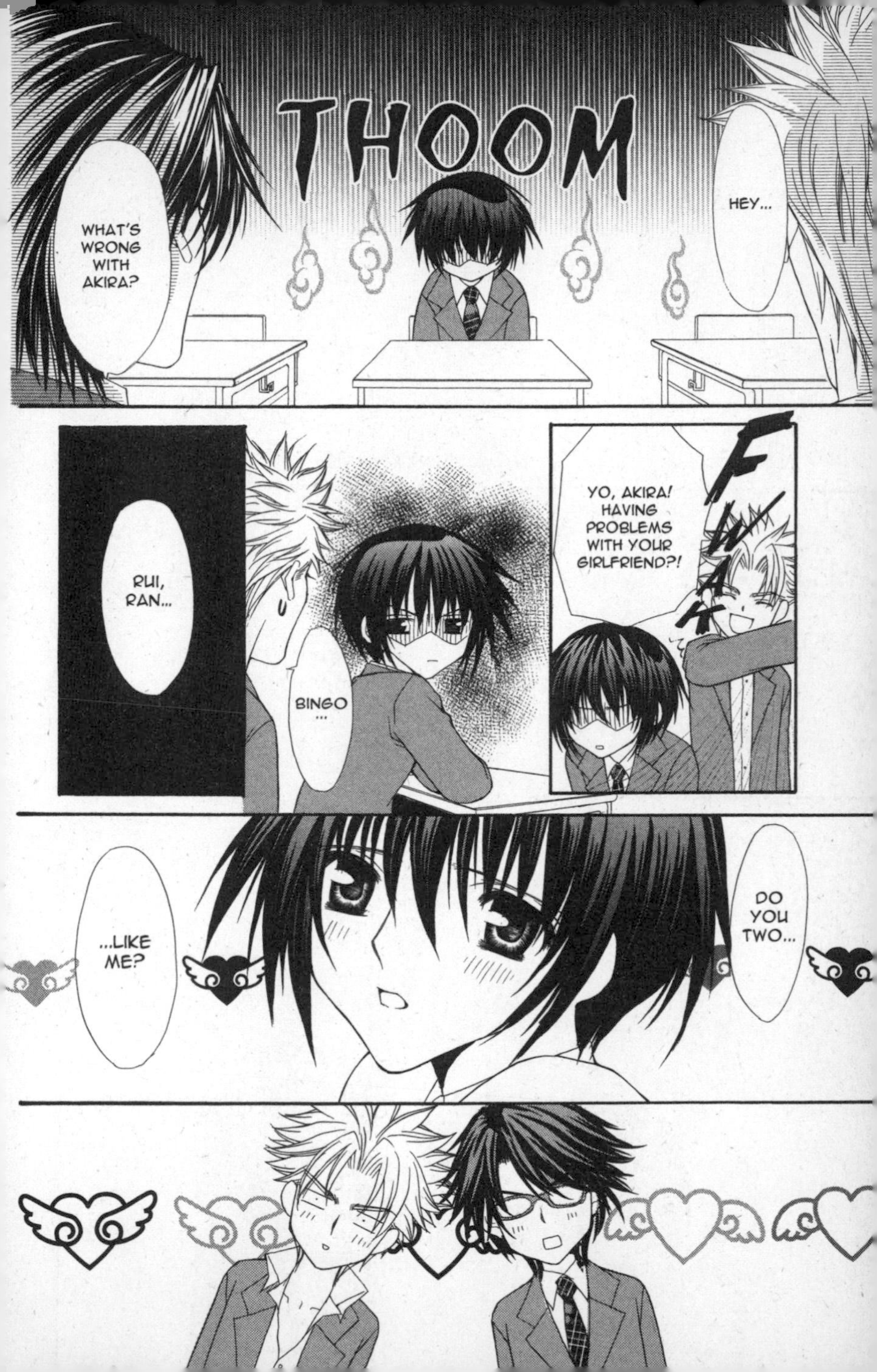
THOOM
HEY...
WHAT'S WRONG WITH AKIRA?
FWAK
YO, AKIRA! HAVING PROBLEMS WITH YOUR GIRLFRIEND?!
BINGO...
RUI, RAN...
DO YOU TWO...
...LIKE ME?

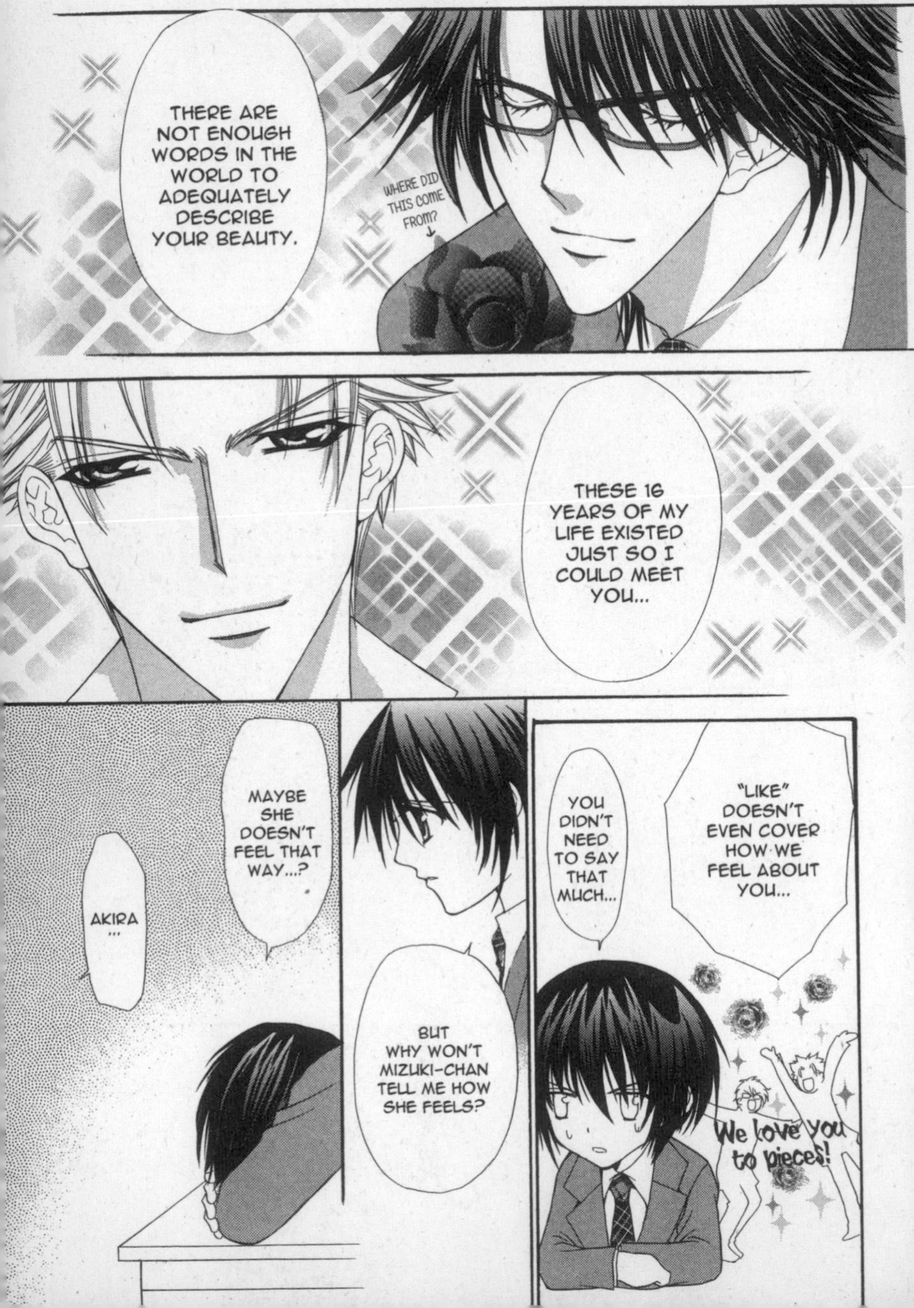
THERE ARE NOT ENOUGH WORDS IN THE WORLD TO ADEQUATELY DESCRIBE YOUR BEAUTY.
WHERE DID THIS COME FROM?
THESE 16 YEARS OF MY LIFE EXISTED JUST SO I COULD MEET YOU...
"LIKE" DOESN'T EVEN COVER HOW WE FEEL ABOUT YOU...
YOU DIDN'T NEED TO SAY THAT MUCH...
We love you to pieces!
BUT WHY WON'T MIZUKI-CHAN TELL ME HOW SHE FEELS?
MAYBE SHE DOESN'T FEEL THAT WAY...?
AKIRA ...

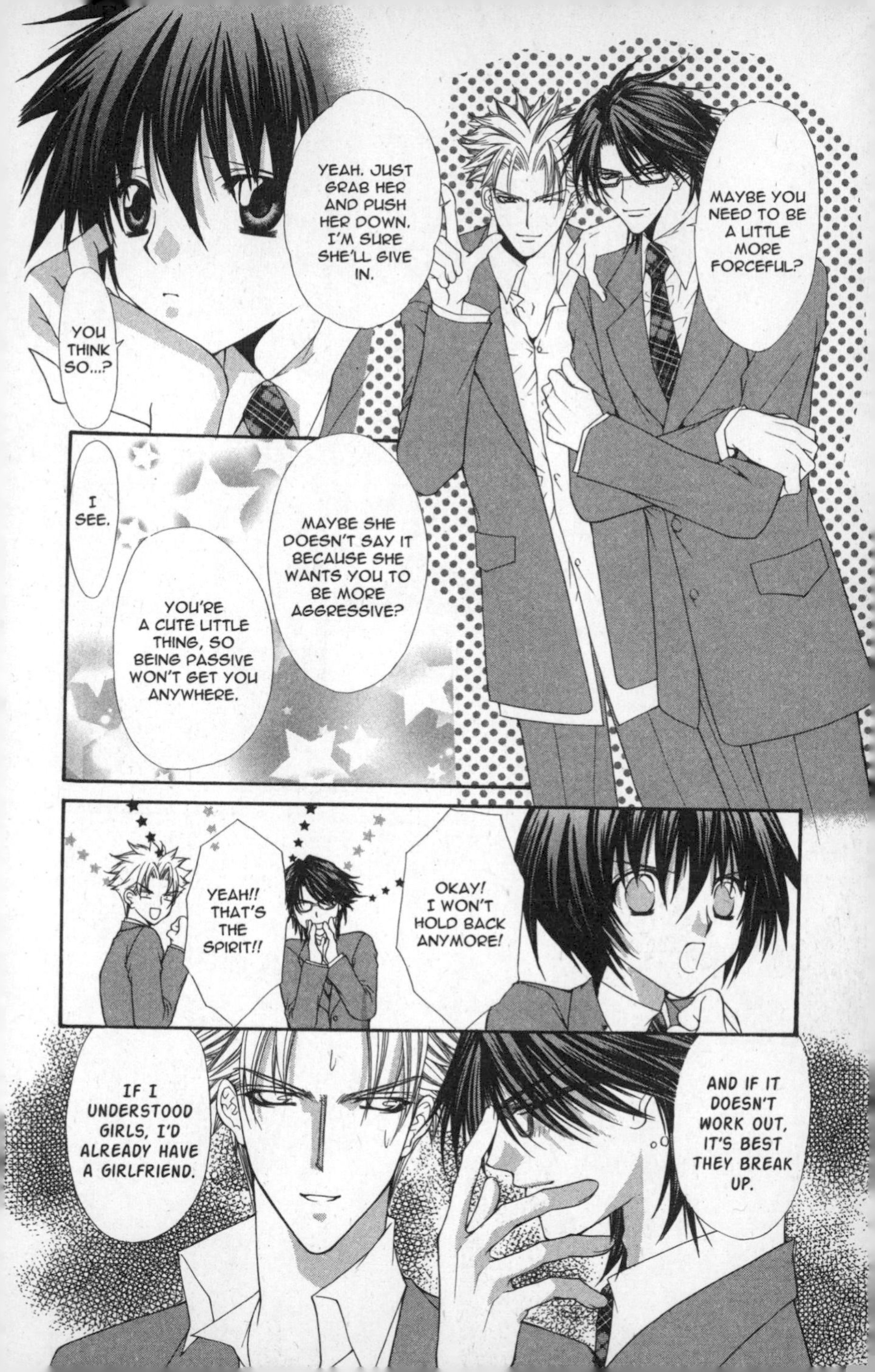
MAYBE YOU NEED TO BE A LITTLE MORE FORCEFUL?
YEAH. JUST GRAB HER AND PUSH HER DOWN. I'M SURE SHE'LL GIVE IN.
YOU THINK SO...?
MAYBE SHE DOESN'T SAY IT BECAUSE SHE WANTS YOU TO BE MORE AGGRESSIVE?
YOU'RE A CUTE LITTLE THING, SO BEING PASSIVE WON'T GET YOU ANYWHERE.
I SEE.
OKAY! I WON'T HOLD BACK ANYMORE!
YEAH!! THAT'S THE SPIRIT!!
AND IF IT DOESN'T WORK OUT, IT'S BEST THEY BREAK UP.
IF I UNDERSTOOD GIRLS, I'D ALREADY HAVE A GIRLFRIEND.

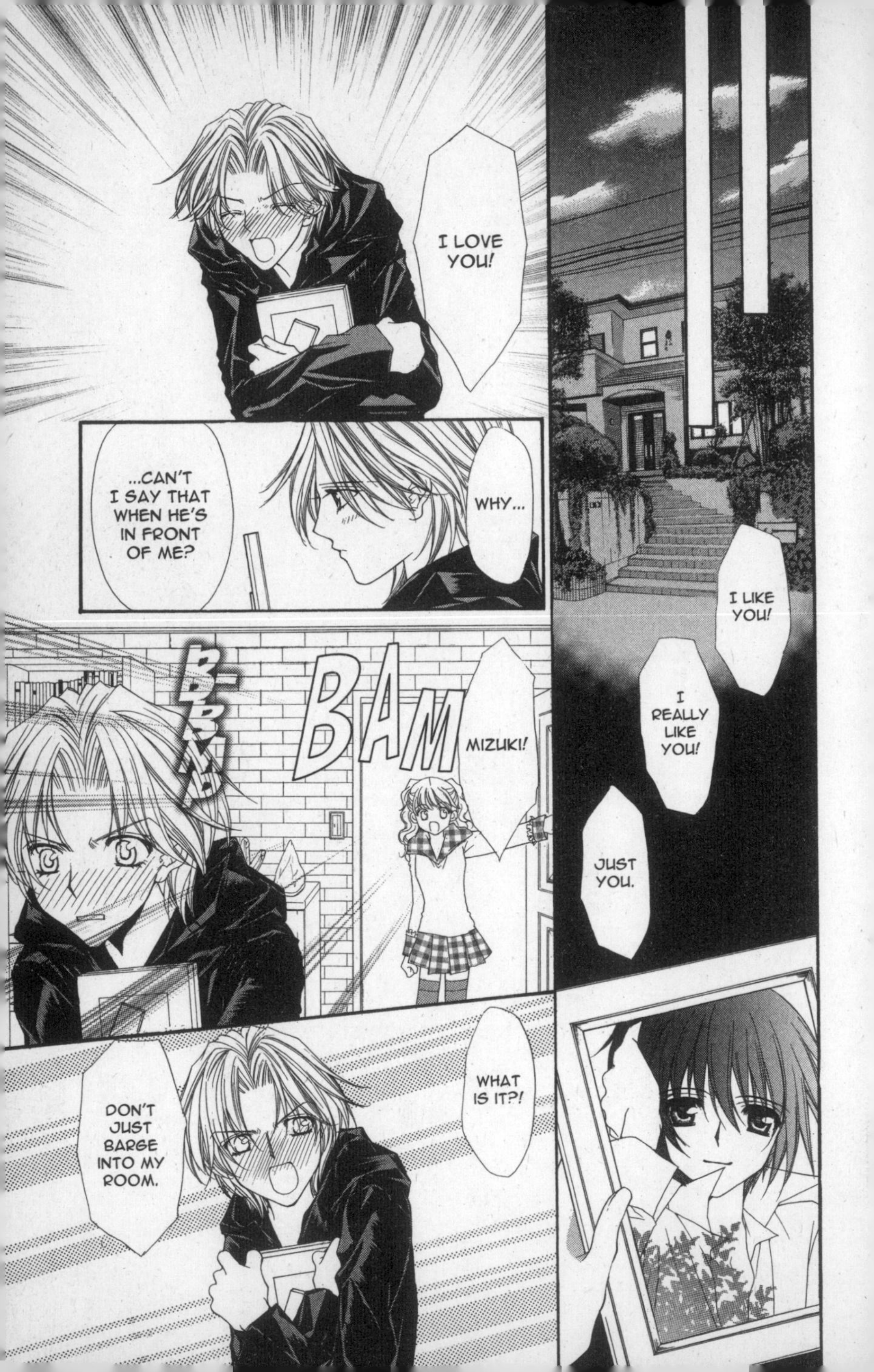
I LIKE YOU!
I REALLY LIKE YOU!
JUST YOU.
I LOVE YOU!
WHY...
...CAN'T I SAY THAT WHEN HE'S IN FRONT OF ME?
BAM
MIZUKI!
B-BAM
WHAT IS IT?!
DON'T JUST BARGE INTO MY ROOM.

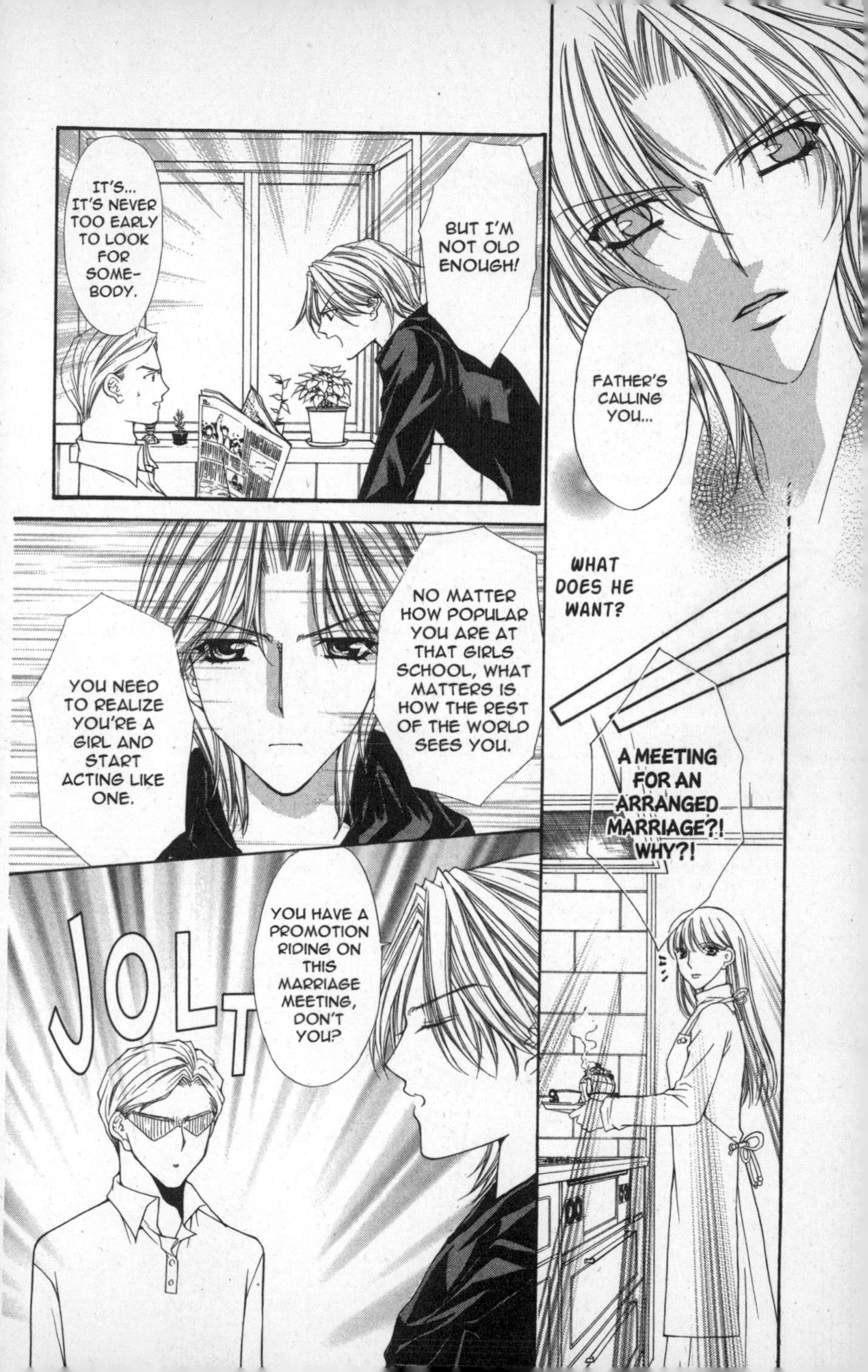
FATHER'S CALLING YOU...
WHAT DOES HE WANT?
A MEETING FOR AN ARRANGED MARRIAGE?! WHY?!
BUT I'M NOT OLD ENOUGH!
IT'S... IT'S NEVER TOO EARLY TO LOOK FOR SOMEBODY.
NO MATTER HOW POPULAR YOU ARE AT THAT GIRLS SCHOOL, WHAT MATTERS IS HOW THE REST OF THE WORLD SEES YOU.
YOU NEED TO REALIZE YOU'RE A GIRL AND START ACTING LIKE ONE.
YOU HAVE A PROMOTION RIDING ON THIS MARRIAGE MEETING, DON'T YOU?
JOLT

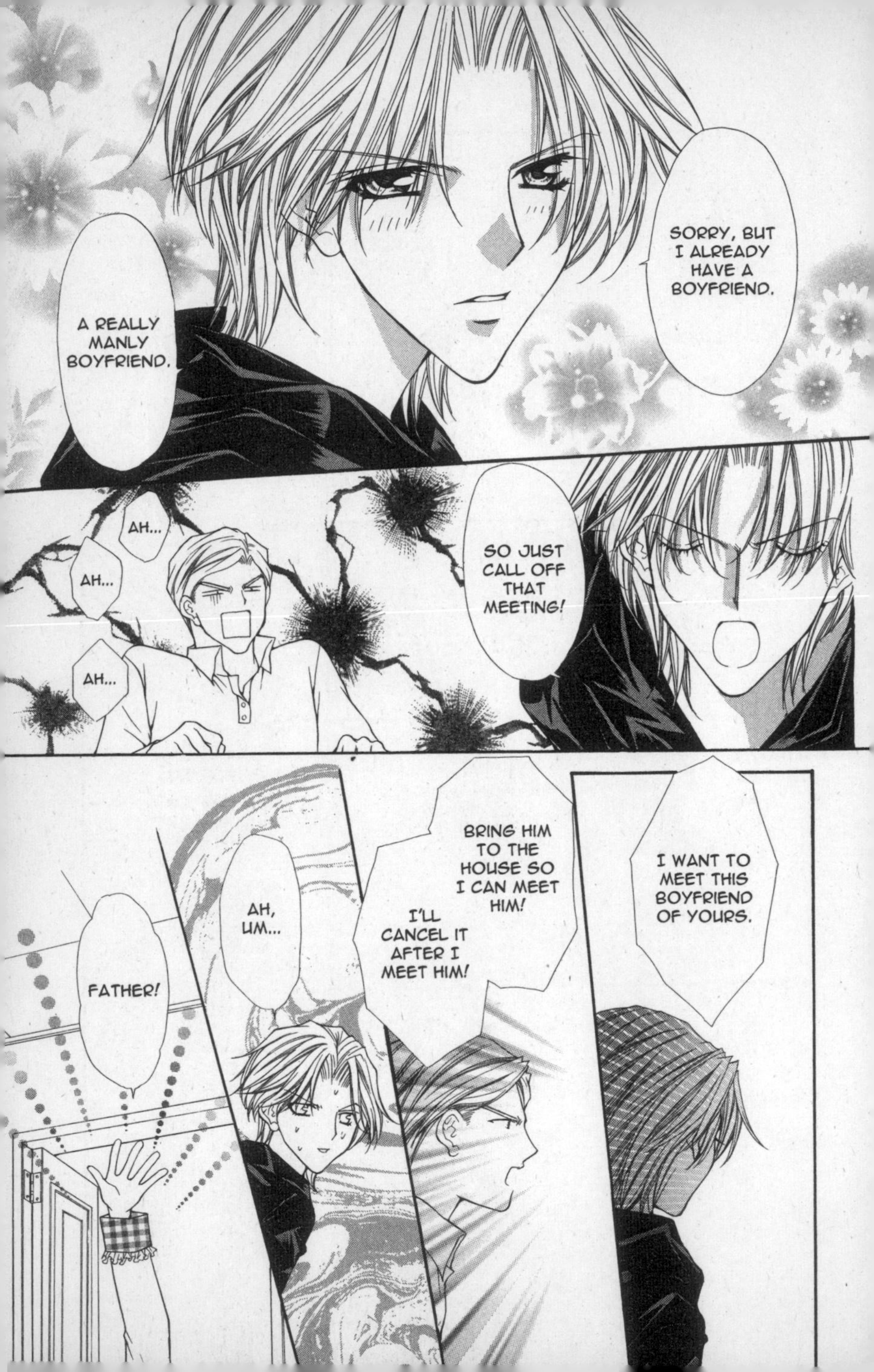
SORRY, BUT I ALREADY HAVE A BOYFRIEND.
A REALLY MANLY BOYFRIEND.
SO JUST CALL OFF THAT MEETING!
AH...
AH...
AH...
I WANT TO MEET THIS BOYFRIEND OF YOURS.
BRING HIM TO THE HOUSE SO I CAN MEET HIM!
I'LL CANCEL IT AFTER I MEET HIM!
AH, UM...
FATHER!

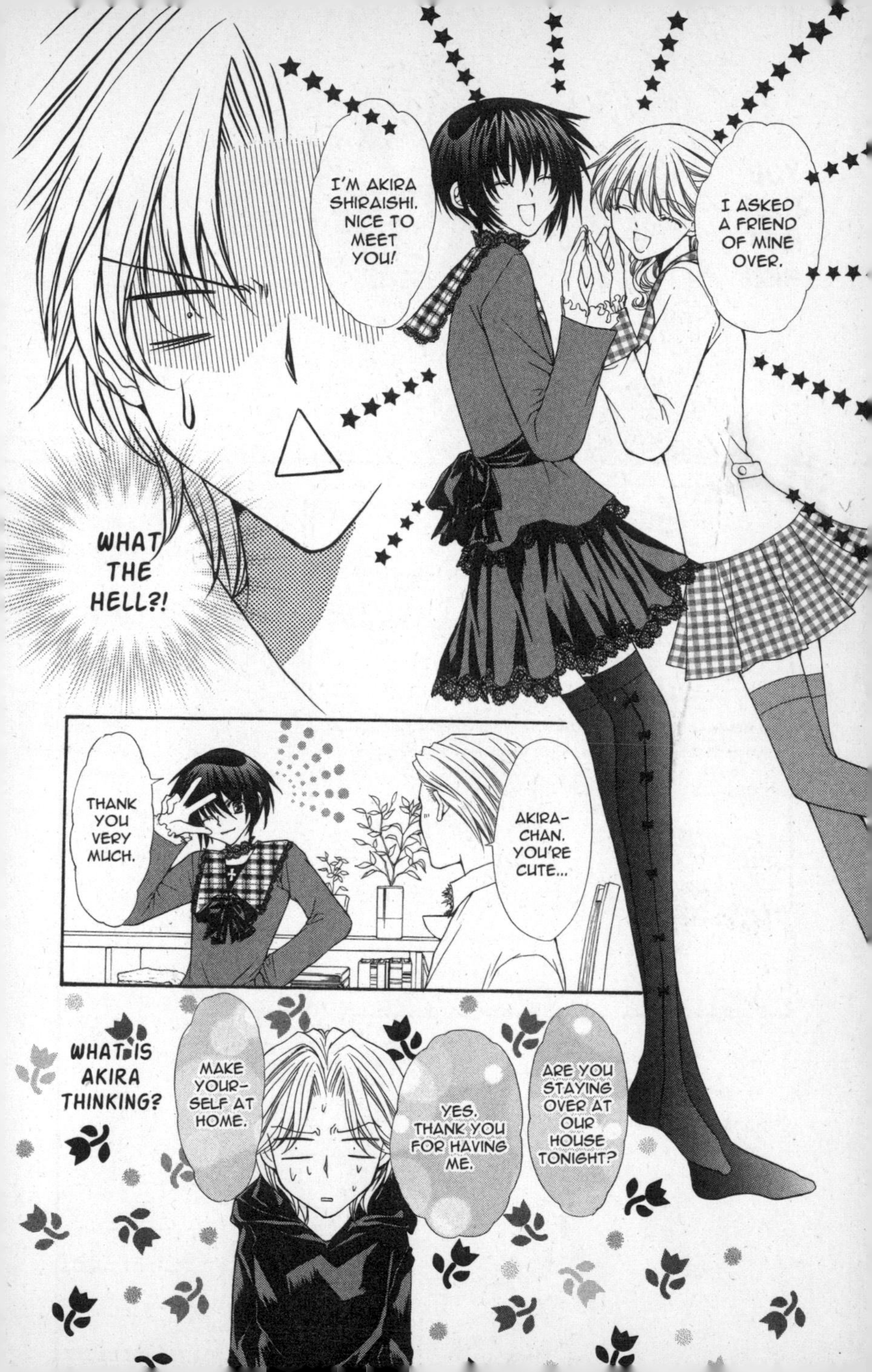
I ASKED A FRIEND OF MINE OVER.
I'M AKIRA SHIRAISHI. NICE TO MEET YOU!
WHAT THE HELL?!
AKIRA-CHAN. YOU'RE CUTE...
THANK YOU VERY MUCH.
ARE YOU STAYING OVER AT OUR HOUSE TONIGHT?
YES. THANK YOU FOR HAVING ME.
MAKE YOUR-SELF AT HOME.
WHAT IS AKIRA THINKING?

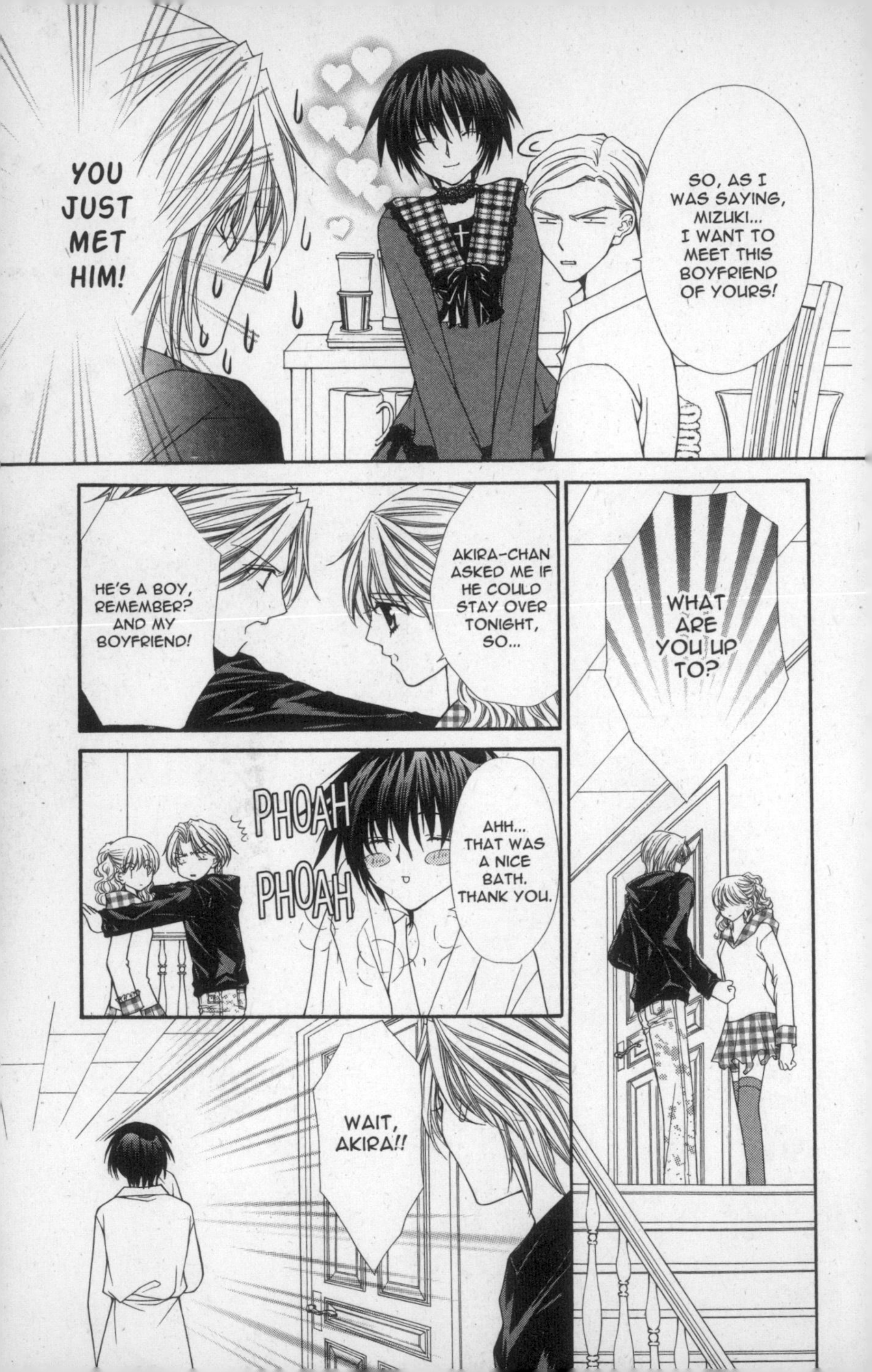
SO, AS I WAS SAYING, MIZUKI... I WANT TO MEET THIS BOYFRIEND OF YOURS!
YOU JUST MET HIM!
WHAT ARE YOU UP TO?
AKIRA-CHAN ASKED ME IF HE COULD STAY OVER TONIGHT, SO...
HE'S A BOY, REMEMBER? AND MY BOYFRIEND!
AHH... THAT WAS A NICE BATH. THANK YOU.
PHOAH
PHOAH
WAIT, AKIRA!!

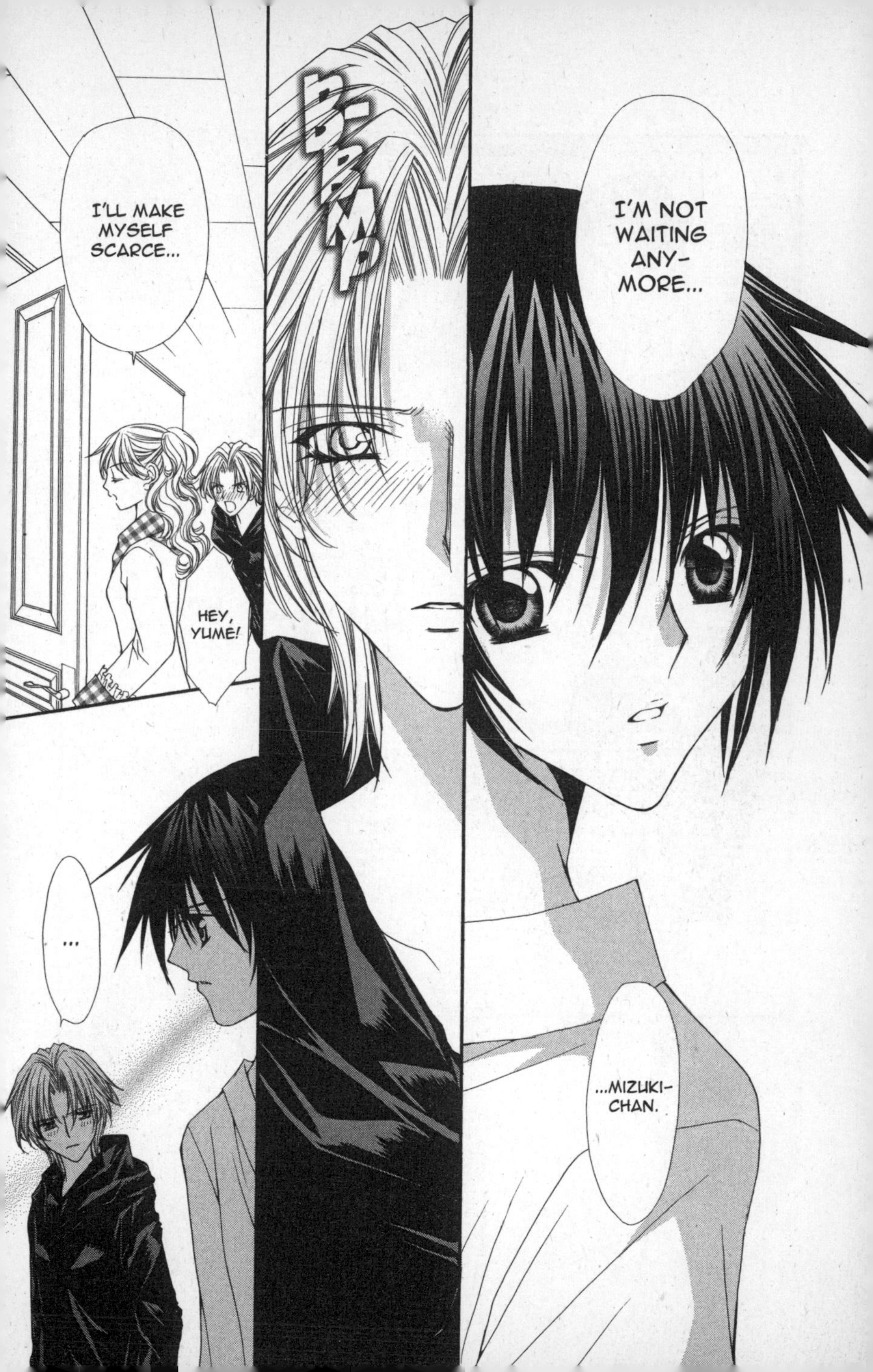
I'M NOT WAITING ANY-MORE...
...MIZUKI-CHAN.
B-BMP
I'LL MAKE MYSELF SCARCE...
HEY, YUME!
...

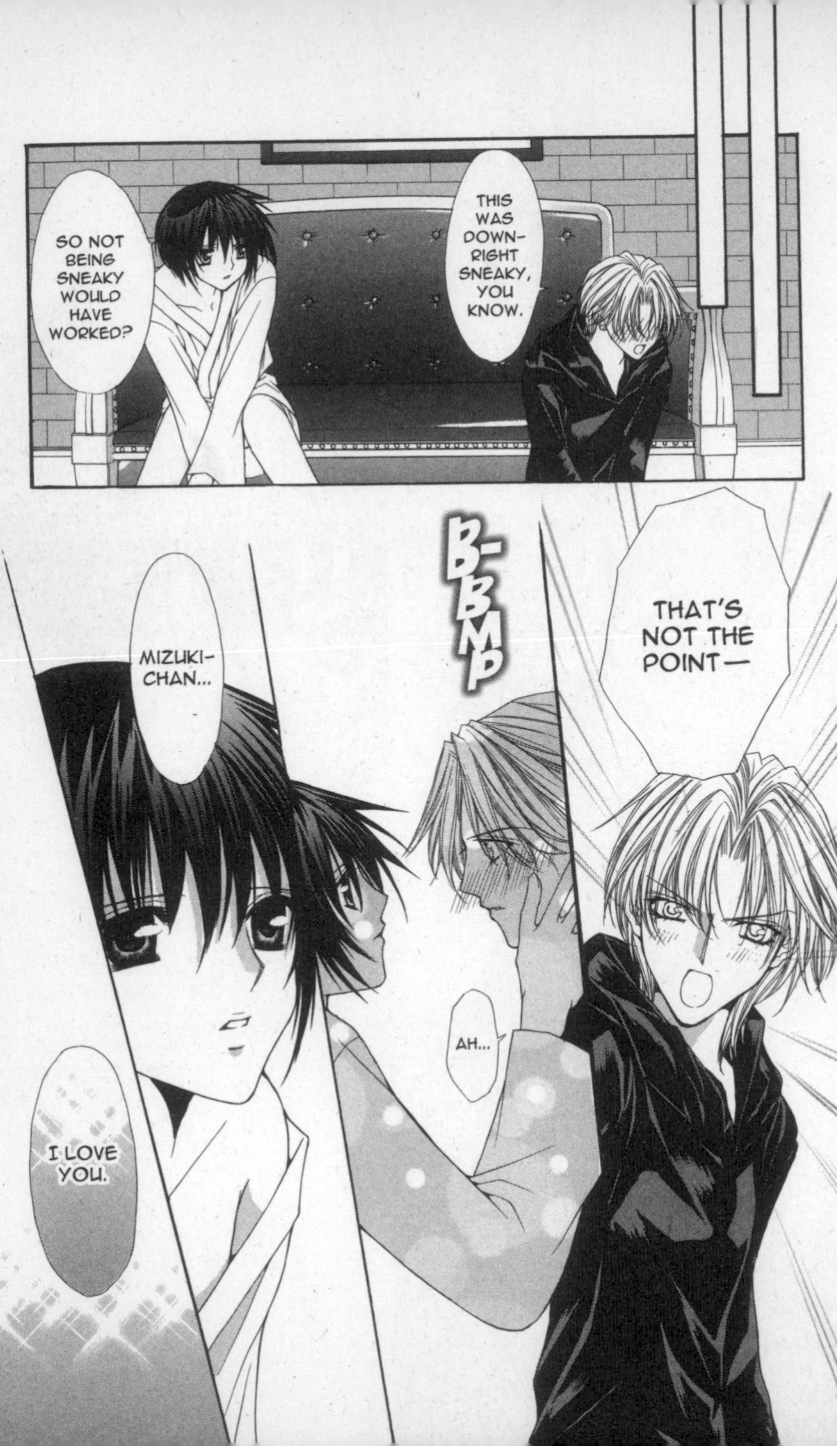
THIS WAS DOWN-RIGHT SNEAKY, YOU KNOW.
SO NOT BEING SNEAKY WOULD HAVE WORKED?
THAT'S NOT THE POINT—
B-BMP
AH...
MIZUKI-CHAN...
I LOVE YOU.

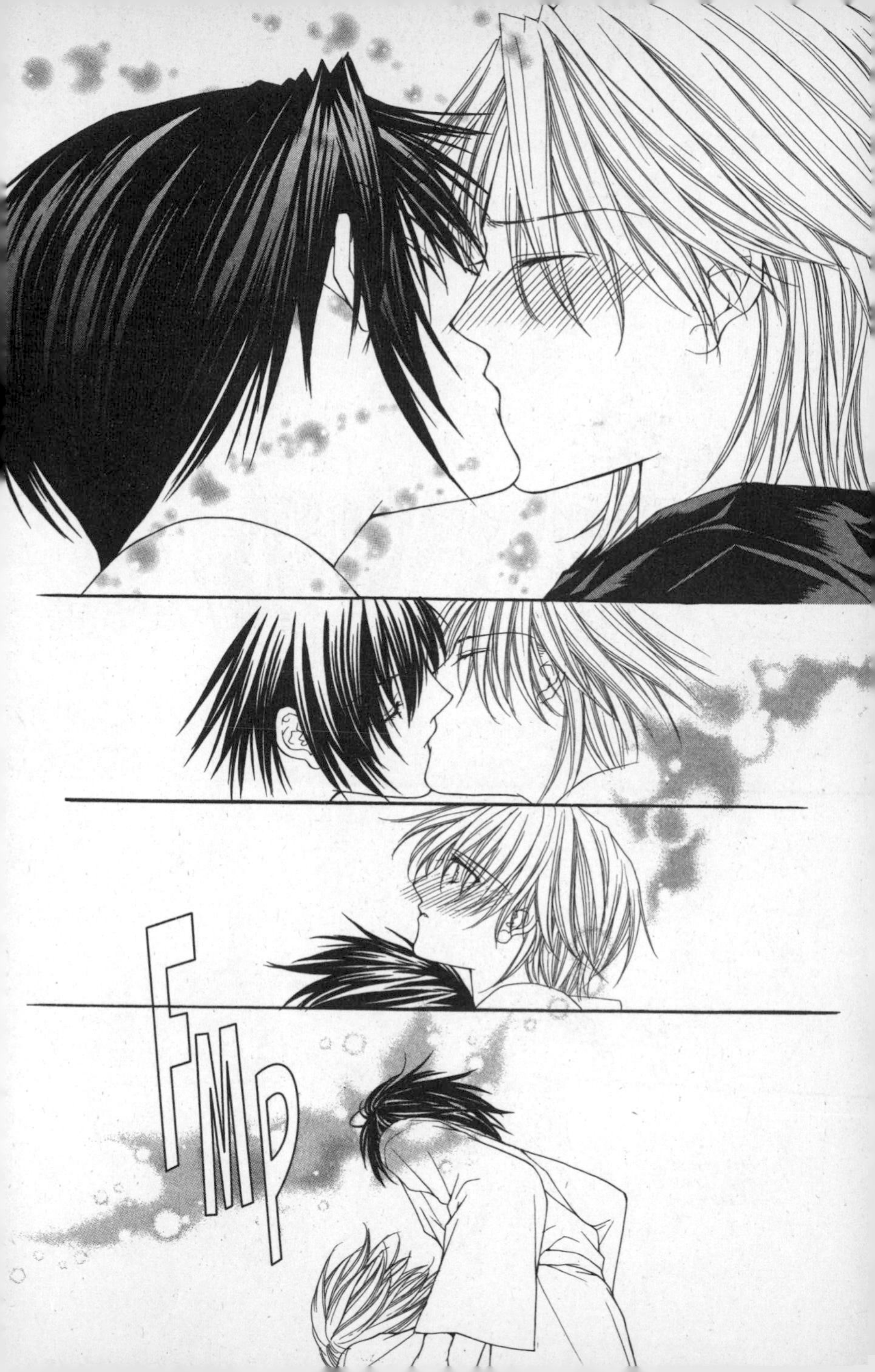
FMP

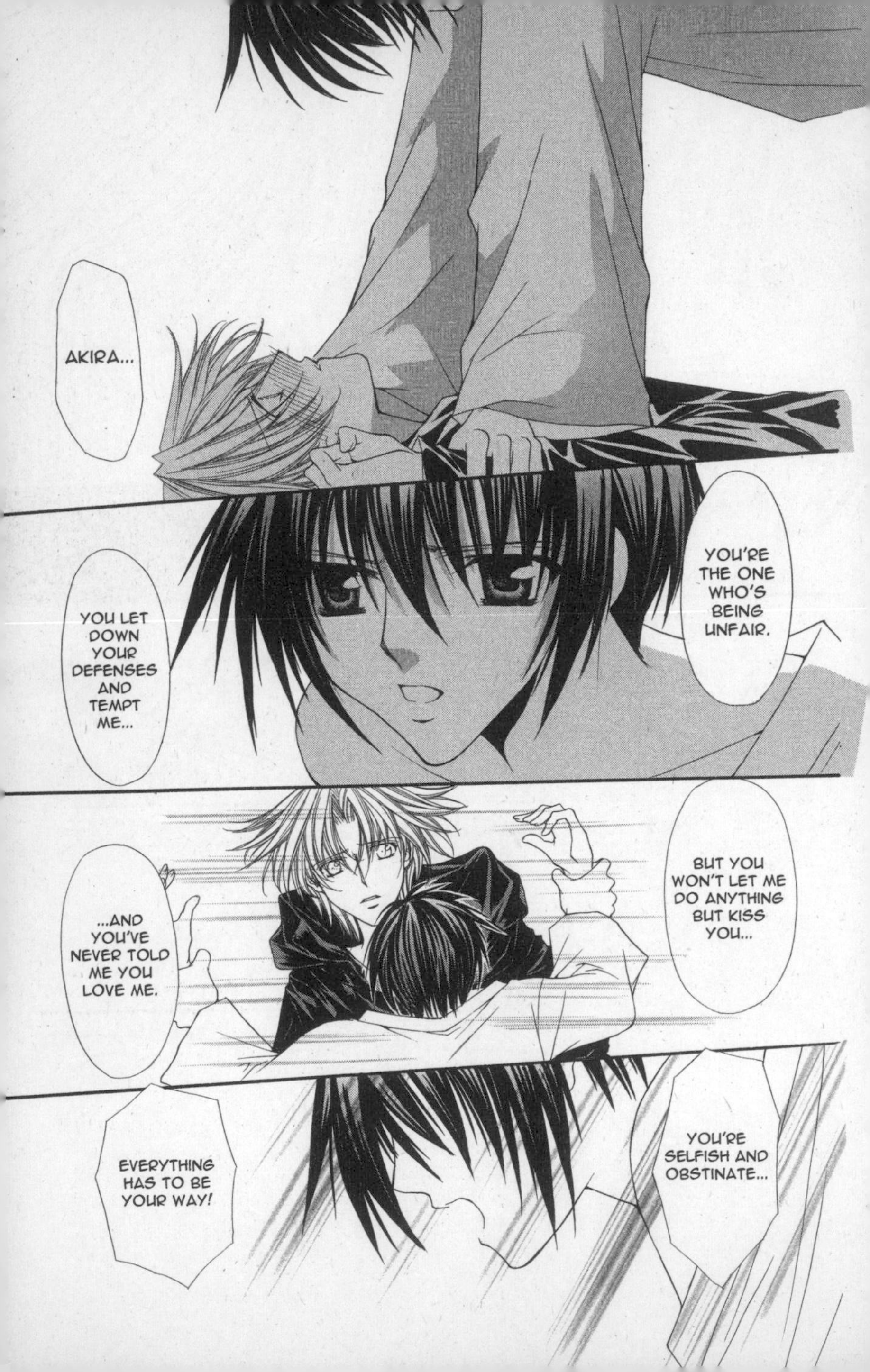
AKIRA...
YOU'RE THE ONE WHO'S BEING UNFAIR.
YOU LET DOWN YOUR DEFENSES AND TEMPT ME...
BUT YOU WON'T LET ME DO ANYTHING BUT KISS YOU...
...AND YOU'VE NEVER TOLD ME YOU LOVE ME.
YOU'RE SELFISH AND OBSTINATE...
EVERYTHING HAS TO BE YOUR WAY!

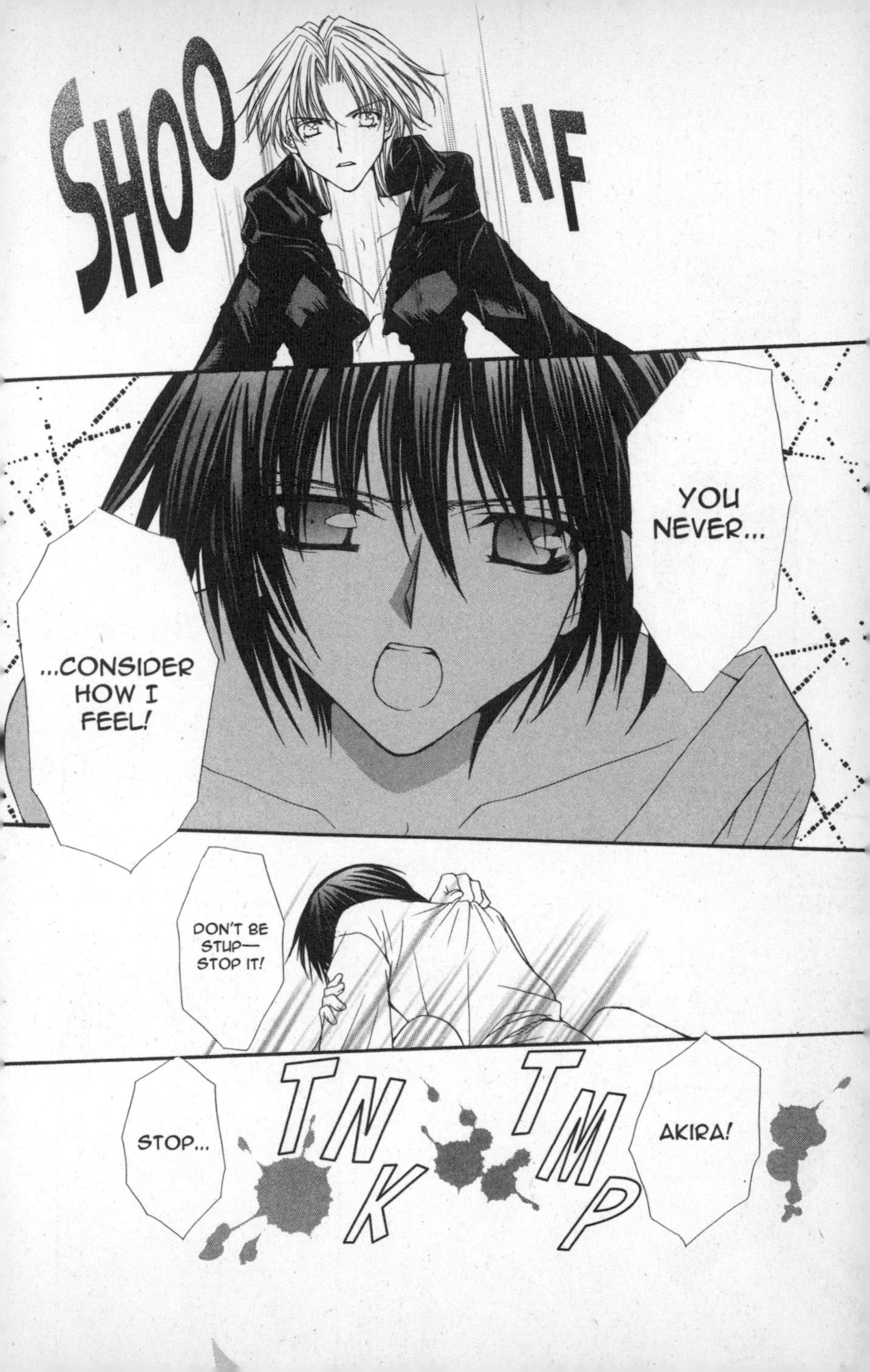
SHOO
NF
YOU NEVER...
...CONSIDER HOW I FEEL!
DON'T BE STUP— STOP IT!
AKIRA!
TMP
TNK
STOP...

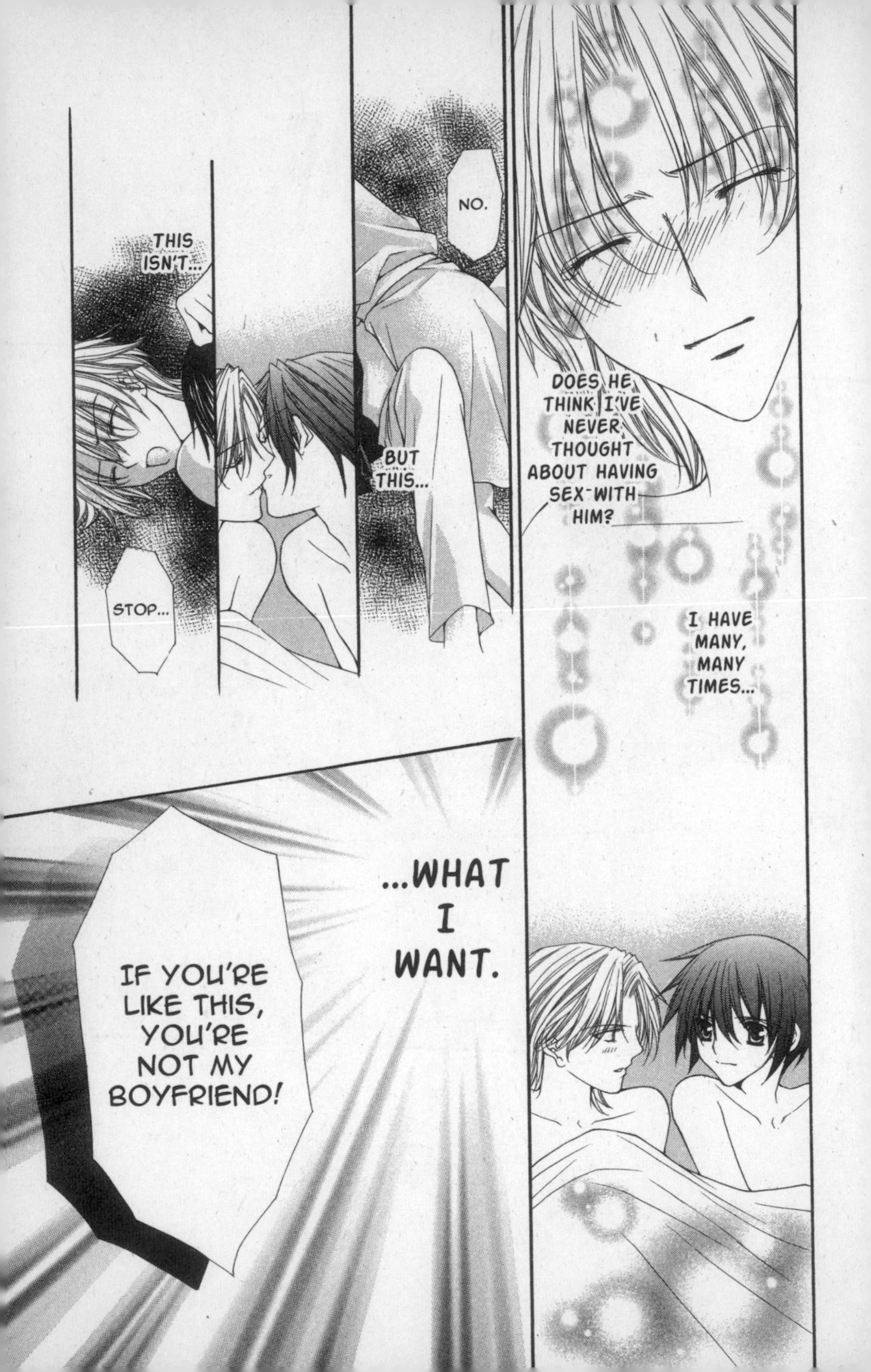
DOES HE THINK I'VE NEVER THOUGHT ABOUT HAVING SEX WITH HIM?
I HAVE MANY, MANY TIMES...
NO.
BUT THIS...
THIS ISN'T...
STOP...
...WHAT I WANT.
IF YOU'RE LIKE THIS, YOU'RE NOT MY BOYFRIEND!

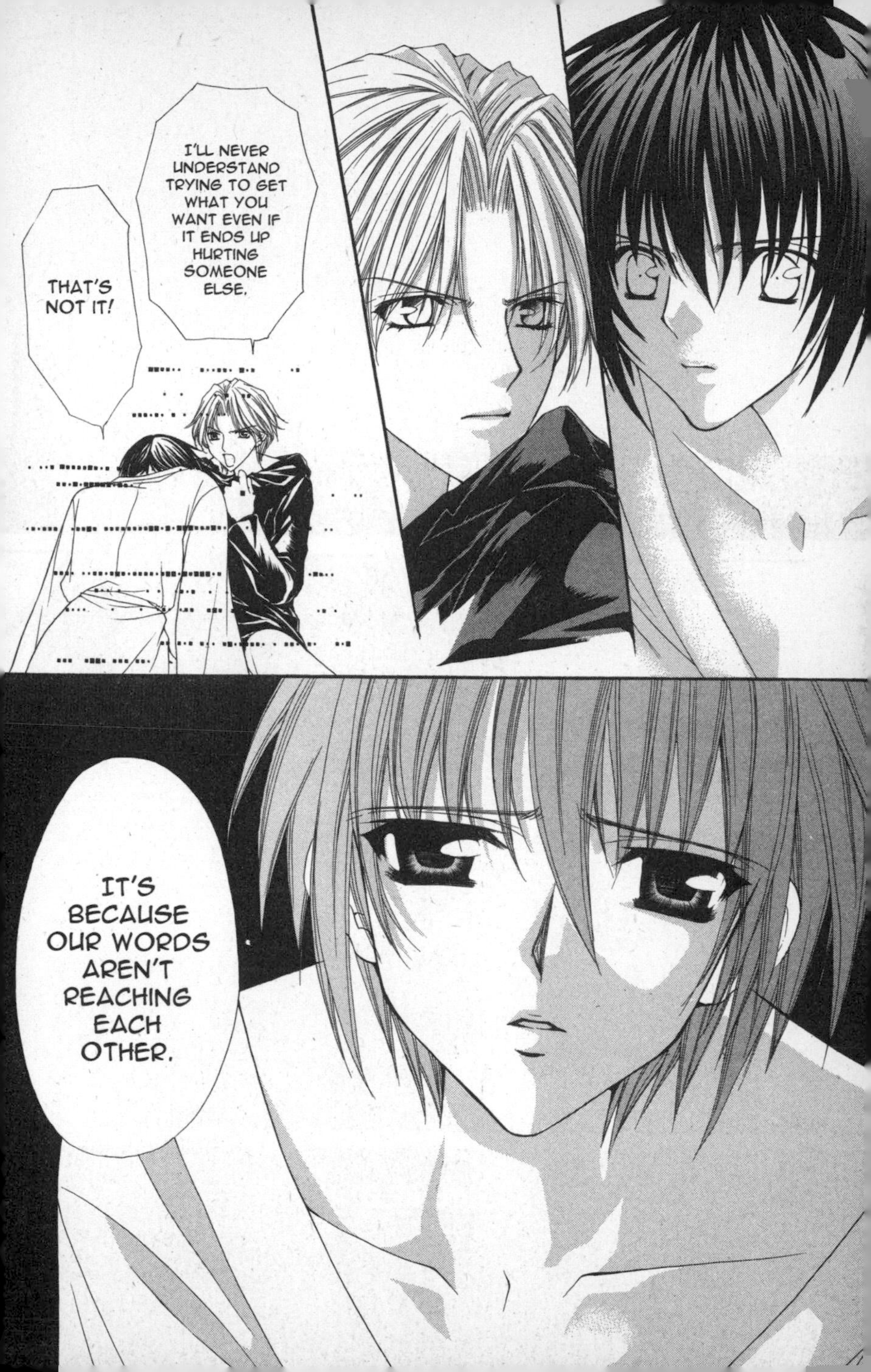
I'LL NEVER UNDERSTAND TRYING TO GET WHAT YOU WANT EVEN IF IT ENDS UP HURTING SOMEONE ELSE.
THAT'S NOT IT!
IT'S BECAUSE OUR WORDS AREN'T REACHING EACH OTHER.

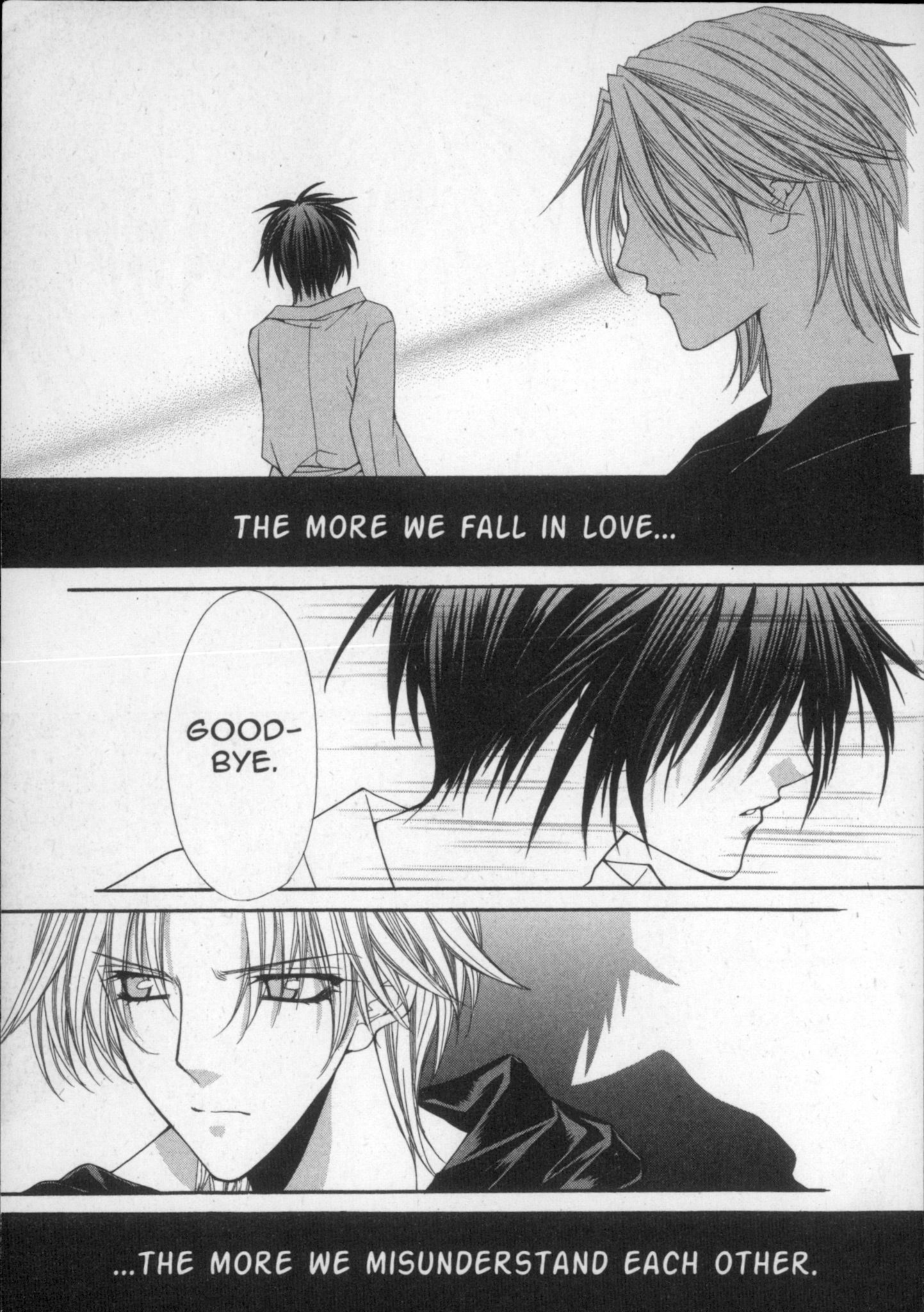
THE MORE WE FALL IN LOVE...
GOOD-BYE.
...THE MORE WE MISUNDERSTAND EACH OTHER.

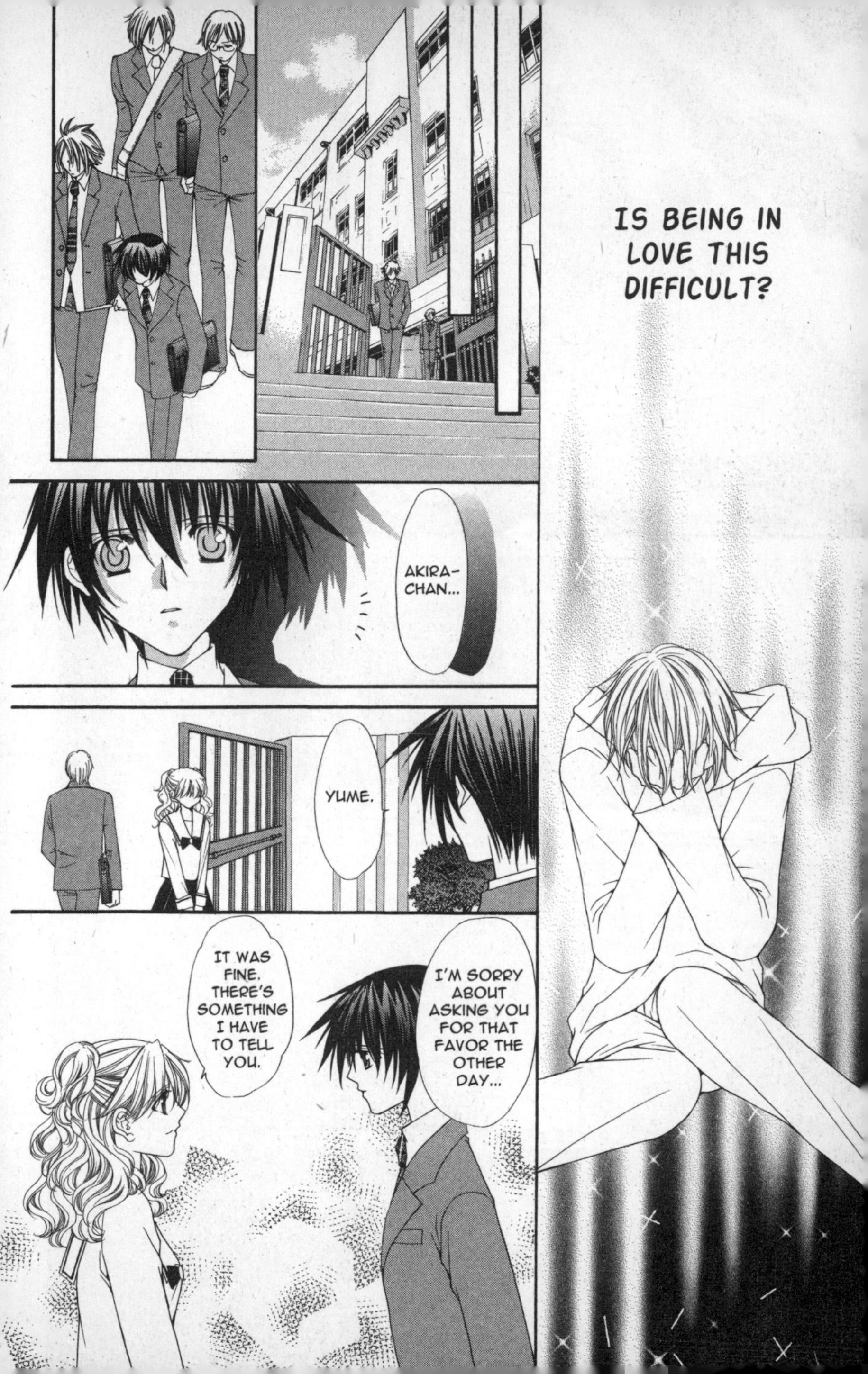
IS BEING IN LOVE THIS DIFFICULT?
AKIRA-CHAN...
YUME.
I'M SORRY ABOUT ASKING YOU FOR THAT FAVOR THE OTHER DAY...
IT WAS FINE. THERE'S SOMETHING I HAVE TO TELL YOU.

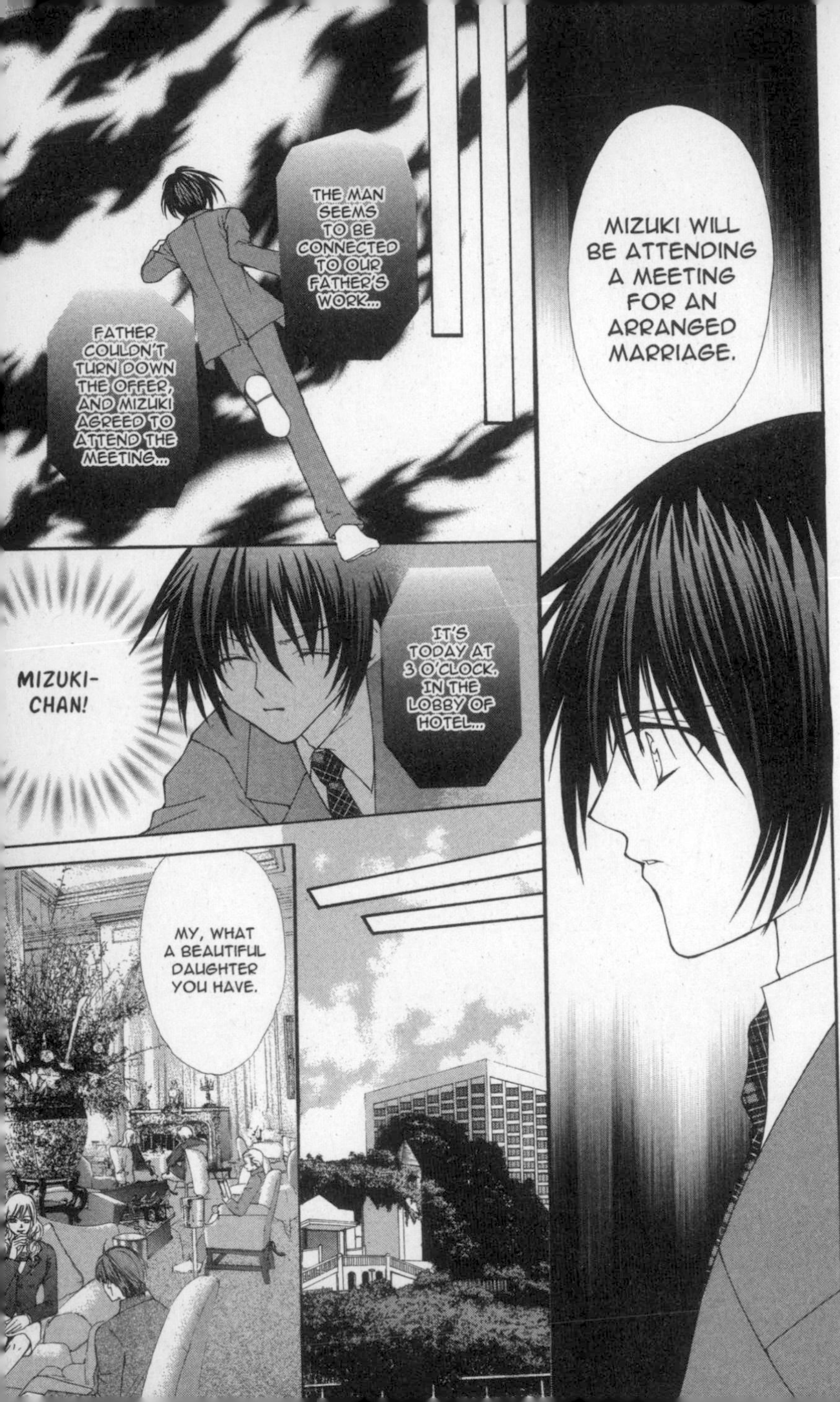
MIZUKI WILL BE ATTENDING A MEETING FOR AN ARRANGED MARRIAGE.
THE MAN SEEMS TO BE CONNECTED TO OUR FATHER'S WORK...
FATHER COULDN'T TURN DOWN THE OFFER, AND MIZUKI AGREED TO ATTEND THE MEETING...
IT'S TODAY AT 3 O'CLOCK, IN THE LOBBY OF HOTEL...
MIZUKI-CHAN!
MY, WHAT A BEAUTIFUL DAUGHTER YOU HAVE.

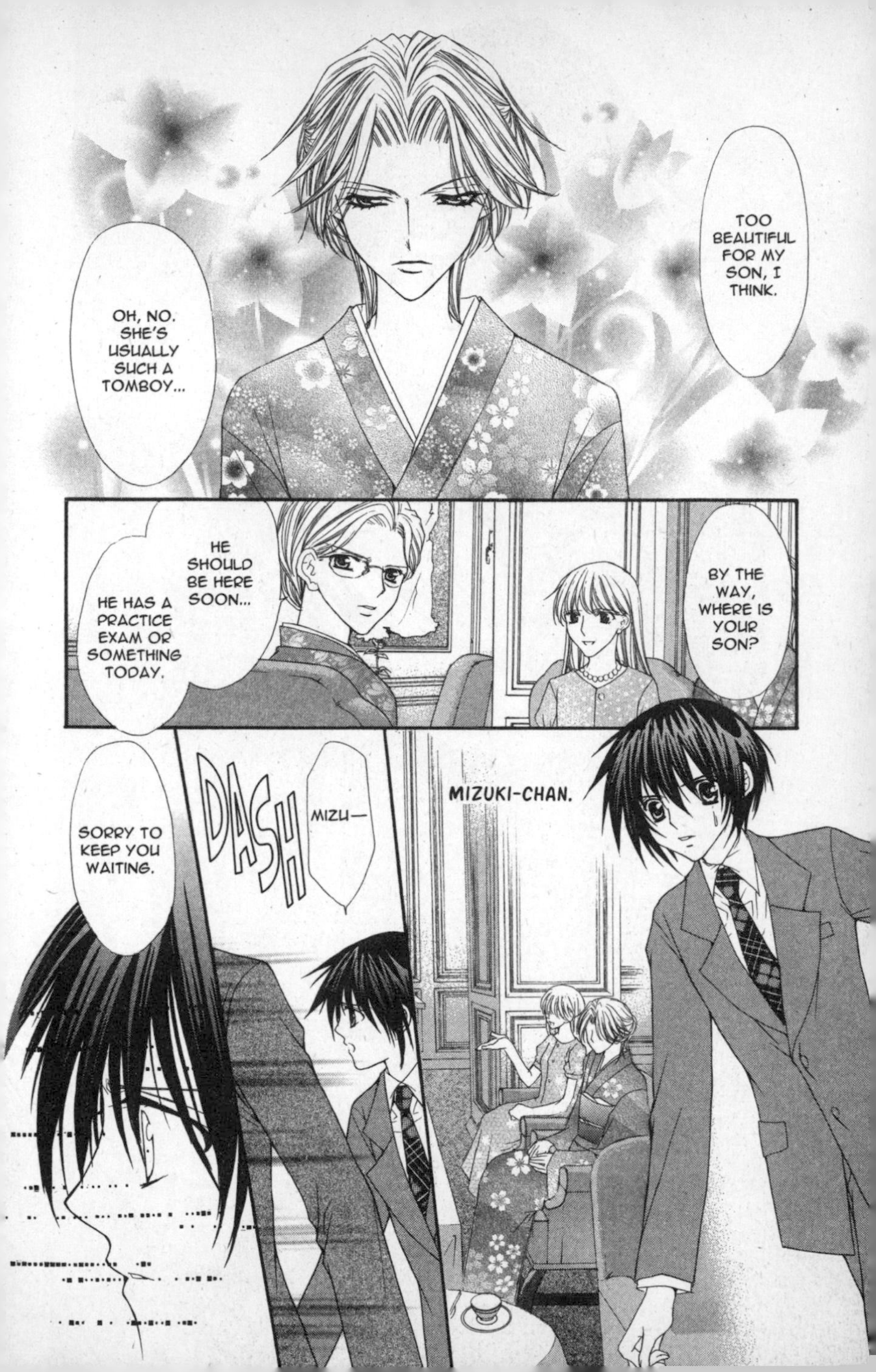
TOO BEAUTIFUL FOR MY SON, I THINK.
OH, NO. SHE'S USUALLY SUCH A TOMBOY...
BY THE WAY, WHERE IS YOUR SON?
HE SHOULD BE HERE SOON...
HE HAS A PRACTICE EXAM OR SOMETHING TODAY.
MIZUKI-CHAN.
MIZU—
DASH
SORRY TO KEEP YOU WAITING.

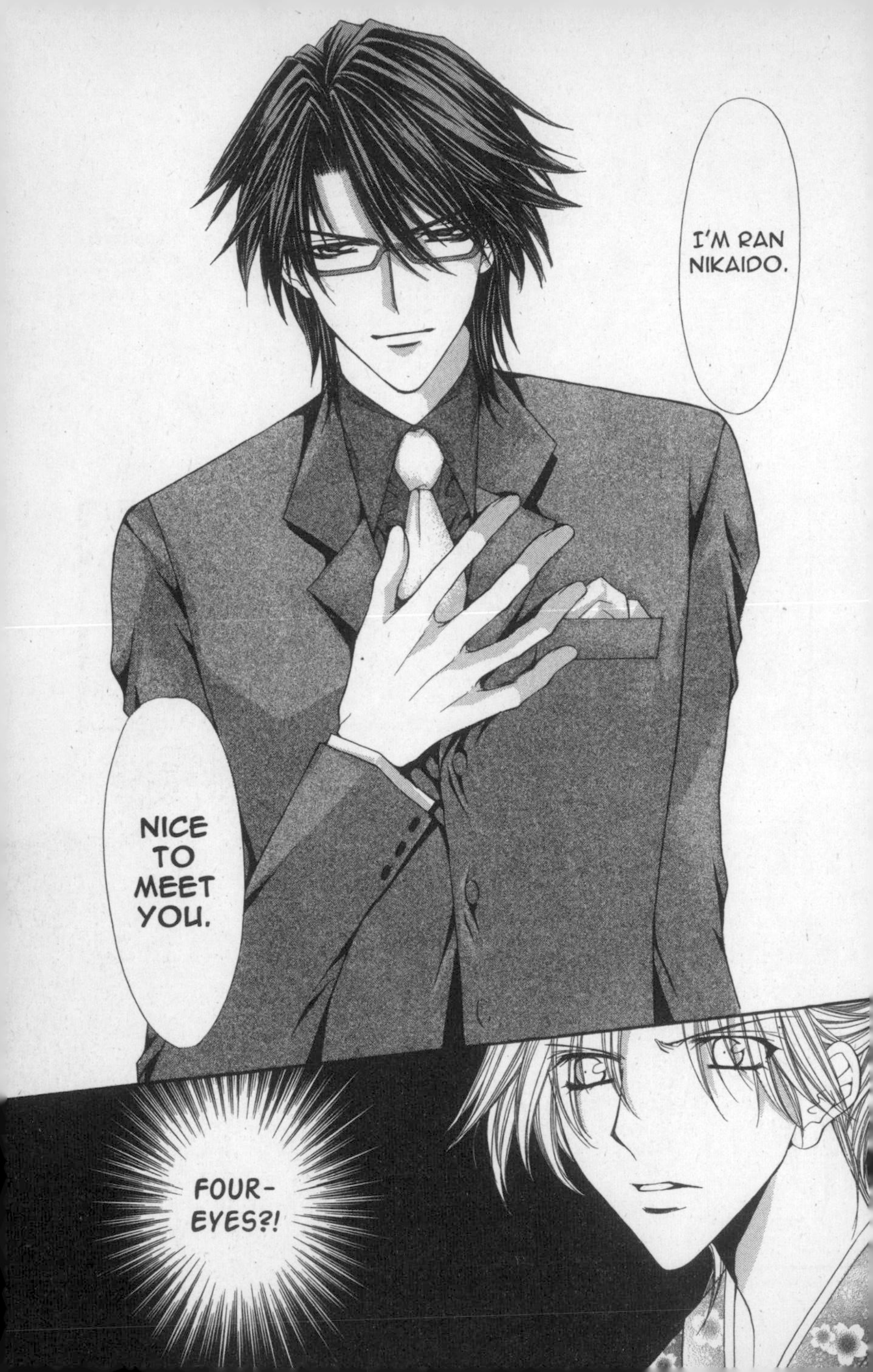
I'M RAN NIKAIDO.
NICE TO MEET YOU.
FOUR-EYES?!

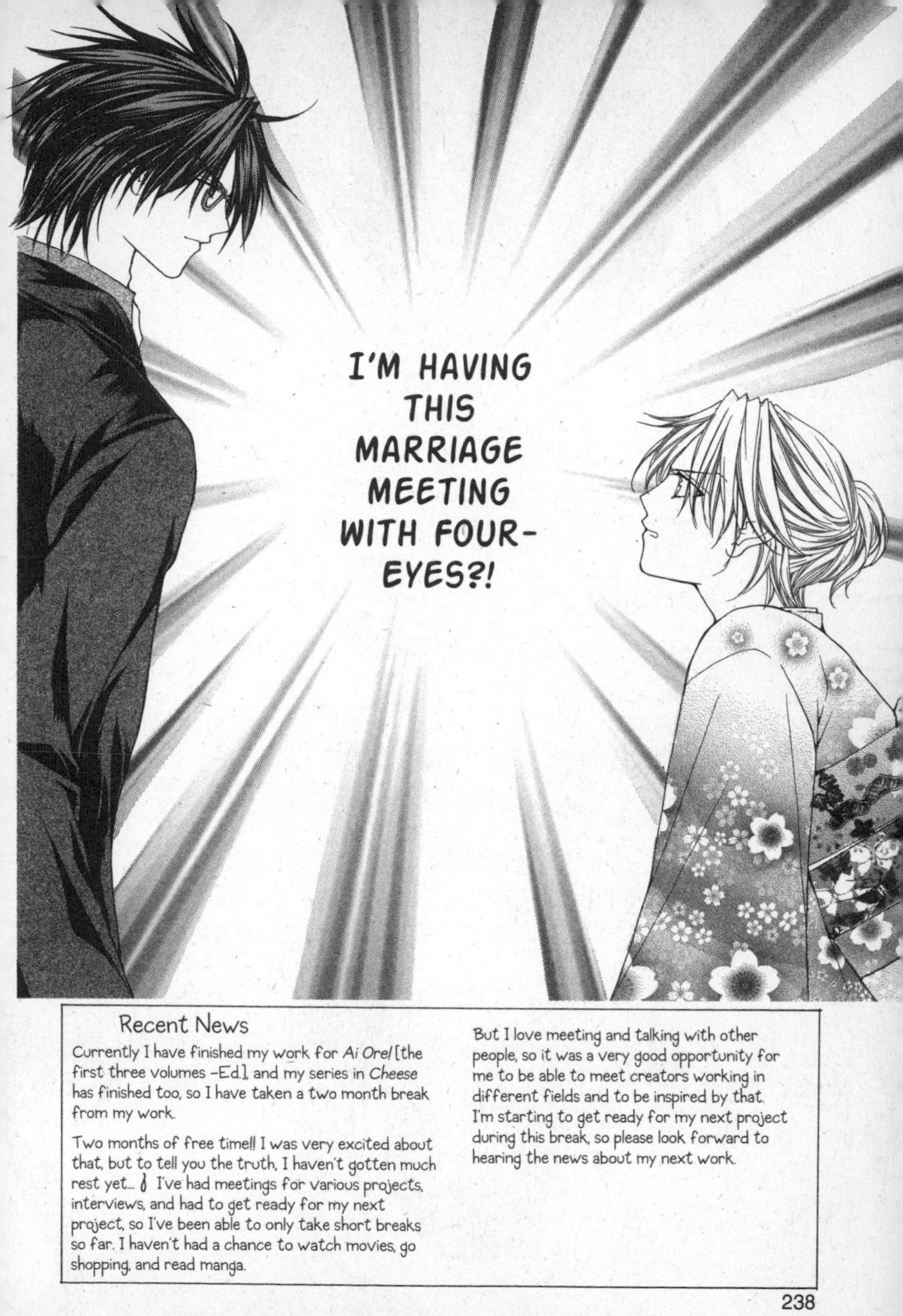
I'M HAVING THIS MARRIAGE MEETING WITH FOUR-EYES?!

Recent News

Currently I have finished my work for *Ai Ore!* [the first three volumes –Ed.], and my series in *Cheese* has finished too, so I have taken a two month break from my work.

Two months of free time!! I was very excited about that, but to tell you the truth, I haven't gotten much rest yet... I've had meetings for various projects, interviews, and had to get ready for my next project, so I've been able to only take short breaks so far. I haven't had a chance to watch movies, go shopping, and read manga.

But I love meeting and talking with other people, so it was a very good opportunity for me to be able to meet creators working in different fields and to be inspired by that. I'm starting to get ready for my next project during this break, so please look forward to hearing the news about my next work.

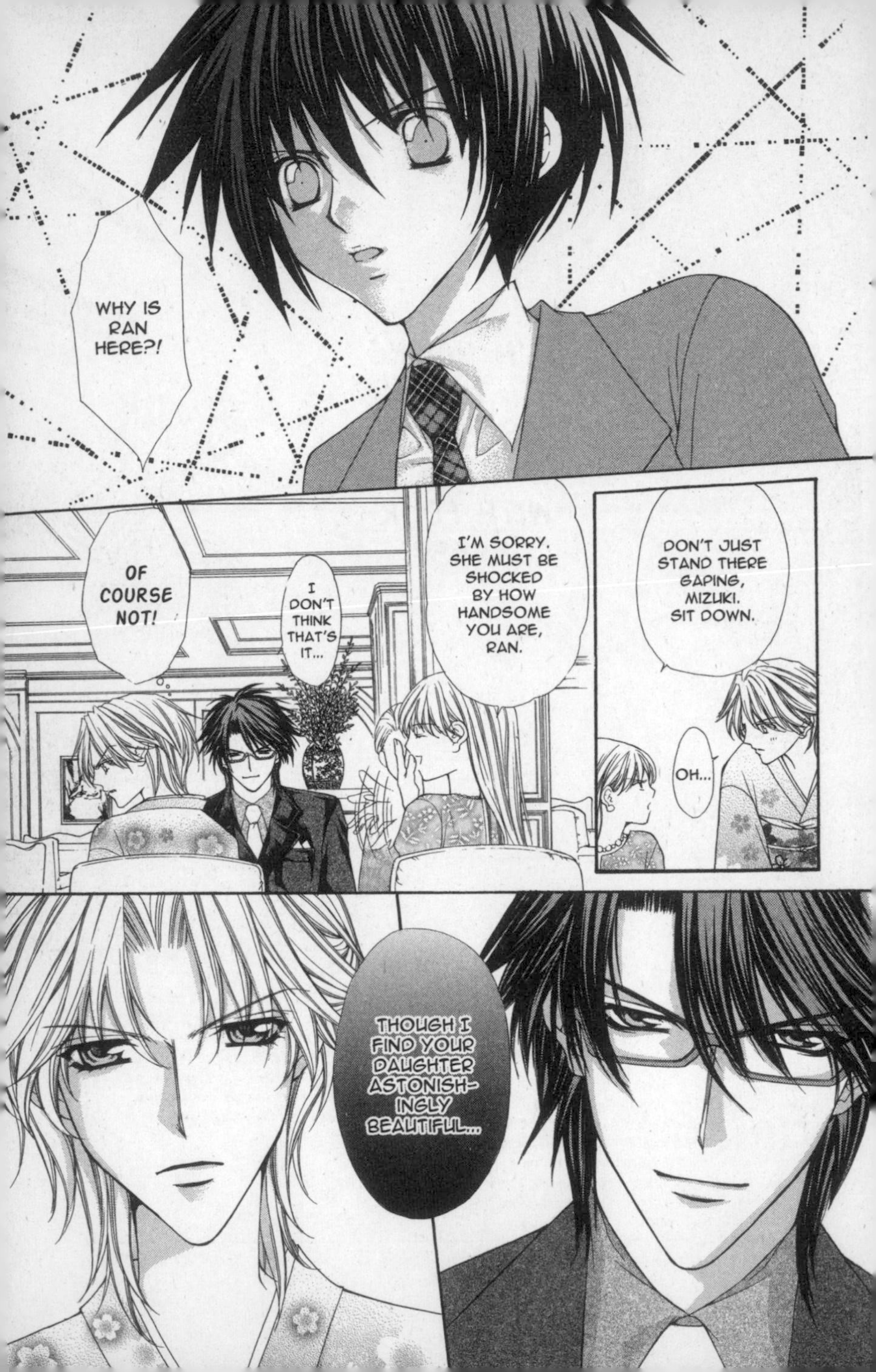
WHY IS RAN HERE?!
DON'T JUST STAND THERE GAPING, MIZUKI. SIT DOWN.
OH...
I'M SORRY. SHE MUST BE SHOCKED BY HOW HANDSOME YOU ARE, RAN.
I DON'T THINK THAT'S IT...
OF COURSE NOT!
THOUGH I FIND YOUR DAUGHTER ASTONISH-INGLY BEAUTIFUL...

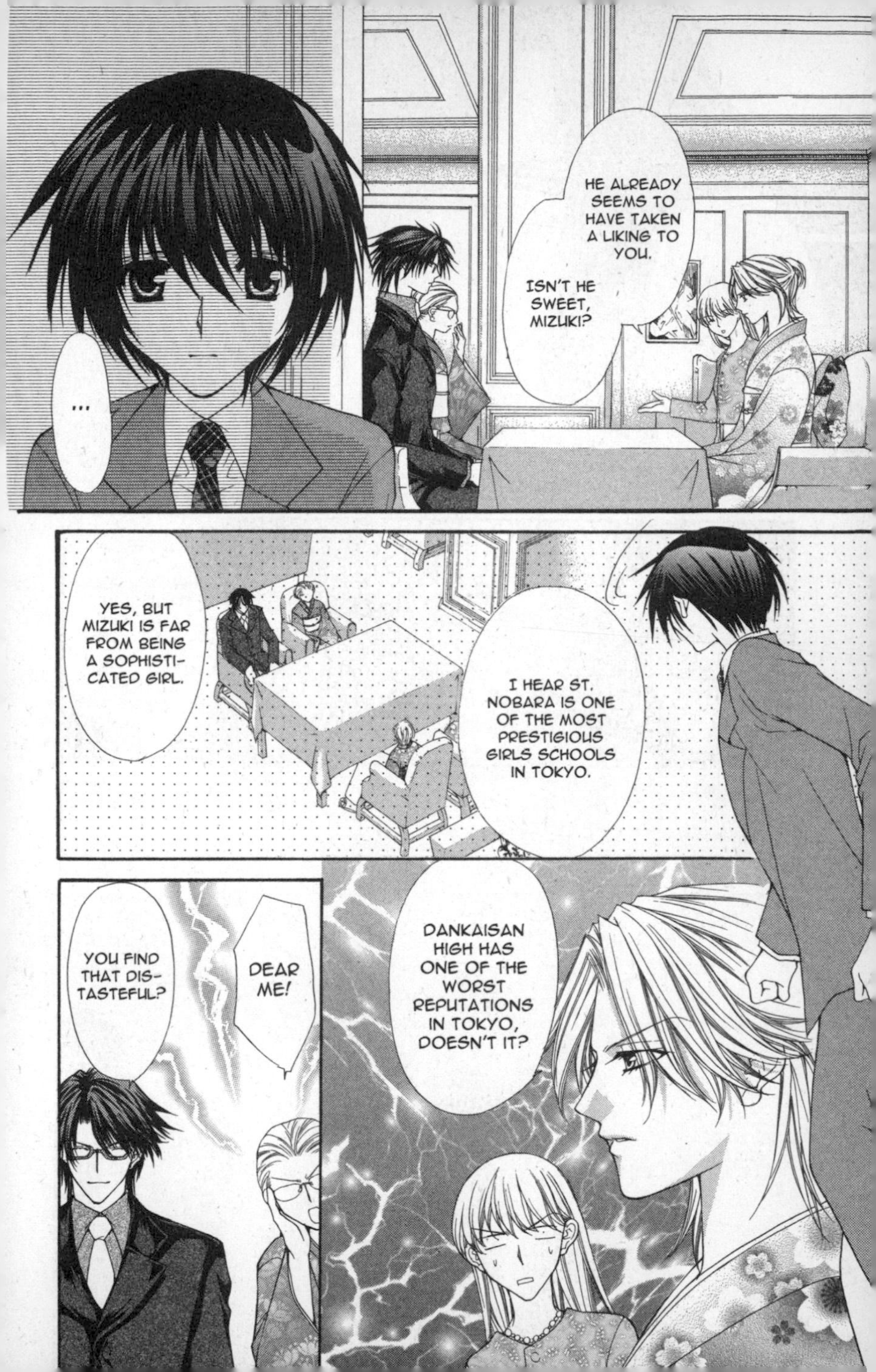
HE ALREADY SEEMS TO HAVE TAKEN A LIKING TO YOU.
ISN'T HE SWEET, MIZUKI?
...
I HEAR ST. NOBARA IS ONE OF THE MOST PRESTIGIOUS GIRLS SCHOOLS IN TOKYO.
YES, BUT MIZUKI IS FAR FROM BEING A SOPHISTI-CATED GIRL.
DANKAISAN HIGH HAS ONE OF THE WORST REPUTATIONS IN TOKYO, DOESN'T IT?
DEAR ME!
YOU FIND THAT DIS-TASTEFUL?

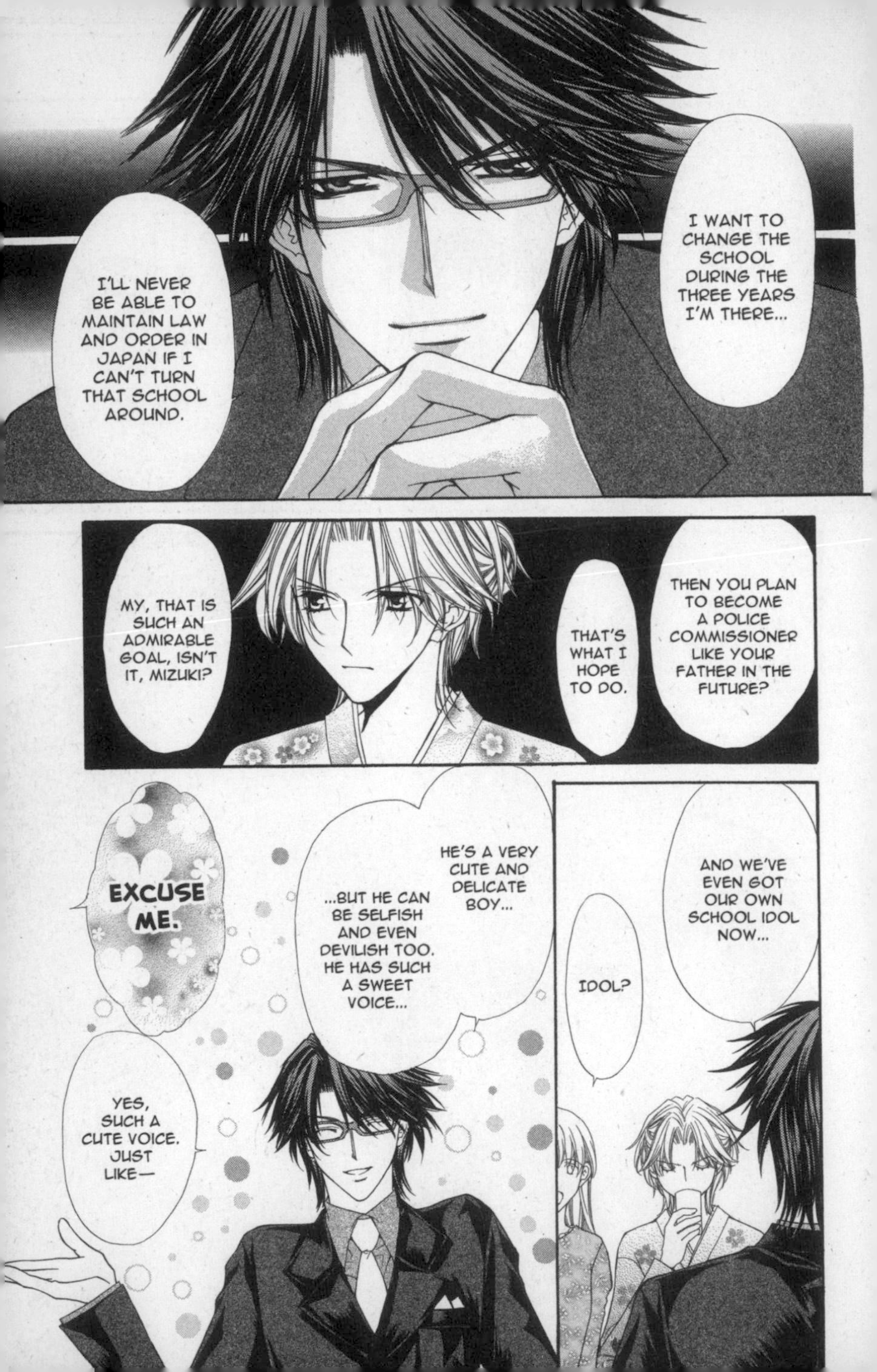
I WANT TO CHANGE THE SCHOOL DURING THE THREE YEARS I'M THERE...
I'LL NEVER BE ABLE TO MAINTAIN LAW AND ORDER IN JAPAN IF I CAN'T TURN THAT SCHOOL AROUND.
THEN YOU PLAN TO BECOME A POLICE COMMISSIONER LIKE YOUR FATHER IN THE FUTURE?
THAT'S WHAT I HOPE TO DO.
MY, THAT IS SUCH AN ADMIRABLE GOAL, ISN'T IT, MIZUKI?
AND WE'VE EVEN GOT OUR OWN SCHOOL IDOL NOW...
IDOL?
HE'S A VERY CUTE AND DELICATE BOY...
...BUT HE CAN BE SELFISH AND EVEN DEVILISH TOO. HE HAS SUCH A SWEET VOICE...
EXCUSE ME.
YES, SUCH A CUTE VOICE. JUST LIKE—

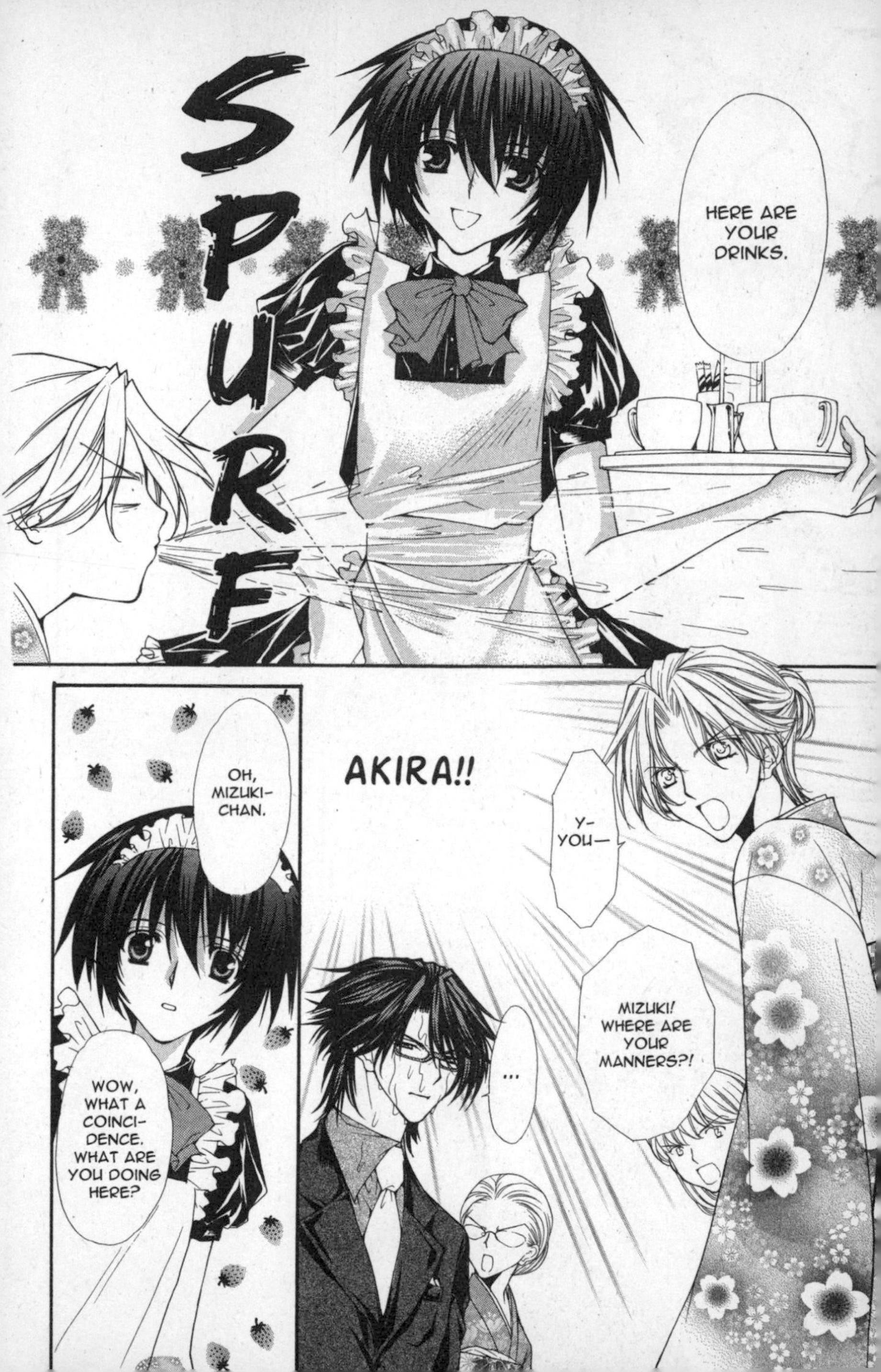
HERE ARE YOUR DRINKS.
SPURF
Y-YOU—
AKIRA!!
MIZUKI! WHERE ARE YOUR MANNERS?!
...
OH, MIZUKI-CHAN.
WOW, WHAT A COINCIDENCE. WHAT ARE YOU DOING HERE?

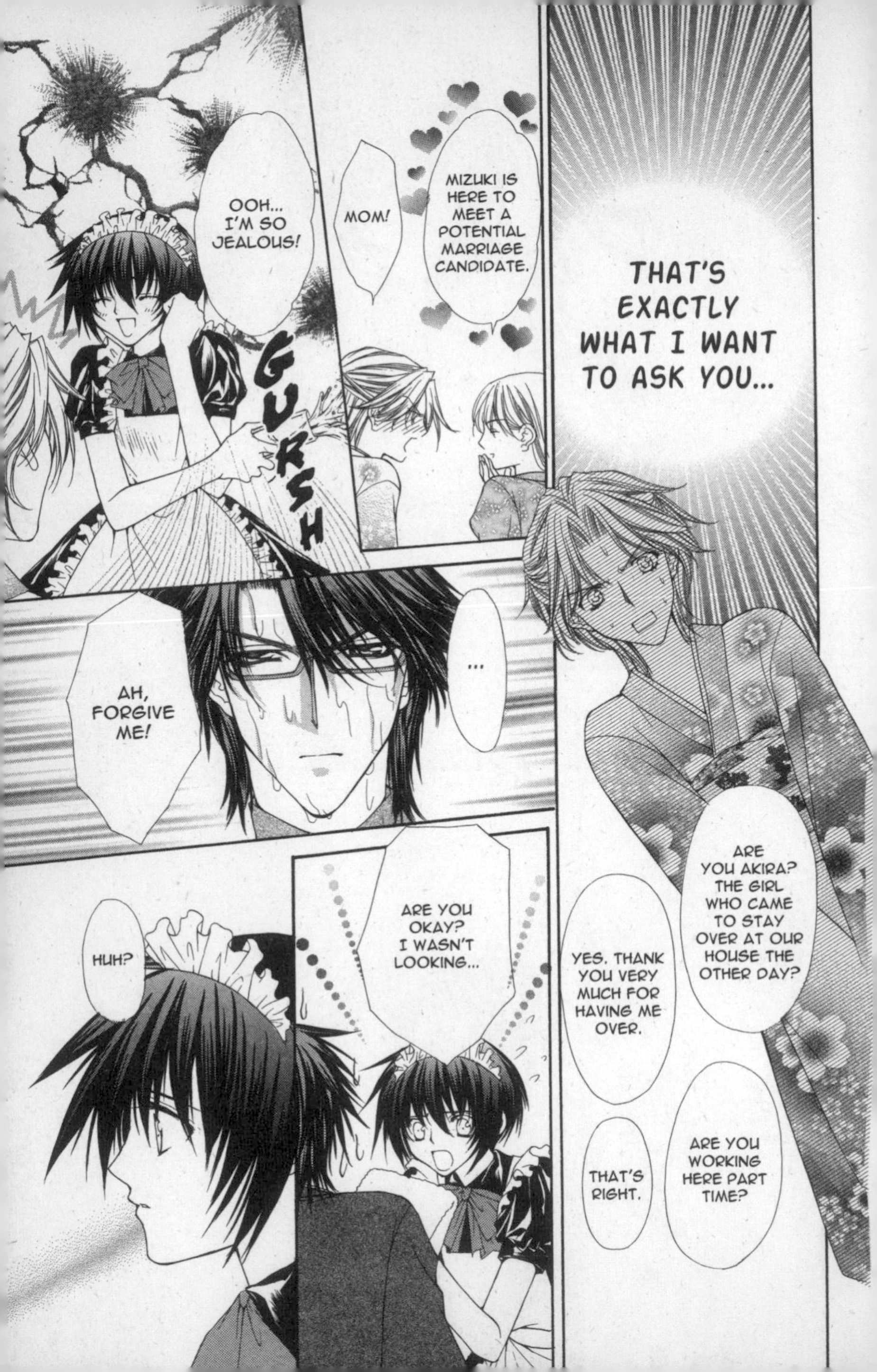
THAT'S EXACTLY WHAT I WANT TO ASK YOU...
ARE YOU AKIRA? THE GIRL WHO CAME TO STAY OVER AT OUR HOUSE THE OTHER DAY?
YES. THANK YOU VERY MUCH FOR HAVING ME OVER.
ARE YOU WORKING HERE PART TIME?
THAT'S RIGHT.
MIZUKI IS HERE TO MEET A POTENTIAL MARRIAGE CANDIDATE.
MOM!
OOH... I'M SO JEALOUS!
GURSH
...
AH, FORGIVE ME!
ARE YOU OKAY? I WASN'T LOOKING...
HUH?

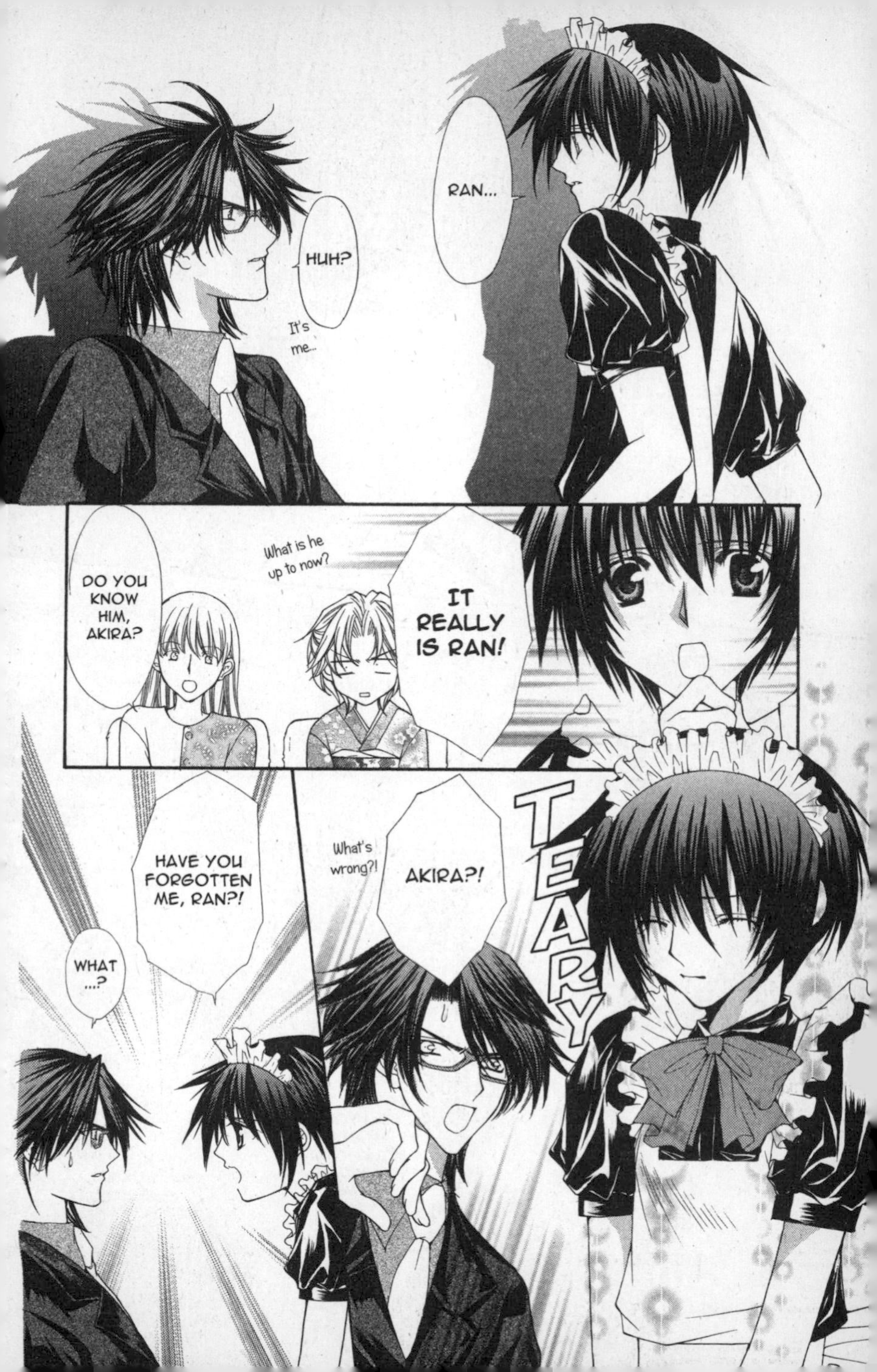
RAN...
HUH?
It's me...
IT REALLY IS RAN!
What is he up to now?
DO YOU KNOW HIM, AKIRA?
TEARY
AKIRA?!
What's wrong?!
HAVE YOU FORGOTTEN ME, RAN?!
WHAT ...?

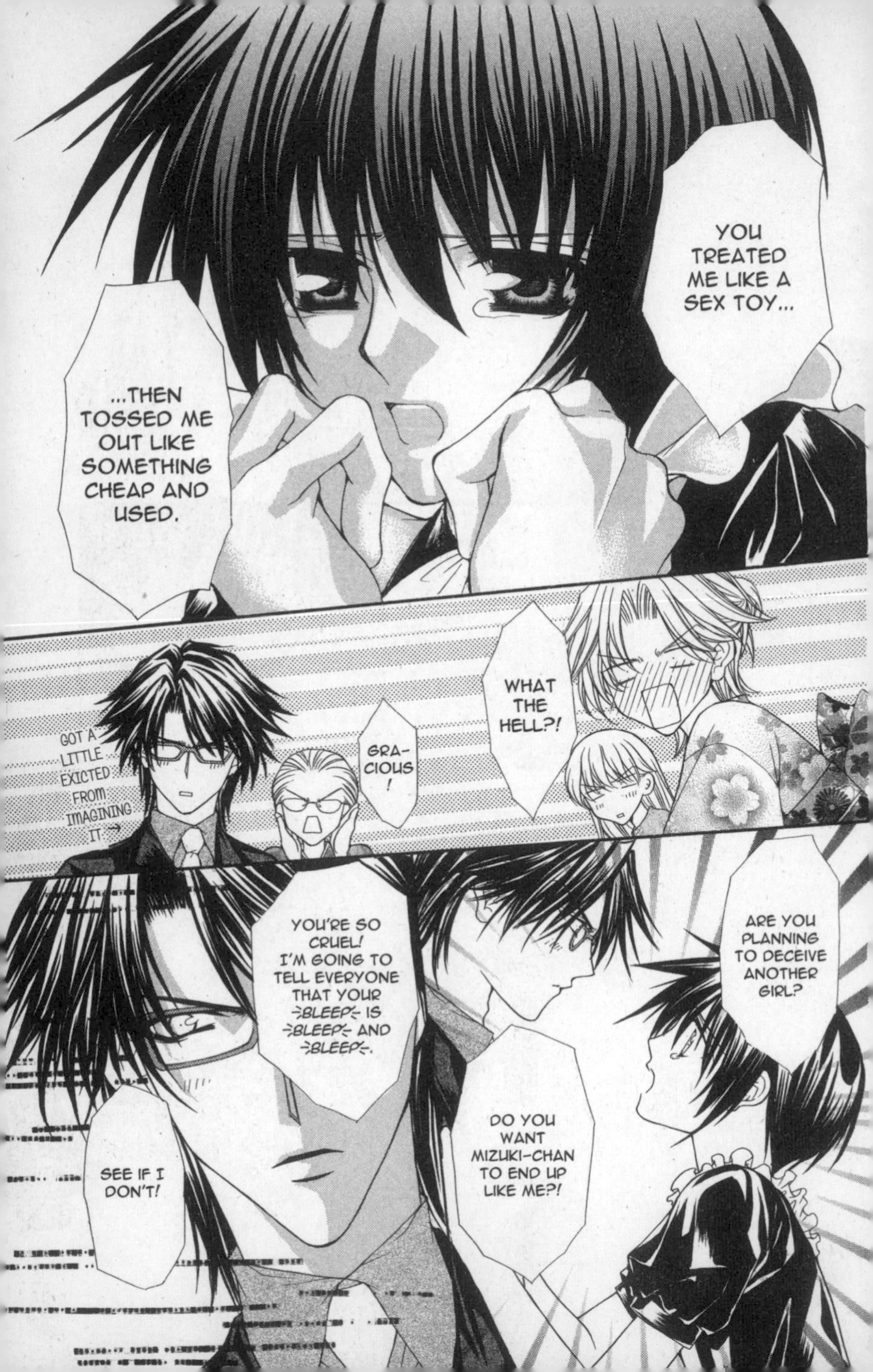
YOU TREATED ME LIKE A SEX TOY...
...THEN TOSSED ME OUT LIKE SOMETHING CHEAP AND USED.
WHAT THE HELL?!
GRA-CIOUS!
GOT A LITTLE EXICTED FROM IMAGINING IT.→
ARE YOU PLANNING TO DECEIVE ANOTHER GIRL?
DO YOU WANT MIZUKI-CHAN TO END UP LIKE ME?!
YOU'RE SO CRUEL! I'M GOING TO TELL EVERYONE THAT YOUR -BLEEP- IS -BLEEP- AND -BLEEP-.
SEE IF I DON'T!

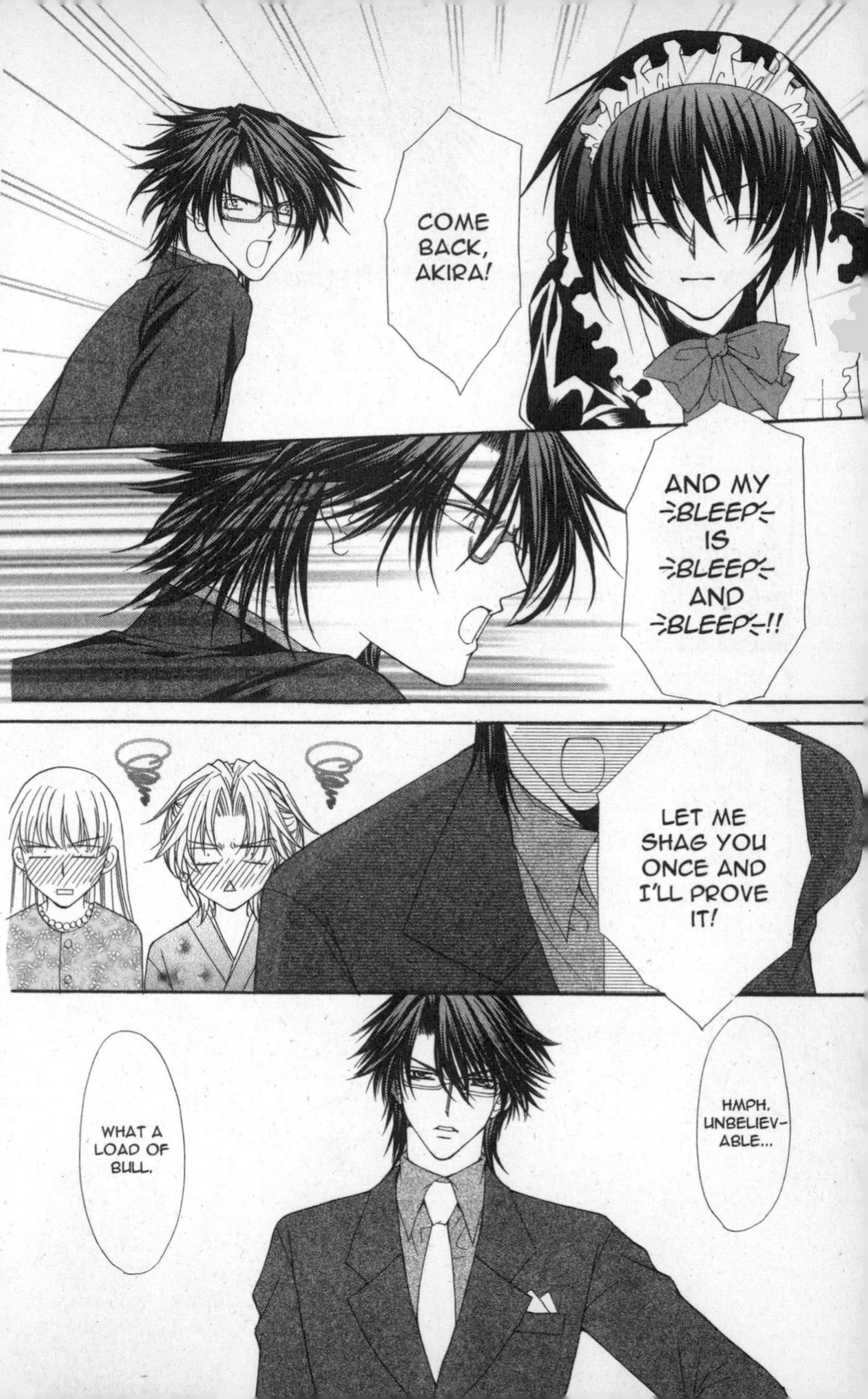
COME BACK, AKIRA!
AND MY BLEEP IS BLEEP AND BLEEP!!
LET ME SHAG YOU ONCE AND I'LL PROVE IT!
HMPH. UNBELIEV-ABLE...
WHAT A LOAD OF BULL.

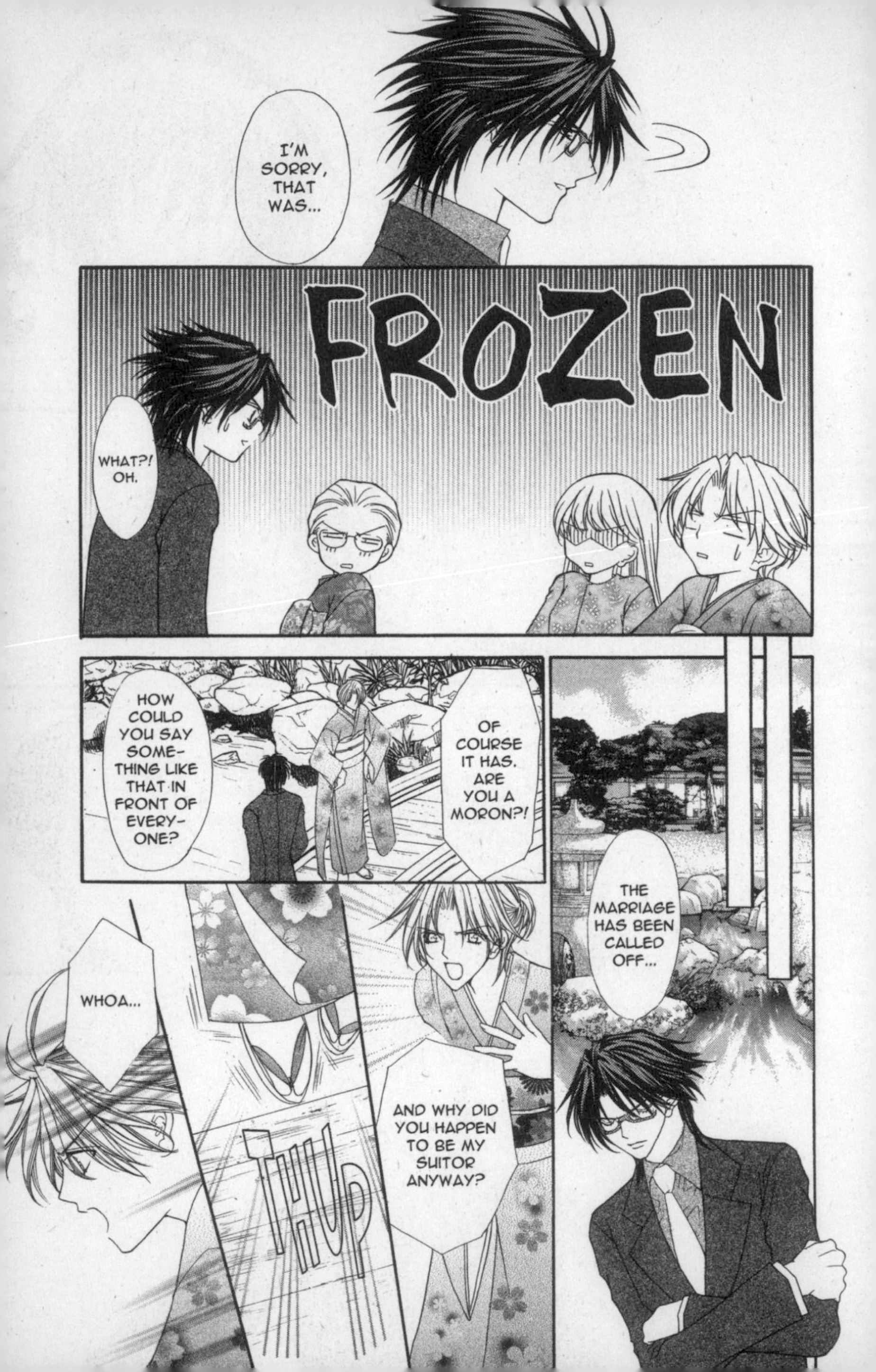
I'M SORRY, THAT WAS...
FROZEN
WHAT?! OH.
THE MARRIAGE HAS BEEN CALLED OFF...
OF COURSE IT HAS. ARE YOU A MORON?!
HOW COULD YOU SAY SOME-THING LIKE THAT IN FRONT OF EVERY-ONE?
AND WHY DID YOU HAPPEN TO BE MY SUITOR ANYWAY?
THUP
WHOA...

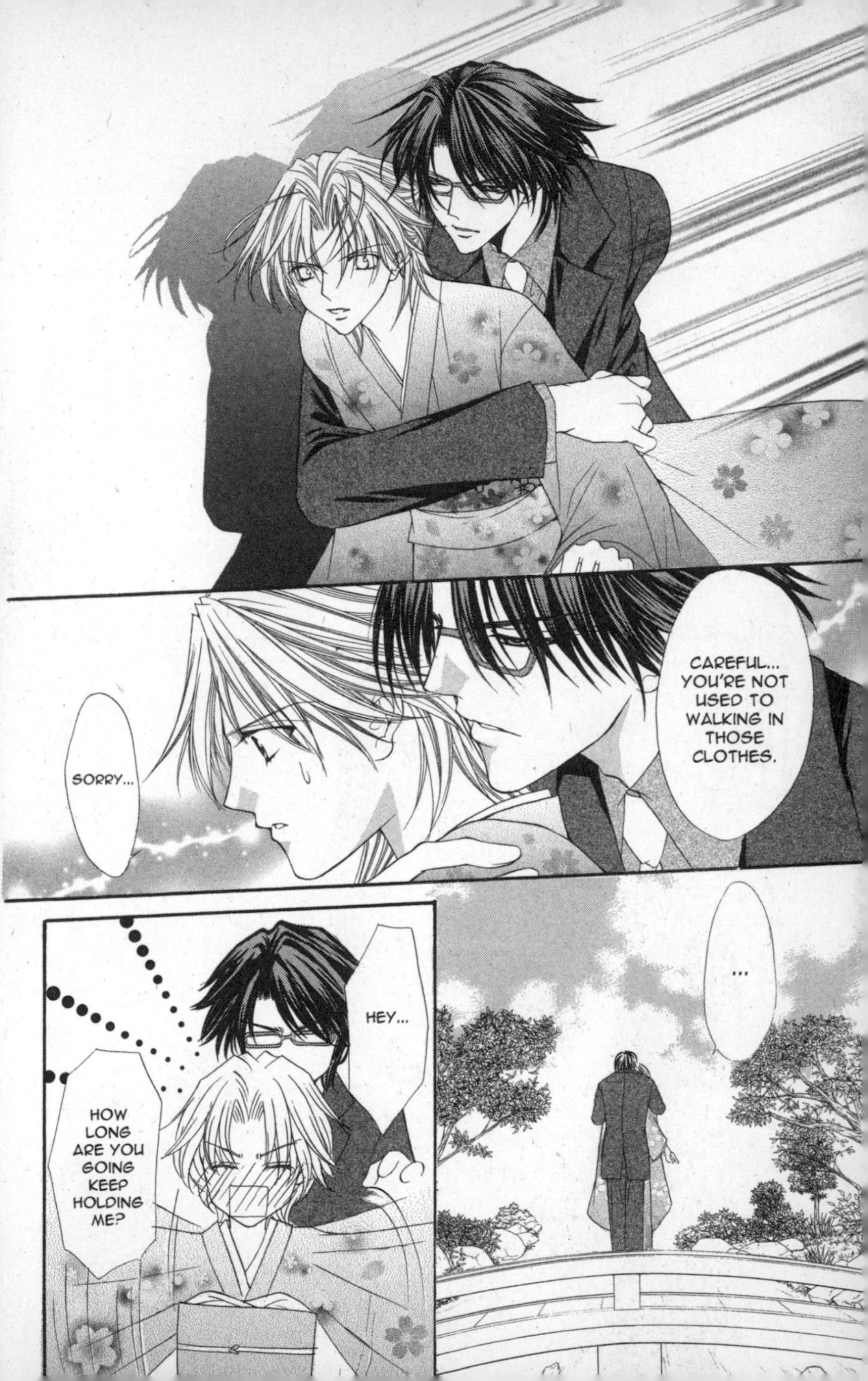
CAREFUL... YOU'RE NOT USED TO WALKING IN THOSE CLOTHES.
SORRY...
...
HEY...
HOW LONG ARE YOU GOING KEEP HOLDING ME?

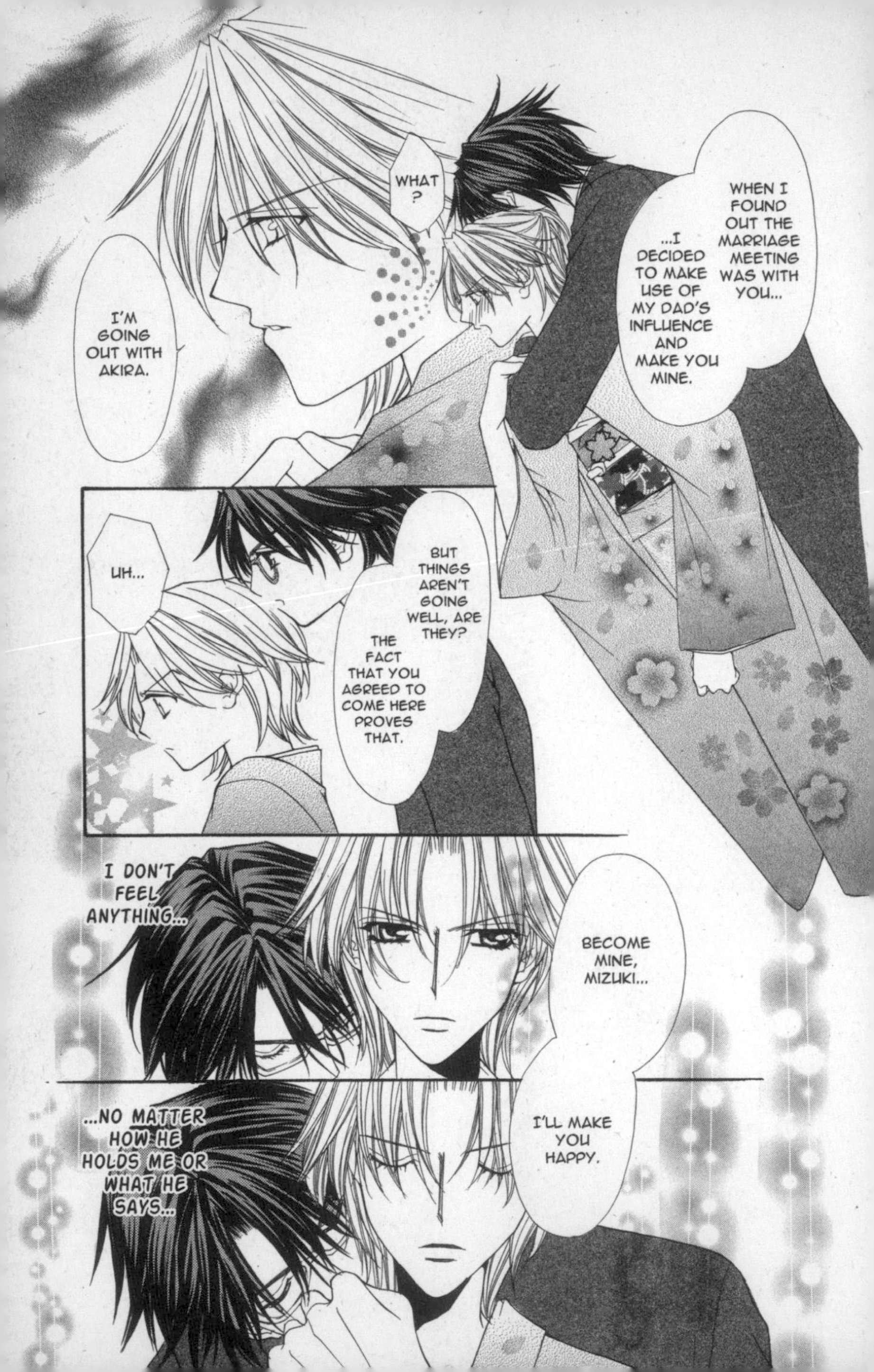
WHEN I FOUND OUT THE MARRIAGE MEETING WAS WITH YOU...
...I DECIDED TO MAKE USE OF MY DAD'S INFLUENCE AND MAKE YOU MINE.
WHAT?
I'M GOING OUT WITH AKIRA.
BUT THINGS AREN'T GOING WELL, ARE THEY?
THE FACT THAT YOU AGREED TO COME HERE PROVES THAT.
UH...
BECOME MINE, MIZUKI...
I DON'T FEEL ANYTHING...
I'LL MAKE YOU HAPPY.
...NO MATTER HOW HE HOLDS ME OR WHAT HE SAYS...

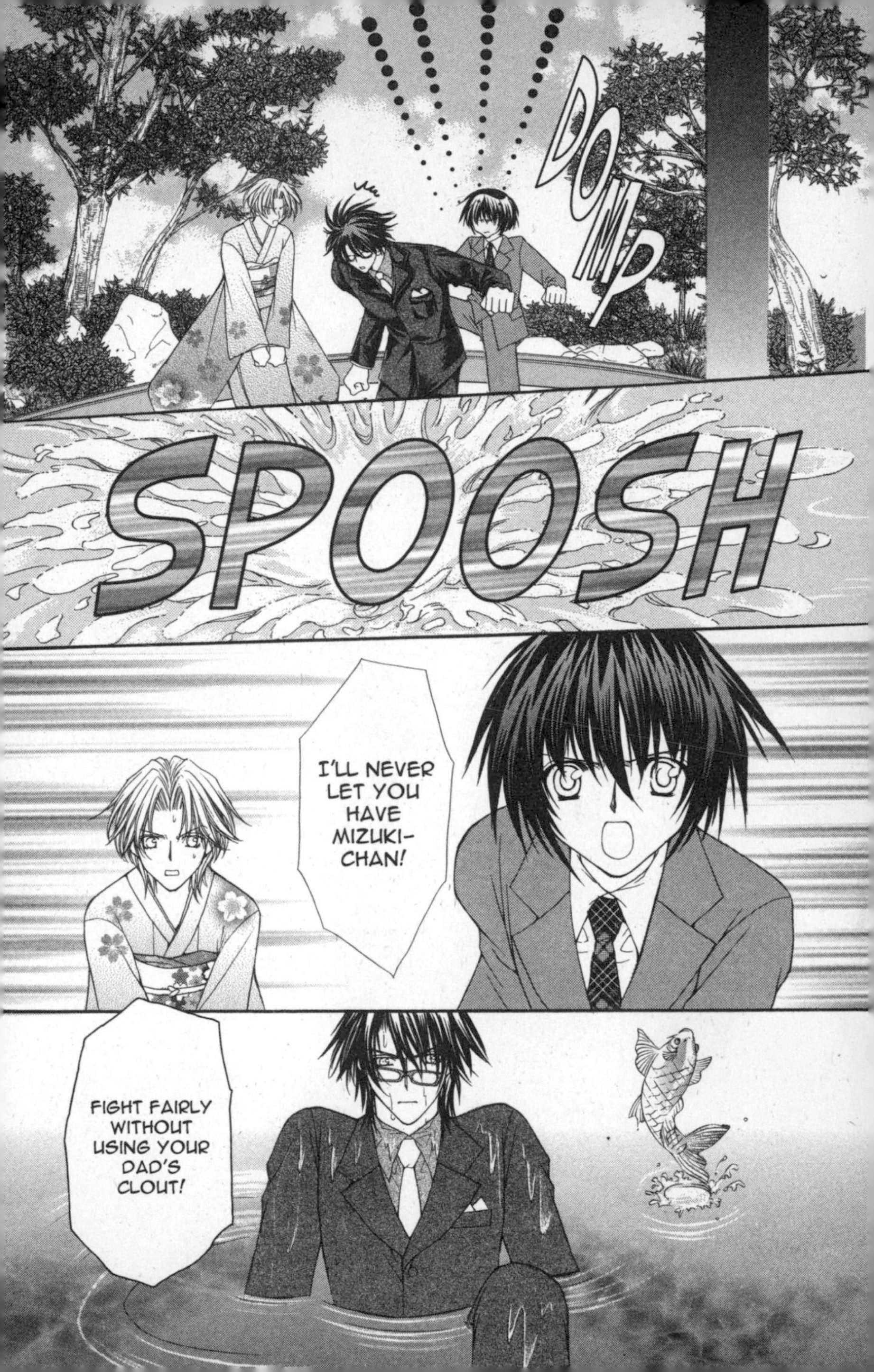
DOMP
SPOOSH
I'LL NEVER LET YOU HAVE MIZUKI-CHAN!
FIGHT FAIRLY WITHOUT USING YOUR DAD'S CLOUT!

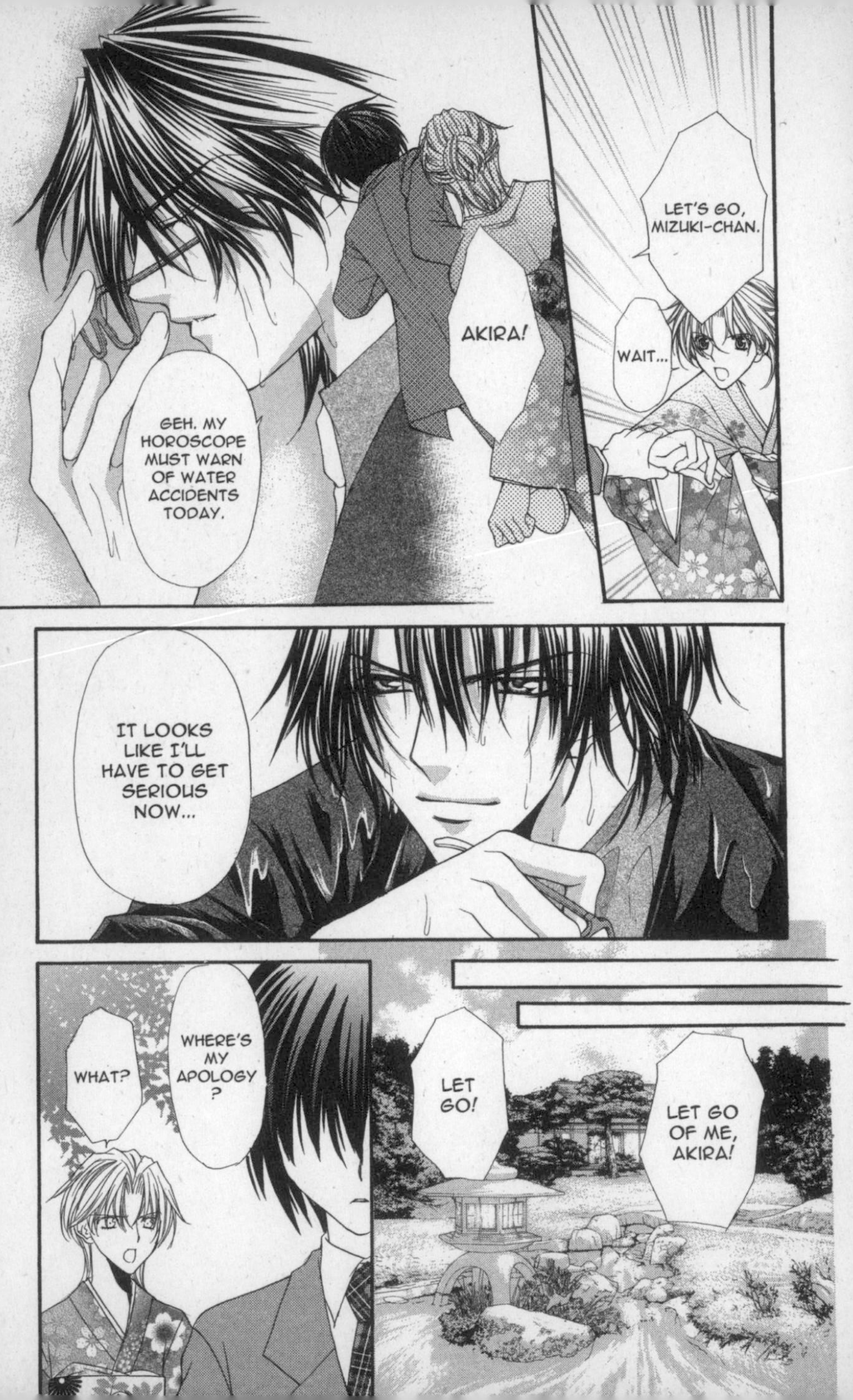
LET'S GO, MIZUKI-CHAN.
WAIT...
AKIRA!
GEH. MY HOROSCOPE MUST WARN OF WATER ACCIDENTS TODAY.
IT LOOKS LIKE I'LL HAVE TO GET SERIOUS NOW...
LET GO OF ME, AKIRA!
LET GO!
WHERE'S MY APOLOGY?
WHAT?

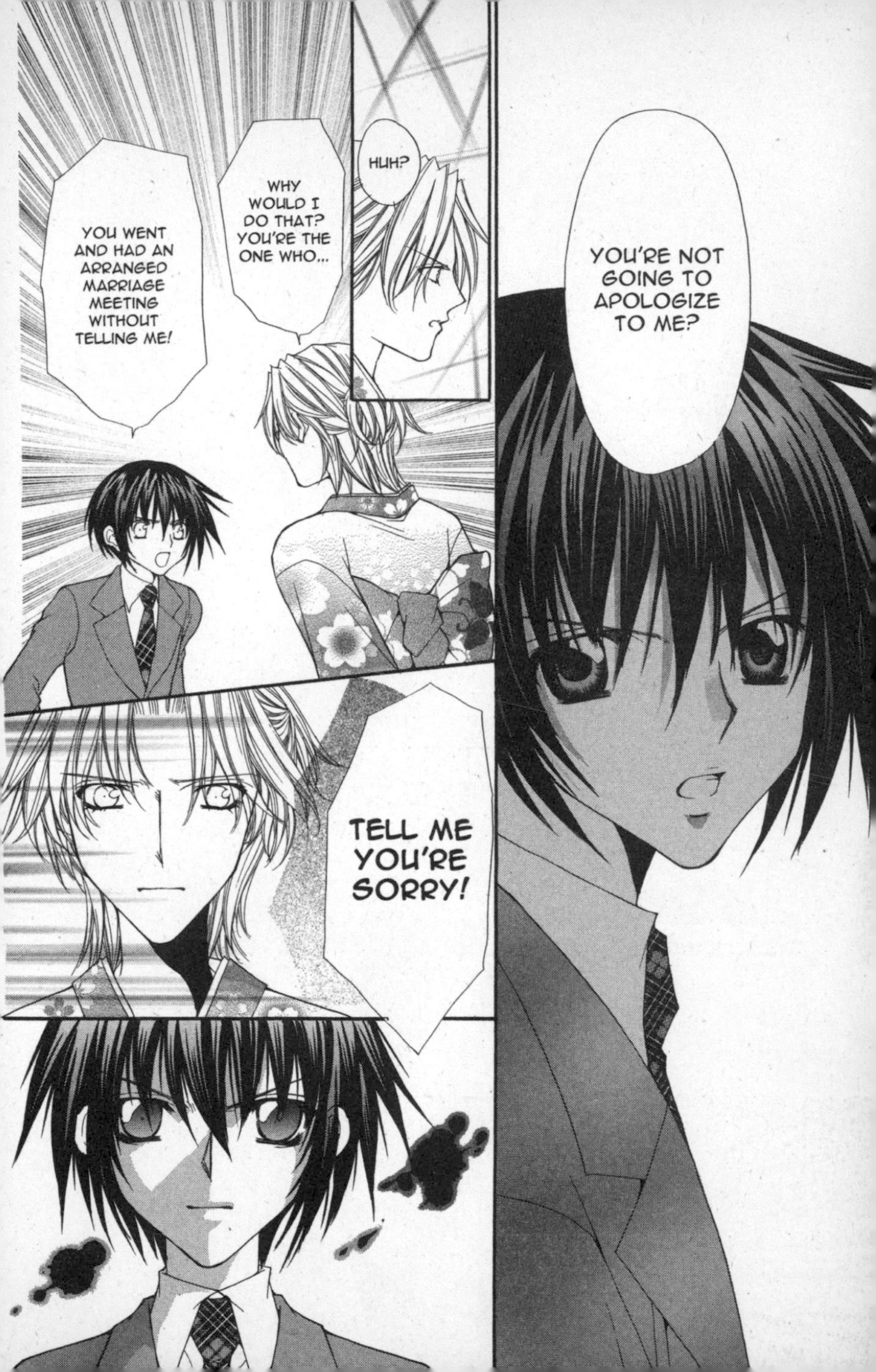
YOU'RE NOT GOING TO APOLOGIZE TO ME?
HUH?
WHY WOULD I DO THAT? YOU'RE THE ONE WHO...
YOU WENT AND HAD AN ARRANGED MARRIAGE MEETING WITHOUT TELLING ME!
TELL ME YOU'RE SORRY!

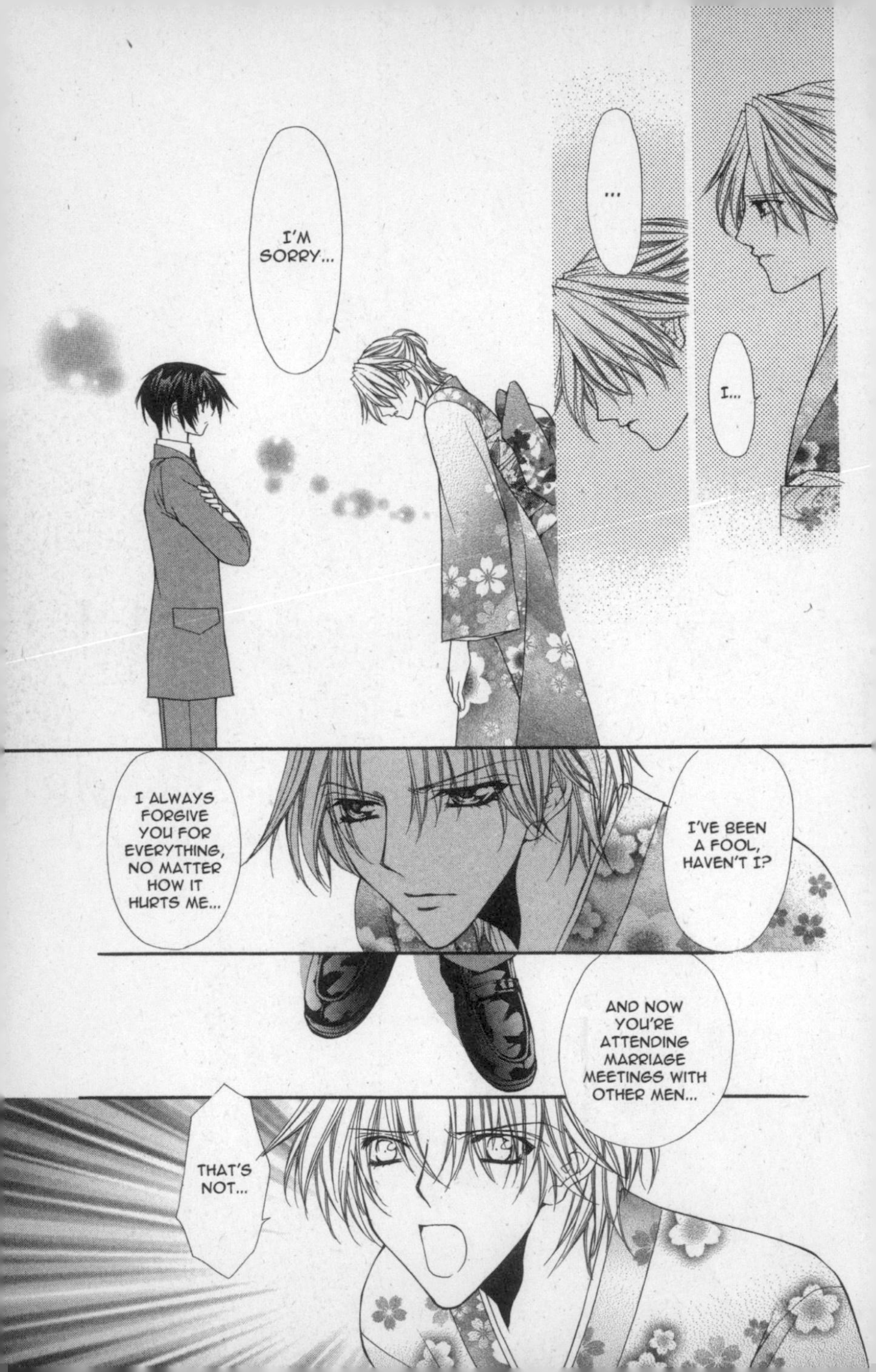
I...
...
I'M SORRY...
I'VE BEEN A FOOL, HAVEN'T I?
I ALWAYS FORGIVE YOU FOR EVERYTHING, NO MATTER HOW IT HURTS ME...
AND NOW YOU'RE ATTENDING MARRIAGE MEETINGS WITH OTHER MEN...
THAT'S NOT...

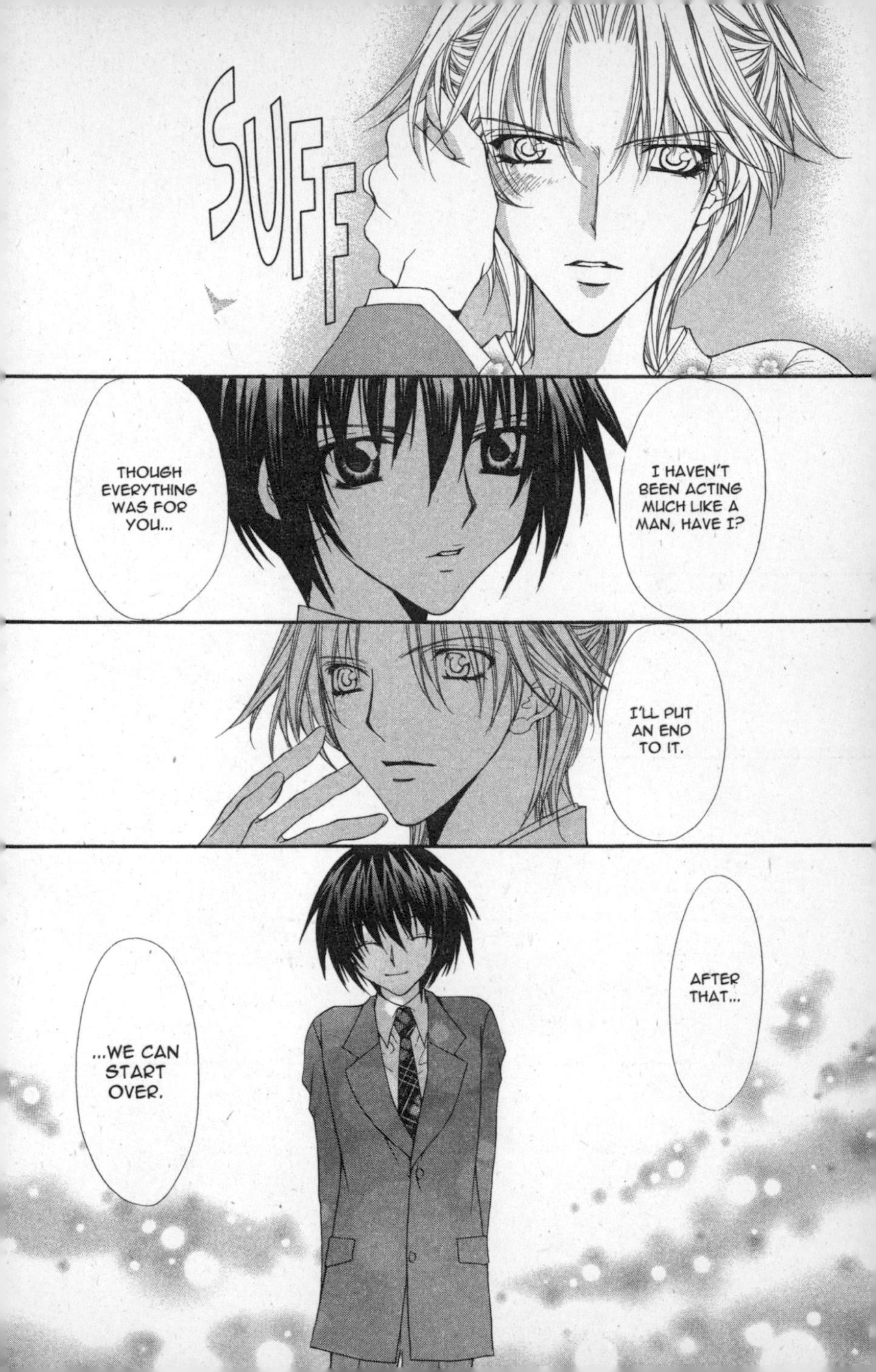
SUFF
I HAVEN'T BEEN ACTING MUCH LIKE A MAN, HAVE I?
THOUGH EVERYTHING WAS FOR YOU...
I'LL PUT AN END TO IT.
AFTER THAT...
...WE CAN START OVER.

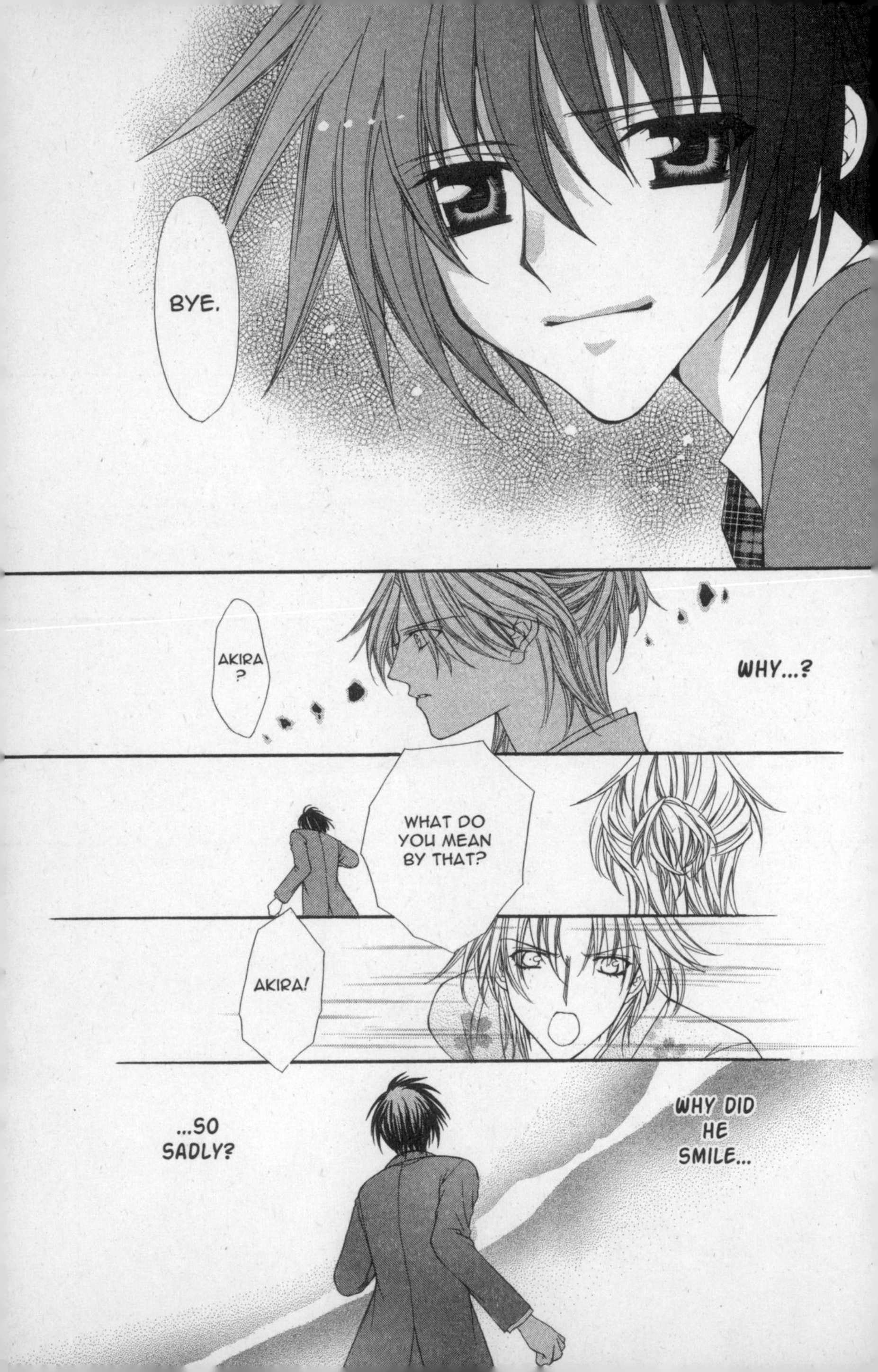
BYE.
WHY...?
AKIRA ?
WHAT DO YOU MEAN BY THAT?
AKIRA!
WHY DID HE SMILE...
...SO SADLY?

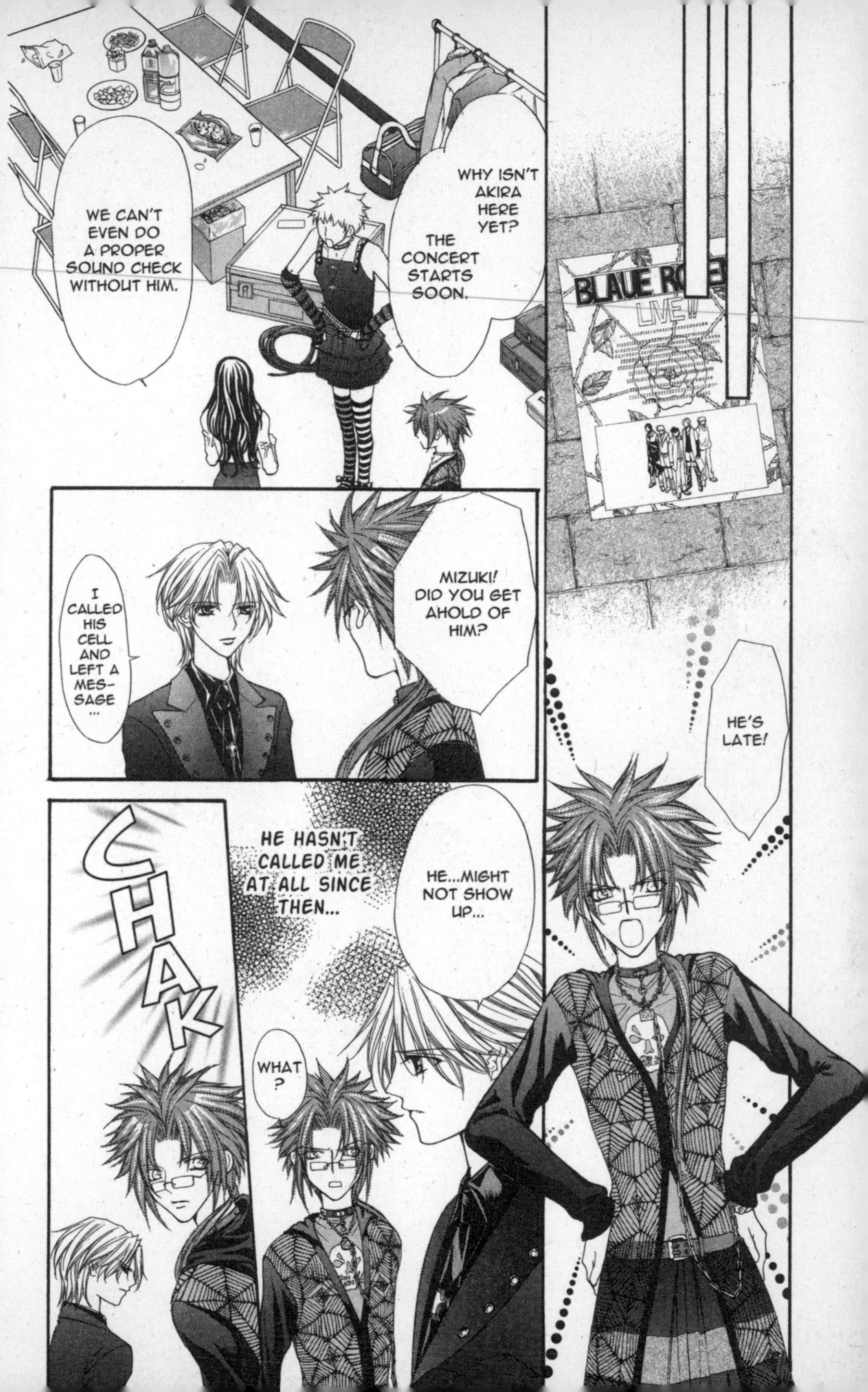
BLAUE RO
LIVE!!
WHY ISN'T AKIRA HERE YET?
THE CONCERT STARTS SOON.
WE CAN'T EVEN DO A PROPER SOUND CHECK WITHOUT HIM.
MIZUKI! DID YOU GET AHOLD OF HIM?
I CALLED HIS CELL AND LEFT A MES-SAGE...
HE'S LATE!
HE...MIGHT NOT SHOW UP...
HE HASN'T CALLED ME AT ALL SINCE THEN...
CHAK
WHAT?

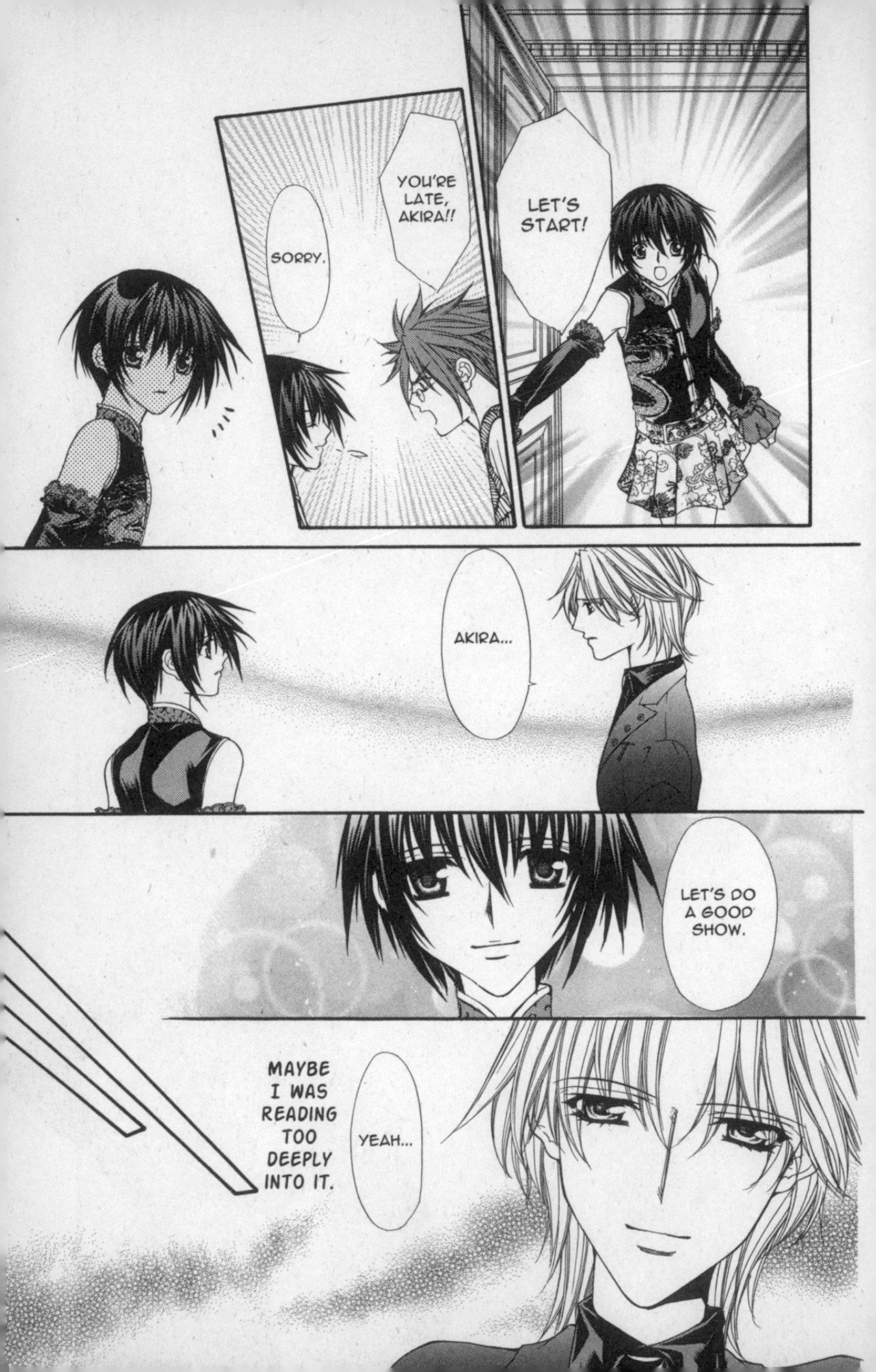
LET'S START!
YOU'RE LATE, AKIRA!!
SORRY.
AKIRA...
LET'S DO A GOOD SHOW.
YEAH...
MAYBE I WAS READING TOO DEEPLY INTO IT.

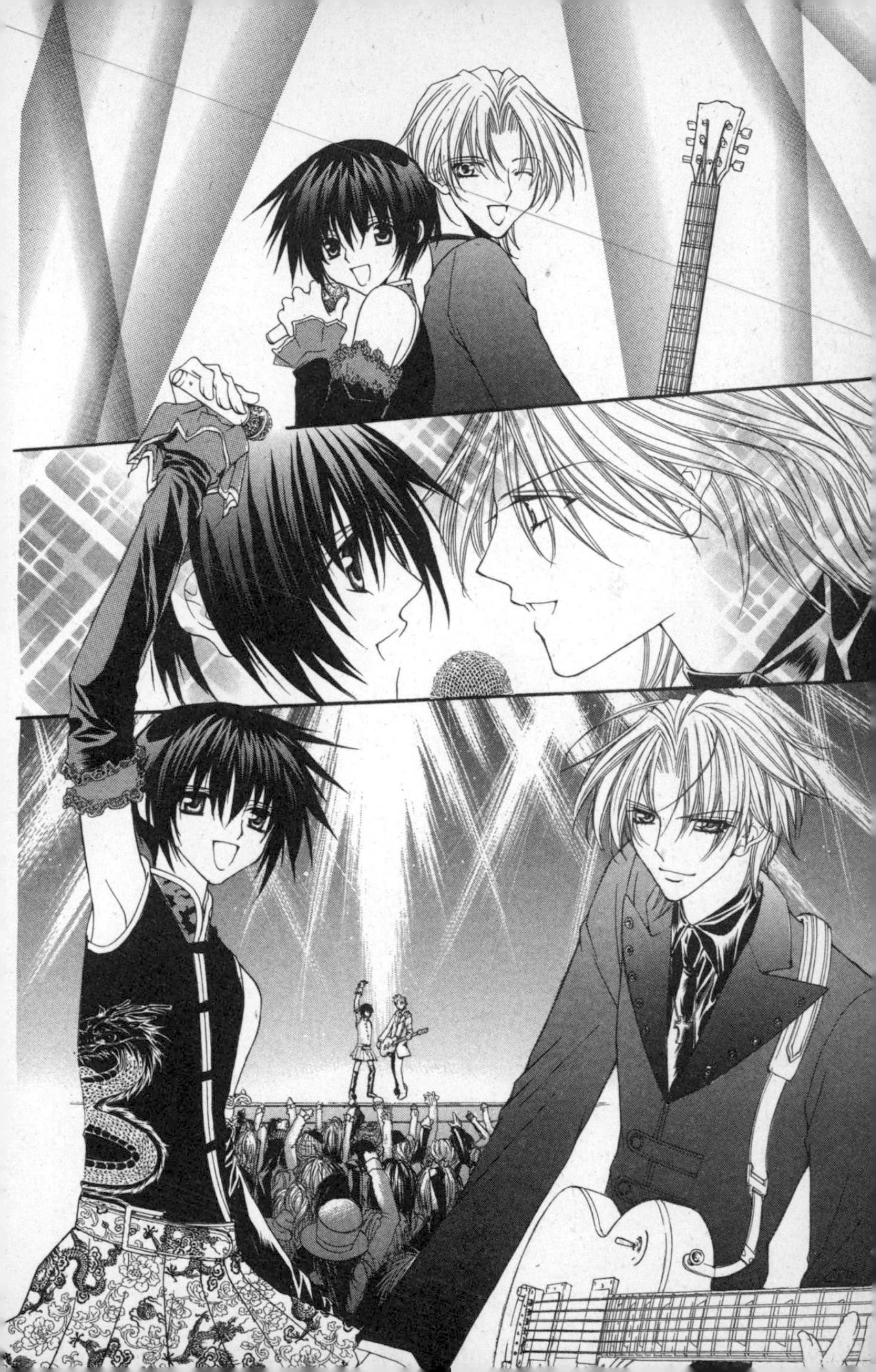

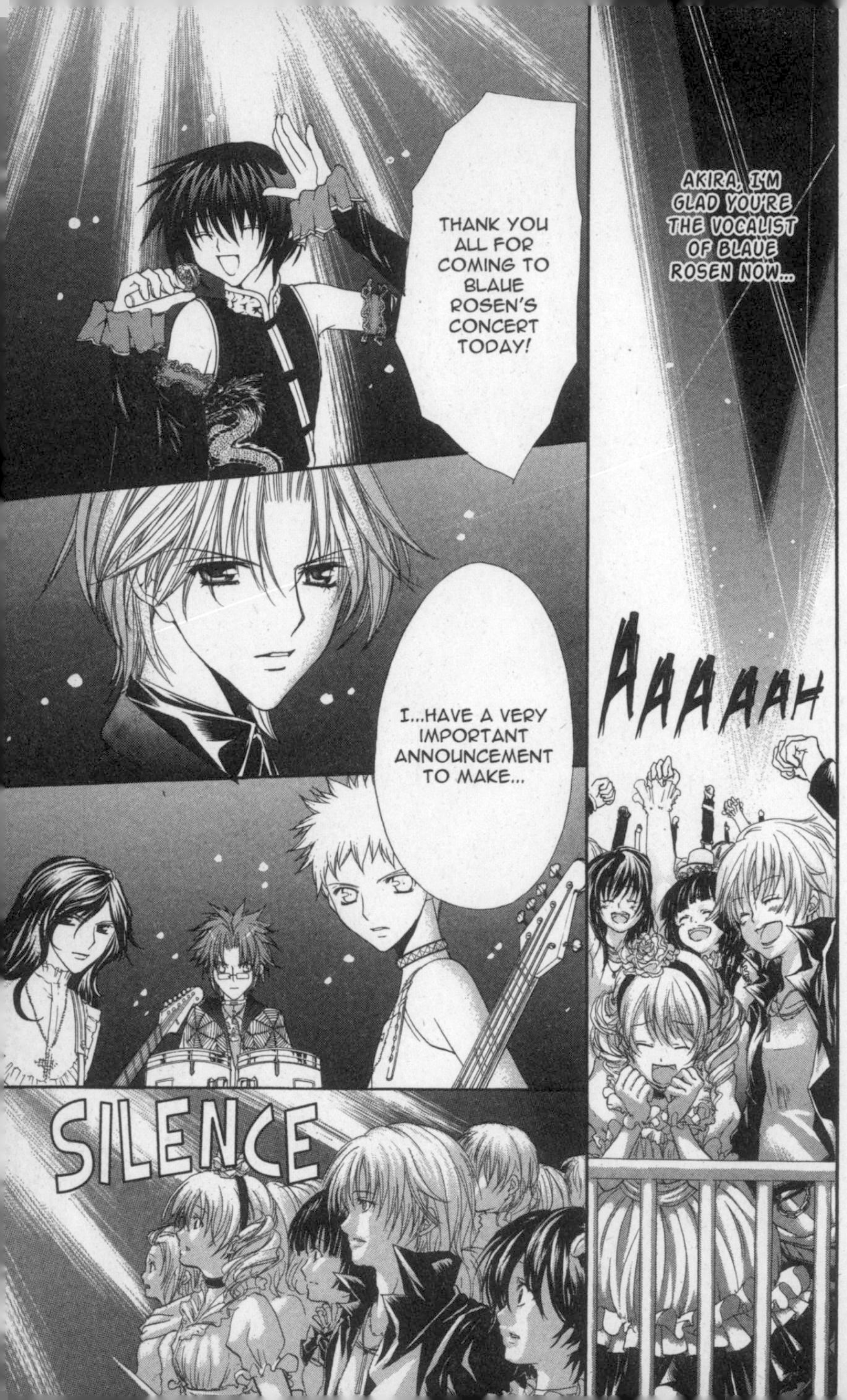
AKIRA, I'M GLAD YOU'RE THE VOCALIST OF BLAUE ROSEN NOW...
AAAAAH
THANK YOU ALL FOR COMING TO BLAUE ROSEN'S CONCERT TODAY!
I...HAVE A VERY IMPORTANT ANNOUNCEMENT TO MAKE...
SILENCE

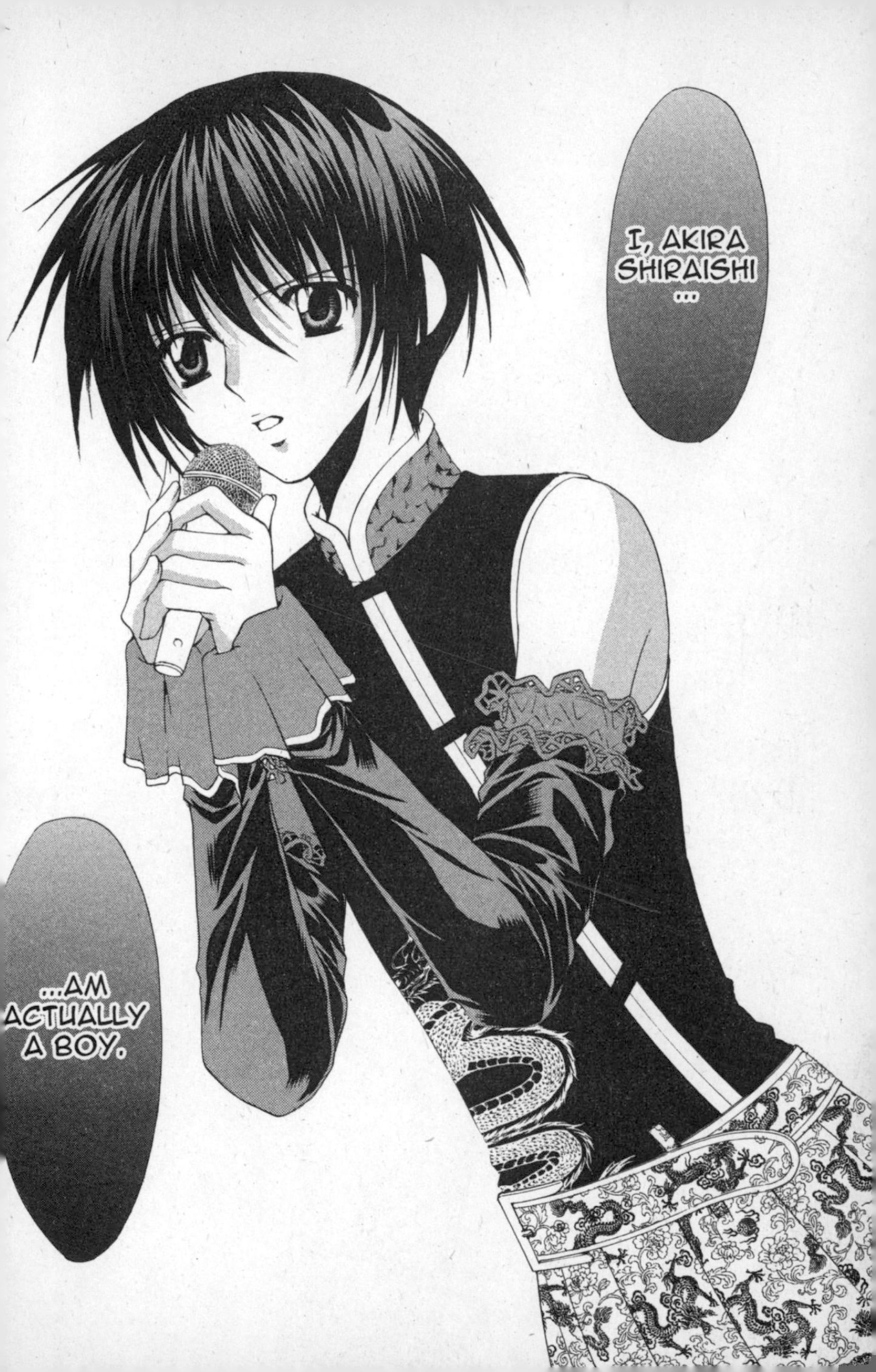
I, AKIRA SHIRAISHI ...
...AM ACTUALLY A BOY.

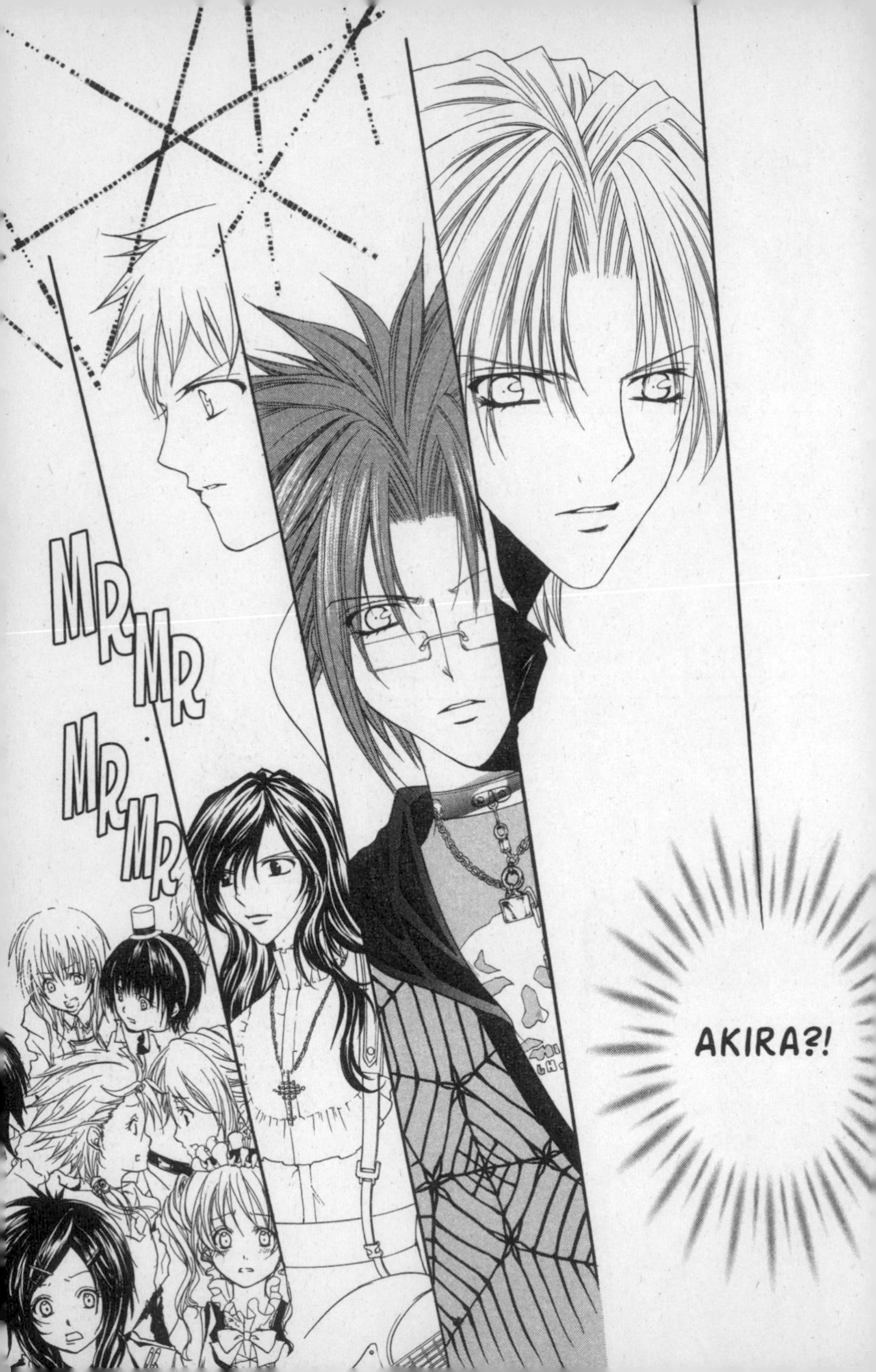
AKIRA?!
MRMR MRMR

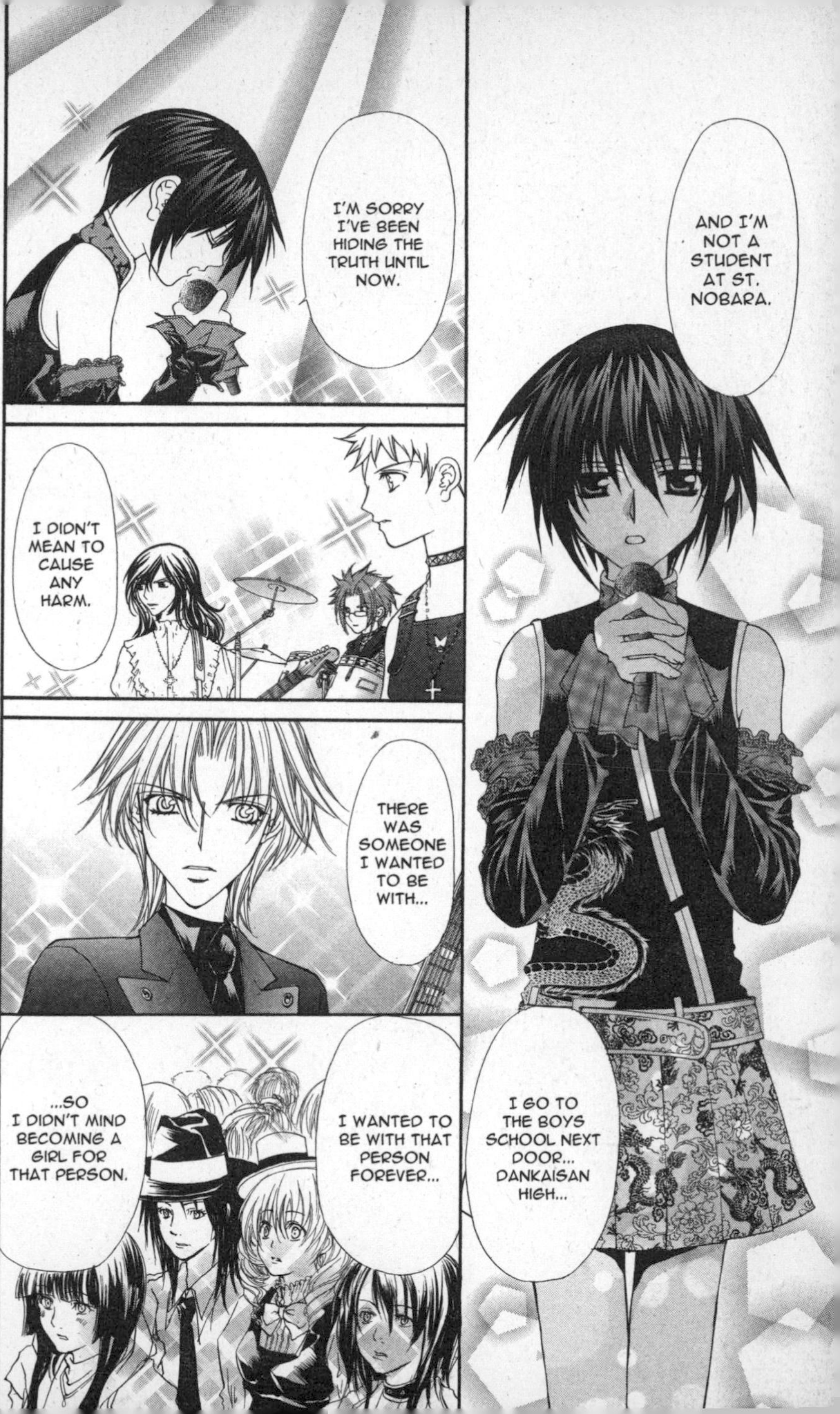
AND I'M NOT A STUDENT AT ST. NOBARA.
I GO TO THE BOYS SCHOOL NEXT DOOR... DANKAISAN HIGH...
I'M SORRY I'VE BEEN HIDING THE TRUTH UNTIL NOW.
I DIDN'T MEAN TO CAUSE ANY HARM.
THERE WAS SOMEONE I WANTED TO BE WITH...
I WANTED TO BE WITH THAT PERSON FOREVER...
...SO I DIDN'T MIND BECOMING A GIRL FOR THAT PERSON.

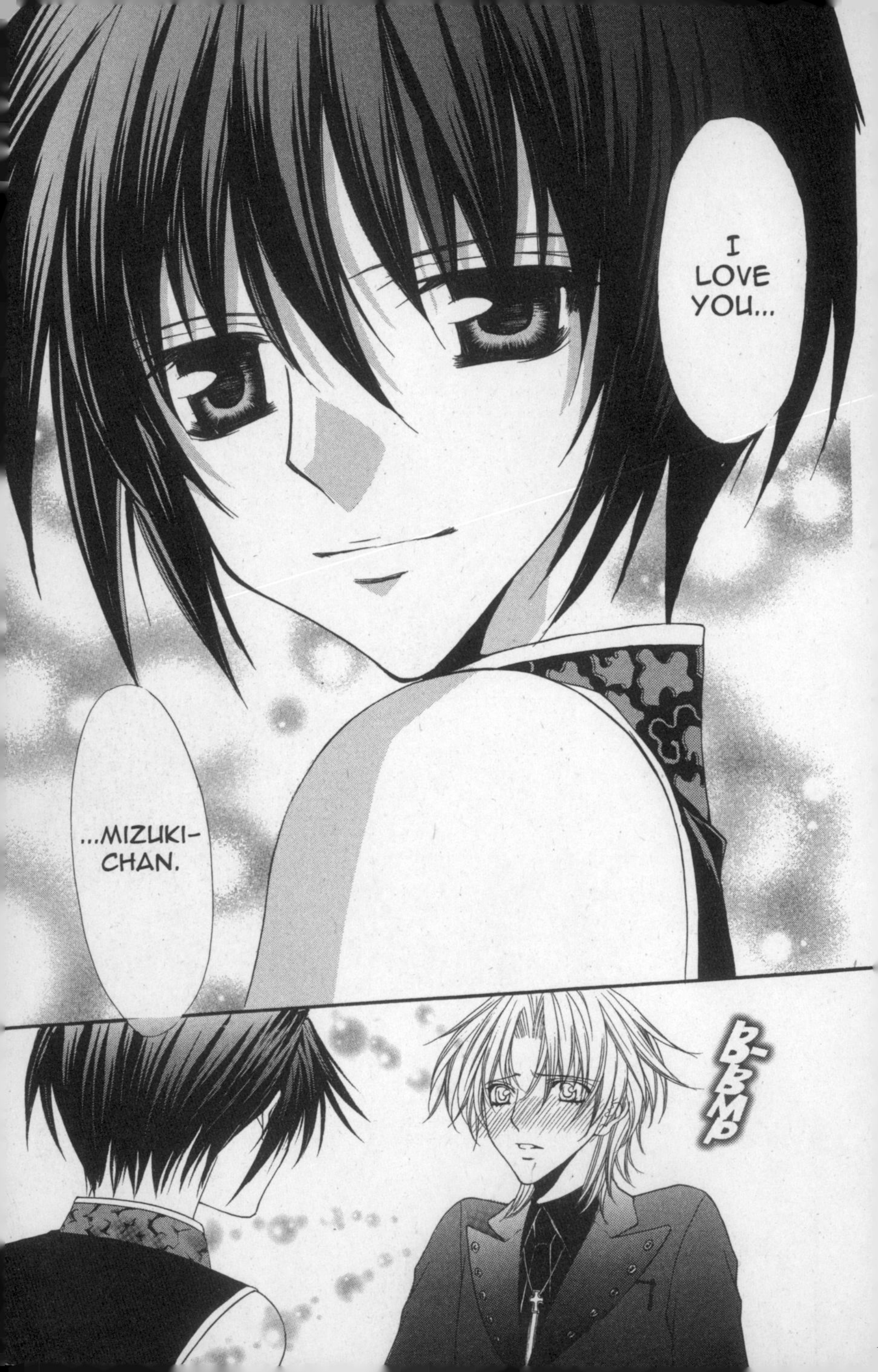
I LOVE YOU...
...MIZUKI-CHAN.
B-BMP

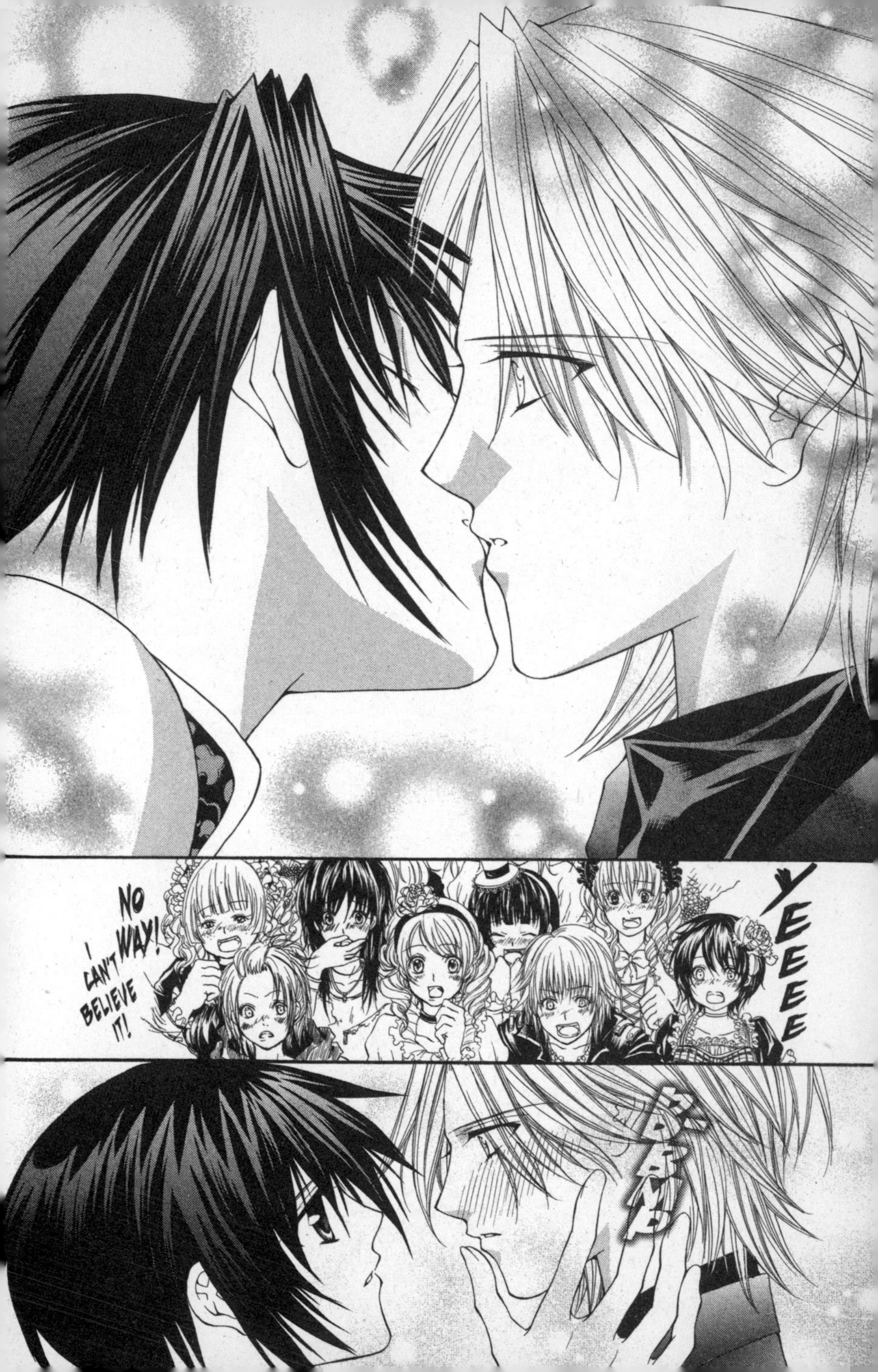
YEEEE
NO WAY!
I CAN'T BELIEVE IT!

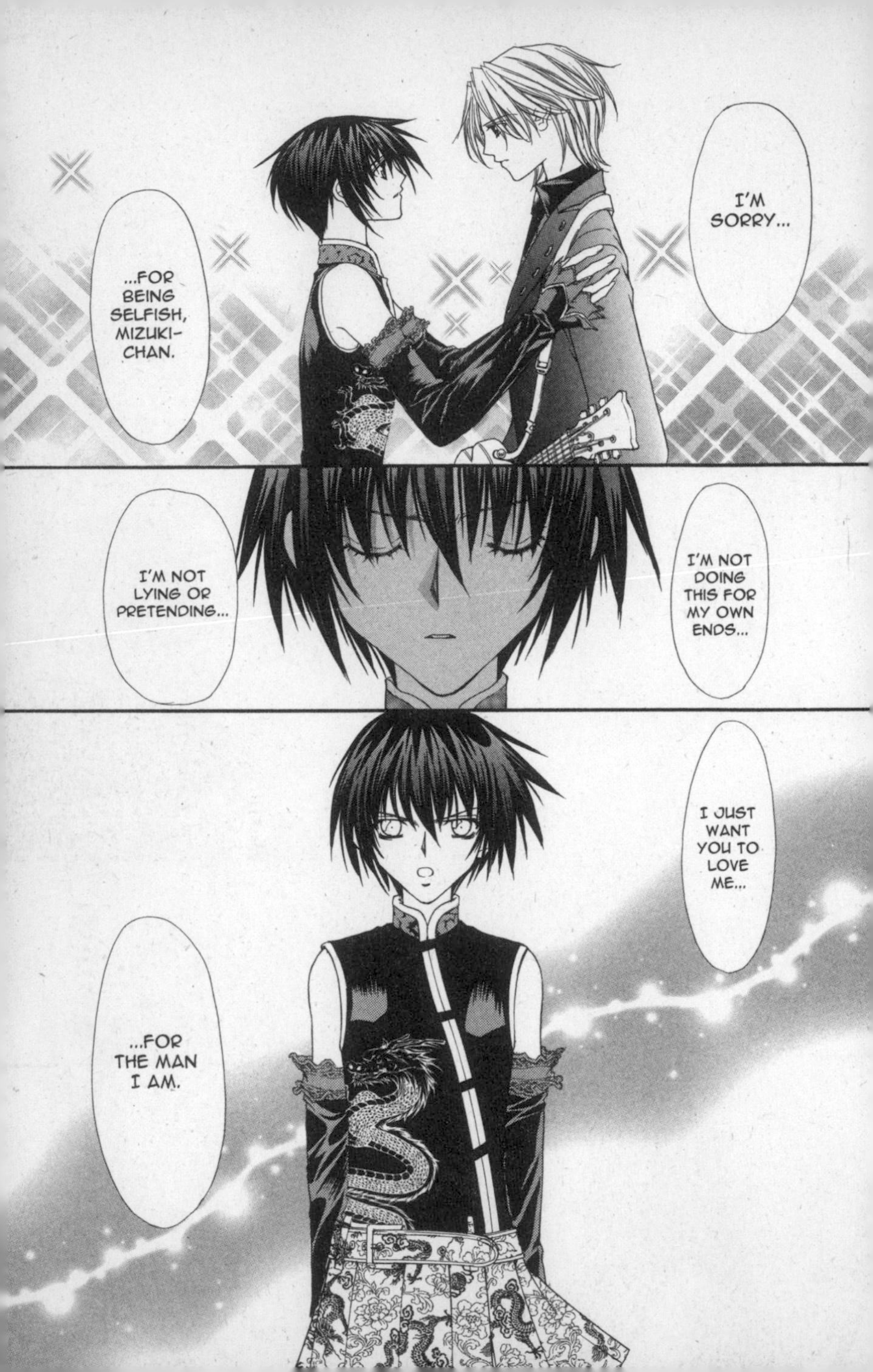
I'M SORRY...
...FOR BEING SELFISH, MIZUKI-CHAN.
I'M NOT DOING THIS FOR MY OWN ENDS...
I'M NOT LYING OR PRETENDING...
I JUST WANT YOU TO LOVE ME...
...FOR THE MAN I AM.

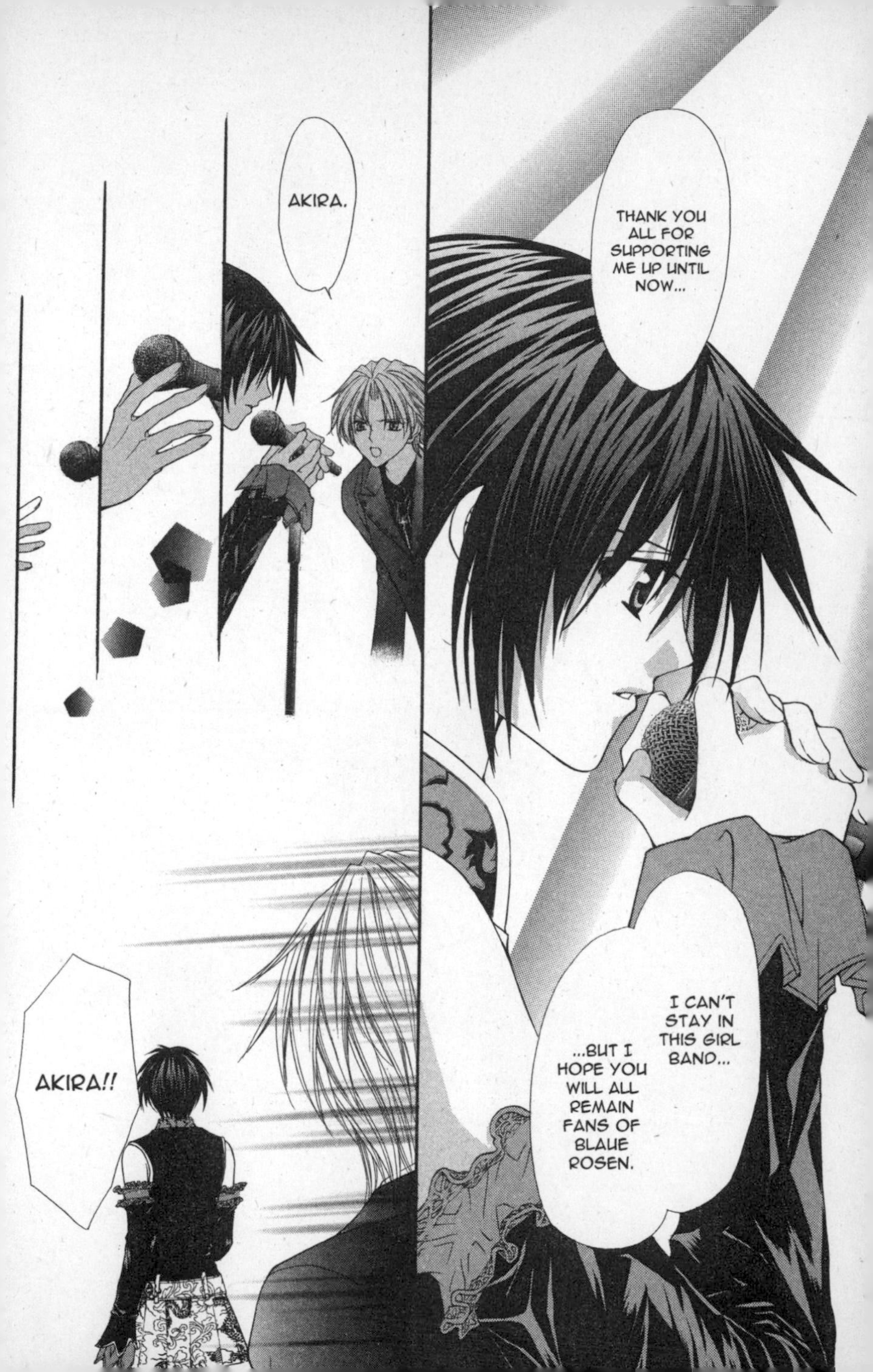
THANK YOU ALL FOR SUPPORTING ME UP UNTIL NOW...
I CAN'T STAY IN THIS GIRL BAND...
...BUT I HOPE YOU WILL ALL REMAIN FANS OF BLAUE ROSEN.
AKIRA.
AKIRA!!

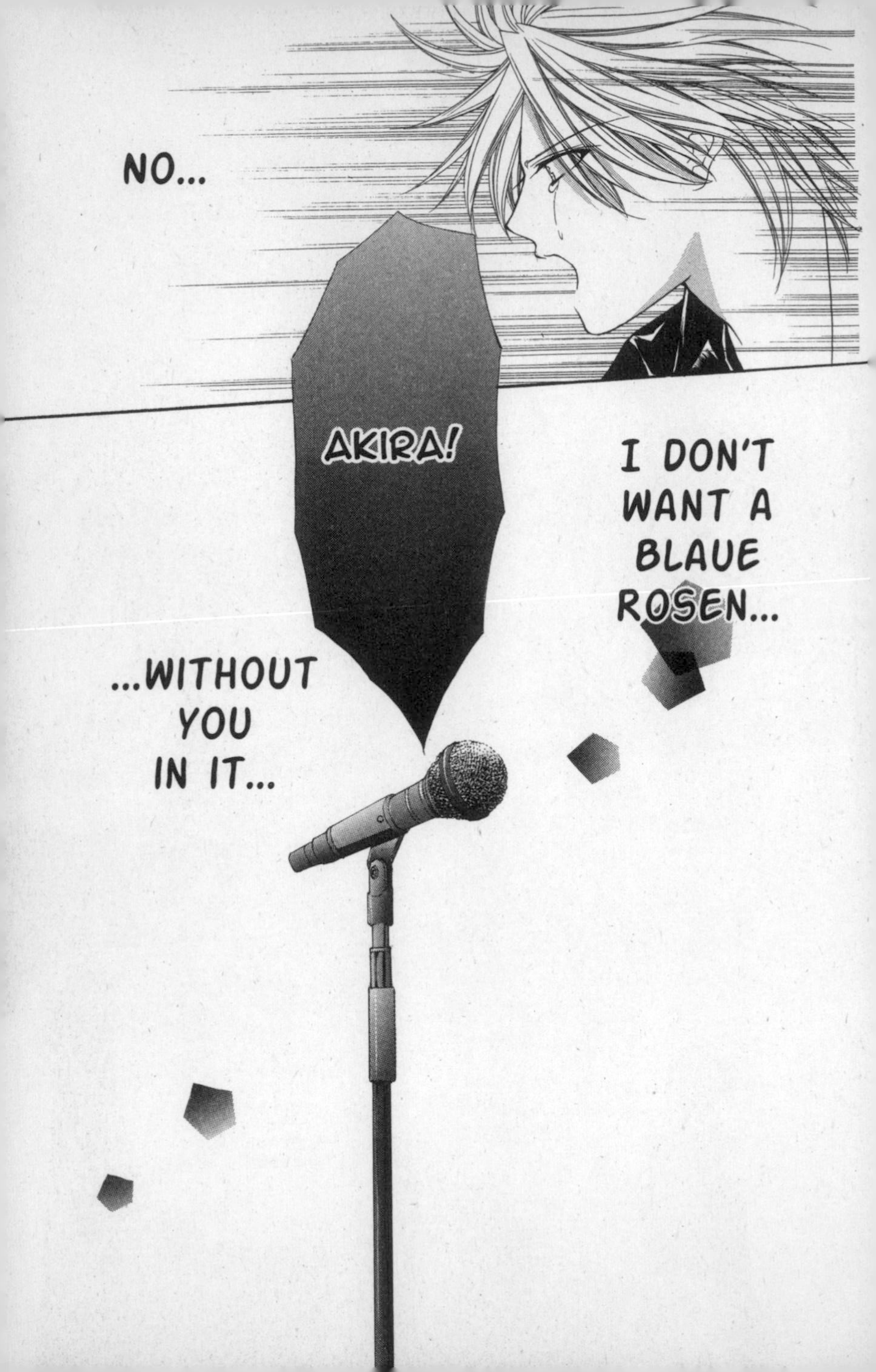
NO...
AKIRA!
I DON'T WANT A BLAUE ROSEN...
...WITHOUT YOU IN IT...

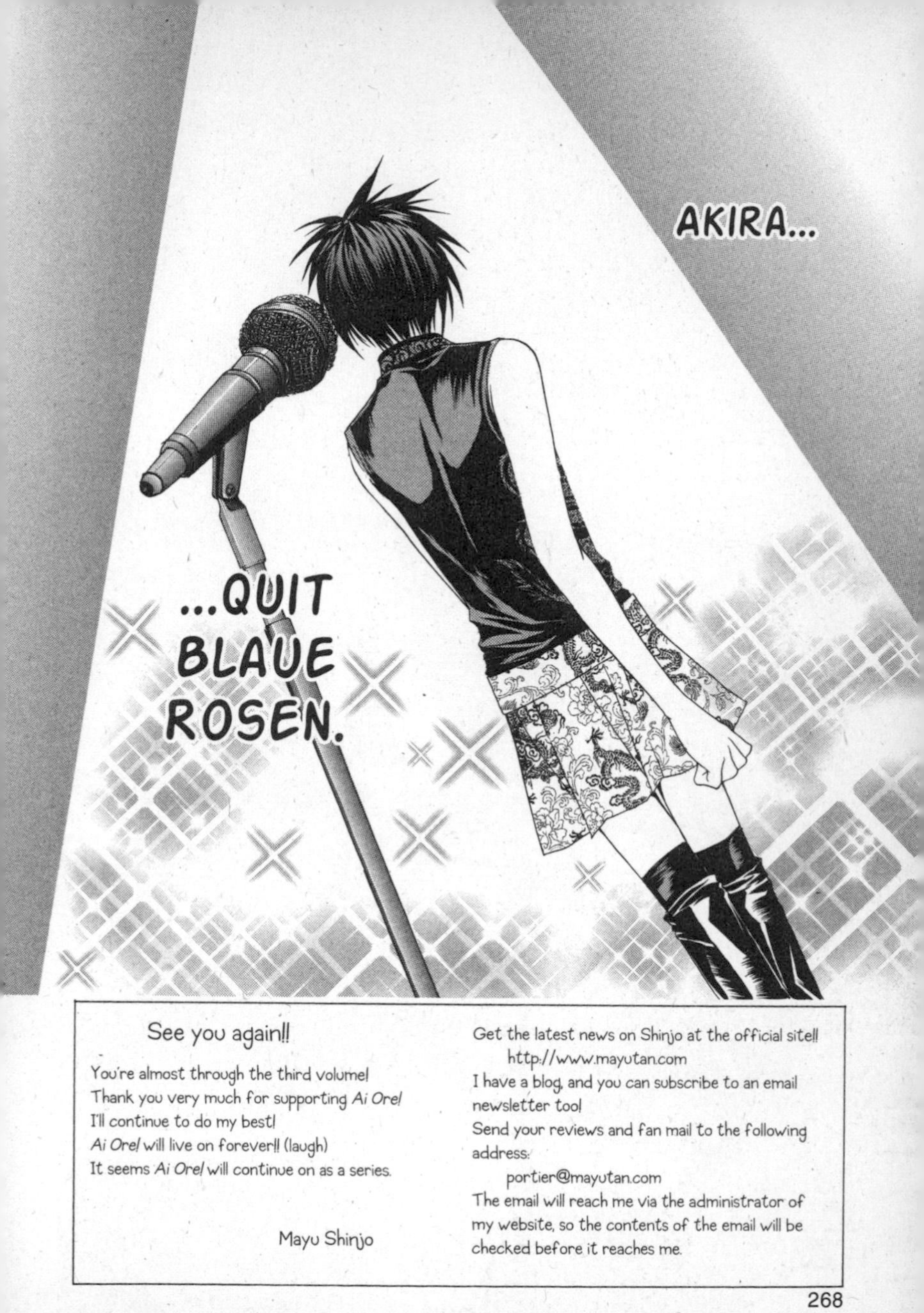
AKIRA...
...QUIT BLAUE ROSEN.

See you again!!

You're almost through the third volume!
Thank you very much for supporting *Ai Ore!*
I'll continue to do my best!
Ai Ore! will live on forever!! (laugh)
It seems *Ai Ore!* will continue on as a series.

Mayu Shinjo

Get the latest news on Shinjo at the official site!!
http://www.mayutan.com
I have a blog, and you can subscribe to an email newsletter too!
Send your reviews and fan mail to the following address:
portier@mayutan.com
The email will reach me via the administrator of my website, so the contents of the email will be checked before it reaches me.

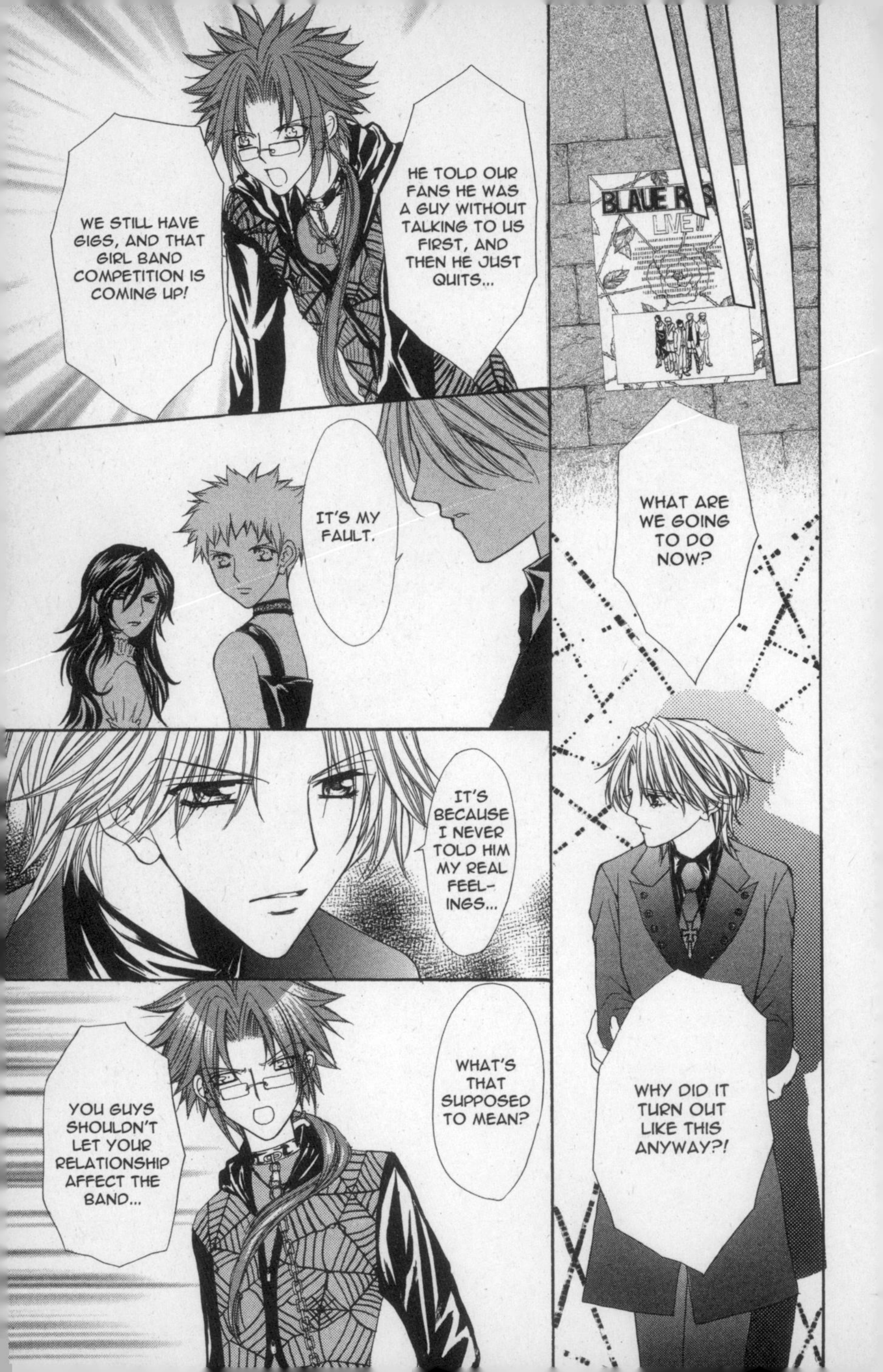
LIVE!!
WHAT ARE WE GOING TO DO NOW?
WHY DID IT TURN OUT LIKE THIS ANYWAY?!
HE TOLD OUR FANS HE WAS A GUY WITHOUT TALKING TO US FIRST, AND THEN HE JUST QUITS...
WE STILL HAVE GIGS, AND THAT GIRL BAND COMPETITION IS COMING UP!
IT'S MY FAULT.
IT'S BECAUSE I NEVER TOLD HIM MY REAL FEEL-INGS...
WHAT'S THAT SUPPOSED TO MEAN?
YOU GUYS SHOULDN'T LET YOUR RELATIONSHIP AFFECT THE BAND...

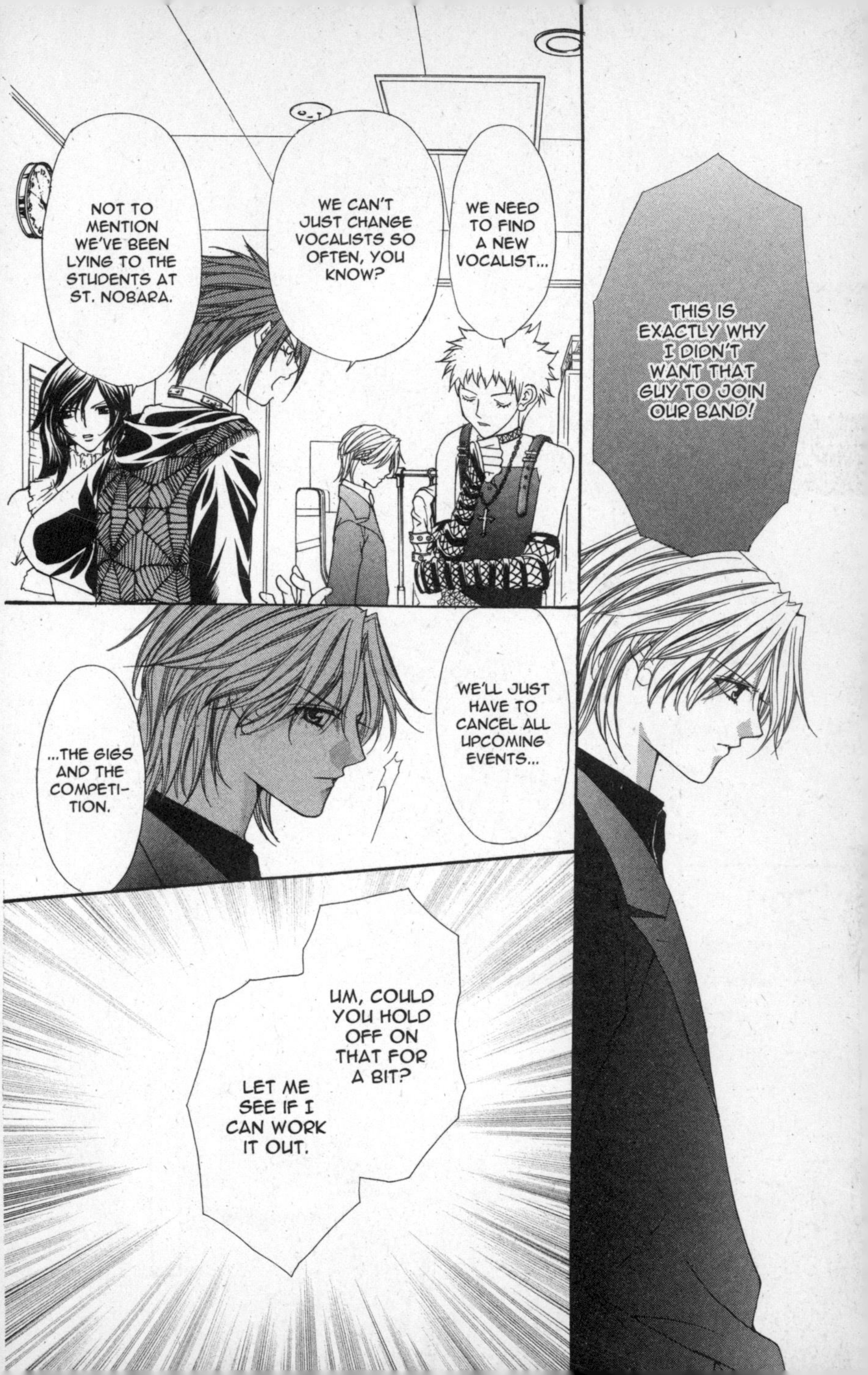
THIS IS EXACTLY WHY I DIDN'T WANT THAT GUY TO JOIN OUR BAND!
WE NEED TO FIND A NEW VOCALIST...
WE CAN'T JUST CHANGE VOCALISTS SO OFTEN, YOU KNOW?
NOT TO MENTION WE'VE BEEN LYING TO THE STUDENTS AT ST. NOBARA.
WE'LL JUST HAVE TO CANCEL ALL UPCOMING EVENTS...
...THE GIGS AND THE COMPETI-TION.
UM, COULD YOU HOLD OFF ON THAT FOR A BIT?
LET ME SEE IF I CAN WORK IT OUT.

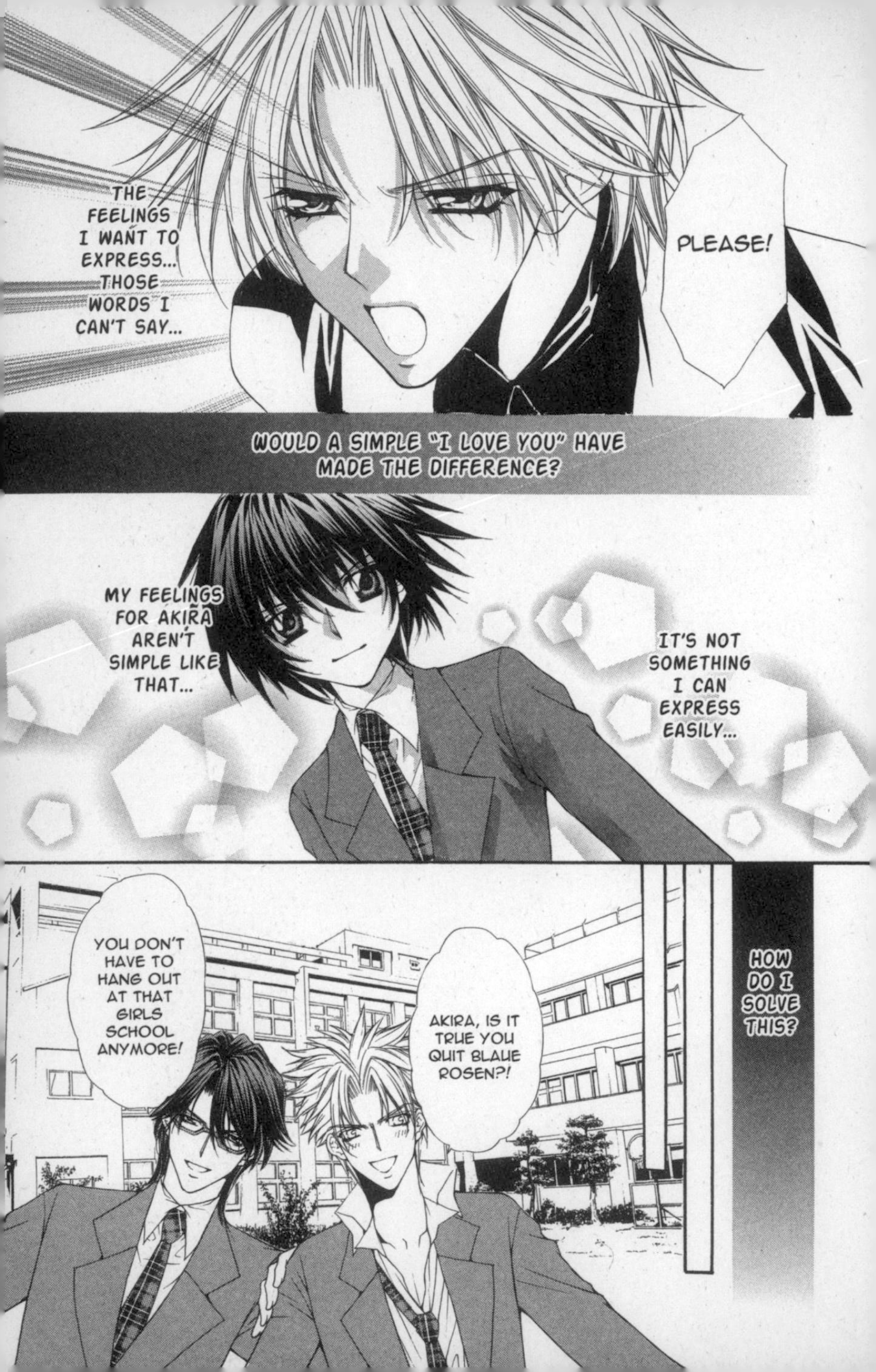
PLEASE!
THE FEELINGS I WANT TO EXPRESS... THOSE WORDS I CAN'T SAY...
WOULD A SIMPLE "I LOVE YOU" HAVE MADE THE DIFFERENCE?
MY FEELINGS FOR AKIRA AREN'T SIMPLE LIKE THAT...
IT'S NOT SOMETHING I CAN EXPRESS EASILY...
HOW DO I SOLVE THIS?
AKIRA, IS IT TRUE YOU QUIT BLAUE ROSEN?!
YOU DON'T HAVE TO HANG OUT AT THAT GIRLS SCHOOL ANYMORE!

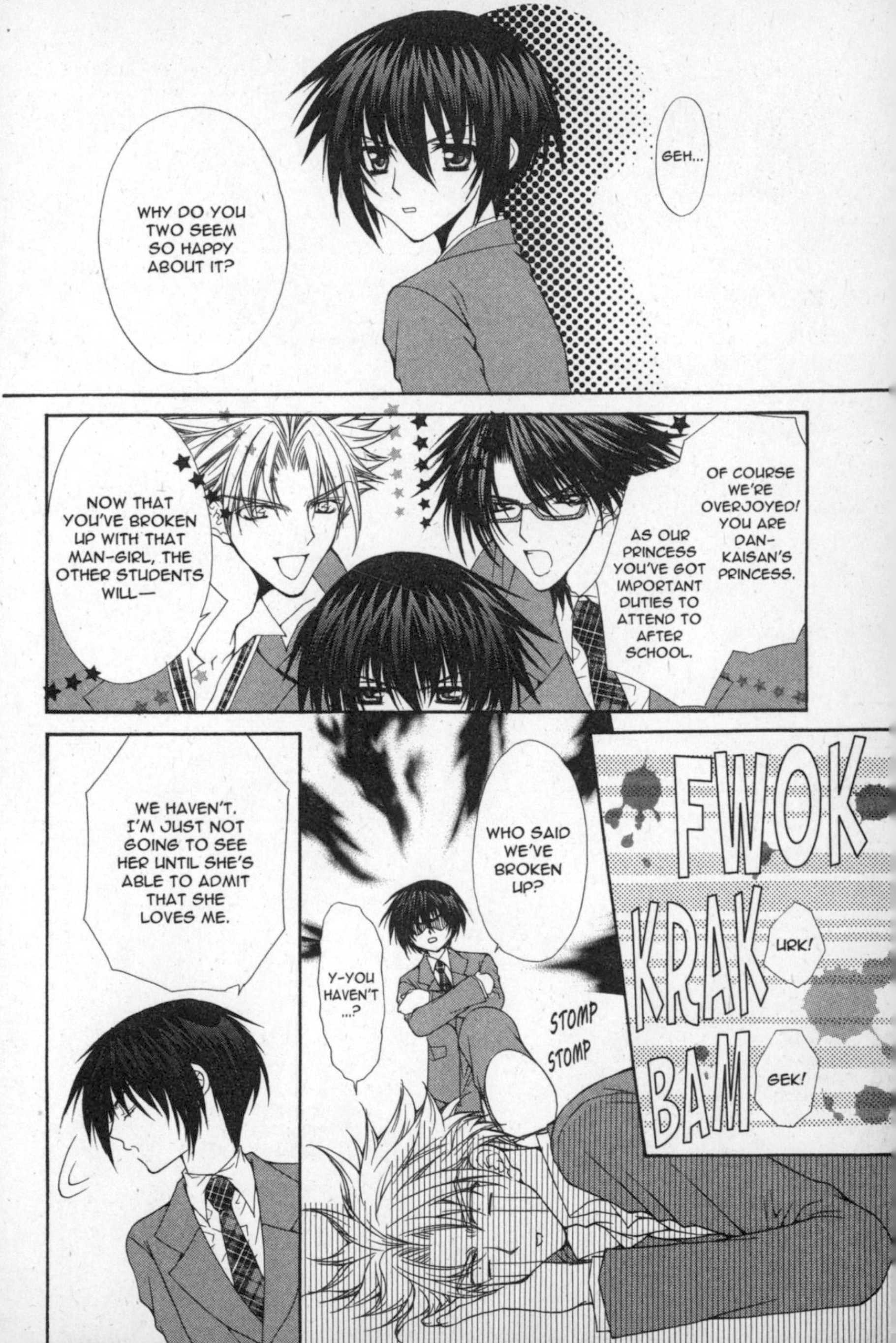
GEH...
WHY DO YOU TWO SEEM SO HAPPY ABOUT IT?
OF COURSE WE'RE OVERJOYED! YOU ARE DAN-KAISAN'S PRINCESS.
AS OUR PRINCESS YOU'VE GOT IMPORTANT DUTIES TO ATTEND TO AFTER SCHOOL.
NOW THAT YOU'VE BROKEN UP WITH THAT MAN-GIRL, THE OTHER STUDENTS WILL—
FWOK
KRAK
URK!
BAM
GEK!
WHO SAID WE'VE BROKEN UP?
STOMP STOMP
Y-YOU HAVEN'T ...?
WE HAVEN'T. I'M JUST NOT GOING TO SEE HER UNTIL SHE'S ABLE TO ADMIT THAT SHE LOVES ME.

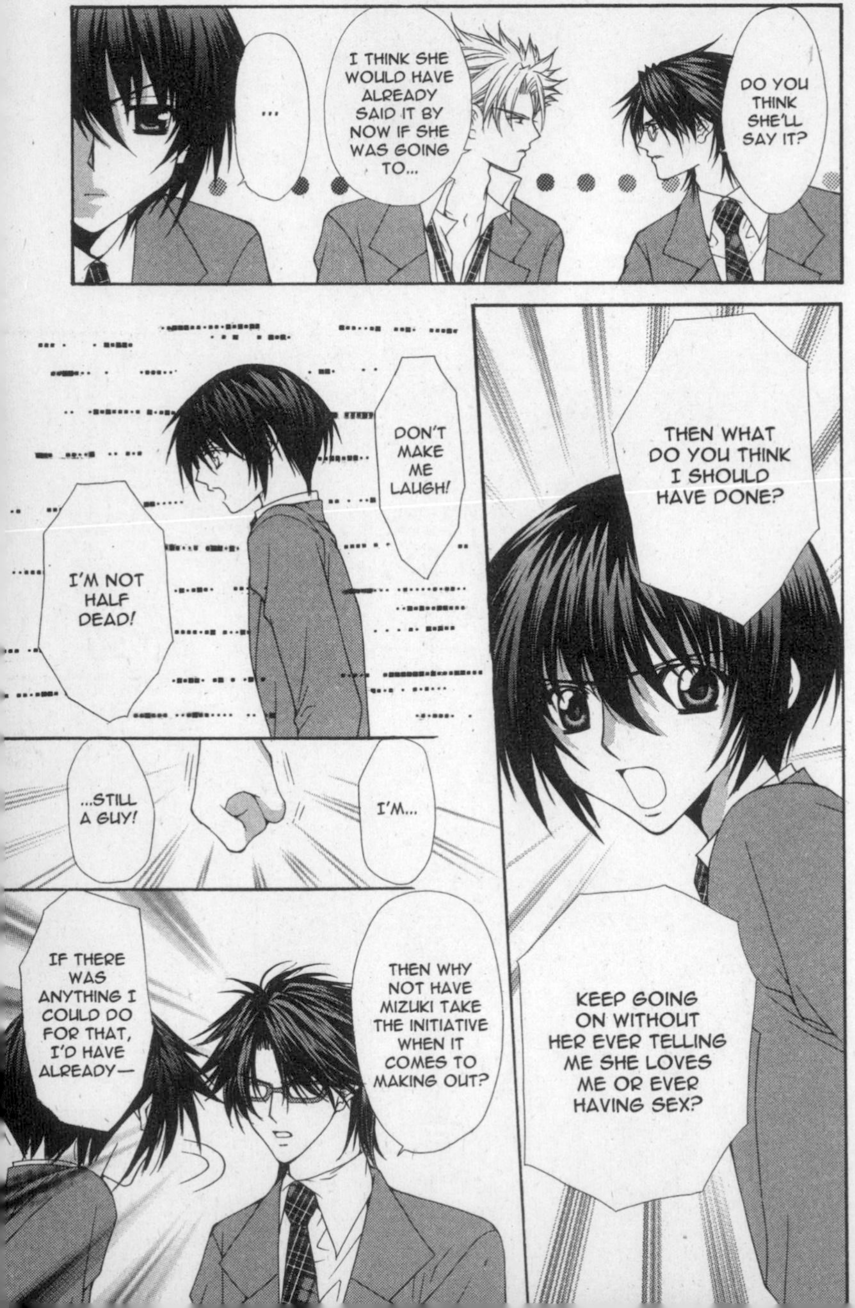
DO YOU THINK SHE'LL SAY IT?
I THINK SHE WOULD HAVE ALREADY SAID IT BY NOW IF SHE WAS GOING TO...
...
THEN WHAT DO YOU THINK I SHOULD HAVE DONE?
KEEP GOING ON WITHOUT HER EVER TELLING ME SHE LOVES ME OR EVER HAVING SEX?
DON'T MAKE ME LAUGH!
I'M NOT HALF DEAD!
I'M...
...STILL A GUY!
THEN WHY NOT HAVE MIZUKI TAKE THE INITIATIVE WHEN IT COMES TO MAKING OUT?
IF THERE WAS ANYTHING I COULD DO FOR THAT, I'D HAVE ALREADY—

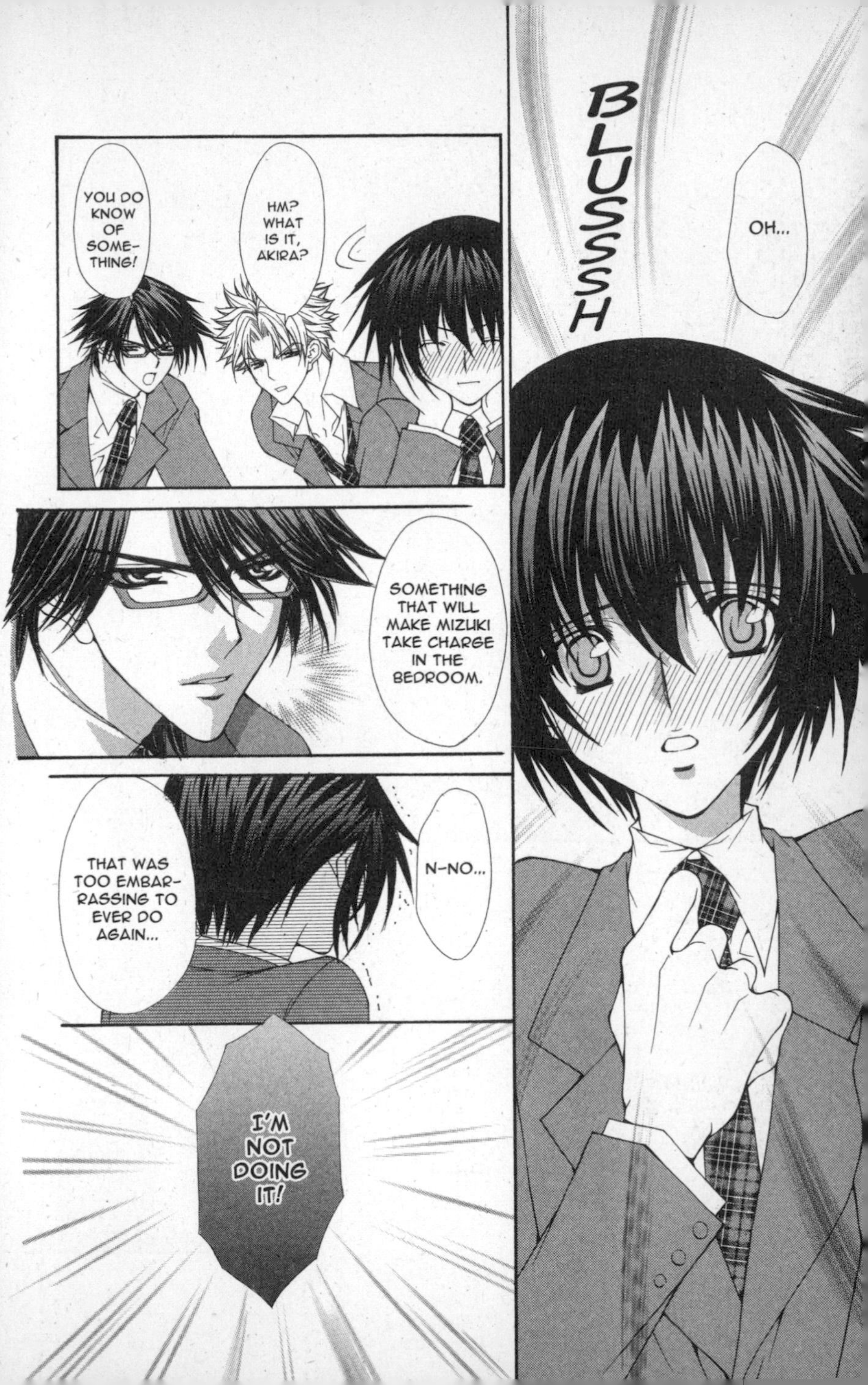
OH...
BLUSSSH
HM? WHAT IS IT, AKIRA?
YOU DO KNOW OF SOME-THING!
SOMETHING THAT WILL MAKE MIZUKI TAKE CHARGE IN THE BEDROOM.
N-NO...
THAT WAS TOO EMBAR-RASSING TO EVER DO AGAIN...
I'M NOT DOING IT!

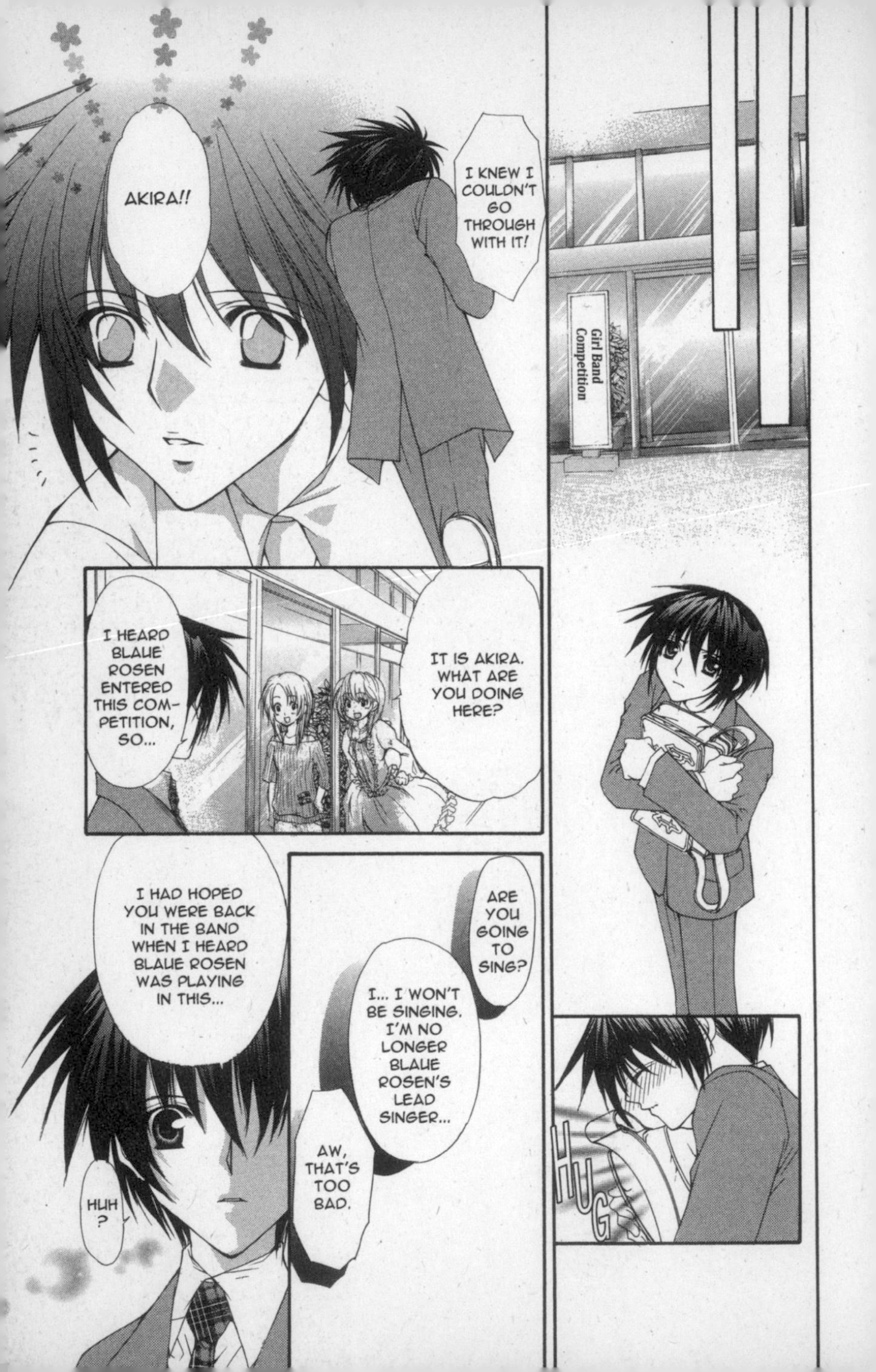
Girl Band Competition
I KNEW I COULDN'T GO THROUGH WITH IT!
AKIRA!!
IT IS AKIRA. WHAT ARE YOU DOING HERE?
I HEARD BLAUE ROSEN ENTERED THIS COMPETITION, SO...
ARE YOU GOING TO SING?
I... I WON'T BE SINGING. I'M NO LONGER BLAUE ROSEN'S LEAD SINGER...
AW, THAT'S TOO BAD.
I HAD HOPED YOU WERE BACK IN THE BAND WHEN I HEARD BLAUE ROSEN WAS PLAYING IN THIS...
HUH?
HUG

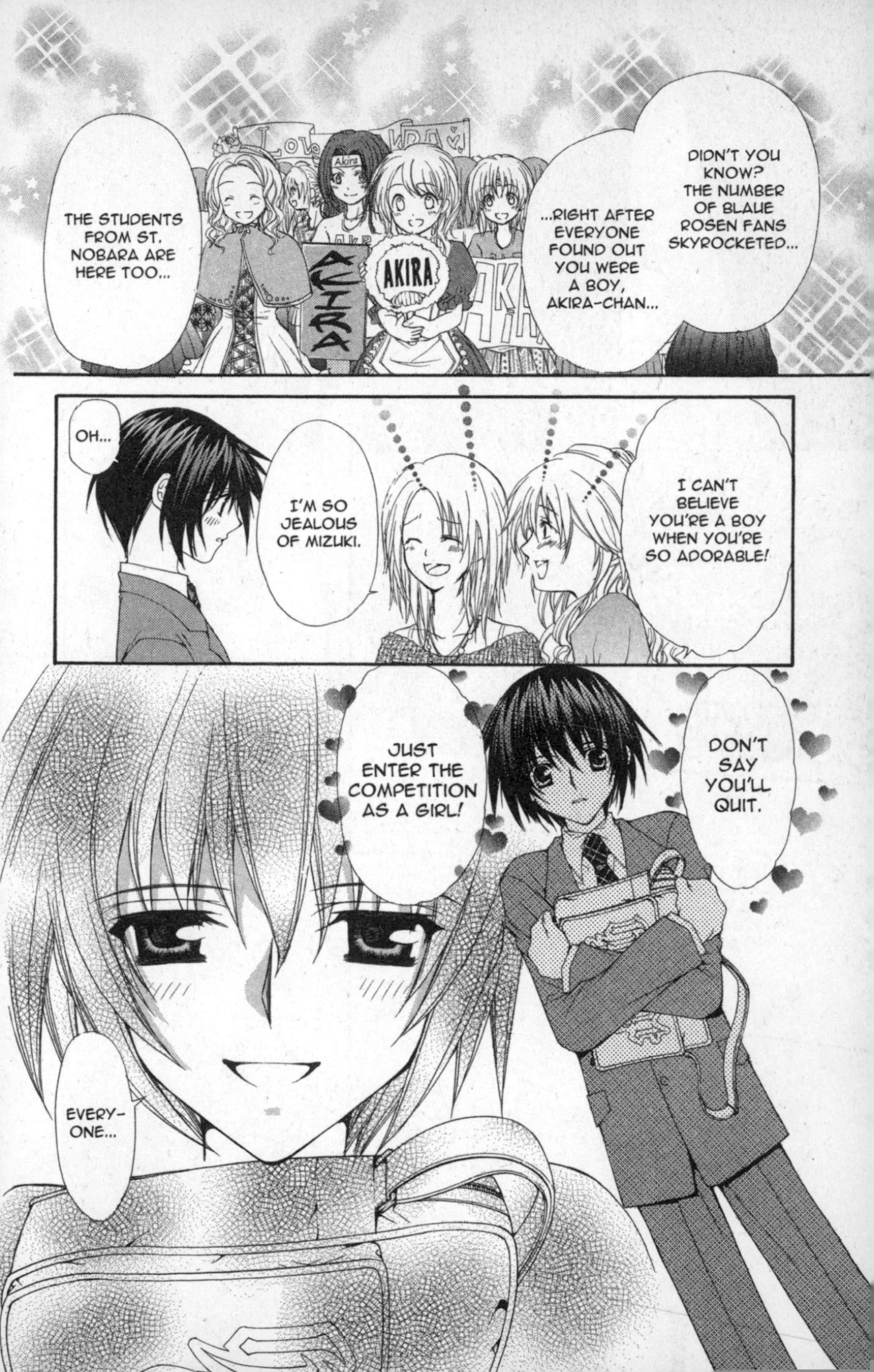
DIDN'T YOU KNOW? THE NUMBER OF BLAUE ROSEN FANS SKYROCKETED...
...RIGHT AFTER EVERYONE FOUND OUT YOU WERE A BOY, AKIRA-CHAN...
AKIRA
THE STUDENTS FROM ST. NOBARA ARE HERE TOO...
I CAN'T BELIEVE YOU'RE A BOY WHEN YOU'RE SO ADORABLE!
I'M SO JEALOUS OF MIZUKI.
OH...
DON'T SAY YOU'LL QUIT.
JUST ENTER THE COMPETITION AS A GIRL!
EVERY-
ONE...

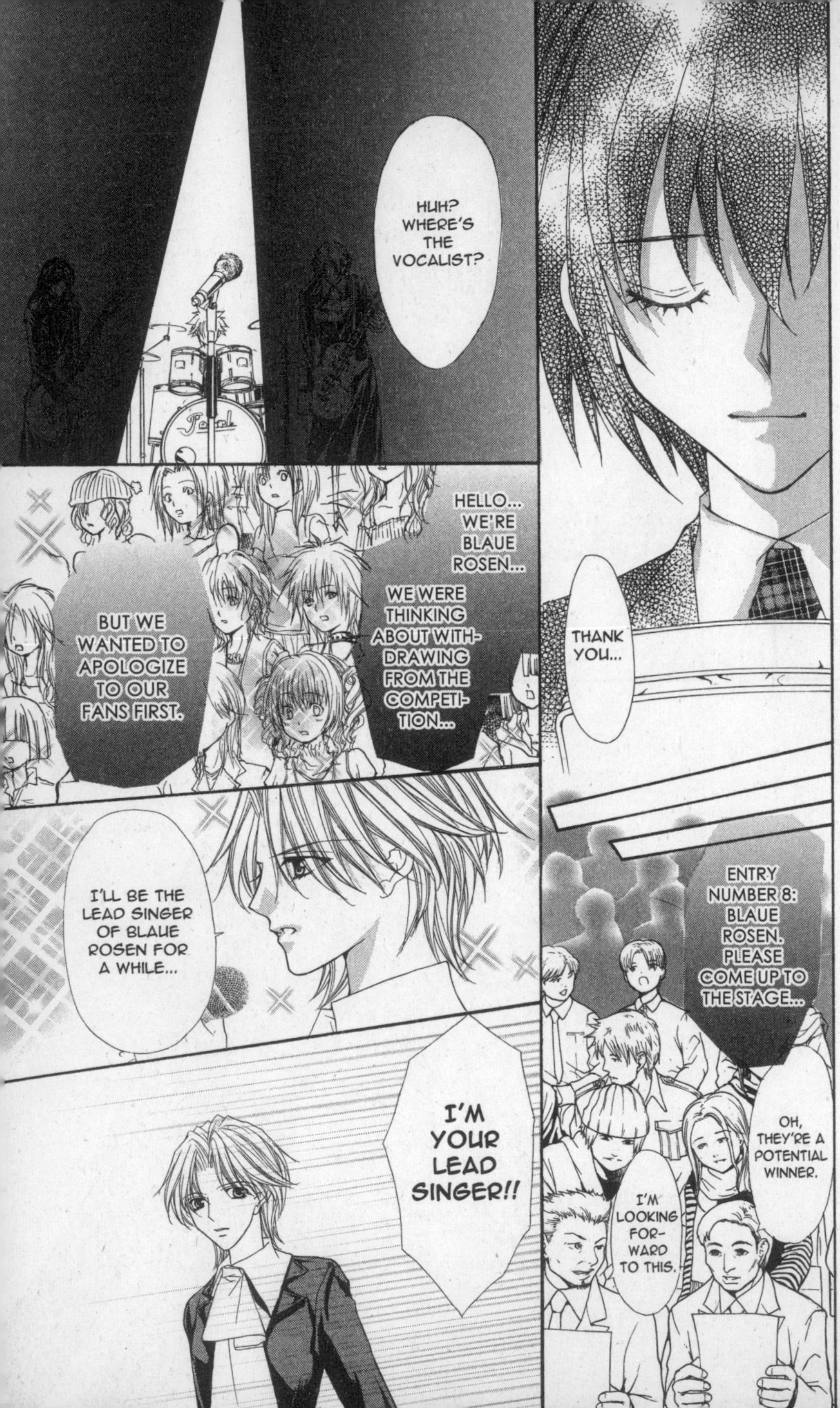
THANK YOU...
ENTRY NUMBER 8: BLAUE ROSEN. PLEASE COME UP TO THE STAGE...
OH, THEY'RE A POTENTIAL WINNER.
I'M LOOKING FOR-WARD TO THIS.
HUH? WHERE'S THE VOCALIST?
HELLO... WE'RE BLAUE ROSEN...
WE WERE THINKING ABOUT WITH-DRAWING FROM THE COMPETI-TION...
BUT WE WANTED TO APOLOGIZE TO OUR FANS FIRST.
I'LL BE THE LEAD SINGER OF BLAUE ROSEN FOR A WHILE...
I'M YOUR LEAD SINGER!!

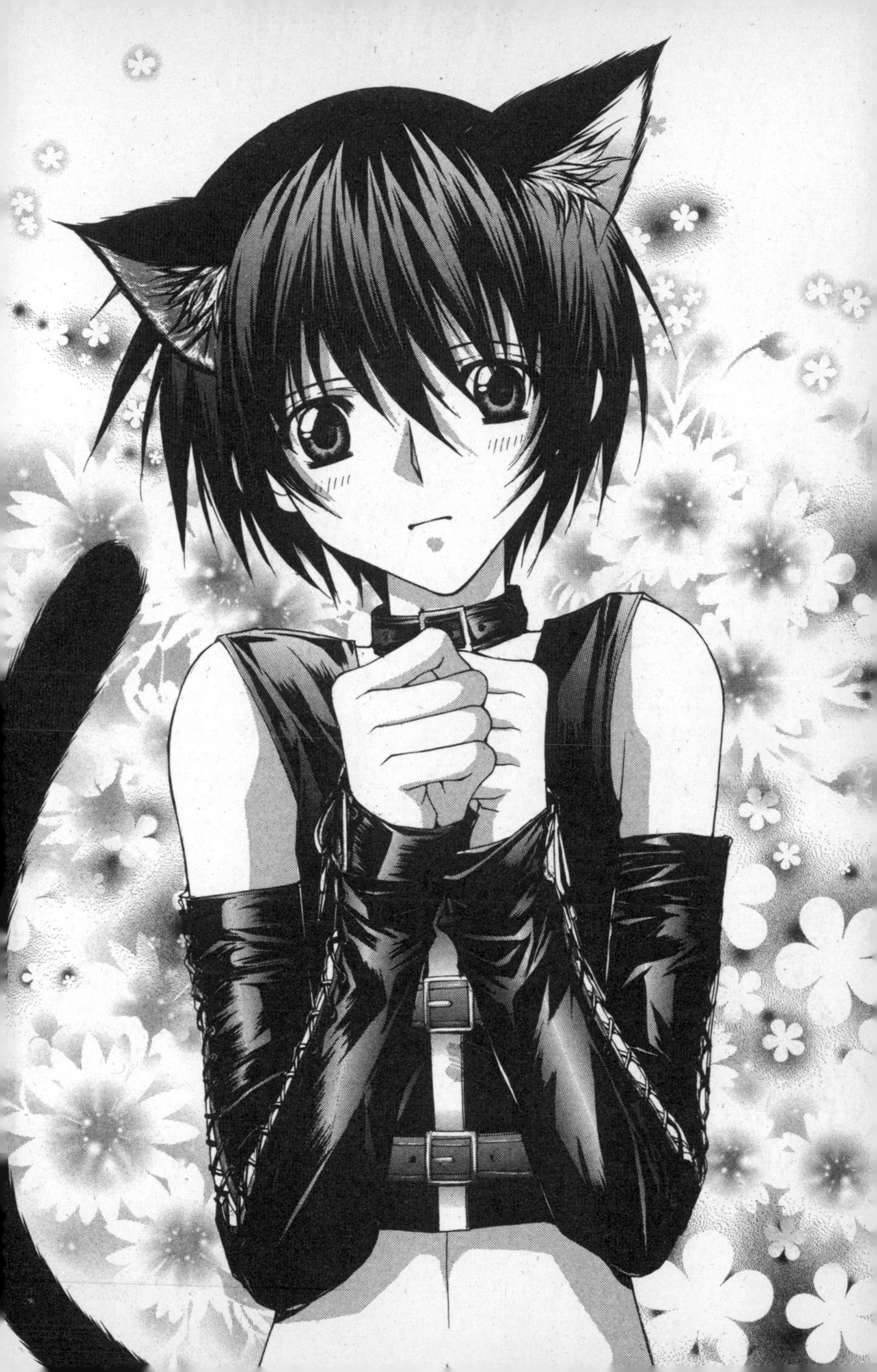

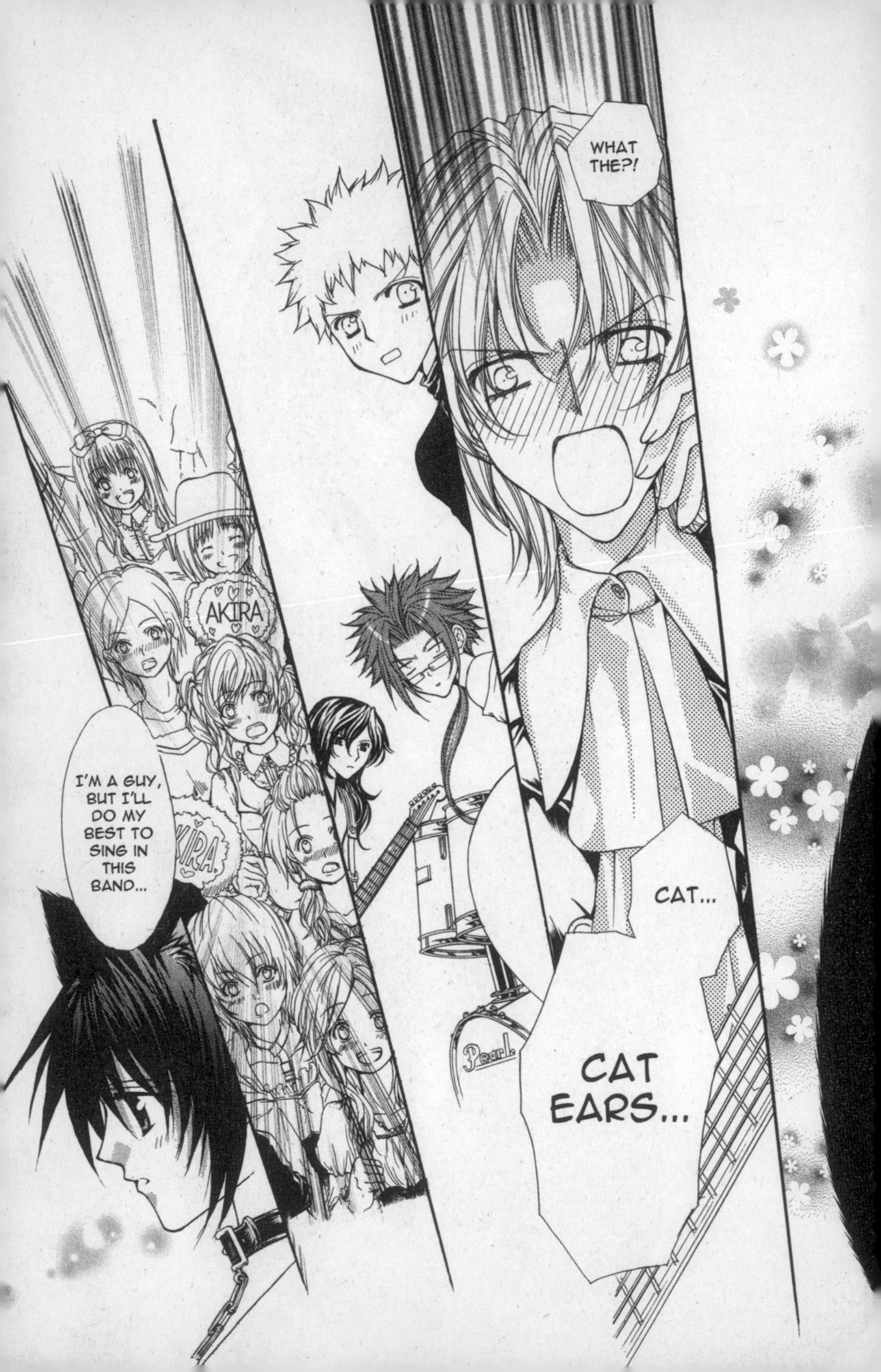
WHAT THE?!
CAT...
CAT EARS...
Pearl.
AKIRA
I'M A GUY, BUT I'LL DO MY BEST TO SING IN THIS BAND...

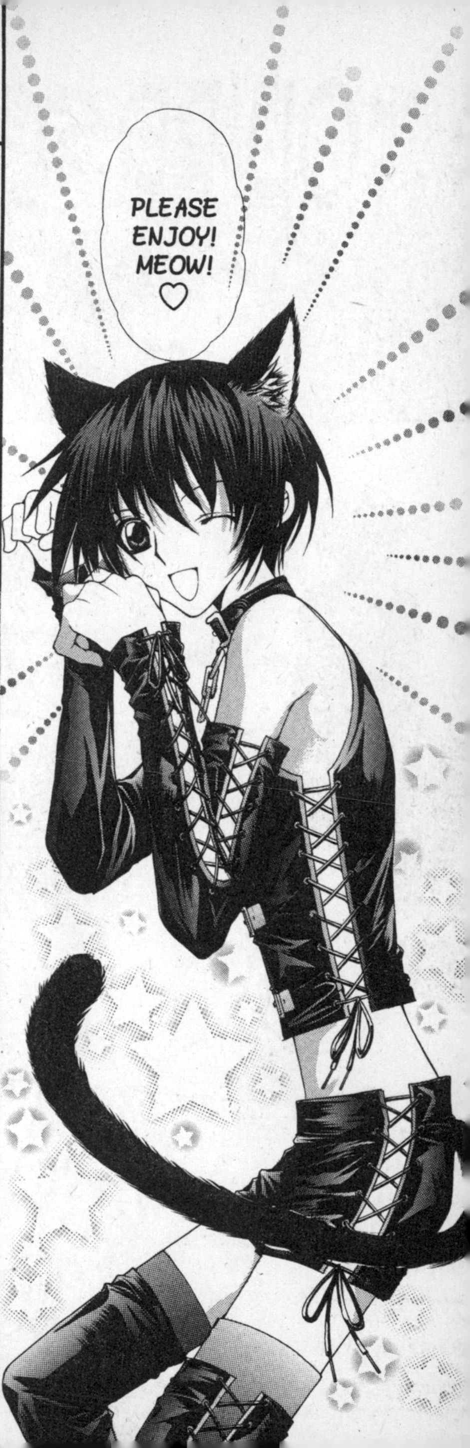
PLEASE ENJOY! MEOW! ♡

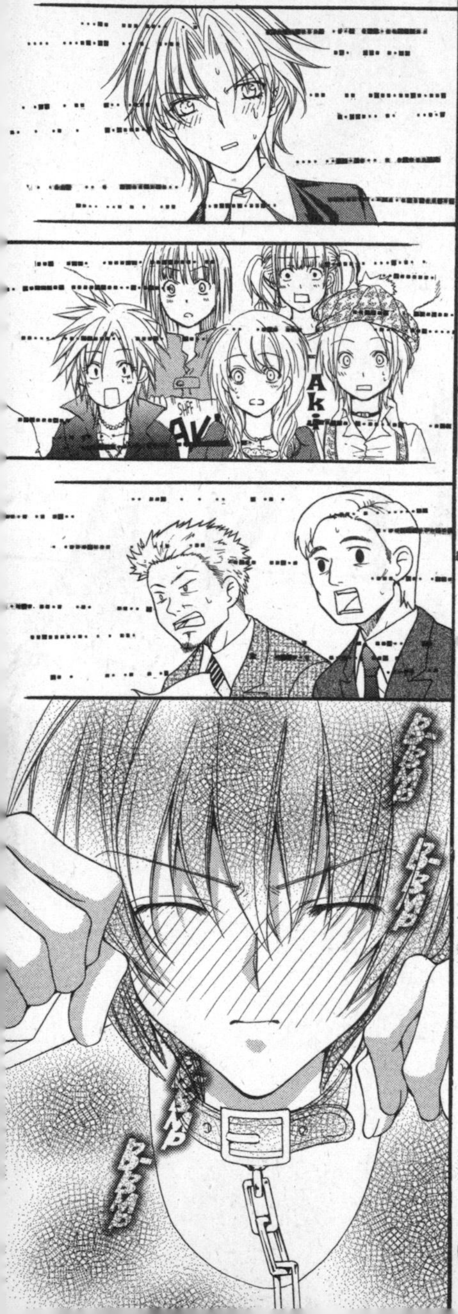
SHFF

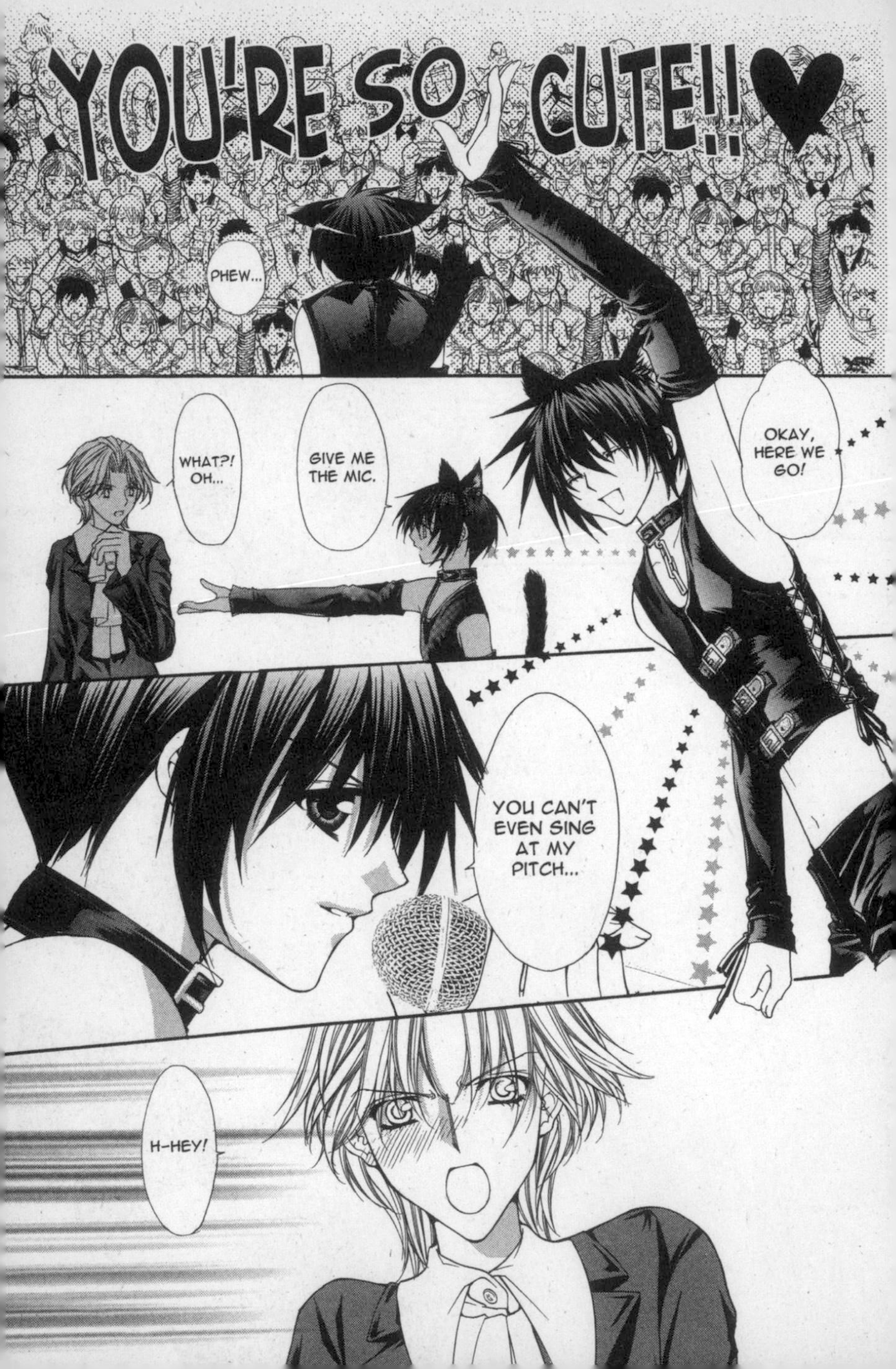
YOU'RE SO CUTE!! ♥
PHEW...
OKAY, HERE WE GO!
GIVE ME THE MIC.
WHAT?! OH...
YOU CAN'T EVEN SING AT MY PITCH...
H-HEY!

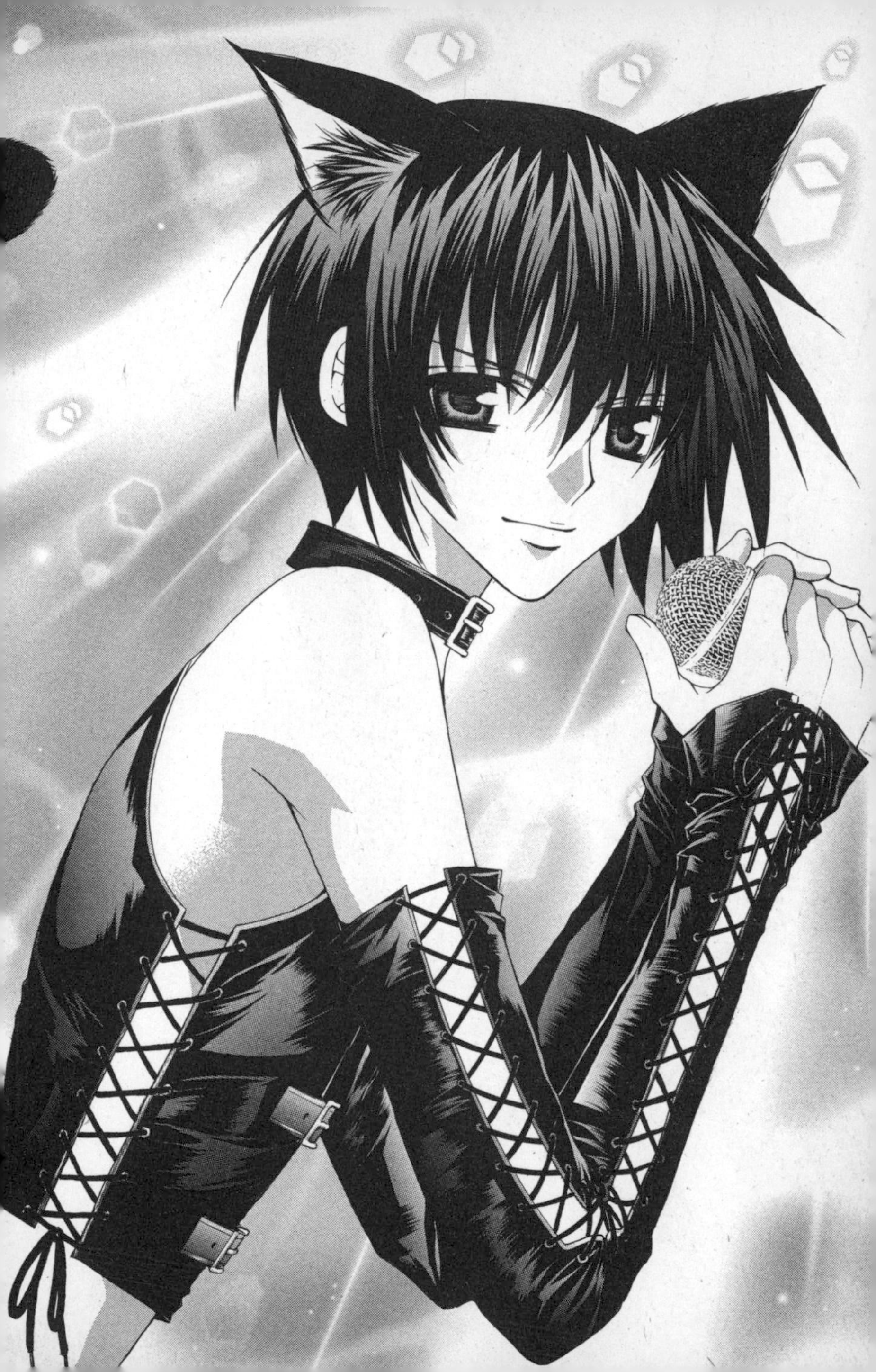

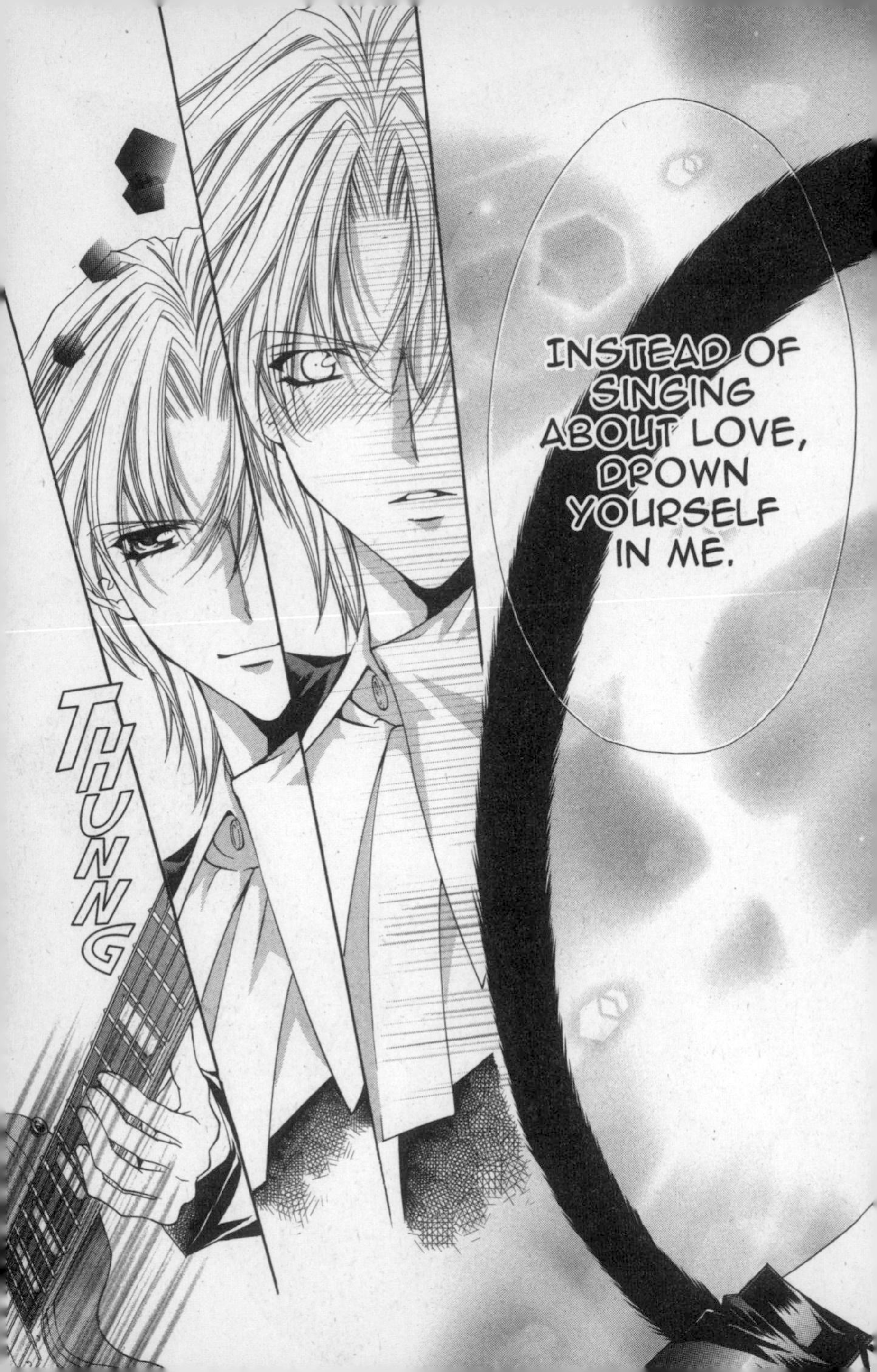
INSTEAD OF SINGING ABOUT LOVE, DROWN YOURSELF IN ME.
THUNNG

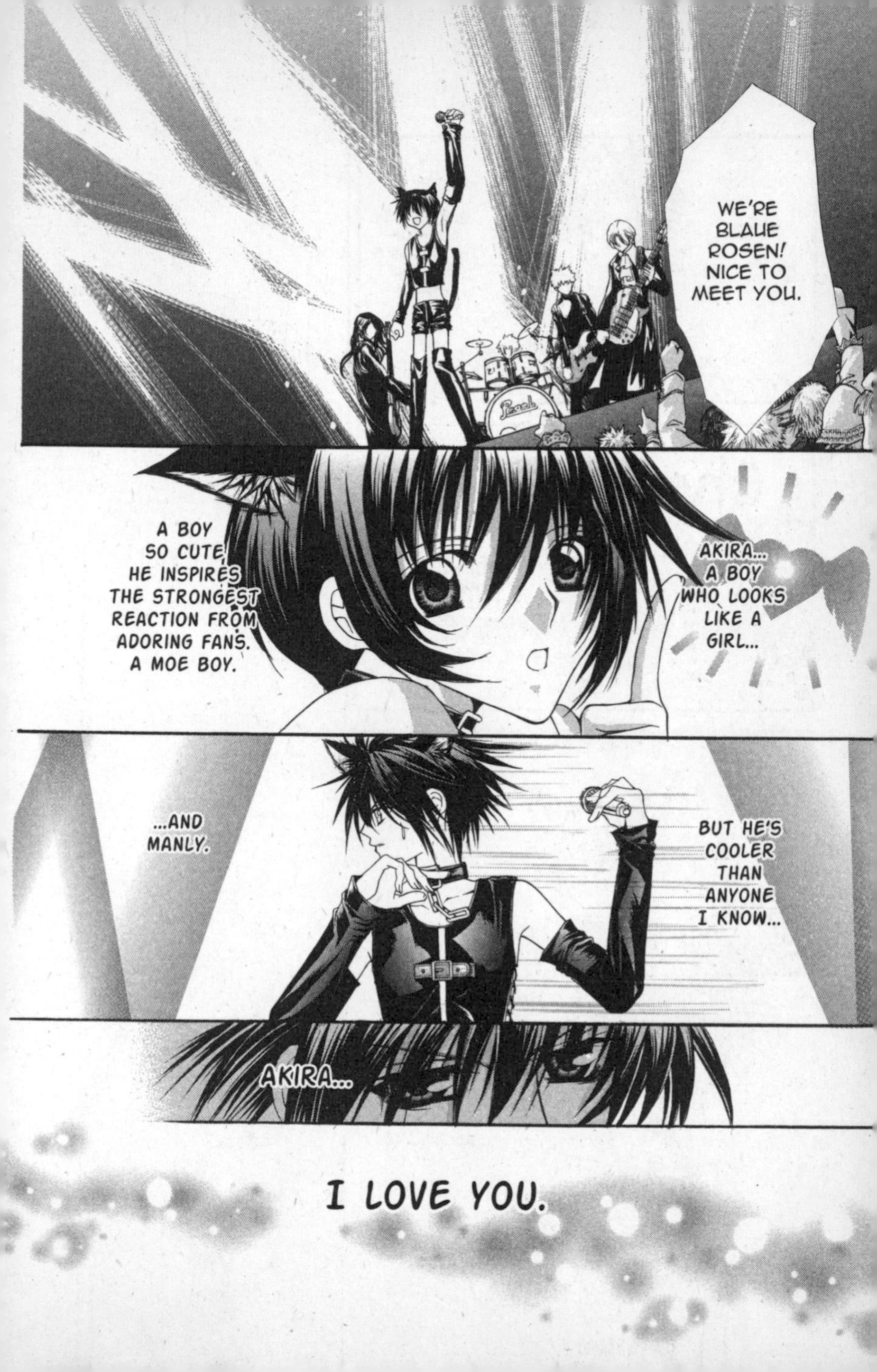
WE'RE BLAUE ROSEN! NICE TO MEET YOU.
AKIRA... A BOY WHO LOOKS LIKE A GIRL...
A BOY SO CUTE, HE INSPIRES THE STRONGEST REACTION FROM ADORING FANS. A MOE BOY.
BUT HE'S COOLER THAN ANYONE I KNOW...
...AND MANLY.
AKIRA...
I LOVE YOU.

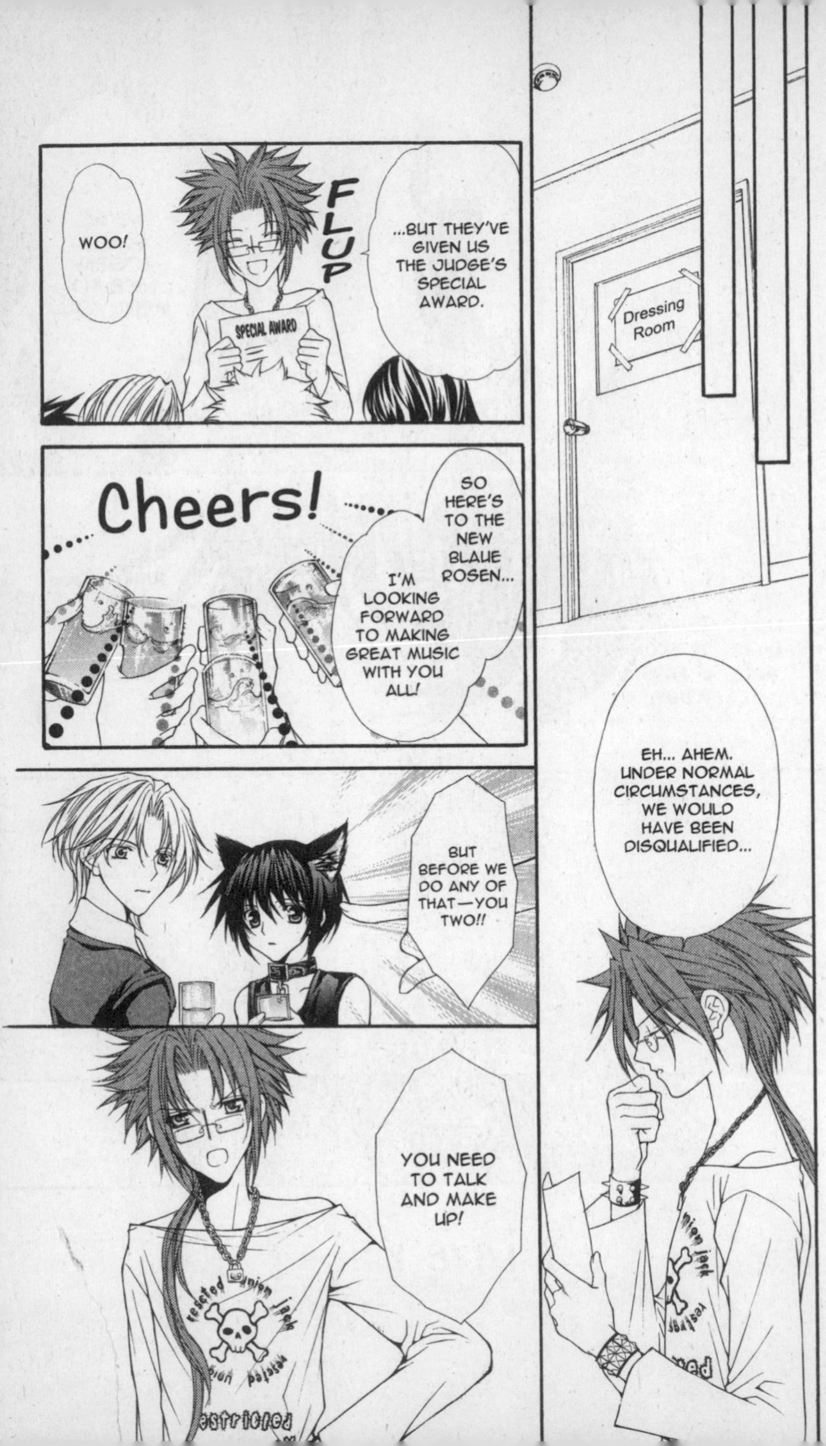
Dressing Room
EH... AHEM. UNDER NORMAL CIRCUMSTANCES, WE WOULD HAVE BEEN DISQUALIFIED...
...BUT THEY'VE GIVEN US THE JUDGE'S SPECIAL AWARD.
FLUP
SPECIAL AWARD
WOO!
SO HERE'S TO THE NEW BLAUE ROSEN...
I'M LOOKING FORWARD TO MAKING GREAT MUSIC WITH YOU ALL!
Cheers!
BUT BEFORE WE DO ANY OF THAT—YOU TWO!!
YOU NEED TO TALK AND MAKE UP!

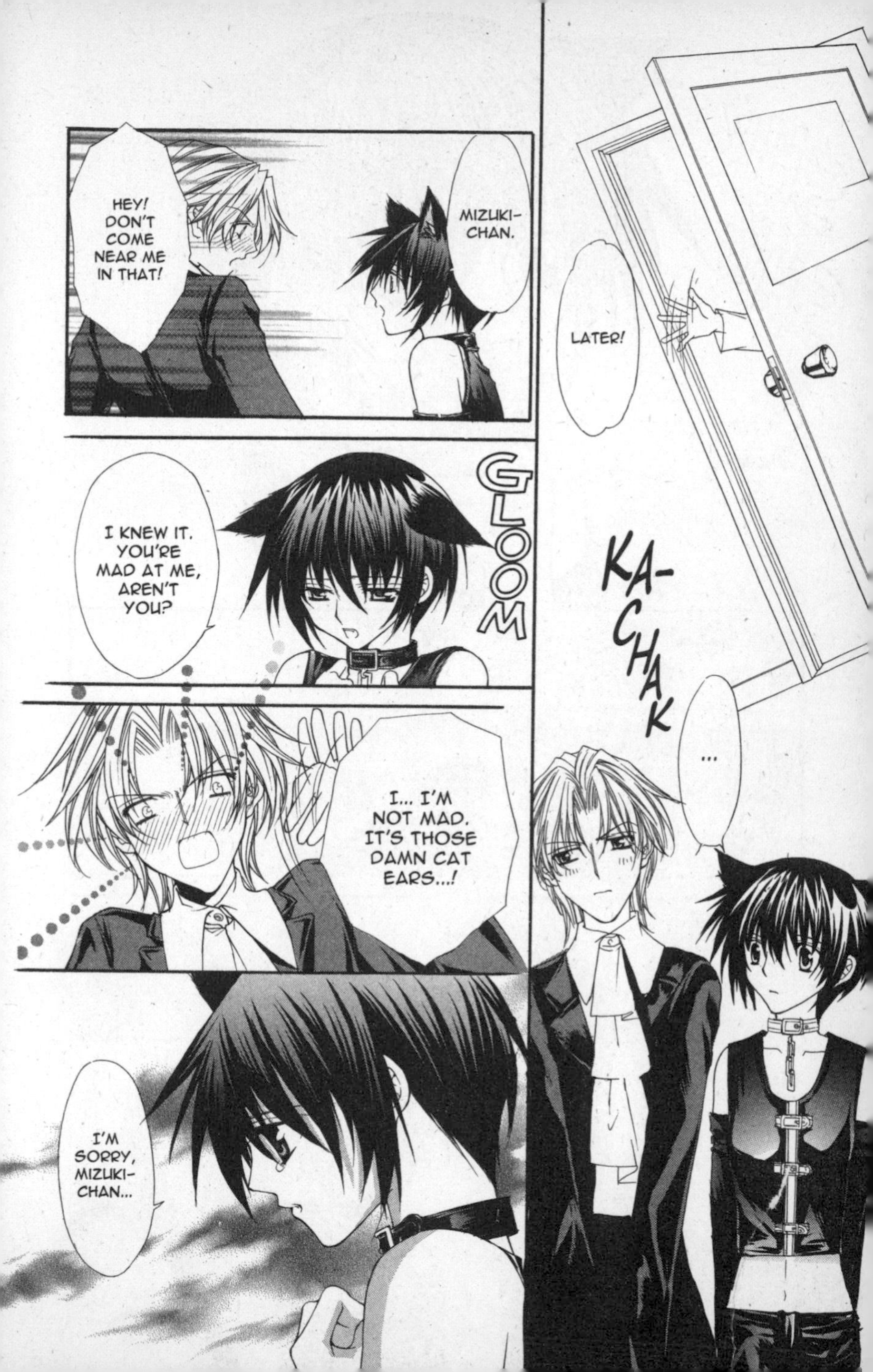
LATER!
KA-CHAK
...
MIZUKI-CHAN.
HEY! DON'T COME NEAR ME IN THAT!
GLOOM
I KNEW IT. YOU'RE MAD AT ME, AREN'T YOU?
I... I'M NOT MAD. IT'S THOSE DAMN CAT EARS...!
I'M SORRY, MIZUKI-CHAN...

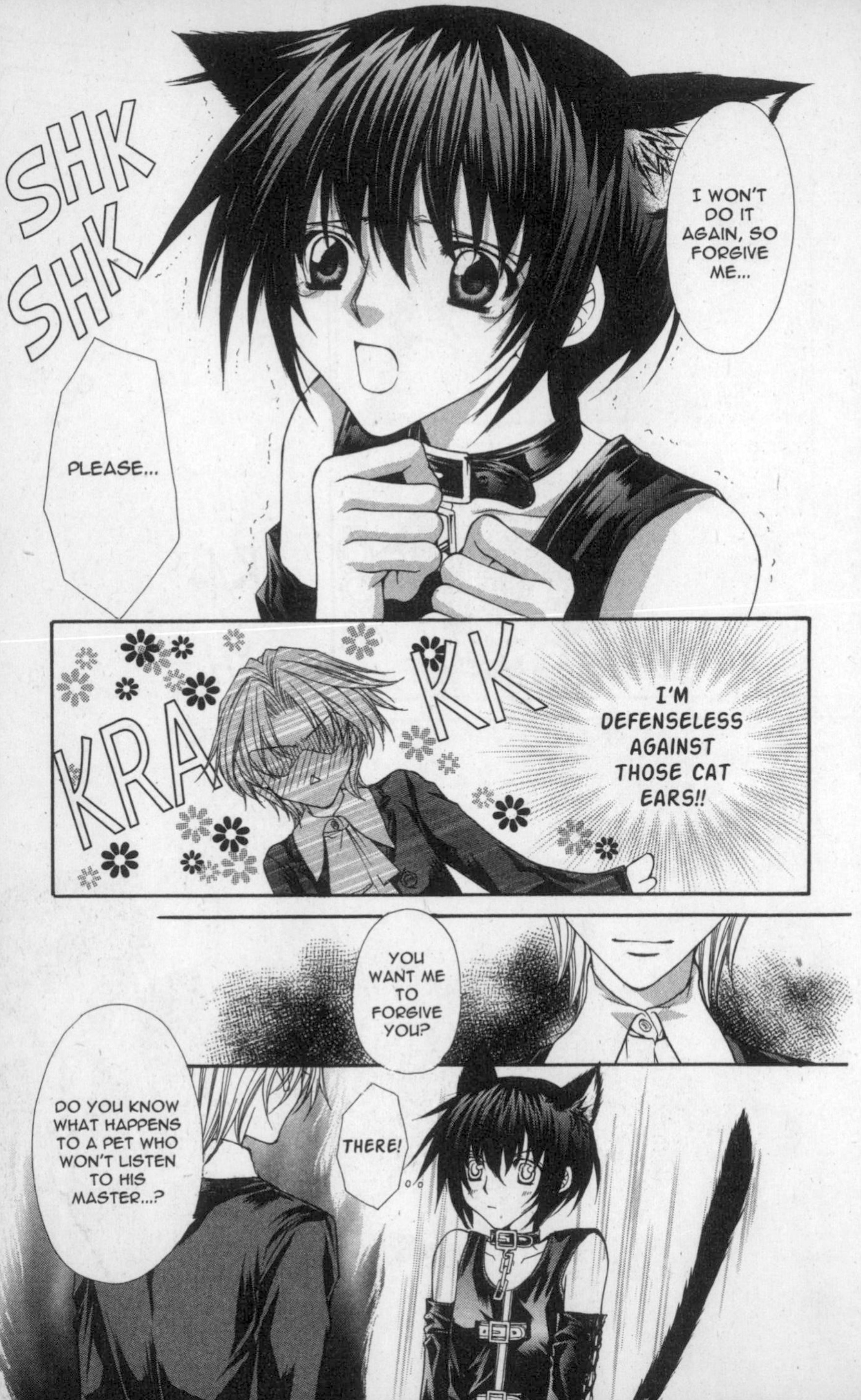
I WON'T DO IT AGAIN, SO FORGIVE ME...
SHK SHK
PLEASE...
I'M DEFENSELESS AGAINST THOSE CAT EARS!!
KRAKK
YOU WANT ME TO FORGIVE YOU?
THERE!
DO YOU KNOW WHAT HAPPENS TO A PET WHO WON'T LISTEN TO HIS MASTER...?

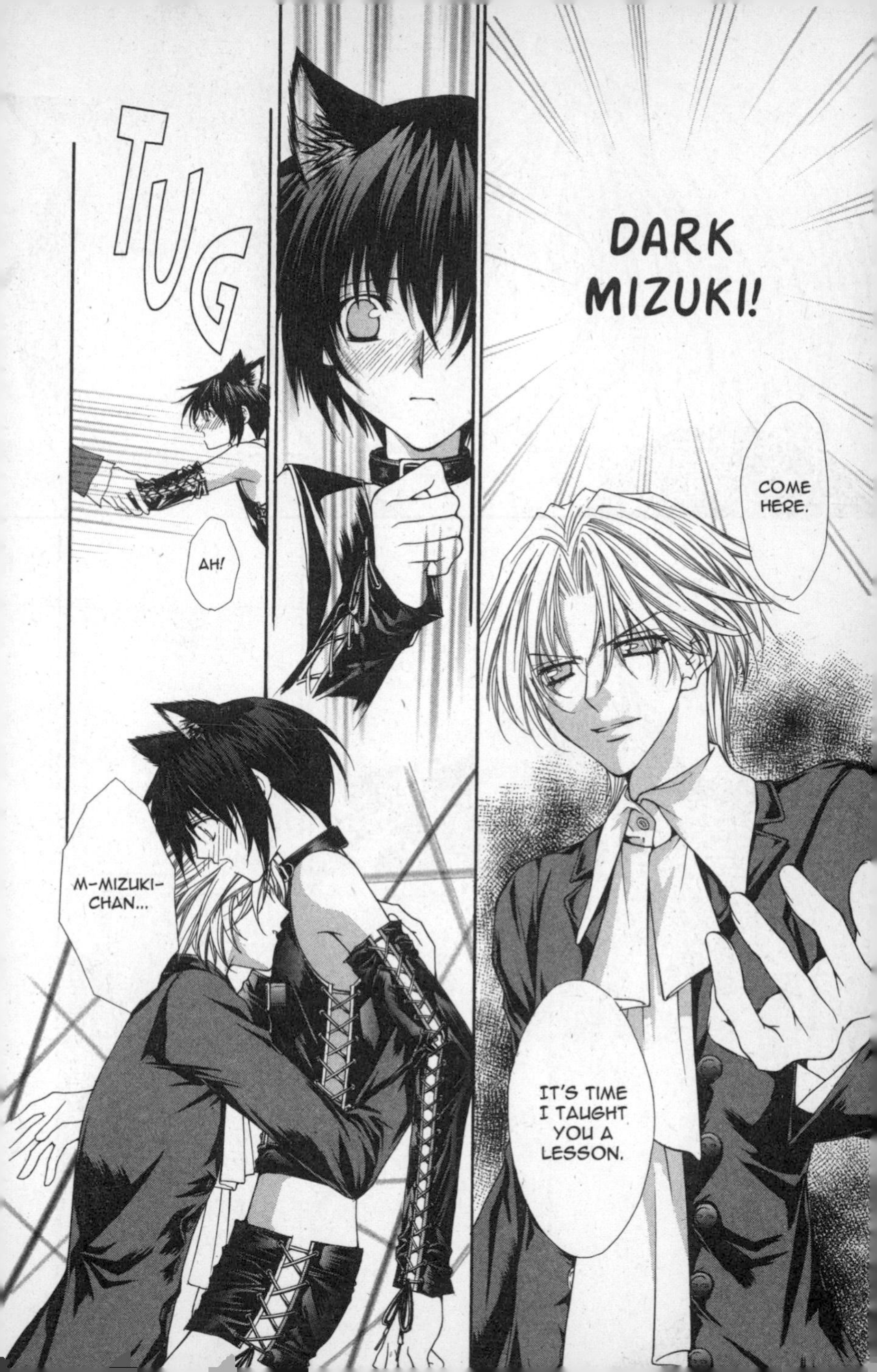
DARK MIZUKI!
COME HERE.
IT'S TIME I TAUGHT YOU A LESSON.
TUG
AH!
M-MIZUKI-CHAN...

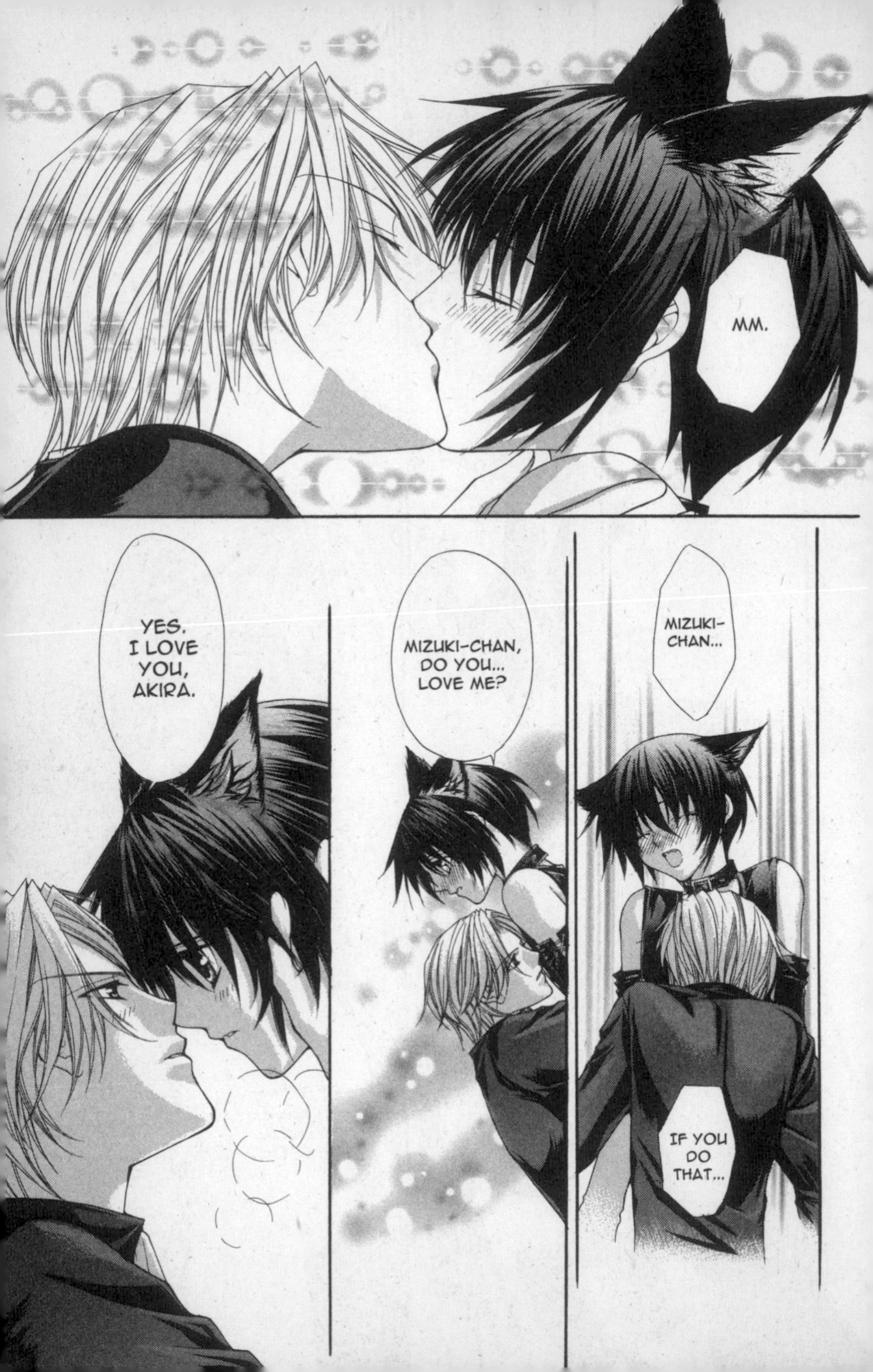
MM.
MIZUKI-CHAN...
IF YOU DO THAT...
MIZUKI-CHAN, DO YOU... LOVE ME?
YES. I LOVE YOU, AKIRA.

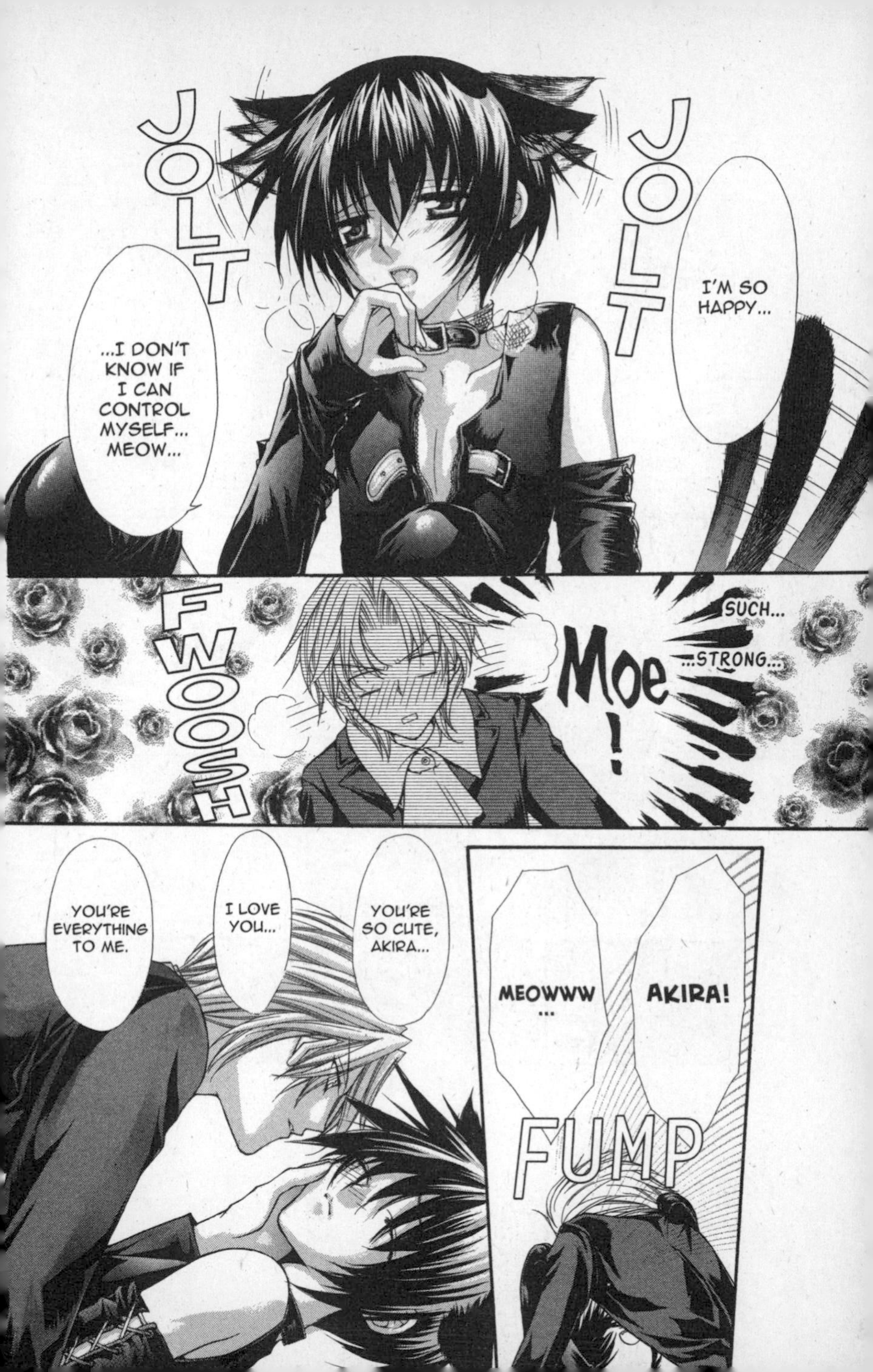
JOLT
I'M SO HAPPY...
JOLT
...I DON'T KNOW IF I CAN CONTROL MYSELF... MEOW...
SUCH...
...STRONG...
Moe!
FWOOSH
AKIRA!
MEOWWW ...
FUMP
YOU'RE SO CUTE, AKIRA...
I LOVE YOU...
YOU'RE EVERYTHING TO ME.

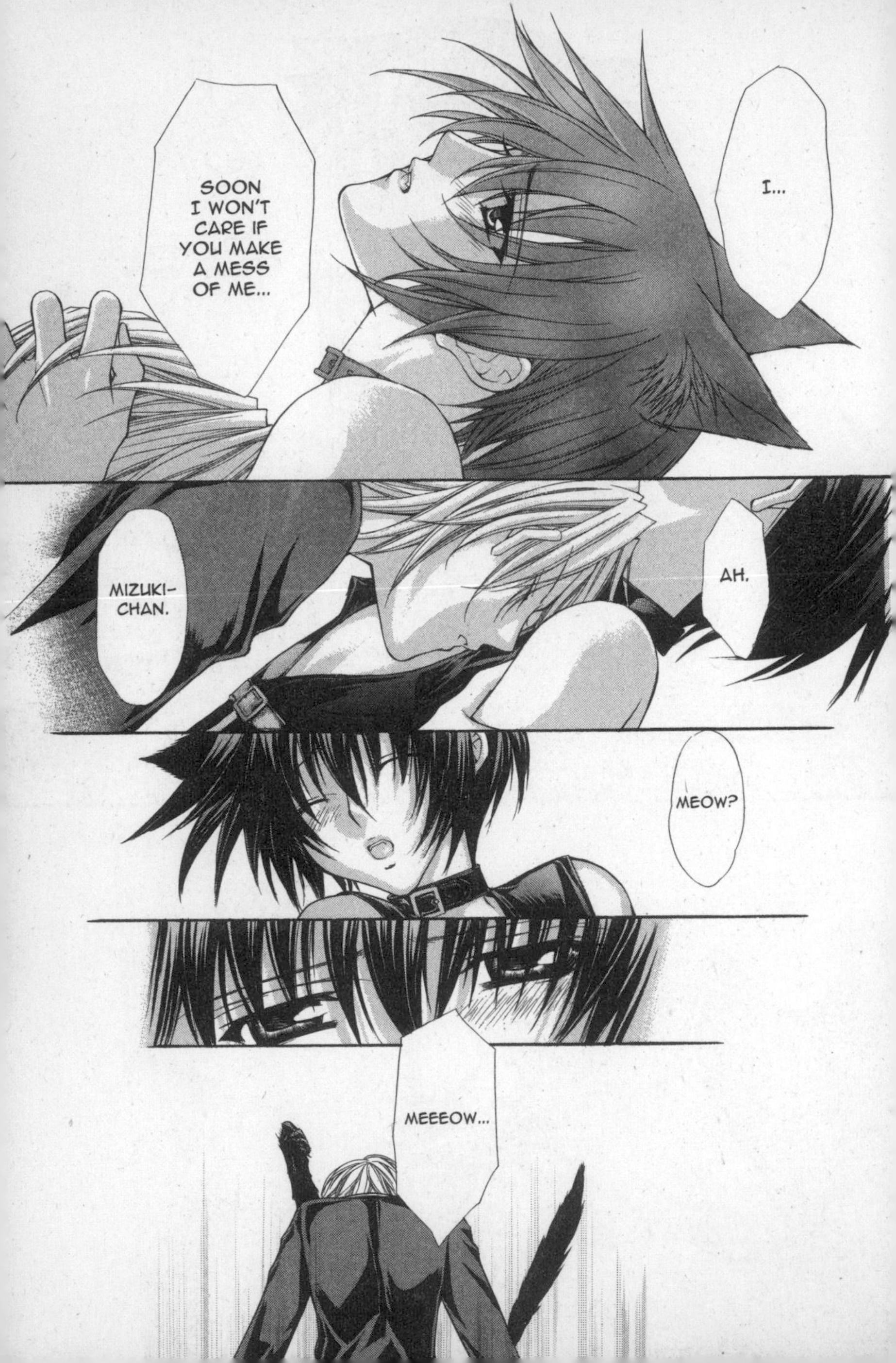
I...
SOON I WON'T CARE IF YOU MAKE A MESS OF ME...
AH.
MIZUKI-CHAN.
MEOW?
MEEEOW...

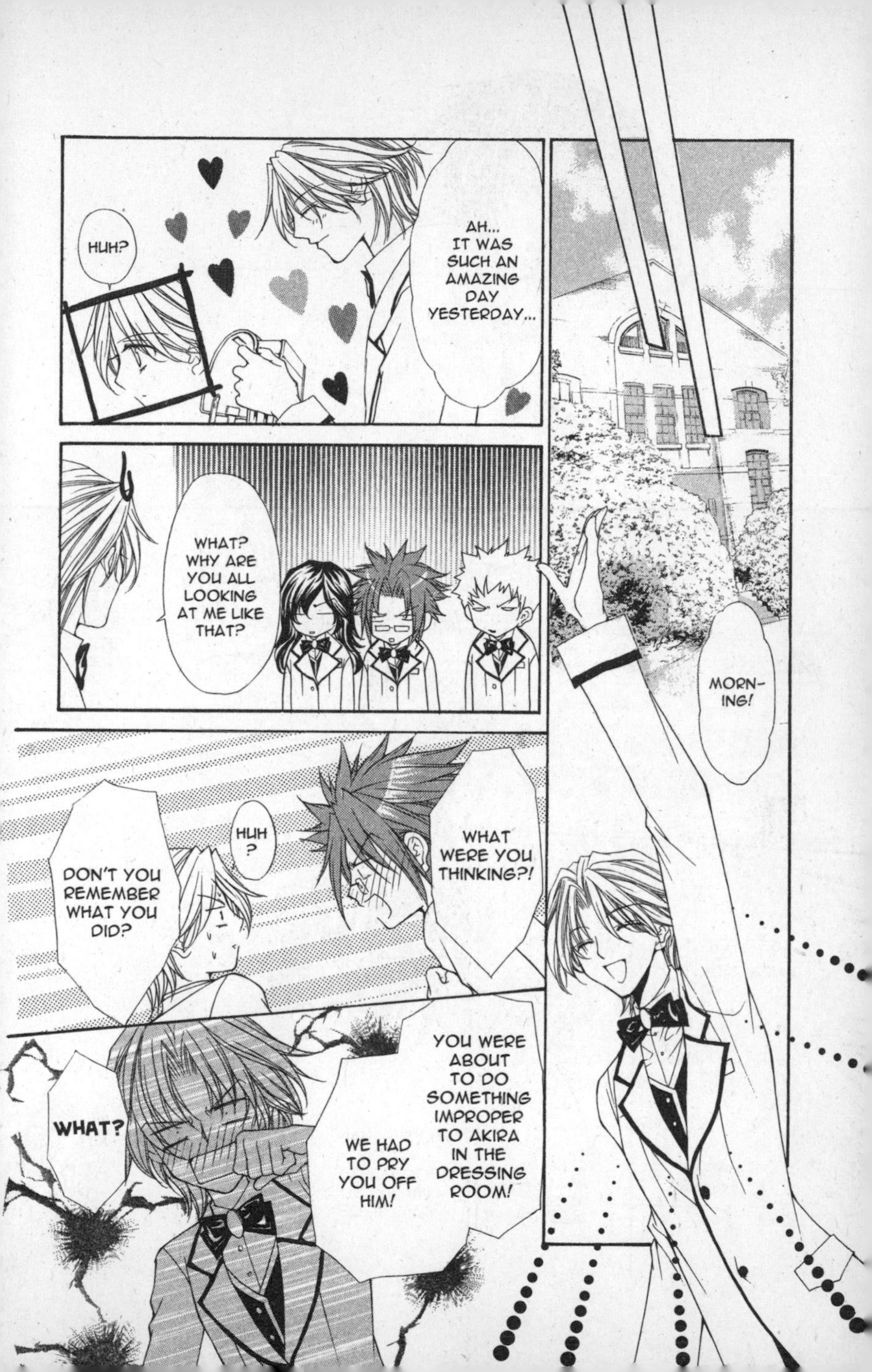
MORNING!
AH... IT WAS SUCH AN AMAZING DAY YESTERDAY...
HUH?
WHAT? WHY ARE YOU ALL LOOKING AT ME LIKE THAT?
WHAT WERE YOU THINKING?!
HUH?
DON'T YOU REMEMBER WHAT YOU DID?
YOU WERE ABOUT TO DO SOMETHING IMPROPER TO AKIRA IN THE DRESSING ROOM!
WE HAD TO PRY YOU OFF HIM!
WHAT?

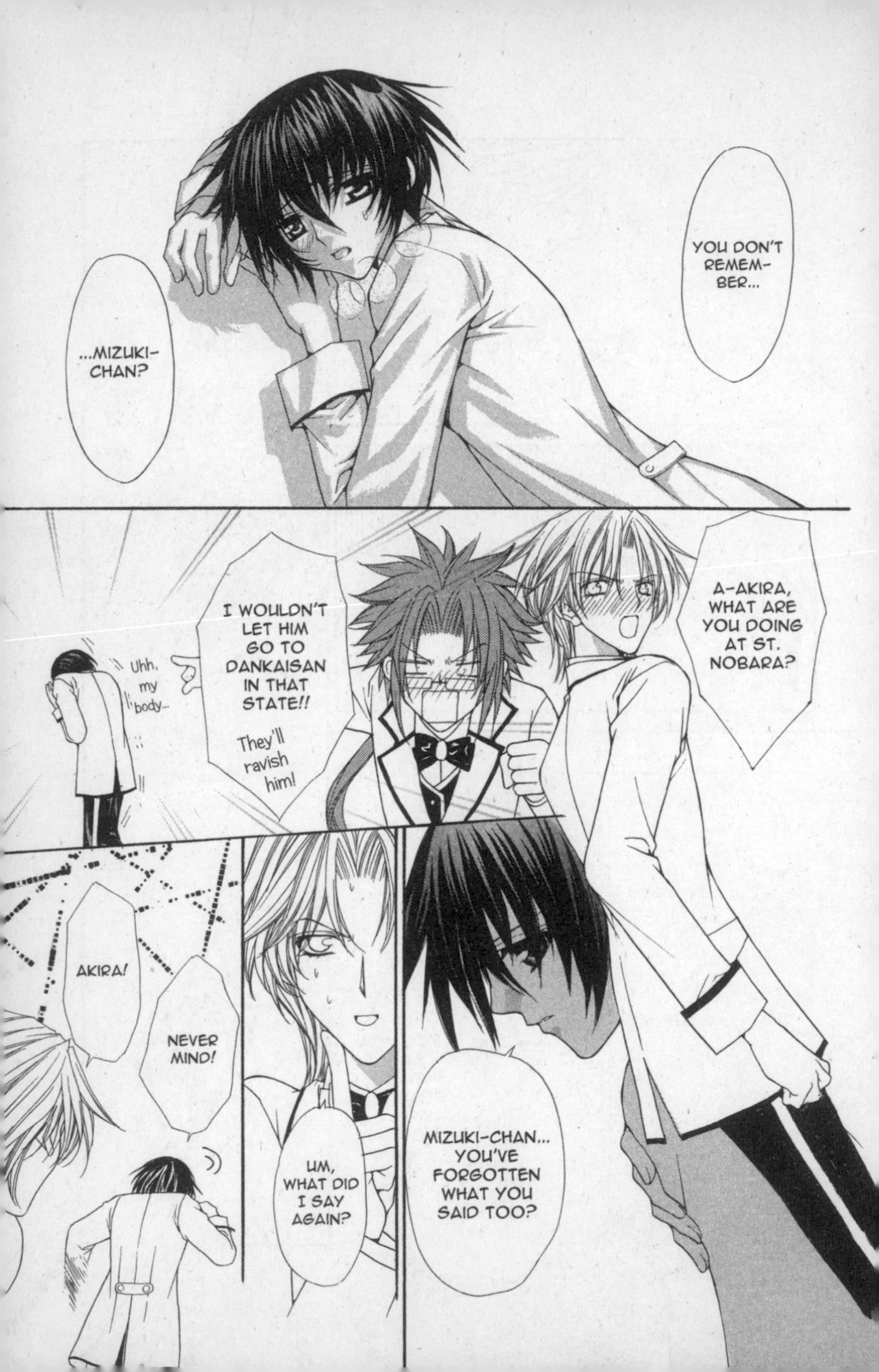
YOU DON'T REMEM-BER...
...MIZUKI-CHAN?
A-AKIRA, WHAT ARE YOU DOING AT ST. NOBARA?
I WOULDN'T LET HIM GO TO DANKAISAN IN THAT STATE!!
They'll ravish him!
Uhh, my body...
MIZUKI-CHAN... YOU'VE FORGOTTEN WHAT YOU SAID TOO?
UM, WHAT DID I SAY AGAIN?
AKIRA!
NEVER MIND!

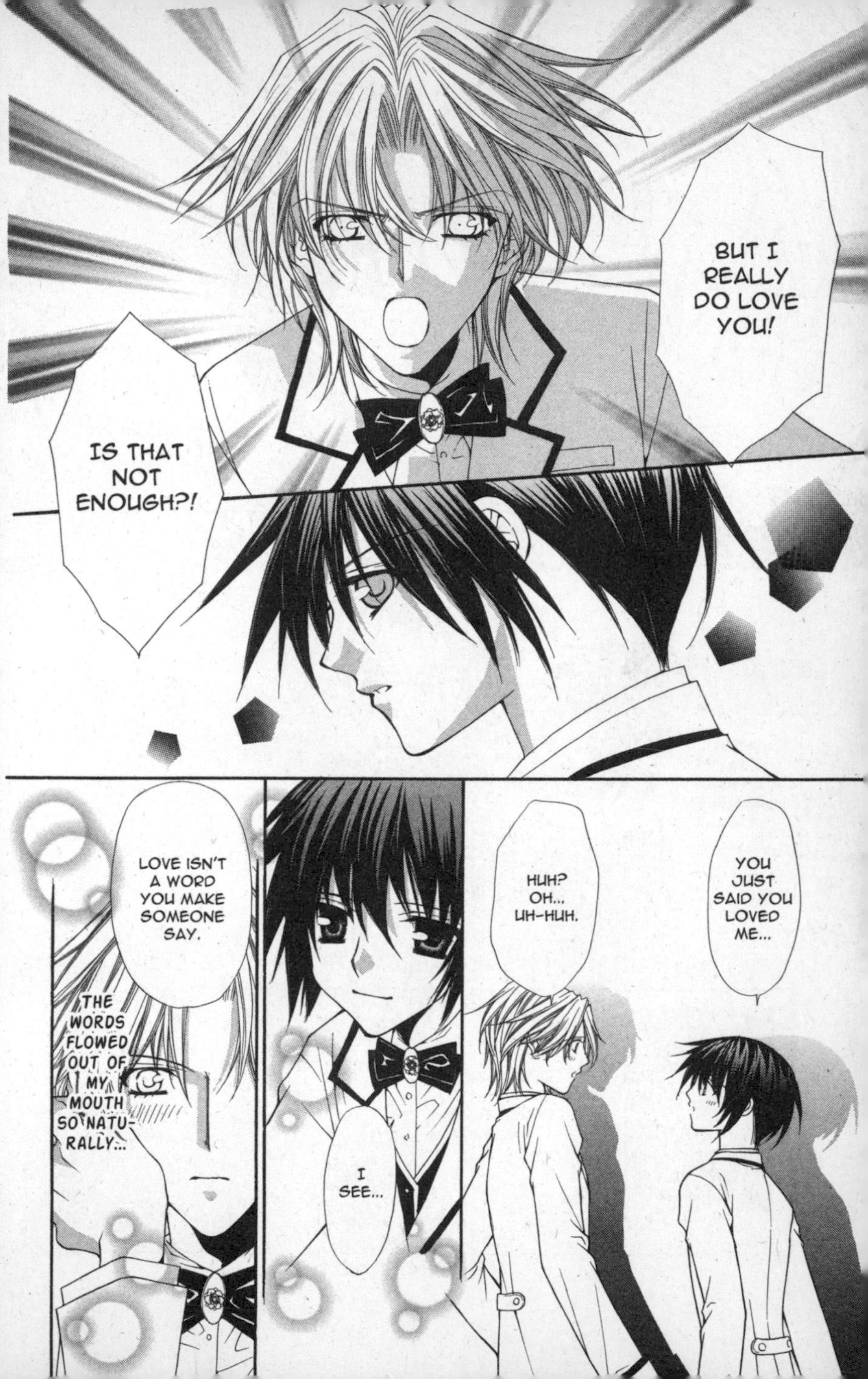
BUT I REALLY DO LOVE YOU!
IS THAT NOT ENOUGH?!
YOU JUST SAID YOU LOVED ME...
HUH? OH... UH-HUH.
I SEE...
LOVE ISN'T A WORD YOU MAKE SOMEONE SAY.
THE WORDS FLOWED OUT OF MY MOUTH SO NATU-RALLY...

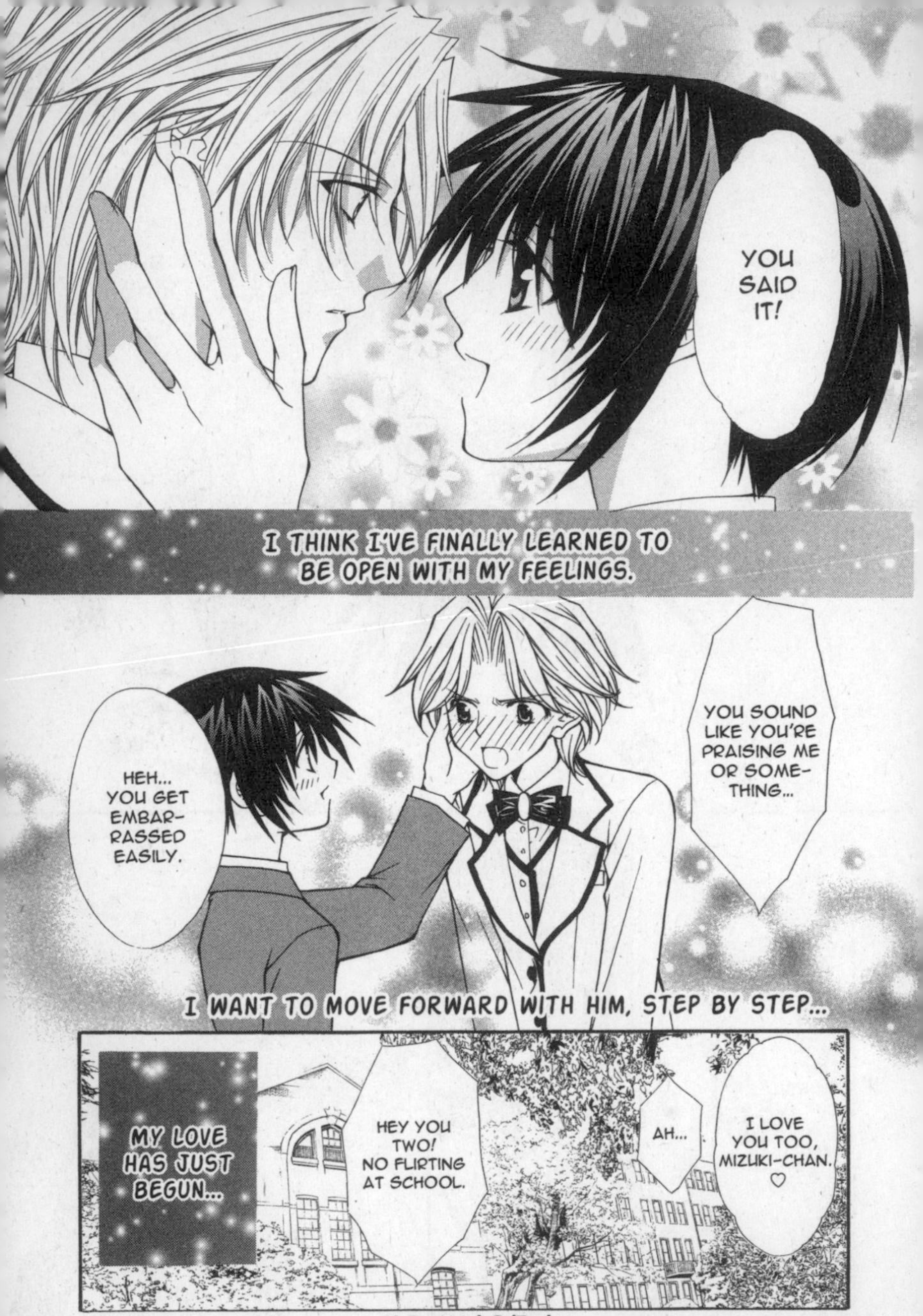
YOU SAID IT!
I THINK I'VE FINALLY LEARNED TO BE OPEN WITH MY FEELINGS.
YOU SOUND LIKE YOU'RE PRAISING ME OR SOME-THING...
HEH... YOU GET EMBAR-RASSED EASILY.
I WANT TO MOVE FORWARD WITH HIM, STEP BY STEP...
I LOVE YOU TOO, MIZUKI-CHAN. ♡
AH...
HEY YOU TWO! NO FLIRTING AT SCHOOL.
MY LOVE HAS JUST BEGUN...

Ai Ore! Vol. 3/End

Illustration Gallery

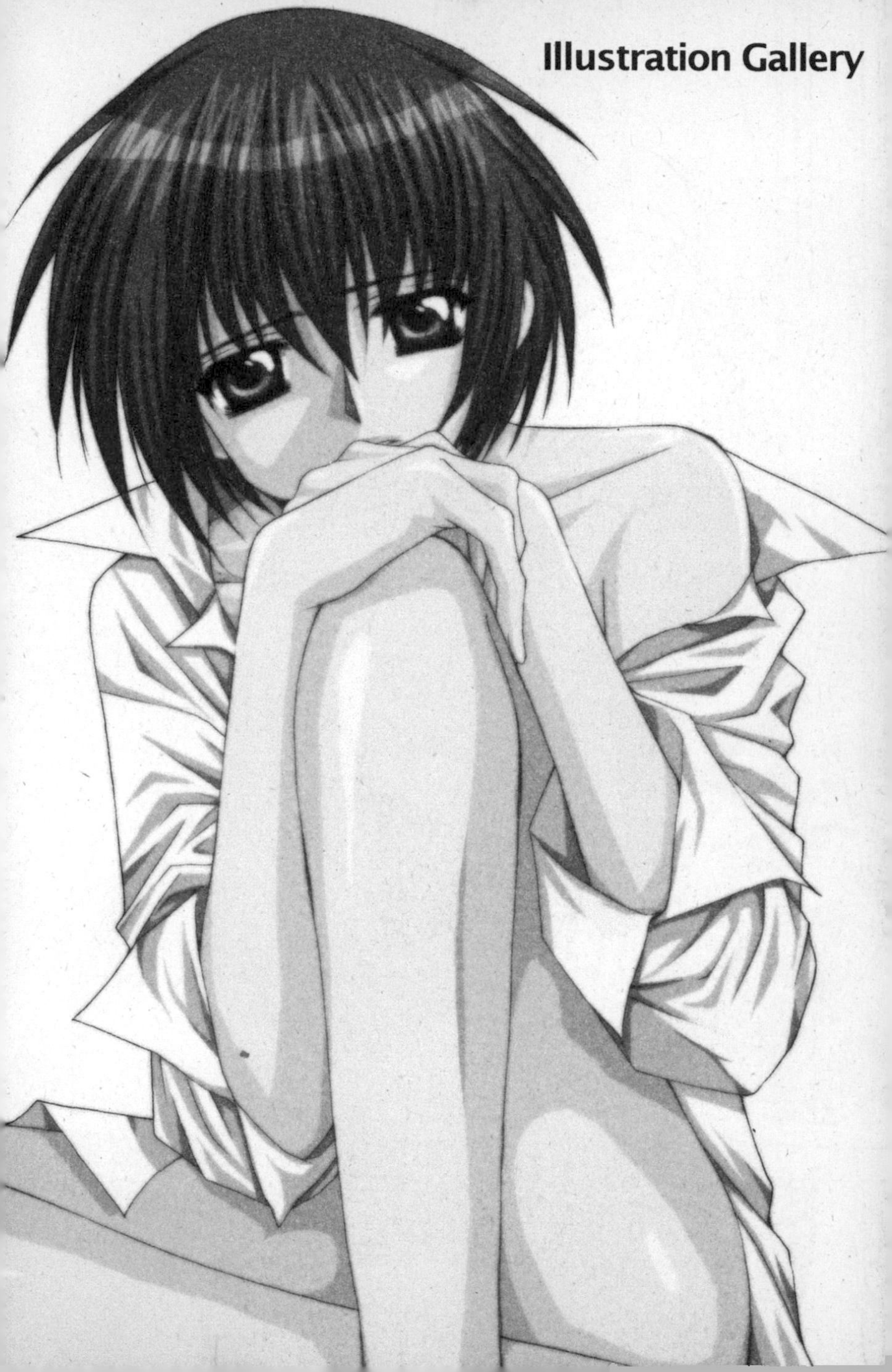

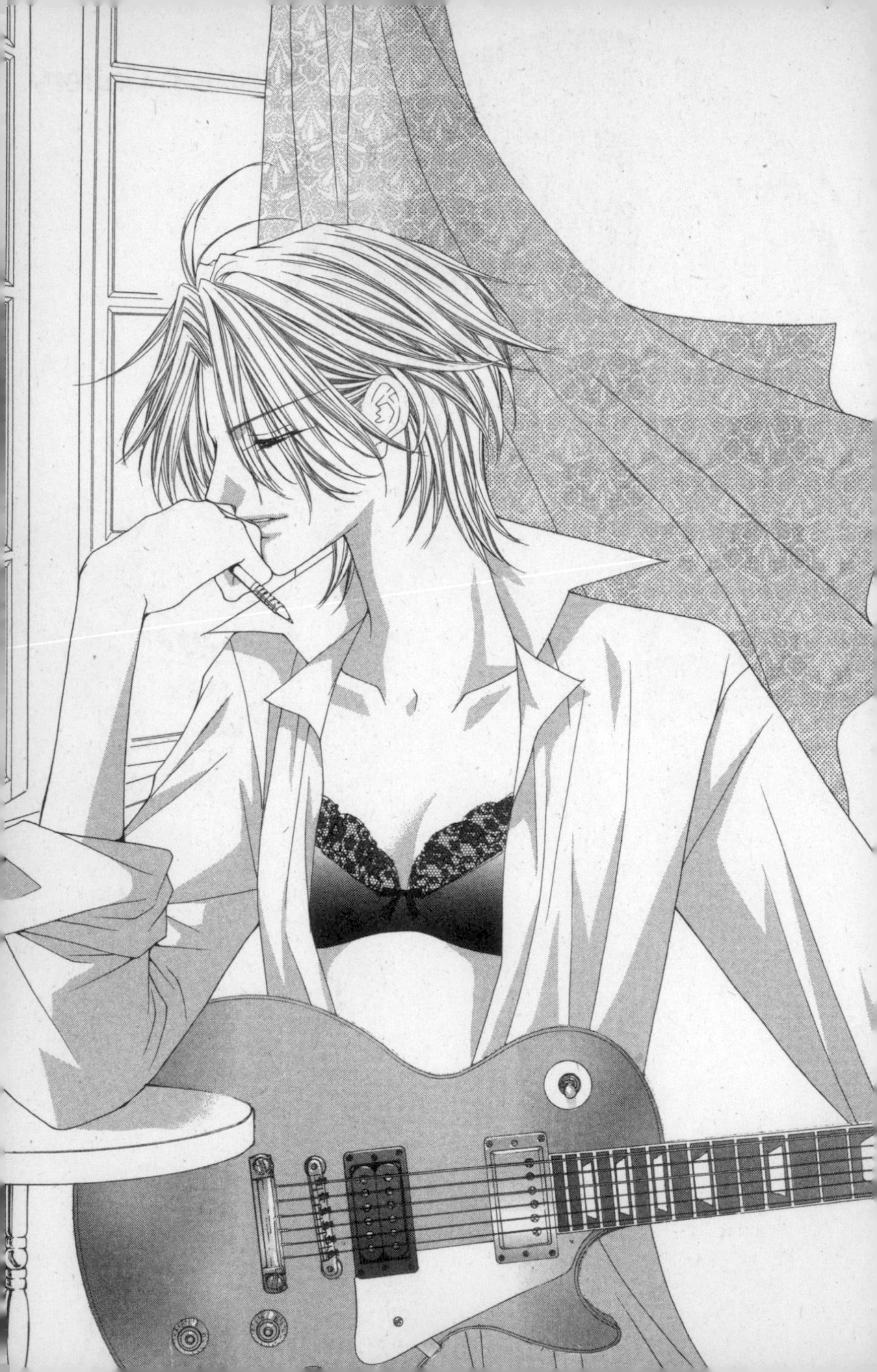

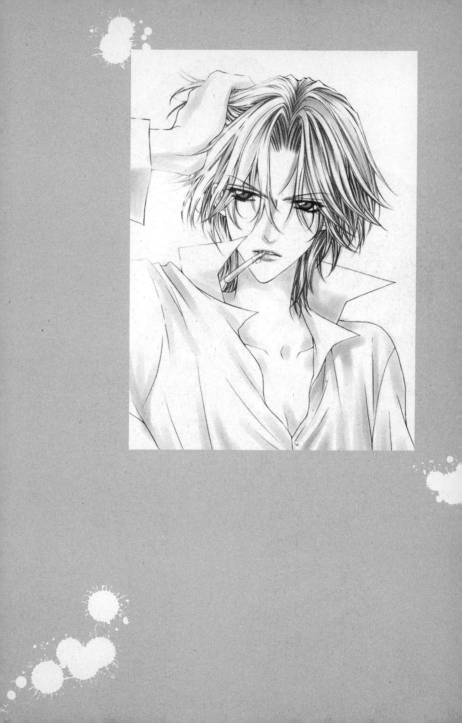

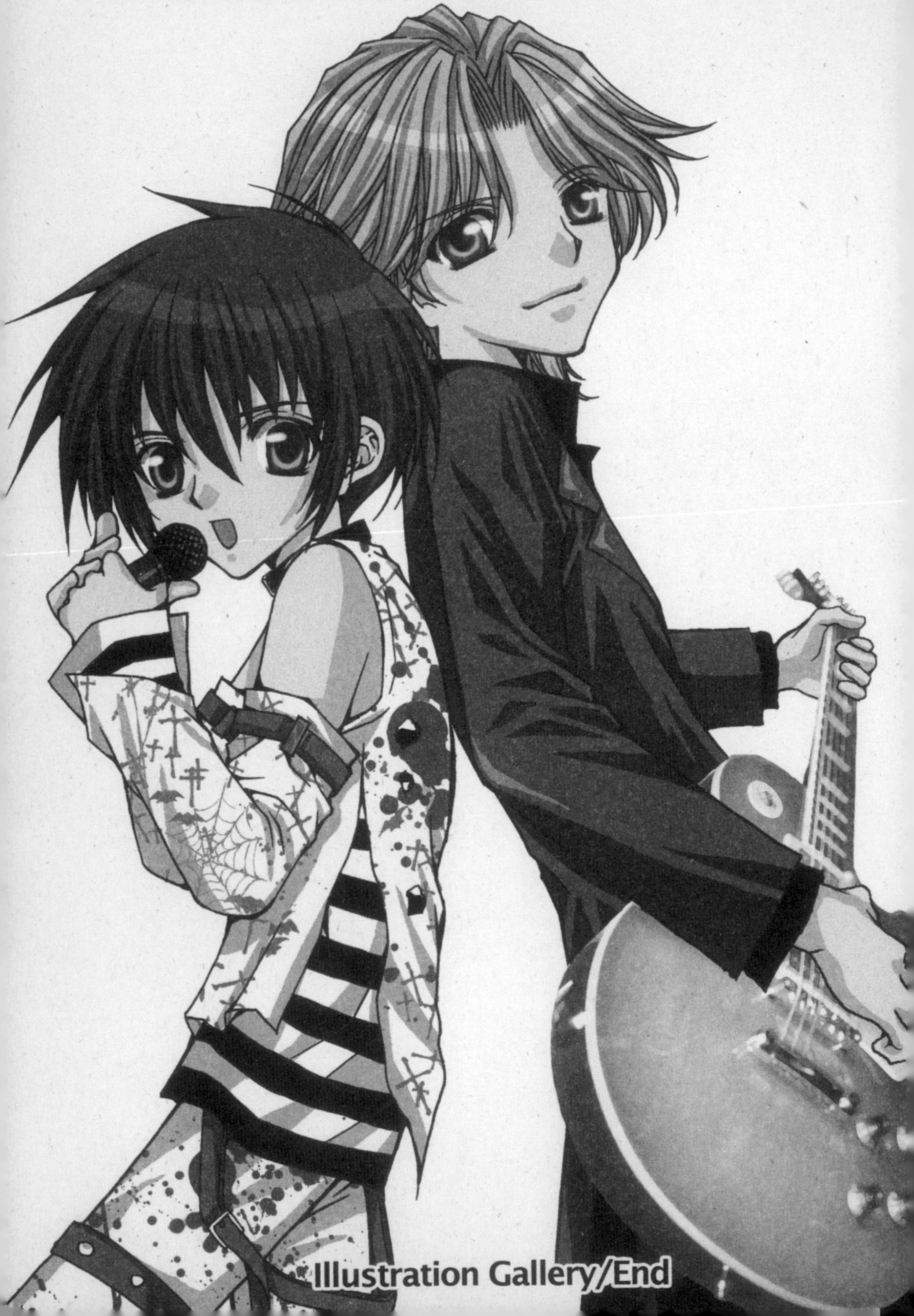

Illustration Gallery/End

I was extremely stressed when I created the chapters in this volume, so I hardly remember the contents of it, but I do remember this piece of work and its characters being very dear to me. I also have memories of fighting against many things. I just hope that even a small portion of those feelings have reached you by reading this.

-Mayu Shinjo

Mayu Shinjo was born on January 26. She is a prolific writer of shojo manga, including the series *Sensual Phrase*. Her current series include *Ai-Ore!* and *Ayakashi Koi Emaki*. Her hobbies are cars, shopping and taking baths. Shinjo likes The Prodigy, Nirvana, U2 and Glay.

Ai Ore!

Volume 3
Shojo Beat Edition

STORY AND ART BY
MAYU SHINJO

Translation/Tetsuichiro Miyaki
Touch-up Art & Lettering/Inori Fukuda Trant
Design/Yukiko Whitley
Editor/Nancy Thistlethwaite

Aiwo Utauyori Oreni Oborero! Volume 3

First published in Japan in 2010 by KADOKAWA SHOTEN Co., Ltd., Tokyo.
English translation rights arranged with KADOKAWA SHOTEN Co., Ltd., Tokyo.

Printed in Canada

Published by VIZ Media, LLC
P.O. Box 77010
San Francisco, CA 94107

10 9 8 7 6 5 4 3 2 1
First printing, November 2011

RATED T+ FOR OLDER TEEN
PARENTAL ADVISORY
AI ORE! is rated T+ for Older Teen and is recommended for ages 16 and up.
ratings.viz.com

www.viz.com

www.shojobeat.com

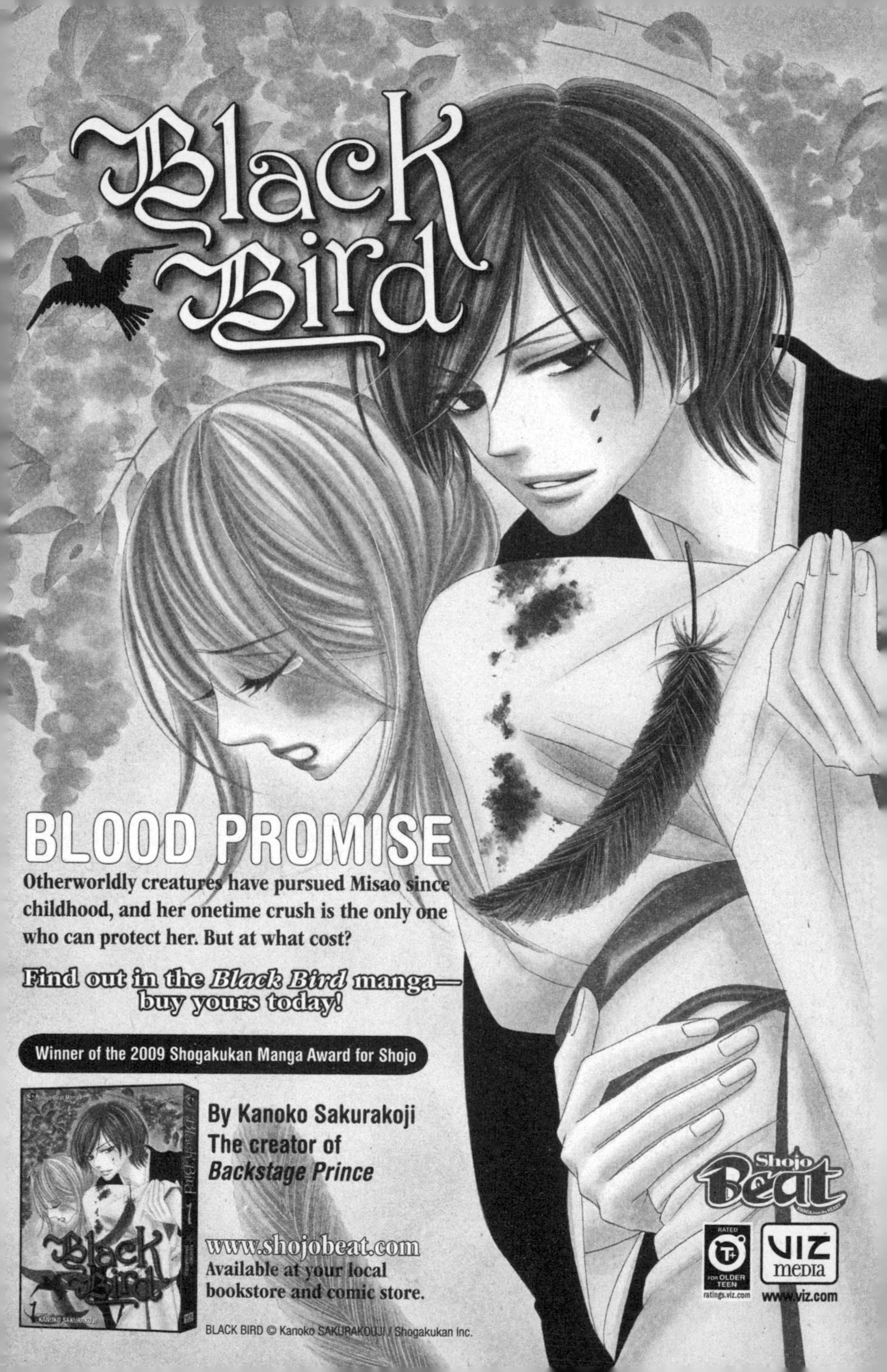
Black Bird
BLOOD PROMISE
Otherworldly creatures have pursued Misao since childhood, and her onetime crush is the only one who can protect her. But at what cost?
Find out in the Black Bird manga—buy yours today!
Winner of the 2009 Shogakukan Manga Award for Shojo
Black Bird
By Kanoko Sakurakoji
The creator of Backstage Prince
www.shojobeat.com
Available at your local bookstore and comic store.
Shojo Beat
RATED T+ FOR OLDER TEEN
ratings.viz.com
VIZ media
www.viz.com
BLACK BIRD © Kanoko SAKURAKOUJI / Shogakukan Inc.

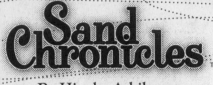
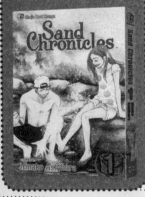

LAND OF *Fantasy*

MIAKA YŪKI IS AN ORDINARY JUNIOR-HIGH STUDENT WHO IS SUDDENLY WHISKED AWAY INTO THE WORLD OF A BOOK, *THE UNIVERSE OF THE FOUR GODS*. WILL THE BEAUTIFUL CELESTIAL BEINGS SHE ENCOUNTERS AND THE CHANCE TO BECOME A PRIESTESS DIVERT MIAKA FROM EVER RETURNING HOME?

THREE VOLUMES OF THE ORIGINAL *FUSHIGI YŪGI* SERIES COMBINED INTO A LARGER FORMAT WITH AN EXCLUSIVE COVER DESIGN AND BONUS CONTENT

EXPERIENCE THE BEAUTY OF *FUSHIGI YŪGI* WITH THE HARDCOVER ART BOOK

ALSO AVAILABLE: THE *FUSHIGI YŪGI: GENBU KAIDEN* MANGA, THE EIGHT VOLUME PREQUEL TO THIS BEST-SELLING FANTASY SERIES

TAKE A TRIP TO AN ANCIENT

FUSHIGI YÛGI

FROM THE CREATOR O
ABSOLUTE BOYFRIEND
ALICE 19TH, *CERES:*
CELESTIAL LEGEND,
AND *IMADOKI!*

VIZ media **The VIZ Manga** some new fr...

The world's best manga is now on
the iPad,™ iPhone™ and iPod touch™

To learn more, visit viz.com/25years

From legendary manga like *Death Note* to
Absolute Boyfriend, the best manga in the
world is now available on multiple devices
through the official VIZ Manga app.

- **Hundreds of volumes available**
- **Free App**
- **New content weekly**
- **Free chapter 1 previews**

HEROES OF MANGA